Employee Relations

John **Gennard** is Professor of Human Resource Management at the University of Strathclyde, and is the CIPD Chief Examiner for Employee Relations.

Graham Judge is Group Human Resources Director for Yattendon Investment Trust plc. He is an Associate Examiner (Employee Relations) for the CIPD and a Fellow of the CIPD.

The CIPD would like to thank the following members of the CIPD Publishing Editorial Board for their help and advice:
- Pauline Dibben, Middlesex University Business School
- Edwina Hollings, Staffordshire University Business School
- Caroline Hook, Huddersfield University Business School
- Vincenza Priola, Wolverhampton Business School
- John Sinclair, Napier University Business School

Employee Relations

4th edition

John Gennard and Graham Judge

Chartered Institute of Personnel and Development

Published by the Chartered Institute of Personnel and Development, 151 The Broadway, London, SW19 1JQ

First published in 1997, Reprinted 1998
Second edition published 1999, Reprinted 2000
Third edition published 2002, Reprinted 2002, 2003, 2004
This edition published 2005
Reprinted 2006 (twice)

Design and typeset by Fakenham Photosetting, Fakenham, Norfolk
Printed in Great Britain by The Cromwell Press, Trowbridge, Wiltshire

British Library Cataloguing in Publication Data
A catalogue of this publication is available from the British Library
ISBN 1843980630

Chartered Institute of Personnel and Development, 151 The Broadway, London, SW19 1JQ
Tel: 020 8612 6200
E-mail: cipd@cipd.co.uk Website: www.cipd.co.uk
Incorporated by Royal Charter. Registered Charity No. 1079797

Contents

List of figures and tables

Acknowledgements

We would like to thank the following individuals for their help and assistance with this book: Ruth Lake; Geoff Hayward for his valuable input, particularly on matters relating to Europe; Debbie Campbell, John's secretary, and Jennie Allan, Graham's secretary. John would like to thank Anne for her support, while Graham would like to thank Kim for her invaluable help and assistance.

John Gennard
Graham Judge
December 2004

Foreword

I am very pleased to be offered the opportunity to introduce the latest (the fourth) edition of *Employee Relations* by John Gennard and Graham Judge. The book offers a systematic and comprehensive review of employee relations, with a substantial amount of up-to-date information and analysis provided by two highly experienced writers who, between them, have a wealth of knowledge about how employee relations really works. Chapters deal with the key elements in employee relations; management objectives and strategies within the context of business needs and forces in the external environment; the parties, including employers and employers' organisations, trade unions and ACAS; the processes, such as employee involvement and collective bargaining; the outcomes, in terms of pay levels or numbers of grievances, as well as the impact of effective employee relations on organisational performance; employee relations skills, such as how to handle a disciplinary case or take part in a negotiating exercise. This final section clearly differentiates Gennard and Judge from most other books on employee relations, and it provides advice about how HR practitioners can offer timely and value-adding contributions to their management teams.

The book has been written specifically for practitioners, particularly those in the HR function or with responsibility for HRM, who need to know more about how to manage employee relations. Advice is offered as to whether or not it is beneficial for individual employers to join an employers' association, set up a non-union establishment or deal with unions, or how to develop effective procedures for handling grievance and disciplinary issues. It follows closely the CIPD professional standards both in terms of its contents and its philosophy. Of course, this is to be expected as Professor Gennard has been its Chief Examiner for Employee Relations for a number of years and has had a major influence on the development of the CIPD's professional standards in the area. He has also been a highly active and influential researcher in employee relations, with an international reputation in issues to do with trade unions in the print industry, the career paths of HR Directors and collective bargaining. Graham Judge is a senior practitioner who has worked in HRM for many years and acts as one of the Professor Gennard's examining team for the CIPD Employee Relations professional standards. Between them, their knowledge of the subject is immense and students will gain a considerable amount from reading what they have to say about the subject that should help them with their exams and in their work as HR practitioners.

Whilst the book's strong practical focus makes it different from many other texts in employee and industrial relations, it is certainly not devoid of theory. Quite the reverse in fact, but it just so happens that theoretical ideas are woven into the substantive material in each of the chapters in a way which provides a terrific grounding for students who want to know more about *why* employee relations takes such a variety of forms in different organisations. Cases and examples help to embed this understanding more effectively within the CIPD framework. Moreover, compared with the first edition, which was written nearly a decade ago, this book goes way beyond a UK-oriented approach to employee relations, drawing heavily on the legal and political environment in which employers now operate and making readers aware that all organisations operate within an increasingly global economy.

In short, students will find this book satisfies all their needs if they are doing a CIPD course on employee relations as it covers the professional standards much more systematically than any of the competitors. The insights it provides for those working in employee relations are also significant, and practitioners ought to find it invaluable after they have completed their studies and are looking for solutions to organisational problems. Try to think of this as a book for life, not just for your studies!

Professor Mick Marchington
Professor of Human Resource Management, Manchester Business School, The University of Manchester and Chief Moderator, Standards for the CIPD

Introduction

CHAPTER OBJECTIVES

There are a number of key themes associated with this book. The key ones are:

- the difference in perspective between the CIPD Practitioner Standards and an academic qualification

- the identical relevance of employee relations in non-union environments as in unionised ones

- the unforeseen impact of changes in the corporate environment on the balance of bargaining power between the employers and employees, and on the employee relations policies adopted by an organisation

- the influence of Europe and European institutions on the employment relationship, and the need for practitioners to be aware of, and understand, this influence

- the important requirement for management to behave in a fair and reasonable and consistent manner

- the need to evaluate whether new employment practices introduced into one organisation can be successfully transplanted into another

- the day-to-day grind of intra- and inter-management negotiations.

THE CIPD PRACTITIONER STANDARDS

This book is written to meet the needs of the students seeking to reach the Chartered Institute of Personnel and Development's Practitioner Level Standards in employee relations. This is the criterion against which the relevance of this book must be judged. It does set out to cater for the needs of those students seeking to gain a Master's degree in human resource management. Other employee relations textbooks (see below) provide for this need better than this one. The expected outcomes of a Master's degree and those of the CIPD Practitioner Level Standards have a difference in emphasis between theory and practice. The former places greater emphasis on theory and the latter on practice.

The CIPD Professional Standards set out what an employee relations practitioner should be able to do and should be able to understand and explain if he or she is to operate at a professional level. Central to the Standards is that employee relations professional practitioners acquire and develop the skills to add value to the organisation that employs them by:

- making a contribution, directly or indirectly in circumstances of corporate difficulties
- helping the organisation to make progress towards its vision and its strategic goals
- working in alignment with the organisation's mission
- customer-focused continuous improvement

- personal flexibility both when reacting to change and stimulating it
- genuinely influencing corporate strategy and contributing to the bottom line.

The employee relations professional practitioner requires knowledge and understanding, but they are of limited value if he or she lacks the competencies to apply them to solving problems. The student reaching the CIPD Practitioner Standards, whether via an educational, NVQ/SVQ or the professional assessment route, should have acquired and developed 10 core competencies. These are:

1 Personal drive and effectiveness: the existence of a positive 'can do' mentality, anxious to find ways round obstacles and willing to exploit all of the available resources in order to accomplish objectives

2 People management and leadership: the motivation of others (whether subordinates, colleagues, seniors or project team members) towards the achievement of shared goals not only through the application of formal authority but also by personally role-modelling a collaborative approach, the establishment of professional credibility, and the creation of reciprocal trust

3 Business understanding: adoption of a corporate (not merely functional) perspective, including an awareness of financial issues and the accountabilities of business processes and operations, of 'customer' priorities, and of the necessity for cost/benefit calculations when contemplating continuous improvement or transformational change

4 Professional and ethical behaviour: possession of the professional skills and technical capabilities, specialist subject (especially legal) knowledge, and the integrity in decision-making and operational activity that are required for effective achievement in the personnel and development arena

5 Added-value result achievement: a desire not to concentrate solely on tasks, but rather to select meaningful accountabilities – to achieve goals that deliver added-value outcomes for the organisation, but simultaneously to comply with relevant legal and ethical obligations

6 Continuing learning: commitment to continuing improvement and change by the application of self-managed learning techniques, supplemented where appropriate by deliberate, planned exposure to external learning sources (mentoring, coaching, etc)

7 Analytical and intuitive/creative thinking: the application of a systematic approach to situational analysis, the development of convincing, business-focused action plans, and (where appropriate) the deployment of intuitive/creative thinking in order to generate innovative solutions and proactively seize opportunities

8 'Customer' focus: concern for the perceptions of personnel and development's customers, including (principally) the central directorate of the organisation; a willingness to solicit and act upon 'customer' feedback as one of the foundations for performance improvement

9 Strategic thinking: the capacity to create an achievable vision for the future, to foresee longer-term developments, to envisage options (and their probable consequences), to select sound courses of action, to rise above the day-to-day detail, to challenge the status quo

10 Communication, persuasion and interpersonal skills: the ability to transmit information to others, especially in written (report) form, both persuasively and urgently; to display listening, comprehension and understanding skills, plus sensitivity to the emotional, attitudinal and political aspects of corporate life.

The employee relations professional practitioner thus requires business orientation, application capability, knowledge and understanding of employee relations activities and persuasion and presentational skills. Individuals with the CIPD graduate membership qualification should be capable of adding value for the business. They cannot do this on their own. They need to collaborate with others, both within and outside the organisation, in order to make a value-adding organisation contribution.

These outcomes are not what academics would emphasise in a Master's degree programme. Here students would be expected to be aware of the plurality of perspectives on employee relations issues and theories and be able to evaluate critically the behaviour of the employee relations players. Skills development to solve employee relations problems would have much less emphasis. So, for students on a CIPD-accredited postgraduate Master's course in HRM at a university, this textbook is essential reading. However, students seeking to gain the graduate membership of the CIPD in an institute that has no degree-awarding powers do need to read one of the more theoretically centred employee relations textbooks – such as:

- Hollinghead S., Nichols P., Tailby S. and Leat M. (2003) *Employee Relations*, 2nd edn. Prentice Hall/*Financial Times*
- Rose E. (2004) *Employment Relations. Financial Times*/Prentice Hall
- Salamon M. (2004) *Industrial Relations: Theory and practice*, 4th edn. *Financial Times*/Prentice Hall.

It is important to be aware of contemporary research by academics as well as practitioners and policy-makers in the field of employee relations.

THE RELEVANCE OF EMPLOYEE RELATIONS TO ALL ORGANISATIONS

It is a misunderstanding to believe employee relations is only a relevant management activity if the organisation deals with trade unions. In non-union environments, as in unionised ones, collective relationships exist. In non-union firms there are employee representative bodies (for example, Employee Councils, Works Councils, Joint Consultative Committees) and just as in unionised environments employee grievances have to be resolved, disciplinary matters processed, procedures devised, implemented, operated and monitored. In addition, in non-unionised situations, as well as unionised ones, the support and loyalty from one's management colleagues, at all levels of seniority, has to be gained by using inter alia negotiating, interviewing and communication skills. Employee relations knowledge, understanding and skills acquisition is just as relevant to non-union environments as unionised environments.

As we shall explain, an important employee relations concept is the relative balance of bargaining power between the buyers and sellers of labour services, and the knowledge that important determinants of this relationship are external to the organisation – for example, government economic and legislative policies. One result of this is that the key employee relations policies and practices can be rendered irrelevant, illegal or more expensive to operate because of legislative intervention. Instances include the changes in representational rights in grievance and disciplinary procedures and the statutory recognition procedures contained in the Employment Relations Act (1999), and the changes in maternity leave, disciplinary procedures, etc, introduced by the Employment Act 2002. The professional employee relations manager has to be capable of offering advice as to how his or her organisation might deal with such situations that stem from decision-making sources over which companies have no direct control. This book is designed to help in this regard.

Changes in the corporate environment by influencing the balance of bargaining power, help explain changes over time (for example, the present decade relative to the 1970s) in the employee relations behaviour of employees and employers in terms of processes used, the subject of rules, regulations and agreements and their authorship. In the 1970s when the corporate environment was very different from today, trade unions grew steadily, strike action was more frequent and higher wage increases were gained by employees from their employers. In today's corporate environment, trade union membership has fallen, strike action has fallen, employers are able to decide unilaterally on the rules and regulations governing employment, and – courtesy of low inflation – wage increases are much smaller. Employee relations managers-professionals require an understanding of the impact of changes in the corporate environment on management employee relations strategy, policies and agreements in order to predict the impact of possible external changes on the organisation's employee relations and to discern how they might seek to mitigate them.

In conducting their employee relations activities, professional managers should behave in a fair and reasonable manner – and seek to persuade their management colleagues to behave in a like manner. This means acting with just cause (for example, having a genuine reason to dismiss a worker or for selecting an employee for redundancy) and behaving in procedural terms via a series of stages in which behaviour is compatible with the standards of natural justice – for example, a statement of the complaint against the individual is drawn up, a proper investigation is undertaken, the accused is given the opportunity to cross-examine witnesses, there is sufficient time made available for the accused to prepare their defence, an appeals procedure exists, and different individuals are involved at the different stages in the operation of the procedure.

It is important for personnel/HR managers to appreciate that the underlying principle of employee relations procedures is that they establish standards of behaviour which will pass the tests of reasonableness. However, personnel/HR managers must appreciate not only what constitutes fair and reasonable behaviour but why such good practice is essential to protecting and advancing management's interests – namely, the avoidance of adverse financial consequences through the payment of compensation to individuals wronged by such action, and of damaging the organisation's labour market image in the eyes of the sellers of labour services. As we have already indicated, managers by behaving in a fair and reasonable manner (best practice) help to add value to the business. This is a key theme of the book.

Change and innovation in employee relations policies and practices to gain a competitive advantage or to deliver a service at a higher quality is essential in a modern competitive-based economy. New and developing management practices (for example, performance-related pay, single-union-no-strike agreements) of the 1980s have been successfully introduced into organisations. However, employee relations practitioners cannot assume that such practices can automatically be transferred successfully to their own organisation, which may be operating in very different environments. They must be able to evaluate whether practices successfully introduced in one organisation can be successfully transplanted into their own. Organisations cannot change policies and practices constantly without any reference to the organisational needs of existing practices. A further assumption of this book is that 'new initiatives' in management practice have to be evaluated in a rational manner as to whether they can be introduced with equal success into another organisation.

Yet another theme of this book is how important it is for personnel/HR professional practitioners to understand why negotiating skills are necessary for the effective solution of people management problems. They need to be able to identify the different negotiating situations (grievance-handling, bargaining, group problem-solving) in which managers may find themselves, appreciate the different stages through which negotiation may proceed and take account of the skills required in different negotiation situations.

THE INFLUENTIAL MANAGER

If personnel/HR professional practitioners, at any level of seniority, are to be pro-active and to have influence in an organisation, they must demonstrate certain abilities (see Figure 1). First, they require a successful record of professional competence in the personnel/HRM field, which is recognised by their

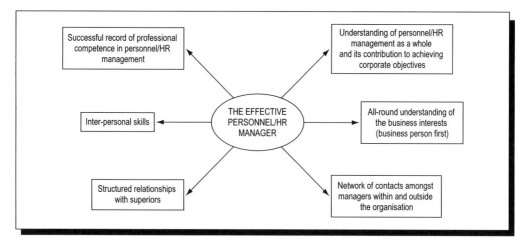

Figure 1 *The abilities required of a personnel/HR professional practitioner*

managerial colleagues both within and outside the personnel/HRM function. Second, they must demonstrate an understanding of the personnel/HRM function as a whole and how its separate components integrate. Third, they must understand the interests of the business/organisation as a whole and that these take preference over those of any management function as a whole or their component parts. Fourth, they must develop a network of contacts with managers, both within and outside the personnel/HRM function, in their own organisation and with managers in other organisations, including employers' associations and professional bodies such as the Chartered Institute of Personnel and Development (CIPD) and the British Institute of Management (BIM). Fifth, they also require to build fruitful relationships with their superiors and, sixth, to possess excellent inter-personal skills, particularly with respect to communications and team-building. Each of these six abilities is a necessary condition for an effective and influential personnel/HRM professional practitioner, but each is an insufficient ability on its own.

All people managers regardless of their seniority (personnel assistant, officer, manager, executive, etc) must understand the nature of the business of the organisation in which they manage in terms of its mission, objectives, strategies and policies. In the private sector, the effective and influential personnel/HRM professional practitioners will understand the 'bottom line' for the business and be able to contribute constructively, at the appropriate level of decision-making (department, section, management team, working party, etc), to discussions on how the business might be developed and expanded. In the public sector, the effective and influential personnel/HR practitioner will understand the objectives of efficiency, effectiveness, economy, 'value for money' and the quality of service delivery to the customer or client.

The effective personnel/HRM professional practitioner can explain how the various components of resourcing, development, reward and relations contribute to the achievement of the objectives of the personnel/HR function. This means that he or she must fully understand how the strategies and policies of the components of the personnel/HR function link together to achieve the goals of the function. The horizontal integration of the personnel/HRM function will not be new to you because it has been a central theme in your people management and development studies. It is important during your employee relations studies that you understand such vertical and horizontal integration.

The effective personnel/HRM professional practitioner in a management team has a proven competence recognised by his or her management colleagues in employee relations as well as employee resourcing, training and development and pay and reward. It is essential, therefore, if personnel/HR practitioners are to be effective, that they have an adequate knowledge and understanding of employee relations and have acquired the appropriate skills to apply that knowledge and understanding to solve employee relations problems in order to enable the organisation to achieve its commercial and/or societal objectives. An implication of this statement is that not only do existing, and prospective, personnel/HR professional practitioners need to acquire employee relations knowledge, understanding and skills but so do all managers, regardless of their seniority or specialism.

The personnel/HRM practitioner who lacks professional competence in employee relations will be a less effective manager. The trend in many organisations to devolve their personnel/HRM function across management teams reinforces this view. Devolution often means that the services of a personnel/HR professional practitioner with a specialism will not always be required. However, the activities of the employee relations function (for example, communications policy, handling employee grievances, dealing with disciplinary matters and the adjustment of the size of the workforce) must nevertheless be delivered to the management team. Generalist personnel/HR practitioners with employee relations skills are therefore essential to any management team. Specialist personnel/HR practitioners are less attractive to a management team.

This book therefore aims to provide the generalist personnel/HRM professional practitioner – and any other managers who have to manage people – with the appropriate employee relations knowledge, and to provide them with the understanding and skills they require to apply that knowledge and understanding to solving people management problems. This in turn will contribute to the organisation's achieving its commercial and/or social objectives. It will have the additional advantage of enhancing the creditability of the personnel/HRM practitioner in the eyes of his or her managerial colleagues both within and outside the personnel/HRM function.

A central theme of the book is that 'good practice' in the delivery of the personnel/HRM strategy and policies adds value to the business and thereby contributes to the achievement of the corporate-organisational economic and social objectives. It explains not only what constitutes good practice (that this is acting with just cause and behaving fairly and reasonably) but why operating to good practice standards is sound business practice – for example, avoiding falling foul of industrial tribunal decisions in terms of having 'bad' practices exposed and thus embarrassing the organisation. The book also aims to help personnel/HR professional practitioners develop and acquire skills, not only to solve their people management problems but also to develop and improve their inter-personal skills and thereby the quality of their relationships with superiors.

If HR practitioners are to be effective and influential, they require to be 'generalist' *not* 'specialist' personnel/HR managers. Generalist personnel managers require an adequate knowledge, understanding and skills of employee relations. If they neglect this and concentrate exclusively on development, or resourcing or reward, they will be less effective managers.

EMPLOYEE RELATIONS ACTIVITIES

The purpose of employee relations activity is to determine the 'rules' that will govern the employment relationship. These rules reconcile the different interests of the buyers of labour services (employers) and of the sellers of labour services (employees), and in so doing assist the organisation to achieve its business and/or social objectives. This difference of interests revolves around the 'price' (including the quality and quantity) at which labour services are bought and sold. Although there is this difference of interests, both management and employees have a common interest in reconciling these differences. The alternative is mutual destruction of the organisation. The closure of the enterprise is of no benefit to employers or employees. There is mutual advantage to both employers and employees in making rules to resolve their differences as buyers and sellers of labour market services. These employment rules take the form of agreements and regulations and are made through the use of various employee relations processes – employee involvement, collective bargaining, unilateral imposition by management, joint consultation, arbitration, mediation and conciliation and Parliamentary legislation.

The agreements and regulations express the price at which labour services are bought and sold and are made at different levels (workplace, company, industry) and have different degrees of authorship. Some are written solely (imposed) by the employer with little or no influence from the employees, whereas others, usually as a result of collective bargaining, are jointly authored by the employer and representatives of their employees. Agreements and regulations cover two broad range of issues. One is substantive issues (pay, holidays, hours of work, incentive schemes, pensions, sick pay, maternity leave, family-friendly policies, etc) and the other is procedural issues. Employee relations procedures provide fair and reasonable standards of behaviour to resolve in a peaceful manner issues over which employers and employees have differences. Such procedures normally cover issues such as employee complaints against the behaviour of employers (known as grievances), employer complaints about the behaviour of employees (referred to as disciplinary matters), the need to reduce the size of the workforce (redundancy), employee claims that the responsibilities of their job have increased (job grading), and employee requests for union representation (union recognition procedures).

The content of agreements and regulations and the employee relations processes used to secure them reflect the relative balance of bargaining power between employers and employees. This balance is heavily influenced by changes in the corporate environment in which an organisation undertakes its employee relations activity. The major facts of shaping the external corporate environment are the economic and legal policies of national governments and the European Union political decision-making institutions. In an attempt to enhance their economic interests, both employers and employees, via representative organisations, spend relatively large sums of money on the political lobbying process to persuade the government to introduce appropriate economic and legal policies. A further factor in the external corporate environment that influences employee relations is the implementation, by employers, of technological change.

The balance of bargaining power is a central concept that must be understood by the employee relations professional practitioner. It helps to explain the constraints in which managements can exercise their power. Abuse of power to obtain one's aims is not professional behaviour. It inevitably leads to pressure for legal restraints to be imposed to curb the abuse. Unprofessional behaviour which suggests that 'might is right' will result in employees behaving in that way when the balance of bargaining power shifts away from management towards the employees. Professionalism requires tackling matters in a systematic and careful manner. The fact that at a point in time the state of the balance of bargaining power means that management can 'succeed' without behaving in this way is no excuse for managers not to behave in a professional way. Good practice dictates that they behave in a professional manner, gaining consent by discussion, consultation, negotiation and involvement – not by the crude exercise of power.

However, personnel/HR professional practitioners require more than just knowledge and understanding of employee relations parties, processes, agreements and regulations and the external environment in which these activities take place if they are to solve effectively people management problems. Employee relations problem-solving also requires the development and application of certain skills, of which the most significant are communication (oral and written), interviewing, listening, negotiating, evaluating and analysis.

This book thus endeavours to widen and develop the employee relations knowledge and understanding you acquired in your core people management and development studies. It provides sufficient knowledge, understanding and skills for employee relations practitioners and for those who manage people in other management functions to operate as professional people managers in a number of different situations, including both union and non-union environments. The book also aims to introduce you to how essential it is for employee relations professionals practitioners to become effective and influential in the organisation by understanding the concepts of good practice and the balance of bargaining power, and acquiring and developing the general management skills referred to above.

THE BOOK AND THE CIPD PRACTITIONER STANDARDS

The CIPD Professional Development Standards on employee relations are arranged under five headings:

- employee relations management in context
- the parties in employee relations
- employee relations processes
- employee relations outcomes
- employee relations skills.

In this book, sections that fall within *employee relations management in context* describe the corporate environment in which organisations undertake their internal employee relations activities. A growing and important part of this external environment is the evolution of the 'social' dimension (Social Chapter, Social Charter) of the European Union. This section of the Standards also covers the role of the national government as an economic manager and as a law-maker, as well as of 'state agencies' such as the Advisory, Conciliation and Arbitration Service (ACAS), the Central Arbitration Committee, the Certification Officer and the Health and Safety Commission. The employee relations management in context part of this standard is covered by Chapter 1 (Employee relations: an overview), Chapter 3 (The economic and corporate environment), Chapter 4 (The legislative framework) and Chapter 5 (The importance of the European Union).

The sections of the Standards on *the parties in employee relations* deal with management objectives and styles, employee relations strategies, gaining employee commitment and participation, and managing with or without unions. They also cover the changing role and functions of employers' associations (such as the Confederation of British Industry and the Engineering Employers' Federation) and management associations organised at the level of the European Union. The parties section of the Standards which covers employee organisations (trade unions, professional associations, staff/employee associations, etc) is dealt with in Chapter 6 (Employee relations institutions). Chapter 2 looks at management strategy and policies, together with issues such as management style and the management of change.

There is a wide range of *employee relations processes* which impact on employment relationships in organisations: joint consultation, employee involvement schemes, third-party intervention (arbitration and conciliation), collective bargaining, industrial sanctions (lock-outs, suspension, collective dismissals) and Parliamentary legislation. This part of the Standards is covered by Chapters 7 and 8.

The *employee relations outcomes* component of the Standards covers the various dimensions of agreements (both collective and individual), their types (substantive and procedural), their authorship (joint or singly by employer), the levels at which they are concluded, and their scope (the subjects covered by agreements, rules and regulations). This section of the syllabus is dealt within Chapter 6.

The *employee relations skills* section of the Standards covers the definition of negotiations, the different types of negotiating situations and the various stages involved in the negotiating process. It also covers the skills required by managers in preparing for and conducting bargaining, in presenting claims/offers and counter-offers, in searching for the common ground, in concluding the negotiations, and in writing up the agreement.

The Practitioner Standards also cover the skills required by an employee relations professional practitioner in handling employee complaints against management behaviour (commonly referred to as grievances), in handling disciplinary proceedings, in managing a redundancy situation, and in managing health and safety. It additionally covers management skills and the knowledge and understanding required in devising, reviewing and monitoring procedural arrangements.

Chapter 9 deals with negotiations in general terms (that is, its definition, its different types and its component stages) and bargaining collectively with the workforce. The chapter places great stress on the skills required of management in the preparation stages of grievance handling and bargaining, and in particular identifying the common ground with the other party via the use of techniques like 'if and then' and the 'aspiration grid'.

Chapter 10 deals with handling employee behaviour and performance issues (including disciplinary proceedings), and stresses the importance of management behaving in a fair and reasonable manner (good practice); Chapter 11 covers grievance-handling. Chapter 12 centres on managing redundancy situations and the devising, reviewing and monitoring of redundancy procedures. Chapter 13 concentrates on the management of health and safety and emphasises the need for this subject to be taken seriously and integrated with other people management policies.

We hope you enjoy reading this book. If you can acquire and develop a deep understanding and appreciation of its contents, you have an excellent chance of reaching the CIPD Practitioner Professional Standards in employee relations.

John Gennard
Graham Judge

Employee relations: an overview

CHAPTER 1

CHAPTER OBJECTIVES

This chapter introduces the components of a typical employee relations system at an international, national, company or enterprise level:

- the different, and common, interests of the 'buyers' (the employers) and the 'sellers' of labour services (employees) in the management of employees: these are the 'players' (the participants) in the employee relations game

- the processes (mechanisms) available to employers and employees whereby they agree rules and regulations to govern the employment relationship and at the same time accommodate their differing interests

- the rules, regulations and agreements made (and by whom) to regulate the employment relationship (the outcome – output – of the employee relations game): these rules are the 'price' at which labour services are exchanged in the labour market

- the relative balance of bargaining power between employers and employees, and how this influences the mechanisms used to establish employment rules, etc, and the content of those rules, regulations and agreements: this relationship is influenced by the internal and external context (environment) of the organisation, of the sector of the economy and of the national economy in which the game of employee relations is played.

INTRODUCTION

Twenty-five years ago, the conventional approach to employee relations centred on trade union behaviour, collective bargaining, industrial disputes and UK government-trade union relationships. Trade unions were regarded as workplace adversaries negotiating with employers and also as social partners expressing an 'employee view' on economic and social matters, particularly through the Trades Union Congress, to governments.

Collective relationships were seen as adversarial. The employer/individual employee relationship was perceived as secondary. The context in which the employee relations game took place was one of full employment. If this led to increasing inflation, the UK government of the day sought to contain it by interfering directly with the collective bargaining process through the imposition of an incomes policy designed to limit the rate of increase in money wages. Although the extent to which this employers-propose/unions-oppose approach squares (or squared) with reality can be questioned, there is no doubt the perspective is seen as of lesser relevance to today's employment relationship. The institutions of trade unions, collective bargaining procedures and arrangements, strikes and tripartism have declined steadily over the last 25 years. Indeed, the 1998 Workplace Employee Relations Survey reported that 47 per cent of workplaces have no union members at all.

Attitudes to work and relationships at work have certainly changed since the late 1970s. The driving forces for this have been a marked change in the context in which the game of employee relations has been played. The last 25 years have seen increased product and labour market competition, reductions in international trade barriers, the imposition of public sector financial constraints, pressures for better value for money, the implementation of rapidly changing and easily transferable technologies and increasing demands by customers that products and services are customised to their needs. In this changed environment, the focus of employee relations has changed. There is now greater focus on the individual employee rather than on the employees as a collective body. Collective relationships are now based on relatively more co-operation in which both parties are motivated to add value to the organisation. Such employment relationships are seen as based on:

- the success of the enterprise
- building employee trust, feelings of fairness and greater commitment
- enhancing the satisfaction employees get from their work
- providing all employees with a voice to influence, and be involved in, decisions that are likely to affect their interests (employee voice). The form of this employee voice is no longer solely that of a trade union. There are now others – for example, Works Councils, business enhancement forums and quality circles
- helping the organisation to improve productivity, profitability and efficiency.

These changing approaches to employee relations are reflected in the management-led changes in communication methods (for example, team briefing), in work organisation (quality circles, teamworking and single status), in changes in payment systems (for example, performance-related pay), in changes in employees' representative systems (business-focused consultation arrangements), in the recognition of the employees' need for employment security (training and development of employees), in attitudes towards trade union recognition, in patterns of working (part-time, shift work, annualised hours) and in employment status (temporary/agency workers, fixed-term contract).

Although the context in which employee relations takes place changes over time, giving rise to different behaviour by the parties and different outcomes, the basic purpose of the game remains the same. The purpose of employee relations is to establish rules, regulations and agreements to regulate the employment relationship. The priority given to the individual employment relationship as opposed to the collective employment relationship within companies depends on management's view of what is in the best interests of the business/organisational employee relations. It is concerned with how to gain, in a number of different situations, employees' commitment to the achievement of an organisation's business goals and objectives. It is also about changing attitudes so that the organisation establishes rules, regulations and agreements which enable an organisation to implement organisational change successfully.

An Institute of Personnel and Development (IPD) Position Paper in 1997 advocated an employee relations system in which the regulatory rules, etc, encouraged the achievement of higher skill levels, better skill utilisation, greater co-operation within the workplace and the acceptance by the workforce of initiatives to develop higher added value through differentiated goods and services. In this model of employee relations, organisations are seen to succeed by:

- raising the skills of their employees
- providing high-quality services and products
- giving excellent customer service.

These, in turn, generate high profits, high earnings and a relatively more secure future for employees. In practical terms, the model embraces effective performance, good people management practices based on trust, fairness and delivery of the deal, a knowledge and understanding of employees' aspirations, and attention to the 'employee voice' obtained through a variety of channels (for example, employee involvement and participation, and trade union representatives).

EMPLOYEE RELATIONS SYSTEMS' COMPONENTS

Employee relations systems in any organisations have a number of components. These are shown in Figure 2. First, there are the 'players' of the employee relations game. The principal 'players' are:

- individual employers
- individual employees
- employee representative bodies (staff associations, trade unions, works councils, etc)
- employers' associations
- private companies
- public bodies
- voluntary organisations (for example, the Save the Children Fund).

These 'players' operate in a labour market in which they attempt to protect and advance their economic interests relative to each other. Although sellers (employees) in the labour market have interests that are different from the buyers (employers) both have a common interest in finding their opposite number. Both employees and employers have a common interest in the survival of the employing enterprise even though they may disagree on how any surplus generated by the sales of its products or services should be divided amongst themselves. They have a mutual interest in resolving this problem because not to do

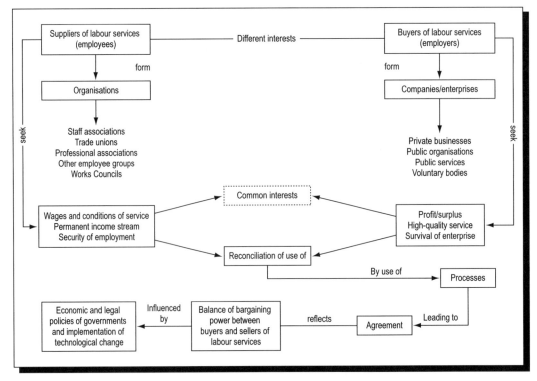

Figure 2 *Employee relations: the reconciliation of interests – players in the game*

so will result in mutual destruction. An analysis of the interests of the 'players' in the employee relations game is thus a central concern of employee relations.

The employee relations 'players' also have expectations of how each will behave towards the other. This is referred to as the 'psychological contract', which has been described by Schien (1978) as "a set of unwritten, reciprocal expectations between an individual employee and the organisation". It is based on the notion that, in addition to the formal employment contract, employees develop a set of informal unwritten assumptions and expectations from their employing organisation. These are said to depend on employee trust, perceptions of fairness and reliable delivery of the deal over a range of issues such as job satisfaction, career progression, reward, relationships with managers, well being (employment security, involvement via voice to the employer and skills development) and technology upgrading. It is a concept that enables conclusions to be drawn about the quality of the employment relationship in the UK (IPD, 1998).

The second component is the mechanisms available to the buyers and sellers of labour services to agree rules and regulations to govern the employment relationship and at the same time arrive at an accommodation of their different economic interests. The mechanisms by which the employee relations game is played include:

- consultation
- employee involvement and participation
- communication processes
- collective bargaining
- conciliation, mediation, arbitration and enquiry
- legal regulation by the UK Parliament and the European Union.

The third component is the agreements and regulations (ie the rules) that govern the employment relationship for an individual and/or group of employees and that result from the use of these mechanisms. These rules are also a statement of the rights, responsibilities and obligations employers and employees have towards each other.

The context

The fourth component is the context in which the employee relations game is played. The game does not take place in a vacuum. It takes place within an organisation that operates in product and labour markets, has product and/or service delivery mechanisms, and has its own culture, values, past experiences and internal politics. All these factors have an influence on the employee relations processes used in that organ-isation and the outcomes of the use of the processes. In short, they influence the relative power relation-ship between the employee relations players in the organisation (see below). The employee relations game in any organisation is also influenced by the external environment in which the organisation operates. In this respect, the macro-economic and employment law initiatives of the UK government are crucial. With respect to employment law initiatives, the actions of the European Union are becoming increasingly more important.

Employment legislation stipulates the redress one party can seek from the other if it steps outside the minimum standards of behaviour set down in the appropriate legislation. The UK government's economic and legal policies (also those of the EU) influence, at the macro level, the relative bargaining power between the buyers and sellers of labour services, which then affects the choice of employee relations processes used as well as the outcomes from their use. If UK government economic and legal policies are more favourable to the interests of employees (for example, by pursuit of full employment policies), it will be reflected in the content of the 'rules' regulating the employment relationship.

The mechanism used and the output (ie the rules, regulations and agreements) of the employee relations game in any organisation is also influenced by the balance of bargaining power at the multi-sector, sector and enterprise level. This requires the employee relations professional to analyse variables such as the strategic position workers hold in the production or service provision process and the availability of an alternative workforce to the one currently employed. If a group of workers has the power to stop an organisation's activities, is willing to exercise that power, and has exercised it successfully in the past, the group will have a relatively greater bargaining power than the employer and will be able to obtain a 'price' for its labour services that is closer to its ideal economic objectives than it is to the economic objectives of the employer.

What are the four main components of the employee relations game in any organisation?

THE EMPLOYER'S INTERESTS IN THE LABOUR MARKET

Employee relations is a management problem-solving activity designed to establish the rules, regulations and agreement by which the services of employees are bought and sold – that is, the 'price' at which labour services are to be exchanged in the labour market. The word 'price' is in quotation marks because employers seek to secure labour services on the most advantageous terms they can through offering a package of employment conditions that contains monetary (pay, paid holidays, etc) and non-monetary (opportunities for career development, good working conditions, colleagues) advantages and disadvantages.

The employer's employment package

The monetary considerations taken into account by an employer in purchasing labour services include:

- pay
- hours of work
- paid holidays
- sick pay schemes
- incentive schemes
- pension arrangements
- the provision of family-friendly policies such as childcare facilities, flexible working arrangements, etc.

In return for provision of these items, employers expect their employees to provide, depending on the skill and status of the job:

- flexibility between tasks (functional flexibility)
- minimum standards of competence in the task for which they are being hired, as expressed in qualifications, training received and the employee's experience
- a willingness to change (aptitude and adaptability)
- an ability to work as a member of a team
- a capability to show initiative
- a talent to give discretionary effort
- a demonstrable commitment to the organisation's objectives.

In recruiting labour services, the employer trades off items in a package of conditions. A management that would, for example, like to be able to hire and fire labour services at will (numerical flexibility) may be willing to offer potential employees – depending on the state of the labour market – a higher financial reward to compensate for the reduced job security. However, if jobs are scarce, an employer may not have to make such a trade-off. Employers who prefer to deploy any labour services they purchase, thereby requiring flexibility between various tasks, are likely to offer a package of higher financial rewards in order to attract employees who can adapt relatively easily to change.

If employers wish to purchase high-quality labour services in terms of skills, attitude, etc, they may offer a package of financial rewards that is more advantageous than those being offered by employers who are happy to purchase lower-quality labour services. In every sector of the economy there are some employers who are more prepared than their competitors to invest in better employment conditions. The argument is that the higher financial rewards given the employees are more than offset by the increased productivity, lower labour turnover, greater motivation, etc, that results from purchasing higher-quality labour services.

In purchasing labour services, employers cannot ignore the longer-term interests of their organisation. Although employers may like to hire and fire employees at will, they nevertheless require a core of permanent employees to provide continuity and some stability if they are to survive in the marketplace. The size of this core workforce, in relation to those hired and fired at will, is a matter for commercial judgement by each organisation.

The package offered, and accepted, by the suppliers of labour services, may be minimal, consisting of low wages, long hours, few opportunities to acquire and develop skills and little employment security. The suppliers of labour services may be prepared to accept such a package because the alternative is unemployment. However, suppliers of labour services who work under such an employment package are likely to have low morale, perform at standards below their capability and feel no commitment or loyalty to the purchaser of their labour services. Low morale and low commitment have adverse consequences for an organisation's economic performance and/or the quality of service offered to customers. In the long run, the employment of a 'poor' quality of labour services increases an organisation's costs, reduces its competitiveness in the product market and puts at risk its very survival.

In purchasing labour services, the package of conditions the buyers will have to offer is influenced by the relative balance of bargaining power between the buyers and sellers. If the relative bargaining power favours the buyers, the buyers will purchase labour services for a lesser package of conditions than if the power relationship were reversed. But if the buyers of labour services abuse this market power by offering unacceptably low wages and conditions, pressures will develop for the state to restrain – by legal regulation – the misuse of such power. It was such behaviour – admittedly, on behalf of a small number of employers – that led to the imposition by the UK government from 1 April 1999 of a national minimum wage to be paid to all those in employment aged over 18. So in offering a package of conditions to employees employers must have regard to longer-term considerations and not merely to what can 'be got away with' in the short run.

Consider a group of employees in your organisation. What package of monetary and non-monetary employment conditions does your organisation offer to attract that group to come to work for it, and to continue to work for it? Why that package?

EMPLOYEE INTERESTS IN THE LABOUR MARKET

In the labour market, the sellers of labour services seek from employers (the buyers) the best possible available package of monetary and non-monetary employment conditions available. The monetary aspects include wage/salary rates, hours of work, paid holidays, pension schemes, sick pay arrangements, incentive schemes, childcare facilities and flexible working arrangement opportunities. The non-monetary elements involve such items as:

■ employment security

■ the opportunity to work with good colleagues in a sociable atmosphere

■ the potential for advancement and promotion

■ access to training and development opportunities to upgrade skills, acquire new skills, etc

■ being treated as a human being, not merely a commodity

■ job satisfaction in relation to job design, the degree of control over the job (empowerment)

■ family-friendly employment policies (eg flexible working arrangements), which enable a balance to be achieved between being a family person and the need to take paid employment to provide for that family

■ fair and consistent treatment by managers relative to other employees

■ influence on the day-to-day operations at the workplace and at policy level (a voice heard by management).

Like the buyers of labour services, employees also give different weight to the items in the package of employment conditions on offer. They may, for example, be prepared to work for 'lower' wages if this is compensated by greater employment security. Some employees may, for example, stay with an organisation even though it pays below the market rates because it practises employee involvement and empowerment by vesting decision-making with the team leaders or promotes self-managing teams.

It is impossible to tell what a 'standard mix' of benefits sought from employment by employees would include. Motivation theory postulates that each individual is stimulated by his or her own package and that as economic and social conditions change, the pressures on employees alter with them. The balance between the various items in the package depends on many factors, including age, family circumstances, local and industry-specific employment conditions, and the national scene. Nevertheless, employees – like any seller in a marketplace – seek the best possible package of monetary and non-monetary employment conditions.

> What is your monetary and non-monetary package of employment conditions? Which are the most important to you? Why?

THE EMPLOYMENT RELATIONSHIP

The employment relationship has some similarities with all transactions. A golden rule of buying is to purchase goods or services of acceptable quality at the lowest price obtainable. The seller (the employee) wishes to sell at the highest possible price. To reach agreement, employees must accommodate each other's interests and establish an appropriate price.

However, the employment relationship is more stable and longer-term than that between the buyer and seller of a commodity such as a house or piece of equipment, furniture, etc. In that kind of activity, the buyers and sellers engage in a one-off and immediate exchange relationship. The parties involved in the labour market, on the other hand, are entering what is expected to be a long-term relationship involving terms that will be reviewed periodically and amended if necessary. In short, a particular feature of the employment relationship is that it has a future.

Different interests within management

There are differences of interest within management at all levels of an organisation, including the workplace. Although working to a common end, management is not a united whole. Managers have differences which, like those between the employers and employees, have to be reconciled if corporate objectives are to be achieved.

In larger organisations, common management activities are divided into different functions – for example, marketing, production-operations, personnel and finance. These management interest groups have a common interest in the survival and growth of the business but often have different and competing interests at the same time. While the common aim of all is to ensure that the products or services reach their destinations at the right time and are of the right quality, internal power struggles (management politics) and competition for shares of a finite budget often play off one management interest against another.

The main aim of production-operations management is usually the achievement of production targets, and to this end they may consider the organisation's best interests are served by employment policies that permit the hiring and firing of labour and the granting of employee demands to prevent production-service disruptions. This approach conflicts with that of people managers who believe the organisation's interests are best served by recruiting, selecting and/or dismissing employees in accordance with good personnel practices, and rewarding them on objective criteria rather than in order solely to meet market demand at any costs.

Differences between interest groups within management are resolved by negotiation between themselves or by arbitration by a more senior manager. Using persuasion and perhaps making constructive compromises, managers seek to gain the commitment of their managerial colleagues to their proposed course of action. Should managers at the same level of seniority be unable to settle their differences by negotiation, a senior manager will arbitrate and decide the appropriate course of action to be adopted.

Employee relations professionals cannot take it for granted that what they propose will be accepted at once and without question by other managers. However, differences between managers have to be reconciled in a constructive, not a destructive, manner. Most management differences can be resolved quickly. As an employee relations professional, you will find yourself frequently negotiating with your management colleagues (at the same, a lower or a higher level of seniority) to resolve differences over what constitutes 'good' employee relations policies and practices to be implemented if the organisation is to achieve its objectives.

> When did you last have a difference with a colleague over how a problem should be resolved? What was the problem about? What were the differences between you? What was the resolution of the difference? Why was there a difference in the first place?

Different interests among employees

Just as there is a plurality of interests within and between groups of managers, so there is within and between groups of employees. In a workplace, different types of employees (technical, clerical, administrative, craft manual, semi-skilled and unskilled, etc) are employed and have different interests from each other. Non-manual employees usually expect a positive employment conditions differential over manual workers. Skilled manual workers see their interests, relative to those of lesser-skilled workers, best served by pay differentials expressed in percentage terms. If this percentage figure is reduced, skilled manual workers usually demand improvements in pay and conditions to re-establish accepted percentage differentials.

Lesser-skilled manual workers (who also tend to be low-paid) view their interests relative to skilled manual workers best served by pay differentials expressed in money terms. They oppose percentage increases in pay on the grounds that such increases widen monetary differentials. Such differences between the various groups of employees continue. These differences of interests between various groups of employees often make it difficult for them to support each other in differences with employers.

Recognition of different interests

Employee relations aims to resolve differences between the various interest groups regardless of whether these groups comprise different categories of managers or employees. The bottom line is that the activity of the organisation has to continue even if the behaviour to make it happen must alter, depending on the current situation and the underlying climate of employee relations. In organisations, whether non-union or unionised, where the emphasis is on problem-solving, consultation and communications procedures, differences of interests between employers and employees are formally recognised in written statements of policy and procedures and/or in collective agreements with trade unions. For example, Clauses 2.3 and 2.4 (General Principles) of a union recognition procedural agreement at a carpet manufacturing firm in the West Midlands state:

> 2.3   The union recognises management's responsibility to plan, organise and manage the company's operation.
>
> 2.4   The company recognises the union's responsibility to represent the interests of its members and to maintain or improve their terms and conditions of employment and work within the constraints imposed on the plant by corporate policy and finance.

Another example can be drawn from a procedural agreement between a food manufacturer in the west of Scotland and AMICUS which states in its preamble:

> The company recognises the union as the sole collective bargaining agent in respect of the categories of employees coming within the scope of this agreement.
>
> The union recognises management's responsibility to manage its establishments and accepts that the company must continue with new and improved methods of work and that the company must be able to make free and intelligent use of its labour force to achieve the highest quality of service and obtain maximum efficiency ...

Yet another example of the recognition of the difference of interests between employers and employees is to be seen in the recognition agreement between an electricity cable manufacturer in north-east England and the Transport and General Workers Union, which contains the following :

> 3   General Principles
>
> The company has the right to manage the business and direct its affairs and workforce in the efficient pursuit of the organisation's business.
>
> The company recognises the union's responsibility to manage its affairs and to represent the interests of its members.
>
> Both parties agree the need to maintain open and direct communications with all employees on matters of mutual interest and concern.

The aim of employee relations is to resolve areas of conflicting interests and to identify and pursue areas of common interest so as to maintain the business organisation. We now turn to these common interests.

EMPLOYER-EMPLOYEE COMMON INTERESTS

Unless the organisation keeps running, there is nothing to manage, no profit to be made, no service to provide and no pay for work done. Although, as buyers and sellers of labour services, employers and employees have different interests, they have a common interest in ensuring that their different interests are reconciled. There are strong economic pressures on employers and employees to accommodate each other's interests rather than to perpetuate their differences.

Costs to employers

If employers fail to reconcile their different interests with their employees, a number of costs arise:

- The employer has no goods/services to sell in the marketplace.
- The employer cannot earn a profit or provide services at value for money.
- Goods and services cannot be supplied to the marketplace at the right price, at the right time and at the right quality.
- Customer needs cannot be satisfied.
- Factories, offices and shops, etc, lie idle or close down.
- Customers take their business to competitor firms.

Costs to employees

The consequences for employees who fail to resolve their different interests from employers are equally obvious :

- They do not remain in employment.
- They do not receive a steady income stream.
- They have no power as consumers.
- They cannot enter into long-term financial commitments (eg mortgages, bank loans, hire purchase contracts).
- They accumulate no employment benefits based on continuity of employment (eg paid holidays, sick pay entitlement and pension payments).
- There is no certainty as to the future level of income.

If employees gain no income from employment, they become dependent on the state for a minimum level of income to satisfy their basic needs of housing, heating, lighting, food, etc.

The recognition of common interests

Both employers and employees have an enlightened self-interest in ensuring that their differing interests are reconciled. Enlightened self-interest also helps produce a bottom line beyond which it is not worth pushing for one's own self-interest against the interests of the other party. Interest reconciliation potentially brings mutual gain. Employers secure the survival of their enterprises, gain profit or provide services at value for money, and satisfy the needs of their customers. Employees obtain job security and benefit from more income security, consumer power and status from being employed. Both employers and employees have a common interest in ensuring that companies/enterprises are successful. However, there are occasions when this common interest might not seem very common to employees, especially when told by management they are to be made redundant because cost cuts are required to re-establish the viability of the enterprise.

The recognition of this common interest is important and is frequently formally stated in agreements between employers and employees. For example, the 2004 National Agreement between the Scottish Print Employers Federation and the Graphical, Paper and Media Union says:

> 2   Unit Cost and Competitiveness
>
> The parties recognise that the whole basis of the market for printed products is changing rapidly, posing new challenges for everyone engaged in the industry. It is of fundamental importance that those challenges are met with a positive response from employers and employees in order to secure the future of Scottish printing in the face of intensifying domestic and international competition. The parties willingly accept the need for companies to attain the highest standards in meeting customers' requirements, in particular the need for continuous improvement in increasing efficiency at reducing unit costs.
>
> It is therefore agreed that at individual company level, management and chapel [workplace] representatives will co-operate fully in identifying, discussing and implementing any changes necessary to achieve increased output and lower unit costs through the most effective use of people, materials and machines.
>
> It is further agreed that where practical, managements and chapels will agree and implement efficiency and productivity measures sufficient to offset in full additional costs arising from the national wages and conditions settlement. Such measures can be wide-ranging in scope.
>
> No person will be made redundant as a direct result of implementing this clause . . .

Similarly, the Constitution and Memorandum of Agreement between the Transport and General Workers Union and the Road Haulage Association Ltd for the Road Haulage Industry (Hire and Reward) contains the following paragraph:

> Objects and functions:
>
> 3   The objects of the Council should be to promote joint action for their mutual benefit by organisations of employers and working people.

Clauses 6.2 and 6.3 of Section 6 entitled 'Competitive Advantage' of the pay and conditions agreement between Scottish Power, Power Systems, Scotland and AMICUS, GMB, the Transport and General Workers and UNISON state:

> 6.2   A key part of the competitive advantage strategy will be continuous improvement in all Power Systems activities to ensure that changing business demands can be rapidly met and best working practices, identified through benchmarking and other means, are safely implemented within the normal joint processes so that competitive advantage can be developed and maintained.
>
> 6.3   The Division and the Trade Unions agree that to achieve and maintain competitive advantage, continuous improvement and the changes which will result will be implemented on an ongoing basis, subject to the normal joint processes.

A further example of the mutual recognition of employers and trade unions and employees of common interest can be seen from the following clause, which is taken from a recognition and procedural agreement in the further education sector:

> College management, trade union and staff representatives have a common objective in the long term of ensuring the efficiency and effectiveness of the college in the interests of the students and the staff . . .

The common requirements between employers and employees to reconcile their different interests to mutual advantage was stressed in the 1997 Trade Union Congress document *Partners for Progress: Next steps for the new unionism*, in the following paragraph:

> 3   The theme of this statement is partnership, a recognition that trade unions must not be seen as part of Britain's problems but as part of the solution to the country's problems. At the workplace, social partnership means employers and trade unions working together to achieve common goals such as fairness and competitiveness; it is a recognition that although they have different constituencies, and at times different interests, they can serve these best by making common cause wherever possible. At the national level, partnership means government discussing issues with employers and trade unions on a fair and open basis where a common approach can reap dividends – for example, attracting inward investment and promoting training and equal opportunities.

One of the methods by which the different labour market interests of employers and employees are accommodated is by negotiation, which involves two parties (employers and employees) coming together to make an accommodation (agreement) by purposeful persuasion (the use of rational argument) and by making constructive compromises (identifying the common ground for a basis for agreement) towards each other's position. There are different types of negotiating situations (see Chapter 9) but the most usual of those that involve employers and employees are:

- grievance-handling to resolve a complaint by an employee that management behaviour has infringed his or her employment 'rights'
- bargaining, during which employers and employees 'trade' items within a list of demands they have made of each other
- group problem-solving, in which the employer settles the details upon which the employees will co-operate with a request from management to assist in obtaining information to help solve a problem of mutual concern.

Why do you think it is essential for employees and employers to reconcile their differences?

Alternative interest resolution mechanisms

There are, however, other ways in which the conflict of interests is accommodated. In some cases, individuals who find their aspirations (for example, for promotion or for higher pay) cannot be met with their present employer, resign their employment and go and work for another where their interests can be, or are more likely to be, better accommodated. Although labour turnover represents a peaceful method of resolving the differences of interests between employers and employees, management has to keep voluntary disengagements in such circumstances to manageable proportions, for labour turnover is not without cost to the employer.

In other circumstances accommodation may be achieved by the employer dismissing the employee. Here the employer says that it is not in the interest of the company to continue to employ the individual concerned. The employee, however, is virtually bound to hold the opposite view and see his/her interest best advanced by continuing in employment with that employer. Such opposing positions cannot be reconciled, so the employer forces the issue by dismissing the employee – who may or may not respond by complaining to an employment tribunal that he/she has been dismissed unfairly. The tribunal must then come to a decision in favour of the employer or the employee – a decision that may or may not stipulate reinstatement, re-engagement or financial compensation. Ultimately, the tribunal resolves differences of interest between the employer and the employee.

Table 1 *Distribution of workplaces and employment by workplace size*

Workplace size	Percentage of all workplaces	Percentage of all employees
25–49 employees	52	17
50–99 employees	25	16
100–199 employees	12	16
200–499 employees	8	22
500 or more	3	30

Source: 1998 Workplace Employment Relations Survey

In collective disputes, on rare occasions it can prove impossible to reconcile the interests of employers and employees. During the coal mining dispute of 1984/85 there were many skilled and patient hands at work trying to obtain a compromise settlement. However, none of their efforts sufficed to forestall the 'starvation' of the miners into returning to work after a 12-months-long strike on the same employment conditions prevailing before the dispute began in March 1984. No acceptable compromise proved available to the parties.

WHERE ARE LABOUR SERVICES EMPLOYED?

Workplace size

The 1998 Workplace Employment Relations Survey found that workplaces employing between 25 and 49 employees accounted for 52 per cent of all workplaces but only 17 per cent of all workplace employees. On the other hand, workplaces employing 500 or more accounted for only 3 per cent of all workplaces but almost 30 per cent of all workers, the remaining 70 per cent being fairly evenly distributed across other size bands (see Table 1 above).

Sector distribution

Table 2 below shows the distribution of employers by industry and sector of the economy. Some 18 per cent of workplaces were in the manufacturing sector which was predominately privately owned. This same pattern existed for wholesale and retail distribution. Marked differences were apparent in the workforce composition across the groups.

Workplaces making or doing different things had differing skill requirements and there were substantial differences in occupational composition by industry. For example, 70 per cent of education workplaces employed professional people. Plant and machine operatives were mostly found in manufacturing and transport and communications. Craft and related occupations were mainly employed in public utilities and construction. The 1998 Workplace Employment Relations Survey also reported that some 29 per cent of workplaces employed mainly women employees to the extent that at least three quarters of their employees were female. 27 per cent of workplaces employed mainly male labour services, and 44 per cent employed both male and female employees. Under a quarter of private sector workplaces had a largely female workforce compared to nearly a half in the public sector. Women employees dominated workplace employment in health (84 per cent) and education (63 per cent), whereas men dominated construction (85 per cent), transport and communications (71 per cent) and electricity, gas and water (70 per cent).

Part-time workers – defined as those working fewer than 30 hours per week – accounted for a quarter of all jobs in workplaces with 25 or more employees. 16 per cent of workplaces employed no part-time

Table 2   *Distribution of workplaces and employment by industry and sector*

Industry	Percentage of workplaces in private sector	Percentage of workplaces in public sector	All workplaces
Manufacturing	99	1	18
Electricity, gas and water	85	15	–
Construction	88	12	4
Wholesale and retail	99	1	18
Hotel and restaurants	96	4	6
Transport/communications	78	22	5
Financial services	100	0	3
Other business services	87	13	9
Public administration	–	100	6
Education	13	87	14
Health	57	43	13
Other community services	72	28	100
All workplaces	72	28	100

Source: 1998 Workplace Employment Relations Survey

workers, whereas in 26 per cent of workplaces, part-timers formed the majority of the workforce. Substantial proportions of workplaces in manufacturing, the public utilities and construction used no part-timers at all, while similarly high proportions of workplaces in wholesale and retail, hotel and restaurants, education and health employed a majority part-time workforce.

The number of employees in June 2004 (Labour Market Trends, 2004) was 26.1 million of which 4 million (17 per cent) were employed in the manufacturing sector. In 1971, manufacturing employed 8.1 million (36.3 per cent) of the workforce. In 2004, the service sector employed 22.6 million, which was 85 per cent of the total workforce. In 1971, the share of service sector employment was almost 53 per cent. In 2004, 6.4 million (more than in the whole of manufacturing) were employed in public administration, education and health, 2 million in banking, finance and insurance, and 5 million in retail and wholesale distribution, hotel and restaurants.

INTEREST-ENHANCING INSTITUTIONS
Employers
Employers seek to maintain and enhance their interests by organising themselves into companies or enterprises, of which there are four main types:

- private businesses, in which a distinction can be made between:
  - the private company owned by either an individual or a family and which has no shareholders. Such a company retains control of the decision whether to sell itself to another company

  and

  - the private company owned by shareholders but controlled by managers. Such a company can be acquired by other companies with the agreement of the shareholders irrespective of the views of the managers
- public corporations
- central and local government
- voluntary bodies.

Private businesses employ some 18 million people. Although there are large numbers of small incorporated businesses, the most common form of organisation is the registered company. A major feature of the corporate sector is the concentration of output into a small number of very large private limited companies (many of which have production or service capacity in more than one country) alongside a substantial but growing number of much smaller private firms serving local 'niche' markets. This concentration of output into fewer enterprises is the result of corporate acquisitions within countries and across national boundaries.

There is, in large, private sector businesses, a divorce of ownership by individual and institutional shareholders (such as banks and pension fund managers) and management control, which lies with a team of professional managers who are accountable to the owners for the performance of the company. Corporate strategy and its associated policies are normally decided by an executive group selected by the chief executive officer/managing director. This strategy is then taken to the plc board of directors for approval, modification or rejection. Senior, middle and junior managers are appointed to implement the policies in order to achieve the corporate strategy. In private corporations, the authority chain is from the top downwards through management structures.

Public sector organisations can be divided into public corporations, central government and local authorities. Public corporations, which include organisations such as the Royal Mail and NHS Trusts, in 2004 employed some 1.5 million people. In the same year central government employed just over half a million people, of which a half worked for the Civil Service. The numbers employed in local authorities in 2004 was some 2.1 million. By 2004, employment in the public sector had fallen to its lowest level in the post-World-War-II period.

Voluntary bodies are usually small not-for-profit organisations with social rather than economic objectives. They do, however, include some large organisations such as Oxfam, the Save the Children Fund, the British Heart Foundation, local housing associations and the Red Cross. The voluntary sector also contains worker or producer co-operatives where an enterprise is owned and controlled by its members. In 2002 it was estimated that some 500,000 were employed in voluntary organisations.

Employers associations were also used by employers to protect and advance their interests. The Annual Report of the Certification Officer, 2003/04, reports that in 2004 there were 85 such associations. Some of these are national bodies covering a whole industry (for example, the Engineering Employers' Federation); others are specialised bodies representing a segment of an industry (for example, the Newspaper Society, which represents the interests of provincial newspaper employers in England, Wales and Northern Ireland); and yet others are local associations representing geographically based industrial interests (for example, the Lancashire Textile Manufacturers Association). Employers associations' major activities fall into the following areas:

- assistance to member firms in the resolution of disputes with their employees
- general help and advice on good practice in employee relations matters
- representation of members' interests to political decision-makers at all levels
- representation of members' interests at employment tribunals
- in some cases, negotiation of collective agreements with trade unions.

The ways in which employers' associations can assist the employee relations specialist in his or her everyday job is outlined in Chapter 6.

Employees

Some employees attempt to strengthen and enhance their interests in the labour market by presenting a collective face to the employer, notably in relation to minimum conditions on which they are content to supply their labour services to the employer. The most common employee labour market organisations are:

- professional associations
- staff associations
- trade unions.

In enterprises where such organisations do not exist, employers often create a collective employee organisation (sometimes called an employee council, a Works Council, a representative committee, a business involvement group, etc) so that they can obtain a collective and representative voice from their employees. It is only in very small firms that a truly individual and personal relationship can exist between employer and employee. Once an organisation grows, in employment terms, beyond a critical size, the views of the employees are best collected (in time and efficiency terms) through some representative organisation. It becomes too time-consuming to talk to each separate employee. An employer's interests may therefore be enhanced by the employees having a representative body. However, employers' attitudes differ over what form of collective employee organisation best serves the company's interests (see Chapter 2).

Professional associations

Professional associations are not central employee relations players. They usually control the education and training of new members to the profession by acting as 'qualifying associations'. They also establish, maintain and review professional and ethical standards for their members. In addition, they advance the standing and status of the profession in the wider community. However, some professional associations – especially those whose members are mainly employed in the public sector – also protect and improve their members' employment interests in pay bargaining. In the health service, for example, there are groups of professional employees, such as nurses and midwives, who use their professional associations in the dual capacity of a professional and bargaining body.

Staff associations

Staff associations are in some cases the creation of employers who wish to keep their business non-unionised. The majority, however, are independent of the employer. Despite low membership subscriptions and lack of militancy, staff associations can, and do, for many employees provide an acceptable alternative to trade unions. This is particularly true of certain white-collar groups. Nevertheless, most staff associations are characterised by weak finances and a narrow membership base confined to a single employer (see Chapter 6).

Larger staff associations tend to acquire their own staff and premises and rely less on the employer for services and facilities. In 2004, the Certification Officer's list of employee organisations contained some

25 staff associations concentrated mainly in the financial sector, of which 15 were recognised to be independent of employer influence and domination. These staff associations are characterised by high membership density, often exceeding 75 per cent.

Trade unions

Trade unions are the best-known form of employee representative organisation. They were formed to protect and advance the interests of their members against employers and members of other trade unions. In the UK, trade unions have different recruitment strategies. Occupationally based unions (for example, BALPA and ASLEF) focus on recruiting employees who perform certain jobs. Other unions confine their recruitment to all grades of employees employed in a particular industry. These are referred to as industrial unions, although few, if any, such exist presently in the UK. General unions, such as the T&GWU and GMB, organise workers across the boundaries within and between industries. They take into membership any worker regardless of the job he or she does and the industry in which he or she does it.

In the UK, trade union organisation is characterised by a large number of small unions co-existing with a very small number of large trade unions. In 2004, 153 of the total number of trade unions registered with the Certification Officer had memberships of less than 5,000. On the other hand, 16 of the unions had memberships in excess of 100,000.

Unions represent different interests in terms of jobs, types of workers, industries, services and public and private sectors of the economy. They also have different interests within them (skilled, unskilled, non-manual workers, etc) but these are accommodated through their decision-making procedures, which are based on the principle of representative democracy. Trade unions in the UK are characterised by:

- being job-, not class-, centred
- preferring to achieve their objectives by industrial methods (for example, collective bargaining) rather than political means (for example, industrial action against government measures they dislike)
- being pragmatic rather than principled.

All the above issues surrounding trade unions are described in more detail in Chapter 6.

EMPLOYEE RELATIONS PROCESSES

In the game of employee relations, the accommodation of the interests of employers and employees is achieved by the players using various employee relations processes (mechanisms), of which the most important are:

- unilateral action
- employee involvement and participation schemes
- collective bargaining
- third-party intervention
- industrial sanctions.

In addition to these processes, the state can interfere with the buying and selling of labour services by establishing minimum terms that the employer must offer to his or her employees. It does this by way of legal regulation. Unlike the other processes listed above, management has no direct control over what legal regulation the government and/or the European Union introduces. However, management does try to influence such regulation by means of political lobbying activities. For example, in 1998 the employers succeeding in persuading the Labour government to alter its original proposal, contained in its White Paper *Fairness at Work*, that there should be no limit on the amount of compensation that could be awarded to an individual who is unfairly dismissed by his or her employer. As a result of employer pressure, the government restricted its increase to the limit on such compensation from £12,000 to £50,000.

Unilateral action

Unilateral action is where the employer is the sole author of the rules, agreements and regulations that govern the conditions under which employees work. In deciding employment conditions in this way, the employer may or may not give attention to the views (voice) of the employees. It is a methodology that was formerly associated with non-union companies, but in the last 25 years there has been an increase in the number of employers who unilaterally impose employment conditions (and changes in them) on their employees. They have justified this on the grounds of business efficiency and management's right to manage. However, even in highly unionised organisations (for example, commercial television companies and the NHS Trusts) there have been examples of the unilateral imposition of changes by management on issues such as overtime opportunities, and changes in job descriptions. At the extreme, managers who unilaterally impose changes to their employees' employment conditions are effectively saying 'Accept these new terms or consider yourself dismissed. Take it or leave it.'

Another area in which employers exercise unilateral action is the devising of company rules which are applicable to all employees and set out in the company handbook/rule book. If employees breach these rules, serious consequences – including dismissal – can arise. Such rules usually include the steps to be followed in the event of an accident, directions on maintaining security, safety and/or hygiene, the dress code, and an obligation on employees to report to the employer a change of address.

It is difficult to find out exactly how many management-imposed changes are made to the employment conditions of employees since there is no regular source of such information. The Workplace Industrial Relations Survey series, however, provide some information with respect to pay determination (see Chapter 9). The 1998 Employee Relations Survey revealed, over the economy as a whole, that more than 70 per cent of employees had their pay determined by non-collective-bargaining mechanisms, and that 30 per cent of employees (compared with 21 per cent in 1984) had their pay determined by workplace management. For a further 25 per cent (11 per cent in 1984) pay was determined by a higher level (than workplace) of management in the organisation. In 1998, in the private manufacturing and extraction sector, 48 per cent of employees (as opposed to 33 per cent in 1984) had their pay determined by workplace management and a further 24 per cent (11 per cent in 1984) by a higher level of management in the organisation. In private services in 1998, 39 per cent of employees had their pay settled by workplace management and 36 per cent by a higher level of management in the organisation. In the public sector, on the other hand, in 1998 only 2 per cent of employees had their pay determined by management at the workplace and 6 per cent by a higher level of management in the organisation. The 1998 Employee Relations Workplace Survey concluded that in 32 per cent of the workplaces it surveyed there was an absence of any formal structure for employees to make their voice heard by their employer.

Employee involvement

Employee involvement is a broad term that covers a range of processes designed to enable employees to voice their views to the employer and so have an involvement in management decision-making and the feelings of participation involvement in the development of the business. There is, however, no commitment on the part of management to act on the employees' views. These processes include indirect forms of participation, such as consultative committees or Works Councils, as well as direct communication forms, such as regular workforce meetings between senior management and the workforce, problem-solving groups that discuss aspects of performance (for example, quality) and briefing groups, which usually involve regular meetings between junior managers and all the workers for whom they are responsible.

Consultation is different from communication because it invites the participation of staff by seeking views, bringing individuals into the decision-making process and delegating a measure of autonomy through empowerment. Consultation can take place either directly with staff or through a representative forum (such as a Works Council), or some other form of joint consultation machinery.

Each of the elements of the employee involvement mix is linked. It is not always clear where communication ends and consultation begins. Organisations which pursue employee involvement typically use a wide range of differing activities to develop the mix needed to achieve success in the marketplace. Employee involvement is analysed in greater detail in Chapter 7.

In joint consultation, management seek views, feelings and ideas from employees and/or their representatives prior to making a decision. Although joint consultation may involve discussion of mutual problems, it leaves management to make the final decision. There is no commitment to act on the employees' views. Issues dealt with by joint consultation vary from social matters, such as the provision of canteen or sports facilities, to issues such as the scheduling of production.

The Workplace Employee Relations Survey (1998) provides information on the extent of joint consultative arrangements in establishments employing 25 or more employees. It revealed that 23 per cent of workplaces had a functioning joint consultative committee at the workplace. These committees were responsible for discussing a range of topics rather than a single issue such as health and safety. In the private sector, only 20 per cent of workplaces had a JCC compared with 32 per cent in the public sector. Workplace committees are much more frequent among large workplaces, and higher-level committees – through which management prefers to consult with employees on a multi-site basis rather than have a consultative committee for each establishment – are more frequent in larger organisations. All in all, some 67 per cent of employees work in places with joint consultative arrangements at either the workplace or a higher level in the organisation.

Collective bargaining

Collective bargaining is not only an employee relations process for determining employment conditions but also a system of industrial governance whereby unions and employers jointly reach decisions concerning the employment relationship. The process involves employees – via their elected representatives and unions – participating in the management of the enterprise. Collective bargaining is a problem-solving mechanism but can only take place if employees are organised and if the employer is prepared to recognise the trade union(s) for collective bargaining purposes.

In practice, the outcome of collective bargaining is not confined to union members. Unionised companies apply collectively bargained terms and conditions of employment to their non-union employees as well as their unionised ones. Companies that do not recognise unions have regard to collectively bargained rates in their industry or in comparator firms when deciding on their own employees' employment conditions if they are to remain competitive in the labour market. Many non-unionised companies (for example, Marks & Spencer, IBM, Mars) seek to retain union-free workplaces by paying above the union-negotiated pay and other employment conditions. This means that such companies must have an interest in the outcome of collective bargaining although they are not direct parties to it.

Over the period 1984–1998 inclusive, collective bargaining as part of the employee relations game declined sharply. The 1998 Workplace Industrial Relations Survey revealed that overall the proportion of employees covered by collective bargaining was 70 per cent in 1984, 54 per cent in 1990 and 41 per cent in 1998. In the public sector, the coverage of collective bargaining in 1998 was 63 per cent compared with 80 per cent in 1990. In private manufacturing, the corresponding figures were 51 per cent and 46 per cent respectively. The largest proportionate fall in collective bargaining as an employee relations process has been in private services, with a fall from 33 per cent in 1990 to 22 per cent in 1998.

> What are the main processes used to regulate employment conditions in your organisation? Why are these the main processes, rather than others?

Third-party intervention

In situations where the players in the employee relations game are unable to resolve their collective differences, they may agree voluntarily to seek the assistance of an independent third party. Third-party intervention can take one of three forms:

- conciliation
- mediation
- arbitration.

In the case of disputes between an employer and an individual employee over unfair dismissal, non-payment of a termination of employment payment or commission or sex, race, equal pay and disability discrimination, the law requires the Advisory, Conciliation and Arbitration Service (ACAS) to attempt a conciliated settlement before the claim can proceed to an employment tribunal.

In conciliation, the role of the third party is to keep the two sides talking and assist them to reach their own agreement. The conciliator acts as a link between the disputing parties by passing on information that the parties will not pass directly to each other, from one side to the other until either a basis for agreement is identified or both parties conclude there is no basis for an agreed voluntary settlement to their problem. Conciliation permits each side to reassess its situation continually. The conciliator plays a passive role and does not impose any action or decision on the parties.

A mediator listens to the argument of the two sides and makes recommendations on how their difference(s) might be resolved. The parties are free to accept or reject these recommendations. On the other hand, the arbitration process removes from employers and employees control over the settlement of their differences. The arbitrator hears both sides' case and decides the solution to the parties' differences by making an award. Both parties, having voluntarily agreed to arbitration, are morally bound, but not legally obliged, to accept the arbitrator's award. Pendulum arbitration is a specific form of arbitration which limits the third party to making an award which accepts fully either the final claim of the union or the final offer of the employer. It reduces arbitration to an all-or-nothing win-or-lose outcome for the disputants. By creating an all-or-nothing expectation, pendulum arbitration is said to provide the incentive for bargainers to moderate their final positions and reach a voluntary agreement.

Third-party intervention is facilitated by ACAS, established as a Royal Commission in 1974 and put on a statutory basis by the Employment Protection Act (1975). Mediation and arbitration is undertaken by an independent person (or occasionally persons) selected jointly by the parties to the dispute, from a list held by ACAS of competent arbitrators made up of academics, trade union officers and employers. The listed members of this panel are all experienced and knowledgeable in employee relations. There is also the Central Arbitration Committee which is a standing independent arbitration body. Originally established as the Industrial Court in 1919, it can deal with issues relating to industrial disputes, to a single employer or to a particular employee group. As well as providing voluntary arbitration in trade disputes, it arbitrates on unilateral claims by trade unions over alleged failure of employers to disclose information for collective bargaining purposes, in disputes over the establishment of European Works Councils and in disputes over trade union recognition. These are all areas in which the law permits one party to take the other against its wishes to arbitration. In short, arbitration in these issues is not voluntary. The roles of ACAS and the CAC are examined more fully in Chapter 6.

Third-party intervention is little used by the players of the employee relations game. The number of completed collective conciliation cases handled by ACAS fell from 2,284 in 1979 to 1,245 in 2003/04. Mediation is rarely used. In the whole of 2002/03 there were eight mediation hearings arranged by ACAS, while in 2003/04 there were only six. Throughout the 1990s the number of arbitration hearings arranged by ACAS fell. In 1990 there were 190 such hearings, but in 2003/04 there were only 63. The process of third-party intervention in the employee relations game is described in more detail in Chapter 6.

Industrial sanctions

To resort to the imposition of industrial sanctions is costly to both employers and employees. The main sanctions available to the employer are:

- locking out some, or all, of the workforce
- closing the factory
- relocating operations to another site
- dismissing employees who participate in industrial action.

The main industrial sanctions that employees can impose on employers are:

- a ban on overtime
- working to rule
- the imposition of a selective strike
- holding an all-out strike.

The threat of the imposition of industrial sanctions can be important in bringing about a reconciliation of the different interests of employers and employees. The threat that one player might impose industrial sanctions, with their ensuing costs, on the other may be as important as if sanctions were imposed. It is the threat effect that can oblige players to adjust their position and negotiate a peaceful settlement. Both parties will be reluctant to go ahead and impose industrial sanctions because of their associated costs. However, their existence means the employee relations players have to have regard to them and adjust their behaviour accordingly.

Employers and employees have to think carefully before imposing or threatening to impose industrial sanctions. There is little to be gained in imposing industrial action if it is unlikely to be successful, especially if economic pressures may quickly mount as the organisation's product market competitors take advantage of its industrial problems to poach its customers. It is pointless to relocate operations to another site unless an alternative competent workforce is available (or can be recruited) at the new site. To impose sanctions that fail to bring further concessions from the other player undermines, at a future date, the credibility of the threat to use them.

The extent of industrial action

In the UK, official statistics on the use of industrial sanctions relate only to strikes (see Table 3). They measure three dimensions of strike activity – their numbers (how frequent they are), their size (the number of workers involved) and their duration (the number of working days lost). This last measure is often distorted by a few big strikes. For example, in 1979 an engineering industry-wide strike accounted for 55 per cent of 29.5 million working days lost. In 2003 the number of working days lost in the UK was 499,000.

However, disputes still happen – for example, a series of one-day stoppages in 2002 on the railways over the widening of pay differentials between drivers, who were in short supply, and other railway employees. The dearth of drivers meant that the railway employers wanted to give them higher pay rises than other staff. The latter then went on strike because of the smaller increases offered to them. It meant that the pay differentials were increasing. The year 2003 also saw strikes in teaching in London, and threatened strikes in local government, in the fire service and the Royal Mail.

Although dispute levels have declined in the 1990s and early 2000s, there are signs that some managers have been performing inadequately in managing their employee relations in that there has been, over the same period, a dramatic growth in the number of complaints to employment tribunals. In the 1980s, the number of complaints reported to ACAS averaged about 45,000 per annum – but the number increased in every year in the 1990s. In 2004 the annual number of such complaints exceeded 102,000. This would suggest a rising sense of individual grievance among people at work.

Legal intervention

The processes described above used in the employee relations game are private means by which the interests of employers and employees are accommodated. Employers have some choice over which of these processes they will use. However, on occasions, the state interferes in these private relationships and sets minimum employment conditions that employers must provide for their employees. Although employers have no control over Parliamentary legislation, they can, by political lobbying, attempt to influence the details of proposed legislation to maximise its positive effects on their economic interests or to minimise its negative impact on their interests.

UK Parliament regulation

In the UK today, legal intervention comes from two sources – the UK government and the European Union. Since 1997, Labour Governments have introduced new minimum standards of protection for employees at the workplace. In April 1999 the National Minimum Wage Act (1998) introduced a national minimum wage. The Employment Relations Act (1999) gave individual employees the right to be represented for collective bargaining purposes by a trade union where a majority of the relevant workforce wish it. It also created the right for individuals to be accompanied by a fellow employee or trade union representative during grievance and disciplinary procedures, over serious matters. The Employment Act (2002) provided individual employees with the right to request more flexible working arrangements and imposed on all organisations, regardless of size, statutory discipline and grievance procedures laying down minimum standards in terms of the number of stages, etc (see Chapters 10 and 11).

The European Union

The European Union is committed to establishing a 'level playing field' of minimum social and employment standards in its Single European Market in which goods, capital, people and services can move freely. In 1997 the UK government accepted that more social and employment measures could be harmonised between member states, through the use of the EU's qualified majority voting procedure. One implication of this has been that an employee relations professional in the UK has experienced increasing legal regulation from the European Union. Chapter 5 shows how the EU has impinged on the work of the employee relations profession in the areas of equal opportunities, employment protection and working conditions, information and consultation rights, and health and safety.

AGREEMENTS, RULES AND REGULATIONS

The outcome of the employee relations game is the establishment of rules, regulations and agreements by which employment relations are governed. These rules may relate to a group of employees or may be the result of bargaining between an employer and an individual employee resulting in a personal contract. The distinguishing characteristic of such contracts is that none of its terms has been bargained collectively. The employee has negotiated as an individual – although in doing so he or she may have received assistance from a third party.

However, in practice, few personal contracts are genuinely individualised. At British Telecom, for example, all terms and conditions for senior managerial staff used to be standard across all personal contracts. The only difference was that pay was determined 'individually' with no published rates (and thus there was no transparency in the criteria) by which pay increases were given to individuals.

Types of agreements

It is conventional to divide the rules, regulations and agreements stemming from the employee relations game into two broad types. First, there are substantive rules which cover the money aspects of employment conditions (pay, hours of work, paid holidays, shift premiums, etc). An example of a substantive agreement is shown below.

AGREEMENT BETWEEN:
UNION OF SHOP, DISTRIBUTIVE AND ALLIED WORKERS (USDAW)
and
ABC LIMITED

The following has been agreed between USDAW and ABC Limited, regarding the 2002/03 Pay and Conditions claim.

The following are the rates of pay which now apply for a 39-hour week and are effective from Monday 5 June 2002.

Rates of pay

Boners	£170.82
Butchers	£156.47
M/c Op/Prep	£151.23
Gen Worker 'A'	£146.66
Gen Worker 'B'	£146.66
Drivers	£152.57

Nighshift premiums
Will be increased from their present levels to 18.5% of basic hourly rate.

Working hours, with immediate effect to become:

Dayshift	Monday to Friday	6.00 am until 2.30 pm
	or	8.00 am until 4.30 pm
Nightshift	Sunday to Thursday	9.00 pm until 5.18 am

Breaks – During each shift the following breaks will apply:
    1 × 30-minute lunch break
    1 × 15-minute tea break
    2 × 10-minute tea breaks

Service day holidays
Qualification periods for 5 days' holiday to be reduced to 13 years.

Death in service
Sum assured benefit increased to £10,000.

Holidays
5 days of public holiday to become annual holiday commencing 1 April 2003.

Second, there are procedural rules (agreements) which set standards of conduct to be met by employers and employees in resolving specific differences. In this sense, they provide the 'law and order' for the workplace. They constitute criteria by which reasonable, fair and consistent behaviour by employers can be judged by employees and outside institutions, such as employment tribunals. Procedural 'rules' also send a message to all employees as to how they will be treated should the specific issue arise.

In practice, employers have a wide range of procedural arrangements and agreements that cover such specific issues as:

- disputes
- employee grievances
- discipline
- redundancy
- union recognition
- grading
- health and safety
- promotion
- staff development and career review.

An example of a procedural agreement (Appeal against grading) is shown below. The 1998 Workplace Employee Relations Survey reported that in 92 per cent of establishments surveyed there was an individual grievance procedure, and that a similar proportion of workplaces operated formal disciplinary procedures.

CLERICAL STAFF PROCEDURE AGREEMENT
SECTION FIVE – APPEALS AGAINST GRADING

1 INDIVIDUAL RIGHT TO APPEAL
Where an employee is dissatisfied with the decision of the University at the annual review concerning an application for regrading on the grounds of increased duties and responsibilities, he/she may apply in writing within three weeks to the Director of Personnel to have his/her case considered by an Appeals Panel constituted as below.

2 APPEALS PANEL – MEMBERSHIP
The Appeals Panel shall consist of five members, as follows:
(a) Two members nominated by the University
(b) Two members nominated by the Association
(c) One member, who shall act as Convenor, acceptable to the University and the Association.

PROCEDURE FOR APPEALS

(i) Persons involved in the hearing
(a) The appellant
(b) A colleague or Trade Union representative of the appellant if he/she wishes
(c) A Personnel Officer
(d) The Head of Department or his/her nominee.

(ii) Prior to the hearing
(a) The Panel shall have available to it all the original documentation
(b) Each party shall make available a written statement of case to the Panel
(c) Written statements and supporting documents, if any, should be in the hands of the Personnel Officer eight working days prior to the hearing. These together with copies of all the original documents will be circulated to the members of the Panel four working days prior to the hearing.

(iii) The hearing of the appeal
(a) The appellant or his/her representative may, if they wish, present a short summary of the case to the Panel
(b) The members of the panel may then ask questions of any of those present
(c) The appellant will withdraw from the hearing
(d) The Personnel Officer will be asked to present the University's case
(e) The Head of Department or his/her nominee will be asked to present the departmental view of the merits of the case and the members of the Panel may ask questions.

(iv) Consideration of the appeal
(a) The Panel will then consider its decision after all parties have withdrawn
(b) The decision will be by a simple vote of the Panel. The decision of the Panel is binding on all parties.

Select three procedures which operate in your organisation. Explain how they demonstrate that management behaves fairly and reasonably in operating these procedures.

The legal status of collective agreements

Rules that are set out in collective agreements have a unique status in the UK in that they are not legally binding on the parties who have signed them. If either the union or management acts contrary to the agreement, the other party cannot enforce its rights outlined in the agreement via the courts. Collective agreements are binding in honour only. In almost every other democratic society, collective agreements between unions and employers are legally binding and enforceable through the courts.

A consequence of non-legally-binding collective agreements is they are not comprehensive and their wording can be relatively imprecise. This reinforces the requirement for employers to have a disputes procedure to resolve differences with their employees over whether the agreement is being applied properly. The style of UK collective agreements also reflects that they are normally subject to review and renegotiation on an annual basis.

Dimensions of agreement rules

Employment rules can be analysed by their dimensions. The main dimensions are:

- scope (ie subjects covered)
- formality (ie whether they are written or unwritten)

- level
- bargaining units (ie the employees covered).

The scope (ie the subjects covered) of employment regulation rules varies widely but normally cover some, or all, of the following:

- pay levels and structure
- overtime and shift payments
- incentive (bonus/performance-related pay) payments
- hours of work and paid holidays
- working arrangements and productivity
- training and retraining opportunities
- the means of resolving disputes, individual grievances, etc.

It is traditional for pay rates and working arrangement rules to be reviewed and amended annually by the signatories to the agreement. Hours of work and paid annual holidays are normally reviewed and changed at less frequent intervals. Procedural arrangements can remain unchanged for many years.

Rules and regulations governing employment conditions can also be analysed in terms of their formality. The vast majority of rules are written out in full, but there are some which do not exist in written form. Such rules are held to remain in force through 'custom and practice'. The employees have operated the working practice for many years. The employers have gone along with this behaviour although they have never formally agreed it with their employees. The practice has become accepted and if management were to try to change it, the employees are likely to expect something in return.

Employment regulation rules can operate at different levels. Some apply only to the place where those covered by them work; others apply to all workers in the company, as is seen in the Ford Motor Company and ICI. Some rules cover a group of workers in an enterprise whereas others relate to all (or to certain grades of) workers in an industry. Over the past 25 years, many employers have withdrawn from operating under national agreements, often supplemented by local bargaining, preferring to bargain collectively (especially over pay) with their employees at a more decentralised level, considering this necessary to recruit, motivate, retain and reward the right calibre of employees if the success of the business is to be secured.

The rules resulting from the employee relations game can also be analysed in terms of the number of workers they cover. In the case of collectively bargained agreements, that number is referred to as the 'size' of the bargaining unit. In some unionised organisations, management operates by concluding separate agreements with separate trade unions that represent different groups of employees and that thus have a multiplicity of bargaining units and collective agreements.

However, other companies prefer to have a single set of rules and regulations to cover all relevant groups. They have one unit covering significant numbers of employee and possibly a different number of trade unions or employee representative groups. In unionised situations this is referred to as 'single-table bargaining', in which all recognised trade unions sit at the same table with the employer. Yet other managements may believe the business objectives to be more achievable if they have one employing 'unit' in which all employees are represented by a single representative body – a situation that is known in unionised companies as a 'single-union agreement' situation.

Non-union companies, like unionised ones, have substantive and procedural sets of rules, but these rules will have been authored by the employer and only the most professional of employers will have consulted with its workforce in doing so. In non-union companies, employment rules can also be analysed in terms of their scope (ie issues covered by information and consultation arrangements) and the number of workers to which they apply. Some information and communication systems apply to all workers in the enterprise, whereas others apply only to some groups. Quality circles, on the other hand, are usually confined to small groups from the same work area who carry out similar job tasks and activities. Performance-related pay schemes often will apply to certain occupational groups (eg managers in strategic positions) within an enterprise or workplace. Financial participation schemes again differ as to the workers covered. Some embrace all employees (eg profit sharing and profit-related pay) while others are confined to certain occupational groups (eg share option schemes). Although the practices used in non-union companies may not be directly based on trade union organisation, they often parallel practices in unionised companies.

Workforce agreements

The Working Time Regulations (1998) have given rise to a new form of agreement called a 'workforce agreement'. The Regulations allow for some of the measures to be adopted through agreements between workers and employers so as to allow flexibility in order to take account of the specific needs of local working agreements. Employers and workers are expected to come to a consensus on which of three types of agreements – collective agreements, workforce agreements and relevant agreements – is the most appropriate to their circumstances.

Workforce agreements permit employers to fix working time arrangements with workers who do not have any terms or conditions set by a collective agreement. Workforce agreements allow employers to decide for themselves how to use the flexibilities permitted in the implementation of the Regulations. A workforce agreement may apply to the whole of the workforce or to a group within it. Where it is to apply to a group of workers, the group must share a workplace function or organisational unit within a business.

THE BALANCE OF BARGAINING POWER

It was pointed out earlier in this chapter that the employee relations game does not take place in a vacuum. It takes place in an organisational setting, which in turn operates within constraints imposed by the behaviour of organisations external to that organisation. This internal and external context influences the relative balance of bargaining power between employers and employees.

Whether the outcome of the employee relations game results in employment rules that are closer to satisfying the interests of the employers or of the employees is influenced heavily by the relative balance of bargaining power between them. Issues relating to the relative balance of bargaining power are relevant to employers who bargain individually with their employees as well as to those who bargain collectively with their workforce. The balance of bargaining power is a key employee relations concept, which influences, inter alia, the employer's preferred employee relations process, the subject matter of agreements, rules and regulations, whether job regulations are jointly authored by employers and employees or solely written by one of the parties, and the actual content of the employment rules.

The macro level

The factors in the environment external to the organisation that influence the relative balance of bargaining power between employers and employees, and therefore the outcome of the employee relations game, are:

- economic
- legal
- technological.

The government's economic and legal policies have major implications for the outcome of employee relations activities. Economic policies that are directed towards the creation of full employment and the maximising of economic growth weaken the bargaining power of the employer relative to that of the employees. In an expanding economy the demand for labour services increases, causing the price of those labour services to rise. The substantive rules thus become more favourable to employees. On the other hand, if macro-economic policies are directed at restraining economic activity, the demand for labour services falls, resulting perhaps in redundancies and rising unemployment. In such circumstances the balance of bargaining power of the employer is strengthened relative to that of employees, and the substantive rules become more favourable to employers.

If the government introduces legislation favourable to employers' interests – for example, by restricting the circumstances in which trade unions may instruct their members to take industrial action without the employer being able to seek redress through the courts, for instance, for compensation for a downturn in sales, etc – the bargaining power of employers relative to employees is strengthened. The Conservative governments of 1979 to 1997 inclusive enhanced employers' bargaining power relative to that of the employees by passing nine pieces of parliamentary legislation that regulated the labour market activities of trade unions progressively more tightly. As a result, strikes fell dramatically and substantive rule changes were favourable to the employer.

If a government introduces legislation favourable to the interests of individual employees and trade unions, the bargaining power of employees relative to employers is increased. The present Labour government via its Employment Relations Act (1999) and the Employment Act (2002) together with legislation from the EU has enhanced employee/trade union bargaining power relative to the employer.

The implementation of new technology also impacts on the relative bargaining power of employees and employers. Technological developments based on computers, lasers and telecommunications have in some sectors of the economy destroyed jobs – for example, those of compositors (typesetters) in the printing industry – de-skilled jobs, blurred demarcation lines between existing jobs and industries, and created for employers an alternative and lower-paid workforce. These impacts have increased the bargaining power of the employer relative to the employee.

However, in other sectors of the economy, by creating new jobs and new skills and making some industries more capital-intensive, the implementation of technological change has strengthened the bargaining power of employees relative to the employer. For example, the growth of telephone banking services has created a new business, which in part replaces the jobs lost in traditional banks.

The economic and legal environment surrounding an employee relations system influences the relative bargaining power between employers and employees at the macro level. This is why employer and employee organisations spend large sums of money in lobbying political decision-makers.

> What factors determine at the national level the relative bargaining power between employers and employees? Explain, with appropriate examples, how the balance of bargaining power influences employer or employee behaviour in employee relations.

The micro level

An analysis of the relative bargaining power at the macro level cannot explain why some groups of employees retain their bargaining power vis-à-vis the employer despite recession and high unemployment, or why some employers are in a relatively weak bargaining position despite depressed economic activity. To explain these situations we have to examine the relative bargaining power at the individual organisation level.

At this level the balance of bargaining power is influenced by some of the following factors:

- whether employees can inflict costs on the organisation (for example, are the employees concerned at a crucial/key point in the production/service provision process?)
- whether there is an alternative workforce available to the employer (ie within the organisation or external to the organisation)
- the product market situation of the organisation (ie are sales increasing or decreasing?)
- whether the group of employees is aware of its potential power
- whether the group of employees has previously exercised its power
- whether, if the group has previously exercised its power, was the outcome favourable – did the employees feel they had gained something they would otherwise not have got? For example, in assessing the relative bargaining power of a group of its employees, management has to consider how crucial the group is to the workflow production/service supply process. The more central the group is to workflow, the greater is its potential power within the organisation. Its staff, for example, are in strategic positions to disrupt workflow.

The bargaining power of a group of employees relative to management is strengthened if there is a lack of an appropriate alternative workforce available to undertake the group's work on an individual or a departmental basis. In short, a group of workers it is difficult to substitute has greater bargaining power relative to the employer than a group whose services are easily replaceable. These relative differences in bargaining power will be reflected in the rules operated to regulate the employment relationship and the process whereby those rules are made.

SUMMARY

- This chapter identified the main components of the employee relations game at the organisation, sector or national level:
  - the players (employers and employees) and their different and common interests
  - the processes whereby the game is played
  - the outcome/output of the game (viz rules to regulate employment relationship)
  - the internal and external environments to the organisation in which the game is played. These contexts influence the relative power relationship between employers and employees and thereby the outcome of the game.
- The main processes whereby the employee relations game is played are unilateral action by management, employee involvement and participation schemes, communication processes (including employee voice), collective bargaining, third-party intervention, industrial sanctions and legal regulation by the UK government and the European Union.
- The employee relations game produces rules which govern the employment relationship. It is conventional to group these rules into two broad categories – those covering substantive issues (pay, holidays, hours of work, pensions, family-friendly benefits, etc) and those relating to procedural matters. The latter set of rules lays down the standards of behaviour to be met by employers and employees in resolving specific differences.
- The employee relations game takes place in an organisational context (the internal context), and the organisation itself has to operate against the behaviour of institutions (eg governments) external to itself. These contexts influence the relative bargaining power between employers and employees. The balance of bargaining power is a key employee relations concept which influences, inter alia, the employee relations processes the parties use, the scope and authorship of the rules, agreements and regulations resulting from the employee relations game. In short, changes in the

context in which employee relations takes place influence the behaviour of the players and the outcome of the game both at any point in time and over time.

FURTHER READING

ADVISORY, CONCILIATION AND ARBITRATION SERVICE *Annual Reports*.

CENTRAL ARBITRATION COMMITTEE *Annual Reports*.

CERTIFICATION OFFICE FOR TRADE UNIONS AND EMPLOYERS' ASSOCIATIONS *Annual Reports of the Certification Officer*.

CULLY, M., WOODLANDS S., O'REILLY A. and DIX G. (1999) *Britain at Work, as Depicted by the 1998 Employee Relations Survey*. London, Routledge.

FARNHAM D. (2000) *Employee Relations in Context*. London, Institute of Personnel and Development; chapters 1, 2, 3, 6, 8 and 10.

GUEST, D. E. and CONWAY, N. (1998) *Fairness at Work and the Psychological Contract*. London, Institute of Personnel and Development.

INSTITUTE OF PERSONNEL AND DEVELOPMENT (1995) *People Make the Difference*, an IPD Position Paper, January.

INSTITUTE OF PERSONNEL AND DEVELOPMENT (1997) *Employment Relations into the 21st Century*, an IPD Position Paper, December.

INVOLVEMENT AND PARTICIPATION ASSOCIATION (1997) *Towards Industrial Partnership: New ways of working in British companies*, February.

MARTIN R. (1992) *Bargaining Power*. Oxford, Oxford University Press; chapter 3.

MILLWARD N., BRYSON A. and FORTH J. (2000) *All Change at Work? British Employment Relations 1980–1988 as Portrayed by the Workplace Industrial Relations Survey Series*. London, Routledge.

SCHEIN, E. H. (1998) *Career Dynamics*. London, Addison-Wesley.

TAYLOR R. (2000) *The Future of Employment Relations*. Economic and Social Research Council.

TRADES UNION CONGRESS (1997) *Partners for Progress: Next steps for the new unionism*.

Employee relations strategies and policies

CHAPTER 2

CHAPTER OBJECTIVES

When you have completed this chapter you should be aware of and able to describe:

■ what strategy is and the role that strategy plays overall in defining employee relations strategies and policies

■ how strategic choices can be driven by the values, preferences and power of those who are the principal decision-makers

■ why the choice of particular employment policies is often a strategic decision

■ the concept of management style and its importance to the process of employee relations

■ why some organisations continue to embrace collective relationships and others prefer to remain non-union or anti-union.

INTRODUCTION

In Chapter 1 the main components of employee relations were identified, and we noted that the balance of bargaining power is affected by the economic, legal and technological environments, and that this in turn can influence prevailing management style. In following chapters we will develop these issues further as we examine the corporate environment, the legislative framework and the European Union, and how these are important to employee relations professionals. In this chapter we shall discuss the importance of employee relations strategies, and the type and style of employment policies that flow from such strategies.

The management of people is one of the most challenging areas of business management and most organisations would argue that it is taken very seriously. Nonetheless it is, in many organisations, the poor relation in terms of importance and profile. This is despite the large amount of research and analysis that shows how important it is in differentiating between organisational performance.

Writing in *People Management* in 2001, Simon Caulkin pointed out that there had been over 30 studies conducted in the USA and UK since the early 1990s that had left little doubt that the management and development of people has one of the most powerful effects on overall business performance, including overall profitability.

Reviewing the evidence on behalf of the CIPD, Caulkin stated that

> it would be hard to overestimate the importance of this finding. The empirical results that prove the business case slot the final piece into a new business model that has people squarely at its centre. It completes a historic transition from a mechanistic view of the company to one that sees it as a living system where Tayloristic task management gives way to knowledge management; the latter seeking to be cost efficient by developing an organisation's people assets, unlike the former which views labour as a cost to be minimised.

Caulkin believed that the findings opened up

> huge opportunities for competitive improvement through learning, managing and developing people more effectively. The same goes for the UK economy as a whole, where people management has the potential to turbo-charge investment in skills, R&D and new technology, offering a way to jolt the economy out of its low-skills/low-quality equilibrium and claw back the productivity advantage held by its competitors.

The work reviewed by Caulkin has been further underpinned by a report by John Purcell *et al* and published by the CIPD in 2003. The report *Understanding the People and Performance Link: Unlocking the black box* was the culmination of six years of study and was developed to overcome criticism of earlier studies, which were seen as flawed because they 'had been carried out in manufacturing where issues such as productivity were easier to manage'.

The Institute therefore developed a programme of work with three specific aims:

- to improve the evidence linking people management to business performance or organisational competitiveness
- to provide accessible information on which managers can act through effective choices and decisions
- to improve understanding of why and how people management practices influence business performance.

Despite the plethora of research into the HR/business performance link, one of the most difficult tasks facing personnel professionals is opening the minds of their management colleagues to adopting different, but proven approaches, to managing people. An earlier CIPD report *Voices from the Boardroom* by David Guest *et al* noted that 'most senior executives are, at best, only dimly aware of recent research on people management and performance'. Such a lack of awareness carries the danger that the employee relations specialist, who ought to be aware of new ideas and approaches, will attempt to implement a new idea without ensuring that his or her management colleagues have a full understanding of what is proposed. That is why, in this book, and in the employee relations exam, great stress is laid on gaining commitment from colleagues to employee relations initiatives. Yet gaining commitment is not something that happens in isolation. In order to obtain it you have to ensure that a proper business case is made for the adoption of new techniques or new approaches. It is easy to be critical of managers for not embracing new ideas, but if they are simply invited to buy into them as an article of faith, they will not make available the necessary investment in time and resources.

So before seeking to change people management processes within an organisation, there has to be a business case made that will demonstrate that such change is necessary. In making this business case it is important to show that there is a link between the delivery of business performance, human resource management generally, and, in the context of this book, employee relations specifically.

To be successful the business case must flow from the organisation's overall strategy. And to understand this connection we need to look at the whole concept of strategy, a subject that has, in recent years, become the subject of intense discussion and debate, and become increasingly more important to managers in both the public and private sector. This has happened because although organisations have always had strategies, 'only since the 1960s has it been common to address explicitly the question of what their strategy should be' (Kay, 1993; page 6). One of the reasons for the change in emphasis, as we shall demonstrate in Chapter 3, is that economic fluctuations and intense competition have forced organisations to recognise that there is a need to continually change themselves – not necessarily revolutionary change, but certainly a process of evolution. Such evolutionary change has to be managed and requires that organisations develop clear business strategies that will then drive functional strategies, one of which is human resources generally and more specifically the management of employee relations. However, it is not only senior managers who need to concern themselves with the strategic direction of an organisation: it is essential for all levels of management.

If the 1980s and 1990s taught us anything, it is that the pattern of employee relations has, for the most part, changed. Twenty years ago employee relations was dominated by the relationship between management and unions. That is no longer the case. Not only have unions declined in terms of membership, they have also changed in terms of attitude and approach. Similarly, managers have also changed, and where unions are recognised, they are seen more as partners than opponents.

The reality of this changed relationship has, quite clearly, been the impact of the pace of change to which most businesses have been exposed, and which has created a need for directors and senior managers to look more carefully at their approach to employee relations management, both strategically and through day-to-day management activities. They have come to accept that there are advantages to be gained in identifying employee attitudes through enhanced communication, and then attempting to re-shape those attitudes for the benefit of the organisation and the people that work in it. Such attitudinal change is of particular importance as organisations, in both the public and private sectors, have sought to maximise efficiency as a means of securing a competitive advantage. Such advantage is now as important an issue for the public sector as it is for the private sector, particularly if the levels of public spending that have been agreed for sectors such as health and education are to continue. Public sector organisations have had competition forced upon them as successive governments have insisted on their being more customer- and quality-focused, while private sector organisations have had their own challenges. As we will see in the next chapter, these are very often linked to new technology or to the growth of the global economy. Whatever the challenge, it will impact on and dictate the type of employment policies that the management of an organisation will seek to implement.

WHAT IS STRATEGY?

The overall purpose of strategy is to influence and direct an organisation as it conducts its activities. There are many definitions of strategy, and students of employee relations must be aware that there is no model answer. Notwithstanding this, it is hard to argue against the view (Tyson, 1995) that:

> Strategy may be described as the attempt by those who control an organisation to find ways to position their business or organisational objectives so that they can exploit the planning environment and maximise the future use of the organisation's capital and human assets.

Clearly this is but one definition of strategy and many writers have attempted to offer their own definition, but two writers stand out in the way that they have sought to define strategy in a way that is relevant to all tiers of management.

Johnson and Scholes (2003) have tried to provide an understanding of what corporate strategy is and why strategic decisions are important. They view corporate strategy in two ways – as a matter of economic analysis and planning, and as a matter of organisational decision-making within a social, political and cultural process. In the latest edition of their book they have introduced the concept of viewing strategy through three separate lenses: a very traditional 'design' view of strategy; the idea that strategy can derive from experience and culture; and, thirdly, that strategy is the product of emergent ideas.

Overall the two authors have identified a number of characteristics that are usually associated with the terms 'strategy' and 'strategic decisions', and these are:

- Strategic decisions are likely to be concerned with or affect the long-term direction of an organisation.

- Strategic decisions are about trying to achieve some advantage for the organisation – for example, over the competition.

- Strategic decisions are sometimes conceived of, therefore, as the search for effective *positioning* to give such advantage in a market or in relation to suppliers.

- Strategic decisions are likely to be concerned with the scope of an organisation's activities.

- Strategy can be seen as the matching of the activities of an organisation to the environment in which it operates.

- Strategy can be seen as building on or stretching an organisation's resources and competences to create opportunities or capitalise on them.

- Strategies may require major resource changes for an organisation.

- Strategic decisions are likely to affect operational decisions.

- The strategy of an organisation will be affected not only by environmental forces and resource availability, but also by the values and expectations of those who have power in and around the organisation.

Overall, Johnson and Scholes would say that if a definition of strategy is required, the above characteristics provide the basis for the following one:

> Strategy is the *direction* and scope of an organisation over the *long term*: which achieves *advantage* for the organisation through its configuration of *resources* within a changing *environment*, to meet the needs of *markets* and to fulfil *stakeholder* expectations.

If they are correct in the way they describe these characteristics, it means that the whole process becomes very complex. This is particularly true if the organisation operates in a wide geographical area – a multinational, for example – or has a wide range of products, or operates in the public sector – a health trust, for example. Throughout this text we make the point that employee relations cannot stand alone, that it has to be integrated with other management and personnel functions. The same is true of strategy: it also requires, as Johnson and Scholes point out, an integrated approach to managing the organisation:

> Managers therefore have to cross functional and operational boundaries to deal with strategic problems and come to agreements with other managers who, inevitably, have different interests and perhaps different priorities.

As we will explain in Chapter 9, this will often involve negotiation over the use of resources with management colleagues and is one of the reasons why negotiation skills are so important.

Strategic formulation

To understand further the nature of strategy it is helpful to gain some understanding of the process of strategy formulation, and we can identify a number of different approaches. One of the oldest and most influential portrays strategy as a highly rational and scientific process. This approach is based on one of the characteristics identified above – namely, the importance of the fit between an organisation and its environment. Analyses are made of a firm's environment to assess likely opportunities and threats, and of its internal resources to identify strengths and weaknesses. This process is often referred to as a SWOT analysis, and it is argued that through rigorous planning, senior managers can predict and shape the external environment and thus the organisation itself.

Other approaches to strategy formulation argue that the complexity and volatility of the environment may mean that a SWOT analysis is both difficult and inappropriate. This evolutionary approach believes organisations are at the mercy of the unpredictable and hostile vagaries of the market. The environment in which they operate may be changing so frequently that any data they use, either historical or current, may be worthless.

Some writers argue that it is not possible to apply either a rational or evolutionary label to the process of strategy formulation, but that it is behavioural. That strategic choice results from the various coalitions that are to be found within organisations. The most dominant of these coalitions will be at senior management level, and that it is they who have to 'create a vision of the organisation's future' (Burnes, 1996; page 168).

The extent to which managing people is given a high profile within the organisation will be driven by the values, ideologies and personalities of those in positions of power and influence and those individuals who formulate strategy and the long-term direction of the organisation. When we talk about the organisation in strategy terms, we very often mean the Chief Executive, whose values and beliefs will ultimately shape the culture of the organisation and will consequently decide the type and style of employee relations policies that it tries to follow. In essence what we are talking about here is leadership – that strategy is moulded by the personality of an individual or individuals and the way in which they are able to motivate people to change

Similarly, the values and beliefs of such Chief Executives will have a significant impact on the long-term direction of a business, and there are those who believe that leadership is a key success factor. However, not everybody takes this view. David Butcher and Mike Meldrum (*People Management*, 28 June 2001) question whether leadership is really important in business. They suggest that 'where chief executives do preside over successful businesses, it is sometimes because they are the beneficiaries of decisions taken long before they landed the top job'. Sometimes this issue of leadership is linked to particular organisations that are the flavour of the month and are perceived to be doing something different. As Butcher and Meldrum point out:

> The reason that companies such as Virgin, Cisco Systems, Dell, easyJet and other 'different' enterprises have been so keenly observed is that each has, in its own way, pioneered a new business and organisational model. They have eschewed tried and tested industry practices and ignored the rules of the game. That is why these companies are celebrated by management gurus.

From this brief description it is clear that there is no one right way of formulating strategy. There are a number of approaches that can be adopted by an organisation. Jenkins and Ambrosini suggest that:

> a useful way to examine the needs of a strategic approach is to consider the different elements of strategy and use these to form an agenda that gives managers a reasonably clear set of concepts.

They identify eight primary subjects (the eight Cs) which cover the diverse and complicated aspects of strategy that can be considered by an organisation.

THE EIGHT ESSENTIAL ELEMENTS OF BUSINESS STRATEGY

Context

Issues concerned with an organisation's external environment: how the external environment is perceived, how it is studied, what the organisation can do to control it and to change it. Context also refers to industry and market structure, and strategic groups.

Competing

Issues concerned with how organisations gain customers, how they identify their competitors and how they outperform them. This section is also about the competitive strategies organisations can implement to achieve sustainable advantage, and about co-operation and collusion.

Corporate

Corporate strategy typically addresses the multi-business context. So this heading deals with questions of alliances, diversification, mergers, globalisation, corporate parenting, etc.

Choice

Issues concerned with decision-making and the degrees of freedom for an organisation to determine a particular strategy. This section deals with questions and issues surrounding the choices made by firms in following a particular trajectory.

Competences

Issues concerned with the organisation's resources, such as skills, knowhow, organisational knowledge, routines, competences and capabilities. This section focuses on the role of a resource in an organisation, and in generating competitive advantage. It also deals with issues such as the transferability and the immutability of resources.

Culture

Issues concerned with an organisation's internal environment. It includes the role of organisational culture, its importance and its influence on employees. This heading also covers how culture is created or changed, and how employees perceive organisational culture.

Change

Issues concerned with the types of change an organisation can implement, and how change can take place, or how change is constrained. This section also includes the reasons for change, the change process, and the possible outcomes of change programmes.

Control

Organisational structure, power relationships and the *way* managers control what is happening in their organisation. Control describes the role of managers in the organisation, the extent to which they can 'manage' what is happening inside organisations, and the extent to which they know what is happening around them.

Source: *Strategic Management: A multi-perspective approach, ed. M. Jenkins and V. Ambrosini*

Whatever method of strategy formulation is adopted, it is important to understand that it will be constrained by societal, environmental, industry-specific and organisational factors, many of which will conflict with each other. Take, for example, societal factors. There can often be significant national differences in the way people approach work, and with the growth in multinational companies and internationalisation this can have a major impact on workplace culture. It is often the case that changes in society have a greater impact on organisations than changes in management.

The environment within which any organisation operates will, without doubt, constrain strategic choice. This may be a relatively stable and predictable environment in which planning and predicting the future is not a particularly hazardous exercise. Alternatively, it may be a hostile, unpredictable and uncertain environment in which planning is almost impossible. Whatever the environment, most organisations have to operate in a constantly changing world and their fundamental challenge is to cope with a scenario where they develop an appropriate strategy and then the world steps in and changes the rules. This external interference, whether it comes from currency exchanges, increases in energy prices or terrorism, often has a far bigger impact on companies than managerial issues. The name of the game is how quickly they can adapt their business model to those changes, because it is the change process that provides the link between business strategy and employee relations strategies. And while environmental considerations may provide the stimulus for change, there is a clear consensus that the success or otherwise of individual change programmes is governed by the people in each organisation.

> Consider the environment in which your own organisation has to operate. How would you describe it?

LEVELS OF STRATEGY

It is important to consider not only the sort of strategic choices that organisations can make but also the levels of strategic decision-making. There are three levels with which we need to concern ourselves (Burnes, 1996):

- corporate-level strategy, which concerns the overall direction and focus of the business
- business-unit-level strategy, which is concerned with how to compete in a particular market
- functional-level strategy, which is concerned with individual areas such as personnel, marketing, etc.

All these levels are interrelated, but equally, each of them has its own distinctive strategic concerns. We now need to look at them in a little more detail.

Corporate-level strategy

Corporate-level strategy concerns itself with a number of questions and is usually formulated at board level. One of these questions will be about the overall mission of the organisation: what is the game plan? How should the business portfolio be managed? Should you make acquisitions or dispose of parts of the business? What priority should be given to each of the individual parts of the business in terms of resource allocation? How is the business to be structured and financed?

In the CIPD research conducted by Purcell *et al* they noted that:

> one of the keys to the HR-performance link is the existence of a 'big idea', a clear mission underpinned by values and a culture expressing what the organisation stands for and is trying to achieve.

Of the organisations that they studied, the 'big idea' in Jaguar Cars was quality, whereas in the Nationwide Building Society it was 'mutuality'. According to Purcell *et al*, organisations with a big idea displayed five common characteristics – the idea was embedded, connected, enduring, collective and measured-and-managed. The big idea therefore means more than just having a formal mission statement. It means that the values are spread throughout the organisation so that they are embedded in policies and practices. These values interconnect the relationships with customers (both internal and external), culture and behaviour, and provide the basis upon which employees should be managed.

However, even taking on board the processes espoused by Purcell *et al*, the mission will fail unless it is capable of being achieved. This means that three things are necessary. Firstly, the mission must be expressed in language that is understandable to the bulk of employees, which means that attention must be paid to the communication process (see Chapter 7). Secondly, it must be attainable. That is, employees should recognise that the organisation has some chance of achieving the objectives it has set itself. Thirdly, the mission must be challenging. It needs all of those involved in its achievement to be stretched, for their individual performances to be a condition of the mission's overall success.

> If the organisation in which you work has a declared mission, how does it fit with the criteria we describe? If it doesn't fit those criteria, how would you express a mission for it that does meet the need to be understandable, attainable and challenging? Alternatively, if no mission has been articulated, what do you think it should be (again fitting it with our declared criteria)?

Business-unit-level strategy

Competitive or business-unit-level strategy is concerned with the way a firm or business operates in particular markets – what new opportunities can be identified or created? Which products or services should be developed? In this context strategy is concerned with gaining an advantage over the competition. Porter (1985) sees this as seeking to obtain a sustainable competitive advantage – which markets should the organisation attempt to compete in, and how does it position itself to achieve its objectives? How does it achieve some form of 'distinctive capability' (Kay, 1993)? What should its product range or mix be? Which customers should it aim for? Decisions about products, markets and customers were central to some of Porter's (1985) theories about strategy. He argued that there are only three basic strategies that dictate the choice to be made. These are:

- cost leadership that aims to achieve lower costs than your competitors without reducing quality
- product differentiation based on achieving industry-wide recognition of different and superior products and services compared to those of other suppliers
- specialisation by focus – in effect seeking out a niche market.

This type of distinction is fine in the private sector, but what about the public sector? All the decisions that Porter says are important have an effect on employee relations in that they impact on the way that the organisation structures itself internally and on the way that relationships are managed. For this reason it is important for public sector organisations to adapt these principles to their own service in order to create their own business strategies.

Functional-level strategy

Functional-level strategy is, in a sense, fairly straightforward. At this level strategy is concerned with how the different functions of the business (marketing, personnel, finance, manufacturing, etc) translate corporate- and business-level strategies into operational aims. As Johnson and Scholes describe it:

> how the component parts of the organisation in terms of resources, processes, people and their skills are pulled together to form a strategic architecture which will effectively deliver the overall strategic direction.

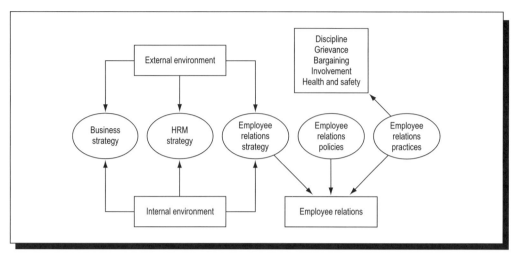

Figure 3 *Strategic employee relations management: an overview*

In Figure 3 above, we demonstrate how employee relations strategy is formulated – that business strategy drives HRM strategy, which in turn drives employee relations strategy, and that from this process are derived the practices and policies that influence the employment relationship. Once you have reached down to this level of functional strategy it is important that the various functions pay attention to how they organise themselves, not only in order to achieve their aims but to ensure synergy with the rest of the business. We can now turn specifically to the strategic issues concerning the management of people.

What external factors over the next five years are likely to impact on corporate strategy, both in the wider business context and in the specific challenges that your own organisation is likely to face? How, if at all, will these impact on your employee relations strategy?

People strategy

One aspect of strategy concerns the match between an organisation's activities and its resources. These resources can be physical (equipment, buildings) or they can be people. Strategies in respect of physical resources may require decisions about investment or even about the ability to invest. Strategies about people also require decisions to be made about investment, but it is a different type of investment decision – not the type that fits easily into the process usually reserved for capital expenditure. It is more likely to be the sort of investment that we examine in Chapter 3, such as investment in skills development.

Research carried out by the Institute of Work Psychology and the Centre for Economic Performance, and published by the IPD (1997) and by Deloitte & Touche (1998) shows a clear link between the adoption of human resource management practices and business performance. This demonstrates how much of the variation between companies in change in productivity and profitability is attributable to focusing on key people management issues – that significant improvement in both productivity and profitability can be achieved by focusing on:

- ensuring that people are satisfied with their jobs, rewards, working conditions and career prospects
- developing commitment by encouraging people to move beyond the contractual commitment to emotional commitment, by which they develop a strong sense of loyalty to the organisation, its customers and clients, and will not only see what needs to be done for the benefit of the organisation but will initiate action and urge action from colleagues

- managing organisational culture through focusing on all the key cultural dimensions
- adopting an integrated approach to human resource management programmes and processes that will develop satisfaction and commitment.

The research then goes on to show that the use of human resource management practices and effective job design can have more impact on productivity and profitability than other fundamental business activities.

This research is of some significance in that it provides very clear evidence that concentrating on people is one of the keys to success, and therefore that an effective strategy for their management is a key requirement for any business.

But what makes an effective strategy for managing people?

The Deloitte & Touche survey in 1998 identified 12 key factors in five main areas of management activity that differentiate between high-growth businesses and low-/no-growth businesses. The five main areas of management activity are:

- taking a strategic view of managing people
- involving people in the business
- investing in communication
- managing people's performance
- focusing on employees as individuals.

Some of these activities are covered in much greater detail in Chapter 7, but because they are key features in the development of strategy we will summarise them here.

In *taking a strategic view of managing people* it is imperative that people are at the centre of strategic planning for the organisation. Key questions about the organisation's people must be addressed in planning business strategy. Are the right knowledge, skills and competencies available within the organisation, and if not, can they be acquired? Are people capable of taking forward new directions in business strategy? Can the knowledge, skills and competency available be deployed in a way that opens up new business opportunities?

It is also important in developing strategy to take account of company culture. This is a complex area, says the Deloitte & Touche survey, and requires a focus on:

- the artefacts and symbols of the organisation, such as the layout of the working environment, the technology used, the use of information and reporting
- the stories and myths that are commonly shared in the organisation and indicate success and failure
- the rites and rituals that reinforce behaviour patterns and demonstrate the organisation's values
- the rules, systems and procedures that set the parameters for behaviour and action
- the organisational heroes and heroines that act as role models for people
- the beliefs, values and attitudes that are expressed and displayed in everyday activity
- the ethical standards that guide the boundaries of what is acceptable and not acceptable
- the basic assumptions that are made about human behaviour, human nature, relationships, reality and truth.

Involving people in the business requires careful job design with a particular emphasis on teamworking whereby teams have a high degree of autonomy and freedom for self-management. To be effective, teams would need clear objectives and targets and the autonomy to plan and undertake work, acquire resources, and improve processes, products and services. Parameters must be specified so that integration with the organisation as a whole is not compromised, but these must be as wide as possible.

There are very few managers who would disagree with the third main activity, *investing in communication*. Successful businesses invest heavily in communications and there are three aspects of communication that distinguish high-growth businesses from the less successful. These are:

- communicating business strategy to all employees
- regularly giving feedback on performance measures to all employees
- using a wide range of communication methods.

The fourth activity, *managing people's performance*, is also self-evident, but failing to pay sufficient attention to this area can cause significant employee relations problems. People perform best if they know what they have to do, how well they are doing it, what they have to improve, and how the improvement is going to be achieved. Setting clear, individual objectives for employees is a critical element in any successful organisation. For people not to know what is expected of them can lead to dissatisfaction, low morale, high labour turnover and high levels of absenteeism – all of which are classic employee relations problems.

The final activity is *focusing on employees as individuals*, and while the use of terms such as 'human resources' and 'human capital' encourages a view of an organisation's employees as a homogeneous group, they can diminish the view of employees as individuals. Yet high-performing organisations do focus on people as individuals and use techniques of involvement that are designed to encourage satisfaction and commitment (see Chapter 7).

All of the activities identified by Deloitte & Touche are important in formulating strategy, but they must not be viewed in isolation, as the following two examples – one from an educational establishment and one from a private sector organisation – demonstrate. It has not been possible to publish both documents in full, but the extracts from both strategy documents show that it is vital to ensure that the whole range of people management activities – recruitment and selection, reward and recognition, training and development, and employee relations – are integrated into the strategic planning process.

Example 1 Private sector organisation (with several subsidiaries)

HUMAN RESOURCES PLAN 2004–2008

Executive summary
The environment in which all our companies have to operate continues to be very competitive and in this context, it is important to recognise the importance of the 'people contribution' . . .

People's contribution is influenced by the way that they are managed and whether they perceive that they are valued for their individual contributions. To this extent it is vitally important that managers, at all levels, acquire, and develop, expertise and knowledge in management skills. . . . To achieve these aims means that we must:

- take a strategic view of managing people

- involve people in the business
- continue to invest in communication
- manage people's performance effectively
- focus on employees as individuals.

If we do these things, we are much more likely to develop enhanced employee commitment. In turn, this will mean that individuals are encouraged to move beyond their basic contractual commitment and develop a strong sense of loyalty to the organisation. Creating the climate where people are prepared to give more by 'going the extra mile' will ensure that their contribution to the business is maximised. But, by itself, this is not enough. We need to concentrate on certain key factors which can be summarised as follows:

1 **Employee reward systems**

   Our basic reward system is primarily a combination of basic pay, performance or profit-related bonus (for some individuals) and an optional pension benefit. If we want to motivate individuals to deliver our declared business strategies, we have to build on our current reward system so that it is capable of meeting individual employee aspirations. To achieve this we need to ensure that we have a reward system that is both flexible and fair and that is perceived as such by employees.

2 **Recruitment and selection**

   There are two major issues that we need to be concerned with. One is to ensure that the level of labour turnover in each part of the business is properly managed and kept within acceptable norms. The second is the need to attract sufficient numbers of high-calibre candidates for declared vacancies. Because of the changing nature of the labour market we need to consider what changes we need to make in our employment practices if we are to meet this objective.

3 **Performance management**

   Reducing the incidence of poor performance, and improving organisational performance generally, will continue to be a key priority. This is a complex process with no easy solutions and there are number of steps that can be taken to enhance both individual and collective performance. . . .

4 **Career development**

   If we are to retain competent employees within our workforce we need to develop the process of career planning. While this will not be appropriate for everyone, it will be an important factor for some in deciding whether to remain in our employment. Added to this will be a continuing requirement to develop the skills of all our employees. Every business should have a training plan and appropriate budgets for this purpose which should be driven by the appraisal process. Beyond this, there is also a need to develop those individuals who might have the capability of taking on senior management roles in the future. Our annual succession planning exercise is crucial to meeting this objective, but we also need to provide a senior management development programme.

5 **Employee relations**

   It is clear that developments in employment law will not slow down and during the lifetime of this plan further changes will be introduced that will have a direct impact on our businesses. In particular, there will be legislation on employee involvement and consultation, and equal opportunities. It is therefore important that we gain the commitment and trust of the majority of our employees. This can be achieved if we invest in techniques of employee involvement.

Overall, our human resource activities over the lifetime of this plan have to meet the following objectives:

- to generate commitment of all employees to the success of the organisation
- to enable the business to better meet the needs of its customers and adopt to changing market requirements
- to help the business to improve performance and productivity, and adapt to new methods of working
- to improve the satisfaction that employees get from their work
- to provide all employees with the opportunity to influence and be involved in decisions which are likely to affect their interests.

Example 2 Educational establishment

STRATEGY FOR HUMAN RESOURCE MANAGEMENT AND DEVELOPMENT

1 The context for the human resource strategy

1.1 The human resource strategy

The initiative to develop the HR strategy starts from the importance and value of the College staff. The effective management, engagement, development, participation and motivation of its staff are key to the success of the College. The human resource culture, values and the managerial leadership within the College will play a major influence on the quality of staff performance and the quality of the learning experience and achievement of its students. The various elements of HR strategy and the related policies and practices must be managed in an integrative way and not as a series of unrelated events.

1.2 The strategy is derivative from the College's vision and corporate objectives

The strategy identifies key aims and success criteria which determine the operational objectives and the priorities that underpin the College's continuous development.

2 College vision statement and the key elements of an HR strategy

2.1 In summary the College's vision is to enrich lives through various actions, including being a dynamic, responsive and well-run organisation, developing and training its staff.

2.2 A key human resource challenge is to bring together the continuous development of staff with the growth and aspirations of the College. This means that the human resource strategy takes a view of how skills and abilities need adapt and be proactive to address staff development needs as the College progresses. It also requires a review of systems and processes that have become moribund in whole or in part and to ensure that they are more responsive to development needs identified.

2.3 It is recognised that continuing development and innovation requires a flexible and responsive approach with accuracy. This will require consistent advice and support from the HR team.

2.4 The human resource culture must recognise, value and encourage achievement and ambition through constructive criticism, creative thinking and problem-solving skills. The College as a dynamic learning organisation will create and nurture conditions where staff have opportunities to take forward the challenge to develop the learning environment in line with the corporate objectives.

3   The human resource section – key aims

3.1 The key aims of the human resource section are to:

- provide a professional service through accurately and consistently reflecting best employment practice in all its activities
- be outward-looking and reflective on developments outwith the College and apply these dispositions with sensitivity to the College context to achieve the College's strategic objectives
- operate successfully within the time-scales of the operational and strategic plans delivering efficient service, helping to deal with day-to-day issues and problems.

The importance of adopting an integrated approach, as demonstrated above, is supported by the research carried out for the CIPD and others. This confirms that companies which are achieving the best results in productivity, profitability and growth have people management strategies that make a real difference. The conclusions of Purcell *et al* are compelling. They state that

> the most successful organisations were those that could sustain their performance over the long term and demonstrate a robust association between people management and performance.

Strategy and employment policies

Having examined the process of strategy formulation we now turn to look at how this links into employee relations in particular – but not forgetting that there must be a link with other aspects of the employment relationship: employee resourcing, employee reward, employee development.

Whatever means organisations choose for formulating their strategy, either at corporate or business level, maximising the organisation's competitive advantage has to be a major issue. This inevitably means that an organisation must constantly re-evaluate itself in order to sustain any necessary improvements. Organisations are therefore concerned with the design and management of employment policies and processes that will deliver and sustain business improvement. The process of change, and its impact on the development of strategy, presents many challenges for the employee relations professional. For example, as we discuss later, there is the issue of trade unions and the provisions on recognition. Where trade unions already exist and are recognised within an organisation, the trends towards individualism, as opposed to collectivism, means that strategic choices must be made about whether those unions are encouraged or marginalised. Where they do not exist and requests for recognition are received, are these resisted or accepted voluntarily?

Overall, strategies and policies on employee relations must have a direct relationship with the business strategy and must be imaginative, innovative, clear and action-oriented. They need to be formulated by a continuing process of analysis to identify what is happening to the business and where it is going. In this context, the relevance of clear business objectives, as expressed through the medium of a mission statement, cannot be overstated. The key is to develop an employee relations strategy that is responsive to the needs of the organisation, that can provide an overall sense of purpose to the employee relations professional and assist employees to understand where they are going, how they are going to get there, why certain things are happening, and most importantly, the contribution they are expected to make towards achieving the organisational goals.

A classic example of this can be found in the example of Britannia Building Society, as featured by Persaud in *People Management*, Volume 9, No.17, August 2003. When Karen Moir, the director of organisational development, took her seat on the Britannia board she had a clear message for her fellow directors, which was that she wanted 'to introduce a people strategy that could be woven into Britannia's wider business goals and propel the society forward'.

Moir believed that 'people policies could not be separated from other aspects of business strategy'. The Society's business strategy is to maintain and improve its place in the market. Central to this is the need for the organisation to be more customer-focused and internally more people-focused. To this end Moir and her team began a series of changes aimed at transforming values. The organisation is introducing a series of measurements for every part of the business.

> Employee satisfaction, customer satisfaction, individual performance and business performance will all be quantified, replacing the intuitive thinking and rumour that Moir says used to determine performance.

In order to sustain the changes they are trying to drive through, Britannia have developed a new communication model called 'Mutual understanding'. As we say repeatedly in this text: without good communication, people strategies will either fail or wither and die. But even with good communication, unless people strategies are understood by those affected, they will be of little value. As Moir concludes:

> For the first time we understand what an HR strategy is and the part it needs to play in the business. . . . Unless HR delivers the business requirements, it has no right to play a part. It has to constantly fulfil its role.

As the Britannia experience demonstrates, once it is clear what the overall philosophy of an organisation is, the employee relations specialist can use this knowledge to put together the employee relations policies for the business. The needs of an organisation in terms of its employee relations policies are potentially infinite, but could emanate from two specific areas. One, the 'management of change', could encompass issues as diverse as improving productivity, greater employee involvement, changing reward systems or introducing teamworking. The second is the organisation's attitude towards trade unions.

Future challenges

If we examine some of the challenges facing the personnel specialist both now and in the future, we can identify some of the important links between the various personnel disciplines. In the area of employee resourcing, organisations face continuing challenges in developing policies on recruitment and selection. In employee reward there are continuing and continuous challenges to the personnel practitioner. Stimulating employee commitment, motivation and enhancing job performance are matters which will be discussed in Chapter 7, but among the issues that must be considered is the balance between pay and non-pay rewards and individual versus collective bargaining. But reward policies must (Armstrong, 1996) be

> developed and managed as a coherent whole. . . . They need to be integrated with one another and, importantly, with the key business and personnel processes of the organisation.

So far as employee development is concerned, the personnel practitioner faces three challenges, all of which impact on employee relations. Firstly, is it in the company's interests to buy in or develop their own staff? Where do the long-term interests of the business lie? If you get the balance wrong and buy in too much labour, there is a risk that existing employees will become disillusioned and assume that the organisation is not interested in investing in their future.

Secondly, what sort of employees are required? Generalists or specialists? Personnel professionals have a significant role to play in helping to identify what value there is to the organisation in particular types of employee. Although it is popular to support the idea of multi-skilling, this concept does not always serve the organisation's best interests. Too many people may want to be trained in specific skills, some of which may never be fully utilised. This can then lead to resentment or resistance to further training interventions.

Finally, if investment is to be made in employee development, is it simply a question of training people to carry out the current tasks that they are required to fulfil, or is it strategically valuable to create a 'learning environment', as many organisations have done?

All of these challenges are strategic issues that are interlinked and have an impact on employee relations. In each case they will be conditioned in their scope and their impact by the type and size of the organisation.

What challenges will your organisation face over the next five years, and how will these impact on employee relations strategy?

You should have looked at any trends in your organisation's business strategy that might have an impact, such as:

- *plans for expansion*
- *proposals for new investment*
- *the need to improve profitability or productivity.*

You need to consider the impact of changes to your employee relations strategies on the other policy areas – for example, resourcing, reward, health and safety, development. Finally, you need to consider the impact of external influences such as political (a change of UK government, or even Prime Minister), economic (interest rates, inflation, joining the euro, unemployment), societal (demographic trends, the age profile of the population), new technology, and any possible changes in legislation, particularly European influences.

MANAGEMENT STYLE

We said above that the organisation's attitude to trade unions could have a significant impact on employee relations strategy. We have already noted the impact that the values and preferences of organisations' dominant management decision-makers have on strategy formulation. These values and perceptions will in part be determined by whether the organisation adopts a unitary or pluralist approach to its employee relations. The unitary approach emphasises organisations as harmonious and integrated, all employees sharing the organisational goals and working as members of one team. The pluralist approach recognises that different groups exist within an organisation and that conflict can, and does, exist between employer and employees.

These are broad definitions, and it must be noted that simply because an organisation is described as unitarist does not mean that management and employees share the same agenda. Unitarist organisations can be either authoritarian or paternalistic in their attitudes, and this can have a major impact on management style. Pluralism, while generally used to describe an organisation that embraces collective relationships, can emphasise co-operation between interest groups, not just conflict. It is this distinction in approach to the management of people that leads to variations in employee relations policies, ranging from the paternalistic no-union approach of Marks & Spencer through the single-union no-strike philosophy of Japanese firms like Nissan, to the multi-union sites of companies like Ford.

Although external constraints on employee relations policy formulation are an important element, the internal constraints are probably of greater significance. Factors that often determine management style are organisational size, ownership and location. Style can be an important determinant in defining an employee relations policy, and is as much influenced by organisations' leaders as is business strategy. Since Fox first categorised management and employee relations as unitarist or pluralist, others have sought to define the topic in greater detail. In particular Purcell and Sissons identified five typical styles:

- authoritarian
- paternalistic
- consultative
- constitutional
- opportunist.

The *authoritarian* approach sees employee relations as relatively unimportant. Although policies and procedures may exist, they are often there because of some legislative necessity (eg grievance, discipline), and as a consequence people issues are not given any priority until something goes wrong. Typically, firms with an authoritarian approach can be small owner-managed businesses, and it is not unusual to find that the things that go wrong revolve around disciplinary issues. In many of the small firms that we have contact with, complaints against them of unfair dismissal are a common problem. For example, an employer who has paid little attention to setting standards of performance dismisses an employee who makes a mistake, and then finds that the dismissed employee wins a tribunal claim for compensation. This is usually because no previous warnings were issued and no disciplinary procedure is followed. An analysis of the size and ownership of organisations appearing in tribunal cases would support this view.

Paternalistic organisations share many of the size and ownership characteristics of the authoritarian type, but they tend to have a much more positive attitude towards their employees. Employee consultation is a high priority, irrespective of whether unions are present in the workplace, and staff retention and reward are seen as key issues.

The type of *constitutional* organisation described by Purcell and Sissons assumes a trade union presence. Although sharing some of the characteristics of the previous types of organisation, management style in employee relations is often more adversarial than *consultative*.

In the *opportunist* organisation, management style is determined by local circumstances. These would determine whether it was appropriate to recognise trade unions or not, or the extent to which employee involvement was encouraged.

Purcell (1987, page 535) moved the analysis of 'management style' forward and redefined it as:

> the existence of a distinctive set of guiding principles, written or otherwise, which set parameters to and signposts for management action in the way employees are treated and particular events handled.

This principle of setting parameters is of vital importance in the management of people. Hilary Walmsley (*People Management*, April 1999, page 48) argued that 'to get the most out of people, managers need to adapt their styles to fit different situations'. However, she went on to say that

> Managers typically use the same personal style to handle a range of situations. Usually they do this out of habit. Some are not clear about the array of potential styles available to them. Even those who are aware that there are, for example, different ways of developing and motivating people, or of approaching problem-solving, often fail to apply this knowledge to their day-to-day activities. Those who do want to apply new styles can feel confused about where and when they should try them.

Our own research would suggest that the Purcell definition is still valid, but that very often the 'guiding principles' to which he refers will be those of the Chief Executive. The style employed by these individuals is very closely linked to the issue of leadership.

Individual and collective dimensions

Purcell suggested that management style has two dimensions, individualism and collectivism, each dimension having three stages. Individualism is concerned with how much policies are directed at individual workers and whether the organisation takes into account the feelings of all its employees and 'seeks to develop and encourage each employee's capacity and role at work'. The three stages in the individual dimension are:

- commodity status
- paternalism
- resource status.

In the first, the employee is not well regarded and has low job security; in the second, the employer accepts some responsibility for the employee; in the third, the employee is regarded as a valuable resource.

The collectivist dimension is, in a sense, self-explanatory. It is about whether or not management policy encourages or discourages employees to have a collective voice and collective representation. The three stages in this dimension are:

- unitary
- adversarial
- co-operative.

At the unitary stage, management opposes collective relationships either openly or by covert means. The adversarial stage represents a management focus that is on a stable workplace, where conflict is institutionalised and collective relationships limited. The final, co-operative, stage has its focus on constructive relationships and greater openness in the decision-making process.

Can you identify the management style that operates within your organisation? Do you think that it changes to meet different needs, or is it static?

Remember, identifying a particular management style is not simply a question of labelling an organisation 'individualist' or 'collectivist'. Purcell points out that the interrelationship between the two is complex, and that simply because an organisation is seen to encourage the rights and capabilities of individuals does not necessarily mean that it is seeking to marginalise any representative group.

Selecting employee relations policies

The ability to identify which policies are suitable and which are unsuitable for particular types of organisations is an important skill for the employee relations professional to develop. Two issues that must be taken into account in drafting employee relations policies and then implementing them are external and internal factors and their influences. We identified some of the external factors in earlier chapters, in particular existing and future legislative constraints, but there are other influences. It is important to be aware of the type of policies other employers in your sector or industry are pursuing. These may have an impact in your own organisation – for example, the other organisations' taking a particular stance on employee involvement as a means of retaining key employees could impact on your own ability to retain staff.

Then there is the question of what is considered to be prevailing 'good practice'. In this context 'good practice' means identifying those acts or omissions that distinguish the good employer from the perceived 'bad' employer. For example, if you fail to operate your disciplinary procedure in line with natural justice, you may find that your ex-employees constantly file complaints against you with tribunals, and not only that but they win compensation as well. Many employers when drafting policies and procedures only scratch the surface. They either do not consider how the policy might operate in practice and whether it will meet the needs of their employees, or are careless in its operation, with the result that it fails to meet the criteria of 'good practice' – which is a standard that we pursue throughout this book. Whatever the policy, therefore, it is important to incorporate monitoring mechanisms within it so that checks can be made on its effectiveness.

All organisations need to have policies on grievance, discipline, health and safety, pay and benefits, and sickness absence, and these should always be written down and consistently applied. It is also important to acknowledge that although each of the policies mentioned above might differ in scope and depth from one organisation to another, no one, irrespective of the type of organisation that he or she worked in, would seriously question their selection in the range of employment policies adopted.

However, where we do need to examine questions of selection seriously is in respect of those policies which have a clear impact on corporate and business strategies and which can severely affect relationships at work. That an organisation's approach to strategy formulation – and thus its approach to employee relations – will continue to be influenced by UK government actions and also by consumer preferences will impact on its decisions on the way that it manages people and the policies that underpin these management processes.

In Chapter 1 and Chapter 3 we note that, for well over a decade, the main thrust of industrial, economic and legislative policy has been to create a market-driven economy, and that 'from an industrial relations perspective, the most telling feature of this policy has been the successive pieces of legislation designed to limit the role and rights of trade unions' (Guest, 1995; page 110). Because the question of why some firms willingly recognise trade unions and others do not is so important to employee relations, it is dealt with separately within this chapter. For the moment we will concentrate on policy choices in other areas.

For many organisations that try to link policy choices in employee relations to their business strategies, the real issue is not about individualism or collectivism but about ensuring that their workforce is committed to the organisation. Obtaining employee commitment is one of the principal ways organisations can position themselves in order to achieve a competitive advantage – one of the necessary prerequisites of a successful business. However, employees will only give their commitment if they feel secure, valued and properly motivated – a sense of wellbeing that is in part derived from the type of employment policies that are adopted. Such policies must be capable of 'adding value' to the business. For the employee relations professional who may be trying to decide on the advice he or she gives in respect of a particular policy, this is of some importance.

An interesting example of how commitment must be obtained to the introduction of people management policies can be seen in the case of Surrey County Cricket Club, as revealed by Allen in *People Management*, Volume 9, No.8, April 2003. Having spent some years achieving very little success, the club decided in 1996 to appoint a new Chief Executive. Paul Sheldon, who had a publishing rather than a cricket background, arrived with 'a reputed aptitude for detecting management weaknesses and instigating solutions'. As the case study said:

> poor morale, financial problems, a negative culture, no clarity of responsibility and more self-serving committees than a small democracy – not to mention a lack of cricketing success – made his task a challenging one.

Many of the non-playing staff were sceptical of new policies such as team-building and personal development, but one of those who was quickly converted to the new ideas accepted that 'aspects of the way it [the club] was run were poor'. Sheldon accepts that when he took over his strategy was high-risk, but one of his benchmarks, success on the field, has certainly been achieved.

In respect of trade unionism, the question is not about pro- or anti-union stances, it is whether entering into a relationship with an appropriate trade union can add value to the business. It would be wrong to assume that the answer to this question will always be no. The search for competitive advantage and employee commitment are key issues and are linked to the management of change in an organisation.

Managing change may require variations in organisational culture, the introduction of flexible working practices, empowerment or some form of teamworking. If any of these routes, or a combination of them all, are followed, the devising and implementation of policies to support them will be required. This is where the involvement of the employee relations professional can be of crucial importance – and before we examine the subject of change, it is important to recognise that the process of designing and implementing policies to support change requires the employee relations professional to develop certain skills. It may be that you have been asked by the board to establish whether a particular initiative will be suitable for your organisation, and proper evaluation is of critical importance because there is a danger that organisations will invest in new ideas that are not suitable for them.

MANAGING CHANGE

The management of change is something that most organisations have to undertake at some time or other, and during the change process employee relations can be under tremendous stress. In most change programmes it is safe to assume that no more than 25 to 30 per cent of people will be in favour; that up to 50 per cent will probably sit on the fence to see what happens; and that up to a quarter of people will actively resist any changes. That is why, as Machiavelli said,

> There is nothing more difficult to plan, more doubtful of success, nor more dangerous to manage than the creation of a new system. For the initiator has the enmity of all who profit by the preservation of the old institutions, and merely lukewarm defenders in those who would gain by the new ones.

But why does change fail? After all, most organisations that embark on a change programme do so with honourable motives. They want to make life better, both for the organisation and for the people who work in it. Although it is always dangerous to generalise, the cause of the failure comes from within the company. The reasons are varied, but examples include:

- misunderstanding what change is
- lack of planning and preparation

- no clear vision
- looking for quick fixes
- poor communication
- a legacy of previous change programmes.

Given the importance of people to the change process, it is essential that management are able to articulate a clear vision of the objectives of the change programme. To gain commitment to change, that vision has to be expressed clearly and unambiguously so that commitment can be obtained if management take the right steps in managing the process.

The type of steps we have in mind would include the managers' persuading the employees of the need for change. We have acknowledged that a consensus cannot always be achieved when change becomes necessary, but it is a basic principle of good employee relations that consent, however grudgingly given, is better than force. In this context managers might have to accept that change will sometimes have to be negotiated, with or without trade unions. Even without negotiation, it is absolutely true that seeking employee thoughts about the change is much more likely to lead to effective implementation than the management's adopting an attitude of 'We know best.'

Organisations of all shapes and sizes are embroiled in change, and increasingly that includes changing the established culture. This means asking questions such as how can we get our people to be more innovative, more focused, more assertive, more in line with our values? In some cases a whole new culture is needed in order to fit a new set of values to meet the organisation's intentions.

The experience of Selfridges is a case in point. They were one of the organisations studied as part of the research carried out by Purcell *et al* to which we referred earlier in this chapter. As the authors of the study state, in *People Management*, Volume 9, No.10, May 2003, 'the Selfridges story is one of reinvention and growth, in which people management has played a vital role in creating a highly successful retail chain'. It was, until the mid-1990s 'the embodiment of Grace Brothers', the fusty old department store depicted in *Are You Being Served?* The renewal process began with the appointment of a new senior team whose objective was to make Selfridges 'a store for the next century'. The store now brands itself as the 'House of Brands' and 'in transforming its employment culture to complement the change, it adopted a series of new HR initiatives'. As Selfridges recognised, 'there are a number of means at our disposal to change culture (by which we really mean behaviour and perspective). These include:

- training, mentoring and coaching – all these can help people see where they are not meeting the requirements or values of the company, and help them to change
- performance measurement – if we start to measure the things that demonstrate the right behaviours or culture, that deliver the right results, then people will pay them more attention, and if the measurement is brought into performance reviews, the associated actions will gather momentum
- reward and recognition – if in addition we allocate rewards according to key behaviours and actions, we are bound to affect the culture (We cannot resist a word of warning about those clever people who will find ways of extracting the maximum reward for the least effort, however!)
- recruitment and retention – if we build in processes in which key capabilities and behaviours are favoured, we can stimulate what we need in terms of culture change.'

However, as with many of the issues that we have covered in this chapter, managing change, altering behaviour and creating a new culture requires clear leadership. An article in *Director* magazine summarised some research on leadership conducted by Alan Hooper of Exeter University. Five key themes emerged from the research:

- Effective leaders create an understanding in the company about why change is necessary. They are clear thinkers and highly effective communicators, able to define a clear strategy, but with the flexibility to adapt to changing circumstances. Very good listeners, they are aware of the importance of unlocking others' potential, and are passionate and motivating.

- They set a personal example, demonstrating integrity, truth, openness and honesty. When Archie Norman took over as chief executive of the struggling supermarket chain Asda in 1992, he adopted an open communication policy and always spoke his mind. During the early days of restructuring this won him grudging respect and then a growing momentum of support.

- Good leaders ensure good succession. Jack Welch spent 15 to 20 per cent of his time on leadership development at GE.

- They share their experiences with their people. For example, Ken Keir, the managing director of Honda UK, spends three and a half days a week in the factory with his workforce.

- Effective leaders are self-pacing, more akin to a marathon runner than a sprinter. This means good time-management, discipline, effective delegation and a good work-life balance. They are also sensitive to the effect of change at work on the people they are responsible for.

It seems clear that the way in which an organisation is led has a major impact on the management of change. In the same way, the decision-making process is also important. Because the introduction of most new initiatives will be an evolutionary process, overseeing the pace of change is an increasingly important issue for successful management, and this requires effective decision-making. Decision-making in this context is both an end to achieve and a mechanism that can be used deliberately to shift people's behaviour and perspective over time.

Unfortunately, in many organisations, the expectation of change creates an uncertainty regarding the immediate and long-term future that can be difficult to manage or placate. If left to manage itself, this uncertainty can quickly fester to become an institutionalised insecurity that can undermine effective decision-making and create a range of employee relations problems. We are not suggesting that a focus on decision-making alone will mean the effective management of change, but clear decision-making with specific decisions allocated to relevant roles will underpin the support employees need to cope with it.

A further factor to be taken into account is that during the change process responsibilities might have to be altered and the boundaries of jobs clarified. This may mean examining organisational structure because some change programmes will challenge traditional hierarchies – a change that can give rise to considerable resentment and individual resistance. It is also important to ensure that other policies that might be required to underpin change are themselves in place – for example, equal opportunities or single-status workforce. With any new policy there will always be those who oppose it, sometimes openly and sometimes covertly, and the employee relations professional will recognise this. He or she will not assume that the process is complete just because an initiative has been properly evaluated and then properly communicated to all employees. He or she will monitor implementation and seek ways to reinforce the initial communication about the policy change.

MANAGEMENT AND TRADE UNIONS

Although the influence of trade unions has been declining steadily since 1978, the question of trade unionism *per se* is very important to the employee relations professional in trying to determine policies and procedures for his or her own organisation. Some companies seem to manage extremely well by being 'non-union'; some organisations appear to be happy to embrace unions; some actively resist them. And, as we have already noted, one of the policy choices an organisation can make is the question of its relationship, or not, with a trade union. Moreover, as also noted elsewhere in this chapter, management style and philosophy will cause different managers to have different approaches to the role of and involvement of unions. This will range from encouragement to active resistance and refusal – but the 1999 Employment Relations Act now makes it more difficult, if not impossible, to say no.

However, before making the assumption that some existing non-union firms will become unionised, we must understand what we mean by the term 'non-unionism'. Salamon (1998) explains that the term can be used to explain two different types of organisation:

> Type A: where an organisation has a policy not to recognise unions for any employees or for particular groups of employees (such as managers) and, therefore, it is a distinct aim or element of management's employee relations strategy to avoid any collective relationship (ie non-unionism results from management decision);
>
> and
>
> Type B: where union membership within the organisation or group of employees is low or non-existent and, therefore, unions are not recognised because of the absence of employee pressure for representation (ie non unionism results from the employees' decision not to join unions).

Clearly, type B organisations have little to fear from current union recognition legislation unless something happens in the working environment that fundamentally alters the status quo. If for example the company has a history of treating its employees badly and those employees have now succumbed to the blandishments of a union recruiting drive, something will have changed for the worse in the employment relationship. If it is possible to identify a causal act, can something other than union recognition remedy it? Suppose that in a type B organisation there was sudden rush to join a trade union, the organisation would have to ask itself some very searching questions. Have recent redundancies created a climate of uncertainty? Has there been a change in management style? Have grievances been ignored or badly handled? Any of these could trigger a change in employee attitudes to collective representation such that if management want to remain non-union, they will have to consider how such issues are managed (Judge, 1997).

Non-union organisations

One of the unsubstantiated myths in employee relations has been the idea that non-unionism is the panacea for business success, with organisations such as Marks & Spencer and IBM put forward as prime examples of the concept. The shareholders and customers of M&S might take a contrary view, given that organisation's depressed performance over the past five years. There will always be a debate between those who see trade unions as a negative influence and those, like most of our European partners, who see rights at work (including trade union membership and collective bargaining) as part of an important social dimension to working relationships. It is this polarisation that results in many politicians and business leaders being antagonistic towards the social dimension of the European Union. Post-World-War-II industrial relations has allowed some commentators the opportunity to promote non-unionism as the ideal state to which all businesses should aspire, and to suggest that to allow interventions from Europe would be a massive step backward.

While the debate about unionism versus non-unionism continues, the real question tends to be ignored. That is, is it easier to manage with unions or without unions? Personal prejudice should not to come into the process of effective management, but many managers' attitudes towards trade unions have been conditioned either by their own negative experiences during the 1970s and 1980s – a period when the unions contributed to their negative image with some self-inflicted wounds – or by a perception that unions somehow stop managers managing. In some cases the negativity is a result of union representatives being allowed to take the initiative because of poor management. There may be two reasons for this:

- poor training in core skills like negotiation, communication and interviewing
- a lack of clear policy guidance.

It is because this lack of skills can have such a negative impact on the whole process of employee relations that the second part of this book concentrates on the development of skills such as bargaining, negotiating, managing grievances and handling discipline.

As personnel practitioners ourselves we have received many requests for help from organisations who are having difficulty in managing their employee relations in a collectivist environment. In almost all the cases, blame is laid at the door of the union and there is no recognition that poor management might also bear some responsibility. When appropriate training interventions have been agreed and implemented we find that there is a complete turnaround. Not only do managers seize responsibility but they find that they are able to do so with little or no union resistance. In truth, union representatives have merely been filling a vacuum that nobody else was interested in. These experiences have caused many managers to become very biased against unions, and many of those that we speak to believe genuinely that without the unions business success would be guaranteed.

This faith in managing without unions has meant that some of the larger non-union firms within the UK have become the focus of attention for developments in employee relations. Companies like Marks & Spencer and IBM have always been held up as exemplary non-union employers, but now others have joined the list. At the risk of over-generalisation, the generic characteristics of these non-union companies tend to be 'a sense of caring, carefully-chosen plant locations and working environments, market leadership, high growth and healthy profits, employment security, single status, promotion from within, an influential personnel department, competitive pay and benefit packages, profit sharing, open communications, and the careful selection and training of management, particularly at the supervisory level' (Blyton and Turnbull, 1994; page 234). How many of the companies who yearn for non-union status would be prepared to make the investment in people management that the organisations that they envy have done? The real issue is how well a business is managed – that is what determines success.

Notwithstanding the influence of large organisations, data from the 1998 Workplace Industrial Relations Survey (WIRS) found that non-union establishments are more likely to be small single-plant establishments located in the private services sector. This result is not that surprising given the great encouragement that the small firms sector has received and continues to receive. The number of business start-ups has risen, and many of the new organisations have not been able to see the relevance of trade unions. Many of their employees may have been the victims of redundancy in older, traditionally unionised, industries and a reluctance to embrace the supposed cause of industrial decline (trade unions) may be understandable.

However, one must also question how active trade unions have been in trying to recruit from new industries and the new workforce. Have the unions been so busy defending the interests of their existing members that they have not been able to devote sufficient resources to recruitment? Another question that ought to be asked is, how will employees' feelings of insecurity about their long-term job prospects act as a feeding ground for trade union recruiters?

These and other questions link back to the questions of policy choice. If a business wishes to be, or to remain, non-union, it must be clear about the relationship it will have with its employees. To be a Marks & Spencer you need to be very people-oriented, with great importance placed on respect for employees. This means highly developed and effective leadership skills – and this requires an investment in people. Gaining commitment and becoming a harmonious and integrated unitary workplace requires more than words: it can mean changing the established order.

Alternatively, a business can be a type A organisation as identified by Salamon. These organisations must be prepared to deal with a request for recognition. While the idea might be anathema to an anti-union organisation, having an identifiable policy relating to trade unionism and trade union recognition could be very helpful. We are certainly aware of organisations that have been traditionally non-union, who are taking steps to prepare for a recognition claim – by, for example, training their managers in bargaining skills.

Union recognition

The 1998 Workforce Employee Relations Survey (WERS) found that in 47 per cent of workplaces there were no union members at all – 'a substantial change from 36 per cent of workplaces in 1990'. The survey found that there are 'strong associations between the type of union presence and workplace employment size', but as we have noted elsewhere, 'even stronger associations with management attitudes towards union membership'.

By the end of the 1990s trade union recognition had fallen to the point where only 45 per cent of workplaces recognised trade unions, compared to 66 per cent in 1984 and 53 per cent in 1990. But, as we have noted elsewhere, particularly in Chapter 6, the decline in union membership seems to have been halted. For some, this is a consequence of the Employment Relations Act 1999, but Gregor Gall (*People Management*, 14 September 2000) considers that 'the industrial relations landscape had already begun to change' before the ERA became law. Noting that between 1995 and mid-2000 there were nearly 800 recognition agreements signed, Gall points out that this is not simply a numbers game. For him,

> The kinds of new deals being signed – and where, by whom and under what conditions – are also important. They will influence not only the conduct of industrial relations in those organisations themselves, but also the behaviour of other organisations.

Clearly, the numbers of recognition deals that have been signed owes something to the influence of the ERA, but according to Gall,

> Increasing numbers of employers are realising that there is a positive business case for dealing with their workforces through unions, and that it is more efficient, effective and democratic than treating employees as a collection of atomised individuals.

Taking such a stance is clearly a strategic choice for many businesses, who recognise that signing a voluntary deal allows them much more influence over the content of the agreement and saves a damaging confrontation with their workforce.

What is clear is that membership gains have been achieved and unions are now poised to take advantage of the provisions of the ERA in order to reassert their influence in the workplace. How employers respond will be a mixture of strategic choice and policy formulation.

Obtaining union recognition

The Employment Relations Act (1999) sets out the basis on which employees can obtain recognition. In summary, those provisions are:

- One or more independent trade union seeking recognition must apply to the employer in writing requesting recognition. The employer has 10 working days in which to respond. If, by the end of the 10-day period, the employer has not responded or has rejected the request, the union may apply to the Central Arbitration Committee (CAC) for a decision on the 'appropriate bargaining unit' and/or whether a majority of the workers support recognition for collective bargaining.

- If, however, the employer indicates during the 10-day period that, while not accepting the request, he is prepared to negotiate to agree the bargaining unit and recognition for it, a negotiation period of 20 working days (or longer, if mutually agreed) is available. If these negotiations fail, the union may apply to the CAC as above, but may not apply if it has rejected or not responded within 10 days to an employer proposal for ACAS to assist.

- Once a recognition claim is referred to the CAC, it must try to help the parties reach agreement within 20 working days (or such longer appropriate period as it may determine). If agreement is not reached within that period the CAC then has 10 days (or a longer period where it specifies the reasons for extension) to decide the appropriate bargaining unit.

- In respect of an application to decide the appropriate bargaining unit and whether the union(s) has the support of the majority of the workers in it, the CAC must not proceed unless it decides that:
  - members of the union (or unions) constitute at least 10 per cent of the workers constituting the proposed bargaining unit, and
  - there is *prima facie* evidence that a majority of the workers constituting the proposed bargaining unit would be likely to favour recognition of the union(or unions) as entitled to conduct collective bargaining on behalf of the bargaining unit.

- In deciding the appropriate bargaining unit, the CAC must take these matters into account:
  - the need for the unit to be compatible with effective management
  - the matters listed in sub-paragraph (4), so far as they do not conflict with that need.

Those matters are:

- the views of the employer and of the union (or unions)
- existing national and local bargaining arrangements
- the desirability of avoiding small fragmented bargaining units within an undertaking
- the characteristics of workers falling within the proposed bargaining unit and of any other employees of the employer whom the CAC considers relevant
- the location of workers.

If the union(s) shows that a majority of the workers in the bargaining unit are members of the union(s), the CAC must declare the union(s) recognised, *unless* one of the following three conditions applies:

a) the CAC is satisfied that a ballot should be held in the interests of good industrial relations

b) a significant number of the union members within the bargaining unit inform the CAC that they do not want the union (or unions) to conduct collective bargaining on their behalf

c) membership evidence is produced which leads the CAC to conclude that there are doubts whether a significant number of the union members within the bargaining unit want the union (or unions) to conduct collective bargaining on their behalf.

If the union(s) cannot show majority membership – or can, but one of the three conditions above applies – the CAC must arrange (through a qualified independent person) a secret ballot of the workers in the bargaining unit, asking whether they wish the union(s) to conduct collective bargaining on their behalf.

If the ballot result shows that the union is supported by a majority of those voting and at least 40 per cent of those in the bargaining unit, the CAC will declare the union(s) recognised.

Note that the CAC must not proceed with a recognition application from more than one union unless:

- the unions show that they will co-operate with each other in a manner likely to secure and maintain stable and effective collective bargaining arrangements, and
- the unions show that if the employer wishes, they will enter into arrangements under which collective bargaining is conducted by the unions acting together on behalf of the workers constituting the proposed bargaining unit.

Where the CAC declares a union(s) recognised, the parties have a negotiating period of 30 working days (or longer if mutually agreed) to agree a method for conducting collective bargaining. If they have not reached agreement then, they can seek CAC assistance during a further period of 20 working days (or longer if mutually agreed with the CAC). If they still cannot agree, the CAC must specify the method by which the parties must conduct collective bargaining (which they can vary by written agreement) and which will be a contract legally enforceable through the courts, by orders for specific performance, with which failure to comply will constitute contempt of court.

Employer concerns

Writing in *People Management* (January 1999; page 54), Mike Emmott, IPD Policy Adviser on Employee Relations, stated that 'one thing is clear beyond any doubt: most employers are opposed to the idea of a law on trade union recognition'. Many of these concerns centred on the time-scales within the recognition procedure, but this has been less of an issue owing to the overwhelming number of voluntary recognition deals that have been struck. Of more concern is the perception that many organisations have about the CAC – about whether the CAC adopts an even-handed approach to union recognition claims. The fact that its approach in some disputed cases has been criticised is not necessarily surprising – organisations that have resisted union claims are unlikely to be favourably disposed to the body that granted the disputed recognition. Whether the CAC does give trade unions preferential treatment is largely a matter of perception, but if it is to maintain the confidence of organisations, it must ensure that its independence is clearly maintained.

The government, as is to be expected, takes a much more benign view of the legislation. They see unions, 'where they are run efficiently along modern lines, as important partners for employers in promoting competitiveness and good practice' (Ian McCartney, *People Management*, 17 September 1998; page 38). This view is supported by Gall, who believes that

> the Labour government has helped to engender a climate in which many employers are less inclined to behave unilaterally, and this has legitimised a union role in organisations.

This may of course have little to do with the government, but may be more a pragmatic reaction, from employers, that the legislation on union recognition is here to stay, at least for the foreseeable future.

Notwithstanding this, the negative view of the CAC will not necessarily diminish, and as Gall and Cooper report (*People Management*, 12 July 2001) the 'unequivocal legal backing [given to the CAC in the first disputed case to reach the courts] may deter other aggrieved employers from going down this costly avenue'. There is certainly a danger that employers will grant recognition in the belief that the CAC is pro-union, and this will have a consequential negative effect on employee relations.

Employers and their use of the law

The laws that are now on the statute book impact on employee relations in a number of ways, and changes in legislation have meant that trade unions are much more responsible for the actions of their members than they used to be. This means that it is potentially much easier for employers to seek a legal remedy when industrial action is taken against them. There is a much stricter definition of what constitutes strike action, and it can only be lawful if it follows a properly conducted ballot, relates wholly or mainly to matters such as pay and conditions, and takes place between an employee and his direct employer. This is intended to rule out sympathy or secondary action by those not involved in the main dispute.

Other provisions in the legislative package include restrictions on the numbers of people that can mount a picket outside a workplace, and compulsory ballots to test union members' support for contributions to a political fund. The law has also outlawed the closed shop – which is not to say that *de facto* closed shops do not still exist, because they do, most notably in the printing industry.

Against this background we must consider the employers' use of such laws. Why do some employers seek legal assistance in the resolution of disputes and others do not? Much has been made of the rights that employers now have to take legal action against their employees, either to sue for damages caused by industrial action or to seek injunctions prohibiting action taking place.

Although the occasional high-profile case hits the headlines, there is no evidence to suggest that employers seek to exercise their legal rights every time they are faced with disruptive action. Indeed, there is probably more evidence to suggest that most employers resist the temptation to use the law. This is because they enjoy reasonably good employee relations and are more interested in maintaining those relationships in the long term than they are in short-term victories. This is not to say that some organisations, in industries such as transport, set out deliberately to alienate their workforce. It is simply that there are often other considerations. If they were not seen to challenge 'unnecessary' strikes, they would run the risk of losing, perhaps permanently, many of their customers. For this reason, any employer faced with the threat of industrial action would have to take seriously concerns voiced by its customers and seek to balance these against its long-term relationship with its workforce.

The circumstances in which an employer might have to consider using the law usually follow a breakdown in negotiations with a recognised union. Such a breakdown could lead the union to seek a formal mandate from their members supporting industrial action, or there could be some form of unofficial industrial action encouraged by lay officials. The response that an employer makes in such circumstances is extremely important and can have a critical effect on employee relations.

> Consider how you would respond to a ballot for industrial action in your organisation and what factors you would take into account.

Industrial action ballots

If, for whatever reason, negotiations with a recognised union have broken down, there is every possibility that the union will seek to organise a ballot of its members. The union may do this not just because members have a desire to take industrial action but because a positive vote can be a very useful means of forcing the employer back to the bargaining table. If you are faced with a ballot for industrial action, there are a number of steps to be taken to check that it complies with all the legal requirements. Firstly, was the ballot conducted by post? Before any form of industrial action can commence, all those employees who it is reasonable to believe will be called upon to take part in the action must have been given a chance to vote. Secondly, were you as the employer given seven days' notice before the ballot took place? Thirdly, has the union appointed independent scrutineers to oversee the ballot? Finally, did you receive notice of the result, and was this at least seven days before any proposed action?

Let us assume that all the legal requirements have been complied with. What are the legal options? Can any action be taken against the union? Not really, unless it can be demonstrated that the proposed action would not be a lawful trade dispute within the meaning of the legislation. There used to be a right to take sanctions against individuals, but the 1999 Employment Relations Act has changed this. The legislation makes it automatically unfair to dismiss workers taking part in protected (lawful) action within eight weeks of the action beginning. Furthermore, after eight weeks it will still be unfair to dismiss if the employer has not followed an appropriate procedure for the resolution of the dispute – an 'appropriate procedure' being one established in a collective agreement. What happens when the union or its members are in breach of an agreed procedure?

Now let us examine a second scenario. Let's say that the ballot for industrial action was not conducted properly. In these circumstances, and before seeking a legal remedy, it is important to consider all the options. Decisions on using legal intervention should never be taken without a full and extensive evaluation. Firstly, it might be appropriate to sit down with those who organised the ballot to discuss concerns about its validity. It is possible that they are already aware of its flaws, but are merely seeking to demonstrate the depth of feeling about a particular issue in order to get a resumption of negotiations. Alternatively, it might be appropriate to talk to those who might have been excluded from a ballot. They may be prepared to back the company in any dispute and it is possible their votes, in a re-run ballot, might overturn the original result. The third option is to seek an injunction against the union restraining its members from taking any action until a proper ballot is conducted. Again this can be a high-risk strategy because in a re-run ballot those who previously voted against the union might vote with them on the basis of solidarity.

Ultimately, as with many aspects of employee relations, whether particular employers choose to seek a legal remedy to constrain the actions of their workforce will depend on management style and whether there is a desire to maintain good working relationships.

SUMMARY

In this chapter we have looked at the link between corporate and business strategies and functional activities such as personnel. This has allowed us to see the relationship between the decisions of the board and the role of line managers in translating those decisions into actionable policies. We have looked at the process of strategy formulation and have seen that a number of different approaches are available. The methodology employed will, inevitably, differ and it is important that you understand the various models and their critical components. Equally, it is important that the HR professional understands the goals of his or her organisation and what his or her role is in contributing to the strategic agenda. This will require some more detailed reading of both the texts that have been referred to and the various case studies that have been highlighted. In the next chapter we will be looking, in some detail, at the type of environments in which organisations operate, and this – together with the markets they operate in – will have a clear impact on strategic choice. We also pointed out that employee relations, like every other function within the business, does not operate in a vacuum. This means that there has to be a relationship with employee development, reward and resourcing.

The chapter has also examined some of the issues that must be taken into account when drawing up an employee relations policy and managing change. We looked at the skills required in selecting and applying particular policies to the organisation, and the skills needed to manage change effectively. In the context of gaining commitment we highlighted a number of core skills that we feel are an absolute necessity for the professional personnel practitioner.

We noted that different organisations have different approaches to the role and involvement of unions, and we examined the causes of non-unionism. We looked at some examples of non-union firms and whether their success was owing to good management or the fact that they kept unions at arms' length.

We concluded that good management was the most important factor. We identified the role that the law can play in management/union relationships and what factors employers must consider before they used the legal processes against trade unions or trade union members.

Key points

- There has to be an alignment between business needs and the HR needs in order to develop the HR strategy and determine what HR interventions are required.

- It is important to incorporate monitoring mechanisms into employee relations policies and instigate a robust performance review process.

- It is important to evaluate new initiatives and ideas and gain overall commitment to particular policies before seeking to implement them.

- Management style has a major role to play in the determination of an employee relations policy in respect of trade unionism, union recognition, or non-unionism.

- Decisions on whether, and when, to use the law against trade unions or trade union members can be quite complex and should not be taken lightly.

FURTHER READING

ALLEN D. (2003) Testing times, *People Management*, Volume 9, No.8, April.

ARMSTRONG M. (1996) *Employee Reward*. London, Institute of Personnel and Development.

BLAKSTAD M. and COOPER A. (1995) *The Communicating Organisation*. London, Institute of Personnel and Development.

BLYTON P. and TURNBULL P. (1994) *The Dynamics of Employee Relations*. London, Macmillan.

BURNES B. (1996) *Managing Change: A strategic approach to organisational dynamics*. London, Pitman.

BUTCHER D. and MELDRUM M. (2001) Defy gravity, *People Management*, Volume 7, No.13, June.

CAULKIN S. (2001) The time is now, *People Management*, Volume 7, No.17, August.

DELOITTE & TOUCHE (1998) *Business Success and Human Resources*. Management Survey.

EMMOTT M. (1999) Collectively cool, *People Management*, Volume 5, No.2, January.

GALL G. (2000) In place of strife, *People Management*, Volume 7, No.18, September.

GALL G. and COOPER C. (2001) Court upholds CAC recognition award to steel union, *People Management*, Volume 7, No.14, July.

GUEST D. (1995) Human resource management, trade unions and industrial relations, in Storey J. (ed.) *Human Resource Management: A critical text*. London, Routledge.

GUEST D., KING Z., CONWAY N., MICHIE J. and SHEEHAN-QUINN M. (2002) *Voices from the Boardroom* – A Research Report. London, Chartered Institute of Personnel and Development.

INSTITUTE OF PERSONNEL AND DEVELOPMENT (1997) *The Impact of People Management Practices on Business Performance*.

JENKINS M. and AMBROSINI V. (2002) *Strategic Management: A multi-perspective approach*. London, Palgrave.

JOHNSON G. and SCHOLES K. (2003) *Exploring Corporate Strategy*, 6th edition. London, Prentice-Hall.

JUDGE G. (1997) United firms stand, but divided they fall, the *Guardian*, 29 April.

KAY J. (1993) *Foundations of Corporate Success*. Oxford, OUP.

MARCHINGTON M. and WILKINSON A. (1996) *Core Personnel and Development*. London, Institute of Personnel and Development.

McCARTNEY I. (1998) In all fairness, *People Management*, Volume 4, No.18, September.

MILLWARD N., STEVENS M., SMART D. and HAWES W. R. (1992) *Workplace Industrial Relations in Transition*, the ED/ESRC/PSI/ACAS Surveys. London, Gower.

PERSAUD J. (2003) Mutual appreciation, *People Management*, Volume 9, No.17, August.

PORTER M. (1985) *Competitive Advantage: Creating and sustaining superior performance*. New York, Free Press.

PURCELL J. (1987) Mapping management styles in employee relations, *Journal of Management Studies*, Volume 24, No.5, page 535.

PURCELL J., KINNIE N. and HUTCHINSON S. (2003) They're free!, *People Management*, Volume 9, No.10, May.

PURCELL J., KINNIE N., HUTCHINSON S., RAYTON B. and SWART J. (2003) *Understanding the People and Performance Link: Unlocking the black box* – A Research Report. London, Chartered Institute of Personnel and Development.

SALAMON M. (1998) *Industrial Relations Theory and Practice*, 3rd edition. London, Prentice-Hall.

SCARBROUGH H. and ELIAS J. (2002) *Evaluating Human Capital* – A Research Report. London, Chartered Institute of Personnel and Development.

TYSON S. (1995) *Human Resource Strategy: Towards a general theory of human resource management*. London, Pitman.

WALMSLEY H. (1999) A suitable ploy, *People Management*, Volume 5, No.7, April.

The economic and corporate environment

INTRODUCTION

In a 1997 statement on employee relations the IPD drew attention to the need for every organisation to continually improve its performance because of the challenges that were constantly being imposed by the corporate environment. Whether those challenges derived from intensifying product market competition, from changes in the world economy, or from the spending controls that continue to characterise the public sector, the pressure is much the same for all organisations. That statement is as true today as it was in 1997 – and the pressures to which it refers are unlikely, in the short term, to decrease.

These pressures are external to the organisation, and the purpose of this chapter is precisely to examine those factors which, when taken together, are referred to as the external corporate environment in which all organisations have to operate. It matters not whether the organisation is a large multinational, a National Health Service Trust or a medium-sized service company, its employee relations are influenced, and shaped, by the way in which the external corporate environment impacts on the workplace.

CONTEXT

In Chapter 1 we noted that the corporate environment must be examined in the context of economic management, political/legal influences and technological changes. The legislative influences are more fully considered in Chapter 4, so this chapter will concentrate more on the economic, political and technological factors. These three issues are important to understanding employee relations and why organisations choose to adopt particular policies and how such policies have changed, or might change, over time.

The business environment in which employee relations professionals operate is constantly changing, and it is important for them not only to be aware of specific shifts in employee relations policies resulting from such changes, but to monitor the external environment to anticipate possible changes and developments, and draw up a plan to deal with these expected changes as and when they arise. Employee relations policies devised and implemented in this context have both a reactive and proactive role – a strategic role that is central to the organisation's growth and survival.

Although each of the elements is crucial in determining the employee relations practices of individual employers, the response of each employer to the impact on his or her own business or organisation is likely to be different. For example, a traditional non-union company such as Marks & Spencer is unlikely to have responded in the same way to the legislative changes introduced during the 1980s as a company that was traditionally heavily unionised. Equally, non-union organisations may react in a completely different way to changes introduced by the Employment Relations Act (1999). The statutory rights on union recognition contained within the Act have caused many organisations to fundamentally rethink their attitudes towards collectivism and the role the workforce may play in the process of change. The 1980s changes to the laws on strikes, picketing and closed shops opened the door to employers who wanted to force through change, and had a major impact on trade union membership and influence.

As Zoe Roberts (*People Management*, 11 September 2003) reported:

> The unions have had a roller-coaster ride over the past quarter of a century. After membership levels reached record highs during the late 1970s, the 1980s saw a dramatic decline which led some commentators to predict the death of the movement.

To many employee relations specialists, particularly those whose organisations/industries had always recognised unions, this prediction seemed less than credible, and as Cathy Cooper (*People Management*, 12 July 2001) said:

> The UK's unions seem to have at last broken out of their decline – with union membership rising and the number of recognition deals exceeding TUC expectations.

What is interesting about this change has been employers' willingness to enter into voluntary recognition arrangements rather than be forced into recognition by the new statutory framework. According to research from Incomes Data Services (IDS), nearly 500 voluntary recognition deals were signed in the two years to June 2001. This is partly explained by the concern that many employers have about whether the Central Arbitration Committee (CAC) adopts an even-handed approach to union recognition claims. Its approach in some disputed cases has been criticised because it is felt that it gives trade unions preferential treatment, even though the legislation is not drafted in this way. Since the legislation came into force in June 2000, the ratio of voluntary to statutory recognition has been 4:1 in favour of voluntary. Fraser Younson (*People Management*, 7 March 2002; page 19) suggests that 'A voluntary agreement is more likely to be in a form an employer can live with.'

Although Incomes Data Services reported some significant gains in trade union membership in the years following New Labour's election victory in 1997 – up by 50,589 in 1997/98, and by 105,000 in 1998/99 – a Department of Trade and Industry Report in 2003 suggested that the post-1997 election bounce has not been sustained. The key findings of the DTI report are shown in the box opposite, and they would imply that, relative to the 1960s and 1970s, there is no evidence to suggest that trade unions will attract back the missing millions in their membership numbers.

DEPARTMENT OF TRADE AND INDUSTRY

TRADE UNION MEMBERSHIP 2003

Key findings

- Both the number of trade union members in the United Kingdom and the rate of trade union membership were little changed in autumn 2003 when compared with a year earlier.

- In autumn 2003 an estimated 7.38 million people *in employment* in the United Kingdom were members of a trade union. This was an increase of 0.4 per cent or around 27,000 people, compared with levels recorded in autumn 2002. Despite this modest increase in union members, the rate of union membership remained unchanged from a year earlier at 26.6 per cent of all people in employment.

- The number of *employees* who were trade union members in the UK fell by around 10,000 to 7.068 million in autumn 2003, compared with 2002. However the rate of union membership increased slightly, from 29.2 per cent in 2002 to 29.3 per cent of employees in autumn 2003.

- This was the first increase in employee union density since this series began in 1989. However, it was solely due to growth in the *proportion* of UK employees who worked in the public sector, rather than to an increase in the rate of unionisation in private or public sectors.

- Less than one in five private sector employees in the UK is a union member. In 2003 union density remained unchanged from 2002 at just 18.2 per cent of private sector employees.

- Almost three in five public sector employees in the UK are union members. Public sector union density fell to 59.1 per cent of employees in autumn 2003, from 59.7 per cent in 2002. Despite this fall in density the number of public sector union members rose by around 40,000 in 2003, as the size of the public sector grew.

- The number of male employees who were union members fell by around 48,000 in 2003, while female employees in trade unions rose by around 37,000. Male union density remained unchanged at 29.4 per cent, while for women it increased from 29.0 to 29.3 per cent.

- The hourly earnings of union members averaged £11.06 in autumn 2003, 17.7 per cent more than the earnings of non-union employees.

- Almost half of UK employees (48.8 per cent) were in a workplace where a trade union was present. However, union presence was much lower in the private sector (34.4 per cent) than the public sector (87.4 per cent).

- The number of UK employees covered by a collective agreement was 8.66 million in autumn 2003, or 35.9 per cent of all employees.

The inability of the trade unions to make any significant improvements in their membership base is underlined by their continuing failure to attract younger workers. As Zoe Roberts noted in her *People Management* article (see above):

> Figures from the 2001 Labour Force survey show that while 48 per cent of 18- to 29-year-old public sector workers are union members, this figure falls to just 11 per cent in the private sector. And unfortunately for the unions, 83 per cent of this age group work in the private sector.

Notwithstanding that there has been no significant gain in their membership, many employers still have real fears that the gains made in the last 20 years in eliminating outdated working practices are beginning to be eroded. There is concern that the resurgence in trade union membership will result in a return to militant behaviour by some sections of the workforce and lead to an increase in industrial action. For example, the National Union of Journalists, which has campaigned heavily against low pay in the regional newspaper sector, has supported a series of strikes by its members in support of its objectives. Most students should be familiar with the long-running dispute in the Fire Service, and the government's pledge to cut up to 100,000 civil service jobs may herald an increase in militancy in the public sector generally.

But, says the TUC in a study called *Bargain or Bust?* (www.tuc.org.uk/publications), 'substantial numbers of employers are using consultants to counter union activity'. The TUC claims that the failure of the Communication Workers' Union to win a ballot for union recognition at T-Mobile in 2003 was partly owing to a publicity campaign among employees orchestrated by external consultants.

> Have you perceived any growth in union membership within your own organisation, or one with which you are familiar? If there is such growth, has it resulted in any increase in union militancy?

Change in organisations

All employers have their own objectives, their own styles of employee relations and their own structures of organisations and associations. These structures have changed in recent times, and it is important that the employee relations professional keeps up to date with new trends and developments. For example, the role of employers' organisations (see Chapter 6) has declined in recent years in response to moves to decentralise the levels at which collective bargaining takes place. In the private sector there is now little national bargaining, while in the public sector some local authorities have decentralised traditional systems of bargaining in favour of local wage determination.

Organisational structure has changed in both the public and the private sectors. The structure of the National Health Service today is radically different from what it was 20 years ago. This has meant changes in the way that it manages its employee relations. Changes have also occurred in respect of employees and their organisations. The UK government economic policy and changes in legislation alter the relative balance of bargaining power between employers and employees. This can explain, inter alia, changes in the level of membership of unions, causing individual unions to change their strategies to protect and advance their members' interests – for example, merging with other unions to create 'super-unions'. These issues are discussed in greater detail in Chapter 6.

The role of the state in influencing employee relations has also changed. It has always been a major employer in its own right, and the post-World-War-II expectation was that it would be a 'model employer' by:

■ encouraging collective bargaining

■ ensuring that the pay of its employees was in line with that of the private sector

■ resolving differences with its employees by arbitration and not through the use of industrial sanctions.

This concept has now changed as the whole nature of public sector employment has altered, former civil servants now working for quasi-private-sector employers. The growth of executive agencies, the outsourcing of local authority services and the spread of privatisation has further diluted the concept of the public servant. This dilution is set to spread as the concept of the public/private sector partnership is widened and expanded.

Most of this change resulted from the objective of successive Conservative administrations during the 1980s and 1990s to reduce the influence of government on people's lives. They saw the role of the UK government as staying outside the employee relations arena, and although the state remains a large employer, it no longer views collective bargaining, pay comparability and arbitration as central to its employee relations policies. There continues to be strong encouragement to relate pay increases of government employees to improvements in individual performance. Although the present Labour government is not as outwardly anti-union as its Conservative predecessors were perceived to be, there is significant evidence that the Labour Party's traditional links with the union movement are regarded as less important by Ministers than once they were. There is certainly no suggestion that government will actively promote an increase in collective bargaining in its employee relations policy towards those employees whose terms and conditions of employment it directly or indirectly finances.

All this change has impacted on the nature and style of employee relations processes. As the impact of collective bargaining, and thus collective agreements, has declined, there has been a growth in the use of other employee relations processes. Joint consultation, while not a new concept, has undergone a resurgence and employee involvement schemes (for example, two-way communication, encouraging employees to contribute their knowledge and experience to operational decisions) have become much more important. This process is likely to be further strengthened when the EU Directive on information and consultation (which we examine in more detail in Chapter 4) comes into effect from 2005.

The concept of the balance of bargaining power, and how important it is to the selection by the employer of appropriate employee relations processes, was introduced in Chapter 1. This balance is conditioned by changes in the economic, political and technological elements which taken together make up the corporate environment. In this chapter the concept is examined in greater detail and linked directly to the economic, legal and technical environment in which organisations exist and compete. The concept of the balance of power is also significant in helping explain changes in the employee relations system over time – for example, why employee relations behaviour now is different from what it was in the 1970s.

> List the economic, legal/political and technological factors that have impacted on your organisation in the last five to 10 years.

ECONOMIC MANAGEMENT

The economic environment is influenced by the macro-economic policies a particular government chooses to implement. In the context of the UK, government policies regarding the levels of:

- employment
- inflation
- taxation
- interest rates
- exchange rates

have a direct effect on employee relations. This is because they have an impact on the relative balance of bargaining power between the buyers and sellers of labour services and thereby the rules and regulations that govern employment conditions. For example, if we are in a period of high inflation, high levels of taxation and high interest rates, the stability of business is threatened. This can in turn lead to higher levels of unemployment and a consequent worsening in employment conditions or redundancies and lay-offs. Even when individuals are in work, a less favourable economic climate will alter their perception of continuing job security and will also have an impact on the relative balance of bargaining power.

However, it would be a mistake to assume that the UK government has a completely free hand in deciding what economic policies to implement. Like businesses, it is affected by external events. Even before the catastrophic events of 11 September 2001 there was concern that a downturn in the global economy would have an adverse effect on Britain. Large parts of the US economy had ground to a halt, and Japan and other Far East economies were in difficulties. This situation clearly worsened after 11 September, and in the aftermath of the terrorist attacks the financial markets went into what some described as 'panic mode'. The Dow-Jones and FTSE plunged as investors took fright, moving their cash out of shares and into safe havens like government bonds, and oil prices soared as the world feared a long-drawn-out war. Fortunately, within six months some of the panic subsided and share prices began to recover – but not before thousands of jobs were lost worldwide, primarily in airlines and other associated businesses.

There is no doubt, however, that the aftermath of 11 September has influenced the foreign policy of all governments, and that this in turn will influence economic thinking not just in the UK but also worldwide for some considerable time. The decision to go to war in Iraq is a case in point. Oil prices, which at the time of writing were at an all-time high, show no signs of any significant reduction. In the view of many analysts they will remain high for some considerable time and will influence both consumer and public spending. This in turn will impact on the labour market and thus employee relations.

In addition to the influences that worldwide events have, UK macro-economic policy will also be affected by any decisions the UK government makes regarding European Monetary Union. Now that the euro is a reality – and irrespective of whether the UK joins or stays out – the economy will not be immune from its impact. Many organisations have made arrangements to deal in euros and have set up systems that would allow their employees to be paid in the new currency. Some banks are establishing euro accounts for customers who want them, and many retail businesses have made it clear that they will accept the new currency. All of this could feed down into employee relations practices and policies at the workplace, particularly if the pro-euro campaigners are proved right and the eurozone economies grow at a faster rate than a non-euro UK, thereby putting pressure on jobs and wage rates.

> If the UK were to join the euro, what do you consider would be its impact on the employment relations policies of your organisation? Why do you think so?

However, whatever the degree of outside influence, the UK government has the role of an economic manager. Although different political parties may have different ideologies and policies, the objectives of economic management – whichever party is in power – have been broadly similar. These have been:

- price stability
- full employment
- economic growth
- a balance of payments surplus.

Yet the priorities given to these four objectives have differed between governments. The Conservative governments (1979–1997) gave the greatest priority to price stability, while the Labour governments (1974–1979) put the greatest emphasis on the full employment objective. The objective of the Labour government from 1997 onwards has been slightly different. Although it has adopted many of the economic disciplines of its predecessor Conservative governments, its principal aim has been to establish a stable economy. One of the difficulties that Britain has endured since World War II is a propensity to 'boom and bust' in the context of the economic cycle. In order to achieve their objectives governments have taken a number of steps, some of them reasonably straightforward, like controlling public spending, and some of them very radical, such as surrendering control of interest rates to the Bank of England. Monetary policy was subcontracted to the Bank of England immediately after the 1997 General Election and has, since then, broadly been perceived as a success by all the main political parties. The Bank's monetary policy committee now makes decisions on interest rates, and this has helped to provide a degree of stability in Britain's financial markets.

Of course, not everybody can always be satisfied, whoever sets policy, because it is possible to make a good argument for cutting rates, increasing them, and keeping them the same. Some commentators would argue that our present system is good news for Britain because, unlike the members of the eurozone, at least we still have control over monetary policy. Other member states' interest rates are dictated by the European Central Bank (ECB), which has to sustain a policy that suits the whole of the zone. This may not necessarily be in the interests of individual countries whose economies may be growing at a faster rate than some of their euro partners'. This difficulty is used by the anti-euro camp to support its stance over non-membership.

Even though the two main political parties may have similar economic objectives when in government, the policies they implement to achieve them are likely to be different. The employee relations professional must therefore understand that the economic policies of a Conservative government are likely to differ from those of a Labour government, and that these distinctions in policy can have differing impacts on the relative balance of bargaining power. There are some politicians who believe Britain should follow a policy of full employment, and that the achievement of this goal justifies a degree of direct UK government intervention into the affairs of public and private enterprises. When this approach has been adopted, the outcome has been to give organised labour a relative advantage in the balance of relative bargaining power.

An important aspect of economic policy is the level of public expenditure. The International Monetary Fund (IMF) has repeatedly warned that financial market confidence and long-term interest rates are adversely affected if governments pay insufficient attention to the need to reduce the public sector borrowing requirement. Despite such warnings, the present Labour government has signalled its intention to increase the level of public spending in order to deliver on its promise to improve public services. This could mean that spending rises faster than output for the first time since Labour came into power – which for supporters of Keynesian economic theories is good news. Keynes taught that fiscal policy should be counter-cyclical. But there are dangers in this approach. External influences can impact on government economic policy, and if there a series of adverse events were to impact upon the UK economy, the government's spending plans might be unsustainable and cause a consequent rise in interest rates and unemployment.

The really important policies that might help insulate us are structural ones. We must keep ourselves more attractive than our rivals as a place to work and invest. The government recognises this, and has made it clear it will develop policies that stimulate entrepreneurship. But many such policies are slow-burn. Starting a business that will be successful and create jobs does not happen overnight. It takes time. There are, however, some things that can be done. The key one is not to stifle growth where it wants to take place – for example, easing planning restrictions and giving fast-track clearance to companies that are trying to bring in skilled workers from overseas. This process may be helped following the accession, in May 2004, of a further 10 members of the European Union. Along with the Irish Republic, the UK will offer relatively unhindered access to its jobs market for nationals from the new member states, which will, according to the Home Office, help fill up to 500,000 job vacancies in sectors such as IT, construction and hospitality and catering.

Despite signalling an intention to invest in public services, the principles for this government remain the same: keep public borrowing under some control because of the impact on inflation of not doing so. Translated into employee relations terms, this usually means keeping a tight control over increases in public sector pay. Among private sector employers there is always concern over the possibility of any government's taking a soft line on public sector pay. For example, the desire to improve rewards for groups such as nurses, the police or teachers in response to public opinion can create a knock-on effect across the board. If the government is unwilling, or unable, to keep a tight control over public sector pay settlements, any appeals to the private sector to show restraint will fall on deaf ears. That is why one of the most important skills for the employee relations professional is the art of scanning the political and environmental landscape to establish the extent to which policy shifts may have an impact on employee relations in the future.

The present government has repeatedly stated that it wants the UK to be a 'knowledge-based economy' – that it is human capital in the form of employees who help to create wealth – and therefore it is of fundamental economic importance to create significant numbers of new jobs. If, through initiatives like the New Deal, the government is successful in reducing the numbers of unemployed and creating a significant number of new skilled jobs, then there could be a swing in the balance of power towards employees and away from employers. Evidence from the Audit Commission suggests that the New Deal has not been particularly successful to date, and that most new jobs would have been created without such an intervention. However, if unemployment decreases and if skill shortages increase, organisations could find themselves under pressure to increase wages in order to counteract this.

> Consider what occupational types, either within your own organisation or externally, could be in short supply in such circumstances. It is important that your organisation plans sufficiently far ahead in respect of its manpower requirements.

There is evidence that many organisations have, over time, failed to invest sufficiently in training. Once the pool of available labour decreases, its 'price' goes up. These and other effects are not necessarily the immediate results of a change of UK government, but over time the needs of economic management changes and shifts. The strategic employee relations professional monitors and anticipates such changes, to support and inform the organisation's future plans and objectives.

Globalisation

In economic terms, a further impact on employee relations comes from the growth in multinational companies and the expansion of the global marketplace. 'Globalisation' is a word that is much in evidence today, but it is difficult to define. A possible all-embracing definition is 'the process of developing markets in new parts of the world for products and services developed in another part of the world, with the intention of increasing profit and spreading opportunity for return on "investment"'. Using the benefits of technology it is possible to migrate employment around the world to the place where conditions are most ideal for the producer – development in the 'first world', software in India, production in the third world, and a global sales team based in Brussels. Globalisation is said to be breaking down old world divisions and creating new.

The globalisation of markets, products and businesses has been a driver of major change over the past 50 years. Supporters of globalisation would argue that for both consumer and employee it has built bridges, created a greater sense of global community, and provided employment and opportunity for millions, and that this stimulus for change has created actions and events that have, on the whole, had a major positive benefit for mankind. Opponents of globalisation would refute this. Their argument is that, on the whole, companies have invested in the third world in order to take advantage of cheap labour and increase profits that have benefited Western societies. It is not our intention to agree or disagree with either of these views: our concern is with the impact globalisation has on employee relations.

Competition (which usually underpins the urge to globalise) breeds insecurity. Employees have a tendency to feel unsafe when they know that their employer is competing in the global marketplace. At any time a new process, product or service can undermine the very basis of their jobs, and this can breed insecurity. It is certainly true that we live in a world of multinationals and that the intricacies of international finance have effects on employee relations at the local level. Indeed, they can influence the location of new employment opportunities and, in some cases, the underlying culture of employee relations practices.

Multinationals see wage rates, expansion and investment in the context of the global market, in much the same way that a national company makes decisions after taking into account subsidies from enterprise areas, development corporations, and so on. International competition affects employee relations in other ways. Firms from the USA and Japan who set up in the UK look for qualities such as flexibility and adaptability. This has caused some of the traditional demarcation lines in industry to become blurred or removed to a great extent. The negotiation of such methods of working makes them important in the area of employee relations.

To understand how the UK government's role as an economic manager can affect employee relations and the relative balance of bargaining power between employers and employees, it is important to review and understand the two principal economic theories that have been applied to the management of the UK economy since the end of World War II – not least because a reversal of the economic policies that are currently being applied could result in a high-wage high-inflation economy.

The full employment/economic growth era

For nearly 30 years after World War II successive UK governments, regardless of their political complexion, were committed to a policy of full employment. During this period economic management was heavily influenced by the views of the economist John Maynard Keynes, whose basic ideas included:

- The general level of employment in an economy is determined by the level of spending power in the economy.
- The overall spending power in the economy depends upon the amount of consumption and investment undertaken by individual households and employing organisations, as well as UK government expenditure on health, education, social security, defence, industrial assistance, etc.
- Full employment is achieved by the government's regulating overall spending power in the economy through its fiscal [tax], monetary [interest rates], exchange rates [value of the pound relative to other currencies] and public expenditure policies.
- If unemployment rises owing to a lack of overall spending power in the economy, the government should inject spending power by reducing taxes on private and corporate incomes, property, expenditure (VAT, excise duties); by lowering interest rates; and/or by increasing its own expenditure.

Application of the Keynesian model of economic management led to economic growth, increased public provision (in such areas as housing, education and the National Health Service) and personal prosperity for the majority of households. From the perspective of trade unions, full employment provided them with increased bargaining power which, in many instances, led employers to concede inflationary wage settlements. Many of the craft unions – for example, printers and engineers – operated policies aimed to restrict the number of new entrants to their particular craft, which was said to delay the introduction of new working methods or technology. This behaviour created labour shortages in certain occupations and in others led to overstaffing. Attempts to resolve this problem led to considerable organisational conflict and the perception that management were unable to implement effective policies to counteract many of these restrictions. This led, inevitably, to a worsening of management-union relationships.

However, notwithstanding the increase in the overall standard of living, the general level of performance of the British economy was one of slower economic growth compared to the advance of its major competitors. This relative economic underperformance had many downside effects, one of which was less than constructive employee relations. By the latter part of the 1960s the effect of high wage settlements, together with union defensive attitudes and poor management, caused many commentators to take the view that this deterioration in competitiveness was a direct consequence of poor workplace industrial relations (Nolan and Walsh, 1995). It was a view supported by the report in 1968 of the Royal Commission on Trade Unions and Employers' Associations, which had been established in 1965 under the chairmanship of Lord Donovan. The reform of workplace industrial relations thus became a major public policy priority. However, opinions on the type of reform, and how best to implement it, differed – particularly the notion of using the law as a catalyst for bringing about change. Nonetheless, the need for reform was not questioned.

So by the mid-1960s the concerns about the prevailing system of employee relations and its adverse impact on economic competitiveness via relatively higher UK prices and lower labour productivity levels than those of our economic competitors became central to the political agenda. The Labour government under Harold Wilson, which was elected in 1964, decided to try to re-establish UK economic competitiveness by direct intervention into the outcome of employee relations through a productivity, prices and incomes policy designed to control inflation by ensuring that income increases were linked to increases in productivity and not to changes in the rate of inflation or what other workers were receiving.

For followers of Keynesian economics, if creating full employment gave rise to inflation, the implementation of a productivity, prices and incomes policy was necessary. Because wage costs account for such a significant proportion of employers' total costs, excessive rises in wage levels affect the inflation spiral. As inflation rises, economic policy-makers are tempted to regulate economic activity by stifling demand – which, in turn, can lead to rises in unemployment. Keynes argued that increasing unemployment to control inflation could be avoided, and that full employment could be maintained by the introduction of a productivity, prices and incomes policy.

The history of incomes policy over the period 1948–1979 shows that in the short term such policies were successful, but that after two or three years they broke down, usually in the face of a strike in support of a pay increase in excess of the policy. By the 1970s such policies were proving politically explosive. Such attempts to limit wage settlements were seen by some as a deliberate measure to shift the balance of bargaining power towards the interests of employers, and were resisted by the unions to the point of industrial disputes, the most famous being the miners' strikes of 1972 and 1973/74 and the 'winter of discontent' in 1978/79.

Although not an incomes policy in the accepted sense of the term, the Irish government's Programme for Prosperity and Fairness (PPF) was, nevertheless, an attempt by the state to influence the scale of wage increases (*People Management*, 11 January 2001). The PPF, which was signed in January 2000, was a 33-month national pay agreement that allowed for a first-phase increase of 5.5 per cent, a further rise of 5.5 per cent for the second 12 months, and a final increase of 4 per cent for the remaining nine months. It was the successor to a series of tripartite agreements that had started with the Programme for National Recovery in 1987 – a rescue package for a nation then facing unemployment, declining living standards and unchecked public spending. As with so many incomes policies and similar initiatives, it came under severe strain less than six months after it was signed when the rate of inflation rose above the predicted level of 3 per cent. This resulted in the unions calling for an early review of the agreement. The government initially stalled on their demands, but eventually, following six months of industrial unrest, it entered negotiations with the Irish Congress of Trades Unions and employers represented by the Irish Business and Employers Confederation. These talks produced a 3 per cent top-up on the original deal. The top-up allowed for a further 2 per cent rise on the first phase and a 1 per cent lump-sum payment in April 2002, in effect making an increase of almost 18 per cent. The Irish Business and Employers Confederation agreed to the revisions in return for renewed union commitments on industrial peace.

Despite the scepticism of many, and the opposition of most of the larger private sector unions, a new agreement 'sustaining progress' was signed in 2003. This three-year agreement, billed as a social partnership, included a 7 per cent increase in wages over an 18-month period.

It is possible that Irish employers will find their new agreement advantageous, but the CIPD Ireland director Michael McDonnel (*People Management*, April 2003), while accepting that 'most members saw the benefit of retaining the social partnership [because] the deal was as good as, if not better than, what could be achieved in a free-for-all situation with headline-setting local agreements', believed that 'the real negotiations will be next year, when we see how the economy shapes out'.

This problem of economic performance is of vital importance when considering any sort of long-term pay deal, whether this is a government-imposed incomes policy or a freely negotiated two- or three-year pay deal. If the economy fails to perform in the way that was indicated when the deal was struck, the participants will want to re-examine it. In the 1960s and the 1970s UK management was not always impressed by the arbitrary imposition of government pay norms, particularly when interest rates and inflation were running at very high levels, and they were often happy to work with their employees to find ways round them. Private sector employers were more interested in the continuation of production, and some were prepared to pay higher wages to avoid industrial action. Although we now live in a highly competitive world economy, where maintaining some form of competitive advantage is essential for most businesses, this was not always the case in the three decades after World War II. During that period a much greater proportion of an organisation's customer base was static relative to today, and organisations therefore had a much greater ability to pass on increased wage costs in the form of increased prices. In the case of the public sector, there was no serious long-term attempt to limit the growth in public expenditure, and companies and enterprises therefore learned to live with high inflation and its consequent impact on wages and prices.

> Explain the main tenets of the Keynesian approach to macro-economic management. What are its implications for employee relations at the workplace level? Give some appropriate examples.

'Irresponsible union behaviour'

Circumventing pay norms was but one example of a wider malaise. By the beginning of the 1960s the balance of power was firmly with the trade unions and, particularly in the car industry, shop stewards at plant level were increasingly exercising this power. They were reluctant to abide by disputes procedures and to subject themselves to control by full-time officials, particularly those national trade union leaders who were prepared to co-operate with some form of pay restraint. Some industries like those in ship-building, car manufacture and the ports had their own agendas that tended to be parochial, and in the opinion of many employers were motivated by political and not industrial objectives. Many employers also questioned whether shop stewards in calling unofficial (not supported by the union) and unconstitutional (failing to follow all the stages of an agreed procedure) strikes truly represented the wishes of all their members. Such views about the internal democracy of trade unions were given credence in that many industrial action decisions were based on voting by a show of hands at mass meetings rather than by a secret ballot of those being asked to become involved.

One common theme of the 1960s and 1970s was the perception – based partly on strike statistics and partly on the trade unions' links with the Labour Party and therefore Labour governments – that trade union leaders were more powerful than UK government Ministers. Given that poor workplace industrial relations were judged to have had a negative impact on economic performance, unions and their alleged 'irresponsible' use of power were seen as major contributors to the UK's relative lack of economic competitiveness. If businesses were not investing sufficiently, this, it was claimed, was the fault of the unions. If new technology was not embraced sufficiently quickly, again the unions were seen as the basis of the problem. If inflation was out of control, it was the fault of the unions. Although any objective examination of employee relations during this period would show the unions' having to accept a large part of the blame, weak management performance during the period was also a contributory factor. There was insufficient investment in training and development, and then, as now, insufficient investment in innovation and research.

The debate about skills levels within UK organisations relative to our international competitors is still ongoing. Despite the investment in Training and Enterprise Councils, National Vocational Qualifications, and the National Curriculum that took place in the 1990s, there has been continuing concern that some employers do not see any value in investing in people. A continuing redesigning of the training infrastructure does not help this, now that Training and Enterprise Councils have been replaced by Learning and Skills Councils, who themselves devolve some of their work to the Business Link network. Although it is always laudable that governments should try to underpin training and development with some form of statutory intervention, continual tinkering with the infrastructure is confusing for employers and is likely to result in less, not more, training. And while there has been some success in raising skills levels over the past two decades, a report commissioned by the Department for Trade and Industry and the Economic and Social Research Council by Michael Porter of Harvard Business School stated that:

> an emphasis on skills, innovation and enterprise is needed to ensure that the UK makes the transition to a new phase of economic development.

Porter set out six key areas for improving competitiveness:

- *Public investment*: increase investment in research and development and boost education and transport spending.
- *Regulatory context*: improve competition policy, develop a strategy for training in advanced man-agement skills and improve university/business links.
- *Clusters*: institute a sustained programme of cluster development so that businesses in similar fields benefit from the proximity of partners, suppliers and research.
- *Regions*: decentralise power and address planning issues.
- *Roles and institutions*: form new collective institutions to help the private sector lead development, while the government lessens its role.
- *Management*: managers must boost innovation and quality with increased investment in R&D, skills, modern production and IT.

The full report can be seen by visiting the DTI website www.dti.gov.uk, but the findings underpin much of the research over the past 10 years, which indicates that UK managers at middle and junior levels are less skilled than their counterparts in other competing economies.

The rise of monetarism

The 1978/79 so-called 'winter of discontent', when low-paid public sector employees took strike action to gain pay increases in excess of the then Labour government pay increase norm, coincided with the end of the five-year electoral cycle. The incumbent Labour government knew it had to call a General Election during 1979, and although it sought to postpone it for as long as possible, an election was duly held in May 1979. The Conservative Party campaigned promising better management of the economy, lower income taxes, lower government expenditure and the curtailment of union power, all of which it claimed would help the UK economy regain competitiveness. The Conservatives committed themselves to introducing legislation designed to ensure that trade unions acted responsibly.

During their period in opposition (1974–1979) a growing faction within the Conservative Party had begun to question the ability of Keynesian economic policies to provide price stability (commonly referred to as 'sound money'). Instead, what Keegan (1984; page 66) refers to as the 'economic evangelists' began to embrace the concept of monetarism as the means to control inflation and improve economic competitiveness. While monetarism can mean different things to different people, its basic propositions are:

- If the general level of purchasing power in the economy as a whole grows quicker than the increase in the general level of goods and services produced in the economy as a whole, then firms and households will have more money to purchase goods and services than are available in the economy as a whole.

- There is a position where there is 'too much money chasing too few goods and services' – when demand is greater than supply. Shortages arise and market prices start to increase as consumers compete with each other for this reduced supply.

- Increasing inflation arouses expectations that future inflation rates will be even higher, resulting in (a) higher wage demands and settlements, and (b) a wages-prices inflationary spiral, resulting in an increase in the general level of unemployment as the competitiveness of firms declines and workers 'price themselves out of jobs'.

- To prevent inflation, the increase in overall level of purchasing power in the economy as a whole must match the rate of increase in the general output of goods and services in the economy as a whole.

- If the increase in the economy-wide level of purchasing power exceeds the increase in the general level of the supply of goods and services in the economy as a whole, spending power (demand) must be decreased by raising interest rates and reducing the level of UK government (public) expenditure.

For monetarists, unemployment will only fall, in the longer term, if the productive capacity of the economy is increased. Measures to achieve such an increase are usually referred to as 'supply-side' economics. The key to reducing unemployment and controlling inflation is enhancing the ability of the economy to increase the supply of goods and services to the market more efficiently by:

- creating an environment conducive to private enterprise
- creating incentives for individuals to work
- creating incentives for firms to invest, produce goods and services and employ workers
- liberalising product markets
- privatise public-owned enterprises
- reducing taxation
- deregulating labour markers.

The Conservatives won the 1979 election and began the process of applying monetarist policies to the management of the UK economy. These policies have now been applied in one way or another since that time, and are being continued by the present Labour government. However, it believes competitive advantage comes from quality and added value and the provision of minimum standards of protection for employees – for example, the minimum wage. It may be that the application of economic policy is now less doctrinaire than in the past. There is a view that New Labour endorses and understands the concept of human capital much more than the Conservatives. By spreading opportunities through education and injecting more social justice into the equation it hopes the UK can become a 'knowledge-based economy' capable of competing with the best.

LABOUR MAKES CHANGES

The make-up of the UK economy changed radically in the last quarter of the twentieth century. One of the visible results of this, for the employee relations professional, has been a much more deregulated labour market. The reforms to the labour market have seen a move from employment in manufacturing to employment in the service industry, which has accounted for an increase in non-manual jobs at the expense of manual ones. Part-time employment has increased, while full-time employment has decreased. The rise in part-time employment, when converted to full-time equivalence, does not compensate for this downturn in full-time work. Although it would be an oversimplification to blame all the changes in the labour market on monetarist policies, those policies were the engine by which the reforms were driven.

Higher unemployment relative to the 1960s and 1970s has had a major impact on employee relations. While trade union influence is lower and industrial disputes have declined, there has been a growth in employee insecurity and – if the number of cases being dealt with by ACAS and employment tribunals is any guide – a rise in the number of workplace grievances. In their report for the period 2003/04 ACAS reported receipt of 176,505 applications in respect of their various jurisdictions, of which 102,559 were IT1s in respect of such issues as unfair dismissal, redundancy, etc. Although over 66,000 of these were either settled or withdrawn before reaching a tribunal, it represents a very high level of employee dissatisfaction. It also means that over 100,000 employees felt so concerned about their treatment at work that they wanted to seek the assistance of an external body, whether ACAS and its more general powers of intervention or an employment tribunal. Such high levels of employee insecurity are not helpful if organisations are endeavouring continually to improve their performance. The feelings of insecurity expressed by many employees are a major concern to employers, and thus to employee relations professionals. A full copy of the ACAS annual report can be viewed on its website, www.acas.org.uk/publications.

> Do you monitor the indicators of employee insecurity, such as a rise in grievances, individual or collective, rises in labour turnover, or increases in sickness absence?

The labour market

Some commentators have argued that the relative growth in jobs in the service sector relative to the manufacturing sector has led to an increase in 'McJobs' – part-time, badly paid and with low status – which has contributed to the decline in trade union membership and influence. It is argued that the lack of security offered by this type of employment has made people less inclined to join trade unions because they are afraid to challenge their employer. The decline in traditional union strongholds such as mining and shipbuilding has had an effect, but as with most things in employee relations, the reality tends to be more complex.

If we are to understand the significance that the labour market has on employee relations, we must understand more about the composition of the UK workforce. The 1998 Workplace Employee Relations Survey (WERS) provides useful data. As its authors point out: 'Commentators looking at the British labour market often highlight the issue of flexibility,' and they therefore considered it valid to look at the extent to which workplaces contract out different services [because] if the extent of contracting out has been on the increase, it may have led to a reduction in direct employment in workplaces.

The Survey asked whether workplaces had contracted out services that would previously have been undertaken by people directly employed in the organisation, and found that a third of respondents said this was the case. Furthermore, one third were using former employees of the workplace as the contractors. They found that 11 per cent of employers had transferred some employees to a different employer in the five years preceding the publication of their report, and that this proportion was far higher (22 per cent) in the public sector than in the private sector (6 per cent).

Another area which has had a major impact on the labour market is non-standard employment. This is generally defined as anything that is not permanent full-time work, and embraces part-time working, the use of freelancers, outworkers and temporary and fixed-term contract employees.

Critics of labour market reforms have argued that there has been a growth in the use of part-time labour to the detriment of full-time jobs. The WERS provides information on the extent of part- time employment, which is defined is as working fewer than 30 hours per week. The Survey found that part-time workers accounted for a quarter of all jobs in workplaces with 25 or more employees, but that their distribution varied enormously across workplaces of different kinds.

The WERS revealed that the use of freelancers (13 per cent) and outworkers (6 per cent) is reasonably significant, but provided some revealing data about temps and fixed-term contract employees. There has been a widely held perception that employers have placed a greater reliance on the use of temporary and fixed-term contract employees. Table 3 below shows that this is not the case and that the majority of workplaces do not use temps or employ people on fixed-term contracts.

Table 3   *The use of temporary agency workers and workers on fixed-term contracts, by occupation*

Occupation	Temporary agency workers	Fixed-term contracts
	% of workplaces employing	% of workplaces employing
Managers and administrators	1	6
Professional	5	15
Associate professional and technical	5	6
Clerical and secretarial	17	13
Craft and related	2	3
Personal and protective service	2	5
Sales	0	4
Plant and machine operatives	4	2
Other occupations	5	6
None of these workers used	72	56

Base: workplaces with 25 or more employees. Figures weighted, based on responses from 1,921 managers.

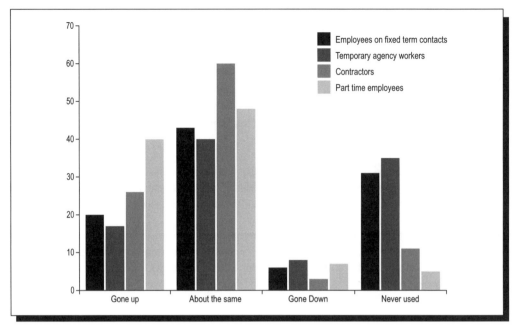

Figure 4   *The change in the use of different forms of labour*

Whatever the statistics, there is no doubt that

> the ability of managers to adjust the size of their workforces in line with requirements and demand – usually referred to as 'numerical flexibility' – appears to be widespread.

Figure 4 above shows that during the 1990s there was an increase in the use of non-standard employment.

Whatever type of organisation you work in, the impact of the labour market changes will have affected the way you do your job. In organisations that still rely on a greater proportion of traditional permanent full-time employees there is likely to be pressure for change. Employment costs are still, for most businesses, the most significant item in the management accounts and provide one of the better opportunities to make savings. In the near future, as competition heightens, some form of the 'flexible firm' will have to become a reality for all organisations – but this is not necessarily bad news ... although the pessimistic view of the reformed labour market remains the 'McJobs' thesis.

A 1999 report by the Institute for Employment Research (IER) at Warwick University suggested that the reality is more encouraging. It predicted that over the period 1997 to 2006 1.4 million new jobs would be created, and because this figure was higher than the expected increase in the population of working age, it would enable unemployment to stay low. While the report acknowledged that many of the new jobs would be part-time and employ women, some of the biggest increases in demand would be for professional and technical staff.

JOB CREATION

Although it is acknowledged that part-time jobs will account for most of the net job creation and that the proportion of women in the workforce will continue to rise, it would be wrong to interpret this as establishing a second-class labour market. A closer look at the forecasts contained in the Warwick report shows job creation taking place in two broad categories. One is in 'personal and protective services', which includes security guards and carers. Although this could be made to fit the pessimistic thesis, the impact of the minimum wage, the Working Time Regulations, and the part-time work and temporary workers and fixed-term contract work Directives should help to mitigate some of the abuses of long hours and low pay.

The second category is in managerial, professional and technical jobs, demanding high levels of education and skill. The report predicted that by 2006 there will on average be 171,000 more jobs a year in these categories, compared to 77,000 a year in the personal and protective services category. The IER predicted big increases in retailing and tourism which, while they would require plenty of part-time labour, were also in the process of upskilling available jobs. This forecast will have been affected by a number of events that have taken place since it was made, most notably the 11 September terrorist attack and subsequent conflicts in Afghanistan and Iraq, so the pace of growth in these economic sectors may be less pronounced. For example, in the month after the Twin Towers atrocity, business travel fell by 40 per cent, and although there has been a recovery since then, job losses – particularly in the airline industry – indicate that the recovery still has some way to go. British Airways alone shed 5,000 jobs and is planning further cuts. Paradoxically, security firms enjoyed an unexpected boom as nervous companies asked them to vet new staff or test their safety procedures. These seismic events demonstrate all too clearly how economic planning and economic forecasts can be blown off course by external events.

Furthermore, evidence from the Labour Force Survey would suggest that the number of newly created managerial, professional and technical jobs predicted in the Warwick report are masking a greater proliferation of lower-skilled lower-paid jobs. In discussing the role that the 'new economy' will play in both job creation and the changing nature of work, Peter Nolan (*People Management*, 27 December 2001) made some very valid points. He said:

> The new economy may yet succeed in transforming the future world of work, but all the signs today are pointing to the emergence of an hourglass economy. The selective proliferation of highly-paid jobs, whose incumbents enjoy substantial discretion over the hours, places and patterns of their work, has helped to spur the growth of low-paid, routine and unglamorous jobs in the very same sectors commonly associated with the thriving new economy. For every entrepreneur, software engineer and professional net worker there are thousands of support staff stuffing envelopes, stacking shelves and distributing products to people's homes.

GREATER FLEXIBILITY

But what does all this structural change in the labour market mean at the level of the individual firm? What is its impact on employee relations? Many of the changes that have taken place over the last two decades have been driven by the increase in the global marketplace and by the need to develop organisations that can respond flexibly to the rapidly changing demands of that market. This has given rise to the concept known as the 'flexible firm', but the data from WERS indicates that the movement towards changing work patterns is at best mixed. Stredwick and Ellis (1998) identified a number of surveys that 'throw light on the reality of the movement towards flexible working'. They conclude that

> the evidence is strong all round that the move to greater flexibility is gathering pace, and that organisations see it as a means of achieving competitive advantage.

Evidence concerning the employees' attitude to flexible working arrangements is thin, but Emmott and Hutchinson (1998) note that 'generally they are perceived as a good thing [but] that there are negative implications'. This ties in with Stredwick and Ellis's conclusion that 'employees are not always fully co-operative in these ventures', and that it is this lack of co-operation which is likely to present the greatest challenge to the employee relations professional. If, as Stredwick and Ellis state, employees are given little choice over embracing flexibility, this will have a major impact on their sense of security and wellbeing. Furthermore, if Stredwick and Ellis are right that few organisations are embracing flexibility for strategic reasons, this could enhance the ability of trade unions to recruit workers as a means of resisting change.

The debate over the future of work will continue, and the major project The Future of Work, launched by the Economic and Social Research Council in October 1998 with a budget of £4 million, will help to rectify the gaps in our knowledge. As those who are responsible for the research point out, much of the debate about the labour market has been dominated by speculation rather than empirical research. The aim of the project is to provide evidence to enhance public understanding of the critical developments most likely to impact on people's working lives. A key objective of the programme is to deepen accounts of the future of work by producing a systematic mapping of past and present shifts and continuities. As Moynagh and Worsley ask (*People Management*, 27 December 2001): is the workplace revolution over? Are the biggest changes – the shift from manufacturing to services, more women in work and more part-timers – behind us?

As part of The Future of Work project, the Tomorrow Project has completed a programme of study and consultation and has concluded that there are even bigger changes ahead that will raise major strategic issues for employers, one of which will be a phase of radical outsourcing. We noted above that the WERS had revealed that a growing number of organisations acknowledged outsourcing some activities and, as Moynagh and Worsley predicted, outsourcing has been taken further. Nowhere is this more apparent than in the financial services sector, where significant call centre activity has been shifted to the Indian subcontinent. This shift has been influenced by the low wage costs and the high educational standards in India, but it has not received universal approval – particularly from employees whose job security in the UK is threatened, but also from customers who complain about a lack of product knowledge or cultural awareness. Jane Simms (*People Management*, June 2004) reports on research commissioned by Alliance and Leicester which found that 'only 5 per cent of people are happy to have their bank accounts serviced by an overseas call centre'.

One organisation that has resisted the move to go offshore is the Royal Bank of Scotland, which has made a policy decision to base its operations where its staff and customers live. Others, however, take a different approach – as the example of the Prudential demonstrates.

Case study

Prudential

The Pru's decision to open a call centre in Mumbai was motivated by customer service rather than cost, according to Russell Martin, HR director at Prudential UK and Europe.

This, he says, has allowed the Pru to apply consistent industrial relations policies, HR practices and training across all its sites and, crucially, make Indian staff feel involved in the company.

High turnover is one of the biggest problems with call centres generally, usually because staff are treated as a dispensable commodity and perform monotonous work in grim surroundings. But the Pru's 16 per cent turnover compares favourably with the standard 35 per cent in outsourced off-shore call centre operations.

'The profile of the Indian call centre workforce is very different from that in the UK or US,' says Martin. 'Ninety per cent of our staff are between 21 and 24, more than 95 per centre of them have

---

one degree, and another 3 per cent have a second degree. You have to press different buttons to engage and motivate them than you would in the UK, where the age range is between 18 and 60 and the level of education and intelligence much more variable.'

Given the heavy premium placed on career paths, further education and job titles in India, the Pru provides structured career progression and opportunities to study for an MBA. The HR business model is the same in India as in the UK, with the local management team (comprised of Indians) reporting through UK functional lines.

The call centre also has its own radio station run by employees, Pru FM, and it organises regular social events, designed and created by employees, which last four or five hours on a Saturday evening. 'They perform the most amazing shows, and the events generate huge buzz, enthusiasm and commitment,' says Martin. When staff were shown a video recently celebrating the Pru's 150th anniversary, they all roared every time the Pru's name was mentioned. 'There is real passion and excitement – a sense that they have really got somewhere,' he says.

Outsourcing, however, is but one of the options open to employers who want to change how things are done. As The Future of Work website, www.leeds.ac.uk/esrcfutureofwork, notes:

> Visionaries of the future portend a radically different workplace from the past. They anticipate a new world in which job structure and broader macro-conditions which provided many workers with a measure of security and career continuity will have a greatly diminished salience.

It goes on to say:

> The stable employment relationships which have come to serve as a reference point for the future are said to be collapsing as the forces of globalisation, privatisation and new technologies are propelling organisations to redefine the rhythms, contractual terms and spatial patterns of work.

Even if the workplace of the future is not as radically different as the visionaries referred to above believe, there will be change – not least because the flexible labour market has been central to UK government policy since 1979 and remains an integral part of ongoing policy decisions.

The state as an employer pre-1979

During the post-World-War-II period, the state always sought to give a lead to the private sector as a model and good employer as expressed in the implementation of particular employee relations policies. Collective bargaining was considered a good and desirable activity. Union membership was encouraged, and this led to high levels of unionisation in the public sector. Nine out of ten white-collar trade unionists were employed in the public sector. When industries were taken into public ownership there was an obligation on the public corporation created to recognise, consult and negotiate with trade unions. The state also sought to ensure that its staff received comparable pay and conditions to those doing the same or similar work in the private sector.

Comparability was thus the basis of wage claims and adjustments. For example in the Civil Service, the civil servants were given a Pay Research Unit to look at rates of pay, to compare pay with private sector employees and to provide information to the negotiators.

Increasing the supply side

Conservative governments post-1979 had a different approach to economic management and pursued a twin-track policy to achieve their objectives. They eschewed the prevailing postwar consensus in areas such as the welfare state, UK government intervention in industry, incomes policy, tripartite discussions and keeping unemployment in check, even at the risk of rising inflation. Instead, they made clear their intention of letting the market decide.

Monetarist policies were introduced as a means of reducing inflation, which meant sharp increases in interest rates and in indirect taxes (especially VAT) and cuts in public expenditure. The result was large increases in unemployment, especially in the country's manufacturing industries such as ship-building, motor cars and steel. By allowing unemployment to rise, the UK government was making it clear that radical measures were needed if the British economy was to re-establish its competitiveness.

In addition, Conservative governments sought the encouragement of an enterprise culture by the de-regulation of product and labour markets, the privatisation of nationalised industries and the regulation of trade unions' industrial activities. As Blyton and Turnbull (1994; page 145) saw it:

> The objectives of UK government policy in the 1980s could be simply stated: namely, to encourage enterprise through the de-regulation of markets, especially the labour market.

They noted that the foundations of Conservative governments' policy under Mrs Thatcher could be found in the writings of free market economists such as Milton Friedman and, in particular, Friedrich Hayek. Of the UK economists who subscribe to the monetarist philosophy, the work of Patrick Minford is a good indicator of why the policy agenda has been developed as it has. Minford argued that trade unions used their power to raise wages above the market rate, which then caused price inflation, which in turn caused further rises in unemployment. This process, he argued, reduced both the efficiency of individual firms and the economy as a whole through the imposition of restrictive practices, demarcation, etc. For the monetarists, then, if employment was to increase, the labour market behaviour of trade unions had to be regulated. Trade unions had to be restrained from abusing market power, and it was for this reason that Conservative administrations over the period 1979–1997 introduced legislation to free up labour markets from trade union, employer association and government influence.

The restriction on trade union behaviour was two-pronged. The Conservatives made it clear that they were no longer prepared to promote the government's traditional role as a 'model employer'. The idea that the state should be a model to the private sector remained, but the notion of what constituted a 'model employer' changed, and in 1981 the government ended the civil service comparability agreement which had operated since 1951.

The UK government became less favourably disposed to collective bargaining and instead argued that employees should be rewarded as individuals. They sought to act against the collective voice, because they subscribed to the view that it led to over-priced jobs and consequently unemployment. The state ceased to encourage people to become members of trade unions or to take part in collective bargaining. Conversely, they also discouraged the traditional role of employers' federations in national wage bargaining. Comparability of pay for public sector employees was terminated because it was thought that pay increases should be related to the ability to pay and the availability of labour resources. The pay of an occupational group should thus not necessarily be the same in different parts of the country. Differentials should reflect the scarcity of that labour. Wage negotiation at operating unit levels, where the ability to pay and scarcity of labour factors could more easily be taken account of, were thus encouraged and the traditional 'going-rate' argument discouraged.

Outline three main functions of the state in employee relations.

PUBLIC EXPENDITURE

The UK Conservative government argued that inflation was the result of the money supply's increasing faster than the increase in the output of goods and services in the economy. Money supply is the total spending power in the economy as a whole, but a major component in this is public expenditure. Given that the UK government was responsible directly or indirectly for the wages of one third of the employees in the country, and given that pay is an important part of public sector expenditure, UK governments cannot adopt a neutral stance on public sector settlements. So although the UK Conservative government made it clear that a formal incomes policy with norms and enforcement agencies was not on its agenda, it was prepared to ensure effective controls over the pay rises for public sector employees by the simple expedient of limiting the rise in public expenditure. This approach brought the UK government into conflict with a number of public sector unions – for example, schoolteachers – who had their collective bargaining rights removed by Act of Parliament.

The labour market reforms since 1979 have seen a progressive diminution of the welfare safety net for unemployed workers. Governments considered that over-generous welfare provision meant that people have less incentive to work and therefore remained unemployed for longer than was necessary. This so-called dependency culture was tackled by changing the basis on which an individual was eligible for unemployment benefit and by reducing the length of time such benefit was payable. Because of the fear of unemployment, such changes in the welfare system meant that employees became less resistant to employer control and were less likely to seek reviews of their terms and conditions of employment for fear of losing their jobs.

Although the present Labour government has not reversed the policy initiatives of its predecessors, it has, through a series of interventions, sought to make work pay for a greater number of people, thus reducing the dependency culture. A report by the Institute for Fiscal Studies (IFS) assessed government changes to the tax and benefits system and the introduction of the national minimum wage. It concluded that the package of measures would make work pay by between £7 and £13 a week extra. This report, together with the Warwick report referred to above, suggest that we are in the process of creating a labour market in which employers are creating new jobs and people are more willing to take them.

THE IMPACT OF TECHNOLOGY

All organisations operate within certain technological constraints which impact on its size and structure. In turn, the size and structure of an organisation will undoubtedly have an influence on its culture. Because culture affects relationships between people, it can be seen that technology and technological development are important factors in employee relations.

It is important for employee relations professionals to understand the term 'technology'. If it merely implies some form of process or engineering, does it have any relevance outside of manufacturing? Technology is more than an engineering process. From the perspective of an organisation it is about the application of skills and knowledge. It is therefore both relevant and necessary to understand it.

In the context of employee relations it is possible to identify three perspectives from which to view the impact of new technology. First, new technology, because of its impact on traditional skills, acts as both a de-skilling agent and a creator of unemployment. The second perspective is that new technology is a positive force in that it creates new opportunities for employees who have the chance to learn new skills. The third perspective sees technology as the means by which previously unpleasant or repetitive tasks can be eliminated. For example, the introduction of robotics into the car industry removed the need for employees to carry out mundane operations, with a consequent improvement in the climate of employee relations in an industry previously dogged by labour problems. Each of these three perspectives is, to some degree, correct, but the impact of new technology varies from industry to industry and from organisation to organisation.

Although most people acknowledge that in general terms technological development has reduced the demand for certain types of labour, it is clear that it has presented some significant opportunities for job creation. One example is the large growth in the use of call centres, particularly in the financial services sector. They are clearly technology-driven, rely on a combination of complex computer-driven communications technologies and employ in excess of 200,000 people, but this figure could alter dramatically if the shift offshore, to which we refer above, continues.

Technological development based on computers, lasers and telecommunications not only has the capacity to de-skill jobs, it can blur demarcation lines, create an alternative lower-paid workforce for an employer and provide the impetus for changes in work patterns.

It is important for the employee relations professional to recognise where technology requires changes in working patterns or processes, and to identify appropriate and available training opportunities. A commonly held view on the impact of technological change is that it creates problems, particularly where trade unions are represented in the workplace, and is often resisted. Of course, when change is on the agenda, both trade unions and employees generally will have fears over job losses, de-skilling and increased management control. The skill of the employee relations professional lies in understanding these concerns and seeking ways of mitigating them. Personnel professionals should have a vested interest in the management of change, not just the imposition of change.

Whatever the nature of the technology, its impact – and therefore the response to it by all stakeholders – is inevitably linked to the UK's poor record in skills development and productivity. The government was so concerned about the lack of skills development that the Performance and Innovation Unit (PIU) at the Cabinet Office set up a task force to examine the problem and recommend policies to overcome it.

The task force, which reported in November 2001, concluded that 'workforce development' (WfD) can 'help to raise labour productivity and increase social inclusion'. It described WfD as 'a relatively new term for training and skills development [sitting] between training (which has a narrow focus) and education (which is broad), and is firmly grounded in business need'. The PIU adopted the following definition:

> Workforce development consists of activities which increase the capacity of individuals to participate effectively in the workforce, thereby improving their productivity and employability.

The full report of the task force can be seen on the web at www.number10.gov.uk/output, but the key points were:

- A relatively high proportion of the UK population of working age lacks basic and intermediate skills.
- The benefits of education and training are, in large part, captured by individuals through increased earnings and by firms through increased productivity.
- Without basic skills – literacy and numeracy – individuals cannot start to develop a career path and may be trapped in a low pay/no pay cycle.

So far as productivity is concerned, there continues to be anxiety over Britain's productivity deficit relative to the performance of other advanced economies. The government enquiry on competitiveness which we referred to above suggested that

> the sluggish pace of managerial innovation might partly cause and be the result of other shortcomings, such as low investment in capital, research and development and workforce skills development –

and because many modern management techniques are thought to rely on the availability of skilled workers and state-of-the-art machinery, these will not be in place if investment is low.

> This cocktail could explain the persistent productivity gap and the low level of innovation ... relative to the US and the leading continental European economies.

> C. Mahony, People Management, May 2003; page 10

This productivity gap means that British workers produce around 20 per cent less for every hour they spend at work than those in France, Germany and the USA. This, the government maintains, is not about a lack of competence on the part of UK workers but is the consequence of decades of under-investment in plant and machinery and in skills development. Raising the skills levels and closing the productivity gap is a central theme of government economic policy, and is another example of how its management of the economy impacts on the employee relations specialist.

This is because whatever skills organisations require in the future, employee relations professionals will have to recognise that changes in the balance of skills will have a significant impact on their work. In some organisations investment in improved technology may lead to both staff development and staff redundancies. In some organisations such investment may cause difficulties in recruiting sufficient skilled labour, with the consequent pressure that this can bring, particularly in respect of unit labour costs. Overall, it is important to remember that new technology varies in its impact. This is based on a number of variables including the nature of the product or service, the type of organisation involved, the management strategy employed, and the attitude of trade unions (where they are represented) and employees.

> What changes in technology do you expect to affect your organisation, or the sector in which you oper-ate, in the next five years? What is their likely impact on employee relations behaviour?

THE BALANCE OF BARGAINING POWER

In Chapter 1 we introduced the concept of the 'balance of bargaining power' and said that it was this bal-ance that determines whether employers or employees feel that their interests have been satisfied. We also said that the balance of bargaining power operates at both a macro and a micro level. At the macro level the combination of economic management and political, legislative and technological change influences the overall conduct of employee relations, while at the micro level these factors can have totally different impacts.

The government's economic and legal policies have major implications for the outcome of employee relations behaviour. Economic policies that are directed towards the creation of full employment and the maximising of economic growth weaken the relative bargaining power of the employer but strengthen that of the employee. A high level of demand for goods and services in the economy as a whole generates demand for labour to produce/provide those goods and services. If the demand for labour services is excessive relative to their supply (ie shortages develop), the 'price' employers will have to pay to secure those services will increase.

If, on the other hand, government economic policies give the highest priority to reducing inflation by lowering household and corporate spending and reducing public expenditure, demand (spending power) in the economy will fall, and as a consequence so will that for labour. The result will be labour 'surpluses', giving rise to redundancies and increased unemployment. The effect of the supply of labour's exceeding demand is downward pressure on the 'price' of labour services, or if labour prices are inflexible downwards, less labour will be employed than previously (unemployment) at the same price. In such situations the relative balance of bargaining power of employers will be strengthened and that of the employees weakened.

If the government introduces legislation favourable to employers' interests, the bargaining power of employers relative to employees is strengthened. This is what Conservative governments did during the period 1980–1997 by introducing a series of labour law reforms. If a government introduces legislation favourable to the interests of employees and trade unions, the bargaining power of employees relative to employers is strengthened. Some employers have real fears that the introduction of the statutory recognition procedures contained in the Employment Relations Act (1999) will swing the balance of power towards trades unions, particularly in industries like the media and communications. Legislation, by setting standards of behaviour by employers to regulate (for example, the right not to be unfairly dismissed) the relationship between an individual employee and his or her employer, also influences the relative balance of bargaining power between employers and individual employees.

The implementation of new technology further impacts on bargaining power. For example, developments in communications have helped to produce global markets which have increased product market competition. This can lead to downward pressure on the 'price' of labour services and a shift in bargaining power towards the employer. The reverse can also be true. By creating new jobs and new skills and by making some industries more capital-intensive, the implementation of technological change has strengthened the bargaining power of employees. One only has to look at the advertised vacancies for a whole range of IT jobs to identify one sector where this is true.

The influence on bargaining power of the wider economic and legal environment surrounding an employee relations system cannot be underestimated, and in this regard the decision-making bodies of the European Union have become increasingly important. The role of the UK government and the European Union Council of Ministers (see Chapter 5) in this context means that representative bodies of employers and employees participate in the political lobbying process to persuade the political decision-makers to introduce economic and legal policies favourable to their interests.

The micro level

So far, the relative bargaining power between the buyers and sellers of labour services has been analysed on the macro level. However, analysis at this level cannot explain why some groups of employees retain their bargaining power vis-à-vis the employer despite low growth or high unemployment, and why some employers are in a relatively weak bargaining position despite the economic climate's being in their favour. In many respects what matters for employers is their bargaining power relative to particular groups of workers at the enterprise level. This is the relative bargaining power at the micro level.

Consider a situation in which the national picture is unfavourable to employees in general. Unemployment is rising steeply, redundancies are occurring every day, employers are seeking to restrict wages and general employment conditions, and new, small firms are replacing more established businesses. However, your organisation could be in a sector where the product or process has a limited shelf-life. If you also have a collective relationship with a well-organised trade union, it would be aware of how a trade dispute could have an immediate and costly effect on customer confidence or income generation. Alternatively, your company could be non-union but very high-tech and experiencing rapid expansion. It requires highly skilled, highly trained and committed employees to produce its products. However, these skills are in short supply because the major employers in the area are in the information industry and other new companies seeking the same skilled labour are continuing to move into the area.

In both these situations employees would perceive that, notwithstanding the national (macro) picture, the relative balance of bargaining power was very much in their favour. This situation could be made even worse if the management of the business had no clear employee relations strategy or policies and procedures were non-existent or out of date.

> Consider the work groups in your organisation and ask yourself the following questions. Which have the most potential power to disrupt the organisation? What is the basis of their power? Do they realise they have this power? If not, why not? Do you think they would be willing to use their power?

BARGAINING POWER AND MANAGEMENT BEHAVIOUR

In general terms, the balance of bargaining power has been in favour of employers over the past years because of the legislative and economic policies of successive governments. When this is the case it is important that power is exercised in a responsible and not an arbitrary manner.

If the balance of bargaining power favours management, it may achieve its objective despite adopting a management style that is unprofessional and based on an attitude of 'Take it or leave it', 'Go and work for somebody else, then' and 'There are plenty of other people who would be only too willing to work here.' In such situations the workforce complies with, but is not committed to, management's action and policy. The employees are cowed, have no respect for management and store up grievances that will come to the surface with a vengeance when the relative balance of bargaining power turns in favour of the employee. There is some anecdotal evidence that some of the claims for union recognition have gained the support of a majority of the affected workforce as a response to previous (bad) management behaviour.

Managing in such a way that employee commitment is not forthcoming is non-sustainable in the longer term. It inevitably relies on a crude abuse of power, and this in the long term will be detrimental to the business, which in turn will experience high labour turnover, low employee morale and depressed productivity levels. The employee relations professional manages on the basis of just cause for action, consults and discusses with employees and treats them in a fair, reasonable and consistent manner. Managing on this basis, regardless of the relative balance of bargaining between employers and employees, normally gains the respect of the latter even though management invariably gains what it wants.

A further reason why an employee relations professional should not act in an arbitrary manner is that if the bargaining pendulum can swing one way, it can swing back. If you fail to exercise power responsibly when it is in your favour, you should not expect responsible behaviour from employees when they have the advantage. Bargaining power, as we have noted, is influenced by economic policy and legal intervention. If those policies are changed, a number of variables may be affected. For example, if the predicted increase in managerial, professional and technical jobs becomes a reality and employers do not invest sufficiently in skills training, skills shortages will raise the price of certain types of labour. Statutory rights to union recognition could provide employees with greater bargaining power

> Can you discern where the relative balance of bargaining power lies in your organisation? Is this balance static, or is there potential for any significant shift in power?

SUMMARY

In the period since 1979, but particularly in the last 15 years, changes in legislation, closer integration with Europe and rapidly changing economic circumstances have led to a re-examination of patterns of employee relations. The way in which the employment relationship is managed has changed; managers are now much more aware of the value of good communication and employee involvement in decision-making. We know, from the 1998 Workforce Employment Relations Survey and other sources, that there has been, and continues to be, a decline in collective bargaining, but that the unions seem to have halted, for now, the decline in their overall membership. All of this change has been influenced by the 'corporate environment'. This chapter has examined the role of the UK government as an economic manager in terms of the objectives of macro-economic policy and how employee relations is affected by the way in which that policy is implemented. In particular, we examined the contrast between the Keynesian and monetarist approaches to economic management and the impact that the change to monetarism has had on the UK economy since 1979.

We noted how the rise in multinational companies and the growth of globalisation has had an impact on both economic management and individual organisations. And we saw that globalisation has provided the spur to organisations to take tough decisions, confront performance issues and create new products so that they compete the world over. However, we also highlighted the insecurity that can be a by-product of the drive to do things in new and better ways.

We looked at the role of the UK government as an employer and examined the way in which the concept of the government as a 'model employer' has changed over time. In the immediate postwar years there was encouragement of collective bargaining and an attempt to ensure comparability of pay between the public and private sectors. From 1979 the emphasis was on a more individual approach to the employment relationship, with a clear discouragement of national pay bargaining.

Finally, we looked at the impact of technological change on the corporate environment and acknowledged that it influences employee relations in a number of ways. We also discussed the need to generate enthusiasm for skills development and to raise UK productivity levels so that they match those of our competitors. We also saw that technology can have negative as well as positive effects – it can create unemployment, it can provide the opportunity for employees to learn new skills, and it can generally improve the working environment.

From whatever perspective you view the corporate environment, there is no doubt that over the last 20 years there has been a radical change in our system of employee relations. This change has manifested itself in changes to working practices and changes in the labour market with an increase in part-time and temporary working. Reward systems have also changed, issues like performance-related pay, reward for teams and profit-related pay becoming more prevalent.

Changes in legislation, closer ties with our European partners, rapidly changing economic circumstances all have an impact on the corporate environment and in turn on the established patterns of employee relations.

Key points

- Changes in economic management and reforms to labour law can cause trade union power and strike activity to decline/increase, and such changes have a marked effect on the balance of bargaining power.
- The role of the state in employee relations has changed: it no longer seeks an active role in promoting particular practices.

- The way in which the economy is managed has a direct impact on employee relations because it influences such things as price stability, growth, investment and employment levels.

- The continuing globalisation of markets will be a major influence on organisational change and thus on employee relations.

- Technological innovation will continue to influence the workplace and will therefore impact on employee relations practices.

- Management power should be exercised in a responsible manner, and not arbitrarily.

FURTHER READING

BLYTON P. and TURNBULL P. (1994) *The Dynamics of Employee Relations*. London, Macmillan.

DONALDSON P. and FARQUHAR J. (1991) *Understanding the British Economy*. London, Penguin.

EMMOTT M. and HUTCHINSON S. (1998) Employment flexibility: threat or promise?, in Sparrow P. and Marchington M. *Human Resource Management: The new agenda*. London, Financial Times/Pitman.

FARNHAM D. (1995) *The Corporate Environment*. London, Institute of Personnel and Development.

GREENFIELD S. (2003) Flexible futures, *People Management*, Volume 9, No.21, October; pages 52–3.

INSTITUTE FOR EMPLOYMENT RESEARCH (2000) *Review of the Economy and Employment 1998–1999*.

INSTITUTE FOR FISCAL STUDIES (1998) *Entering Work and the British Tax and Benefit System*.

KEEGAN W. (1984) *Mrs Thatcher's Economic Experiment*. London, Penguin.

LEWIS D. and SARGEANT M. (2004) *Essentials of Employment Law*, 7th edn. London, CIPD.

MAHONY C. (2003) UK firms need more innovation, *People Management*, Volume 9, No.10, May; page 10.

MOYNAGH M. and WORSLEY R. (2001a) Prophet sharing, *People Management*, Volume 7, No.25, December; pages 24–9.

MOYNAGH M. and WORSLEY R. (2001b) *Tomorrow's Workplace*. London, CIPD.

NOLAN P. (2001) Shaping things to come, *People Management*, Volume 7, No.25, December; pages 30–1.

NOLAN P. and WALSH J. (1995) The structure of the economy and labour market, in Edwards P. (ed.) *Industrial Relations – Theory and Practice in Britain*. Oxford, Blackwell.

O'DOWD J. (2003) A new deal, *People Management*, Volume 9, No.10, May; pages 38–40.

ROBERTS Z. (2003) Crossing the divide, *People Management*, Volume 9, No.18, September; pages 29–32.

SIMMS J. (2004) Home or away?, *People Management*, Volume 10, No.11, June; pages 35–9.

STREDWICK J. and ELLIS S. (1998) *Flexible Working Practices: Techniques and innovations*. London, Institute of Personnel and Development.

TAYLOR R. (2003) Generation next, *People Management*, Volume 9, No.18, September; pages 38–40.

The legislative framework

CHAPTER 4

CHAPTER OBJECTIVES

When you have completed this chapter you should be aware of and able to describe:

■ the importance of the employment contract

■ the legislative process

■ the principal functions of the law

■ how the law impacts on relationships at work

■ the nature and jurisdiction of employment tribunals

■ recent developments in the law.

INTRODUCTION

There has always been a significant role for the law in the conduct of employee relations, but relative to the last 100 years the present employment law regime now imposes itself on every facet of the employment relationship. However, it is important that the employee relations professional does not view the law as simply a process of compliance. Good employee relations will not be achieved by waving a legal rulebook and stating what people cannot do. Good employee relations will be achieved by the positive actions that employers take to win the trust and confidence of their workforce.

Notwithstanding this approach, we have to recognise that from recruitment to departure, every act of the employer is measured against a particular legislative standard. Whether that standard is 'not to discriminate', 'to act reasonably', or to provide a certain level of 'care', it means that employee relations professionals and line managers have to stop and think before taking particular actions. The sheer amount and complexity of employment law can often overwhelm even the most experienced of practitioners, and for this reason its range and impact must be clearly understood.

It is not our intention to provide a detailed explanation of every piece of legislation, and we will not do that. Textbooks like Lewis and Sargeant's *Essentials of Employment Law* (2004) and the CIPD Employment Law Service can do that job in a much more effective way. Our purpose is to examine the legislation in the context of employee relations and to explain how relationships can be influenced by the way in which individual employers apply legislative rules and standards.

THE LEGISLATIVE PROCESS

There are now two principal sources of employment law that the employee relations professional must be concerned with: legislation that derives from a political decision of the governing party and legislation that derives from Europe. Notwithstanding this, it is important to recognise that the UK Parliament will be the source of most laws that the employee relations specialist needs to be concerned with, even though the actual legislation might have been directed by, or influenced by, Europe. In Chapter 5 we describe the process by which European legislation is decided and give numerous examples of EU Directives that have been or will be transposed into UK law, and it is not necessary to repeat that detail here. We will, however, be looking at some of the developments in European law. Lewis and Sargeant provide a detailed explanation of the 'sources and institutions of employment law', but generally, the process by which the legislation is enacted is as follows.

The government of the day might issue a 'Green Paper' followed by a 'White Paper' followed by a 'bill' which, after the parliamentary process has been exhausted, becomes an 'Act of Parliament'. The first two stages are not obligatory, and governments can by-pass them if they so wish.

The Green Paper is a consultative document and is used by the government to obtain the views of interested parties to proposed legislation. This can apply irrespective of whether the proposal is driven by Europe or results from a political decision. Views might be submitted by employers' organisations, trade unions and organisations such as the CIPD. Even individuals can contribute to the consultative process. Recent examples on which the government has entered into consultation include new tribunal rules and procedures, the information and consultation Directive and the new dismissal and grievance procedures, all of which we discuss later in this chapter.

Once the consultation is complete, the government will usually issue a White Paper, setting out its policy and intentions. A bill is then introduced into Parliament and, assuming it survives the scrutiny of both the House of Commons and the House of Lords, the agreed bill becomes an Act – for example, the Employment Rights Act 1996.

One recent initiative, which should be of great value to employee relations specialists, is a decision by the Department of Trade and Industry (DTI) to implement changes in employment law on two specific dates each year. These two dates are 6 April and 1 October, and the harmonisation of commencement dates is intended to ensure that changes to employment policy are made in a co-ordinated fashion and to provide businesses, employee representatives and individuals with greater clarity and awareness about when changes will be made.

At present this initiative is limited to legislative changes on which the DTI is the lead department, and it will therefore not necessarily include changes emanating from the European Union or other government departments. In addition to harmonising dates, the DTI will also issue an annual statement of forthcoming employment regulations, which will comprise four sections. Section A will detail changes that are due to commence on 6 April; section B will detail the changes due on 1 October; section C will detail changes arising from Europe when the coming into force date is different and not aligned to either common commencement date. Finally, section D will provide details of other key DTI activity that will impact on the employment law framework in the current year and beyond. This section will be of particular benefit to those charged with drafting employee relations strategies and policies as part of an organisation's long-term planning process. Details of the current annual statement can be found on the DTI website at www.dti.gov.uk.

> Explain the key stages in the UK legislative process at which employers can attempt to influence the contents of legislation.

Sometimes the distinction between a politically driven development and one that is Europe-driven is not easily identified (Bercusson, *European Labour Law*, 1996):

> The dynamic of national labour laws is no longer determined solely or even mainly by domestic developments. It is not merely that UK labour law is required to incorporate EU norms: EU norms are themselves the reflection of the national labour laws of member states.

It is also the case that legislators will often merge these two influences in an attempt to maximise the use of parliamentary time. For example, the Employment Relations Act 1999 contains provisions – part-time workers, parental leave, etc – that derived from the European process as well as provisions deriving from the political process – trade union recognition and the right to be accompanied at disciplinary and grievance hearings. For HR and personnel practitioners a classic example of how the source of legislation can become confused is demonstrated by the Minimum Wage Act 1998. The proposal for a minimum wage was a clear manifesto commitment of the Labour Party prior to the 1997 General Election and was, in part, a product of their close relationship with the trade union movement. Once they were elected it became one of their priorities for legislation – and yet many practitioners remain convinced that the minimum wage was introduced because of a European Union Directive. Similarly, the current rules concerning statutory union recognition were politically rather than Europe-driven.

The law and employee relations

Employee relations specialists do not need to be lawyers, but they do need to understand the interaction between the law and employee relations. They need to understand that because of the many legal development over the past 30 years and because we live in a more litigious age, every employee relations decision is potentially capable of legal challenge. Hence, in 2003/04 over 170,000 applications were received by employment tribunals. In the following part of this chapter we have attempted, by reference to some of the principal areas of law, to identify where these challenges are most likely to occur and how employee relations policies and processes must be capable of managing them.

For example, the psychological contract – seen by many as a key element in the employment relationship – can be seriously affected by how existing and new rights are implemented. Simply doing the minimum required might avoid legal challenge, but might leave individual employees feeling vulnerable or undervalued. Equally, using the statutory provisions as a baseline from which to offer enhancements – such as providing paid rather than unpaid parental leave – can, in appropriate circumstances, pay major dividends in employee commitment to the organisation.

THE CONTRACT OF EMPLOYMENT

The most important and major influence in employment law is the contract of employment, and the first Contracts of Employment Act was placed on the statute book in 1963. Although that act has now been repealed, its provisions have been incorporated into the Employment Rights Act 1996 and it is vital that the employee relations professional understands its impact. This is because it defines and regulates the relationship between the employer and the employee. Being an 'employee', or in recent years, a 'worker', is the key determinant in the types of rights an individual enjoys, and thus it is an area which has given rise to a large amount of litigation and case law.

In any business the categories of workers used may include any one or more of the following:

- employees, either full- or part-time
- independent contractors
- agency workers
- casual workers
- fixed-term contract workers
- home-workers.

However, in the UK only certain of these individuals are entitled to all the protection afforded by current employment legislation. These distinctions, while they might seem pedantic, are of crucial importance to the management of individuals. 'Workers' might not have all the rights that 'employees' have, but failure to observe good practice in the management of such individuals could be costly if, for example, they allege that they have been unlawfully discriminated against. In many cases it will be absolutely clear that a person is an employee, but in between these two certainties there exists a wide variety of relationships that exhibit characteristics of both employment and self-employment, and it is *in relation* to these relationships that the difficulties lie.

Section 230(1) of the Employment Rights Act 1996 defines an 'employee' as an 'individual who has entered into or works under (or, where the employment has ceased, worked under) a contract of employment'. Section 230(2) provides that a 'contract of employment' means 'a contract of service or apprenticeship, whether express or implied, and (if it is express) whether oral or in writing'. This definition does not provide any guidance as to when an individual may be said to work under a contract of service (as opposed to a contract for services) and in order to determine whether a particular relationship is one of employment (contract of service – referred to in the old cases as a 'master and servant' relationship) or self-employment (contract for services or 'independent contractor') it is therefore necessary to refer to the case law.

There have been many attempts by the courts to provide a simple and easily understandable definition, but in *Montgomery v Johnson Underwood Limited*, the Court of Appeal confirmed that in determining whether a contract of employment exists the 1968 case of *Ready Mixed Concrete (South East) Limited v Minister of Pensions and National Insurance* offers the best guidance. In the *Ready Mixed Concrete* case it was held that a contract of employment exists if three conditions are fulfilled.

The first condition is that there exists a *'mutuality of obligation'* between the parties. If an individual agrees to provide his or her own work (ie personal service) and skill for the employer when the employer requires him or her to do so, and the employer in return agrees to provide work for the individual and pay a wage or other remuneration for that work, then there will exist a mutuality of obligation. The second condition is that the individual is *under the control* of the employing company. Some of the relevant factors to be considered when determining whether an individual is under the control of the employing company are whether the individual:

- is under a duty to obey orders
- has control over his or her hours
- is subject to the company's disciplinary procedure
- is supervised as to the mode of working
- provides his or her own equipment
- has to comply with the company's rules on the taking of holiday
- works regular hours
- can delegate his or her duties
- can work for others at the same time as working for the particular company
- is integrated into the employer's business – eg is he or she responsible for issuing management instructions, and does he or she have the power to discipline the company's workers?

Finally, and if the first two tests are satisfied, there is the condition that the *other provisions of the contract are consistent with its being a contract of service*. Relevant factors include who has responsibility for tax and National Insurance and whether the individual is in receipt of sick pay/holiday pay. Notwithstanding that these factors may be present, the first two factors (mutuality of obligation, and control) are the 'irreducible minimum' required for a contract of employment. Once these tests have been satisfied and it is clear that an individual is employed under a contract of employment, he or she effectively has the following full rights under all current employment legislation:

- protection from unfair dismissal
- statutory redundancy payment
- maternity leave and statutory maternity pay
- statutory sick pay
- parental and urgent family leave
- minimum period of notice, and
- a written statement of particulars of employment.

Nevertheless, there will be occasions when employers will dispute that an individual is an employee, and in such cases it will be necessary to look at the prevailing case law. A useful source of reference in such circumstances would be the CIPD Employment Law Service.

Unfortunately, such has been the development in individual employment rights that it is now necessary to look beyond the distinction of employee and non-employee to determine what entitlements an individual might have and to take into account the relatively new concept of 'worker'. Section 203(3) of the Employment Rights Act 1996 sets out the definition of a 'worker', but a general definition can be broken down in three parts so that a 'worker' is someone who:

- works under a contract
  - to carry out personal services
    - for another party to the contract.

This definition potentially covers a wide range of individuals who provide personal services under a contract. The great majority of agency workers, home-workers, casuals and freelancers are likely to be workers. Someone who falls within the definition of a 'worker' enjoys rights under the following legislation (rights which are, of course, also conferred on employees):

- Working Time Regulations 1998
- National Minimum Wage Act 1998
- Health and Safety at Work Act 1974
- Public Interest Disclosure Act 1998
- The Part-Time Workers (Prevention of Less Favourable Treatment) Regulations 2000, and
- Part 11 Employment Rights Act 1996 (the right not to have unlawful deductions made from wages)
- Section 10 Employment Relations Act 1999 (the right to be accompanied at disciplinary and grievance proceedings)
- Race Relations Act 1976, Sex Discrimination Act 1975 and Disability Discrimination Act 1995.

How would you explain to a line manager the importance of issuing employees with a written statement of their terms and conditions of employment?

Aside from the issue of employment status, one area where the contract of employment is of vital importance is in the management of change. In Chapter 2 we examined change in the context of employee relations strategies – but there is also a legal dimension to this process because, in many instances, the desire for change within an organisation might involve a variation to an individual's contract and how this variation is managed can have a very significant impact on the employment relationship.

In a strictly legal sense neither employer nor employee can unilaterally change the terms and conditions of employment because a contract can only be changed by mutual agreement. Realistically, organisations change their employees' terms and conditions quite frequently, and very often there are little or no discussions about the change. Certainly, it would sometimes be hard to identify where and when the 'mutual agreement' happened. It is also wrong to believe that such agreement can be implied simply because the employer gives 'notice' of an intent to make changes. The key is consent. Consent can be gained by either individual or collective negotiation or can be implied by the conduct of the parties. Implied consent could be deemed to have occurred if an individual remains at work for a considerable period after a change has been imposed. Where a unilateral change is imposed, and the employee makes it clear that it is unacceptable, he or she is entitled to treat the contract as repudiated. In such circumstances he or she could argue that he or she has been been 'constructively dismissed' and seek a suitable remedy from an employment tribunal.

But, as Lewis and Sargeant (2004; page 136) state:

> Developments in the law of unfair dismissal make it very difficult for an employee to resist a unilateral variation. Suffice it to say at this stage that employers can offer, as a fair reason for dismissal, the fact that there was a sound business reason for insisting on changes being put into effect.

Provided that the manager, or managers, dealing with the change process operate from a 'good practice' perspective, they should find it relatively easy to satisfy a tribunal that they have acted reasonably. This is particularly true if the majority of employees affected had been prepared to go along with the employer's proposals. There is one caveat to this – the amount of consultation that took place. While it is not possible to specify what amounts to a 'reasonable' amount of consultation, 'good practice' and common sense would indicate that any consultation would require that employees knew what the changes meant to them personally; what, if any, impact the changes would have on their remuneration, their working time and working arrangements; and what other options were available to them. It would also be expected that they would have sufficient time to consider the proposals and voice any objections. Common sense should tell any manager that presenting somebody with a *fait accompli* is hardly likely to be classed as reasonable.

This may well be the legal reality, and there will be unscrupulous employers who believe that imposing change asserts management's 'right to manage'. They could not be more wrong. There is now overwhelming evidence that individuals work harder, and smarter, when the 'psychological contract' is in a state of high maintenance. Forcing change on people may well be possible, but does it pay dividends? We think not. In this book we have emphasised time and again the need for 'good practice' in employee relations. To use the law as a blunt instrument to drive through change could never be described as 'good practice'. Then again, neither are we naïve – some individuals will always resist change, no matter how much you seek to negotiate or consult with them. In such circumstances, and as a last resort, change might have to be imposed, but at least the employer is seen to have acted in good faith and in the interests of the business.

THE FUNCTION OF THE LAW

Notwithstanding the fact that the contract of employment underpins the legal relationship between employers and their employees, this is not, as we have said, a legal text. In the context of employee relations, therefore, we must consider the law in a much broader framework. Otto Kahn-Freund in his classic book

Labour and the Law (1972) stated that the 'principal purpose of labour law [was] to regulate, to support, and to restrain the power of management and the power of organised labour', and he outlined three functions of the law in regulating employee relations that would achieve this purpose. These were:

- the auxiliary function, where the law is designed to promote certain behaviour (for example, collective bargaining) towards certain ends or else the law, in the last resort, will regulate behaviour. The statutory recognition procedures contained in the Employment Relations Act 1999 are a classic example of this function, as the number of voluntary arrangements made since the Act came into force will testify

- the regulatory function, where the law regulates management's behaviour towards their employees and trade union officers' behaviour towards their members. This is the area of individual employment rights and the rights of individual trade union members

- the restrictive function, where the law establishes the 'rules of the game' when employers and employees are in the process of making agreements. This type of legislation effectively lays down the circumstances in which employers and trade unions can impose industrial sanctions on each other without the parties having redress to the legal system.

In this chapter we will be linking these three functions to various pieces of employment law so that it is evident how the legislative framework develops over time.

The auxiliary function of the law

From the end of World War II and throughout most of the 1950s and 1960s there was tacit support, by both the main political parties and through the legislative process, for the principle of collective bargaining. However, from the late 1960s and throughout the 1970s, employers and some politicians began to challenge this principle because of what they considered an excess of trade union power. This recognition that collective bargaining, and its manipulation by some trade unionists, was a factor in our low productivity, low output economy was the reason that some people started to lobby for change. The lobbying was certainly successful, and the idea that the law should be used to promote collective bargaining was anathema to successive Conservative governments from 1979 to 1997. Certainly, the auxiliary function of the law as described by Kahn-Freund did not figure highly in their legislative programme during this period. In fact, the 1980 Employment Act repealed a statutory trade union recognition procedure that had been introduced in 1975 by the Employment Protection Act, and further legislation during this period actively discouraged the process of collectivism. The Employment Relations Act 1999 – which is examined in more detail in later chapters – has, with its provisions for statutory recognition and opportunities for trade union representation at discipline and grievance hearings, to a degree reversed this process.

The regulatory function of the law

This second function of the law has provided the foundations for a series of statutory rights individual employees have, relative to their employer. These began to emerge in the early 1960s. Parliament justified providing such rights on the grounds that private arrangements (for example, by collective agreement) had failed to provide an adequate minimum acceptable level of protection to individual employees against certain behaviour by their employers. Interestingly, the trade unions were initially opposed to such initiatives as the Redundancy Payments Act because they believed it undermined their own role. At the same time, the introduction of individual rights at work sent a clear message to employers that they must act with just cause and be 'fair and reasonable' in the treatment of their employees on those matters where statutory minimum standards were being established for their employees.

A floor of legal rights was created, which has since been expanded and developed by successive UK governments and the courts, who have been sympathetic to the view that there should be a basic level of employment protection below which no employee should be permitted to fall. These minimum levels can be enhanced by private agreements – for example, via collective bargaining or simply by employers wishing to offer a more attractive employment package. Many organisations now offer maternity pay and leave that goes beyond the statutory minimum, for instance, because they need to attract women back to work after the birth of a child. But this is a matter of policy for individual organisations (see Chapter 2). What is important for the employee relations professional is to understand the range and importance of these individual rights.

DISCRIMINATION

Discrimination law in all its guises continues to be one of the most dynamic and complex areas of employment law. With no cap on the level of compensation payable and with potentially damaging publicity arising out of high-profile cases, employers would be wise to regard the eradication of discrimination, harassment and inequality as a high priority – not just because of the high costs involved but because unlawful discrimination in any form makes it impossible to foster a climate of good employee relations.

In the UK it is unlawful to treat people less favourably on the ground of their sex or their race, or because they have a disability. Basically, there are two categories of discrimination, *direct* and *indirect*. Direct discrimination occurs when people are treated less favourably because of their sex, race or other protected characteristic as set out in the various pieces of legislation that apply, such as the Race Relations Act and the Sex Discrimination Act. Indirect discrimination occurs when people are treated the same way as everyone else, but they do not, or cannot, comply with a rule, condition or requirement of employment that applies to everyone because of their race, sex, marital or family status, religious beliefs, etc, and a higher proportion of people who do not have that characteristic do, or can, comply with it and there is no valid reason for the rule or requirement. For example, a policy of only hiring people who were able to relocate at short notice may disadvantage people who have family responsibilities – eg persons with young children (women employees).

The requirement not to discriminate applies before and during the employment relationship (and to a limited extent after employment), and would therefore cover less favourable treatment in recruitment, performance review appraisal, training, a compensation package, promotion, or selection for redundancy. Unlike claims of unfair dismissal, in which the level of compensation is capped, discrimination claims are unlimited in the potential amount of the financial award. Moreover, employers can, in appropriate cases, be required to pay compensation for injury to feelings and personal (psychological) injury as well as being required to discharge aggravated or exemplary damages. On top of this, interest can be added to the award of compensation.

For this reason the eradication of discrimination requires a knowledge and understanding of the key legal principles, the ability to monitor changes and developments in the law, and the will to take on board the practical lessons to be learned from decided cases. Since the Equal Pay Act 1970, Sex Discrimination Act 1975, Race Relations Act 1976 and Disability Discrimination Act 1995 came into force, there have been some 700 significant decisions by the appellate courts which have been reported in *Industrial Relations Law Reports* (IRLR), one of the most widely used series of law reports in the field of employee relations, interpreting the statutory provisions.

One of the reasons we are devoting a significant amount of this chapter to the subject of discrimination is because discrimination cases have assumed increasing prominence and – although they represent only 15 per cent of cases that go to employment tribunals compared to 27 per cent for unfair dismissal – now represent the largest subject area that goes before the appellate courts. This has been owing to the influence of EU law, a rise in the number of appeals and the introduction of a major new jurisdiction in disability discrimination. Added to this, the year 2003 saw some major changes in statute law with the Race Relations Act (Amendment) Regulations and the Equal Pay Act (Amendment) Regulations coming into force. There were also changes to the definition of indirect discrimination and the burden of proof in the Race Relations Act, together with changes made to the Sex Discrimination Act by the Burden of Proof Regulations. These regulations arose from the EU Burden of Proof Directive, which states that:

> Member states shall take such measures as are necessary in accordance with their national judicial systems to ensure that where the plaintiff [the discriminated employee] establishes before a court or other competent authority facts from which discrimination may be presumed to exist, it is for the defendant [the employer] to prove that there has been no contravention of the principle of equality.

An example of the minefield that is discrimination law can be seen in the case of *Garry v London Borough of Ealing*, CA 2001. One of the key elements an applicant must prove if he or she wishes to succeed in a discrimination complaint is the existence of a detriment. Ms Garry, a Nigerian, worked in the housing department of LBE dealing with housing benefits. In 1996 her manager learned that in a previous employment with another London borough, Ms Garry had been investigated for housing benefit fraud. Further, another Nigerian employee had recently been dismissed for housing benefit fraud with LBE. The Council initiated a covert special investigation into Ms Garry which she only became aware of in May 1997. This special investigation was a departure from the more usual form of internal investigation.

Ms Garry was interviewed by an audit officer on 30 June, whose findings were reported to the director of housing. He decided that there was insufficient evidence to justify disciplinary action but regrettably failed to inform either the applicant or the special investigator. It appears that the investigator continued the investigation for almost another year until the applicant became suspicious and asked what was happening with the enquiry – at which point she was informed that no further action would be taken.

Ms Garry complained of race discrimination on the basis that a special investigation had been commenced and that it had been continued without her knowledge long after the Council had concluded it should have halted. It was held by the tribunal that the special investigation was initiated because of the applicant's race (the tribunal observed that it was open to the Council to invoke a quicker and more modest form of internal investigation), but the question of whether she had actually suffered a detriment became the subject of an appeal – first to the Employment Appeal Tribunal and then to the Court of Appeal.

The Court of Appeal had little hesitation in holding that it was no defence to say that ignorance is bliss – ie that without knowing about the continuing investigation the applicant had suffered no distress or concern. The reality was that some of the applicant's colleagues were at the time, or subsequently became, aware of the continuing investigation and therefore it was perfectly possible that some stigma or career damage could arise. Accordingly, the tribunal's finding of discrimination was upheld.

This case underlines the fact that applicants in race (and by implication, sex and disability) claims have a low threshold to clear in terms of establishing detriment. It also reminds ER practitioners that mere ignorance of potentially discriminatory words or conduct on the part of the employee concerned will not prevent a claim arising should that person become aware of it at a later date.

The cost of dealing with complaints of discrimination and harassment and resultant tribunal claims can, relative to claims for unfair dismissal, be prohibitive. Generally, there is more evidence to be gathered, more witnesses to be heard and, of course, no cap on the possible compensation to be awarded. There are also a number of business risks – firstly to the organisation's reputation, particularly if the case is covered by the press. Secondly, a discrimination claim is also likely to be personally embarrassing and in all likelihood distressing for those managers named in the claim. If they are found to have discriminated, harassed or bullied, managers are likely to be subject to disciplinary action, may be dismissed and may well find that the claim continues to blight their career. Finally, there is the issue of management time. Frequently in discrimination claims an employer will be served with a discrimination questionnaire. The time taken to respond to these questionnaires together with the time taken to properly prepare for and attend at a tribunal hearing can be substantial.

Employers and individual line managers are most at risk of allegations of discrimination when making key decisions that will impact on employees on subjective grounds. What this means in practice, of course, is that when making key decisions about employees, employers must as far as possible base them on objective criteria. By far the best means of minimising the risk of claims is to act proactively and stop claims being brought in the first place. In order to do this it is essential that employers are sensitive to potential issues of discrimination and harassment within the workplace, and that steps are taken at an early stage when a potential problem arises.

It is, therefore, particularly important that employers watch out for the warning signs of discrimination/harassment, which are likely to include the following:

- grievances (which may themselves seem somewhat petty)
- 'personality clashes'
- high levels of absenteeism
- ill health (particularly any stress-related illness)
- poor performance (particularly where there has been a sudden downturn in performance following some change in the working arrangements)
- negative comments through the peer evaluation/appraisal process
- high levels of staff departures
- negative comments during exit interviews.

There are very few employers or individual line managers who do not genuinely want to eradicate discrimination and harassment from their workplace. If asked to pinpoint where employers/line managers with the best of intentions have gone wrong, the majority of employment lawyers would tell you that they have waited too long before obtaining advice and assistance from their own personnel specialist. If line managers are facing a difficult personnel issue, are having to make 'high-risk decisions' or believe they have spotted the warning signs of a potential dispute within their team, clearly the first action they should take – rather than seeking to resolve it themselves – is to pick up the phone and call for help. But for this to happen the ER specialist must ensure that he or she enjoys the confidence of line manager colleagues – confidence that is gained through offering reliable, consistent advice.

Time and again the cases indicate that if action is taken at an early stage, potential problems can be resolved. Often problems can be resolved using an employer's internal grievance procedure, particularly if this allows any grievance to be dealt with confidentially. If, however, potential problems are not dealt with at an early stage, there will be an increasing risk of claims being brought, potential liability and the costs already outlined. For this reason organisations must not only have equal opportunities policies that are more than just bland statements, they must have a means by which people can raise issues of concern – as the following example, taken from an actual employee handbook, illustrates.

PROCEDURE FOR HANDLING EQUAL OPPORTUNITY PROBLEMS

This procedure explains what to do if you have an equal opportunities problem, issue or complaint.

At **Smith & Co. Limited** we understand that it may be hard for you to work to your full capacity if you are being treated unfairly or harassed at work. That is why we support equal opportunity (EO) in this workplace.

If you bring a problem to us it will be handled **confidentially, impartially and speedily**.

We have outlined the procedure for handling problems in steps. Not all of these may apply to you, or you may follow them in a different order than shown here.

Step 1: Talk to the person/people involved
If you can, it's best to try and resolve issues yourself and to do so as soon as possible after the incident. We understand that you may not always feel comfortable doing so, particularly if you have a problem with your supervisor or line manager.

Step 2: Talk to the person responsible for EO
If you would like to talk over an issue or find out what your rights are, make a time to talk to our company's EO representative who will meet with you as soon as possible. In general they will not discuss your problem with anyone else without your permission. The only exception to this is if you tell them something that may affect someone's safety.

Depending on what you decide and after taking details from you, the EO representative will arrange for the other person(s) involved in the issue to be seen (preferably within two workdays of meeting with you) to obtain their side of the story.

We strongly encourage timely complaint resolution and we will aim to deal with matters as expeditiously as possible. The EO representative will speak to witnesses if they need further information. Witnesses may include people who didn't actually see what happened but who observed your reaction or other related behaviour.

The EO representative will then decide if they have enough information to know whether your allegation happened (using the standard proof that it is more likely than not to have happened). They will then submit a report to the Managing Director or other director with a recommendation about what, if any, further action is needed.

Although our intention is to deal with all complaints in a timely manner, there may be times – during holidays, for example – when the time-scales set out above cannot be adhered to.

Where allegations are proved, the company will resolve the problem by:

- bringing everyone together for a meeting to reach an agreement/resolve issues if the allegation is not of a serious nature
- taking appropriate disciplinary action (such as requiring an apology, counselling, an official warning, transfer, demotion) against the person(s) responsible if the allegation is serious.

They may also arrange training on EO issues for all staff to ensure that everyone knows what is and isn't acceptable.

Step 3: Contact the Group Human Resources Director
If you are unsatisfied with the decision reached under this procedure, or you do not feel comfortable bringing it to our attention, you can contact the Group Human Resources Director for information and advice about your issue at [*insert details*]

How will our company handle your problem?

We will handle your problem:

Confidentially
Only those directly involved in your issue or complaint (including anyone helping to sort it out) will have access to information about it. Information about the problem will only go on an employee's file if they are disciplined in relation to it.

Impartially
Everyone involved in the issue will get the chance to tell their side of the story, and will be treated as fairly as possible. The person handling the issue or complaint will not make a decision or take any action until all relevant information has been gathered.

Speedily
We will handle all issues or complaints as quickly as possible. Where possible, we will try to resolve all issues within 4 weeks.

We will not tolerate:

Victimisation
Less favourable treatment or disadvantage of anyone involved in an issue or complaint being handled under this procedure will be disciplined. Malicious use of this procedure (for example, to lie about someone) will also be a disciplinary matter.

We will not take any action without proof. We will investigate all issues before making a decision and/or taking action. We will only take action if we believe that it is more likely than not that what is alleged actually happened.

Does your organisation have an equal opportunities policy? What are the business case arguments you would use to justify such policies?

DISMISSAL AND REDUNDANCY

Although discrimination law might be one of the most dynamic and complex areas of employment law, the law relating to unfair dismissal and redundancy continues to provide the bulk of the practitioner's workload. In Chapters 10 (Employee performance and behaviour) and 12 (Managing redundancies) we look at the skills that are required to manage these two important issues in much greater detail, but in the context of Kahn-Freund's regulatory function these individual rights are a key area for any employee relations professional.

By virtue of section 94 of the Employment Rights Act 1996, an employee who at the effective date of termination (EDT) of employment has had continuous service of one year or more with the employer has a right not to be unfairly dismissed and is afforded the right to present a complaint to an employment tribunal. In order to successfully defend an employee's claim for unfair dismissal, an employer must be able to satisfy an employment tribunal of three things:

- that the real or principal reason for the dismissal was one of the potentially fair reasons as set out in section 98(2) of the Employment Rights Act 1996
- that it was reasonable to dismiss in all the circumstances of the case, and
- that the employer followed a fair procedure.

The potentially fair reasons for dismissal are:

- incapability (including ill health) or lack of qualifications
- misconduct
- redundancy
- contravention of statute (eg no work permit for the employee), or
- 'some other substantial reason'.

Concerns often arise when employers seek to attach a label to the 'reason' that they are dismissing an employee, and this is especially true in, for example, cases of persistent short-term absences. Where employees have been dismissed on these grounds, some employers have sought to justify their actions by classifying the dismissal as being for incapability (an 'issue of capability') arising from the sickness whereas others have classified the dismissal as being on the basis of conduct relating to the employee's attendance. Understandably, this has caused employers some anxiety in that they had difficulty in satisfying themselves that they had a potentially fair reason for dismissal. To their relief, the Employment Appeals Tribunal (EAT) sought to resolve this difficulty in the case of *Post Office v Wilson*, in which they indicated that tribunals should consider whether any of the reasons set out in section 98(2) apply to the facts before them but that if none of these categories fitted the facts, the tribunal must then consider whether the employer has established 'some other substantial reason for dismissal'. The burden of proof in establishing the reasons for dismissal lies squarely with the employer, although in most cases this burden is not difficult to discharge.

However, there are a number of circumstances where an employee's dismissal will be held to be automatically unfair, which include where the employee can show that the real reason for dismissal was:

- health- and safety-related
- maternity-related
- related to dependant care/parental leave
- related to the employee's assertion of a statutory right
- related to the participation by the employee in industrial action where it is within the first eight weeks of industrial action
- related to the employee's membership or non-membership of a trade union or to his or her participation in trade union activities
- redundancy, where the employee was selected for redundancy for any of the reasons set out above
- relating to protected shop workers and betting workers who may not be dismissed for refusing to work on Sundays

- relating to employees appointed as member-nominated trustees of their pension fund, under the Pensions Act, who may not be dismissed for exercising their function as such

- relating to employees elected (or seeking election) as employee representatives for the purposes of consultation over collective redundancies or transfers of undertakings, who may not be dismissed for performing, or proposing to perform, any such functions or activities

- connected with a business transfer to which the Transfer of Undertakings (Protection of Employment) Regulations 1981 applies

- related to the employee's spent conviction or failure to disclose it, or

- related to a disclosure qualifying under the Public Interest Disclosure Act 1999, or exercising rights under the Working Time Regulations 1998, the National Minimum Wage Act 1998 or Tax Credits Act 1999.

Individual employees enforce their rights on discrimination, redundancy, unfair dismissal and a range of other matters via employment tribunals. We will examine the nature and jurisdiction of tribunals later in the chapter, but suffice to say here that they are independent judicial bodies set up with the objective of dealing with employment disputes quickly, informally and cheaply.

The sheer variety of potentially unfair reasons for dismissal, or claims for discrimination, indicates that for the employee relations professional there is no room for complacency. An incorrectly handled dismissal, a

Table 4 *Applications made to employment tribunals: all jurisdictions*

Nature of claim	2003/04		2002/03	
	Number	%	Number	%
Unfair dismissal	47,682	27	49,424	30
Wages Act	40,928	23.2	39,656	24
Breach of contract	28,471	16.1	29,206	18
Redundancy pay	8,707	4.9	8,478	5
Sex discrimination	13,778	7.8	7,713	5
Race discrimination	3,418	1.9	3,624	2
Disability discrimination	5,490	3.1	5,380	3
Working time	7,506	4.3	6,420	4
Equal pay	3,073	1.8	2,665	2
National minimum wage	569	0.3	803	0.5
Flexible working	201	0.1	–	–
Other	16,682	9.4	9,562	6
Total	**176,505**		**162,932**	

failure to deal with a complaint of discrimination, an ill-advised decision in respect of a business transfer or health and safety issue, can mean an appearance before an employment tribunal. Even when things are done properly, the area of law dealing with individual rights at work can still give rise to a vast amount of litigation. The statistics on the number of complaints bought by employees continues to rise and is, as we said earlier, in excess of 170,000 cases per year. Table 4 above demonstrates how the number of applications to tribunals rises on a year-by-year basis, and although many of the applications made are not proceeded with, they still represent a degree of work for the employee relations specialist.

Some employers believe the law prevents them from sacking employees. Does it? If not, explain how it doesn't. If it does, explain how it does.

THE RIGHTS OF UNION MEMBERS

As well as a statutory floor of rights for employees, union members have their own statutory rights. These rights, which were considerably extended under the post-1979 Conservative governments, have been justified on the grounds that trade unions needed to be more democratic and more accountable to their members, and to exercise their power more responsibly. As the climate of UK industrial relations worsened in the 1960s and 1970s there was a widespread belief that trade union leaders were, without collecting the views of their members, coercing them to undertake labour market activities (for example, undertaking industrial action) harmful to their employment security. In short, that much strike activity was the result of political idealism on the part of trade union officials, rather than the consequence of a breakdown in collective bargaining.

This view resulted in the enactment of a series of measures to provide positive rights for union members to participate in or restrain union decision-making on specific issues. The main trade union member rights are:

- to participate in regular secret postal ballots, at least once every 10 years, to decide whether or not their union should establish, or retain, a political fund financed by political fund contribution, independent of the normal union subscription
- to elect all voting members of their union's executive (including its president and general secretary) by secret postal ballot at least once every five years
- to participate in a secret ballot before a union takes organised industrial action against an employer
- not to be called upon to participate in industrial action not supported by a properly conducted secret ballot
- not to be disciplined unjustifiably by their union
- to inspect their union's accounting records.

As a means of helping individual union members enforce their rights, the Employment Act 1988 provided the means by which they could seek assistance if they were considering or taking legal action against their union.

The restrictive function of the law

Ever since 1871 trade unions have, except when they were undermined by the *Taff Vale* decision in 1901, enjoyed immunity from actions for civil damages. That is, they have been protected from being sued simply because they took, or were taking, industrial action. The basic immunity framework was contained in the Trade Disputes Act 1906, and this remained in force until 1971, when the Conservative government introduced the Industrial Relations Act. This limited trade union immunity by the introduction of the concept of 'unfair industrial practices' which, if unions committed them, gave those affected by the action the right to sue for damages.

The Trade Union and Labour Relations Act 1974 repealed the Industrial Relations Act 1971 and re-established the trade unions' immunities position back to that provided by the Trades Disputes Act 1906. The Trade Union and Labour Relations (Amendment) Act 1976 extended trade union immunity to the breach of all contracts for which trade unions were responsible when they called their members out on industrial action. This gave trade unions licence to persuade their members to take secondary industrial action. Secondary action is that taken against an employer with whom the trade union has no dispute but who might, for example, be a key customer of an employer with whom they currently do have an industrial dispute. By taking this type of industrial action the union hopes the secondary employer will put pressure on the employer involved in the main dispute to settle the dispute on terms more favourable than presently on offer.

By 1976, trade unions had a very wide immunity from legal action in the case of industrial disputes. They could call, without a legal liability arising, for industrial action in connection with any kind of industrial dispute, no matter how remote those taking the action were from the original dispute. Nobody seriously challenged this union legislative position until 1979 when, as we mentioned above, there were moves to clamp down on the unions' abuse of their power. Legislation came at regular intervals, and between 1980 and 1993 there were seven Acts of Parliament designed to restrict trade union activity and behaviour:

- The Employment Act 1980 removed the unions' immunity if their members engaged in picketing premises other than their own place of work.
- The Employment Act 1982 narrowed the definition of a trade dispute, outlawed the practice of pres-suring employers not to include non-union firms on tender lists, and enabled employers to sue trade unions for an injunction or for damages where they were responsible for unlawful industrial action.
- The Trade Union Act 1984 introduced pre-strike ballots.
- The Employment Act 1988 effectively outlawed the closed shop.
- The Employment Act 1990 removed unions' immunity if they organised any type of secondary action in support of an individual dismissed for taking unlawful action.
- The Trade Union and Labour Relations (Consolidation) Act 1992 brought together in one piece of legislation much of the law relating to collective provision.
- The Trade Union Reform and Employment Rights Act 1993 made some amendments to existing requirements, most particularly in relation to ballots for industrial action.

These pieces of legislation substantially increased the grounds on which an employer can take legal action against a union. The circumstances in which unions can claim immunity from civil action have been tightened and now include provisions which requires full-time officials to repudiate the actions of lay officials if they take actions that are contrary to the legislation. If immunity is to be maintained, such repudiation has to be meaningful, and the courts can require unions to present evidence of the steps they have taken to bring their members within the law.

> Outline, with appropriate examples, the functions of the law in employee relations.

There is now no serious argument that these reforms were both necessary and timely. Requiring unions to hold a pre-strike ballot of their members prior to taking industrial action has now become part of the employee relations landscape and is not seriously questioned. Similarly, the requirement that full-time officials should be subject to periodic re-election has become part of the fabric of trade union organisation.

THE NATURE AND JURISDICTION OF EMPLOYMENT TRIBUNALS

Employment tribunals are independent judicial bodies, 'inferior courts' within the meaning of the Rules of the Supreme Court. For administrative convenience the country is divided into regions, each of which has its own regional chairman and regional office. Individual tribunals usually comprise three members: a legally qualified chairman (a solicitor or barrister of seven years' qualification), an employer representative, and an employee representative (usually a trade union representative). They also have jurisdiction in a wide range of matters derived from various statutory provisions (see Table 4 above). Each matter is begun by an application which is subject to its own time limit but which the employment tribunal usually has a discretion to extend, and applications are made to the appropriate tribunal regional office.

The employment tribunal is a statutory body and its composition is governed by the Employment Tribunals Act (ETA) 1996 as amended by the Employment Act 2002, and as a consequence of the 2002 Act, the rules for its administration are now set out in the Employment Tribunals (Constitution and Rules of Procedure) Regulations 2004, which came into force on 1 October 2004. These Regulations incorporate recommendations made by the Employment Tribunal System Taskforce, a strategic body set up by the government in 2001, and are intended to clarify and simplify the previous procedural regime. They also unify the separate rules of procedure that previously existed in Scotland with those applicable to England and Wales.

One of the key aspects of the new Regulations is in their structure, which should mean that they are easier to follow. They are also in 'plain English', which means that terminology that employee relations professionals have been used to for many years has changed (see box below). Notwithstanding the intent to simplify matters, there are still 61 rules of procedure which the employee relations specialist will need to be familiar with and for which the Department of Trade and Industry have provided a set of guidance notes.

PLAIN ENGLISH

Previously current term	New term
Applicant	Claimant
Originating application	Claim form
Notice of appearance	Response form
Directions hearing	Case management discussion
Preliminary hearing	Pre-hearing review

The application process

Proceedings are commenced by an applicant presenting a claim form, which has to provide details about the claimant and the respondent and other information that will help determine whether the claim can be accepted by the employment tribunal.

Once the application is received, and has been accepted by the Secretary to the Tribunals, it is registered and a copy sent to the respondent and, in defined circumstances, to ACAS. With the copy that is sent to the respondent the tribunal will send details of how to respond to the claim, the deadline, and the consequences of not replying. The respondent has 28 days to return the response form.

Once a claim has been received and properly responded to, the tribunal chairman, under rule 10, has powers to manage the proceedings in order to ensure the smooth and efficient running of the case. He or she can issue directions on any matter that he or she thinks is appropriate either from the parties' application/response or at a pre-hearing review.

Either may apply, or the tribunal may order, that one or other party must provide further and better particulars of any grounds upon which it relies, or any facts or contentions that are relevant to its claim. The essence of further particulars is to enable a party to know in advance the nature of the case that it must meet at the hearing. Failure to provide further particulars can result in the claim's being struck out. In keeping with the need to provide further and better particulars, a tribunal can order the disclosure and inspection of documents and set a time and a place for compliance. As with further particulars, disclosure ('discovery') is an important step in the process of enabling the parties to know the nature and extent of the case they have to respond to. The rules of procedure allow tribunals the power to strike out applications, or award costs, when a party to the proceedings does not comply with a directions order. This change has meant that the importance of compliance with any directions made is greatly increased. Costs can be awarded if a party, or its representative, has conducted proceedings vexatiously, abusively, disruptively or otherwise negatively. Costs can only be awarded if a party to the proceedings is legally represented, but there is also a provision within the rules for preparation time orders to be made when there is no legal representation. These orders may be particularly beneficial to those employers who prefer to present their own cases because they also cover the issue of vexatious claims.

ACAS conciliation

Since its inception, one of the roles that ACAS has played in employee relations is conciliation in tribunal claims. ACAS officers receive details of claims to tribunals and then contact the parties to assess whether a settlement is possible. The fact that a significant number of claims do not get to a full hearing is testament to their success in this area. Prior to the introduction of the 2004 rules of procedure, the tribunal office would continue with the arrangement for the hearing, and even set a date, irrespective of whether ACAS was continuing with its conciliation attempts. That has now changed, and ACAS's duty to conciliate will become limited to a fixed period in all but discrimination and equal pay cases (owing to their complexity). There will be two fixed periods. The short conciliation period of seven weeks will apply to pure money claims, such as breach of contract and statutory redundancy payments. The standard conciliation period of 13 weeks will apply to all claims not falling into the short or unlimited categories. The conciliation period in all cases will run from the date when the claim is sent to the respondent. During the conciliation periods it will not be permissible for a tribunal hearing to take place.

The intention is that the time limits will help to focus the parties' minds about settlement well in advance of the tribunal hearing. However, they may be detrimental to all parties, particularly as ACAS has indicated that it will apply them strictly. However, most practitioners will appreciate that it is often in the days leading up to the tribunal hearing, or at the tribunal door itself, that settlement between the parties is reached. At such point ACAS may no longer be able to play an active role in the settlement process in any event.

The hearing and the decision

The parties should ensure that their witnesses are ready and willing to attend at the tribunal, and that they, through the process of discovery, have in their possession all necessary and relevant documents. Every encouragement is given to the parties to agree documents, and tribunals much prefer that the parties prepare an agreed 'bundle' of documents for use during the hearing.

Individual applicants may appear before a tribunal without representation or may be represented by a lawyer, a trade union official or any other person of their choice. If they are unrepresented, the tribunal does what it can to assist them while ensuring that there is no bias.

Although there is no specific rule that dictates the order in which evidence is given, it usually depends on who had the burden of proof. In unfair dismissal cases, where dismissal is admitted, the respondent employer begins. If dismissal is not admitted, or it is incumbent upon the applicant to prove his or her case – for example, in constructive dismissal – the applicant begins. In order to speed up the process of evidence-giving, tribunals encourage the production of witness statements which can then be read out at the hearing.

Once a witness has given his or her evidence, he or she may be cross-examined by the other side and may also have to answer questions put by the tribunal members. Then, when the parties have called all their witnesses they are given an opportunity to make their final submissions. It is generally the case that the party that presented their evidence first will have the final word. Finally, the tribunal will withdraw to make its decision. Tribunal members will usually indicate whether they can announce their decision on the day of the hearing, or whether it will be given in writing in due course to the parties. When the applicant is successful, there is often a need for the parties to make further submissions in respect of the size of any compensation payment or the type of relief to be granted.

> You are asked by your line manager to explain the procedure used in employment tribunal hearings. What would you tell him or her, and why?

ACAS ARBITRATION SCHEME

ACAS was empowered by the Employment Rights (Dispute Resolution) Act 1998 to operate an arbitration scheme as an alternative to employment tribunal hearings. The implications of the scheme are far-reaching, and before submitting to arbitration the parties should therefore be aware of the process involved.

The central features of the arbitration scheme are that it is:

- voluntary
- speedy
- informal
- confidential, and
- free from legal arguments.

With these aims, it was thought by many that the scheme would herald a return to the idealism of the original tribunals of the mid-1960s. The scheme is currently only available for unfair dismissal complaints and referral must be by the mutual consent of both parties.

Arbitration under the scheme is on standard terms only. These cannot be varied. If the arbitrator, having regard to the ACAS code of practice, found the dismissal to have been unfair, the rewards may be reinstatement, re-engagement or compensation.

The hearing

The arbitrator is responsible for the conduct of hearings. The general principles lay out that the language of the proceedings is English, there are no oaths or affirmations, and parties are free to engage representatives and bring witnesses if they wish. Note that no special status will be accorded to legally qualified representatives. The arbitrator decides on procedural and evidential matters. His/her approach is inquisitorial and there is no direct cross-examination. Questions between the parties may be addressed only through the arbitrator.

The applicant may withdraw from the process at any time, provided it is done in writing to ACAS or the arbitrator. The parties are also free to reach a private agreement to settle the dispute before the end of the hearing. The arbitrator can endorse such an agreement but not interpret or ratify it in any way. This power is limited to agreements which are in his/her remit – eg unfair dismissal disputes.

The arbitrator's decision is in writing, includes references to general considerations and reasoning taken into account in reaching his decision, and is sent to both parties at the same time within a three-week deadline. The amount of any awards of compensation will be reasonable in the circumstances, taking into account the established practice of and statutory limits imposed on employment tribunals. The arbitrator's decision will not be published nor lodged with the employment tribunal, which makes the process very attractive where the issue is of a sensitive nature or publicity would rather be avoided. Given the apparent attractiveness of the scheme, it is strange that it has been woefully under-utilised. In the year 2003/04 there were only eight applications to the scheme, which would indicate that parties prefer the established employment tribunal route.

> Explain three advantages and disadvantages to an employer in agreeing to have alleged unfair dismissal claims decided by voluntary arbitration rather than at an employment tribunal.

THE HUMAN RIGHTS ACT (HRA)

The Convention for the Protection of Human Rights and Fundamental Freedoms ('the Convention') was signed by the UK in 1950, and in 1951 the UK was the first to ratify it – but it is only recently that it has been supported by specific legislation. The Human Rights Act 1998, which came into force on 2 October 2000, states in its preamble that it is 'an Act to give effect to the rights and freedoms guaranteed under the European Convention on Human Rights ...'. Although it is not specifically a piece of employment legislation, it impacts on employment law in three ways:

- Courts and employment tribunals are obliged to construe domestic legislation compatibly with the European Convention on Human Rights (ECHR) so far as it is possible to do so.
- Courts and employment tribunals must themselves act compatibly with the ECHR, save where they are prevented from doing so by primary legislation.
- Public bodies must act compatibly with the ECHR (this will include in relation to their employment policies and procedures), again save where they are prevented from doing so by primary legislation.

The impact of the Act on different types of employer

The position in an employment context can be summarised as follows. A pure public authority such as central government or the police is required to act at all times compatibly with Convention rights. Insofar as an employer has acted in breach of a Convention right in respect of a particular employee, that employee can issue proceedings. So far as private employers are concerned, they are not required to act compatibly with Convention rights, regardless of what capacity they are acting in.

The impact of the Act on courts and tribunals

It would be a mistake, however, to assume that the Act does not have implications for a private sector employer or for a public/private sector employer acting in a private context. The Act is still relevant to the actions of such an employer because of its impact on UK courts and tribunals. The Act impacts on UK courts and tribunals in the following ways:

- Courts or tribunals are required to act compatibly with Convention rights (this is because for the purposes of the Act 'public authority' is expressly defined as including courts and tribunals).

- Courts and tribunals are required to take into account European Court of Human Rights jurisprudence when considering an issue relating to a Convention right.

- Courts and tribunals are required to interpret UK legislation in a way that is compatible with Convention rights 'so far as it is possible to do so'.

It is, however, early days in the operation of the Act, and it is realistic to say that its impact will be felt over a much longer period.

Examples of the implications of the Act in an employment context

The exact impact of the Act and particular Convention rights will depend upon how UK courts and tribunals interpret their role under the Act and how they interpret particular Convention rights. Notwithstanding this, it is possible to identify potential implications, and although there has been little case law to date, it is probable that, as the law develops, litigants and their lawyers will seek to link Convention rights to employment rights.

For example, Article 6, which provides for 'the right to a fair trial', might be used to include the admissibility or otherwise of evidence in tribunal hearings. Tribunals will have to consider whether to admit evidence such as evidence from phone-tapping or searches of a company's e-mail system, where that evidence has been obtained in breach of Article 8, 'the right to respect for private and family life'.

In this context, the Court of Appeal has recently adjudicated in an unfair dismissal case in which the applicant claimed that his rights under Article 8 had been infringed. The case (*X v Y* [2004] IRLR 625) concerned a charity youth worker dismissed after failing to inform his employers that he had been cautioned for gross indecency in a public toilet. His claim that the dismissal was unfair because it amounted to a breach of his Convention right to respect for his private life failed before the Court of Appeal, as it did in the EAT, on the basis that a criminal offence which happens in a place to which the public has access cannot be regarded as taking place in private. The Court of Appeal acknowledges, however, that if a dismissal was on grounds of an employee's private conduct within Article 8, and was an interference with the right to respect for private life, it would be relevant to the determination of an unfair dismissal claim. This is because under section 3 of the Human Rights Act, an employment tribunal, so far as it is possible to do so, must read and give effect to section 98 and other relevant provisions of the Employment Rights Act in a way that is compatible with Convention rights. 'There would normally be no sensible grounds for treating public and private employees differently in respect of "unfair dismissal",' Lord Justice Mummery says in the leading decision. Therefore 'it would not normally be fair for a private sector employer to dismiss an employee for a reason which was an unjustified interference with the employee's private life'.

During the course of the decision, Lord Justice Mummery laid down guidelines on the correct approach to be adopted when Human Rights Act points are raised in unfair dismissal cases:

1) Do the circumstances of the dismissal fall within the ambit of one or more of the articles of the Convention? If they do not, the Convention right is not engaged and need not be considered.

2) If they do, does the state have a positive obligation to secure enjoyment of the relevant Convention right between private persons? If it does not, the Convention right is unlikely to affect the outcome of an unfair dismissal claim against a private employer.

3) If it does, is the interference with the employee's Convention right by dismissal justified? If it is, proceed to 5) below.

4) If it is not, was there a permissible reason for the dismissal under the ERA, which does not involve unjustified interference with a Convention right? If there was not, the dismissal will be unfair for the absence of a permissible reason to justify it.

5) If there was, is the dismissal fair, tested by the provisions of section 98 of the ERA reading and giving effect to them under section 3 of the HRA so as to be compatible with the Convention right?

Other issues which might come before the courts include Article 10, 'freedom of expression'. This might be used by employees to sound the death knell for employers' dress codes. But potentially the most contentious issue might arise over Article 11, 'freedom of assembly and association'. Article 11's principal significance is in relation to trade unions and their activities. The provisions of the Trade Union and Labour Relations (Consolidation) Act 1992 (TULRCA) will have to be interpreted in a way that is compatible with Article 11 insofar as this is possible – although the general view of commentators is that by and large it *should* be possible.

Particular areas in which it is felt that Article 11 is likely to be relevant include picketing where the issue is likely to depend upon whether the existing provisions within section 220 TULRCA and the Code of Practice on picketing (Code of Practice: Picketing (1992)) strike a reasonable balance between the right to protest and the interests of those affected by protest. In particular, it has been suggested that although in general these provisions may do this, there may be room for argument that certain provisions – such as, for example, provisions limiting the number of pickets to six – go beyond this. A further issue concerns the right to be a member of a particular trade union/not to join a trade union. It has also been argued that because Article 11 gives a right to form and join trade unions for the 'protection of interests', this must necessarily involve a right to representation. Finally, there is the matter of the 'right to strike'. It has been held that the right to strike is one of the rights protected by Article 11 – but the consensus is that it is likely to be reasonable for a state to impose significant restrictions on this right. However, there is a real possibility that trade unions and their lawyers will seek to use Article 11, particularly if there is any attempt by future governments to limit their rights to picket, strike and represent their members.

Has the Human Rights Act made any impact on your organisation or one with which you are familiar?

DEVELOPMENTS IN THE LAW

For personnel practitioners, dealing with the law should be second nature and taking account of the law in decision-making ought to be automatic. However, throughout the 1960s, 1970s and 1980s the scope of the law was relatively narrow and could be neatly categorised as individual or collective. Latterly, however, that scope has widened. New pieces of legislation continue to be introduced, and this requires the employee relations professional to be particularly vigilant in monitoring them. In the concluding part of this chapter we look at some of these developments and seek to identify what their probable impact is likely to be.

Age discrimination

We have already said that discrimination law is one of the most dynamic and complex areas of employment law, and its scope and coverage has changed dramatically over the past few years. A major reason for this has been the influence of the European Anti-Discrimination Framework Directive.

The government always indicated that there would be separate items of legislation for each of the strands in the Directives in order for there to be sufficient time for consultation and preparation. Legislation on race, sexual orientation and religion has thus already been implemented, and we are now awaiting the final piece of the jigsaw in the form of legislation on age discrimination. This has to be in place by October 2006, but as yet the government has not made up its mind about the shape and form of any legislation. Unfortunately for the employee relations practitioner, this is very unsatisfactory.

We know that legislation is coming, we know that it will outlaw some recruitment practices, and we know it is likely to see the end of compulsory retirement ages. But other than reviewing existing polices to take account of these factors there is very little that can be done, apart from recognising that age discrimination is not 'good practice' and can be very detrimental to organisational performance.

> What will be the business implications for your organisation in complying with any age discrimination legislation?

Employee consultation

In 1998 the European Commission, encouraged by the success of the European Works Council Directive, published a draft Directive on the information and consultation of workers at national level. After some hesitation, the UK government finally signed up to the Directive in 2001, and the Information and Consultation of Employees Regulations will come into force from April 2005 for organisations that employ at least 150 people, from April 2007 for organisations that employ at least 100 people, and from April 2008 for organisations that employ at least 50 people. It looks as if the main elements will be that UK organisations will be required to provide information for and to consult with employee representatives on the following topics:

- information on the recent and probable development of the business's activities and economic situation
- information and consultation on the situation, structure and probable development of employment within the undertaking, and on any anticipatory measures envisaged, in particular where there is a threat to employment within the undertaking
- information and consultation on decisions likely to lead to substantial changes in work organisation or in contractual relations.

This will affect an employer's ability to keep secret mergers, disposals and acquisitions, plans to change terms and conditions of employment, and planned reduction programmes.

There is no single model for how a suitable system for informing and consulting employees should be set up. A degree of variation will be possible, depending upon individual organisations, and requirements can be tailored to the particular circumstances so long as the basic criteria of the Regulations are met.

Undertakings will be expected to set up a consultation body for employees if they receive a request to do so in writing from at least 10 per cent of their workforce – subject to that being a minimum of 15 employees. This means that a relatively small number of employees can trigger the obligations.

Requests can also be made anonymously to the Central Arbitration Committee (CAC). Where 40 per cent or more of the employees in the undertaking endorse the request, employers must seek to reach a negotiated agreement. Once the request has been made, the undertaking must initiate negotiations for an agreement as soon as practicable and in any event within a month.

OTHER DEVELOPMENTS

The developments discussed above concern issue that are, or will be, of direct relevance to employers and employees, but there are always other matters that are not specifically about employment but that nevertheless impact upon the work of the personnel professional and must be taken account of and their significance understood. One of these is the government's plan to replace the three specialist equality bodies – the Equal Opportunities Commission, the Commission for Racial Equality and the Disability Rights Commission – with a single umbrella organisation.

The new body, the Commission for Equality and Human Rights, will not only carry on the work of the existing commissions but also take responsibility for the sexual orientation and religious discrimination laws that came into force in 2003 – plus, eventually, age discrimination.

As well as enforcing the law, the new commission – planned to become operational in late 2006 – will promote equal opportunities in society as a whole, in particular, the provision of public services. It will also aim to provide a 'one-stop shop' for businesses seeking advice and information on diversity strategies.

One of the government's reasons for the umbrella organisation is that 'People don't see themselves solely as a woman or black or gay, and neither should our equality organisations.' Given this mindset, there is every possibility that at some time in the future there might be a harmonisation of existing legislation into a single, cohesive Equality Act encompassing all forms of discrimination.

SUMMARY

In this chapter we have tried to identify the relationship between good employee relations and the law. We have stressed that employee relations is as much about 'good practice' as it is about legal compliance, but we have recognised that the employee relations professional cannot afford to be dismissive of the law. This is because the law impacts on almost every activity in the workplace. Furthermore, individual employees are very much aware of their 'rights' at work and do not hesitate to use the mechanisms open to them (employment tribunals) to assert those rights.

We have explained that legal intervention derives from two main sources: the political choices of the governing party and from developments within Europe. But in addition to this are developments in case law, and as we explained, some of the major developments in discrimination law have been influenced by the decisions of the appellate courts.

We have examined the role of employment tribunals, with particular reference to the revised rules of procedure, and made it clear that the employee relations specialist must understand their scope and complexity. Finally, we have looked at some, but not all, legal and other developments that we believe will impact on the work of the employee relations professional.

Key points

- Because all employee relations decisions have the capacity for legal challenge, it is important for managements to operate 'good practice'.
- The sheer variety of potentially unfair reasons for dismissal, or claims for discrimination, indicates that for the employee relations professional there is no room for complacency.
- Union members have rights allowing them to participate in or restrain union decision-making on specific issues.
- The contract of employment is one of the most important legal influences on the employment relationship.
- Discrimination has to be taken seriously and steps taken to eradicate it.
- The scale of legal development is such that employee relations professionals must continue to monitor changes and develop their own skills.

FURTHER READING

BERCUSSON B. (1996) *European Labour Law*. Oxford, Butterworths.

CIPD Employment Law Service

Employee Relations Act 1999

Employment Act 2002

Employment Rights Act 1996

Employment Tribunals (Constitution and Rules of Procedure) Regulations 2004

Human Rights Act 1998

Information and Consultation of Employees Regulations 2004

IRLR (Industrial Relations Law Reports)

IRS (regularly) *Employment Review – Policy, Practice and Law in the Workplace.*

KAHN-FREUND O. (1972) *Labour and the Law*. London, Stevens.

LEWIS D. and SARGEANT M. (2004) *Essentials of Employment Law*. London, Chartered Institute of Personnel and Development.

O'DEMPSEY D., ALLEN A., BELGRAVE S. and BROWN J. (2001) *Employment Law and the Human Rights Act*. Bristol, Jordan Publishing.

The importance of the European Union

CHAPTER 5

Geoff Hayward, Visiting Professor, Strathclyde Business School

---

CHAPTER OBJECTIVES

When you have completed this chapter you should be aware of and able to describe:

- the influence of the European Union on employee relations management in the UK

- the main developments in the social dimension to the European Single Market

- the key institutions of the European Union

- the legislative processes of the European Union

- the unique role for 'social partner' organisations at the inter-professional and sectoral level to shape, draft and determine the scope of all new EU employment and social legislation (the so-called social dialogue process)

- the Social Chapter of the European Union

- how the Social Chapter of the European Union impinges on the everyday work of the employee relations professional in the fields of equal opportunities, employment protection/working conditions, employee relations and health and safety at work.

INTRODUCTION

The influence of the European Union (EU) on personnel/HR management in the UK cannot be overstated. Its powers to determine the rules and regulations which govern workplace relations between employers and employees have grown dramatically since the mid-1990s. Examples of where the UK has had to take on board EU initiatives in the employment law field include collective redundancies, transfers of undertakings, acquired rights, 'burden of proof' in equality cases, information and consultation, part-time work, fixed-term contracts, pregnancy and maternity leave rights, parental leave, working time and equal opportunities. These are all areas where EU legislation has affected directly the everyday work of the UK personnel professional.

Personnel and HRM specialists have to appreciate that laws made at the EU level take precedence over the domestic laws of member states. This applies to employment legislation just as much as legislation in every other field. However, the most important lesson to be learnt from the innovations since 1993 is that the two sides of industry – employers and workers – are encouraged to participate in the law-making process when legislation is being enacted in the social and employment field.

The TUC, CBI and CEEP (UK) are members of the ETUC, UNICE and CEEP respectively, the trade union and employer organisations at EU level. As officially recognised 'social partners' by the EU, the ETUC and UNICE are given the opportunity to participate in the law-making process by negotiating collective agreements (the social dialogue process) which may then be transposed into legally binding EU Directives. The UK government can, of course, continue to enact whatever social and employment legislation it wishes domestically, provided that such legislation does not undermine the provisions laid down by EU law. The considerable powers given to the social partners by courtesy of the Maastricht and Amsterdam Treaties might well be expected to lead to trade unions and employers playing a much greater role in the determination of social and employment legislation in the future. As a consequence, the TUC and CBI (the UK social partners), as influential affiliates within the ETUC and UNICE, are well placed to have an important say in the determination of any such legislation.

Personnel and HRM specialists should also give thought to the consequences of the UK's joining the European Single Currency (the euro). Although there has been much debate over the economic and political merits or otherwise of the UK's joining the euro, little attention has been given to the impact it will have on employee relations. Currency transparency, for example, will inevitably lead to easier comparisons of productivity and labour costs across member states, which in turn will probably lead to further pressure for harmonisation of minimum employment and social standards across member states. In addition, with the 'enlargement' process completed and the 'EU 15' becoming the 'EU 25', the high-skill and low-labour-cost workforce of Eastern and Central Europe will generate even greater calls for a 'level playing field' in the area of social and employment conditions.

As personnel and HRM specialists, you ought to be aware of the impact that the 'European dimension' has on employee relations and give consideration to how line managers might be persuaded to recognise its relevance.

THE DEVELOPMENT OF THE EUROPEAN UNION

The origins of the European Union date back to the late 1940s and the revulsion which followed the two devastating World Wars. Jan Monnet, an 'ideas' man who had been put in charge of the *Commissariat du Plan* to bring about the economic recovery of France, suggested the pooling of French and German coal and steel production to Robert Schuman, the French foreign minister. Both men were convinced that a pre-requisite to a lasting peace in Europe was the reconciliation of the two great enemies, France and Germany. This proposal formed the basis of the Schuman Plan, which led to the Treaty of Paris (1951). Under its terms, Germany, Italy, France, Belgium, the Netherlands and Luxembourg created the European Coal and Steel Community (ECSC, 1952), whose fundamental aim was to enable these six countries on a joint basis to control the production, development and distribution of coal and steel which were still then major prerequisites for waging war.

Although essentially an economic initiative, both Schuman and Monnet believed that the pooling of French and German coal and steel production would 'immediately provide for the first stage of a European federation'. In short, they saw the ECSC as the first step towards an economic and political federal Europe. Schuman was a pragmatic politician and rejected any 'big bang' approach. He believed the way to European integration was to deal with each sector at a time – hence, coal and steel in 1952, followed by atomic energy in 1957. Ironically, it was the 'big bang' approach that was to succeed. Although we had to wait for some 30 years, the European Economic Community (EEC, 1957) paved the way for the creation of a single integrated European economy in 1987 with the adoption of the Single European Act (SEA, 1987).

The experience of the Coal and Steel Community provided a model for the establishment, via the Treaty of Rome (1957), of two further European Communities – the European Atomic Energy Community (EAEC) and the European Economic Community (EEC), commonly referred to as the 'Common Market' and aimed to develop close co-operation on economic matters.

In 1967, the three Communities and their institutions were rationalised by a Merger Treaty, which created the European Communities (EC). In 1973, the UK, Ireland and Denmark joined the EC, followed by

Greece in 1981 and Spain and Portugal in 1986. The EC became the European Union (EU) in 1993 when the Maastricht Treaty on European Union revised and widened the remit to include inter-governmental co-operation between member states on common foreign and security policy and on justice and home affairs. In 1995, Sweden, Finland and Austria joined the EU. The Treaty of Amsterdam (1997) was marked by the then new Labour government in the UK's signing up to the 'Social Chapter', the terms of which were incorporated for the first time into the main corpus of the treaty. The Treaty of Nice paved the way for further enlargement of the EU, and on 1 May 2004, ten new states became members of the EU (Slovakia, Estonia, Hungary, the Czech Republic, Slovenia, Latvia, Lithuania, Poland, Malta and Cyprus). The 25 member states of the EU constitute the largest economic unit in the developed world, with a population of over 480 million.

Iceland, Norway and Liechtenstein are part of the European Single Market. They are subject to all EU Single Market legislation under the European Economic Area Agreement (EEAA) including some employment legislation. However, they are not full EU members of the EU.

Aims of the European Union

The principal aims of the European Union (EU) are summarised as follows:

> The Community shall have as its task, by establishing a common market and an economic and monetary union and by implementing the common policies or activities referred to in Articles 3 and 3a, to promote throughout the Community a harmonious and balanced development of economic activities, sustainable and non-inflationary growth, respecting the environment, a high degree of convergence of economic performance, a high level of employment and of social protection, the raising of the standard of living and quality of life, and economic and social cohesion and solidarity among member states.
>
> (See Official Journal of the European Commission (OJEC) C 325/40 24.12.2002.)

And – most important from a personnel/HRM point of view – the treaties commit the member states to ensuring that the EU's citizens receive a share of the benefits accrued from economic integration in the form of an upward harmonisation of living standards and working conditions. (See OJEC C 325/92 24.12.2002.)

These along with other aims, objectives and principles are defined in a series of treaties. The treaties also contain details of the structure and operation of the EU (see below). They are the constitution of the EU and provide a legal basis for legislation and other measures. All members have to abide by these treaties and the legislation agreed under them. All the legislation adopted by the EU since 1957 is referred to collectively as the *Acquis Communautaire*, which all countries wishing to join the EU must accept as a condition of membership.

When there are changes to the treaties, they have to be ratified by all member states. This is done either by a referendum of a member state's citizens or by a majority vote in the member state's national parliament. In both cases, the people, or their representatives, have the last word. However, there is always a price to democracy – namely, delay. Ratification normally takes about 18 months to two years. Changes brought about by treaties do not become binding on member states until the ratification process has been completed.

The Treaty of Rome (1957)

The founding treaty of the EU is the Treaty of Rome (the European Economic Community Treaty) of 1957, which provided for the creation of a free trade area by removing barriers to the free movement of goods, labour, capital and services (the so-called four great freedoms) between member states. By integrating the economies of the member states, it was hoped that healthy competition would stimulate innovation, technological development, increased productivity and increased demand. It was envisaged that consumer prices would fall, stimulating even further demand for goods and services. The 'European economy' would thus be firing on all four cylinders, and this 'upward virtuous circle of prosperity' would result in real benefits for everyone within the Common European Market.

Although the bulk of the Treaty of Rome was concerned with removing the barriers to free trade, it did contain an important chapter that dealt with a whole set of social provisions. The Social Chapter contained in the original Treaty of Rome distinguished the EU from all other 'free trade agreements' in so much as it gave it a 'social' as well as an 'economic' dimension. (See Treaty Establishing the European Economic Community (EEC), Title III, Social Policy, 1957.)

The Social Chapter provided for closer co-operation in the 'social and employment field' between member states. One of the tasks it set itself was

> to promote improved working conditions and an improved standard of living for workers so as to make possible their harmonisation while the improvement is being made.

The Chapter also enshrined, as one of its principles, the right to equal pay for equal work between men and women.

The founders of the EU were not creating just a free trade area but a community in which there would be harmonisation of social and employment conditions. There would be free competition within the free trade area, but this would be within the constraints of minimum social and employment standards across member states. As explained above, unlike any other free trade agreements (for example, the North America Free Trade Association (NAFTA)), the EU has always had a social dimension.

The Single European Act (SEA, 1987)

Progress in moving towards a free market was slow, largely because each proposal to achieve this objective required the unanimous agreement of all member states. There was always at least one member state which objected. A way therefore had to be found to prevent any single member state from preventing the rest from getting on with the job of completing the establishment of a free trade market. In 30 years, the Council of Ministers (see below) had hardly been able to adopt a single important measure designed to achieve the Single Market.

In 1985 the Commission (see below) proposed that member states should speed up the creation of the common market and by 31 December 1992 adopt 282 necessary measures to achieve the free movement of goods, capital, labour and services between member states. To achieve this, the Single European Act amended the Treaty of Rome in three important ways.

First, for the first time a deadline – 31 December 1992 – was set for finally achieving the 'four great freedoms'.

Second, it introduced a new legal basis to allow member states to agree measures by 'qualified majority vote' (QMV) rather than unanimous vote. Under this system member states were given a number of votes relating to their populations:

- France, Germany, Italy and the UK: 10 votes each
- Spain: eight votes
- Belgium, Greece, the Netherlands and Portugal: five votes each

- Sweden and Austria: four votes each
- Denmark, Finland and Ireland: three votes each
- Luxembourg: two votes

A 'qualified majority' was 62 of the total 87 votes available. To block proposals a member state had to gather together 26 votes. Put another way, there had to be opposition from at least three member states to block a proposal. Two large states (for example, France and Germany together) could no longer veto proposals. In the absence of at least 26 votes against, a proposal was accepted, and even the member states who abstained or voted against it had to implement it into their national law.

Third, the Act introduced another innovation by formalising the EU's commitment to involve the 'social partners' (employers and trade unions) in its decision-making machinery (see below).

The Single European Act also brought changes to the Social Chapter. It provided that health and safety regulations across the EU member states could be harmonised on the basis of qualified majority voting. This health and safety 'fast track' has been used lavishly (see *Europe: Personnel and Development*, CIPD, December 2000) and was the basis of the Working Time Directive (1993), which was then transposed into UK employment law via the Working Time Regulations 1998 (see below).

The impact of the Single European Act cannot be over-estimated. By removing the veto of a single member state to proposals, it was radical and revolutionary. It meant Europe would never be the same again. It meant the EU law-making mechanisms could actually start to work as envisaged by the authors of the Treaty of Rome. Above all, it meant employee relations professionals had to take Europe seriously because it was now possible to influence the drafting of new EU laws in a way unthinkable within national parliaments.

The Treaty on the European Union (TEU, 1993)

In December 1991, the heads of member states met in Maastricht to agree further steps on the road to greater political, economic and monetary integration amongst member states. The eventual outcome was the Treaty on the European Union (1993), which formally changed the name of the EC to the European Union (EU) and provided for the creation of a common currency (the euro) from 1 January 1999, with national currencies taken out of circulation by the year 2002. The Treaty also reaffirmed the principle of 'subsidiarity' in EU legislation. Although the principle is interpreted in different ways, it basically provides that the EU should take legislative action solely when the objectives of such legislation can only be achieved, or at least achieved better, at the EU level than at national level. Not surprisingly, however, there is little agreement on when this criterion is met.

The Treaty on the European Union also made two important changes to the Social Chapter. First, all member states (excluding the UK) agreed to extend the number of employment and social issues that might be adopted by QMV. As a result of the UK's objections, no new 'social provisions' were incorporated into the main body of the Maastricht Treaty. However, a compromise agreement was reached whereby member states other than the UK could use EU institutions to introduce additional binding legislation within the social field, on the understanding that any such legislation would not apply to the UK. This was done under a separate Social Policy Agreement which listed the specific social issues upon which the rest of the member states could legislate. This agreement was attached to the Social Protocol annexed to the main Treaty spelling out the arrangements just described.

The second innovation was the formalisation of the EU's commitment to involve the 'social partners' directly in its decision-making machinery. It provided for compulsory consultation with the social partners on social and employment proposals, and gave them the option of negotiating Framework Agreements on such issues, which could then be made legally binding on member states by transposing them into a Council Directive.

The Treaty of Amsterdam (1999)

This Treaty introduced changes thought necessary to help prepare the EU for eventual enlargement to the applicant countries of Central and Eastern Europe, to take account of changing political priorities and to give effect to the need for stronger EU action in areas such as employment, social policy and the environment. The key provisions of the Treaty were:

- It developed further the principles of democracy and individual rights and for the first time established a clear procedure to be followed in the event of 'serious and persistent' breaches by member states.

- The Council of Ministers was provided with new powers to take more effective action to combat discrimination based on sex, ethnic origin, religion or belief, disability, age or sexual orientation.

- It pledged to remove all remaining restrictions on free movement of labour between member states by 2004, the only exemptions being the UK and Ireland, which were allowed to retain frontier controls.

- It introduced a new Chapter which related exclusively to employment.

- The Agreement on Social Policy was transferred from the annex and incorporated into the main body of the Treaty and thus becomes applicable to all member states. This was possible only because of the 1997 General Election in the UK, which brought about a Labour government committed to rescinding the 'UK opt-out' and 'signing up' to the Social Chapter.

For the personnel/HR professional, the Treaty was significant for four reasons. First, the UK Labour government agreed to opt into the Agreement on Social Policy annexed to the Treaty of Maastricht. As a result, the provisions governing this area were fully incorporated into the Treaty proper, and the UK again took full part in social policy-making and thus became fully bound by EU legislation in this area. The UK also had to adopt those Directives – on parental leave and on European Works Councils – which had been adopted under the Social Policy Agreement.

Second, the principle of equal pay for equal work was extended to 'work of equal value'.

Third, the Treaty provided the EU with competencies to take action to combat any form of discrimination whether based on sex, racial or ethnic origin, religion or belief, disability, age or sexual orientation. All legislation in this field, however, was subject to the agreement of all member states (the 'unanimity' principle).

Fourth, the Treaty contained an Employment Chapter committing the EU for the first time to take into account the need to achieve high and sustainable employment opportunities when taking decisions related to its commercial and economic objectives. This was the first time the promotion of a high level of employment had been written down as one of the main objectives of the EU. It was to be achieved by co-ordinating the employment policies of the member states to develop a common strategy.

The Employment Chapter

The Chapter is designed to restore balance in the EU by creating a counterweight to its economic and monetary provisions. It asserts that:

- Employment is a matter of common concern.
- The objective of generating high employment is to be taken into consideration when implementing all other common policies.
- The achievement of this objective is closely monitored.
- The EU considers the employment situation in each member state and in the Union as a whole on an annual basis and conducts a detailed examination of the steps taken by individual governments to promote employment.
- An employment committee promotes co-ordination of national measures and encourages dialogue between employers and employees.

The Employment Chapter is important because it makes the EU and its institutions for the first time the guardians of an overall employment policy. It is ambitious in the sense that it provides for permanent and regular collaboration within the EU framework. (See OJEC C 325/88 Title VIII, 24/12/2002.)

The Treaty of Nice (2003)

The Treaty of Nice, which came into force on 1 February 2003, paved the way for 10 new countries to join the EU, thus enlarging the EU from 15 to 25 member states. It extended further the issues that could be harmonised on the basis of qualified majority voting, changed the future size and composition of the European Commission and introduced an 'enhanced co-operation' procedure. (See SEC (2001) 99.)

The Treaty extended the scope of qualified majority voting (QMV): some 27 issues changed over completely or partly from unanimity to QMV. The Treaty also re-weighted member states' voting powers in the Council of Ministers to reflect their larger population size. As from 1 January 2005, a qualified majority vote will be obtained if a proposal passes two – and in certain circumstances – three tests:

- Test number 1: it receives at least 'a specified number of votes' (this number is termed 'the qualified majority threshold').
- Test number 2: it is approved by a 'majority of member states'.
- Possibly, test number 3: a member of the Council may 'request verification' that the proposal has received at least 62 per cent of the total Council votes. If it has not, the proposal will not be adopted. (However, this test only applies if it is triggered by a request from a Council member.)

The Treaty also limits the size of the European Commission (see below) to one Commissioner per member state, which means that the five large member states will have to give up their second Commissioner in 2005. It also decrees that in the event of the EU's eventually expanding beyond 27 member states, a rotation system for appointing Commissioners will be introduced.

The Nice Treaty also introduces a 'second track' system named Enhanced Co-operation. In a nutshell, where there are at least eight member states who wish to proceed further and faster on an issue, they will be able to request a formal proposal from the Commission and – subject to agreement by the Council of Ministers acting by qualified majority voting, as well as the approval of the European Parliament – the measure will become binding on the member states involved. The Commission, when receiving a request for enhanced co-operation, will have to ensure that such co-operation aims to achieve the objectives of the Union, that those objectives could not otherwise be achieved, and that the proposed enhanced co-operation will not undermine the functioning of the Single Market. Opting in to enhanced co-operation will require the new member state to adopt all decisions previously taken under enhanced co-operation.

Explain the difference between qualified majority voting and unanimous decision-making in the European Union.

SUMMARY OF THE DEVELOPMENT OF THE EUROPEAN UNION

1957 – the Treaty of Rome
- creation of a 'common market'
- contains two social measures:
  - freedom of movement of labour
  - harmonisation of social conditions (the Social Chapter)

1987 – the Single European Act
- introduced the qualified majority voting (QMV) procedure
- health and safety to be harmonised on the basis of QMV

1993 – the Treaty on the European Union
- provided for a common currency (euro) from 1 January 1999
- Social Policy Agreement containing Social Protocol extending the social issues to be harmonised by QMV
- greater involvement of social partners in the EU decision-making machinery

1999 – the Treaty of Amsterdam
- introduced an Employment Chapter
- Social Policy Agreement incorporated into the Treaty of Rome as the Social Chapter
- further measures to combat discrimination based on sex, sexual orientation, disability, age, religious belief and racial/ethnic origin
- EU institutions required to encourage social dialogue on issues such as employment, right to work, training, etc

2003 – the Treaty of Nice
- paved the way for enlargement
- re-weighted the votes in the Council of Ministers
- increased the ceiling on the European Parliament from 626 to 732
- capped the size of the European Commission to 27
- increased the number of issues subject to QMV

HOW THE EU WORKS

The Treaty of Rome set up four key institutions to achieve its objectives. These were:

- the European Commission
- the Council of the European Union
- the European Parliament
- the European Court of Justice.

The European Commission

This is the EU's executive body, whose main role is to propose measures and ensure their implementation. There are currently 20 Commissioners made up of the President, two Vice Presidents and 17 members. Commissioners, who are usually senior and distinguished politicians, are nominated by the governments and serve for a period of five years. The President enjoys considerable power and influence and sets the agenda for the weekly Commission meetings where new initiatives for making European law are discussed. The larger member states (UK, France, Germany, Italy and Spain) currently nominate two Commissioners while the others nominate one, although this will change, as we have seen, in 2005 as a result of the Treaty of Nice. The Commissioners think EU-wide and not in national terms. All policy proposals made by a Commissioner must have the support of a simple majority of all Commissioners before they can be launched officially.

Each Commissioner has a personal 'cabinet' of advisory staff, and each is also in charge of one or more of the policy divisions in the Commission called Directorates-General (DGs). These are subdivided into Directorates. They are responsible for drawing up proposals for EU action and monitoring the implementation of agreed measures. The Commissioner for Employment and Social Affairs is responsible for employment (including employee relations), social affairs and equal opportunities.

The Council of the European Union

The Council comprises 25 members – one representing each member state. It is the EU's decision-making body. Its main function is to adopt measures proposed by the Commission for enactment in the member states. The Council is made up of several levels. There is the European Council level – which comprises the heads of government of the EU member states – which meets four times a year to discuss major issues and decide on broad areas of policy.

There is then the level of the Council of Ministers, which comprises a Minister from each member state according to the subject under discussion. Thus, although each country has a permanent seat in the Council, the personalities who fill these seats change in accordance with the subject being considered. For example, if the Council is discussing employee relations matters, then the seats are filled by the respective Employment/Labour Ministers from each of the member states.

There is also the level of the Presidency of the Council, which is held by each member state for a period of six months. As President of the Council, the member state sets Council agendas and can therefore determine, to some extent, which Commission proposals are progressed and given priority. Member states normally run a programme of high-profile events during their Presidency. All Council meetings are chaired and negotiations co-ordinated by the representative of the presiding member state.

The European Parliament

The European Parliament is the EU's main consultative body. Its members have been directly elected since 1979. The number of seats allocated to each member state is in direct proportion to the size of each state's population. Elections to the Parliament are held at five-yearly intervals. Members of the European Parliament (MEPs) take up their seats according to their trans-national political group rather than their nationality. UK MEPs are elected by proportional representation. Labour MEPs sit as part of the European Socialist Group, while UK Conservatives sit with the European People's Party.

The Parliament has a number of specialist committees – such as the Employment and Social Affairs Committee and the Women's Rights Committee – which examine issues in depth. The committees draft opinions on Commission proposals and on other issues within their remit, which are debated at the monthly plenary session of the Parliament.

The European Parliament approves the appointment of the European Commissioners, determines the EU budget and proposes amendments to measures initiated by the Commission. Initially, the European Parliament had few powers and was regarded as nothing more than a talking-shop. However, over the years it has acquired greater influence, and its powers to influence the legislative process vary according to the procedures governing decision-making in any given area (see below). For example, since the introduction of the co-decision procedure by the Treaty on European Union, the Parliament has significant co-legislative powers. Although the Parliament can reject the annual budget prepared by the Commission, it has only exercised this power on two occasions since 1957.

The Parliament – voting by a two-thirds majority – can dismiss the Commissioners but only *en bloc*. They cannot dismiss a single Commissioner. It is 'all of them or none'. (See OJEC C 325/117 24.12.2002.) This power had never been exercised until spring 1999. President Santer and his team of Commissioners resigned *en bloc* – preferring to 'go voluntarily' rather than be 'pushed' by the powers of the Parliament, which on this occasion would most certainly have been used. Santer's Commission collapsed as a result of six cases of mismanagement and petty corruption.

The European Court of Justice (ECJ)

This Court is the supreme custodian of the EU-enacted laws and its decisions take precedence over any laws or judicial decisions taken in the member states. The size of the ECJ is dependent on the number of member states as each is entitled to one judge who is appointed for a six-year term. They are assisted by eight Advocates General who deliver preliminary opinions on cases before they are put to the court. (See OJEC C 325/122 24.12.02.) A subsidiary court, the Court of First Instance, hears many of the more routine cases. Even so, the average time for a case to be heard is 18 months and the procedure can take several years.

The European Court of Justice acts as the final arbiter in disputes over the interpretation of the Treaties, and over the failure of member states to implement EU laws. It can quash any measures introduced by member states which are incompatible with the Treaties.

The Court has been used by UK individuals, groups and organisations to challenge UK employment legislation on the grounds that it contravenes EU law. For example, the UK Equal Pay Act (1970) was challenged. The Act allowed for equal pay for work of equal value where this was shown to be the case by a job evaluation scheme. Claims by women employees were being rejected after the use of job evaluation. However, a complaint was laid before the European Court of Justice that such claims were failing because the job evaluation schemes being used by UK employers contained gender bias factors. The complaint was upheld, and in 1983 the Equal Pay Act (1970) was amended.

Explain the differences in the functions of the European Commission, the Council of Ministers, the European Parliament and European Court of Justice.

Legislative instruments

Most EU employment and social legislation comes in any of three forms which have important differences from each other:

- Regulations
- Directives
- Decisions.

Regulations are the highest and most rigorous form of EU legislation. They comprise detailed instructions which are immediately applicable throughout the European Union once adopted by the Council of Ministers, and are 'directly binding' upon all member states. In other words, Regulations have the same direct status as laws passed by the UK Parliament and must be enforced by the UK courts in the same way. Failure to apply Regulations results in the European Commission making a complaint to the European Court of Justice.

Decisions are more specific in their application (particular member states, sectors or industries) and are immediately binding on those to whom they are addressed. Decisions which impose financial obligations are enforceable in national courts. Decisions are used when the EU wants the full force of European law to apply to individuals, to particular firms or enterprises, or to specific member states.

The 'instruments' that the Commission can use confuse many people, so a few words of explanation might be helpful. In some cases, primary legislation is contained within the Treaty, such as the provisions that safeguard the rules on competition (see Articles 85 and 86, EEC 1957), which the Commission has the responsibility to oversee. Should individuals, enterprises or individual member states breach those provisions, the Commission needs instruments to coerce the offenders into compliance. These may take the form of Decisions, which are directly applicable and binding on those to whom they are addressed. (See Article 90 EEC 1957.) However, in the employment and social field, Directives are the main legislative instruments.

Directives set out specific objectives, and each member state is given time (usually two years) to enact legislation within its own Parliament to ensure that the objectives are achieved. Directives, while being less rigid and allowing more flexibility than Regulations or Decisions, are still binding in all member states. In itself, a Directive does not have legal force in the member states, but particular provisions may take direct effect if the Directive is not duly implemented. In the UK, Directives have been implemented either by being incorporated as they stand into national law or by means of secondary legislation drawn up by the relevant government department or by an Act of Parliament, formulated in the usual way through a Parliamentary Bill.

Softer instruments

In addition to Regulations, Directives and Decisions, which are 'hard legislation' enforced by the EU, there are other 'softer' instruments that attempt to regulate behaviour in the EU. These are:

- Recommendations
- Opinions
- Resolutions
- Declarations
- Communications
- Memoranda.

Though sounding officious, these are not legally binding. They have a moral rather than a legal force, although they can be used as evidence in court. Probably the best known Declaration in the employee relations field is the Community Charter on the Fundamental Rights of Workers, commonly known as the 'Social Charter' (1989).

Implementation of the instruments

Of the three instruments of European Law with real teeth, the most widely used is the Directive. Since 1957, over 60 Directives have been adopted in the social policy field. Over half of these relate to health and safety at work, while the others deal with employment protection/working conditions, equal opportunities, freedom of movement and public health. (See COM (2003) 312 final 2.6.2003.) Almost all of these Directives have been transposed into UK legislation.

If a member state fails to transpose Directives into domestic law by the target date or if EU law is infringed, complaints may be made to the European Commission. Such complaints can be made by individuals, companies, other member states, the European Parliament or pressure groups. The Commission investigates the complaint and asks the member state(s) concerned for an explanation. If this is unsatisfactory, the Commission orders the member states to put the matter right within a specific period of time. If the infringement continues, the matter is referred to the European Court of Justice. If this Court finds against the member state, it passes a judgment with which the member state has to comply. If the failure to comply results in a denial of individual rights, the European Court of Justice may require the member state to pay compensation to the individual. The important thing about the European Court of Justice is that it takes precedence over all the courts within member states. It has the power to overrule the UK judiciary, including the House of Lords. When issues and disputes reach the European Court of Justice, it is the end of the road. Once it makes its judgment, there is no further appeal.

> Outline the difference between a European Union Directive and a Regulation. Which is the more important in employee relations terms?

THE SOCIAL PARTNERS

Following the ratification of the Treaty of Maastricht, the EU-wide representative bodies of employers and employees (referred to as the social partners) now have a role in the EU legislative process. There are three main social partners at the inter-sector level of the EU: the European Trade Union Confederation (ETUC), the Union of Industrial and Employers' Confederations of Europe (UNICE) and the European Centre of Enterprises with Public Participation and of Enterprises of General Economic Interest (CEEP).

The European Trade Union Confederation (ETUC)

The European Trade Union Confederation (ETUC) has a dual structure. Apart from the member states leading national trade union confederations, which are affiliated to the ETUC as full members, it also comprises 11 European sectoral trade unions that until 1995 were called European industry committees but are now known as European Industry Federations (EIFs). These federations represent individual trade unions from a particular sector. They are recognised by the EU institutions as the sectoral (industry) employees' social partners.

The Confederation was formed in 1973, and today its full members include 77 national trade union confederations from 35 countries in Western, Central and Eastern Europe and 11 European sectoral trade union organisations. All in all, the ETUC represents the interests of some 60 million trade union members at European level. There are three decision-making bodies which determine ETUC policy – Congress, the Executive Committee and the Steering Committee. The Congress, the highest body, is held every four years and decides the organisation's policy priorities. The Executive Committee generally meets every three months and takes the policy decisions required to implement the priorities laid down by the Congress. The Steering Committee normally meets eight times a year to decide on urgent action required to implement the strategies laid down by the Executive Committee. The ETUC Secretariat is in Brussels and carries out tasks assigned to it by the Congress, the Executive and Steering Committee. The current General Secretary is John Monks, who is the head and spokesperson of the Confederation. (See www.etuc.org/en.)

The Union of Industrial and Employers' Confederations of Europe (UNICE)

The Union of Industrial and Employers' Confederations of Europe (UNICE) is the official voice of European business and industry in contact with European institutions, and was established in 1958. It comprises 35 members and four observers from throughout Europe, including EU member states, EEA countries and some Central and Eastern states. It has a permanent secretariat based in Brussels. Its aims are to keep up with issues that interest its members by maintaining permanent contacts with European institutions; to promote a framework which enables industry and employers to secure European policies and proposed legislation and prepare position papers; to promote its policies and position at European and national level; and to persuade European legislators to take these into account and represent its members in the dialogue between social partners as provided for in the European Treaties outlined above. It operates through its Council of Presidents and an Executive Committee, which assists in policy formation and suggests actions to be taken. (See www.unice.org.)

The European Centre of Enterprises with Public Participation and of Enterprises of General Economic Interest (CEEP)

CEEP represents the interests of the public sector employers. It was formed in 1961 and has several hundred member organisations from over 20 countries. Although its full members belong to European Union countries, non-EU countries can also join as 'Associate members'. (See: www.ceep.org.) CEEP has its general secretariat in Brussels and National Sections in each member country. For example, public sector employers in the UK would be members of CEEP (UK).

THE LEGISLATIVE PROCESS

Legislative procedures

The Treaty of Amsterdam streamlined the EU's decision-making procedures so that there are now two main procedures for adopting EU legislation: the 'Co-operation (Article 252)' and the 'Co-decision (Article 251)' procedures. In addition, in the social and employment field, a third procedure is used, known as the 'Social dialogue (Article 138) procedure' (see below).

Common to all procedures is that the initiative is taken by the Commission, which has the sole right of initiative. In practice, however, many Commission proposals emanate from direct requests or indirect pressure from member states, other EU institutions or interest groups.

The 'Co-operation (Article 252) procedure'

Under the terms of the Co-operation procedure, legislation may be adopted by QMV in the Council, following two readings by the European Parliament. After the Parliament's first reading, the Council adopts a so-called 'common position'. Parliament may then propose amendments to this common position or reject it outright. If the Council wishes to maintain its common position, despite Parliament's objections, it may only do so unanimously. Following the Parliament's second reading, the Commission will re-examine its original proposal along with the Council's common position and the Parliament's amendments. If the Council wishes to make amendments to this re-examined proposal, it may do so only by unanimity. If it does not wish to do so, the proposal may be adopted by QMV. In short, under the Co-operation procedure the Parliament has the power to reject legislation after the second reading. The Council can, of course, decide to ignore Parliament and still go ahead with the legislation, but it can only do this if it can achieve a unanimous vote amongst all Council members. It only takes one vote against for the legislation to be blocked.

See Figure 5.

135

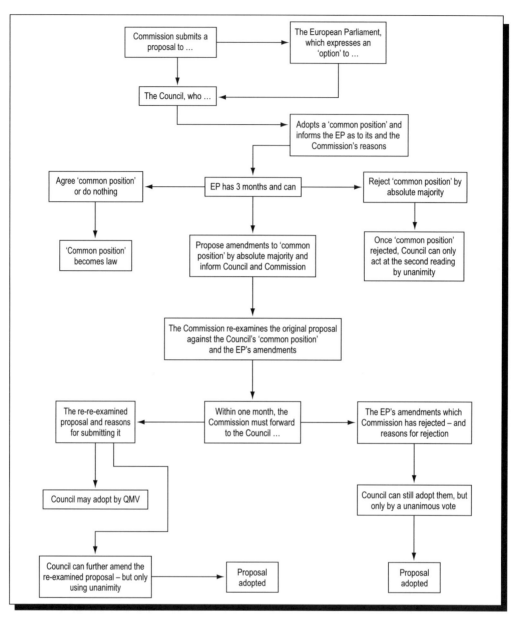

Figure 5 *Article 252, the Co-operation procedure*

The 'Co-decision (Article 251) procedure'

Under the terms of this procedure, the Parliament's legislative powers are significantly enhanced in that the Council can only adopt legislation jointly with the Parliament. The procedure is considerably longer than the Co-operation procedure and it includes a final stage in which an attempt is made to reconcile potentially diverging positions of the Council and the Parliament. To put it more simply, the Co-decision procedure works in the same way as Co-operation – except in one very important way: the Parliament's decision cannot be overruled, even if the Council votes unanimously to reject it! This means that under the Co-decision procedure the Council and the Parliament must seek a compromise which they are jointly prepared to support if a proposal is to become law.

See Figure 6.

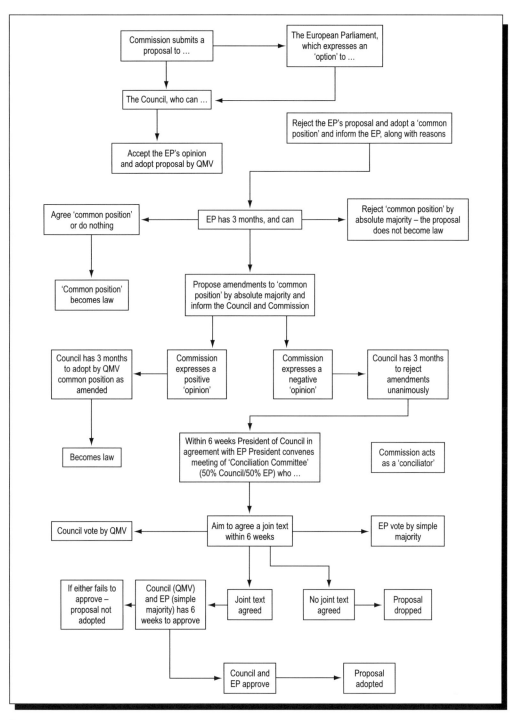

Figure 6 *Article 251, the Co-decision procedure*

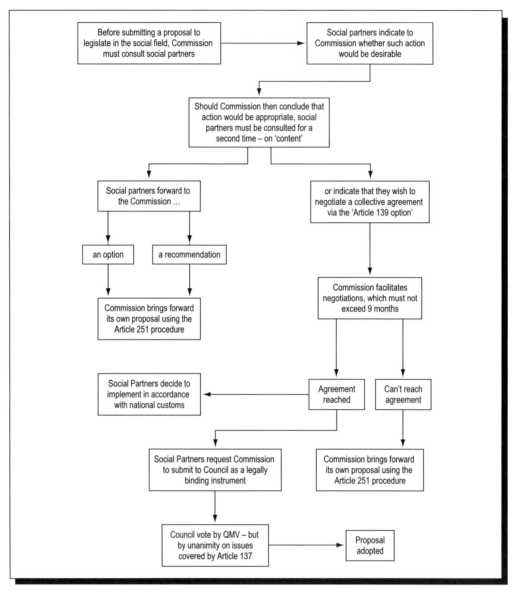

Figure 7 *Article 138, the Social dialogue procedure*

The 'Social dialogue (Article 138) procedure'

See Figure 7.

Inter-sectoral

The Treaty of Amsterdam saw Maastricht's 'Agreement on Social Policy' included in the main body of the Treaty. This stated that the European Commission must consult with the social partners (ETUC, UNICE and CEEP) about both the direction and the content of EU legislation in the social and employment field. The Treaty also provided for the social partners, should they so wish, to negotiate Framework Agreements as a substitute for legislation. The social partners were additionally given powers to engage in negotiations at their own initiative. This process is known as 'social dialogue'. It operates as follows:

- When considering proposed legislation in the social field, the Commission must first consult the social partners on whether there is a need for legislation. The social partners will typically have six weeks within which to submit their views (Article 138, paragraph 2).

- If the Commission, after consultation with the social partners, concludes that a need for legislation exists, it then consults the social partners for a second time with a view to establishing their views on the possible scope of such legislation. The social partners are given the opportunity to negotiate an agreement as a substitute for Commission legislation. This second period of consultation is normally a six-week period.

- If one or both of the social partners reject(s) the negotiations option, the Commission then has the powers to bring forward its own proposals for legislation under the Co-decision procedures. If, however, the social partners opt for the negotiations route, they have a period of up to nine months, with the possibility of extension, within which to negotiate a Framework Agreement.

- If the social partners successfully negotiate a Framework Agreement, they have to submit that agreement to the Commission with a recommendation that it be put forward as a formal legislative proposal to be adopted by the Council of Ministers.

- Should the social partners fail to reach a voluntary agreement, a fall-back position comes into play. The Commission may submit its own proposals under the Co-decision procedure by which the Council of Ministers takes decisions on the basis of QMV.

The negotiation of a EU-wide Framework Agreement has already happened successfully in the case of parental leave (Parental Leave Directive), part-time work (Part-Time Work Directive) and fixed-term contracts of employment (Fixed-Term Contracts Directive).

A fourth Framework Agreement was also negotiated by the social partners which provided protections and laid down regulations governing the working practices of 'teleworkers'. The social partners decided not to ask the Commission to transpose the agreement into a Directive and opted for the 'voluntary' route by which member states would implement the terms of the Agreement in accordance with their own customs and procedures (see Article 139). A fifth attempt to use the social dialogue procedure was with respect to temporary and agency workers. Although indicating a will to reach a Framework Agreement with regard to temporary and agency workers, negotiating between the social partners broke down and the Commission brought forward its own proposals under the Co-decision procedure. At the time of writing this proposal is being delayed in the Council of Ministers by a blocking majority led by the UK.

However, on three issues – European Works Councils, the burden of proof in sex discrimination cases and information and consultation at the national level – the social partners decided not to enter into negotiations on these issues and the Commission brought forward its own proposals, which were eventually adopted by the Council.

Framework Agreement negotiations are arranged and appropriate venues and interpreters provided by the Commission, which also provides a 'chairperson' to facilitate the negotiations between the social partners. All the costs associated with the negotiations – for example, travel, accommodation, etc – are met by the Commission. The employer and trade union sides usually negotiate against very tight 'mandates' from their respective constituents. Once agreement is reached, the social partners' affiliated organisations must ratify the agreement.

Sectoral
The same social dialogue process as exists for inter-sectoral purposes is also available for social partners within the EU industrial sectors to establish minimum social and employment standards for a particular sector. The social partners in the sectoral social dialogue are the European industry federations affiliated to

the ETUC and the sector-based employers' organisations. Sectoral social dialogue has so far led to well over 100 joint texts, covering such issues as vocational training, employment and working conditions. The weight of these texts varies from joint opinions expressing views on Community proposals for legislation and general policy in the sectors to specific agreements on issues reached by collective bargaining. These agreements commit the national partners as members of the signatory organisations, but have no binding force.

An example of a sector-wide Framework Agreement is the agreement limiting annual working time in the civil aviation industry to 2,000 hours and flying time to 900 hours. This was the third agreement of its kind in the transport industry. The other two agreements were negotiated in 1998 and related to sea transport and the railways. In 2002 voluntary guidelines on supporting age diversity in commerce were negotiated by EuroCommerce (employers) and UniEuropa Commerce (trade unions), and in the agricultural sector, a European agreement was made on vocational training. The social partners of the telecommunication sector also concluded the first review of the implementation of their telework agreement, which had been concluded in February 2001. (See the Commission's communication *Scoreboard on Implementing the Social Policy Agenda*, COM (2003) 57 final.)

Framework Agreements have been negotiated at a European level. Briefly explain:

- who the parties are that negotiate such agreements
- how long the parties may take to reach such an agreement
- how such agreements are enforced throughout the member states of the EU.

THE SOCIAL DIMENSION OF THE EU

The Social Chapter

The founders of the European Union did not just create a free trade area in which people, goods, services and capital could move freely. They were establishing a political and economic community in which there would be social regulation/protection in its free trade area. Product and service market competition would take place on a 'level playing-field' of minimum social and employment conditions in all member states. To this end the Treaty of Rome contained a Social Chapter (Title III, Social Policy), subsequently amended by the Single European Act (1987) and the Treaty on European Union (1993) and regrouped under Title XI of the Treaty of Amsterdam with the heading 'Social Policy, Education, Vocational Training and Youth'. The objectives of the Social Chapter are :

> the promotion of employment; improved living and working conditions; proper social protection; dialogue between management and labour; the development of human resources with a view to lasting employment; and the combating of social exclusion . . .

It also commits member states, as a condition of membership, to ensure and maintain the application of the principle that men and women should have equal pay for equal work or work of equal value. The UK became fully covered by the Social Chapter on 1 May 1999 when the Treaty of Amsterdam came into force. That treaty also empowers the EU to take action to combat any form of discrimination whether based on sex, racial or ethnic origin, religion or belief, disability, age or sexual orientation. Finally, when making social policy, the EU may draw inspiration from the European Social Charter signed in Turin on 18 October 1961 and on the 1989 Community Charter of the Fundamental Social Rights of Workers (Article 136) (see below).

The Social Chapter is not a set of detailed regulations. It is a mechanism which allows the member states to make new rules and legislation at the EU level on a wide range of social and employment issues. As we have seen, it allows common rules to be introduced by the Council of Ministers by

- a unanimous vote
- a qualified majority vote
- a Framework Agreement negotiated by UNICE, CEEP and the ETUC and/or their sectoral equivalents

which may then be issued as Directives and transposed into national legislation.

The Framework Agreement procedure limits the power of the European Parliament or member states in the Council of Ministers to make any amendments. This ability of collective bargaining to shape both the direction and content of legislation is considerable and unique. The CBI, CEEP (UK) and TUC are the UK members of UNICE, CEEP and the ETUC respectively. As a result, they have acquired a new and special significance as organisations in the UK. All three organisations are respectively representing the interests of UK companies (private and public) and employees in the drafting of legislation that can then become legally binding in the UK and apply equally to unionised and non-unionised companies/establishments.

Qualified majority items

Under the Social Chapter procedures, legislation in any of the following areas can be adopted by qualified majority voting:

- improvements in the working environment to protect workers' health and safety
- working conditions
- informing and consulting with workers
- the integration of persons excluded from the labour market
- equality between men and women with regard to labour market opportunities and treatment at work (Article 137, paragraph 1).

Unanimous vote issues

The Social Chapter mechanisms can be used to introduce European Union-wide legislation on the basis of unanimity amongst member states in the following areas:

- social security and social protection of workers
- the protection of workers where their employment contract is terminated
- the representation and collective defence of workers' and employers' interests, including co-determination
- conditions of employment for third-country nationals legally resident in the EU.

Excluded issues

However, certain subjects – namely, pay, the right of association, the right to strike and the right to impose lock-outs – are formally excluded from harmonisation by legislation based on Social Chapter procedures (Article 137, paragraph 5).

Critics of the EU nonetheless point out that although some areas are formally subject to unanimity or even excluded altogether, this is by no means a secure safeguard. They argue that past experience suggests EU institutions will seek to apply the broadest possible interpretations in order to maximise the scope for adopting measures by qualified majority voting despite possible objections from individual member states. The Social Chapter mechanisms are seen as bearing the risk of costly, far-reaching and unforeseeable legislation being imposed on the UK. It is viewed by its opponents as mirroring the more interventionist approach common in much of the EU and contrary to a deregulated approach to the operation of labour markets.

The Social Chapter in practice

There are four areas of employee relations management in which EU laws have had, and will continue to have, a direct impact on the work of the UK personnel/HR specialist:

- equal opportunities
- employment protection/working conditions
- employee relations
- health and safety at work.

Employee relations professionals must obtain copies of the actual Directives and the implementing UK legislation in these areas rather than depend on summaries. It must also be borne in mind that many Directives are not simply implemented in UK law by one piece of legislation. For example, in areas such as equal opportunities, the requirements of a Directive have been transposed into several separate legal instruments within the UK.

Equal opportunities

Equal pay

The 1975 Equal Pay Directive sought to improve the effectiveness of equal pay for men and women as laid down in the Treaty of Rome by reducing differences between member states in the application of this principle through approximation of member state laws on the subject. The Directive stated that the principle of equal pay required the elimination of all discrimination on the grounds of sex with regard to all aspects and conditions of remuneration for the same work or for work to which equal value is attributed. It also provided that any job classification (evaluation) system used for determining pay must be based on the same criteria for both men and women, and must be drawn up so as to exclude discrimination on grounds of sex.

In 1983 the Equal Pay (Amendment) Regulations were introduced in the UK to comply with this Directive. These regulations, inter alia, introduced provision for 'independent experts' to undertake job evaluation exercises independently of the employer in the case of claims for equal pay based on work of equal value.

Parental leave

In 1996, the social partners (UNICE, the ETUC and CEEP) concluded a Framework Agreement on parental leave which was then issued as the Parental Leave Directive. It provides an individual right for parents to take up to three months' unpaid leave after the birth or adoption of a child before its eighth birthday. Employees are protected from dismissal for asking for the leave, and have the right to return to work on the same conditions as before. The Directive also entitles individuals to a certain number of days off work for urgent family reasons in the case of sickness or accident. The UK government transposed this Directive into national legislation via the Maternity and Parental Leave Regulations 1999.

Equal treatment

The Equal Treatment Directive (1976) was designed to give effect to the principle of equal treatment for men and women with regard to access to employment, promotion, vocational training and working conditions, including the conditions governing dismissal. As a result of this Directive, the UK had to introduce legislation to equalise the retirement ages for men and women, to remove the difference whereby men could receive statutory redundancy payments up to the age of 65 but women up to 60, and to ensure that occupational pensions were equal for men and women. The provisions of the Directive were made binding in the UK initially under the Sex Discrimination Act (SDA) 1975, and the Equal Pay Act (EPA) which came into force in 1975. Each Act has been amended a number of times since it came into force, the latest amendment to both being in 2003. (See the equal opportunities website www.eoc.org.uk.)

The burden of proof

Measures laid down in respect of the burden of proof in cases of discrimination based on the Sex Discrimination Directive (1997) sought to improve the effectiveness of national implementation of the principle of equal treatment by enabling all persons to have their right to equal treatment asserted by judicial process after possible recourse to other competent bodies. The Directive provides that where a complaint to a tribunal establishes 'facts from which it may be presumed that there has been direct or indirect discrimination', the employer has to prove 'that there has been no breach of the principle of equal treatment'. The Directive thus places the burden of proof on the employer to demonstrate that the principle of equal treatment has not been breached, rather than on the employee to prove that an infringement has taken place. This Directive was implemented in the UK in October 2001 by the Sex Discrimination (Indirect Discrimination and Burden of Proof) Regulations.

Employment protection/working conditions

Part-time workers

In 1997, UNICE, the ETUC and CEEP negotiated a Framework Agreement on part-time work designed to remove discrimination against part-time workers, to improve the quality of part-time work, to facilitate the development of part-time work on a voluntary basis, and to contribute to the flexible organisation of working time in a manner that takes into account the needs of employers and workers. A part-time worker is defined as a worker whose normal average weekly hours of work calculated over one year are less than those of a comparable full-time worker. If no comparable full-time worker exists within the same establishment, reference is made to applicable collective agreements or national law.

The social partners agreed that part-time workers should be treated no less favourably with regard to employment conditions except where justified on objective grounds. Employers are to facilitate the transfer between full-time and part-time work by providing information on available work within the establishment and by greater access to vocational training. Member states and national social partners were urged to identify and eliminate obstacles to part-time work. The Framework Agreement was transposed into a Directive with an implementation deadline of 20 January 2000. In April 1998 this Directive was extended to the UK and came into force in June 2000 under the Part-Time Workers (Prevention of Less Favourable Treatment) Regulations. This gave part-time workers in the UK rights to be treated no less favourably than full-time workers and to receive the same hourly rate of pay, the same access to company pension schemes, the same entitlements to annual leave and maternity/parental leave on a pro rata basis, the same entitlement to contractual sick pay, and no less favourable treatment in access to training. (See DTI website www.dti.gov.uk.)

Fixed-term contracts

In 1999, the EU social partners concluded a Framework Agreement on fixed-term contracts. These negotiations had been initiated by UNICE, who had proposed in February 1998 that the social partners negotiate on fixed-term contracts. This was unique in that it was the first time UNICE had proposed, and initiated, legislation in the social and employment field under the social dialogue provisions. The agreement generated an EU Directive discouraging the promotion of fixed-term contracts and limiting their use. Fixed-term employees are:

- not to be treated less favourably than permanent employees doing similar work for the same employer at the same establishment
- protected against unfair dismissal without a qualifying requirement

- no longer able to waive their right to claim redundancy pay when their contract expires
- entitled to terms and conditions equivalent to permanent staff, on a pro rata basis.

The UK gave effect to this Directive in 2002 via the Fixed-Term Employees (Prevention of Less Favourable Treatment) Regulations.

Redundancy

The Collective Redundancy Directive (1975) introduced the requirement for consultation, in good time, with employee representatives on mass redundancies with a view to reaching an agreement. The consultations must cover ways and means of avoiding collective redundancies or limiting the number of workers affected, and of mitigating the consequences through help for redeployment or retraining workers made redundant. The employer must provide the workers' representatives with certain information – for example, the reason for the redundancies, the number and types of workers to be made redundant, and the criteria proposed for the selection of workers to be made redundant.

This Directive was transposed into UK legislation in the Employment Protection Act 1975. The Directive was amended slightly by a further Directive (1992), which was implemented in the UK in June 1994 in the Trade Union Reform and Employment Rights Act 1993. This ensured that consultation takes place at the workplace affected, even if the redundancy decision has been taken by a controlling body in another country.

Transfer of undertakings

The Transfer of Undertakings/Acquired Rights Directive (1977) sought to protect employees in the event of a change of employer through takeover or merger. It introduced the principle that when a business is sold, employees should transfer to the new owner on the same basic terms and conditions of employment and could not be dismissed for reasons connected with the transfer. In implementing the Directive into UK law (the Transfer of Undertakings and Protection of Employment Regulations – TUPE) the government excluded the public sector.

However, in 1992, the European Court of Justice confirmed that the Directive applied to employees in both the private and non-profit sectors. The UK law was, therefore, amended by the Trade Union Reform and Employment Rights Act 1993 to include public sector employees. In 1998 an amendment to the 1977 Directive was introduced to limit existing law by clarifying that transfer of undertaking legislation applied only when an 'economic activity that retains its identity' is transferred. The UK implemented this amendment in July 2001. A further Directive was adopted in 2001, and it is expected that as a consequence amendments to the TUPE Regulations will follow.

Contracts of employment

The Proof of an Employment Relationship Directive (1992) imposed an obligation on the employer to inform employees of the conditions applicable to the contract of employment relationship. By doing so, it is hoped to provide employees with improved protection against possible infringements of their rights and to create greater transparency in the labour market. The Directive required all employees working over 8 hours per week for more than one month to receive written confirmation of the main terms and conditions of their employment within two months of starting work. Changes to written particulars must be notified in writing within one month. It also required conditions for overseas postings to be provided in writing. Implementation of the Directive in the UK was via the Trade Union Reform and Employment Rights Act 1996.

Insolvency

The Insolvency Directive (1980) requires member states to set up insolvency funds to guarantee reimbursement of outstanding pay to employees if a business collapses. It was implemented in the UK without change to existing law, which was already established by the then Employment Protection (Consolidation) Act 1978. Further protections of employees in the event of their employer's insolvency were provided for in the Employment Rights Act 1996 and the Pension Schemes Act 1993.

Posting of workers

The Posting of Workers Directive (1996) aims to ensure minimum protection of workers posted temporarily to a member state other than the one in which they normally work. It is also designed to ensure fair competition and to provide minimum employment conditions for these employees. A posted worker is guaranteed such terms and conditions as laid down in the law and in applicable collective agreements in the member state to which he/she is posted, in particular, maximum work periods and minimum rest periods; minimum paid annual holidays; minimum rates of pay, including overtime rates; health and safety; the conditions of hiring out workers, particularly temporary employment agencies; protective measures concerning the employment of pregnant women, new mothers, children and young people; equality of treatment between men and women; and other non-discrimination measures.

Member states are required to establish adequate procedures to allow workers and/or their representatives to enforce the provisions of the Directive. A posted worker can bring a claim under the Directive in the host country without affecting any right to do so elsewhere. This Directive was transposed into UK law via the Employment Relations Act 1999 and the Equal Opportunities (Employment Legislation) (Territorial Limits) Regulations (1999).

Employee relations

The European Works Council Directive

This Directive (1994) and its extension to take in the UK in 1998, provides for a Europe-level information and consultation system to be set up in all organisations with more than 1,000 employees in member states and employing more than 150 people in each of two or more of these. A Works Council (or an alternative system) has to be agreed between the central management of the organisation and a 'special negotiating body' (SNB) of employee representatives. If no agreement is reached within three years, a fall-back system applies. This requires the establishment of a European Works Council of employee representatives with the right to meet central management at least once a year for information and consultation about the progress and prospects of the company, and to request extra consultation meetings before certain major decisions are taken affecting more than one member state.

European information and consultation systems already in place before the set deadline implementation date of 22 September 1996 – or 15 December 1999 in the case of the UK – were exempted. Effect was given in the UK to the European Works Council (UK Extension) Directive (1997) by the Transnational Information and Consultation of Employees Regulations (1999).

Information and consultation at national level

The aim of the Information and Consultation Directive (2002) is to establish a general framework setting out minimum requirements for the right to the informing and consultating of employees in undertakings or establishments within the European Community. Its requirements apply to undertakings employing at least 50 employees in any one member state or establishments employing at least 20 employees in any one member state. An 'undertaking' is defined as a public or private undertaking, carrying out an economic activity whether or not operating for gain. An 'establishment' means a unit of business in accordance with national law and practice. In short, a multi-site UK company employing at least 50 individuals across a number of plants in different geographical locations would be deemed an 'undertaking'. An 'enterprise' could be any of these individual plants providing it had a workforce of at least 20 employees. The right to information and consultation covers information on the recent and probable development of the undertaking's or the establishment's activities and economic situation; on the situation, structure and probable development of employment within the undertaking/establishment; and on any anticipated measures envis-aged, in particular where there is a threat to employment; and on decisions likely to lead to substantial changes in work organisation or in contractual relations. This information is to be given at such time, in such fashion and with such content as is appropriate to enable employees' representatives to conduct an adequate study and, where necessary, prepare for consultation.

Under the Directive, consultation should take place at the relevant level of management and employee representation and in such a way as to enable employees' representatives to meet with the employer and obtain a response, and the reasons for that response, to any opinion they might formulate. In addition, consultation must take place with a view to reaching an agreement on decisions within the scope of the employer's powers likely to lead to substantial changes in work organisation or in contractual relations.

Member states also have to provide for appropriate measures in the event of non-compliance by employers or employees' representatives with the provisions of the Directive, and ensure that adequate administrative or judicial procedures are available to enable the obligations deriving from the Directive to be enforced. Member states must also provide for adequate penalties to be applicable in any infringement of the Directive. Such penalties are to be proportionate to the seriousness of the offence.

Member states have until early 2005 to implement the requirements of this Directive. Implementation of the required provisions by a voluntary negotiated agreement between labour and management is permissible. In member states such as the UK and Ireland, where there is no general, permanent and statutory system of information or consultation, or of employee representation at the workplace, the Directive can be introduced in stages as follows:

- Undertakings with at least 150 employees (or establishments with at least 100 employees) are to be covered no later than 23 March 2005.
- Undertakings with at least 100 employees (or establishments with 50 employees) no later than 23 March 2007.
- Undertakings with 50 employees (or establishments with 20 employees) no later than 23 March 2008.

European Company Statute

In October 2001, the EU adopted a Regulation establishing the European Company Statute (ECS) and an accompanying Directive on the involvement of employees in the 'European company'. In terms of the devel-opment of EU social and employment legislation, this event was historic, bringing to a close after 31 years what was probably the longest legislative process in this field. It was in 1970 that the European Commission had first proposed giving companies the option of forming a 'European company' which could operate on a Europe-wide basis and be governed by Community law directly applicable in all member states (rather than national law). For many years the proposal failed to gain approval in the Council of Ministers largely owing to disagreement over the worker-involvement provisions to apply in a European company.

A European company may be formed by two or more EU companies through merger or the formation of a joint subsidiary or holding company, or by the transformation of a single existing EU company. Employee involvement arrangements – information and consultation, plus board-level employee participation in some circumstances – must generally apply in all types of European companies.

Companies participating in the formation of a European company must negotiate with the employees via a special negotiating body (SNB) made up of employee representatives. The negotiations are expected to result in a written agreement on the employee involvement arrangements. If these arrangements include a reduction of existing board-level participation rights that apply to a certain proportion of employees, this must be approved by a two-thirds majority of SNB members (from at least two member states). The SNB may decide not to open talks or decide to terminate talks in progress – in which case existing national information and consultation rules will apply. Where the SNB and the management reach an agreement, the result should see the setting up of an EWC-like 'representative body' or an information and consultation procedure. If the parties so decide, the agreement may also set out rules for board-level participation. SNB negotiations must be completed within a six-month period. This may, however, be extended by mutual agreement to a total of one year. If no agreement is reached, or the parties so decide, a statutory set of 'standard rules' apply, providing for a standard 'representative body'. The standard rules also provide for board-level participation in certain circumstances where this existed in the participating companies.

In October 2003, the DTI published a consultative document entitled *The Implementation of the European Company Statute: The European Public Limited Liability Company Regulations 2004*. The consultation period ended in January 2004, but at the time of writing no proposed legislation has been placed before Parliament. The UK deadline for implementing the Directive was October 2004.

Health and safety at work

Several Directives were adopted in the 1970s and 1980s setting minimum standards for the control of noise, vibration, asbestos and other agents, as well as Directives harmonising safety signs. Today, over 30 Directives have been adopted making health and safety at work the most regulated area of EU social policy. These Directives have largely been incorporated into UK law via the Control of Substances Hazardous to Health (COSHH). However, the majority of these Directives are so-called Daughter Directives, aimed at implementing, in specific areas, the provisions laid down in the 1989 Framework Directive which aims to encourage improvements in the health and safety of workers at work.

An important EU measure in the health and safety area is the Working Time Directive (1993), transposed into UK law via the Working Time Regulations, which became operative on 1 October 1998. The Conservative government (1992–1997) challenged the legality of the Directive before the European Court of Justice, on the basis that it was an 'employment' measure rather than a health and safety issue and thus ought to be subject to unanimous voting in the Council of Ministers rather than by QMV. The rationale behind the challenge was that the UK was exempt at that time from voting when the QMV procedure was operated because of the 'Maastricht opt-out', whereas under the 'unanimity' principle the UK would have been allowed to exercise its vote and thus block the measure. In the event, the ECJ confirmed the Commission's position that 'working time' was indeed a health and safety measure, and the UK was instructed to transpose the Directive into domestic legislation. A further consequence of this ruling was that the ECJ spelt out a new and much wider definition of what was a health and safety issue, opening the door to the Commission's bringing forward many more proposals to legislate on what hitherto would have been considered employment issues, which required 'unanimous' voting. As health and safety measures, such proposals could henceforth be adopted by QMV. (Note that because the UK opt-out still applied at that time, such measures could have been adopted by the Council of Ministers without the UK's being present.)

The Working Time Regulations introduced a range of significant new rights and entitlements, such as a minimum of four weeks' paid annual leave (but which can include Bank Holidays). There is significant scope in the Regulations for employers and employees to enter into agreements on how the working time rules will apply in their own particular circumstances. Collective agreements can be made with an independent trade union, while 'workforce agreements' can be made with workers who are not covered by collective bargaining. Certain activities, or sectors of activities, of workers are excluded from the Regulations. These include those whose working time is under their own control – for example, managing executives, family and religious workers, domestic servants and trainee doctors. However, a new so-called 'Horizontal Amending Directive (HAD)' was adopted by the Council of Ministers extending the

Directive on organisation of working time to the previously excluded sectors and activities (road, rail, air, sea, inland waterways and lake transport, sea fishing, offshore work, and junior doctors). These new measures were scheduled to be implemented over the period 2003/04. At the time of writing, however, the transposition legislation has not yet been adopted by the UK.

Broadly speaking, worker entitlements under the Regulations (eg rest periods and paid annual leave) are enforced by an individual complaint to an employment tribunal. In the case of the mandatory 'limits' on working time (such as the weekly working time and night-work limits), employees' rights are enforced by health and safety authorities (the Health and Safety Executive and local authorities). However, workers have protection against detrimental treatment or unfair dismissals for, among other things, refusing to work in breach of an acceptable working time limit. Employers are required to keep adequate records, going back two years, to show that the working time limits have been honoured. The transposition legislation, which gave force to the original Directive, was the Working Time Regulations (1998). (See the DTI website.)

> Explain, with appropriate examples, the impact of at least three pieces of European Union-derived law on your organisation. What implementation problems did they give rise to? How were these overcome?

European Union Declarations

In the field of employee relations there are two major EU Declarations. These are the so-called Social Charter of 1989 and sections of the Charter of Fundamental Rights of the European Union (2000).

The Social Charter

The Community Charter on the Fundamental Rights of Workers, commonly known as the Social Charter, was adopted by all member states except the UK in December 1989. It was introduced as a result of political pressure to provide benefits for employees as a balance to what was seen as the advantages for companies provided by the Single European Act (1987) and the coming into force of the Single Market on 1 January 1993. The Charter is a Declaration and has no legal force in itself. It is in essence a 'wish list' of social objectives.

The Charter proposes a floor of basic common employment rights and objectives which should be established and implemented without discrimination at appropriate levels across all member states to ensure that:

- The right of free movement in the EU becomes a reality.
- Workers are paid a sufficient wage to ensure a decent standard of living.
- Adequate social security protection is provided by all member states.
- Basic law on working time, provision of contract, treatment of part-time and temporary workers, and collective redundancies is improved and harmonised.
- All workers have the right to join or not to join a union, negotiate collective agreements and take collective action, including strike action.
- All workers have access to continuous vocational training throughout their working lives.
- Equal treatment and equal opportunities between men and women are developed, particularly to enable men and women to reconcile family and work responsibilities.
- Information and consultation are developed along appropriate lines, taking into account national practices, particularly in European enterprises.
- Health and safety protection is improved.

- Young workers are given access to training and fair treatment.
- The elderly are guaranteed an adequate income.
- Measures are taken to improve the social and professional integration of people with disabilities.

The Charter emphasises that the implementation of these 12 principles would contribute not only towards the improvement of living and working conditions provided in the Treaty of Rome (1957) but would also lead to a more effective use of human resources across the EU and therefore improve economic competitiveness and job creation. Although not in itself a legally binding document, the Charter has nevertheless formed the basis for much EU action in the area of social policy – for example, the Working Time Directive, the European Works Council Directive and the Part-Time Work Directive. The Charter's incorporation into the Treaty of Amsterdam strengthens its standing as an important basis for EU social and employment policy (Article 136).

The Charter of Fundamental Rights of the European Union
All member states adopted this Charter, commonly known as the Charter of Fundamental Rights, in 2000. It is a Declaration of Rights for all EU citizens. It sets out 54 rights, of which those especially relevant to employee relations professionals are:

Article 12   Freedom of assembly and of association, which covers the right of every individual to form and join a trade union for the protection of his or her interests

Article 23   Equality between men and women, which covers areas such as employment work and pay

Article 27   Workers' rights to information and consultation within the undertaking

Article 28   The right of collective bargaining and action, which requires that workers and employers have, in accordance with Community law and national laws, the right to negotiate and con-clude collective agreements at the appropriate levels and, in cases of conflict of interests, to take collective action to defend their interests, including strike action

Article 30   Protection in the event of unjustified dismissal

Article 31   Fair and just working conditions, which recognises the right to working conditions that respect the worker's health, safety and dignity.

The Treaty of Amsterdam gives recognition to the Community Charter of the Fundamental Social Rights of Workers, and cites it as a basis for bringing forward measures aimed at 'the promotion of employment, improved living and working conditions' (Article 136).

SUMMARY
This chapter has:

- identified the growing importance of the European Union on employee relations management in the UK
- explained how the European Single Market in which goods, services, people and capital can move freely (the four great freedoms) also has a social dimension, known as the Social Chapter, to pro-vide for the harmonisation of minimum social and employment conditions between member states
- outlined the main role and function of the legislative institutions of the European Commission, the Council of Ministers, the European Parliament and the European Court of Justice
- pointed out how the introduction of the 'qualified majority voting' (QMV) procedure in 1987 removed the veto of member states over Commission proposals in certain areas and meant that Europe

could never be the same again – and that its law-making mechanisms could actually start to work as envisaged in 1957

■ explained how the Treaty of Maastricht (1993) provided for compulsory consultation by the European Commission with the social partners (both at the inter-sectoral and sectoral levels) on any social and employment proposals, and permitted the social partners the option to agree voluntarily to negotiate a Framework Agreement on the issue and for that Agreement to be made binding on member states via its transposition into a Directive

■ noted that Framework Agreements collectively bargained by the inter-sectoral social partners and then issued as a Directive and then transposed into UK legislation have been concluded in four areas – parental leave, part-time work, fixed-term contracts and teleworking

■ described how European Union social and employment legislation comes mainly in the form of Directives which set out specific objectives, and how each member state is given time (usually two years) to enact legislation within its own Parliament to ensure that the objectives are achieved

■ detailed how, under the Social Chapter procedures, some issues (eg working conditions, information and consultation of workers) can be harmonised by qualified majority voting, some (eg the protection of workers where their employment contract is terminated, co-determination) on the basis of unanimity among member states, and yet others (eg the right to association, the right to strike and the right to lock out) are formally excluded

■ spent time outlining how, and where, European Union laws have had, and will continue to have, a direct impact on the work of the employee relations professional in the UK

■ noted above all that UK legislation arising from the European Union exists in the following areas – equal opportunities (equal pay, parental leave, equal treatment and the burden of proof in cases of sex discrimination); employment protection/working conditions (redundancies, transfer of undertakings, insolvency, part-time work, fixed-term contract workers); employee relations (information and consultation with employees in multinational companies within the EU, in European companies and in member-states-based companies); and health and safety (Working Time Regulations).

FURTHER READING

CHARTERED INSTITUTE OF PERSONNEL AND DEVELOPMENT (2000a) *Europe: Personnel and Development*, London, CIPD.

CHARTERED INSTITUTE OF PERSONNEL AND DEVELOPMENT (2000b) *European Update*. This appears 10 times a year and provides invaluable information on EU developments in employment and related areas.

DEPARTMENT OF TRADE AND INDUSTRY (1996) *The Social Chapter – The British and Continental Approaches*.

EUROPEAN INDUSTRIAL RELATIONS REVIEW is a monthly journal covering industrial relations news in the European Union.

EUROPEAN UNION COMMISSION (2000) *Industrial Relations in Europe*.

INDUSTRIAL RELATIONS SERVICES and INDUSTRIAL RELATIONS RESEARCH UNIT, WARWICK BUSINESS SCHOOL, *European Works Council Bulletin*. This is a regular bulletin dealing with developments in European Works Councils.

KELLER B. (2003) Social dialogue – the state of the art after Maastricht, *Industrial Relations Journal*, Volume 34, Issue 5.

PEOPLE MANAGEMENT, a fortnightly journal for CIPD members which covers major developments in employment and social matters in the EU. Legislative matters covering employment arising from EU Directives are included in its Law at Work section.

Employee relations institutions

CHAPTER OBJECTIVES

When you have completed this chapter you should be aware of and able to describe:

- why some organisations join employers' associations and others do not

- how employers' organisations can help personnel professionals in their day-to-day work

- why trade unions behave as they do

- the role and functions of staff associations

- the role of the Advisory, Conciliation and Arbitration Service, the Central Arbitration Committee and the Certification Officer.

INTRODUCTION

This chapter is concerned with the institutions of employee relations – employers' associations or federations, trade unions and staff associations, including their peak organisations the CBI and the TUC, their international and European equivalents (see Chapter 5), and the state organisations of the Advisory, Conciliation and Arbitration Service (ACAS), the Central Arbitration Committee (CAC) and the Certification Officer. Both employers and employees have a range of options open to them by way of external organisations which might be useful to them and about which they have to make choices.

For example, should an employing organisation join its sector association or federation? Should it join peak organisations such as the Confederation of British Industry (CBI) or the Institute of Directors (IoD)? If it does decide to join its sector organisation, does it – assuming that the organisation it is thinking of considering joining is one which gets involved in collective bargaining in the first place – allow that organisation to bargain on its behalf? Does becoming a member bind it to a particular course of action? Even if the reasons for contemplating membership are nothing to do with collective bargaining, what sort of services are available to employers – and how are they paid for?

On the other side of the coin there is a need for employers to hear the voice of their employees so that there is a two-way dialogue enabling staff to influence what happens at work. This in turn raises the question of what institution embodying that employee voice might be appropriate. Is it a trade union? A Works Council? Or should employee voice not be viewed any longer in terms of collective representation? And again, in turn this raises issues such as why employees join or do not join trade unions.

EMPLOYERS' ORGANISATIONS

Employers' associations are voluntary, private bodies which exist to provide information and co-ordination in areas of common interest. There are many different associations, covering overlapping areas of geographical spread and industrial sector, and grouping large or smaller organisations. The *Annual Report* of the Certification Officer (2003) lists 91 employers' associations with a total membership of 226,226 organisations. In 2003, the gross income of employers' associations was £239 million, and gross expenditure was

£234 million. Employers' associations vary in size and influence from the very small with no full-time staff to large and highly influential organisations like the Engineering Employers Federation (over 5,000 member organisations), the Road Haulage Association (9,434 members) and the Retail Motor Industry Federation Ltd (9,330 members).

The 1998 Workplace Employee Relations Survey showed that employers' association membership in industry and commerce fell during the 1980s from 22 per cent of workplaces in 1984 to 13 per cent in 1990. The 1998 results suggested a modest recovery, however, in that 18 per cent of workplaces then reported membership. The recovery was complete amongst the largest workplaces – those that employed 500 or more workers – for whom membership levels in 1998 had returned to the level of 1984.

In common with trade unions, employers' associations who wish to have their legal status confirmed must be registered on a list kept by the Certification Officer (see below). Employers' associations are required to keep proper accounting records, to establish and maintain a satisfactory system of control of their accounting records, and to submit an annual return to the Certification Officer. An employers' association must submit its annual returns and accounts to this Officer before 1 June each year. The Certification Officer can investigate the financial affairs of any employers' association.

Is your organisation in the membership of an employers' association? If not, why not? If it is, why is it?

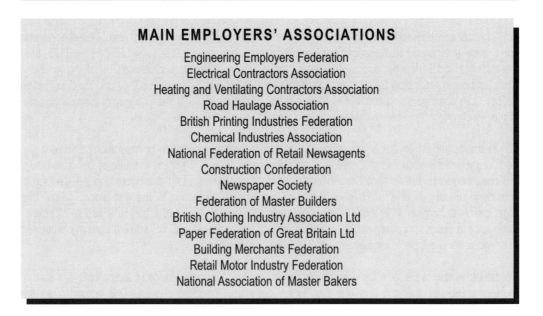

MAIN EMPLOYERS' ASSOCIATIONS

Engineering Employers Federation
Electrical Contractors Association
Heating and Ventilating Contractors Association
Road Haulage Association
British Printing Industries Federation
Chemical Industries Association
National Federation of Retail Newsagents
Construction Confederation
Newspaper Society
Federation of Master Builders
British Clothing Industry Association Ltd
Paper Federation of Great Britain Ltd
Building Merchants Federation
Retail Motor Industry Federation
National Association of Master Bakers

The importance of employers' associations

Employers' bodies, whether in the public or private sector, organise themselves in different ways. The priority each gives to employee relations, as opposed to trade matters, differs according to tradition, the nature of the industry it represents and the degree of unionisation in its particular sector. Generally, it remains true that those associations that are most concerned with employee relations are those involving companies that make use of semi-skilled and skilled labour in areas where there is a high concentration of a single industry, such as engineering or printing.

There are three types of employers' associations:

- national federations to which local employers' associations are affiliated – eg the Engineering Employers Federation (EEF), which is a federation of 12 autonomous organisations
- single national bodies such as the British Printing Industries Federation (BPIF), which is divided into six regions for administrative and representational purposes
- single associations with a national membership, like the British Ceramic Confederation.

Employers' associations consist of companies of varying sizes, from the very small to the very large. The largest are sometimes organised into either autonomous local associations (for example, the EEF West Midlands Association, EEF South and EEF East Midlands Association) or non-autonomous district associations, like the British Printing Industries Federation. Some employers' associations have a similar organisational structure to trade unions such that their ultimate decision-making authority is a national council or the equivalent. The basis of representation on such a council varies from association to association. Except for those with local autonomy, in most employers' associations local and regional associations are consultative rather than decision-making bodies.

Although organisations of employers have existed for a very long time, there is some evidence that in recent years their prominence and influence over employment issues has declined. The 1998 Workplace Employee Relations Survey reported, for example, that in their role as sources of advice and information and as the employers' side of industry-wide or regional negotiating bodies, employers' associations had diminished in importance since the 1980s, indicating that more and more managements seemed to be assuming responsibility for their own employee relations. Nevertheless, there are still a significant number of employers' associations which continue to negotiate collective agreements at national level. In the private sector national agreements still exist, for example, in electrical contracting, paper-making, construction, road haulage and general printing. In the public sector national pay arrangements still exist for doctors and nurses, and the National Association of Health Authorities and Trusts – an employers' body – provides evidence to the appropriate pay review body. Yet in many industries national agreements have become less extensive as the percentage of employees covered by collective bargaining has fallen from 70 per cent of employees in 1994 to 41 per cent in 1998. National agreements tend to remain in industries dominated by small companies that operate in very competitive labour markets. For these companies, which usually do not have the resources to establish a personnel function, the national agreement is still regarded as significant in taking labour out of competition and in providing an employee relations infrastructure to the sector via the procedures (eg disputes and grievances) contained in the agreement.

The Social dialogue procedure at the inter-professional and sector level of the European Union (see Chapter 5) has, however, given an added importance to the collective bargaining role of employers' associations. Employer organisations that wish to influence the social regulation of the labour market in the EU can only do so by joining an employers' association and then trying to shape the policy of that association so that in turn that body attempts to get that policy adopted as the view of its EU-wide equivalent either at the sector or inter-professional level. If British companies wish to influence the position of UNICE (which is the only EU-wide inter-professional private sector employer voice recognised by the EU Commission) on the social regulation of the Single Market, they must be members, directly or indirectly, via the Confederation of British Industry (CBI). If UK engineering companies wish to shape EU social regulation of the EU-wide engineering industry, they have to be members of the EEF, which in turn affiliates to the Western European Metal Trades Employers' organisation, which is the only EU-Commission-recognised EU-wide engineering sector employer voice for consultation and negotiating purposes.

National and other representative bodies

The best-known nation-wide employers' organisation in the UK is the Confederation of British Industry (CBI), whose roots go back to 1915 with the formation of the National Union of Manufacturers, later renamed the National Association of British Manufacturers (NABM). Within five years, two further organis-ations – the Federation of British Industries (FBI) and the British Employers' Confederation (BEC) – were formed. The CBI as an organisation was the result of a merger in 1965 between these three bodies. Its membership includes individual companies and national and regional trades and employers' associations. It sees as its overall task the promotion of policies for a more efficient mixed economy. It is estimated that around half of the total workforce are employed in organisations affiliated to the CBI. An important political lobbying organisation, the CBI's major function is to provide for British industry the means of formulating, making known and influencing general policy with regard to industrial, economic, fiscal, commercial, labour, social, legal and technical questions.

However, although it does not specifically engage in employee relations activities, the CBI's lobbying activities can (and do) have an impact on issues that affect workplace employee relations. In recent years, the CBI has lobbied successfully on behalf of employers on issues such as the national minimum wage, statutory trade union recognition procedures, the reform of the employment tribunal system and the implementation in the UK of EU Directives. As an organisation the CBI does not engage in negotiations with employee representatives but it does maintain a direct working relationship with the Trades Union Congress (TUC) as well as an indirect one via joint membership of bodies such as ACAS and the Health and Safety Executive.

> Outline the main services the Confederation of British Industry provides for its members.

THE ACTIVITIES OF EMPLOYERS' ASSOCIATIONS

Employers' organisations can assist the personnel professional in his or her day-to-day work through the services they offer to their members. These services fall into five areas:

- collective bargaining with trade unions
- assisting in the resolution of disputes
- providing members with general advice
- representing members' views to political decision-making bodies
- representing member companies at employment tribunals.

Collective bargaining

Collective bargaining services carried out for members have declined. Multi-employer bargaining, which had greatly diminished in importance in the 1980s became – according to the 1998 Workplace Employee Relations Survey – even more of a rarity in the 1990s. In workplaces with recognised trade unions, multi-employer negotiations affected the pay of some or all employees in 68 per cent of workplaces in 1980s. By 1990 this had fallen to 60 per cent – but in 1998 it was down to 34 per cent. Over three broad sectors of the economy, the fall over the period 1980–1998 was substantial. In public services, the drop was from 81 to 47 per cent, while in private manufacturing the fall was from 57 to 25 per cent. The most dramatic fall, however, was in private services. In 1984, in this sector, 54 per cent of workplaces were affected by multi-employer negotiations. By 1998 the figure had fallen to just 12 per cent.

The Workplace Employee Relations Survey (1998) reports that when the falling proportion of workplaces with a recognised union is taken into account, the demise of multi-employer collective bargaining is even more apparent. Among all workplaces with 25 or more employees, multi-employer bargaining directly affected 43 per cent of workplaces in 1980, 31 per cent in 1990, and just 14 per cent in 1998. The public sector emerged as the only major sector of the economy in which multi-employer bargaining remained common: in 1998, 41 per cent of public sector workplaces were affected by it. In the private sector, the proportion in 1998 was a mere 4 per cent of workplaces, down from over 25 per cent in 1980. Private sector employers have effectively abandoned acting jointly to regulate the terms and conditions of employment.

Dispute resolution

The provision of dispute resolution services has links with national bargaining arrangements in that most national agreements provide access to an established dispute procedure. Such procedures tend to stipulate a number of stages through which a dispute will be processed. Stage one may include the involvement of a local employers' association representative, a union branch secretary, lay union officials from within the organisation in dispute, and the organisation's management. If the dispute is not resolved at this stage it may – depending on the employers' association and the union involved – move up to a district or regional level. Some of the players will stay the same as at the first stage, but the full-time officials will probably differ. The third stage involves national officials of the employers' association and the appropriate trade unions. If there is no resolution of the differences at this stage, some disputes procedures provide for the involvement of an independent third party whose decision will be binding. Such dispute procedures usually contain provisions stating that 'no hostile action' is to be taken by either side or that the status quo must prevail while the dispute is going through its various stages.

Advisory and information services

During the years when national collective bargaining was in the ascendancy, many employer organisations became bureaucratic and unimaginative. They had a captive membership and paid little attention to membership retention, or to the range of services that they offered members. All this changed as companies began to prefer bargaining at a more local level. This in turn led employers to examine what else they were receiving from their associations in return for not insignificant subscriptions. Some employers' organisations quickly realised that if they were to continue to have an employee relations influence, they had to provide their members with a package of benefits and services to their members that would be seen to add value to businesses. In this context many employers' associations widened their existing advisory services on good practices and model procedural agreements on issues such as disciplinary, dismissal and redundancy procedures. Their ability to market such services has been helped by the growth – particularly in the 1970s and 1980s – of employment legislation that added to employees' 'rights at work': unfair dismissal, health and safety and equal pay are just three examples. In the 1990s and the early years of the twenty-first century, a raft of legislation from the European Union Council of Ministers added to the advisory and information services that employers' associations now provide for their members.

The recruitment literature of any of the larger employers' associations places greatest emphasis on the employment advice and support services it can offer to members. For example, the Construction Confederation offers its members advice and support on wage rates and conditions of employment, disciplinary procedures, redundancy procedures, and representation at employment tribunals, and issues a regular bulletin outlining relevant developments in employment law. Most employers' organisations also provide employee relations information services. Prominently featured in such information are pay and benefits data based on regularly conducted surveys, which are useful for salary and pay comparisons and for use in local negotiations. However, such surveys can be problematic because the associations have no means of enforcing individual returns. Nevertheless, provided that the employee relations professional recognises these limitations, such surveys can be a valuable tool. Other topics on which employers' associations give information include labour productivity and UK government and EU policy developments in employee relations.

Representation of members' interests

A major growth area of activity has also been the representation of members' views to a range of other organisations, particularly political bodies – UK government departments, local authorities, the institutions of the European Union, and political parties. These political lobbying activities may be of particular interest to the large company whose inclination might otherwise be to leave an association if its only purpose was the negotiation of a national agreement. Now that many large organisations operate in a European- and world-wide market, they know that their only means of influencing UK government or European Union policy is through a collective voice. In its 2003 review the EEF reported on its representations to the major political parties to try to ensure the employment policies that they develop meet the needs of the engineering industry (EEF *Annual Review*, 2003). UK governments and the EU Commission find employers' organisations useful in obtaining a collective employer view on a wide range of consultative documents. Examples included the review of the Employment Relations Act 1999, high-performance workplaces and the role of employee involvement in a modern economy (2002), fixed-term contracts regulation, and the review of European Council Directives (2004). Employers' associations also play an important role in representing the interests of their members (especially small companies) at employment tribunal hearings.

Why might organisations wish to be members of an employers' association?

NON-MEMBERSHIP OF EMPLOYERS' ASSOCIATIONS

First, not all organisations view employers' associations in a favourable light. Why is that? Some companies view employers' associations as too restrictive and see membership as an obstacle to independent action to introduce innovation in employee relations policies and practices. Such companies regard innovation, whether in operational matters or people issues, as an essential managerial activity in today's economic climate. They therefore feel the need to be responsible for, to co-ordinate and to control their own employee relations activities. Nevertheless, it is important to remember that even those companies which bargain unilaterally, or independently of the appropriate employers' association, cannot ignore when deciding their own employee relations policies and practices what is happening more generally in the sector in which they are operating. An important part of the employee relations function is to take account of other wage settlements, particularly within the sector in which their organisation operates. Not being aware of such settlements, many of which affect their competitors, could seriously weaken their own bargaining position and impact adversely on their competitiveness.

Second, there are those companies who do not take out membership of an employers' organisation because they see it as incompatible with their non-recognition of trade union policy and philosophy. These companies perceive employers' associations as very much part of a collective approach to employee relations. They prefer to relate to their employees on a more individualistic basis.

There are businesses which, despite their feelings, join employers' organisations because of their more traditional trade association activities. A number have arbitration schemes to resolve differences between supplier and customer, whereas others have the ability to remove an organisation from membership if they do not meet agreed standards on, for example, the quality of service or product provided for the customer. This can be an effective sanction for a company which relies on the 'badge' of the trade association to help secure business, such as in some of the building trades or electrical contractors.

TRADE UNIONS

Purpose and objectives

Trade unions are organised groups of employees who

consist wholly or mainly of workers of one or more description and whose principal purposes include the regulation of relations between workers and employers.

Section 1 of the Trade Unions and Labour Relations (Consolidation) Act

The primary purpose of trade unions is to protect and to enhance the living standards of their members. The principal methods they use to achieve this objective fall broadly into two categories – industrial and political. Industrial methods include the negotiation of agreements with employers and all that belongs to collective bargaining, grievance procedure, industrial action, use of third-party intervention, joint consultation, etc.

Political methods, on the other hand, cover all types of union participation in the political process, including 'pressure group' activities in relation to the UK government and the EU decision-making bodies, whether they are conducted by campaigns, delegations, lobbying or sitting on governmental and EU advisory committees. Pressurising the UK government to pass legislation favourable to trade unions is usually done by the Trades Union Congress (TUC). EU political lobbying is done through the activities of the European Trade Union Confederation and/or the European Industry Federation for the sector (see Chapter 5). Trade unions also lobby the International Labour Office (ILO), which is a United Nations agency, to obtain minimum labour standards on a global scale. This lobbying is undertaken by the International Confederation of Free Trade Unions (ICFTU), which was formed in 1949. Its membership consists of 234 affiliated organisations in some 152 countries on five continents, with a total of 148 million. The ICFTU thus has a close relationship with the International Labour Organisation (ILO), which is made up of government, employer and worker representatives. The ILO has established many minimum labour standards (known as ILO Conventions) to operate globally to protect workers' rights and which all governments in the membership of the United Nations are expected to enact in their national legislation.

What are the main purposes of trade unions?

Trade union membership levels

Overall

Table 5   *Trade union membership 1978–2003*

Year	Membership of TUC	Number of TUC-affiliated unions	Membership of non-TUC unions
1978	11,865,390	112	1,188,206
1979	12,128,078	112	1,084,276
1980	12,172,508	109	463,847
1981	11,601,413	108	709,821
1982	11,005,984	105	738,406
1983	10,510,157	95	789,722
1984	10,082,144	89	691,809
1985	9,855,204	91	963,745
1986	9,580,502	91	1,017,506
1987	9,243,297	87	1,236,853
1988	9,127,278	83	1,259,960
1989	8,652,318	78	1,391,288
1990	8,405,246	78	1,404,773
1991	8,192,662	74	1,292,321
1992	7,786,885	72	1,142,017
1993	7,647,443	70	1,018,501
1994	7,117,436	69	1,113,109
1995	6,894,604	67	1,136,722
1996	6,790,339	73	1,147,874
1997	6,756,544	75	1,044,771
1998	6,638,986	75	1,212,918
1999	6,749,481	77	Not available
2000	6,745,907	76	1,151,612
2001	6,722,118	73	1,057,275
2002	6,685,353	70	1,065,637
2003	6,478,345	70	1,272,655

Source: TUC *Annual Reports*; Certification Officer, *Annual Reports*

Table 5 shows trends in UK trade union membership over the period 1978–2003. Total union membership in the UK peaked at an all-time high of 13.2 million members in 1979, made up of 12.1 million members in TUC-affiliated unions and just over 1 million in non-TUC unions. In 2002/03 the total trade union membership, as reported by the Certification Officer, was 7.8 million. Trade union density is much larger in the public sector than the private sector. In the public sector, three employees in five are trade union members, but in the private it is fewer than one in five (Metcalf, 2004). In the manufacturing sector, union density at 27 per cent is below that for the economy as a whole (29 per cent). However, in the manufacturing sector there is still, especially among skilled manual workers, a high union presence. Trade union membership remains low in private sector services (financial, retail), among private sector non-manual employees, in small firms and in foreign-owned firms.

Trade union membership decline

The traditional explanations for the decline in trade union membership include:

- the composition of workforce and jobs – If employment declines in traditional areas of high union membership, then as a matter of arithmetic, total union membership falls. Booth (1989) attributes over two fifths of the decline in union membership in the 1980s to such competitional factors. That composition factors play a minor part in explaining changes in union membership has been confirmed by Machin (2002)

- the business cycle – Membership is said to increase at times of low and/or falling unemployment

- the role of the state – The state can influence membership directly through laws on recognition and the closed shop, and indirectly by creating the environment in which employee-management relations are conducted. In this way the state can undermine or promote collectivism. Freeman and Pelletier (1990) calculated a 'legislation index' according to how favourable or unfavourable various strands of labour laws were to unions in each year. The changes in the law in the 1980s were held to be 'responsible for the entire decline' in union membership. There are, however, those who argue that the state today so regulates the employment relationship – for example, working time, family-friendly policies – that in both the short run and the long run, the activities of the state undermine the rationale for unions. For example, in the mid-1960s the trade unions opposed the Redundancy Payments Act, arguing that the obtaining of financial compensation for the inevitable loss of a job was the legitimate concern of trade unions, not of the state

More recently, it has become accepted that these three explanations of changes in union membership give insufficient weight to the role of employers, individual employees and unions themselves

- the role of employers – Some argue that employers have become more hostile to unions. To examine this view one could look at plant closures, de-recognition activity and new recognition of trade unions. There is no research evidence to support the hypothesis that union activity has resulted in a higher rate of plant closures among unionised workplaces relative to their non-union counterparts, nor that management embarked on the wholesale de-recognition of trade unions. Research by Machin (2000; 2003), however, demonstrates that union decline is mainly explained by the inability of unions to achieve recognition in newer workplaces (see below)

- the role of individual employees – An important advantage to the individual who joins a trade union is the wage premium compared with an equivalent non-member. In the 1980s, economists estimated the mark-up in wages for a union member relative to a non-member to be around 10 per cent. Today, the premium is estimated at best to be half this level. Indeed, some studies show there is no longer any wage plus to joining a union. The loss of a wage premium is a reason cited by Metcalf (2004) for individuals not to join unions, and that helps to explain why union membership is also falling in those sectors of the economy where unions are recognised

Millward *et al* (2000) argue that workers have lost their taste for belonging to a union, but others (for example, Towers, 1997) believe there is a 'frustrated demand' for membership, which results in a 'representation gap'. Over the last 20 years there has been a large rise in the proportion of the workforce that has never been a union member – up from 28 per cent in 1983 to 48 per cent in 2001 – suggesting that unions are experiencing difficulties in getting individuals to take out membership in the first place. Research also suggests (see below) that younger employees are much less likely to belong to a union than older workers, and that this gap in membership rates by age has grown sharply in recent years. This 'withering of support' for trade unionism thesis has been questioned by Towers (1997), who argues that many non-unionists would join a union if one were available in the workplace

- the role of unions themselves – This involves questions such as: what is the impact on membership gains, for example, of the trend to large conglomerate unions, of the recent emphasis by unions on 'organisation', and of moves away from traditional adversarial industrial relations towards greater co-operation with employers via partnership (Heery *et al*, 1999; and Chapter 8)?

The new workplace/young worker thesis

Machin's research (2000; 2003) shows that union recognition in workplaces with 25 or more employees fell from 64 per cent in 1980 to 42 per cent in 1998. In 1980, establishments under 10 years old had a recognition rate of 0.59, almost as large as the fraction of workplaces aged 10 or more years which recognised unions. He also shows, however, that over the next 20 years, unions found it increasingly more difficult to organise new workplaces. By 1998, just over a quarter of workplaces under 10 years of age recognised a trade union – only half the corresponding figure of older workplaces. This inability of unions to make an impact on new workplaces is not, as often thought, restricted to the private services sector. Only 14 per cent of manufacturing workplaces opened after 1980 recognised a trade union, compared to 50 per cent of those establishments in 1980 or before. This 36 per cent gap in union recognition rates in manufacturing compares with a corresponding figure of 10 percentage points for private services. There is no significant recognition gap for public sector workplaces.

Some of the difficulty in achieving recognition in younger/newer workplaces is owing to the fact that they tend to be small, relatively more female-intensive and more likely to be in the private sector. Machin's (2003) research demonstrates clearly that workplace age is a central factor in explaining the decline in union membership over the past 20 years. It also indicates that lower recognition rates in newer workplaces is not the end of the story, since he also shows that even where union recognition is achieved, union density is some 11 percentage points lower than it is in older workplaces.

Research by Bryson and Gomez (2003) and Machin (2003) shows that young workers are now much less likely to be in a trade union than at any time since 1945. Their 'age of employee' effect corresponds to the 'age of workplace' factor discussed above. In 1975 55 per cent of employees aged 18–64 were union members, but by 2001 this figure had fallen by 29 per cent. Membership rates were lower in both years for employees aged below 30. In 1975 union membership density was only 11 percentage points lower for younger people (48 per cent compared to 59 per cent), but by 2001 the gap had risen to 19 points (15 per cent compared to 34 per cent). Union density among young men has fallen by 39 points over the last quarter of a century, and that for young women by 23 points.

One reason for the increasing gap between membership rates between younger and older workers is said to be the transmission of membership across generations. Machin and Blanden (2003) have shown that there is a 30 per cent higher probability of being a union member if your father is also a union member. Fewer parents are union members today than was previously the case, so – given the cross-generation correlation in trends of taking up union membership – fewer younger people are likely now and in the future to join trade unions.

Table 6 *Trade unions: distribution by size*

Number of members	Number of unions	Member-ship (000s)	Number of unions		Membership of all unions	
			%	cumulative %	%	cumulative %
Under 100	41	1	19.0	19.0	0	0
100–499	40	12	18.5	37.5	0.2	0.2
500–999	25	18	11.6	49.1	0.2	0.4
1,000–2,499	22	40	10.2	59.3	0.5	0.9
2,500–4,999	25	92	11.6	70.8	1.2	2.1
5,000–9,999	9	66	4.2	75.0	0.9	3.0
10,000–14,999	6	69	2.8	77.8	0.9	3.8
15,000–24,999	13	253	6.0	83.8	3.3	7.1
25,000–49,999	14	491	6.5	90.3	6.3	13.4
50,000–99,999	5	309	2.3	92.6	4.0	17.4
100,000–249,999	5	744	2.3	94.9	9.0	27.0
250,000 and over	11	5,656	4.6	5.1	73.0	100
TOTAL	216	7,751	100		100	

Source: *Annual Report* of the Certification Officer, 2002–2003; page 20

Two main features in the decline of trade union membership since 1979 are thus that fewer young workplaces have union recognition agreements and/or arrangements and fewer young workers are members of unions. In sectors of employment dominated by new firms, there is less likely to be a union to join. Younger workers are particularly affected because they are more likely to be employed in young workplaces. In 1998, for example, in workplaces established before 1980, only 10 per cent of the workforce was aged under 25 whereas among those set up in the 1980s and the 1990s, the corresponding figure was 17 per cent. Metcalf (2004) argues that young workers probably are the main factor in explaining falling union density in workplaces where unions are recognised. Between 1983 and 1998, he points out, in workplaces where unions are recognised, unionisation density of those aged 30 remained virtually unchanged at 70 per cent but density of those aged 18–25 almost halved, from 67 per cent in 1983 to 41 per cent in 1998.

The future of unions?

The review of contemporary research on trends in trade union membership indicates that future membership trends of trade unions will depend on unions' ability to persuade employers to recognise them and to convince employees to take up membership. One route by which trade unions might revive their membership is to engage in more intensive organising activities, and another would be to improve their attraction to both employers (for example, by partnership arrangements, see Chapter 8) and potential members. With respect to their organising and servicing of members' activities, trade unions cannot neglect their existing membership. This will involve unions maintaining and advancing their members' terms and conditions of employment, providing them with services such as advice on employment matters, promoting life-long learning, representing their interests in grievance and disciplinary procedures, and representing them before employment tribunals and third-party intervention bodies. Currently, the percentage of workers covered by collective bargaining (see Chapter 8) but who are not members of a union stands at 38. If trade unions are to increase their membership in the future, they will have to make serious inroads into organising this group of workers. Future membership will also be boosted if unions succeed in organising a significant proportion of the estimated 14 million employees who are not presently members and who do not have their terms and conditions determined by collective bargaining.

Heery *et al* (2000) surveyed major unions and found that most have formal organising, recruitment and retention of membership policies, have invested additional resources in organising activity, and have attempted to organise groups of workers whom they had hitherto forgotten. Contemporary research shows, however, that all this organising activity has met with limited success. The impact of the trade union recognition procedures of the Employment Relations Act 1999 has been modest (Gall, 2003; 2004). After gaining recognition relatively easily in the first two years of the operation of the Act, unions are now meeting stronger resistance to recognition demands from employers. The loss of union members from redundancy, plant closures, etc, continues to far exceed the number of new members obtained from organising activity. The future for unions therefore looks bleak.

Explaining trade union behaviour

The classic work of Alan Flanders of some 40 years ago on this question is as relevant today as it was then. For Flanders, union behaviour was characterised by:

- 'sword of justice' objectives
- the advancement of job interests and not class interests
- according the highest priority to delivering their objectives by industrial methods rather than political methods
- pragmatism – dealing with matters in a sensible, flexible and realistic manner rather than being influenced by fixed theories or ideology.

Flanders has demonstrated that throughout their history trade unions have sought for their members not only more income, more leisure time and more security, but also an enhancement of their status by establishing employment rights for them – for example, the right to a certain wage, the right not to have to work longer than so many hours, the right not to be subject to arbitrary dismissal. For this reason, Flanders contended, trade unions can be viewed as a 'sword of justice' seeking fairness of treatment for their members from employers and from the state. This 'sword of justice' behaviour is seen in the impact of trade union behaviour, for example, on pay distribution, on the event of accidents in the workplace, on the provision of friendly-family policies and in the promotion of equal opportunities. Metcalf (2004) has estimated that if there were not trade unions in the labour market, the wage differential between male and female employees would be 2.6 per cent higher than its present level. The corresponding figures he presents for non-manual/manual worker differentials and between white and black workers are +3.0 per cent and +1.4 per cent respectively. An aspect of union behaviour is to seek to be an egalitarian influence on the workings of the labour market.

Flanders (1970) also helps us to understand trade union behaviour when he described them as being 'job-centred' and not 'class-centred'. The basis of trade union membership in the UK is the job the individual performs. The main function of a trade union is to protect the employment conditions and status of their members from 'invasion' by employers, other groups of workers and their trade unions. Trade unions represent a sectional interest in society in that they further the common interests of employees performing certain jobs to the exclusion of other groups of job performers.

One of the consequences of job-centred trade unionism is the existence of different types of trade unions. Although in the light of trade union mergers it is becoming less and less relevant, it is still the convention to divide trade unions in the UK into three broad main types – occupational (or craft), industrial, and general. However, today few occupational unions exist, and those that do are relatively small in size. Examples include the British Air-Line Pilots Association (BALPA), the Associated Society of Locomotive Engineers and Firemen (ASLEF) and the Professional Footballers Association (PFA). Such unions recruit members selectively, on a job-by-job basis, irrespective of where they work. It is the employee's occupational status, job skills and qualifications or training that determine whether or not an individual qualifies for membership, not the industry or the organisation that employs him or her.

Table 7   *Trade unions with memberships of 100,000 or more in 2003*

Union	Membership
UNISON: the public services union	1,272,700
Transport and General Workers Union (T&GWU)	848,809
Amalgamated Engineering and Electrical Union (AEEU)`	728,508
GMB	689,276
Royal College of Nursing (RCN)*	332,691
Manufacturing Science and Finance Union (MSF)	344,192
National Union of Teachers (NUT)	310,377
Union of Shop Distributive and Allied Workers (USDAW)	314,174
Public and Commercial Services Union	279,679
Association of Teachers and Lecturers	186,774
Communication Workers Union (CWU)	281,923
National Association and Union of Women Teachers (NASUWT)	253,584
Graphical Paper and Media Union (GPMU)	170,279
UNIFI	119,993
Union of Construction Allied Trades and Technicians (UCATT)	154,434
British Medial Association (BMA)*	112,872

* Non-TUC affiliate

Industrial unions will organise any workers, regardless of their status and skills, who are employed in a particular industry. They recruit vertically within an industry but will not recruit from groups working in much the same way in a different industry. In short, they recruit members vertically from among all employment grades, normally including both manual and non-manual workers within a single industry. However, in the UK because of the constantly changing and evolving structure of industry, it is not a simple matter to define the boundaries between industries. Examples of single-industry-based unions in the UK are now very few.

General unions will recruit any workers (both manual and non-manual) horizontally across industries and vertically within industries. Such unions seek to regulate labour markets by trying to establish a monopoly over the supply of employees. The two best examples of general unions in the UK are the Transport and General Workers Union and the GMB.

Another consequence of job-centred unionism is the existence of a large number of individual trade unions. In the UK, trade union structure is characterised by a small number of very large unions co-existing with a large number of small unions (see Table 6). In 2003 the *Annual Report* of the Certification Officer declared that there were 216 registered independent trade unions in the UK. Of these, 16 (all with membership of 100,000 or more) accounted for 83 per cent of total trade union membership but accounted for only 7 per cent of the total number of trade unions. 86 trade unions had membership of less than 1,000. They accounted for 49.1 per cent of the total number of unions but only 0.4 per cent of the total membership of trade unions. The 16 largest unions in 2003 are shown in Table 7 above.

Over the last 24 years, as a result of trade union mergers, the number of unions affiliated to the TUC has fallen from 112 in 1979 to 70 in 2003. These mergers have been driven by the implementation of technological change and changing product and labour markets. The impact of the changes has been a loss of trade union membership, continuing employer opposition to recognition in key economic sectors, difficulties in financial viability, and inter-union competition for members. The trend in union mergers is leading to formation of 'mega-unions' aspiring to represent whole sectors of the economy. The union AMICUS is seeking to become the union that represents all the interests of all employees in the private sector of the economy. UNISON has aspirations to become the union that represents the interests of all employees employed in the public sector.

A consequence of the unwieldy trade union structure resulting from job-centred unionism is inter-union conflict over the recruitment of employees (membership jurisdiction) and industrial policy. Skilled workers, for example, prefer to see their wage differential over lesser-skilled workers expressed in percentage terms. The lesser-skilled workers, on the other hand, prefer wage differentials expressed in absolute monetary terms. Equal-percentage increases in wages widen money differentials. Equal monetary increases (commonly referred to as flat-rate increases), on the other hand, narrow percentage differentials.

Job-centredness also results in differences in attitudes to macro-economic policy issues. Trade unions whose members are working in firms engaged very much in foreign trade favour UK entry into the euro currency because this would protect their members from experiencing downward pressures on their employment conditions as the value of the pound fluctuates against that of the euro. Membership of the euro, however, removes from governments the ability to regulate the economy by changing interest rates and devaluing the pound sterling. Euro membership also commits member country governments to keep their debts within 3 per cent of the gross national product. Given these restraints, public sector unions fear that when their economies experience difficulties, governments are likely to react by cutting public expenditure. Such a government policy would not be in the interests of the members for public sector unions. So we can see why private sector-based unions perceive euro membership as favouring the job interests of their members whereas public sector unions, on the whole, see such membership as contrary to the job interests of their members.

Job-centred unionism also has implications for trade union solidarity. There is a tendency to think – especially amongst left-wing romantics – that unions automatically support one another when involved in an industrial dispute with employers. In reality, this is far from the case. Solidarity action only occurs when the job interests of the different trade unions concerned coincide. Then, and only then, do they show support and solidarity for each other. In 2003 the Royal Mail decided to discontinue transporting mail on the railways. The effect of this was to transfer work from the railways to the road. The Rail, Maritime and Transport Union (RMT) members stood to lose jobs from this move. The Communication Workers Union (CWU) members employed by the Royal Mail, stood to gain. The mail carried on the railway network was now to be transported by road in Royal Mail vehicles. When the RMT sought the support of the UCW to get Royal Mail to change its decision, the UCW remained unchanged in its attitude.

Flanders (1970) also showed that unions accord the priority to industrial methods, over political methods, in advancing the interests of their members. This is still as true today. When they have a choice, trade unions invariably prefer to rely on industrial, rather than political, methods to achieve their aims. This does not mean they despise political action. On the contrary, they are as a rule very ready to use political lobbying – but to support and to supplement their industrial methods, never to supplant them. This was seen in the attitude of trade unions to union recognition and the national minimum wage legislation, both of which are supportive – as opposed to being restrictive – of collective bargaining. As a minimum, unions have to engage in political action to obtain freedom from legal constraints upon the exercise of their main industrial functions – freedom of association, the right to undertake industrial action. However, trade unions have enough industrial strength to regulate their relationships with employers by direct negotiation – they do not seek government assistance. If, however, trade unions are too weak to do this, as we witnessed in the 1990s, then they give a higher priority to regulating their relationship with employers by UK and EU legislation.

Why, then, do trade unions prefer industrial methods to political methods to achieve their objectives? Their members join because they value the services trade unions provide in enlarging and protecting their rights in the workplace. There is also the basic point that the vast majority of trade union members are much less interested in political issues than they are in industrial issues. Given this, how many members would trade unions be able to recruit and retain if all they had to offer was their political activities?

THE TRADES UNION CONGRESS

The TUC was established in 1868. In 2004 it had 70 affiliate unions with a total membership of 6.4 million. It performs two broad roles. First, it acts as the collective voice of the UK trade union movement to governments and international trade union bodies. Second, it attempts to influence the behaviour of its affiliated unions. However, the sanctions it possesses to influence its affiliates are limited. When the TUC was established, it was very much the voice of the craft unions, which jealously guarded their autonomy. As a result, in devising the TUC constitution, they were not prepared to devolve much power or resources to it nor to allow it to interfere in their activities. This limitation still remains and the autonomy of affiliated unions is still regarded as paramount, particularly in the area of wages and employment conditions. The TUC has limited authority over its affiliates and little resources. It has to persuade its affiliates of the rightness of its decisions. It is not always successful.

The supreme authority in the TUC is its Annual Congress, which is held in September, and to which affiliated organisations send delegates on the basis of one for every 5,000 members or part thereof.

Congress policy is decided on the basis of motions, submitted by affiliated unions, being accepted by a majority vote of delegates. The implementation of policy decided at Congress is the responsibility of the General Council, which is serviced by the General Secretary. Unions over a certain membership size have automatic representation on this Council. There is also reserved representation for women and black unionists.

The TUC's role

The TUC has authority from its affiliates to act in three areas – industrial disputes, inter-union disputes, and the conduct of affiliates. In the case of a dispute between an affiliate union and an employer, the TUC does not intervene unless requested to do so by the affiliate involved. However, when negotiations break down (or are likely to break down) and the ensuing dispute could result in the members of another affiliated union being laid off, the TUC General Secretary can then intervene to try to effect a settlement.

The TUC can intervene in the case of disputes between affiliated unions over membership and job demarcation issues. A complaint by one affiliate against another is investigated by a Disputes Committee, which can recommend that a union that has poached members from another affiliate must give those members back. If the union fails to comply with recommendations of a Disputes Committee, the General Council can suspend the union from membership until the next Congress, at which it may be expelled from membership.

The TUC can also investigate complaints that an affiliated union is engaging in conduct detrimental to the interests of the trade union movement or contrary to the declared principles or declared policy of the Congress. Should such a complaint be upheld, the General Council will recommend to the union concerned what it must do to put the matter right. Should the union fail to do this, the General Council will recommend its suspension from membership until the next Congress, at which it will be expelled unless it complies with the recommendation.

Outline the main functions of the TUC.

STAFF ASSOCIATIONS

Staff associations are usually established within a single organisation and for a particular group of employees. Their funding and/or office accommodation is therefore often dependent on the employer. They are not regarded as trade unions in the traditional sense, and stand apart from mainstream trade unionism, even if not actually hostile to it. Staff associations included on the Certification Officer's list of independent trade unions have historically been strongest in banking and insurance. However, such staff associations are small in membership size in that more than half have fewer than 500 members. The main causes of the formation of independent staff associations relate to the employees' wish to:

- respond concertedly to a specific event (eg threatened redundancies)
- have their own rather less formal type of union
- replace an existing consultative body with one that has negotiating powers
- establish collective representation where no representative system previously existed.

They also sometimes fulfil employer desires for a management-dominated consultative body or a management-inspired association.

Independent staff associations are characterised by high membership density. For example, the coverage rate within the top 10 building societies typically averages around 70–80 per cent. They typically represent all white-collar employees of a company from managers to clerks and word processor operators. However, a substantial minority limit their membership to specific groups, the two most common being managers and executives, and agents, representatives and sales people.

Although the largest staff associations may act as independent unions, the effectiveness of the smaller ones is limited by their narrow membership base and weak financial resources. Many operate from a modest financial base. The majority of staff associations are recognised by employers for negotiating and representational purposes. Most agreements they conclude follow the normal pattern and cover such issues as recognition, provision of facilities, joint negotiating machinery, consultation, and grievance and disciplinary procedures.

The ability of independent staff associations to represent the interest of their members may be questioned. An organisation whose membership is confined to the employees of a single employer is exposed to pressures that are much less effective against a broad-based organisation. It will also find it difficult to bargain on equal terms with that employer, particularly if the size of the undertaking places strict limits on its membership and financial resources. The fact that senior managers can, and do, belong to a staff association leads some to question their genuine independence from employer interference.

In addition to staff associations which have a Certificate of Independence from the Certification Officer (see below), there are a much larger number of bodies which bear the title of 'staff association' and which make no claim to be a trade union even in an informal sense. Such bodies usually have a consultative rather than a negotiating function, and little or nothing in the way of independent resources. Membership is usually automatic for all non-manual employees, and there is often no membership subscription since the employer meets any expenses incurred by the association.

Explain the difference(s) between a staff association and a trade union.

Professional associations such as the British Medical Association or the British Dental Association often represent the interests of their members in negotiation with the relevant employers but also function as organisations responsible for the education and certification of practitioners and the maintenance of professional standards among members. The dual role of negotiators and professional standard-bearers can sometimes conflict, as the medical and nursing professions have found. It can be difficult to take legitimate action in support of an industrial dispute without coming into conflict with a professional code of conduct.

STATE AGENCIES

In this section we look at those state agencies that have a statutory role in employee relations, whether that role is in respect of individual or of collective issues. In the UK there are three major agencies of this kind: the Certification Office for Trade Unions and Employers Associations, the Advisory, Conciliation and Arbitration Service (ACAS) and the Central Arbitration Committee (CAC).

The Certification Office

The post of Certification Officer was established in 1975. The Officer is appointed by the Secretary of State for Trade and Industry after consultation with ACAS. The office performs the following functions:

- maintaining a list of trade unions
- determining that a trade union is independent of employer control, domination or interference. The principal criteria used by the Certification Officer for this purpose are history, membership base, organisation and structure, finance, employer-provided facilities and negotiating record

- dealing with complaints by members that a trade union has failed to maintain an accurate register of members or failed to permit access to its accounting records; seeing that trade unions keep proper accounting records, have their accounts properly audited and submit annual returns; investigating of the financial affairs of trade unions; ensuring that the statutory requirements concerning the actuarial examination of members' superannuation schemes are observed; and dealing with complaints that a trade union has failed in its duty to ensure that positions in the union are not held by certain offenders

- handling complaints by members that a trade union has failed to hold secret ballots for electing members of its executive committee, its president and general secretary

- ensuring observance by trade unions of the statutory procedures governing the setting up, operation and review of political funds; and dealing with complaints about breaches of political fund rules or about the conduct of political fund ballots, or the application of general funds for political objects

- seeing that the statutory procedures for trade union amalgamations, transfer of engagement and changes of name are observed; and dealing with complaints by members about the conduct of merger ballots

- maintaining a list of employers' associations; ensuring that the statutory requirements concerning accounting records, annual returns, financial affairs, political funds and the statutory procedures for amalgamation and transfer of engagements in respect of employers' association are observed.

The Employment Relations Act 1999 extended the Certification Officer's power to deal with:

- complaints by trade union members that there has been a breach, or that a breach is threatened, of the rules of a trade union relating to the appointment, election or removal of an office-holder

- disciplinary proceedings

- ballots of members other than in respect of industrial action

- the constitution or proceedings of an executive committee or other decision-making meeting.

The Advisory, Conciliation and Arbitration Service (ACAS)

The state provided third-party intervention in industrial disputes long before ACAS was established (Mumford, 1996). Such measures were previously the responsibility of the Department of Employment and its predecessor Ministries (eg the Ministry of Labour). The credibility of third-party intervention depends on the two disputant parties being confident that the third party is independent of government (or any other political) influence and therefore totally independent.

In the 1960s and 1970s, the credibility of government-provided third-party intervention services became seriously compromised. This came about because Ministers – often as a condition of making the third-party services available to the disputant parties – made it clear that they expected the independent arbitrator to have due regard to the government of the day's incomes policy. Indeed, on occasions the Minister refused joint requests from employers and unions for third-party intervention on the grounds that the employer's offer was already in excess of the limits of the government's incomes policy. The clash between the government's role as an industrial peacekeeper and its role as an economic manager became most acute in 1968 when the newly created Department of Employment and Productivity – which was responsible, inter alia, for the provision of third-party intervention services – was also given responsibility for ensuring that the government's incomes policy was applied effectively.

The early 1970s therefore saw increased demands by unions and employers for a third-party intervention service that was formally independent of the state, and in particular of the whims of different governments' prices and incomes policies. The strength of this feeling was seen when the TUC and CBI established their own private third-party arrangements. In September 1974 the then Labour government established the Advisory, Conciliation and Arbitration Service (ACAS) as a Royal Commission. It was established as a statutory body on 1 January 1976 following the Employment Protection Act 1975.

ACAS is independent of direct ministerial intervention, although its sponsoring Ministry is the Department of Trade and Industry. ACAS is governed by an executive body known as 'the Council', which originally consisted of a chairperson and nine ordinary members – three chosen in consultation with the CBI, three in consultation with the TUC, and the remaining three independent people with specialist knowledge of employee relations. In 1992 the Council became 11 ordinary members, the additional two members representing the interests of small businesses and non-TUC unions.

ACAS seeks to:

- promote good practice
- provide information and advice
- conciliate in complaints to employment tribunals
- conciliate in the case of collective disputes
- prevent and resolve employment disputes.

Promoting good practice

ACAS organises conferences and seminars on topical employment and industrial relations issues. For small businesses, ACAS also runs self-help workshops in which employment policies and procedures are discussed. Unlike the other services provided by ACAS, which are free, there is a charge for conferences, seminars and small firm workshops. ACAS also sells a range of booklets offering practical guidance and advice on employment and industrial relations topics – for example, on discipline, job evaluation, recruitment and induction, employee appraisal, hours of work, teamworking and employee communications and consultation. During 2003/04 ACAS ran just over 2,500 events reaching more than 35,000 organisations, the majority aimed at small and medium-sized enterprises (SMEs). The conferences, seminars and workshops make an important contribution to ACAS's objective of disseminating good practice and assisting in the formulation of sound policies for the employment relationship. They are also part of a service ACAS has developed to help SMEs, which because of pressures of work can often find it difficult to keep up to date with good employment practice.

ACAS also has issued three Codes of Practice. Its Code of Practice on Disciplinary and Grievance Procedures provides practical guidance on good practice in disciplinary and grievance matters in employment and is obligatorily taken into account by arbitrators appointed by ACAS to determine cases brought under the ACAS Arbitration Scheme (see Chapter 11).

The ACAS Code of Practice on the Disclosure of Information to Trade Unions for Collective Bargaining Purposes sets out good practice in this area, and its Code of Practice on Time Off for Trade Union Duties and Activities provides guidance on time off for trade union duties, time off for training of trade union officials and time off for other standard trade union activities. It also covers the responsibilities which employers and trade unions share in considering reasonable time off, and outlines the advantages of reaching formal agreements on time off.

These Codes impose no legal obligations on an employer. Failure to observe a Code does not, by itself, render anyone liable to proceedings – the provisions of the Code on Disciplinary and Grievance Procedures may, however, be taken into account in proceedings before an employment tribunal and in an arbitration hearing under the ACAS Arbitration Scheme. The Disclosure of Information Code is taken into account by the Central Arbitration Committee when arbitrating on a complaint that an employer has failed to disclose information for collective bargaining purposes.

Providing information and advice

ACAS provides information and guidance on a wide range of employee relations matters. It does this primarily through the ACAS Helpline, which can be contacted by anyone. It has a team of 110 advisers based throughout Great Britain. The service is free, confidential and impartial, and is designed to assist employers and people at work. It provides a useful and cost-effective advisory service particularly for small firms and individuals to help them clarify the range and increasing complexity of employment legislation, and thereby avoid difficulties at work. Most enquiries are dealt with by telephone, but a small number are answered by letter or personal interviews, usually by prior appointment.

In 2003/04, ACAS Helpline advisers answered 796,649 telephone calls, on every aspect of employment relations. The most frequently asked questions related to discipline and dismissal issues. Other topics of regular questions are requests for flexible working, maternity, paternity and adoption leave, and pay. The

Table 8 *Individual complaints concerning employment rights 1987–2004*

Date	Unfair dismissal	Total complaints received
1987	34,572	40,817
1988	36,340	44,443
1989	37,324	48,817
1990	37,654	52,071
1991	39,234	60,605
1992	44,034	72,166
1993	46,854	75,181
1994	45,824	79,332
1995	40,815	91,568
1996	46,566	100,399
1997	42,771	106,912
1998	40,153	113,636
1999	52,791	164,525
2000/01	51,721	166,153
2001/02	53,994	163,409
2002/03	49,424	162,932
2003/04	47,682	176,505

Source: ACAS *Annual Reports*, 1985–2003/04

Working Time Regulations are also a regular theme of questions. For many organisations the ACAS Helpline is often the first point of contact with ACAS. Sometimes their enquiry raises issues which cannot readily be answered by telephone, and in such cases the problem is addressed by face-to-face contact with ACAS field staff.

Conciliation in individual employment rights disputes

ACAS has a statutory duty to act as conciliator in a wide range of individual employment rights complaints, including unfair dismissal, breach of contract (eg non payment of termination payments or commission) or discrimination on grounds of sex or race or in equal pay or a failure to provide statutory benefits. However, for individuals and organisations to participate in this conciliation is voluntary. It is impartial, confidential, free of charge and independent of the employment tribunals. The number of complaints handled by ACAS concerning alleged breach of employment rights is shown in Table 8 above.

When making a complaint to an employment tribunal, a person must first complete form IT1 and send it to the appropriate employment tribunal office, which then passes a copy to ACAS. The case is then allocated to an ACAS conciliation officer whose responsibility it is to attempt to help the parties settle the complaint without the need for a tribunal hearing if that is their wish and if both parties are willing to accept conciliation. The officer's role is to help in a neutral and independent way, and involves making both parties aware of the option available to them so that they may reach informed decisions on how best to proceed. The conciliation officer explains tribunal procedures and the ACAS Arbitration Scheme (see below) as well as relevant law, but does not make decisions on the merits of the case or impose or recommend a particular settlement. Any settlement terms are the responsibility of the parties concerned. The conciliation officer conveys the views of one party to the other. If there is information one party wishes to keep from the other, then so long as the party explains that to the conciliation officer, the information will not be passed on. Where a case is not settled before the date fixed for the tribunal hearing, the employment tribunal will resolve the matter.

In unfair dismissal cases, the conciliation officers have the statutory duty to explore first the possibility of reinstatement, or of re-engagement on suitable terms, before seeking to promote a monetary or other form of, settlement. The Employment Rights (Disputes Resolution) Act 1998 empowers conciliation officers, if both parties agree, to draw up binding settlements in which the two parties opt out of the employment tribunal system in favour of resolving the employee's complaint of unfair dismissal through voluntary arbitration – the so-called ACAS Arbitration Scheme (see Chapter 11). The underlying principle behind this Scheme is to make the resolving of unfair dismissal claims by voluntary arbitration as similar as possible to the arbitrations currently undertaken by ACAS in settling collective disputes (see below). During 2003/04 there were 7 instances of the use of the ACAS Arbitration Scheme compared with 23 in 2002/03. The main barriers to the use of this Scheme continue to be opposition from the legal profession and a lack of understanding on the part of individuals, trade unions and employers of the benefits of the process and its outcome compared to the more confrontational tribunal process. ACAS also has an Arbitration Scheme for resolving by voluntary arbitration, rather than an employment tribunal, disputes over alleged unreasonable refusal by an employer to grant an employee's request for more flexible working. To date this ACAS Scheme has not been used.

ACAS's role is to attempt to settle cases without the need for a tribunal hearing, recognising that not all cases are capable of a settlement and that some parties may wish to have their cases decided in a legal setting. On average, three out of four claims for employment rights breaches are either settled or withdrawn following ACAS intervention, after which there is no need for a tribunal hearing. In the case of discrimination claims, the withdrawal/settlement rate is over 80 per cent.

ACAS involvement is normally welcomed by the parties because it provides a means of settling their differences without the need for what can be expensive, stressful and lengthy legal hearings. An important part of the conciliation officer's job is to defuse the tension and reduce the acrimony that often exists between the parties so as to enable them to focus realistically on the options open to them.

Nevertheless, an organisation that has acted without just cause against an employee is unlikely to be interested in seeking an ACAS-conciliated settlement with the individual concerned. If the employer had complied with good employment practice, there would after all be no business case for settling the complaint via ACAS conciliation. The organisation would be confident of having its case upheld. Only organisations that for example dismiss employees without complying with good employment practice are likely to see advantages in an ACAS-brokered pre-tribunal settlement.

> How effective do you consider ACAS has been in preventing individual complaints against alleged arbitratory behaviour by an employer going to employment tribunals?

Conciliation and mediation in collective disputes

Collective employment disputes are very costly both to the employers and to the employees, so it is sensible to resolve workplace problems before they develop into disputes. ACAS employs two principal methods to help organisations avoid costly collective disputes:

- workshops in which employer and employee representatives discuss and agree on potential barriers to the achievement of long-term organisational goals. Such workshops are useful for exploring problems where the underlying causes are not clearly known. Once these are identified, courses of action can be agreed to rectify the problems
- joint working parties in which employer and employee representatives work together to devise and implement practical solutions to specific problems by, for example, collecting and analysing information and evaluating options.

ACAS staff will normally chair the working party. However, although prevention is better than the cure, employment disputes inevitably occur. When this happens, ACAS can help the parties by offering:

- conciliation
- mediation
- arbitration.

The conciliation process

Requests for conciliation in collective disputes normally come from employers, trade unions or in organisations where there are no trade unions employee representatives. Before it agrees to conciliate, ACAS checks that the parties have exhausted any internal dispute resolution procedures they may have. In coming to conciliation, no prior commitment is required from the parties, only a willingness to discuss the problem(s) at issue. As in individual disputes so in collective ones. Conciliation is an entirely voluntary process and it is open to either party to bring the discussion to an end at any time – although effectively management remains in control in deciding whether to continue with the process or to withdraw from it.

ACAS conciliators help the parties in dispute settle their differences by agreement and, if possible, in a long-term way. The conciliator remains impartial and independent, makes constructive suggestions to facilitate negotiations, provides information at the request of the parties, and gains the trust and confidence of both parties so that a sound working relationship is developed. The first step in conciliation in a collective dispute is to discover what the dispute is about – a fact-finding process that usually requires the conciliator to meet with both sides separately, although occasionally, information may be obtained at joint meetings. Almost all conciliations involve a mixture of side meetings at which the conciliator explores issues separately with the parties, and joint meetings at which the parties can explain their position face-to-face. The exact mix of side and joint meetings is determined by the conciliator in discussion with the parties.

Where it is clear a settlement might be achieved, the conciliator seeks to secure a joint agreement, usually in the form of a signed document, which finalises the terms of the settlement. Any agreements reached in conciliation are the responsibility of the parties involved, and ACAS has no power to impose or even to recommend settlements. In collective disputes there is no time limit to the conciliation process, and ACAS continues to assist the parties so long as they wish it to and there appears a chance of reaching an agreed settlement. The role of the conciliator is to keep the two sides talking and to help facilitate an agreement.

The mediation process

In a collective dispute, if a settlement is not reached through conciliation, ACAS can arrange for the issue to be resolved through mediation. In this case, both parties agree that an independent person or a Board of Mediation should mediate between them. The process of mediation involves each side setting out its case in writing, followed by a hearing at which the two sides present, in person, their evidence and arguments. Hearings are usually held at ACAS offices or at the premises of the employer or the trade union. The mediator (or the Board of Mediation) makes formal, but not binding, proposals or recommendations to provide a basis for a settlement of the dispute. The parties are free to accept or reject the mediator's proposals or recommendations. In mediation, as in conciliation, the employer remains in control of the situation and can withdraw at any stage. A settlement cannot be imposed by a third party. The employer remains free to accept or reject.

The arbitration process

If the parties to a collective dispute decide to take their differences to arbitration for settlement, they appoint a jointly agreed arbitrator to consider the dispute and to make a decision to resolve it. Occasionally, arbitration may be by a Board of Arbitration with an independent chairperson and two side members drawn from employer and trade union representatives. It is the arbitrator who makes the award resolving the dispute and not – as many seem to think – ACAS. Unlike conciliation and mediation, in arbitration the employer does not retain control, because before ACAS will facilitate arbitration, both parties must agree to abide by the arbitrator's decision. This is a long-established principle of arbitration, and in practice arbitration awards are invariably accepted and implemented.

> Explain the differences between conciliation, mediation and arbitration.

What issues go to the arbitrator?

Table 9 below shows the extent to which conciliation, mediation and arbitration has been used in the UK in collective disputes since 1979. It shows that in general there has been a fall in the use of all three processes. However, the table indicates a slight but irregular rise in the incidence of conciliation since the late 1980s and early 1990s. In the case of mediation and arbitration the figures have been relatively static for a decade. The types of issues that are the subject of arbitration are what are often referred to as disputes of rights, which are issues arising from the parties' rights under collective agreements. Arbitration is rarely used in what are referred to as disputes of interest – issues that arise from the negotiation of new or revised collective agreements.

Table 9 *The use of third-party intervention in industrial disputes*

Date	Completed collective conciliation	Mediation	Number of arbitration hearings
1979	2,284	31	394
1980	1,910	31	281
1981	1,716	12	245
1982	1,634	16	235
1983	1,621	20	187
1984	1,448	14	188
1985	1,337	12	150
1986	1,323	10	174
1987	1,147	12	133
1988	1,053	9	129
1989	1,070	17	150
1990	1,140	10	190
1991	1,226	12	144
1992	1,140	7	155
1993	1,118	7	156
1994	1,162	8	148
1995	1,299	5	136
1996	1,197	4	113
1997	1,166	11	60
1998	1,159	6	55
1999/2000	1.247	1	63
2000/01	1,472	5	55
2001/02	1,371	5	61
2002/03	1,353	9	71

Source: ACAS *Annual Reports*, 1979–2003

An analysis of ACAS statistics (see its *Annual Reports*) over the last 20 years reviewing the types of issues under dispute at arbitration shows a dominance of three – job grading, dismissal and discipline, and pay and other conditions of employment (not annual pay increases). This demonstrates that employers have been prepared to go to arbitration on issues:

- that are important to them – but not so important that they are prepared to impose industrial sanctions on the union
- where the cost of losing is bearable
- where there is unlikely to be adverse publicity from the arbitrator's award.

Why is arbitration so little used?

Arbitration is the accepted instrument of the last resort, but employers – whether in the private or public sector – continue to be sceptical about the principle of arbitration even on disputes of rights, let alone disputes of interests. Trade unions essentially remain pragmatic in their approach to accepting arbitration. They are in the bargaining business and are suspicious of anything that impedes their ability to gain by whatever means the best possible deal for their members. Although many trade unions profess to love 'free and unfettered' collective bargaining, their objections to arbitration are as much pragmatic as principled. However much they might be opposed to it in other circumstances, trade unions whose bargaining power is weak sometimes propose arbitration if and when they sense they could not secure approval for industrial action. In the 1980s and 1990s, unions anxious to maintain or expand their membership base showed a willingness to enter into so-called 'new-style' agreements in which pendulum arbitration (see Chapter 1) was provided as the basis of avoiding the need for strike action.

Employers can also be similarly guided by pragmatism. Whatever the principal argument of companies that they should negotiate within their procedure agreements and then, if there is a final 'failure to agree', stand up to the consequences without third-party intervention, the fact remains that many companies faced with the prospect or reality of industrial action themselves seek the conciliation, and at times arbitration, route.

However, a major reason in employers' reluctance to resort more readily to arbitration is the reputation of the arbitration process itself – that the employer cannot retain control of events and must accept whatever the arbitrator may award, and that the arbitrator will 'split the difference' between the parties. Arbitration is first and foremost a process which transfers the ultimate responsibility for certain key business decisions from management to an independent third party. This is in contrast to collective bargaining, conciliation and mediation, in which each side retains considerable authority over events. Either party can exercise the prerogative of walking away at any time. There is little evidence to support the view that in a dispute of interests the arbitrator always splits the difference. Yet, however undeserved it is, arbitrators have this reputation. Until ACAS can effectively nail this misconception, any extension of the arbitration process into disputes of interests is unlikely to be achieved.

In disputes of interest there is also the criticism that the arbitrator usually improves upon the final offer made by the employer in direct negotiations. In doing this, arbitrators are likely to be acting on two assumptions. First, that the union would not be coming to arbitration unless it felt it could secure more for its members; and second that in agreeing to arbitration, the employer is anxious to avoid the alternative of industrial action and all its associated costs. The employer might well therefore be willing to pay a little more if such action can be avoided. An award handed down by an independent arbitrator holds out greater certainty of this than an improved offer by the employer.

Arbitration will remain a vital and indispensable instrument of last resort in dispute resolution. It can never be ignored – but it is unlikely to become more extensively used.

Explain the circumstances in which an employer might be prepared to go to arbitration to resolve a dispute with their employees. What are the main dangers to an employer of using arbitration to resolve collective and/or individual disputes with employees?

The Central Arbitration Committee (CAC)

The Central Arbitration Committee's roots go back to the 1919 Industrial Courts Act, which established the Industrial Court as a permanent and independent body for voluntary arbitration in industrial disputes. In 1971 the Industrial Court changed its name to the Industrial Arbitration Board, which in turn became the Central Arbitration Committee under the Employment Protection Act 1975. The CAC is a permanent independent body with statutory powers: its main functions are:

■ hearing complaints from a trade union of an employer's failure to disclose information for collective bargaining purposes

■ disposing of claims and complaints regarding the establishment and operation of European Works Councils in Great Britain

■ adjudicating on applications relating to statutory recognition and de-recognition of trade unions for collective bargaining purposes where such recognition or de-recognition cannot be agreed voluntarily

■ providing voluntary arbitration in industrial disputes – this function, however, has not been used for some years.

The Committee consists of a chairperson, ten deputy chairpersons, 16 members experienced as representatives of employers, and 16 members experienced as representatives of workers. All members of the Committee are appointed by the Secretary of State for Trade and Industry after consultation with ACAS. Decisions are made by panels of three committee members appointed by the chairperson and consisting of either the chairperson or a deputy chairperson, one member whose experience is as a representative of employers and one member whose experience is as a representative of workers.

The CAC is thus a specialist body which can approach its legislative responsibilities in a variety of ways, assisting the parties to reach voluntary agreements but making legally enforceable decisions when necessary. It is this flexibility which sets it apart from traditional courts (Burton, 2002). The CAC seeks to ensure that the parties have every opportunity to state their case, and issues decisions that take full account of the parties' views, explaining clearly the reasoning behind every decision. CAC decisions, however, do not and cannot set precedents because each case is different and has to be treated on its merits. No panel of the CAC is bound by a decision of another panel, and decisions are not circulated, although all are available on the CAC website.

In the case of the trade union recognition procedure, the CAC has powers to decide on:

■ whether an application should be accepted

■ which groups are to be included in any recognition agreement (the bargaining unit)

■ whether to hold a ballot and on the conduct of the ballot(s)

■ the method of collective bargaining if the parties cannot agree this themselves.

The CAC arbitrates on disputes between employers and a trade union over whether the appropriate bargaining unit is compatible with effective management. If there is a CAC-imposed bargaining unit and the union still wishes to proceed to obtain recognition, the CAC has to decide whether the union has majority support. Except where the union has already recruited the majority of employees in the bargaining unit, the CAC will arrange for a secret ballot, which can – at the discretion of the CAC – be at the workplace, or be by post to the employees' homes. If the union has a majority on a vote of at least 40 per cent of the whole bargaining unit, the CAC declares the union recognised. If the employer persists in failing to recognise the trade union, the CAC can impose trade union recognition for collective bargaining purposes by means of an agreement that then becomes legally binding on the parties. The CAC also plays a similar role in the trade union de-recognition procedure contained in the Employment Relations Act 1999.

Between June 2000 and the end of March 2003, trade unions submitted 255 applications for union recognition. Of these, 150 were accepted by the CAC, 21 not accepted, and 76 were withdrawn. In 56 cases, the CAC decided the bargaining unit, but in 56 cases the parties agreed the bargaining unit themselves. In 23 cases trade union recognition was granted without a ballot. Of the 58 ballots held in the period June 2000 to 31 March 2003, 35 resulted in a majority in support of recognition, and in 23 the union failed to gain the necessary majority.

Explain the differences between ACAS and the CAC in terms of their roles and functions.

SUMMARY

- The main services employers' organisations offer to their members are assistance in the resolution of disputes, representation at employment tribunals, advisory and information services ('good practice', model agreements, salary data, etc) and the representation of members' views to political and other decision-making bodies.

- The primary purpose of trade unions is to protect the jobs of their members and to enhance their pay and employment conditions principally by the use of collective bargaining and political lobbying.

- The UK trade union organisation is characterised by a small number of very large unions and a large number of very small unions.

- Over the last 20 years trade union membership has declined owing, inter alia, to structural factors (eg switch of employment from manufacturing) and public policy initiatives unsupportive of trade union organisation.

- Although there are those who believe trade unions are in terminal decline, the early 2000s have seen an increase in total trade union membership.

- Staff associations are usually established within a single organisation and are characterised by high membership density.

- The majority of large staff associations are recognised by employers for negotiating and representational purposes, and most agreements to which they are a party cover such matters as recognition, provision of facilities, consultation and grievance and disciplinary procedures.

- In addition, there are a much larger number of staff associations which are employer-dominated and have only a consultative function.

- The Certification Officer performs a number of functions including determining that a trade union is independent of the employer, dealing with complaints by members, seeing that unions' merger procedures are observed, and overseeing trade union political funds.

- ACAS promotes good practice (via Codes of Practice), provides employee relations information and advice, conciliates in individual complaints to employment tribunals, and in the case of collective disputes, conciliates and facilitates mediation and arbitration.

■ The Central Arbitration Committee arbitrates on industrial disputes, on complaints from trade unions of an employer's failure to disclose information for collective bargaining purposes, on complaints over the establishment and operation of European Works Councils in the UK, and on disputes over trade union recognition and de-recognition.

FURTHER READING

ADVISORY, CONCILIATION AN ARBITRATION SERVICE, *Annual Reports*.

BOOTH A. (1989) What do unions do now?, Discussion Paper in Economics, No.8903, Brunel University.

BROWN W. and TOWER B. J. (2000) *Employment Relations in Britain: 25 years of the Advisory, Conciliation and Arbitration Service*. Oxford, Blackwell.

BRYSON A. and GOMEZ J. (2003) Buying into union membership, in Gospel H. and Wood S. (eds) *Representing Workers: Trade union recognition and membership in Britain*. London, Routledge.

BURTON M. (2002) The principles and factors guiding the CAC, *Employee Relations*, Volume 24, No.6.

CENTRAL ARBITRATION COMMITTEE *Annual Reports*.

CERTIFICATION OFFICER *Annual Reports*.

CHARLWOOD K. (2004) The new generation of trade union leaders and prospects for union revitalisation, *British Journal of Industrial Relations*, Volume 42, No.2.

ENGINEERING EMPLOYERS' ASSOCIATION *Annual Reviews*.

FLANDERS A. (1968) What are unions for?, in Flanders A. (1970) *Management and Unions*. London, Faber & Faber.

FREEMAN R. and PELLETIER J. (1990) The impact of industrial relations legislation on British union density, *British Journal of Industrial Relations*, Volume 28, No.2.

GALL G. (2003) Trade union recognition in Britain: developments, issues and prospects, *Human Resources and Employment Review*.

GALL G. (2004) Trade union recognition in Britain 1995–2002: turning a corner, *Industrial Relations Journal*, Volume 35, No.3.

GENNARD J. (2002) Employee relations public policy developments 1997–2001: a break with the past?, *Employee Relations*, Volume 24, No.6.

HEERY E., SIMMS M., DELRIDGE R., SALMON J. and SIMPSON D. (1999) Organising unionism comes to the UK, *Employee Relations*, Volume 22, No.1.

HEERY E., SIMMS M., DELRIDGE R., SALMON J. and SIMPSON D. (2000) Union organising in Britain: a survey of policy and practice, *International Journal of Human Resource Management*, Volume 11, No.5.

INDUSTRIAL RELATIONS SERVICE (1995) Staff associations: independent unions or employer-led bodies?, No.575, January.

MACHIN S. (2000) Union decline in Britain, *British Journal of Industrial Relations*, Volume 38, No.4.

MACHIN S. (2002) Factors of convergence and divergence in union membership, Centre for Economic Performance Discussion Paper No.554, London School of Economics.

MACHIN S. (2003) Trade union decline, new workplaces and new workers, in Gospel H. and Wood S. (eds) *Representing Workers: Trade union representation and membership in Britain*. London, Routledge.

MACHIN S. and BLANDEN J. (2003) Cross-generational correlations of union status for young people, Centre for Economic Performance Discussion Paper No.553, London School of Economics.

METCALF D. (2004) British unions: resurgence or perdition?, Centre for Economic Performance, London School of Economics.

MILLWARD N., BRYSON A. and FORTH J. (2000) *All Change at Work? British Employment Relations 1980–1998, as Portrayed by the Workplace Industrial Relations Survey Series*. London, Routledge.

MUMFORD K. (1996) Arbitration and ACAS in Britain: a historical perspective, *British Journal of Industrial Relations*, Volume 34, No.2.

TAYLOR R. (undated) *The Future of Employment Relations*, Economic and Social Research Council.

TOWERS D. J. (1997) *The Representation Gap: Change and reform in the British workplace*. Oxford, Oxford University Press.

TRADES UNION CONGRESS *General Council Report to Congress*.

Employee involvement

CHAPTER 7

CHAPTER OBJECTIVES

When you have completed this chapter you should be aware of and able to describe:

- the business case for involving employees in the affairs of the business

- the strengths and weaknesses of the main direct employee involvement and participation practices

- the relevance of the main indirect employee involvement and participation practices

- how to advise management of the likely impact of information and consultation with employees on an organisation

- how to devise, and implement, appropriate employee involvement and participation practices for an organisation

- the legal framework surrounding the provision of information and consultation arrangements

- the impact of the implementation of employee involvement and participation practices on organisational performance.

INTRODUCTION

Employee involvement and participation covers a wide range of practices. As defined by Marchington *et al* (1992) these practices are initiated principally by management and are designed to increase employee information about, and commitment to, the organisation. Employee involvement concentrates on individual employees and is designed to produce a committed workforce more likely to contribute to the efficient operation of an organisation. By introducing employee involvement mechanisms, management seeks to gain the consent of the employees to its proposed actions on the basis of commitment rather than control (Walton, 1985). These mechanisms are thus aimed at enabling individual employees to influence management decision-making processes.

Employee participation, on the other hand, concerns the extent to which employees – often via their representatives – are involved with management in the decision-making machinery of the organisation. This includes joint consultation, collective bargaining and worker representation on the board. These systems focus on collective representative structures.

It is management, however, who makes the final decision on whether employees are to be involved, and to participate, in management decision-making. Employee involvement, unlike collective bargaining and worker representation on the board, is not about employees' sharing power (jointly regulating) with management. The decision whether to accept, or reject, the views of the employees rests with management alone.

Explain the difference between the terms 'employee involvement' and 'employee participation'.

WHY INVOLVE EMPLOYEES?

The control-oriented approach to workforce management associated with F. W. Taylor took shape in the early part of the twentieth century in response to the extending division of labour into jobs for which individuals were considered accountable. To monitor and control effectiveness in these jobs, management organised itself into a hierarchy of specialised roles supported by a top-down allocation of authority and status symbols to position within the hierarchy. At the centre of this workforce control method was the desire to establish order and to inculcate efficiency in the employee – who was expected to obey, and not challenge management instructions.

However, increasing international competition and technological change over the last 25 years have meant that higher skills and far greater flexibility are required of the employee. According to Walton (1985), in this environment a commitment strategy towards the workforce is required. Following this strategic approach to managing, the workforce jobs are designed to be broader than before (job enlargement), to combine planning and implementation and to include efforts to upgrade operations, not just to maintain them. The responsibilities of individual employees are expected to change as conditions change (functional flexibility), and teams – not individuals – are accountable for employee performance. The teams control how they will deliver their output objectives. Employees are thus said to be empowered. A commitment strategy therefore involves dispensing with whole layers of management and minimising status differentials so that control depends on shared goals and expertise rather than on a formal position that carries influence with it.

Under an employee commitment strategy, according to Walton, performance expectations are high and serve not to establish minimum standards but to emphasise continuous improvement and reflect the requirements of the marketplace. As a result, pay and reward strategies reflect not the principles of job evaluation but the importance of group achievement and concerns for gain sharing and profit sharing. Equally important, argues Walton, is the challenge of giving employees some assurance of security by offering them priority in training and retraining as old jobs are destroyed and new ones created, and providing them with the means to be heard on such issues as production methods, problem-solving and human resource policies.

Underlying all these policies is a management philosophy that accepts the interests of an organisation's multiple stakeholders – owners, employees, customers and public. At the heart of this approach is an acceptance that growing employee commitment will lead to improved performance. No organisation in today's modern world can perform at peak levels unless each employee is committed to the corporate objectives and works as an effective team member. Employees want to use and develop their skills, enhance their careers and take pride in their work. The commitment strategy involves employees' contributing their own ideas as to how their performance and the quality of product or service they provide can be improved. There is clear evidence that employees want to be part of a successful organisation which provides a good income, and an opportunity for development and secure employment.

The case for employee involvement and participation stems from economic efficiency gains. There are a number of reasons for such an outcome. First, employees generally are better informed about their work tasks and processes than their managers and are therefore better placed to achieve enhanced performance. Second, advocates of employee involvement and participation argue that its associated practices provide employees with greater intrinsic rewards from work than from other forms of workplace management such as collective bargaining. It is said that these rewards will increase job satisfaction and in turn enhance employee motivation to achieve new goals. Then it is also hypothesised that by granting workers greater access to management information, mutual trust and commitment will be increased, thereby reducing labour turnover. In addition, empowering workers reduces the need for complex systems of control, and hence leads to improved efficiency.

There is thus an important assumption behind employee involvement theory – namely, that employees are an untapped resource with knowledge and experience which can be used by employers if they provide opportunities and structures for worker involvement. Wilkinson (2001) has also pointed out that the theory assumes that participative decision-making is likely to lead to better-quality management decisions, so that empowerment represents a win/win situation with gains available to both employers (increased efficiency) and employees (job satisfaction).

Financial forms of employee involvement are said to improve productivity performance for a number of reasons. First, it is argued that employees will work more co-operatively because they can all gain by co-operating with each other rather than competing amongst themselves. Second, some argue that performance-related pay schemes indirectly enhance employee effort and commitment by improving communication about company performance and by educating employees about the significance/importance of profitability. There are also those who suggest that such payment schemes increase employees' identification with the organisation.

The research of Marchington et al (2001) demonstrated that employers in the 18 organisations they studied valued the voice of the employee in contributing to management decision-making because they believed it contributed to business performance. Employee voice (by communication systems, project team membership and joint consultation) was perceived to contribute to business performance via better employee contributions, improved management systems and productivity gains. This was seen to be the result of the number of ideas that emerged through employee feedback and joint problem-solving teams.

THE OUTCOMES OF EMPLOYEE INVOLVEMENT AND PARTICIPATION

The involvement of and participation by employees in any organisation should have these outcomes:

- generate commitment of all employees to the success of the organisation
- enable the organisation better to meet the needs of its customers and adapt to changing market requirements
- help the organisation to improve performance and productivity, adapt new methods of working to match new technology
- improve the satisfaction employees get from their work
- provide all employees with the opportunity to influence and be involved in decisions which are likely to affect their interests.

Ramsay (1996) argues that the improved economic performance stemming from employee involvement participation is the result of employers' being able, on behalf of their employees, to change the employees' attitude, to increase their business awareness, to improve their motivation, to enhance their influence/ownership and to involve their trade unions (see box on Management objectives in introducing employee involvement practices, below). This is not an exhaustive list of variables but nevertheless demonstrates the need for careful definition of these variables. Vague and general definitions like 'changed attitudes' or 'greater incentive' are inadequate for evaluating the causation between employee involvement and participation practices and their outcomes – for example, increased productivity. Ramsay points out there is also potential conflict (or at least strain) between these variables. As he remarks:

To exemplify this last point, a general sense of unity and belonging may sit poorly with the need to sharpen individual competition and incentive, and it may be advisable to use distinct kinds of scheme to achieve each if both require enhancement ...

For Ramsay, if the businesses awareness of employees can be improved, they are more likely to be better and more accurately informed, the 'rumour grapevine' will be reduced and there is a higher probability that they will have greater job interest, improved knowledge and understanding of the reasons for management decisions and greater support for (or resistance to) to management action. The box below suggests that by using employee involvement schemes to increase employee influence/ownership, management is more likely to provide its employees with greater job control and at the same time, via financial participation schemes, create increased employee ownership in the company and enhanced employee ties to company performance and profitability.

MANAGEMENT OBJECTIVES IN INTRODUCING EMPLOYEE INVOLVEMENT PRACTICES

Attitudes
Improved morale
Increased loyalty and commitment
Enhanced sense of involvement
Increased support for management

Business awareness
Better, more accurately informed
Greater interest
Better understanding of reason for management action
Support for/reduced resistance to management action

Incentive/motivation
Passive Accept changes in working practices
          Accept mobility across jobs
          Accept new technology
          Accept management authority
  Active   Improve quality/reliability
          Increase productivity/effort
          Reduce costs
          Enhance co-operation and team spirit
    Personal   Greater job interest
             Greater job satisfaction
             Employee development

Employee influence/ownership
Increase job control
Employee suggestions
Increase employee ownership in the company
Increase employee ties to company performance and profitability

Trade unions	
Anti-union	Keeps union out of company
	Representative needs outside union channels
	Win hearts and minds of employee from union
With union	Gain union co-operation
	Draw on union advice
	Restrain union demands

Source: *H. Ramsay in B. J. Towers (ed.) The Handbook of Human Resource Management, 2nd edn*

Ramsay (1996) also argues that if management can change employee incentive and motivation in a positive direction, it may have passive, active and personal impacts. The employees may benefit from greater job interest, enhanced job satisfaction and increased opportunities to develop themselves. Active advantages may arise for the organisation stemming from improved quality/reliability of the product or service, increased labour productivity and effort, reduced costs and enhanced co-operation and team spirit. Among the probable passive advantages accruing to the organisation that Ramsay notes are a greater willingness on the part of employees to accept changes in working practices, flexibility across jobs, the implementation of new technology and enhanced front/first line management authority.

If management can achieve a positive change in employee attitudes, it is likely to improve not only the morale of employees but also their loyalty and commitment to the organisation. Their sense of belonging and involvement is also likely to be enhanced. In addition, there will be greater probability that employees will give greater support to management's position. Employee involvement practices are thus an important means by which management can bring about organisational cultural change. However, such cultural change can only be achieved in any organisation on an incremental basis – the full benefits to the organisation from cultural change arising from the successful implementation of involvement methods will not accrue immediately. The attitudes of every employee, or manager, will not change in a positive direction at the same moment in time. Some will take longer than others to develop a positive change in attitude towards the actions of management. Management must be aware of this phenomenon of incremental cultural change when reviewing and monitoring the impact of the introduction of employee involvement practices.

Outline the business case for introducing employee involvement practices in an organisation.

EMPLOYEE INVOLVEMENT PRACTICES

The different practices

Marchington *et al* (1992) talk of direct and indirect employee participation practices. Direct participation consists of:

- downward communication practices
  - team briefing
  - workplace-wide meetings
  - staff newsletters
  - cascading of information via the management chain
- upward problem-solving communications practices

- suggestion schemes
- employee/staff attitude surveys
- employee groups established to solve specific problems or discuss aspects of performance or quality
■ financial participation
  - profit-related bonus schemes
  - deferred profit-sharing schemes
  - employee share ownership schemes.

The main form of indirect employee participation is through some form of employee representative structure, such as a joint consultative committee (JCC) or in some multinational companies a European Works Council.

Ramsay (1996), however, divides employee involvement and participation initiatives into four broad types:

■ communications and briefing systems – which include downward and upward communications systems

■ task and work group involvement – which includes teamworking, quality circles and total quality management (TQM) programmes

■ financial participation – which embraces profit sharing, profit-related pay and share ownership schemes

■ representative participation.

In this chapter, the Ramsay classification is used.

The extent of employee involvement practices

The main sources of information on the extent of employee involvement practices are the Industrial Relations Services surveys of 1993 (62 participating organisations), 1996 (26 organisations surveyed) and 1999 (49 participating organisations), and the Workplace Industrial Relations Survey series which relate to 1980, 1984, 1990 and 1998.

The Industrial Relations Services surveys

These surveys (see Table 10 below) show that the incidence of team-based employee involvement initiatives rises as the frequency of collective bargaining falls. In 1993 the most common type of practice included company newspapers (used by over 80 per cent of respondents) and collective bargaining (89 per cent). Three years later, team meetings (mentioned by 88 per cent) were the most frequently used employee involvement strategy. Team briefings (81 per cent) also featured strongly, reflecting the growth of teamworking and more direct, participative working cultures. In common with 1993, company journals (81 per cent) and collective bargaining (77 per cent) emerged as popular employee involvement strategies.

Table 10   *Employee involvement practices: emerging trends 1993–1999*

Practice	Percentage of respondents		
	1993 n = 62	**1996 n = 26**	**1999 n = 49**
Company newspaper	80	81	92
Team meetings	–	88	92
Team briefings	–	81	86
Collective bargaining	69	77	39

Source: Industrial Relations Services surveys on employee involvement

Tables 11, 12, and 13 show the distribution of communications, participation and representation forms of employee involvement in the 1999 survey of 49 organisations. Taking the overall picture, team meetings (92 per cent), company letters (92 per cent) and team briefings (86 per cent) broadly repeat the trends of 1996. However, collective bargaining had slipped down the employee involvement pecking order. Just 39 per cent reported using it, suggesting that traditional union-based representative forms of employee involvement are becoming rarer. The general conclusion from Table 10 is that over the period 1993–1999 there was a shift away from collective representation towards direct participation and involvement practices.

Table 11   *Employee involvement: communications*

Type of communication	Percentage n = 49
Company journal	92
Team briefings (top-down)	86
e-mail	82
Attitude surveys	49
Employee reports	43
Video presentations	18

Source: Industrial Relations Services, *Employment Review*, No.683, July 1999

Table 12   *Employee involvement: participation*

Type of participation	Percentage n = 49
Team meetings	92
Suggestion schemes	45
Customer care initiatives	45
Quality initiatives	39
Recognition programmes	22

Source: Industrial Relations Services, *Employment Review*, No.683, July 1999

Table 13   *Employee involvement: representation*

Type of representation	Percentage n = 49
Joint consultative committee	49
Collective bargaining	39
Works council	12
Company council	10
European Works Council	8

Source: Industrial Relations Services, *Employment Review*, No.683, July 1999

The 1999 survey also revealed that the average number of employee involvement practices operating in the 49 organisations surveyed was 7.2. In addition, it indicated that:

- Employee involvement practices tended to be found mostly in large manufacturing companies that had a tradition of consultation and some form of worker participation in the production process.
- Employee reports and employee attitude surveys were deployed by only about half the organisations in the sample.
- Respondents used a multitude of communications techniques, no single employer using fewer than two different approaches.
- Some 25 per cent of respondents did not use any form of employee representation.
- Unions are generally in favour of the introduction of employee involvement initiatives.

The Workplace Industrial Relations Survey series
Joint consultative committees were the principal channel of employee voice during World War II and the years immediately afterwards. In 1980, 34 per cent of all workplaces had a joint consultative committee – but by the time of the 1998 survey, the proportion had fallen to 29 per cent. These figures include some committees that meet rarely and that provide only limited opportunities for employees to communicate with management. If attention is confined to joint consultative committees that meet at least once every three months, the proportion of all workplaces in 1998 with an effective joint consultative committee was 23 per

cent, compared with 31 per cent in 1990. The proportion of employees in workplaces with an effective joint consultative committee fell from 50 per cent in 1984 to 34 per cent in 1998. Such committees were most prevalent in the public sector and least common in the private services sector. Managements in organisations with a number of different establishments often prefer to consult with their employees on a multi-site basis rather than have a consultative committee for each establishment. In 1998, 56 per cent of workplaces belonging to a larger organisation reported a higher-level committee in their organisation, compared with 48 per cent in 1990 and 50 per cent in 1984. The increase since 1990 has been entirely within the private sector, where the proportion rose from 35 to 48 per cent.

Profit-related pay became much more widespread during the 1980s. In 1984, 19 per cent of workplaces in industry and commerce belonged to enterprises that operated a scheme. By 1990, this percentage had risen to 44, and eight years later to 46. During the 1990s there were significant increases in profit-related pay in the manufacturing sector that brought its overall extent up to the level in the private services sector. Profit-related pay also increased in foreign-owned workplaces and in a small number of publicly owned establishments in the commercial sector. In 1980, 13 per cent of all workplaces in industry and commerce had employees who were participating in a share ownership scheme. This figure had increased to 22 per cent by 1984, and to 30 per cent in 1990. By 1998, however, the figure had fallen to 24 per cent.

Turning to upward communication channels, the Workplace Surveys revealed an increase in the proportion of workplaces holding a regular meeting (at least once a year) between senior managers and all sections of the workforce, from 34 per cent in 1984 to 49 per cent in 1998. With respect to the existence of problem-solving groups which met at least once a month to discuss aspects of performance, the proportion of all workplaces with such groups increased from 35 per cent in 1990 to 49 per cent in 1998. Briefing groups (team briefing) in which junior managers or frontline managers met at least once a month with all employees for whom they were responsible existed in 1998 in 65 per cent of all workplaces, compared to 48 per cent in 1990 and 36 per cent in 1984. The increase in the use of briefing groups practices during the 1990s was confined solely to the private sector, to workplaces without union representation, and to those without an effective joint consultative committee.

Table 14 shows the provision of employees with information by management over the period 1990 to 1998. It reveals that workplace managers have taken on board the need for increased efforts to inform

Table 14 *The provision of employees or their representatives with information by management 1990–1998*

Information about	Percentage of all workplaces							
	Private manufacturing		Private services		Public sector		All sectors	
	1990	1998	1990	1998	1990	1998	1990	1998
Financial position of the establishment	55	58	51	61	67	83	56	67
Financial position of the enterprise	55	56	58	64	51	62	55	62
Investment plans	48	53	38	50	33	65	39	54
Staffing and manpower plans	52	36	49	58	77	84	57	61
None of the above	23	27	28	19	12	4	22	16

Source: N. Millward, A. Bryson and J. Forth, *All Change at Work?* Routledge, 2000; page 69

employees, in that there has been during the 1990s a marked increase in the number of items of information they disseminate to employees and/or their representatives. Increases in the amount of information provided were most noticeable in the public sector.

> What employee involvement practices operate in your organisation, or one with which you are familiar? How, and why, have the various practices been introduced? Has the distribution of the employee involvement practices changed over time? If it has, why? If it hasn't, why hasn't it?

COMMUNICATIONS AND BRIEFING SYSTEMS

Communication systems

Employee communications involves the provision and exchange of information and instructions which enable an organisation to function effectively and its employees to be properly informed about developments. It covers the information to be provided, the channels (both upwards and downwards) along which it passes and the way it is relayed. Communication is concerned with the interchange of information and ideas within an organisation.

Whatever the size of an organisation and regardless of whether it is unionised or non-unionised, employees only perform at their best if they know their duties, obligations and rights and have an opportunity of making their views known to management on issues that affect them. With the trend towards flatter management structures and the devolution of responsibilities to individuals, it is increasingly important that individual employees have an understanding not only of what they are required to do and why they need to do it, but also have the opportunity to influence what happens to them at work. Marchington *et al* (2001) have shown that companies rate the views of their employees as a critical business issue and are establishing mechanisms for listening to their employees – not because they are being forced to do so but because it seems essential if they are to meet business objectives. These mechanisms engender a two-way dialogue which gives employees the opportunity to influence what happens at work.

Good communication and consultation are central to the management process. All managers have to exchange information with other managers which necessitate lateral or inter-departmental communications. Failure to recognise this need is likely to result in inconsistency of approach or application. The ACAS advisory booklet on *Employee Communications and Consultation* lists the advantages of good employee communications as:

- improved organisational performance – Time spent communicating at the outset of new project or development can minimise subsequent rumour and misunderstanding
- improved management performance and decision-making – Allowing employees to express their views can help managers arrive at sound decisions that are more likely to be accepted by the employees as a whole
- improved employee performance and commitment – Employees will perform better if they are given regular, accurate information about their jobs such as updated technical instructions, targets, deadlines and feedback. Their commitment is also likely to be enhanced if they know what the organisation is trying to achieve and how they as individuals can influence decisions
- greater trust – Discussing issues of common interest and allowing employees an opportunity of expressing their views can engender improved management-employee relations
- increased job satisfaction – Employees are more likely to be motivated if they have a good understanding of their job and how it fits into the organisation as a whole and are actively encouraged to express their views and ideas.

Employee communications strategy

When devising an employee communications strategy, the following questions must be addressed:

- Why should the company communicate?
- What is to be communicated?
- Who are the audience(s)?
- How is communication to be handled?
- Who is responsible?
- How will success be measured?

A variety of communication methods (spoken and written, direct and indirect) are available for use by management. The mix of methods selected will be determined by the size and structure of the organisation. Two main methods of communication can be distinguished. First, there are face-to-face methods that are both direct and swift and they enable discussion, questioning and feedback to take place. However, it is often advantageous to supplement these methods with written materials, especially if the information being conveyed is detailed or complex. The main formal face-to-face methods of communications are:

- group meetings – meetings between managers and the employees for whom they are responsible
- cascade networks – a well-defined procedure for passing information quickly used mainly in large or disparately widespread organisations
- large-scale meetings – meetings that involve all employees in an organisation or at an establishment, with presentations by a director or senior managers; these are a good channel for presenting the organisation's performance or long-term objectives
- inter-departmental briefings – meetings between managers in different departments that encourage a unified approach and reduce the scope for inconsistent decision-making, particularly in larger organisations.

Second, there are written methods. These are most effective where the need for the information is important or permanent, the topic requires detailed explanation, the audience is widespread or large, and there is a need for a permanent record of it. The chief methods of written communications include company handbooks, employee information notes, house journals and newsletters, departmental bulletins, notices and individual letters to employees. Electronic mail is useful for communicating with employees in scattered or isolated locations, and audiovisual aids are particularly useful for explaining technical developments or financial performance.

Communications strategies, policies and techniques need senior management support and they require discipline to follow them through. Industry and commerce are littered with communications schemes that have been introduced with the best of intentions before other matters became priorities and a briefing session or a newsletter was missed. The outcome is the development of cynicism among employees. It is also true that strategies, policies and tools tend not to be effective without the support and interest of staff. Think of it this way:

> If I am not a big enthusiast, preferring to laze around the house at weekends, the existence of a toolbox in the house is unlikely to persuade me to put in a couple of shelves. However, if I am very enthusiastic about DIY and very keen to put up the couple of shelves, the fact that I have no toolbox will not deter me. I will simply borrow or buy a toolbox. It is my enthusiasm that is the driver, not the toolbox ...

Monitoring

It cannot be taken for granted that communications systems are operating effectively, nor can it be assumed that because information is sent it is also received. The communications policy and its associated procedures need regular monitoring and review to ensure that practice matches policy, the desired benefits are accruing, the information is accepted, received and understood, and the management communicators know their roles. Monitoring is largely dependent on feedback from employees through both formal and informal channels, although other indicators include the quality of decision-making by management, the involvement of senior management and the extent of employee co-operation. In monitoring and reviewing an organisation's communication policy, the criteria for assessing its effectiveness are related to the outputs from the operation of the policy. For example, has employee morale improved? Has productivity increased? Is there a greater willingness to accept change on the part of employees and managers? Do the employees have an improved understanding of the company and business generally? Review and monitoring should take place on a regular periodic basis – for example, quarterly or annually – depending on the size of the organisation.

Explain the criteria you would use to assess whether an organisation's communications strategy is operating effectively for management's interests.

Briefing groups

The dangers of the use of such groups, from a management perspective, are that as the information 'cascades' down, it becomes watered down, hedged around with rumour, out of date and imprecise. Many communications policies are less effective than they might be because a lot of information passed down from the top to the bottom of the organisation concentrates on the wider perspective, with the result that the local receivers of the information do not take note of it because it relates to issues which to them are remote and marginal to their interests and concerns.

Of all the communication methods in use, team briefing is perhaps the most systematic in the provision of top-down information. Information cascades down through various management tiers, being conveyed by each immediate supervisor or team leader to a small group of employees, the optimum number being between four and 20. In this way employee queries are answered. This takes place throughout all levels in the organisation, the information eventually being conveyed by supervisors and/or team leaders to shopfloor employees. On each occasion the information received is supplemented by 'local' news of more immediate relevance to those being briefed. Meetings tend to be short but designed to help develop the 'togetherness' of a workgroup, especially where different grades of employees are involved in the team.

Each manager is a member of a briefing group and is also responsible for briefing a team. The system is designed to ensure that all employees from the managing director to the shopfloor are fully informed of matters affecting their work. Leaders of each briefing session prepare their own brief, consisting of information that is relevant and task-related to the employees in the group. The brief is then supplemented with information passed down from higher levels of management. Any employee questions raised which cannot be answered at once are answered in written form within a few days. Briefers from senior management levels are usually encouraged to sit in at briefings being given by more junior managers, while line managers are encouraged to be available to brief the shopfloor employees. The employee relations professional will explain management's view to the employees in a regular and open way, using examples appropriate to each workgroup. Although team briefing is not a consultative process and is basically one-way, question-and-answer sessions can take place to clarify understanding. Feedback from employees is very important.

There are, however, practical problems to be borne in mind in introducing team briefing. First, if the organisation operates on a continuous shiftworking basis, is it technically feasible for team briefings to take place, since the employees are working all the time except for their rest breaks? Second, management has to be confident that it can sustain a flow of relevant and detailed information. Third, if the organisation recognises unions, the management cannot act in such a manner that the union(s) believes management is attempting to undermine its influence. Team briefing is highly unlikely to succeed if the relations between management and the representatives of its employees are distrustful.

Employee attitude surveys

These surveys are an important upward channel of communication from the employees to management. Such surveys are questionnaire surveys of staff on a one-off or regular (say, annual) basis designed to discover their levels of satisfaction/dissatisfaction with particular aspects of work. The 1998 Workplace Employee Relations Survey provides evidence of a steady rise in the use, by employers, of employee attitude surveys. In 1998 45 per cent of workplaces that employed 25 or more people said they had conducted an employee attitude survey within the previous five years. This is a sharp rise from the 17 per cent recorded in the 1990 Workplace Industrial Relations Survey. The increased popularity of employee attitude surveys indicates that they are viewed as an effective tool for assessing both employee morale and commitment.

Management normally uses an employee attitude survey to obtain specific data on employee perceptions of fairness, pay systems, training opportunities and employee awareness of an organisation's business strategy and long-term goals. Employee attitude surveys can:

- provide managers with early warning of issues of concern before they lead to major employee relations difficulties
- help managers make internal comparisons of employee morale and behaviour across a number of departments and sites
- provide employee views on specific personnel/HRM policies, such as the operation of the disciplinary and grievance procedures
- provide data that can be used in problem-solving, planning and decision-making.

Many organisations use the information gained from employee attitude surveys to benchmark employee morale and satisfaction against other organisations. Such information is, however, only likely to be helpful if it is used in conjunction with other information obtained in a different way, and not used in isolation.

Two other important forms of upward communications from employees to management are suggestion schemes and project teams. The former are a formal process established to allow employees to communicate their ideas to management on how working methods, etc, might be improved. Employees are rewarded if their ideas are deemed acceptable for implementation. Such schemes can be electronic or paper-based. In project teams, groups of individual employees are brought together on a regular basis (or an ad hoc basis) to consider issues relating to the organisation of work but also wider questions about the vision and mission of the site. They also examine manufacture excellence or a review of operation.

TASK AND WORK GROUP INVOLVEMENT

The objective of these employee involvement and participation practices is to tap into employees' knowledge of their jobs, either at the individual level or through the mechanism of small groups. The practices are designed to increase the stock of ideas within the organisation, to encourage co-operative relations at work and to justify change. Task-based involvement encourages employees to extend the range and type of tasks they undertake at work. It is probably the most innovative method of employee involvement in that it focuses on the whole job rather than concentrating on a relatively small part of an employee's time at work. Such employee involvement practices include job redesign, job enrichment, teamworking and job enlargement. Job enrichment involves the introduction of more elements of responsibility into the work tasks. Job enlargement centres on increasing the number and diversity of tasks carried out by an individual employee, thereby increasing his or her work experience and skill.

Teamworking is perceived by its advocates as a vehicle for greater task flexibility and co-operation as well as for extending the desire for quality improvement. Geary (1994) has remarked that:

> In its most advanced form teamworking refers to the granting of autonomy to workers by management to design and prepare work schedules, to monitor and control their own work tasks and methods, to be more or less self-managing. There can be considerable flexibility between different skills categories, such that skilled employees do unskilled tasks when required and formerly unskilled employees receive additional training to be able to undertake the more skilled tasks. At the other end of the spectrum, management may merely wish employees of comparable skill to rotate between different tasks on a production line or the integration of maintenance personnel to service a particular group of machines. It may not result in production workers undertaking tasks which were formerly the preserve of craft people or vice versa. Thus, flexibility may be confined within comparable skills groupings. In between, there is likely to be a diversity of practice.

The two most advanced forms of teamworking are semi-autonomous groups and fully autonomous groups. In the latter group, the team members work with one another, having responsibility for the specific product or service, jointly decide how the work is to be done and appoint their own team leader. In 1998, only 3 per cent of the workplaces surveyed in the Workplace Employee Relations Survey corresponded to this model. Semi-autonomous groups are characterised by members working with one another, having responsibility for a specific product or service, and jointly deciding how the work is to be done. In 1998, 35 per cent of workplaces operated teams that approximately corresponded to the model. The 1998 Workplace Employee Relations Survey, however, found that in 54 per cent of the workplaces it surveyed, there were teams where members worked with one another and had responsibility for a specific product or service. In 62 per cent of workplaces there were teams where members only worked with one another and had no responsibility for products or services, for deciding how tasks would be done or for selecting their team leader.

Team size is usually seven to ten, although some teams are much larger. Task flexibility and job rotation can, however, be limited, partly by the sheer range of tasks and partly by the nature of the skills involved. Organisations that operate teamworking arrangements see major training programmes as a necessary accompaniment. Teamworking provides a management with the opportunity to remove and/or amend the role of the supervisor and to appoint team leaders. However, research by Gapper (1990) indicates that management time saved in traditional supervision and control may be more than offset by the need to give support to individuals and groups.

What is the extent of teamworking in your organisation? Why is it that?

Quality circles

A quality circle aims to identify work-related problems that are causing low quality of service or productivity in a section of the workplace, and to recommend solutions to those problems. It provides opportunities for employees to meet on a regular basis (eg once a month, fortnightly) for an hour or so to suggest ways of improving productivity and quality and reducing costs. A quality circle typically involves a small group of employees (usually six to eight) in discussions under the guidance of their supervisor. The members select the issues or problem they wish to address, collect the necessary information and make suggestions to management on ways of overcoming the problem.

In some cases the group is itself given authority to put its proposed solutions into effect, but more often it presents formal recommendations for action, which management then consider whether or not to implement. Quality circles encourage employees to identify not only with the quality of their own work but also with the management objectives of better quality and increased efficiency throughout the organisation. Members of a quality circle are not usually employee representatives but are members of the circle by virtue of their knowledge of the tasks involved in their jobs. They are under no obligation to report back to their colleagues who are not members of the circle.

If quality circles are to be effective, a strong commitment from management is necessary. Management does not supply members to a quality circle but allows time and money for its members to meet and provides the members with basic training in problem-solving and presentational skills. A professional management always treats all recommendations from a circle with an open mind, and if it rejects a proposal will explain the reasons for that decision to the circle. If the organisation recognises trade unions, it would be well advised to consult the workplace representatives on the establishment of quality circles and to encourage their support for a device which, if operated properly, contributes to constructive employee relations.

After a dramatic increase in their number such that by the mid-1980s more than 400 such circles were known to be in existence, the popularity of quality circles declined rapidly. Quality circles fail either at their introduction or after a short period of operation mainly because of a lack of top management commitment, because of the absence of an effective facilitator to promote and sustain the programme, because of management reluctance to bear the costs of operating circles in terms of time – including training time for participants, when employees are inevitably off the job – and/or because of lack of any follow-up action by management on suggestions put forward by the circles.

Total quality management (TQM)

Total quality management programmes derive from a belief that competitive advantage comes from excellent and reliable quality, achieved through the associated welding of more stable and mutual relationships between suppliers and customers. The total quality ethic is a philosophy of business management, the aim of which is to ensure complete customer satisfaction at every stage of production or service provision. Although TQM was initially driven by the demands of external customers, the concept evolved into a more wide-ranging principle to encompass internal operations. TQM programmes are designed to ensure that each level and aspect of the organisation is involved in continuously improving the effectiveness and quality of the work to meet the requirements of both internal and external customers.

Whereas quality issues were traditionally assigned to specific departments, TQM requires that the quality of products and services be the concern of every employee. Quality management offers service management an effective way of organising and increasing employees' responsibility while meeting the interests of employees at every level, offering them an opportunity to become more involved in the decision-making process. The Prudential Assurance Company, for example, claimed in the mid-1990s that TQM had produced many benefits for them, including a reduction of 45 per cent in the average time in dealing with a life assurance claim.

Others (for example, Geary, 1994) have pointed out that TQM places considerable emphasis on enlarging employees' responsibilities, reorganising work and increasing employee involvement in problem-solving activities, and that this search for continuous improvement is a central thrust. He further notes:

The manufacture of quality products, the provision of a quality service and the quest for continuous improvement is the responsibility of all employees, managed and manager alike, and all functions. TQM requires quality to be built into the product and not inspected by a separate quality department. Where employees are not in direct contact with the organisation's customers, they are encouraged to see their colleagues at successive stages of the production process as internal customers. Thus, a central feature of TQM is the internalisation of the rigours of the marketplace within the enterprise.

A second feature of TQM follows on from the first. Because each employee and department is an internal customer to the other, problem-solving necessitates the formation of organisational structures designed to facilitate inter-departmental and inter-functional co-operation. A consequence of this is that problems are best solved by those people to which they are most immediate. Employees are to be encouraged and given the resources to solve problems for themselves. Employees, it is contended, will embrace such job enlargement and undertake activities conducive to an improvement in the organisation's efficiency.

Ramsay (1996) argues that total quality management subsumes quality circles or teamwork arrangements into a more integrated approach and concentrates on stressing change throughout the entire organisational system. It is essentially a top-down management-driven process. If total quality management is to succeed, again top management commitment is essential. Departments have to be persuaded that resistance to integration is self-defeating, and the employees must have it clearly demonstrated to them that total quality management is not a cover for job rationalisation and redundancies. In short, the employees require evidence there is a 'stake' for them in the 'total quality management world' – that is that TQM is superior to their 'present world'.

FINANCIAL PARTICIPATION

Offering employees a direct stake in the ownership and prosperity of the business for which they work is one of the most direct and tangible forms of employee involvement. By giving employees the chance to participate in financial success, employees can acquire and develop a greater sense of identity with the business and an appreciation of the business needs. Employers also benefit. It is argued that a financial stake gives employees increased enthusiasm for the success of the organisation and often for a voice in its operation. In its most developed form employee share ownership means that employees become significant shareholders in the business, or even their own employer.

Financial employee involvement and participation schemes link specific elements of pay and reward to the performance of the unit or the enterprise as a whole. They provide an opportunity for employees to share in the financial success of their employing organisation. The main forms of financial participation are:

- deferred profit-sharing schemes, by which profits are put in a trust fund to acquire shares in the company for employees
- profit-related pay
- employer share ownership plans.

Profit sharing

These schemes aim to increase employee motivation and commitment by giving employees an interest in the overall performance of the enterprise. In this way management hopes to raise employee awareness of the importance of profit to their organisation and to encourage teamworking by demonstrating that rewards accrue from co-operative effort even more than from individual effort. Profit-sharing schemes ensure that employees benefit from the organisation making profits.

However, there are practical problems that must be addressed if profit-sharing schemes are to have the desired effect. A scheme has to contain clearly identifiable links between effort and reward. Individuals must not feel that no matter how hard they work in any year, that effort is not reflected in their share of the company's profits. There is also the issue of whether there is a clearly understood formula for the sharing of any profits so that employees can calculate their share. Profits cannot be assessed quickly enough to secure early movements in pay in response to rapidly changing market conditions. Due account has to be taken of employees or there is a risk of inter-group dissatisfaction in that some employees might believe other groups have received the same profit share payment but have made less effort.

Profit-related pay

Profit-related pay is a mechanism through which employers can reward employees for their contribution to the business. It works by linking a proportion of employees' pay to the profits of the business for which they work. Employees are encouraged in this way to strive for commercial success. Employers who have introduced such schemes argue that as well as helping to create a more motivated and committed workforce, profit-related pay provides greater flexibility in the negotiation of pay settlements.

Share ownership

Share ownership takes financial involvement a step further by giving employees a stake in the ownership of the enterprise. It grants them shareholder rights to participate in decisions confined to shareholders who vote at the annual general meeting. Employee share ownership schemes seek to give individual employees a long-term commitment to the organisation and not just to a short-term financial gain from a sharing of profit. Such schemes are usually linked to profit but the employees' portion is distributed in the form of shares, either directly to each individual or indirectly into a trust which holds the shares on behalf of all employees. Distributing shares to employees involves them in a tax liability that has restricted the development of employee share ownership schemes. One way to avoid this tax liability is an employee share ownership plan (known as an ESOP). Such plans were given a boost when the UK government in the late 1980s provided important tax concessions for investment in such schemes.

In employee share ownership plans the company shares are initially bought, using borrowed money, by a trust representing the employees. They may not be required to put down a cash stake. The transfer of a portion of the company profits to the trust over subsequent years, as laid down in the initial agreement, enables the trust to pay off the loan and to allocate shares to individual employees.

Employee share ownership plans are clearly a means of promoting employee involvement in ownership. They give individual employees democratic control over significant holdings of company shares. They also have limitations. Employees may view the shares as simply a source of income and so lose the thread of the 'shared ownership' concept. Financial participation shares money, and on its own is unlikely to give rise to a greater commitment on the part of the individual employee to the interests of the organisation.

> Do you have any financial participation schemes in your organisation? If you do, why were those particular schemes chosen? To what extent and why are they effective? If your organisation does not have any financial participation schemes, why doesn't it?

REPRESENTATIVE PARTICIPATION

The main form of representative participation is joint consultation, which is a process by which management and employees or their representatives jointly examine and discuss issues of mutual concern. It involves seeking acceptable solutions to problems through a genuine exchange of views and information. Consultation does not remove the right of management to manage – management must still make the final decisions – but it does impose an obligation that the views of employees will be sought and considered before that final decision is taken. Employee communication is concerned with the interchange of information and ideas within an organisation. Consultation goes beyond this and involves management's actively seeking and then taking account of the views of employees before making a decision. It affects the process through which decisions are made in so far as it commits management first to the disclosure of information at an early stage in the decision-making process, and second to take into account the collective views of the employees.

Consultation does not mean that employees' views always have to be acted upon – there may be good practical or financial reasons for not doing so. However, whenever employees' views are rejected, the reasons for rejection should be explained carefully. Equally, where the views and ideas of employees help to improve a decision, due credit and recognition should be given. Making a practice of consulting on issues upon which management has already made a decision is unproductive and engenders suspicion and mistrust about the process among employees.

Consultation requires a free exchange of ideas and views affecting the interests of employees. As such, almost any subject is appropriate for discussion. However, both management and employees may wish to place some limits on the range of subjects open to consultation – because of trade confidences, perhaps, or because they are considered more appropriate for a negotiation forum – but whatever issues are agreed upon as being appropriate for discussion, it is important that they are relevant to the group of employees discussing them. If consultation arrangements are to be effective, discussing trivialities is to be avoided. This is not to say that minor issues may be ignored. Although the subject matters of consultation are for agreement between employer and employees, there are a number of laws and regulations that specifically require an employer to consult with recognised trade unions and other employee representatives. These include:

- The Health and Safety at Work Act 1974 places a duty on employers to consult with safety representatives appointed by an independent recognised trade union.

- The Transfer of Undertakings (Protection of Employment) Regulations 1981 provide for trade unions to be consulted where there is a transfer of a business to which the regulations apply. This consultation must take place with a view to reaching agreement on the measures taken.

- The Trade Union and Labour Relations (Consolidation) Act 1992 requires employers to consult with trade unions when redundancies are proposed. Such consultation must be undertaken by the employer with a view to reaching agreement, and must be about any possibilities of avoiding the dismissals, reducing the numbers to be dismissed and mitigating the consequences of any redundancies.

- The Social Security Pensions Act 1975 requires employers to consult with trade unions on certain matters in relation to the contracting out of the state scheme of an occupational pension scheme.

- The Transnational Information and Consultation of Employees Regulations (2000) permit employee representatives the right to meet central management at least once a year for information and consultation about the progress and prospects of the company on a pan-European basis. These Regulations provide for European Union-wide information and consultation machinery to be established in all organisations with more than 1,000 employees in European Union states and employing more than 150 people in each of two or more of them. A works council (or an alternative body) must be negotiated between corporate representatives and those of employees elected from the various EU countries in which the company has productive capacity.

■ The Information and Consultation Regulations (2004) established a general framework setting out minimum requirements for the right to information and consultation of employees employed in organisations employing 50 employees. Employees have a right to be informed about a company's economic situation, and to be informed and consulted on employment prospects and decisions likely to lead to substantial change in how work is organised and on contractual relations. Information and consultation must take place at the relevant level of management. Employers and employees can agree different procedures from those set out in the Regulations via existing agreements on information and consultation. Employees may withhold information if its disclosure would seriously harm the business. Companies employing 150 or more employees must comply with the regulations by March 2005; those employing 100 or more by March 2007; and those with 50 or more by March 2008. The implications of these Regulations for organisations are considered below.

Joint consultative committees

Joint consultative committees (JCCs) have long been used as a means of employee consultation. They are composed of managers and employee representatives who come together on a regular basis to discuss issues of mutual concern. They usually have a formal constitution which governs their operations. The number of members of a JCC varies depending on the size of the organisation. Management in organisations that operate over a number of different establishments sometimes prefer to consult with employees on a multi-site basis rather than have a consultative committee for each establishment. These are referred to as 'higher-level committees'. The 1998 Workplace Employee Relations Survey reported a higher incidence (56 per cent) of such committees than in previous surveys.

However, as a general rule the size of the committee should be as small as possible still to be consistent with ensuring that all significant employee groups are represented. It is necessary, in order to demonstrate management's commitment to consultation, that the management representatives on the committee include senior managers with authority and standing in the organisation and who attend its meetings regularly.

Every meeting of the JCC should have as its focus a well-prepared agenda, and all members should be given an opportunity of contributing to the agenda before it is circulated. The agenda is normally sent out in advance of the meeting so that representatives have a chance of consulting with their constituents prior to the committee meeting. The JCC must be well chaired if it is to be run effectively. It is important that employee representatives know exactly how much time they will be allowed away from their normal work to undertake their duties as a committee member, and the facilities to which they are entitled. Employee representatives should not lose pay as a result of attending committee meetings. If joint consultation is to be effective, the deliberations of the committee must be reported back to employees as soon as possible. This can be done via briefing groups, news-sheets, noticeboards and the circulation of committee minutes.

In some organisations institutions established to inform and consult with employers have titles other than 'joint consultative committee'. Such alternative titles include 'works council' and 'employee representative council'. In Marks & Spencer, consultation arrangements are referred to as 'business involvement groups'. There is such a group in each store and area of business, and the number of representatives on a group reflects the size of the business unit/area/store. Each group is made up of representatives elected by employees and has a clear remit and support across the business. In addition, there are regional business involvement groups made up of the chairpersons for each local group. They meet periodically to share and debate issues and ideas that have a wider impact on the business. Marks & Spencer sees its system of business involvement groups as an important part of the communication and involvement process, a means of ensuring that employees are up to date with key issues and events, an opportunity for employees to contribute ideas that might improve business performance, and a forum to discuss issues that impact on the employees' working lives. In short, the business involvement group system enables employees to become involved in the way Marks & Spencer develops its business in the future.

Do JCCs exist in your organisation? If so, what forms do they take and are they successful? How could they be improved? If there are no JCCs, what mechanisms are in place to consult with the workforce? Would a JCC be useful? Why/why not?

THE INFORMATION AND CONSULTATION OF EMPLOYEES REGULATIONS

These Regulations give effect to the EU Directive establishing a general framework for informing and consulting employees in the European Community. They came into force on a sliding scale, depending on the number of employees in the organisation. From 23 March 2005 the Regulations apply to undertakings with at least 150 employees. From 23 March 2007 they will apply to undertakings with at least 100 employees. From 23 March 2008 they will apply to undertakings with at least 50 employees. Undertakings employing fewer than 50 employees are exempt from the Regulations. An 'undertaking' means a legal entity such as an individually incorporated company, whereas an 'establishment' is a physical entity such as a factory, plant, office or retail outlet. The UK government decided to apply the Directive to undertakings rather than establishments. When calculating the number of employees for the purposes of these thresholds, the average number employed in each month over the previous 12 months is to be taken. Part-time workers may be counted as half a person, although the employer is under no obligation to accept this.

Negotiated agreements

Requests for information and consultation arrangements

The Regulations require that where employees request the establishment of information and consultation arrangements in their undertakings, the request must be made in writing by 10 per cent of the employees in the undertaking, subject to a minimum of 15 and a maximum of 2,500 employees (see Figure 8 overleaf). The Directive itself, however, gives no guidance on trigger mechanisms. The Regulations do allow two or more requests from different parts of the workforce to be combined. In addition, if the employees making the request wish to remain anonymous, they may submit the request via the Central Arbitration Committee or a qualified independent person. An employer has one month in which to challenge the validity of this request. Grounds for such a challenge can include:

- too few employees have made the request
- the request is not in writing
- the undertaking does not fall within the scope of the Regulations.

If there are any disputes about the validity of the employees' request, the final decision rests with the CAC.

Requests in the case of existing agreements

In the case where a valid request has been made by less than 40 per cent of the workforce, but an agreement providing for information and consultation already exists, the employer may, if he or she wishes, hold a ballot of the workforce to determine whether or not the workforce endorses the request. The ballot should be held as early as practicable but no earlier than 21 days after the request was made. If 40 per cent of the

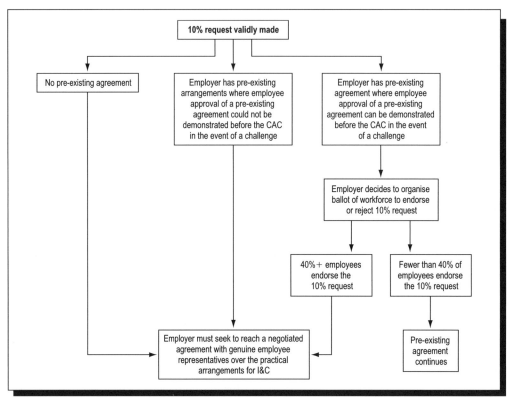

Figure 8   *Procedures for establishing information and consultation agreements*

employees endorse the employee request in the ballot, the employer is obliged to negotiate a new agreement on information and consultation. If less than 40 per cent of employees endorse the request, the employer is under no obligation to negotiate a new agreement. Complaints may be brought to the CAC concerning the fact that there is no valid pre-existing agreement in place or that the ballot requirements have not been met.

The Regulations also permit the employer to take the initiative to enter into negotiations for an information and consultation agreement without waiting for a request from employees. The negotiation process must start within one month of the employer's notifying the workforce of the intent to negotiate an agreement.

The three-year moratorium
There are a number of circumstances in which an employee request (or an employer's notification of an intent to negotiate an agreement) is not valid. These include where there has already been a request which has resulted in a negotiated agreement, or where, in the case of existing agreements, a request was not endorsed by a workforce ballot. Here subsequent requests would not be allowed for a period of three years, unless there are material changes to the organisation or to the structure of the undertaking. This moratorium is intended to avoid repeated request being made by employees and to prevent the employers from unilaterally overturning agreed agreements.

Negotiations
Where a valid request has been made or an employer has notified the workforce that it intends to start negotiations, the employer must take the necessary steps to trigger the process. This includes making

arrangements for employees to appoint or elect negotiating representatives. All employees must be entitled to participate in appointing or electing representatives and must be represented by one of those appointed or elected. Negotiations are required to start within one month of the request/notification and may last for up to six months. This period can be extended without limit by agreement between the negotiating parties. ACAS and other organisations can help the parties in reaching agreements.

The Regulations also set out a number of requirements that negotiated agreements must meet. These are that they must:

- be in writing and dated
- cover all the employees of the undertaking
- set out the circumstances in which employees will be informed and consulted – this may be either directly or via information and consultation representatives
- be signed by and on behalf of the employer
- either be signed by all or a majority of the negotiating representatives and approved in writing by at least 50 per cent of the employees or by 50 per cent of employees who vote in a ballot.

Where the parties do not reach an agreement within the six-month time limit, or any extended period agreed by the parties, standard information and consultation provisions become applicable. The default requirements require the employer to inform/consult elected employee representatives on business developments, employment trends and changes in work organisation or contractual regulations, including redundancies and business transfers. They also require the employer to arrange for a secret ballot to elect one information and consultation representative for every 50 employees or part thereof up to a maximum of 25.

Enforcement

Enforcement of agreements reached under these statutory procedures or of the standard information and consultation provisions where they apply, will be via complaints to the CAC and the Employment Appeals Tribunal. The maximum penalty that can be awarded against employers for non-compliance is £75,000. Employee representatives must not disclose information or documents designated by the employer as confidential. Employers may withhold information or documents if their disclosure could seriously harm or prejudice the undertaking.

Voluntary agreements

The Regulations accept that there is no single static model for information and consultation, no 'one size fits all'. The underlying principle of the Regulations is that UK experience in the area of information and consultation is built up through a wide variety of existing practices all of which should be accommodated. Essentially, individual organisations are encouraged to develop their own arrangements as are tailored to their particular circumstances, by means of voluntary agreements. Accordingly, the general thrust of the Regulations is on voluntarily negotiated agreements. However, in the final analysis if such negotiations fail, employers come under an obligation to inform and consult in accordance with the set of fall-back (default) provisions.

> What do you consider are the implications of the Information and Consultation of Employees Regulations for your organisation?

The Information and Consultation Regulations could potentially change the interface between many employers and their employees substantially, whether they recognise trade unions or not. Employers must make a strategic decision on whether to set up a voluntary arrangement before the Regulations apply to them and to educate management on how such arrangements are expected to operate. Management cannot sit back and do nothing. Existing arrangements can be challenged and the employer find himself or herself obliged to negotiate new arrangements. At the same time, the Regulations contain a procedure whereby existing arrangements can be confirmed. In organisations where no consultation or information arrangements exist, a sensible approach for management would be to negotiate a voluntary agreement, the content of which they would have some control over, rather than have a default agreement imposed upon them.

The Regulations mean that employers will find it more difficult to conduct their relationship with the workforce on a strictly 'need to know' basis instead of talking honestly and openly to employees (or their representatives) about the future of the business. Companies will have to talk to, and consult with, staff in a much more structured manner and in an ongoing way about a broad range of issues, including future employment levels, organisation of work and decisions affecting contractual relations. Employees will be able to seek information from their employers rather than having to be content to receive whatever information management feels is in the best interests of their employees to receive.

A potential problem area for a unionised employer is how the Regulations will impact on collective bargaining machinery. In these situations it is likely that the union(s) will retain their right to negotiate for their members on employment issues. There is also the possibility that the Regulations could strengthen the union's voice at work. In unionised companies, the information and consultation arrangements will see unionised and non-unionised employees sitting alongside each other. This will give an opportunity for the union to have structured contact with the non-unionised sections of the workforce, allowing the former to demonstrate to the latter the logic and benefits of union membership.

THE IMPLEMENTATION OF EMPLOYEE INVOLVEMENT AND PARTICIPATION PRACTICES

General principles

PRINCIPLES UNDERLYING THE IMPLEMENTATION OF EMPLOYEE INVOLVEMENT SCHEMES

- A scheme should be capable of general application to all organisations in which people are employed.
- Arrangements and procedures should be appropriate to the organisation. There is no one best scheme.
- There should be joint employer-employee agreement on participation.
- Where trade unions are recognised, there should be involvement of trade unions.
- Leadership in the scheme should be taken by management.
- The scheme should be inclusive of all employees.
- Education and training should be given to enable participants to fulfil their role in a constructive manner.
- Management must retain the responsibility for business decisions.
- Employees' rights and trade unions' responsibilities may not be prejudiced.

In implementing employee involvement and participation practices, the employee relations business-oriented business performer has to bear a number of basic principles in mind (see box above). Among the most important are:

- The arrangements and procedures should be appropriate to the needs of the organisation.
- Agreement on arrangements should normally be arrived at jointly with the employees.
- The arrangements should involve trade unions where they are recognised by the organisation.
- The lead in establishing, operating and reviewing of arrangements should be taken by management.
- All employees in the organisation should be covered by the arrangements.
- Education and training should be provided to enable those participating in the arrangements to perform effectively.
- Management should retain full responsibility for business decisions.
- Employees' rights and trade unions' responsibilities should not be prejudiced.

The needs of the organisation

The employee involvement and participation practices selected by management should be compatible with the characteristics of the organisation, including the nature of its activities, structure, technology and history. Processes and structures appropriate to older industries will not necessarily match the needs of newer organisations formed in a different social, industrial and commercial context. There is no one way of implementing employee involvement and participation practices, and the sole guiding principle should be that the practices proposed for introduction are compatible with the organisation's circumstances. It is not essential, for example, to introduce employee involvement and participation practices to help improve product and/or service delivery quality if the organisation operates in a product market where competitive advantages rests with price and not the quality and reliability of the product.

Joint agreement

Employee involvement and participation arrangements in organisations are best developed by joint agreement between management and the employees. If arrangements are introduced on a jointly agreed basis, employees have some ownership of them and have a greater commitment to ensuring the success of the schemes. If management imposes the arrangements, the employees have no ownership of them and therefore no stake in ensuring their success. Joint agreement by management and employees means joint commitment to operate the arrangements in good faith and as intended. Both parties have an interest in ensuring that they succeed. It is something they have jointly created. In addition, employees see advantages in their representatives being involved in the management decision-making processes, if for no other reason than to act as the custodians of their interests and to guarantee management accountability. Employees desire that all levels of management take notice of their views and concerns.

It makes sense on the basis of the joint agreement/joint commitment argument that good practice in introducing employee involvement and participation schemes into organisations where trade unions are recognised is that union representatives be involved in deciding the appropriate arrangements and in their operation. This will reassure the trade unions that management's real agenda is not to undermine their influence. In initiating the necessary action to implement effective schemes, the lead must come from management. Employee involvement and participation will not occur or develop of their own accord.

Training and development

Two other key principles are that opportunities be available for all employees, including managers, to participate in employee involvement and participation schemes, and that appropriate training and education be provided for such participants. The former principle involves all employees having the confidence that their views (which are being actively sought) will be taken into account by management before a final decision is made, and not afterwards. An important consideration in this regard is the quality of relationships between individual employees and their immediate superiors and managers. If the quality of decisions made by management is to be improved, they must gain information by listening to what their employees have to say and by asking them appropriate questions. By the same token, employees require information from employers. Both employees and employers require training in communication, presentational and meeting/chairing skills.

Employee involvement and participation arrangements do not relieve management of their responsibility for making business decisions falling within the area of their own accountability or for communicating such decisions, with relevant background information to the employees. The quality of management business decisions is likely to be improved if, before a final decision is made, the views of the workforce are taken into account. However, the employees do not have a veto on management decisions. The prerogative to make business decisions continues to remain with management.

Selecting the practices

Context

There is no single model for the successful implementation of employee involvement and participation practices. Many considerations have to be taken into account by management in deciding which practice(s) to select (see box below). Individual organisations have to develop and adapt arrangements to fit their own needs. These can vary over time as the organisation's size, structure and activities change. There is no single blueprint for success.

FACTORS TO BE CONSIDERED IN IMPLEMENTING APPROPRIATE EMPLOYEE INVOLVEMENT AND PARTICIPATION PRACTICES FOR AN ORGANISATION

Context
- The practices should be introduced as part of a coherent and consistent strategy.
- The practices should preferably not be introduced as 'crisis management'.

Single v multiple arrangements
- The mix can vary.
- A greater mix does not necessarily mean a greater quality of arrangements.

Integration
- There should be integration between the mix of arrangements (horizontal integration).
- There should be integration with the strategic objectives of the organisation as a whole (vertical integration).

Success elsewhere
- Why have such practices been successful elsewhere?
- Could they be transplanted successfully elsewhere?

Legal

- Transnational Information and Consultation Regulations (2000)
- Information and Consultation Regulations (2004)

Good employee relations

- Good employee relations is a necessary precondition.

Commitment by top management

- Top management must demonstrate a belief in employee involvement and participation schemes.

Resources

- Monitor and review arrangements.

Consideration has to be given to the context in which the arrangements will be introduced and operated. If they are to be introduced as part of a coherent and consistent strategy to improve the performance of the enterprise, the proposed arrangements should be the result of a full evaluation of all the possible practices. On the other hand, if they are being introduced to deal with a crisis situation, then it is likely that the arrangements selected will have been ill-thought out and possibly rationalised on the flimsy basis that the proposed employee involvement and participation arrangements have been successfully implemented in other organisations. Without any detailed assessment and evaluation, the management will be assuming that the arrangements can be transplanted successfully into their own organisation. Arrangements introduced without proper analysis and evaluation are unlikely to be successful or to provide management with the advantages that might accrue from the implementation of employee involvement and participation schemes.

A multiplicity of arrangements

Research by Marchington *et al* (1993) into the operation of employee involvement and participation practices revealed that single measures designed to enhance employee commitment to the organisation are much less likely to succeed than the existence of a multiplicity of practices. Nevertheless, whatever the mix of employee involvement and participation practices adopted, they must be appropriate to the organisation's needs as revealed by a thorough assessment and evaluation. Marchington *et al* found, for example, that in some small companies the mix of employee involvement arrangements was no more than one or two different practices, whereas in some larger manufacturing organisations there were as many as eight or nine different schemes for enhancing employee involvement and participation. However, they warn, it is dangerous to assume that the greater the number of employee involvement and participation arrangements an organisation introduces, the greater will be their overall quality. They point out that multiple techniques can lead to potentially conflicting pressures and confusions or communication overload for the staff subject to these arrangements.

Integration

If a multiplicity of different employee involvement and participation schemes is appropriate then not only must they integrate with each other (horizontal integration) but they must be integrated with the strategic objectives of the organisation as a whole (vertical integration). This may require schemes to be customised so that they are relevant and appropriate for the organisation's needs and practices (see below). Since a wide range of employee involvement and participation practices are available to organisations, giving careful consideration to all of them before attempting to implement them makes common sense. If employee involvement and participation arrangements are to make an impact integration with business objectives and consistency with other management practices is essential.

Success elsewhere

Just because employee involvement practices have proved to be successful in one organisation, there is no guarantee they will work as successfully in another organisation which is operating in a quite different context. Copying those arrangements that are perceived to be successful elsewhere is a poor basis for selection. A full analysis and investigation of their appropriateness to another organisation is essential. Information is required on what factors made them successful *in that organisation*. Do these factors exist in 'copying' organisations? Are there factors at one organisation that would prevent the practice from being successfully transplanted in another organisation?

Legal requirements

The business-oriented 'thinking performer' personnel professional must also in implementing employee involvement and participation schemes comply with legal requirements surrounding such practices. This can sometimes be a secondary consideration for the thinking performer since compliance does not give rise to competitive advantage. However, not to comply with legal requirements can give rise to competitive dis-advantage. The major pieces of legislation covering employee involvement and participation schemes have been outlined above and need not be repeated here.

Good employee relations

Employee involvement schemes are more likely to be introduced successfully where there is a willing-ness on the part of both management and employees to be open in their attitude and behaviour. Employee commitment will not be gained in an atmosphere of lack of trust and motivation. Schemes cannot operate effectively in a background of disputes and confrontation. Insufficient motivation on the part of management and employees to make involvement and participation practices work, or insufficient mutual trust to allow them to work, is more likely to be the cause of their failure than the substance of the practices. If management introduces employee involvement and participation schemes but shortly afterwards changes its style to one that is less open and participative, the employees are likely to regard this behaviour as an attempt by management to undermine the schemes. Employee scepticism towards the employee involvement and participation practices under which they work will emerge and the schemes will be less effective.

Good employee relations is thus a necessary precondition for the effective implementation of employee involvement and participation schemes. An open style of management in which employee support for proposed action is gained by consent, and not by coercion, is essential. However, by itself a good employee relations environment is not a sufficient condition for the successful implementation and operation of involvement and participation schemes. It also requires unquestioning commitment from top management.

Commitment by top management

This is a key condition but again is not sufficient on its own to deliver involvement and participation schemes that operate effectively. Such schemes are unlikely, however, to be effective unless top man-agement, by their own behaviour, demonstrate a belief in such schemes. Top management's commit-ment requires not only to be felt positively but also to be seen by employees. All managers should accept the value of employee involvement and participation schemes and not give the impression they are supporting a mere 'fad' in management practice or are speaking rhetoric behind which there is no substance. Whereas a good committee structure may be important for some involvement and partici-pation schemes to be effective, it is totally irrelevant if individual managers are not committed to the schemes' success. Support for introducing employee involvement and participation schemes requires to be secured throughout the whole management structure. If management are not committed to their success, employees will view the arrangements as 'tokenism' and disregard attempts to gain their commitment, loyalty and support.

If managers wish employee involvement schemes to succeed, there can be no loss of momentum following the initial enthusiasm at their introduction. Management commitment has to last longer than just the introduction of schemes, since many are costly in management time if they are not run properly. Nothing destroys employee involvement and participation initiatives more quickly than management action that is inconsistent with the philosophy of worker empowerment. This is particularly so when management's behaviour strongly suggests to the employees that they really consider employee involvement and participation of little significance and something that can be quickly dropped when there is short-term production/service provision pressure to meet the customers' needs. Care must be exercised by management in deciding the timing of meetings. If they are scheduled late on a Friday afternoon and there is, for example, little opportunity to explore issues in sufficient depth, employees will question management's commitment to employee involvement initiatives as a means of improving management decision-making. The same applies if employees feel that their views do not really count since their contributions are dismissed without serious examination.

Two important causes of failure of employee involvement and participation practices are the attitudes of middle and lower managers to such schemes and what Marchington et al (1993) call the 'lack of continuity caused by the dynamic career patterns of managers who are the driving force behind the schemes'. Middle and frontline management often lack commitment to, and fail to support the development of, employee involvement and participation initiatives. Some regard them as mechanisms by which senior/top managers 'pander' to the employees and which at the same time undermine frontline manager authority over employees. They perceive top management's support for the continuation of employee involvement and participation practices as being 'soft' on employees, who they perceive as only too pleased to be paid while not working, and who, as a result, will always have issues they want to discuss with employers.

Frequently in large multi-plant/product firms, senior managers expect to stay at an establishment only for a short period of time, and their duration is regarded as part of their development package en route to senior management positions. Marchington et al refer to this type of character as the 'mobile champion', reflecting a picture of the manager who introduces a scheme then moves on to other duties, generally at another site, or to employment elsewhere. His or her successor often has different priorities and the employee involvement initiatives that were the baby of the predecessor lapse because of operational difficulties or because the successor expects no praise from his/her senior managers for administering another individual's creation.

The introduction of employee involvement and participation arrangements on the basis of fashion and fad will quickly create feelings of disillusionment among employees and a suspicion that management has no real focus to its current and future activities. However, a management committed to the introduction and successful operation of employee involvement initiatives is highly unlikely to select arrangements on the basis of fad over what is appropriate to the organisation's commercial and business needs. Proper analysis of the objectives desired from any employee involvement and participation arrangements before their introduction prevents any possible confusion or conflict between the different practices introduced. This is particularly important when the organisation is introducing a multiplicity of practices. Rather than just select any scheme, it can be helpful if management give extremely careful consideration over how they will apply and modify any schemes introduced to the needs of the workplace. Schemes that are 'customised' (see above) offer better prospects for success than those that are lifted down from the shelf and which may clash with production or service provision considerations.

An all too common mistake by management in introducing involvement and participation scheme initiatives is to become seduced by the prevalence of public relations accounts into believing that any scheme(s) introduced will be a panacea to solve all their product market problems. The impact of employee involvement and participation in securing a positive change in employee attitudes and behaviour is less profound and permanent than is often claimed if the schemes selected turn out to be inappropriate to that organisation's needs. An inappropriate choice of systems is most noticeable, Marchington *et al* (1993) claim, among companies which bring in consultants to advise them on how to implement a new scheme and do so without establishing the relevance or purpose of the scheme. A company might decide, for example, to introduce a system of monthly team briefings. However, it is a waste of time to do so without having assessed whether there will be sufficient information to sustain it on that basis, or whether the frontline manager has the necessary skills or motivation to make it work. This difficult problem becomes further complicated when different management functions or levels in the management structure have a responsibility for introducing employee involvement initiatives, often at the same time and with conflicting objectives. It is a situation particularly current in service sector companies where the issue of customer care often falls within the province of both the personnel and the marketing departments.

A management fully committed to the successful operation of employee involvement and participation practices is going a long way to ensure that those participating in such practices have access to a free flow of information to permit them to operate effectively. This flow of information is most effective if it is up, down and across the organisation. A ready willingness to listen, evaluate and act on views expressed by employees is a sensible approach. There are many pitfalls into which management can fall with respect to the information it makes available in the workplace to participants in the employee involvement schemes. Management need to strike a balance between providing too little information and providing too much information, or employees can become confused. Managers have to avoid too much 'tell and sell', since this triggers employee mistrust of involvement and participation schemes, especially if most information is bad news and is accompanied by rallying calls for belt-tightening and restraint.

The effective operation of employee involvement and participation practices involves two-way communication. To focus on downwards communication carries the risk that employees and/or their representatives might feel they are only being informed of changes or decisions after the event, rather than before. This may seem an obvious statement, but unfortunately for many managers, common sense is not common practice. A further problem management faces is the tendency for employee involvement and participation schemes once implemented to regress, rather than grow and develop, from their original position with respect to their anticipated objectives. Several employee involvement and participation practices that have been successful in one organisation have come apart in another because in the latter their scope collapsed to the level of 'canteen tea discussions'. When the subjects discussed become non-controversial or less interesting, employee indifference – if not scepticism – develops. So despite the fact that employees are the principal objects and recipients of many employee involvement and participation practices, this is potentially the most common cause of failure. A management fully committed to involvement and participation initiatives, introducing it for the right reasons and having selected the schemes appropriate for its business objectives is unlikely to provide opportunities for employee scepticism to arise.

A professional management is motivated to ensure that involvement and participation schemes do not become ineffective because their operation produces adverse impacts on the workings of other employee relations institutions in the organisation. Some of the most successful involvement and participation practices have been established in unionised companies with the joint involvement of management and unions. In contrast, arrangements set up independently of trade unions, where they are recognised and are fully representative of their members' views, have often led to difficulties. This can happen because unions – especially those that are weakly organised – regard the introduction of an independent system of employee involvement as an attempt to bypass them and to undermine their relationship with their members. In strongly unionised organisations employee involvement and participation practices are unlikely to be used to undermine the normal bargaining process with the unions. Attempts to bypass or undermine established trade unions channels are likely to backfire and founder on union opposition taken to the point of withdrawal – for example, a refusal to sit at the same table as non-unionists. In non-union companies, the danger that employee involvement schemes may adversely affect other employee relations institutions is less likely to be a potential hazard for management.

A management committed to the effective operation of employee involvement and participation schemes will adopt an open and participative style of management, select appropriate schemes tailored to the organisation's needs, ensure that there is a full flow of information up, down and across the organisation, and will commit the necessary resources in terms of time, finances, people and equipment to support the operation of the employee involvement and participation schemes.

> Is the management in your organisation fully committed to the successful operation of the employee involvement and participation schemes? Give full reasons for your answer.

Resources

If employee involvement and participation schemes are to operate effectively, resources are required to meet the direct and indirect costs (time lost, production/service foregone, meetings, training, paid leave, etc) associated with introducing, operating and monitoring them. An uncommitted management is likely to regard them as a cost without any benefit and to seek to ensure that there is insufficient business to be discussed by those participating in the schemes. The business-oriented 'thinking performer' employee relations professional has an obligation to persuade his or her colleagues to view employee involvement and participation practices that operate in the organisation in a positive light and to demonstrate to them the value the practices add to the business if they are embraced fully by all levels and functions of management.

The effectiveness of employee involvement practices is often diminished by a lack of skills or knowledge on the part of the participants. It is important for both managers and employees to be provided with training in the skills required to manage employee involvement and participation practices effectively. This involves acquiring and developing the skills of chairing meetings so that employees keep to the agenda and put forward suggestions that are appropriate to the subject matter under discussion. Managers also require training in presentational skills to present information by word of mouth or in writing and by the use of visual aids. In addition, they require interviewing skills to question employees to gain information and/or to seek clarification of employee views. Listening skills are essential, for consultation involves management's listening to what the employees have to say. In participating in employee involvement and participation practices, managers should endeavour to limit their contributions and allow the employees to do most of the talking. By listening, employers acquire additional information. Managers also require the skills of negotiation to gain the commitment of their managerial colleagues at all levels, and in all functions, and of the workforce to the effective operation of employee involvement and participation mechanisms. If the organisation's management does provide training for its managers and employees to prepare them to participate in employee involvement practices, it is sound business sense periodically to evaluate the effectiveness of the training provided.

Spending resources on training for all involved, in the operation of employee involvement and participation practices, represents an investment by management. It demonstrates openly to all concerned their commitment to the schemes. To do otherwise invites employee disillusionment with the schemes. A serious and continuing commitment to employee involvement and participation practices is not easy to achieve and requires significant support from the highest levels of management. The gaining of employee commitment, via employee participation and involvement initiatives, is a time-consuming process. It is much easier to undermine the operation of the schemes than to continue them. Financial resources are necessary to ensure that training is executed effectively and efficiently, and that sufficient time – balanced against production and customer service needs – is set aside for joint consultation meetings, briefing groups and regular management walkabouts.

Management must be aware of the potential problems that face employees working under involvement and participation arrangements. For example, employees may lack knowledge of the subjects under discussion and may have problems coping with the social situation of rubbing shoulders with top management. They may also experience undue pressure from their constituents who have an unreal expectation as to what employee involvement and participation initiatives can achieve in protecting and advancing the interests of the employees. A business-oriented 'thinking performer' employee relations professional assists employee representatives and individual employees to overcome these problems by providing the necessary facilities for them to keep communication channels open between themselves and their constituents. It will add little value to an organisation committed to the successful operation of employee involvement and participation practices to have employee representatives who are unable to represent their members or report back to them, or to have union representatives that suspect management is really opposed to their activities.

Monitoring and review arrangements

The establishment of mechanisms for the regular monitoring and reviewing of the operation of employee involvement and participation practices is essential. Monitoring is a means of assessing whether the schemes are producing the desired outputs of improved efficiency, productivity, quality of service, a greater willingness on the part of employees to accept change, etc. The effectiveness of employee involvement and participation practices is measured against the outputs of their operation in terms of contributing to the achievement of the overall objectives of the organisation.

Assessing effectiveness in this way avoids the simple acceptance by management and employees of a public relations story describing the alleged success of the operation of one group of employee involvement practices. Nevertheless, it is not easy to quantify the contribution of employee involvement and participation practices to the achievement of corporate objectives (see below). There are problems, inter alia, of identifying appropriate benchmarks and isolating the influence of other factors.

The results of any monitoring exercise are best discussed with employee representatives and, where appropriate, recognised trade unions. If the monitoring process exposes weaknesses, remedial action can be taken. Regular monitoring and review also enables an organisation to assess the cost-effectiveness of its employee involvement and participation schemes.

HIGH-PERFORMANCE WORKPLACES

If an organisation implements employee involvement and participation schemes, what does contemporary research and organisational practice tell us about the expected outcome? The potential rewards claim to be substantial. Many organisations have publicised the benefits of the introduction of such schemes. An Industrial Relations Services Survey (1999) of 49 organisations' experiences with employee involvement and participation practices over the period 1992 to 1999 reported that:

■ Around three quarters believed it had enhanced employee commitment and motivation.
■ A similar number considered that their employee relations had improved.

- Approximately six in ten said the quality of products manufactured had improved.

- Over half claimed there had been advances in labour productivity.

- Just under a half believed that their employees' job satisfaction had increased.

- The same proportion claimed that their organisational profits or performance had increased.

- One third said that involving employees had lowered absence rates.

- Just under 30 per cent believed switching to more participative working arrangements had improved their capacity to attract and retain employees.

The Department of Trade and Industry publication *High-Performance Workplaces: Informing and consulting employees* (2003) reported a round-table response of employer and employee representative organisations to the benefit of information and consultation arrangements (see DTI, 2002). At a general level, many employers' response was that commitment, motivation and enthusiasm were the outcome of investing in and valuing the workforce. From that, it was argued, came a sense of shared purpose, ownership and values and a shared interest in the success of the business. The employers also contended that a major ingredient of the success of information and consultation machinery was mutual trust and respect between management and the workforce, and a clear understanding of what was expected from employees. In short, their view was that if the people were not on side, the business plan could not be delivered. Information and consultation was seen by many participants in the round-table discussion as a catalyst for the development of innovative workplace processes and practices in that they helped establish trust and thereby facilitated cultural change. Some respondents stressed the importance of two-way communications – that there was more to it than simply keeping staff informed of what was going on: the decision-making itself could be improved through a process of genuine dialogue in which minds could be changed.

Participants in the discussion were in agreement that there were benefits both to the employees themselves and to the business they worked for in informing and consulting staff. The benefits for employees were said to stem from their having a greater say in the way the business was run. This was viewed as having direct benefits in terms of a better and safer working environment, improved work organisation and working conditions, and better training. By helping staff to feel valued and involved, it was hypothesised, information and consultation machinery could lead to higher employee morale and motivation. In turn, this could lead to fewer recruitment problems, less absenteeism, lower staff turnover, a willingness to take on responsibility and, if necessary, an acceptance of or ability to adapt to changes, whether in ways of working or as a result of larger-scale reorganisation.

Many participants in the DTI round-table discussion believed the benefits of information and consultation for business included improved communications across the organisation, access to a wider pool of knowledge, experience and ideas, staff who better understood what they were doing and how it fitted into the overall business, and a greater responsiveness and less resistance to change. Many respondents accepted that there was a link between information and consultation and improved productivity. Some saw a direct link – for example, employees were perceived to be more responsive to customer demands as a result of information and consultation arrangements. Others considered that better company decisions could be made by tapping into the knowledge and ideas of the wider workforce. Some business organisations, however, urged caution in that there are costs as well as benefits to business – for example, too much consultation can introduce delays and confusion into decision-making, or informing and consulting too early over possible job losses could create uncertainty and hit morale amongst the workforce.

High-performance work systems are said to yield performance levels above those associated with more traditional workplace and employee relations practices (Godard, 2004). According to proponents, these practices achieve this largely by enabling and motivating workers to develop, share and apply their knowledge and skills more fully than do traditional practices, with positive implications for the quality of jobs as well as for performance. In the employee relations literature there are many who argue that the implementation of high-performance systems also create opportunities for union renewal, enabling unions to discard their traditional adversarial role in favour of a new partnership one. As Godard (2004) says:

> Thus the high performance paradigm is best practice not only for employers but also for workers, and, potentially, for their unions ...

A wide variety of practices are associated with high-performance workplaces. To gain the improved productivity over traditional work practices, innovative human resource management practices have to be introduced in certain combinations or 'bundles'. These practices then have an impact on employees – and it is, in large part at least, through this impact that improvements in organisational performance are realised. A high-performance work system strategy entails management ceding a degree of control to employees and introducing a range of progressive methods which increase employee welfare.

High-performance work systems fall into two broad types of human resource practices. The first is often referred to as alternative work practices, and includes autonomous and semi-autonomous work teams, job enrichment, job rotation and participatory practices such as quality circles, problem-solving groups, briefing groups, attitude surveys, profit-sharing schemes, joint consultation machinery and employee share ownership. The second group of practices is referred to as high-commitment employment practices and includes high-quality selection, recruitment and training systems, performance appraisal, job security, Investors in People accreditation and single status. Most supporters of high-performance work systems argue that these practices when successfully implemented are of universal benefit to employers. A general assumption is that the productivity/performance benefit over more traditional employee relations management practices increases with the number of practices adopted. High-performance workplaces are said to gain competitive advantage primarily through the high performance of people stemming from the implementation of a number of different but complementary human resource management practices.

There is, however, a general recognition in contemporary research findings that there is no single template for creating a high-performance workplace. The introduction of the various human resource management practices is not enough by itself. Many other factors are important. They include:

- good leadership
- clear vision
- a commitment to continuous improvement
- a culture that encourages innovation
- capital investment
- customer focus
- a recognition that change is inevitable and must be embraced
- taking a long-term strategy view of where the organisation is going.

The relative importance of these and other factors differs between organisations depending on their individual circumstances, but whatever the mix it is important to be consistent in pursuing them and to keep reinforcing the approach.

Godard (2004), however, argues that the view that high-performance work systems yield superior performance outcomes may be unwarranted, and that their implications for both workers and unions are at best uncertain. Ramsay et al (2000) challenge the view that the superior performance resulting from the implementation of high-performance work practices operates through the incentive and motivation effects captured as 'high-commitment' or 'high-involvement' employee outcomes. They examine an alternative explanation of the relative better performance of high-performance work systems, postulating that the gains arise from work intensification, offloading of task controls and increased job strain. Using data from the Workplace Employee Relations Survey of 1998 they tested models based on high-performance work systems and labour process approaches. They conclude:

> However, the widely held assumption that positive outcomes from HPWS flow via positive employee outcomes has been shown to be highly questionable. Nor do our results suggest we should accept the simple counter-argument that gains to management always come at the expense for labour of degradation of work. On the basis of our analysis, this assumption is no more tenable than that of orthodox theories of HPWS ...

They explain their findings of no adequate explanation for the outcomes of the implementation of high-performance work systems, inter alia, in terms of the limitations of the WERS 1998 data, suggesting that the statistical models of the relationship between high-performance work practices and organisational outcome are perhaps too simple to capture the complex reality of the implementation and operation of such practices.

SUMMARY

- By the introduction of employee involvement initiatives, management seeks to gain consent from its employees for its proposed actions on the basis of commitment rather than control.

- Employee involvement and participation covers a wide range of practices designed to increase employee information about the organisation and thereby to produce a committed workforce.

- It is management, however, who make the final decision as to whether employees are to be involved, or to participate in management decision-making.

- Employee involvement and participation practices are designed to change the attitudes of employees, enhance their business awareness, improve their motivation and enhance their influence in the business.

- Employee involvement and participation practices can be direct (communications, problem-solving groups and financial participation) or indirect (forum of employee representatives).

- The incidence of employee involvement initiatives has risen as the frequency of collective bargaining has fallen.

- In implementing employee involvement practices, a number of general principles apply – the needs of the organisation, the provision of education and training, the multiplicity of arrangements, top management commitment and adequate resources.

- Important initiatives on employee involvement and participation requirements have come from the European Union, in the National Information and Consultative Directive (2000). This has potentially far-reaching implications for all organisations.

- Employee communications mechanisms involve the provision and exchange of information and instructions, which enable an organisation to function effectively and its employees to be properly informed about developments.

- Task and work group involvement schemes encourage employees to extend the range and types of tasks they undertake at work, and teamworking is the best example of such schemes.

- Total quality management is designed to ensure continuous improvement of the effectiveness and quality of the work to meet the requirements of customers.

- Financial participation schemes (profit-related pay/share ownership, etc) enable employees to acquire and develop a greater identity with the business and its needs.

■ The main form of representative participation is joint consultation, which is a process by which management and employees (or their representatives) jointly discuss issues of mutual concern.

■ The introduction of employee involvement and participation schemes with sophisticated HR practices is said to produce high-performing workplaces. Such workplaces are more productive and efficient than workplaces managed by more traditional employee relations practices. Contemporary research, however, suggests that this view may be overstated.

FURTHER READING

ADVISORY, CONCILIATION AND ARBITRATION SERVICE (1995) *Employee Communications and Consultation*.

BEAUMONT P. B. and HUNTER L. C. (2003) *Information and Consultation: From compliance to performance*. London, Chartered Institute of Personnel and Development.

DEPARTMENT OF TRADE AND INDUSTRY (2002) *High-Performance Workplaces: The role of employee involvement in a modern economy*.

DEPARTMENT OF TRADE AND INDUSTRY (2003) *High-Performance Workplaces: Informing and consulting employees*.

GAPPER J. (1990) At the end of the honeymoon, *Financial Times*, 10 January.

GEARY J. (1994) Task participation: employees' participation enabled or constrained?, in K. Sissons (ed.) *Personnel Management*, 2nd edn. Oxford, Blackwell.

GODARD J. (2004) A critical assessment of the high-performance paradigm, *British Journal of Industrial Relations*, 42 (2).

INDUSTRIAL RELATIONS SERVICES (1999) Trends in employee involvement, *Employment Trends*, No.683, July.

MARCHINGTON M., WILKINSON A. and ACKERS P. (1993) Waving or drowning in participation?, *Personnel Management*, March.

MARCHINGTON M., GOODMAN J., WILKINSON A. and ACKERS P. (1992) *New Developments in Employee Involvement*, Employment Department Research Series, Employment Department Publication, No.2.

MARCHINGTON M., WILKINSON A., ACKERS P. and DUNDON T. (2001) *Management Choice and Employee Voice*. London, Chartered Institute of Personnel and Development.

RAMSAY H. (1996) Involvement, empowerment and commitment, in B. Towers (ed.) *The Handbook of Human Resource Management*, 2nd edn. Oxford, Blackwell.

RAMSAY H., SCHOLARIOS D. and HARLEY B. (2000) Employees and high-performance work systems: testing inside the black box, *British Journal of Industrial Relations*, 38 (4).

WALTON R. E. (1985) From control to commitment in the workplace, *Harvard Business Review*, March–April.

WILKINSON A. (2001) Employment, in T. Redman and A. Wilkinson (eds) *Contemporary Human Resource Management: Text and cases*. London, Financial Times/Prentice-Hall.

Other employee relations processes

CHAPTER OBJECTIVES

When you have completed this chapter you should be aware of and able to describe:

■ the main theoretical approaches to collective bargaining

■ the dimensions of collective bargaining in terms of its coverage, scope and level

■ the main types of bargaining arrangements – for example, single table, multi-union

■ the main advantages and disadvantages to employers of partnership agreements

■ the importance of collective bargaining as a pay determination mechanism

■ trends in collective industrial conflict in the UK

■ how to justify the use by employers of conciliation, mediation and arbitration to resolve disputes

■ the processes of conciliation, mediation and arbitration

■ the strategies and policies a management might adopt to minimise the likely effects of the imposition of industrial sanctions against their organisation.

INTRODUCTION

This chapter begins by analysing the employee relations process that is collective bargaining. Second, it examines the options available to a management should it become involved in a collective dispute with its employees. This entails looking at the operation of such conflict resolution mechanisms as disputes procedures, and of such third-party intervention employee relations processes as arbitration, mediation and conciliation. Third, the chapter considers the extent of collective conflict in the UK and possible strategies and policies a management might implement, if a dispute cannot be resolved, to minimise the likely disruption to the organisation should the employees decide to impose industrial sanctions.

COLLECTIVE BARGAINING

Theoretical approaches

The major theoretical approaches to collective bargaining are those of:

■ the Webbs, who in their classic work *Industrial Democracy*, published in 1902, regarded collective bargaining as an economic institution

■ Alan Flanders, who in his classic article entitled 'Collective bargaining: a theoretical analysis' in the *British Journal of Industrial Relations*, November 1968, viewed collective bargaining as a political institution

■ Neil Chamberlain, in his classic 1951 book entitled *Collective Bargaining*. This work produced a generic definition of the institution encompassing twentieth-century developments in its character

- neo-classical economic theory, which sees the effects of collective bargaining as increased unemployment and worker poverty.

The Webbs

For the Webbs, collective bargaining was one of three methods by which trade unions sought to maintain and improve the living standards of their members. It was perceived as an alternative to the methods of mutual insurance (ie providing their members with various benefits such as unemployment, strike and sickness payments) and legal enactment (ie pressing for legislation which favoured their interests). The Webbs did not provide a definition of collective bargaining, arguing that it could best be understood by a number of examples. They put forward the following comparison by way of explanation:

> In organised trades, the individual workman, applying for a job, accepts or refuses the terms offered by the employer without communication with his fellow workmen and without any other consideration than the exigencies of his own position. For the sale of his labour, he makes with the employer a strictly individual bargain. But if a group of workmen concert together and send representatives to conduct the bargaining on behalf of the whole body, the position is at once changed. Instead of the employer making a series of separate contracts with isolated individuals, he meets with a collective will, and settles, in a single agreement, the principles upon which, for the time being, all workmen of a particular group, or class, or grade, will be engaged ...

For the Webbs, collective bargaining was exactly what the words imply – a collective equivalent and alternative to individual bargaining. Where employees were willing and able to combine, they preferred it to bargaining as an individual with their employer because it enabled them to secure better terms of employment by controlling competition among themselves. For the Webbs, collective bargaining is an economic institution.

Flanders (1968) was critical of the Webbs' approach. First, they ignored the employers' interest in collective bargaining and assumed that collective bargaining was something forced upon employers against their will by strikes and other union sanctions. Although this may be true in some cases, it is undeniable that some employers do see advantages in engaging in bargaining (see Chapter 2). Second, Flanders argued that the Webbs were not comparing like with like. The individual bargain (agreement) between the employer and the employee, and which is given legal status in the form of an employment contract, provides for an exchange of work for money (wages and other employment conditions). It sets out the conditions of exchange. A collective agreement, however, as Flanders points out, does not commit anyone to buy or sell labour services. Its function is to ensure that when labour services are bought and sold, the employment conditions offered will, at least, match the terms of the agreement. For Flanders, a collective agreement is essentially a body of rules to regulate the labour market, and as he points out, 'This is a feature which has no proper counterpart in individual bargaining.'

Alan Flanders

For Flanders, collective bargaining is viewed as a political institution. It is, for him, a rule-making and rule administration process. The parties to collective bargaining negotiate procedural as well as substantive agreements (see Chapter 1) to regulate their own relationships as distinct from the employment relationship between the individual employee and his or her individual employer. For Flanders, the joint making of procedural rules is very much part of the collective bargaining process, and he therefore regarded everything concerned with avoiding and/or resolving conflicts between the buyers and sellers of labour services – including grievance settlement – as collective bargaining. Flanders, unlike the Webbs, also regarded collective bargaining as involving a power relationship between organisations. He also saw collective bargaining as being distinct from other rule-making processes, such as legislation and third-party intervention in the authorship of collectively bargained rules. Such rules are jointly determined by representatives of employers and employees who, as a result, share responsibility for their content and observance.

Flanders was also critical of the Webbs for ignoring any consideration of the social achievements of collective bargaining. He argued that for those employees on whose behalf a trade union acts in collective bargaining, the impact of its actions extend beyond the securing of economic advancement to the establishment of rights in industry:

- the right to a defined rate of wages
- the right not to have to work longer than a certain number of hours
- the right to be paid for holidays.

The rules of collective bargaining may also regulate issues such as dismissal, discipline, promotion or training. Rules in a collective agreement, by defining rights (and obligations), are also a means of preventing favouritism, nepotism, victimisation and arbitrary discrimination. In negotiating collective agreements, for Flanders, trade unions are acting jointly with employers as private legislators to promote the 'rule of law' in employee relations. Collective bargaining is perceived as an institution freeing employees from being too much at the mercy of the market.

Flanders also considered the Webbs' approach limited in that they envisaged that the only type of conflict to be settled by collective bargaining was economic. They failed to recognise that unions and employers, when meeting collectively to decide the rules to regulate their relationship, are inevitably involved in resolving other types of conflict. Flanders argued that collective bargainers are interested in the distribution of power between themselves as well as the distribution of income, and so the impact of collective bargaining is not confined to labour markets. In collective bargaining there are also non-material interests at stake – for example, law and order, feelings of equity, employment security, status. A further area of non-economic conflict referred to by Flanders was the role of collective agreements in restraining the exercise of managerial authority in deploying, organising and disciplining the workforce. These issues, he pointed out, are often as much conflicts over values as over interests.

Neil Chamberlain

Chamberlain considered that all the various theories surrounding the nature of collective bargaining could be reduced to three:

> They are that collective bargaining is 1) a means of contracting for the sale of labour, 2) a form of industrial governance, and 3) a method of management . . .

He called them respectively the marketing, governmental and managerial theories. His marketing theory viewed collective bargaining as the process which determines on what terms labour will continue to be supplied to a company by its present employees or will be supplied in the future by newly hired workers. This marketing theory is based on the principle that collective bargaining is necessary to redress the balance of bargaining inequality between employers and employees.

The governmental theory accepts the contractual nature of the bargaining relationship but views the collective agreement as a 'constitution' on the basis of which is established an industrial government for the plant, the company or the industry. The principal function of the 'constitution' is:

> to set up organs of government, define and limit them, provide agencies for making, executing and interpreting laws for the industry and the means for their enforcement . . .

The need for some balance of bargaining power is accepted, but that balance is seen as resting firstly on the mutual dependency of the parties, and secondly on the power of each to veto the actions of the other. So the principle underpinning the governmental theory is the sharing of industrial sovereignty. Collective bargaining is a constitutional system for an industry. The union shares sovereignty with management over the workers and, as their representative, uses that power in their interests.

The managerial theory views collective bargaining as a system in which the union joins the company officials in reaching decisions on matters in which both have vital interests. The presence of the union allows the workers, through union representatives, to participate in the determination of the policies which guide and rule their working lives. Collective bargaining by its very nature involves union representatives in decision-making roles. They are 'actually *de facto* managers'. The principle that underpins this managerial theory is that of mutuality. Once the collective agreement has been concluded, its terms cannot be amended or rescinded except by a renegotiation of the agreement. Union representatives alone are powerless to modify its terms. Management (company) representatives are equally devoid of authority to alter the joint agreement. It is subject to change only by mutual agreement of these two groups of representatives. The managerial theory of collective bargaining recognises that the ownership of property does not give unfettered authority to exercise power in industry. Responsibility towards other stakeholders in the business/organisation provides the basis for insisting that managerial authority be shared with their representatives in the manner collective bargaining can achieve.

Chamberlain's three theories are an attempt to produce a 'generic definition' of collective bargaining. In separating these theories he did not consider them sharply distinguished from one another or that they were mutually incompatible alternatives. He claimed that they represent stages of development of the bargaining process itself, they constitute stages of recognition of what collective bargaining is, they represent different conceptions of what the bargaining process should be, and they suggest different emphases on various aspects of collective bargaining. Chamberlain's three theories are useful tools of analysis in examining employee relations problems and useful guides to explaining union-management relationships.

Neo-classical economic theory

The Webbs, Flanders and Chamberlain all viewed collective bargaining as a good and desirable activity in terms of its content, processes and outcomes, and particularly in its social achievements. Neo-classical economic theory, however, sees the outcomes of collective bargaining as undesirable in that they cause unemployment and the existence of low pay in the non-unionised sector of the economy.

Figure 9 opposite represents the unionised sector. The supply of labour curve (SW) is L-shaped showing that the collectively bargained wage rate is the minimum at which the members of the union will supply their labour services. In the initial equilibrium at the collectively bargained wage rate of OW the employer(s) demands OQ quantity of the union's membership. If the demand for labour falls, the demand curve shifts to D_1D_1.

Because of the terms of the collective agreement, the wage rate is inflexible downwards, so employers are now only prepared to employ OQ_1 of the union's membership. Q_1Q members of the union become unemployed. For OQ of its membership to remain employed, the wage rate would have to fall to OW_1. The union is not prepared for this to happen, so the employer adjusts to the change in labour demand by declaring redundancies among unionised members. Neo-classical economists thus argue that the downward inflexibility in wage rates under a collectively bargained system of pay determination causes unemployment.

Figure 10 represents the non-unionised sector. The sector wage is in equilibrium at a wage rate of OW and an employment level of OQ. The Q_1Q unemployed in the unionised sector now seek employment. Being unable to gain employment in the unionised sector, they seek employment in the non-unionised sector. The supply of labour to the unionised sector thus increases to S_1S_1. The effect of this is to reduce

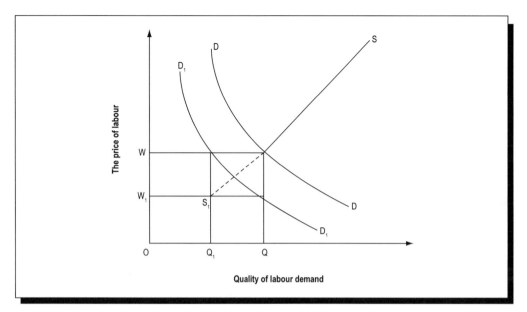

Figure 9   *The unionised sector*

the equilibrium wage rate in the non-unionised sector to OW_1 and to widen the wage differential between the unionised and non-unionised sectors. It is in this way that neo-classical economists argue that collective bargaining causes low pay in the non-unionised sector.

Conditions for collective bargaining

For collective bargaining to exist at any level (see below) four conditions have to be met. First, there must be organisation on the part of the buyers and sellers of labour services (see Chapter 6). Second, there must be a substantive agreement. Third, there must be a procedural agreement (see Chapter 1). Finally, both the buyers and sellers of labour services must be able to impose sanctions (costs) upon each other so that

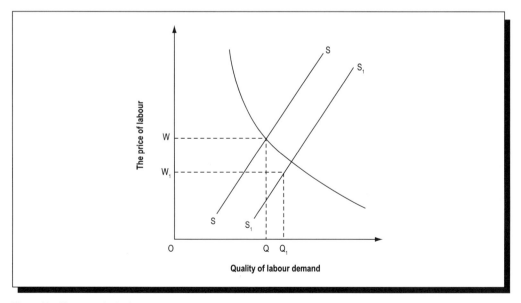

Figure 10   *The non-unionised sector*

they can reassess their positions towards each other in terms of the demands they make of each other (see Chapters 1 and 9).

Coverage

Table 15 shows that the overall level of collective bargaining coverage fell from 70 per cent in 1984 to 54 per cent in 1990, and still further to 40 per cent in 1998. Millward *et al* (2000) show that the fall accelerated in the 1990s, increasing from an annual rate of decline of 2.9 per cent between 1984 and 1990 to an annual rate of fall of 3.3 per cent between 1990 and 1998. The table also shows that whereas in the late 1980s private manufacturing, private services and the public sector experienced similar rates of change, there was a divergence of experiences in the 1990s. Private manufacturing experienced a relatively modest fall from 51 per cent of employees to 46 per cent. Collective bargaining coverage in the public sector declined more rapidly from 78 per cent to 62 per cent. And private sector services witnessed even greater falls – in this sector, the percentage of employees covered by collective bargaining fell by over a third from 33 per cent in 1990 to 21 per cent in 1998: a rate of decline of almost 5 per cent per annum.

Why do you think the coverage of collective bargaining has declined in the last decade? What has happened to collective bargaining coverage in your organisation (or one with which you are familiar)?

Table 15   *Overall collective bargaining coverage, by broad sector and union recognition 1984–1998*

	Percentage of employees covered by collective bargaining			Percentage rate of decline per annum	
	1984	1990	1998	1984–1990	1990–1998
All workplaces	70	54	40	–2.9	–3.3
Broad sector, private manufacturing	64	51	46	–2.6	–1.3
Private services	40	33	21	–2.3	–4.7
Public sector	95	78	62	–2.3	–2.6
Any recognised unions	90	81	69	–1.3	–2.1

Source: *All Change at Work?* Routledge, 2000; page 197

Dimensions of bargaining

The level of bargaining

An important decision for a management which recognises and negotiates with one or more unions centres on the level at which bargaining is to take place. There are a number of bargaining levels available from which to make a strategic choice:

- multi-employer level
- single employer level (ie company level)
- enterprise level
- a combination of all three levels.

Multi-employer bargaining has conventionally combined two levels – bargaining on the establishment of framework terms and conditions at industry level, with bargaining on other matters left to individual companies. The actual distribution of responsibility between the two tiers varies between industries and also changes over time. Company bargaining is where all terms and conditions of employment are negotiated at the central company level. Bargaining at this level enables pay and conditions to be related to the economic circumstances of the company as a whole and provides standardised conditions across the company for similar jobs.

Enterprise bargaining (or plant bargaining) is where terms and conditions are negotiated between management and union representatives at each plant or business unit of the company. Such bargaining tends to be either autonomous to each plant or co-ordinated across all plants. In the former case, each plant has the authority to settle all terms and conditions locally. In the latter case, bargaining is co-ordinated at plant level within limits set by the corporate centre. Enterprise bargaining has the attraction of enhancing management's ability to respond flexibly to employee relations policies by introducing pay, conditions and incentives related to local conditions. On the other hand, it requires management to have a competency in negotiation skills which might not exist at plant level and can increase the danger of claims for wage parity by different groups of workers.

Over the past 25 years, the trend in bargaining levels has been towards decentralised bargaining within organisations. The 1998 Workplace Employee Relations Survey reported that in the latter half of the 1980s some 1 million employees had been moved out of the coverage of industry-wide agreements. Most noticeable in this regard was the collapse of the national agreement between the EEF and the Confederation of Shipbuilding and Engineering Unions in 1990. Today in most of the private sector collective bargaining takes place at either the company or workplace level. The public sector has also witnessed a decentralisation of collective bargaining. The 1984 Industrial Relations Workplace Survey showed that 82 per cent of employees were covered by multi-employer bargaining. By 1998 the percentage had fallen to 39 per cent, or about two workers in every five.

Towers (1996) argues that the choice of bargaining levels can be guided by well-established criteria. He points out that multi-employer bargaining is an attractive option in industries which are geographically concentrated (for example, the ceramics industry), are dominated by a large number of companies of relatively small size (for example, the general printing industry), are faced by strong competitive pressures, have a high degree of trade union membership and have high labour costs. Small employers with limited time, resources and expertise are attracted to bargaining arrangements which secure negotiating skills, limit the influence of the union in the workplace, reduce vulnerability to competitive pay pressures in circumstances of labour intensity and set industry-wide standards. Towers suggests that more generally company (corporate level) bargaining is most likely to be chosen where all or most of the following are present:

- a single product market
- a stable product market
- a centralised organisational structure
- a preference for centralised functions
- standardised terms and conditions across operations
- preference for negotiating with national union officials.

In contrast, enterprise bargaining is likely to be favoured in the opposite set of conditions – for example, in a multi-product company, in the face of unstable product markets, with a multi-divisional organisational structure and with a preference for decentralised functions. The decentralised organisational form allows organisations to respond with sensitivity to different market changes across its product range.

What arguments would you use to convince a line manager that the level of the enterprise (establishment) is the right level at which to conduct collective bargaining?

The scope of bargaining

In 1984 the Workplace Industrial Relations Survey reported that collective bargaining determined pay rates for an average of 90 per cent of employees in unionised workplaces. By the 1990 Survey the figure had fallen to 75 per cent – and the 1998 Employee Relations Workplace Survey estimated the percentage to be 67. However, the 1998 Survey also reported that there were 14 per cent of workplaces in which unions were recognised but no workers were covered by collective bargaining for pay determination purposes. These workplaces were mainly in the private services sector of the economy. This non-pay scope of collective bargaining probably reflects two trends. First, some employers respond to falling or low union density by unilaterally setting employment conditions that treat the union recognition agreement as irrelevant. Second, it may also reflect that employees leave the union when management begins to set wages unilaterally even though the management still formally continues to recognise the union.

Table 16 shows that there has been relatively little change in the scope of bargaining over non-pay issues among establishments that recognise trade unions. Although there has been a substantial increase in the proportion of unionised workplaces where pay bargaining does not take place, no such trend applies to non-pay issues. The table also demonstrates that the percentage of workplaces that bargained over none of the six non-pay issues listed remains small. The mean number of items subject to negotiation fell from 3.8 in 1990 to 3.6 in 1998. It reveals some changes on some items, with reductions in the number of workplaces where recruitment and working hours are regularly on the bargaining agenda, and an increase in the proportion that bargained over the amount of redundancy compensation. Millward *et al* (2000), in their study of British employment relations over the period

Table 16 *The scope of bargaining in workplaces with recognised unions 1990 and 1998*

Items subject to negotiation	Cell percentages and means	
	1990	**1998**
Physical working conditions	80	79
Staffing levels	57	51
Recruitment	44	34
Re-employment within the establishment	70	66
Size of redundancy payments	46	57
Reorganisation of working hours	88	75
None of these	5	7
Mean number of items	3.8	3.6

Source: *All Change at Work?* Routledge, 2000

1980–1998 as portrayed by the Workplace Industrial Relations Survey series, show that the scope of bargaining over non-pay issues declined in private manufacturing and private services but remained the same in the public sector.

Bargaining agreements

Number of unions

Multi-unionism is a feature for a significant number of unionised workplaces, although today the existence of a large number of unions in a workplace is comparatively rare. In 1990, 34 per cent of workplaces with union members had a single union present, 27 per cent had two unions present, 12 per cent had three, and over a quarter (27 per cent) had four or more present. A trend towards single union representation continued during the 1990s such that by 1998 43 per cent of unionised workplaces had a single union. However, more than half of unionised workplaces had two or more unions present. Between 1990 and 1998 the mean number of unions at unionised workplaces fell from 2.7 to 2.4. Even so, a quarter of unionised workplaces had four or more unions present.

Multi-unionism is said by some to have contributed to the UK's labour productivity deficit relative to its major international competitors. Others have argued that it is not multi-unionism as such that has a negative productivity effect but fragmented bargaining structures. In the last 25 years many organisations – especially when opening a 'greenfield site' – have adopted a policy of dealing with one union only or a number of unions collectively. The main planks of this tidying up of bargaining arrangements have been:

- single union arrangements
- single-table bargaining arrangements.

Single union arrangements

Single union arrangements are those that occur where a company recognises only one union for collective bargaining purposes. In workplaces which recognise only one union, this situation has arisen through a formal single union agreement rather than happening simply by chance. The 1998 Workplace Employee Relations Survey reported that about a fifth (17 per cent) of all unionised workplaces had a multiple union presence and negotiated separately with each union. In 25 per cent of all workplaces and in 41 per cent of all unionised workplaces single union bargaining arrangements existed.

Single union arrangements have existed in the UK retail sector for many years. In the 1980s their growth was most prominent on 'greenfield sites'. During this period, their growth was also controversial, especially in circumstances where an employer sought to achieve single union bargaining arrangements by de-recognising existing unions and it turned out the employer's preferred union was chosen after a so-called 'union beauty contest'. In some cases, the selected union had no tradition of membership in the company or industry, and in extreme cases had no members employed at the establishment concerned. Single union arrangements are particularly beneficial in organisations that aim at teamworking, product/service quality and flexibility among its workforce since the presence of one union reduces the likelihood of employee opposition to the introduction of such practices on the grounds that they threaten the job territory claimed by trade unions.

Single-table bargaining arrangements

In single-table bargaining, all trade unions recognised by the management come together to discuss and agree their position before sending a single team representing all the unions' interests to the bargaining table to meet with the employer. This team negotiates on behalf of all employees from each union. Such arrangements save management time and resources and minimises inter-union strife. All this makes for a more efficient operation and for a more effective management of the enterprise. All employees are likely to end up having similar employment deals or single-table arrangements cannot work. Terms and conditions must be at least close in terms of pay, sick leave, holidays, pensions and other fundamentals. Single-table bargaining shortens the communications chain and can be used to unify and to harmonise working conditions as well as making the introduction of new practices – for example, flexible working – more easy to achieve.

However, single-table bargaining is not always the right practice to introduce. There has to be commitment to the concept from top management. In addition, it must be remembered there are specific levels of negotiation which have to be maintained for particular groups below the level of the single table. Managers have to be prepared to open up all employees issues – for example, fringe benefits – which previously may have been restricted to one or two groups.

In 1998, amongst workplaces which recognised two or more unions, the Workplace Employee Relations Survey found that around three fifths (or 62 per cent of all unionised workplaces) conducted joint negotiations with all of the unions. Among workplaces where collective bargaining was the dominant form of pay-setting, the percentage with single-table bargaining arrangements increased from 40 per cent in 1990 to 77 per cent in 1998. By sector the corresponding figures were:

- private manufacturing up from 57 per cent to 80 per cent
- private service up from 57 per cent to 90 per cent
- public sector up from 23 per cent to 70 per cent.

Among unionised workplaces, single union agreements and single-table bargaining arrangements were equally common but found in different types of workplaces. Single-table bargaining arrangements were over three times more likely in the public sector than in the private sector (40 per cent, compared with 12 per cent). Over half the unionised workplaces in the wholesale and retail and financial services and the community services had a single union agreement. The distribution of single-table bargaining arrangements was more evenly distributed, except for the public utilities, where they were especially high.

From the viewpoint of a management which recognises more than one union, what are the advantages of insisting on single-table bargaining?

PARTNERSHIP AGREEMENTS

In the face of increasing global competition, thriving business depends upon improving conditions and upon constant change. To achieve this, the co-operation of all those involved in the enterprise is required. It was shown in Chapter 1 that the idea of management, employees and trade unions working together for their mutual benefit and to secure the future of the enterprise is the very essence of employee relations. In the mid-1990s some trade unions, in an effort to reverse the decline in their membership and to gain the acceptance of employers, began to give greater emphasis to the notion of working together with employers to achieve common goals. This took the form of negotiating partnership agreements with employers.

Principles

Such agreements are a sophisticated form of employee relations in which management and trade unions commit themselves to shared responsibility for meeting business objectives within a framework for jobs, pay security and good conditions of employment. These are six key principles that underpin partnership agreements at the workplace. These are:

- *Principle 1: commitment to success of the enterprise* – Effective partnership agreements are based on a shared understanding of, and commitment to, the business goals of the organisation and of/to its lasting success, including support for flexibility and a willingness to embrace 'good practice' ideas from outside. In some instances, the operation of this principle may mean the replacement of a previously hostile and adversarial atmosphere of employee relations.

- *Principle 2: recognising legitimate interests* – This principle demands a recognition that at any one time there might be quite legitimate differences in interests and priorities between the partners to the agreement, and an acceptance that ultimately each party will respect the other's needs to do its best for its own constituencies. Partnership agreements, if working effectively, should build up trust between the parties and should assist the resolution of differences between the parties.

- *Principle 3: commitment to employment security* – This principle is usually embodied in partnership agreements by a combination of measures to maximise employment security within the enterprise (for example, limiting the use of compulsory redundancy, joint agreement on staffing levels) and measures designed to improve the employability of staff beyond it (for example, by improving the transferability of skills and qualifications).

- *Principle 4: focus on the quality of working life* – This principle is a recognition that successful enterprises should invest in the personal development of their employees by strengthening the talent pool of the enterprise and by opening up opportunities for personal growth (including vocational and non-vocational development) that have hitherto been unavailable to employees.

- *Principle 5: transparency* – If partnership agreements are to be meaningful and not a sham exercise in participation, they must be based upon a real sharing of hard information and on openness to discussing plans about the future when they are at the formulation stage. The process of consultation must be genuine, with the management committed to listening to business cases from the employees for alternative plans.

- *Principle 6: adding value* – This principle is a recognition by the parties to partnership agreements that they should access sources of motivation, commitment and resources that were not accessed by previous employee relations institutions at the workplace. For example, this may involve adding value beyond the immediate workplace through providing the hub of a training process that meets the enterprise's skill requirements but also puts something back into the wider talent pool of the sector.

There are other factors that are essential for successful partnership agreements. One is leadership on both sides. Successful partnerships are often based virtually on the personal leadership skills of a few individuals who often take significant risks in moving relationships on to a new footing. Another factor is a clear understanding of the case for change. Whether the spur is a shift in product markets, the advent of new business goals or the impossibility of continuing a tradition of adversarial employee relations, it has to be closely understood. Building a relationship requires both employees and managers to invest time and effort. Partnership agreements are by definition based on high-trust relationships, and where they supersede antagonism there is no way to shorten this lengthy process.

Extent

Partnership agreements and arrangements are now well established in organisations in every sector of the economy. They exist in many organisations that are household names, including Tesco, the Co-operative Bank, Scottish Power, Legal and General, United Distillers and Vintners, the Inland Revenue, British Gas, UNISYS, Scottish Water and Alstom. It would, however, be wrong to give the impression that partnership is the defining characteristic of a majority of organisations. Partnership agreements and arrangements do not mean the end of conflicts of interest between employers and employees. Conflicts of interest will inevitably remain – but where partnership arrangements exist at the workplace, some would argue that such conflicts will be much easier to resolve where employee relationships are most likely to be based on trust and mutual respect rather than on hostility and suspicion.

Explain the principles that underpin partnership agreements and arrangements at the workplace. Which do you think is the most important? Why?

Benefits

Partnership agreements operating within the unionised context vary in content and style. However, some common issues are covered in all partnership agreements. These include:

- business-focused consultation and communications arrangements
- joint working groups
- employee commitment to business goals
- long-term pay deals
- employment security
- sharing of information
- training and development
- focus on local problem-solving activities
- the harmonisation of employment conditions and single status.

Those who favour the partnership approach to employee relations point to a number of advantages for employers. Involving employees in a partnership arrangement gives them greater say in decision-making and therefore a greater commitment to the enterprise. This in turn should improve the morale of employees and so help employers achieve the increased work performance employers desire. In both the private and public sectors, organisations cannot rise to the challenge of increased competition and demands for improved products and services unless all those working for the organisation feel they have a stake in the success of the business. It is argued, therefore, that partnership agreements will help employees to deliver better products and services.

Advocates of partnership agreements also claim they are an advantage to unionised employers in that they mean that simply saying 'no' cannot be the first response of the workforce to employer proposals for change. They point out that when entering into a partnership, unions must recognise that change is inevitable, that change is not necessarily a threat, and associate themselves with good practice, continuous improvement, high productivity and enhanced competitiveness. Supporters of partnership-based employee relations also point to research which shows that workplaces with partnership agreements are one third more likely than others to achieve average financial success and labour productivity (see *Partnership Works*, TUC; information available at www.tuc.org.uk/partnership/tuc).

Partnership agreements present employers with important challenges, however, the greatest being that partnership agreements allow unions to exercise much more influence over strategic decisions. Partnership also requires some rethinking of management roles – in particular the responsibilities of middle managers. The partnership approach is designed to give workers more autonomy, and this must mean some relinquishing of control by immediate managers, supervisors and team leaders. There is always the danger that some managers may see these developments as a threat rather than a need to move from a culture of direct intervention in relatively simple tasks to a culture of coaching, problem-solving and facilitation.

The outcome of partnership agreements

Views on the actual outcomes of the operation of partnership agreements are divided. Haynes and Allen (2000) argue from their study of partnership agreements in Legal and General and Tesco that these led to a strong workplace union presence and an increase in union membership. Taylor and Ramsay (1998), on the other hand, contend that management may use trade unions, via partnership agreements, to increase the rate of exploitation of workers through their involvement in HRM techniques. Partnership, therefore, they argue does not actually guarantee a strong workplace presence for trade unions.

The debate in the academic research literature is not solely confined to the impact of partnership on trade unions. Kelly (2001) evaluated the actual improvements emerging from partnership in terms of union membership, wages and conditions and union influence. He argued that in terms of membership there are only two partnership companies where this has increased, and that there is little support for the view of the TUC that partnership companies offer 50 per cent higher wages than non-partnership companies. He also claims that job security is not as widely available in partnership companies as supporters would suggest, and that the extent of union influence over decision-making in partnership companies is low.

Oxenbridge and Brown (2002) have analysed the relationship between collective bargaining and what they refer to as the 'new' industrial relations of partnership. Based on case study data, they argue there is a continuum of styles and relations. First, there are those production-oriented companies where relations between unions and employers still focus on conventional bargaining relations. In these situations partnership is mainly implicit and nurtured by the role of formal and informal union-management relations. In contrast, Oxenbridge and Brown also identify companies that used partnership agreements to constrain the influence of trade unions and in which workplace trade unionism was relatively weak. Unions concluded the partnership agreements owing to more aggressive management approaches, and partnership therefore appeared to be related to the enhancement of management control. In short, for Oxenbridge and Brown the outcomes of partnership agreements are less clear-cut than supporters and opponents contend. Johnstone *et al* (2004), on the basis of a case study in a British utility company, reported that management claimed that on balance their partnership agreement had had a positive impact, the benefits including improved industrial relations, quicker pay negotiations and increased legitimacy of decision-making. The trade union representatives also believed that partnership had brought benefits, including greater disclosure of information, greater influence, inter-union co-operation and more local decision-making. The views of employees as to the perceived outcomes of the partnership agreement were found to be more mixed.

The divided views in academic research on the outcomes of partnership agreements have been put down to a number of factors. These include the use of different research methods (for example, the use of case studies as opposed to surveys), the complex interaction of specific contextual factors such as the business context, sectoral differences (for example, relatively negative outcomes in traditional but declining industries and relatively optimistic outcomes reported in expanding sectors such as retailing and finance). There are also definitional problems. There is no one accepted definition of a partnership agreement. For some observers they must conform to the TUC's six principles whereas others include the so-called 'sweetheart' agreements between employers and unions. This raises the possibility that researchers into the outcomes of partnership agreements are not comparing like with like.

COLLECTIVE BARGAINING AS A PAY DETERMINATION MECHANISM

As noted previously, collective bargaining has ceased to be the dominant form of pay determination in the economy as a whole. Table 17 below shows the main mechanisms in 1998 used for determining the pay of non-managerial employees, by sector and workplace size. Just under half of all employees had their pay unilaterally set for them by management, either at a higher level in the organisation or by workplace management. Individual negotiations over pay covered some 2 per cent of non-managerial employees. Of the 36 per cent of non-managerial employees whose pay was determined by collective bargaining, most were

Table 17 *Method determining pay for non-managerial employees, by sector and workplace size 1998*

Sector workplaces: employees	Percentage of employees						
	Collective bargaining			Management at		Pay set by	
	Multi-employer	Single employer	Work-place	a higher level	work-place	individual negotiations	other method
PRIVATE SECTOR							
24–49	4	5	2	39	41	5	3
50–99	4	9	3	30	45	5	4
100–199	10	11	7	29	35	1	6
200–499	5	13	14	29	30	2	6
500 or more	2	25	16	17	37	0	2
all private sector	5	14	9	28	37	2	4
PUBLIC SECTOR							
24–49	30	11	0	16	3	0	40
50–99	30	19	0	10	3	1	36
100–199	37	15	1	11	3	0	33
200–499	43	20	1	8	2	2	24
500 or more	35	16	6	4	2	0	38
all public sector	35	16	3	8	3	0	35
All workplaces	14	15	7	22	26	2	14

Source: Cully et al, *Britain at Work as Depicted by the 1998 Workplace Employee Relations Survey*, Routledge, 1999

covered by arrangements that were organisation- or workplace-specific. The 1998 Workplace Employee Relations Survey revealed that only one in five private sector workplaces engaged in collective bargaining whereas four out of five had pay unilaterally set by management. One in ten employees in the private sector negotiated with his or her employer on an individual basis, whereas in the public sector, two out of every five workplaces surveyed did not engage in collective bargaining.

Table 18 opposite shows that the percentage of workplaces in which collective bargaining was the dominant mechanism for pay determination fell by a half over a period of 14 years, from 60 per cent in 1984 to 42 per cent in 1990 and 29 per cent in 1998. There was also a substantial change to the nature of bargaining in such workplaces, as seen by the decline in the influence of national, regional and industry-wide agreements. In 1984 multi-employer agreements were a feature of pay determination in over two thirds of workplaces where most employees' pay was set by joint negotiation. By 1998 the percentage had fallen below a half (46 per cent). In general terms this means that the percentage of all workplaces in which multi-employer agreements formed some part of the dominant arrangement for pay decreased by about two thirds from 41 per cent in 1984 to 13 per cent in 1998. The proportion of workplaces in which pay was determined unilaterally and influenced to some extent by higher management increased from 16 per cent in 1990 to 25 per cent in 1998.

Table 18 *Locus of pay determination 1984–1998*

Level of pay determination	All sectors of the economy %			Private sector manufacture and extraction %			Private sector services %			Public sector %		
	1984	1990	1998	1984	1990	1998	1984	1990	1998	1984	1990	1998
Collective bargaining	60	42	29	51	33	23	36	29	14	94	71	63
Multi-employer barg'g	41	23	13	21	12	6	17	8	3	82	58	39
Multi-site employer barg'g	12	14	12	11	6	5	14	19	10	11	12	23
Workplace barg'g	5	4	3	17	14	12	3	2	1	n/a	n/a	n/a
don't know	1	1	n/a	2	1	n/a	1	n/a	n/a	1	1	n/a
Non-collective bargaining	40	58	71	49	67	77	64	71	86	6	29	37
External to organisation	7	9	14	4	7	3	13	5	10	3	16	29
Higher managemt in org	11	16	25	11	11	24	19	24	36	1	6	6
Workplace management	21	30	30	33	47	48	31	41	39	n/a	n/a	2
don't know	1	3	2	1	2	2	1	1	2	n/a	6	0

Source: adapted from *All Change at Work?* Routledge, 2000

The proportion of private manufacturing establishments in which pay was determined mainly by collective bargaining fell by nearly a half between 1984 and 1998. In 1984, collective bargaining dominated pay determination arrangements in half of all establishments in private manufacturing. By 1990 this had fallen to one third, and by the turn of the millennium to less than one quarter (23 per cent). In the private services sector, collective bargaining has historically been less extensive than in the manufacturing sector. In the mid-1980s in the private services sector, collective bargaining dominated pay determination in over one third of workplaces. However, in the 1990s the sector witnessed a sharp decline in the joint regulation of pay so that by 1998 only 14 per cent of workplaces negotiated the pay of the majority of their employees with trade unions. Between 1984 and 1998, in the public sector, the proportion of public sector workplaces where pay was mainly determined by collective bargaining declined from 94 per cent to 71 per cent. This is mainly explained by the government's abolition of collective bargaining arrangements for many health service professionals and for schoolteachers in England and Wales. Collective bargaining for these groups was replaced by the establishment of a Pay Review Body. In addition, the privatisation of many public utilities in the 1980s and 1990s removed from collective bargaining coverage important groups of non-manual workers, particularly those employed in middle to higher managerial grades.

INDUSTRIAL ACTION

Large-scale industrial disputes can have a disproportionate effect on the statistics of working days lost. In 1984, for example, the coal mining strike accounted for 83 per cent of the 27,135 days lost. In 1996, one dispute in the transport, storage and communication sector accounted for 61 per cent of the total days lost over the year. Again in 2002, two disputes accounted for 60 per cent of the total days lost over the year.

There was a substantial decline in the strike activity in 1990s. In fact, the number of stoppages has been on a downward trend for over 20 years. In 2002, it fell to 146, beneath the relatively narrow band it had been in since 1992. The number of working days lost per 1,000 employees is the standard method that has been used to convert working days lost into a strike rate that takes account of the size of the labour force. It also enables comparisons to be made across industries and regions that differ in size. Because the number of employee jobs has not changed dramatically over the past 20 years, the rates for the UK as a whole show the same pattern of general decline with occasional peaks that can be seen in the working days lost series. The 1.3 million working days lost in 2002 is equivalent to 51 days lost per 1,000 employees – more than double the strike rate for 2001 and the highest annual rate since 1996.

An alternative way of putting the strike statistics into a wider context is to consider working time lost through strikes as a proportion of time actually worked. In 2002 an estimated 41,600 million hours were worked in the UK. Comparing this with 10.3 million hours lost through strikes shows that approximately one in every 3,900 potential working days was lost through strikes in 2003. The equivalent figure for 2001 was one in every 10,100.

How do we account for the decline in strike activity in the last 25 years? Economic factors have been important. Until the late 1990s economic conditions were characterised by rising unemployment, increased product market competition and changing technological developments. In such economic conditions the probability of strikes occurring is considerably reduced. The ability of the employees to impose economic costs on the employer via the withdrawal of their labour is limited. If strikes occur in such economic conditions, they are likely to last for a long time thereby increasing the economic cost to the striking employees.

Following the re-election of the Blair government in 2001, there was a significant increase in public spending but especially in the health service and education sectors. One effect of this was to increase the demand for labour in the public sector. This quickly led to labour shortages. Excess demand for labour tends to produce economic conditions in which the probability of strikes occurring increases. Such economic conditions are also likely to give a positive outcome for the strikers because the economic costs of imposing industrial sanctions on the employer are high. The employer is more likely to concede. Prior to this expansion in public expenditure, the pay of public sector employees had tended to lag behind that of the private sector. Public sector employees and their unions saw the change in their balance of bargaining relative to their employers as an opportunity to catch up with and preferably overtake pay movements in the private sector. It is not surprising, therefore, that recent years have witnessed significant incidences of industrial action in the public sector. Dispute groups have included local government manual workers, schoolteachers, fire-fighters, nursery nurses and Royal Mail employees.

Another important factor in the decline of strike activity in the last two decades has been the trend in real wages – ie the amount of goods and services that an employee's pay can actually purchase. In periods of rising real wages, strike action tends to fall. The rising expectation of employees for increased living standards can be accommodated. In general, the last 20 years has seen significant increases for those who have remained in real wages.

What factors, other than economic ones, do you believe help to explain the decline in the frequency of collective industrial action in the last 25 years?

MECHANISMS FOR RESOLVING CONFLICT

If agreement cannot be reached in the collective bargaining process and negotiations break down, there are a number of choices available to the employer and the employees. First, the matter can be referred to the disputes procedure (sometimes called the *avoidance* of disputes procedure), which sets out several stages available to attempt to resolve the dispute. If a settlement can be reached using the collective disputes procedure, that procedure may have a final stage providing for third party intervention in the form of conciliation, mediation and arbitration. These processes were explained in Chapter 6. What happens, then, if the parties decide to take their dispute to arbitration?

Arbitration

Terms of reference

If both parties voluntarily agree to arbitration, the first task is to agree terms of reference for the arbitrator. ACAS will assist the parties in this task. The terms of reference are important because they tell the arbitrator what it is the parties wish the arbitrator to do. It sets limits to the arbitrator's powers, which are usually constrained to within the range of the parties' claims. It prevents the arbitrator from wandering into issues that the parties do not wish the arbitrator to get into – for example, commenting on deficiencies in the procedures. In arbitration, the terms of reference are usually worded in a simple manner. Typical terms of reference would be:

'... to decide the daily rate of pay for short-term supply schoolteachers'.

The terms of reference give the arbitrator flexibility within its limits.

However, in the case of pendulum (or final offer) arbitration, the terms of reference confine the arbitrator's award to either the employer's final offer or the employees' (the union's) final claim. The arbitrator must make an 'either/or' decision, and no other settlement can be awarded. This is made clear in the terms of reference.

Below is an example of the terms of reference in a pendulum arbitration case that occurred in the dispute between the Isle of Man Post Office and the Communication Workers' Union (CWU).

The arbitrator is asked to decide between the following differences in the employer's offer and the CWU claim:

The IOM Post Office offer	*The CWU claim*
From 1 January 1999, a 3.1% increase on basic pay, bonuses, overtime and all allowances	From 1 January 1999, a 4.6% increase on basic pay, bonuses, overtime and all allowances

Pendulum arbitration has been favoured by electronics firms where a strike would run the risk of losing markets because adjustments cannot be made quickly enough to product/services in the light of rapidly changing customer demand and technology. Manufacturing companies whose main customers are the large supermarket chains have also favoured pendulum arbitration, believing that a strike runs the risk of a permanent loss of business to what is the company's main customer. Pendulum arbitration is usually written in as the final stage of an agreed dispute procedure. It is argued by those who favour pendulum arbitration that prohibiting arbitrators from occupying the middle ground between a final employer offer and final union claim encourages the parties to make more reasonable offers and claims, since the alternative is to enter a win-all or lose-all situation. Indeed, it is argued that eventually both sides will be so close together that the gap becomes bridgeable in negotiation and arbitration becomes unnecessary. In other words, the main assumption behind pendulum arbitration is that it puts such pressures on the employer and trade union to make an agreement that the process is unlikely ever to be used.

A great disadvantage of pendulum arbitration lies in the assumption that one side is 100-per-cent right and the other is 100-per-cent wrong. Why should compromise be an acceptable and justified principle in the collective bargaining processes and yet be ruled out in the arbitration process? Second, there are longer-term employee relations consequences if one side is found to be comprehensively right and the other just as comprehensively wrong. There are further disadvantages. An arbitrator may be faced with two complicated packages and unless he or she is very lucky he or she will find *both* packages unsatisfactory. If the arbitrator cannot select the best items from each package and award accordingly, he or she has to weigh the two packages and choose the least objectionable.

> What do you consider to be the advantages and disadvantages to an employer of favouring pendulum arbitration over conventional arbitration?

Choice of arbitrator

The next stage in the process is for the two sides to agree jointly on the name of the independent person to arbitrate on their differences. Again ACAS facilitates this by making available to the parties its listed panel of arbitrators, but it does not provide the disputant parties with any information about previous cases. Sometimes the parties are content to allow ACAS to appoint the arbitrator. Mumford (1996) reports that the vast majority of the individuals on the ACAS panel are academics (or retired academics) over 45 years of age and grammar school-educated but interested in the practicalities of industry and employee relations. In short, they do not 'live in ivory towers'. ACAS strives to maintain long tenure amongst its arbitrators in order that they accumulate experience which helps them develop the skills in conflict management that greatly aid dispute resolution. The parties thus jointly determine the independent person to whom they are prepared to hand over the decision on how to resolve their differences.

Written submission to the arbitrator

After the terms of reference have been clarified and the independent person has been selected, the next step in the process is the setting of the date and the venue for the arbitration hearing.

This is agreed between the parties and the arbitrator, although it is ACAS which implements these arrangements. Before the hearing date, both sides submit to the arbitrator a written statement of their case and arguments. The parties also exchange their respective written cases with each other before the date of the hearing. It is essential that all information given to the arbitrator is known to the other side. Written statements, together with any supporting documents and a list of those attending the hearing, are submitted to the arbitrator at least one week before the hearing.

Arbitrators reach their conclusion only after considering all the facts and arguments put to them by the parties, and they always study the written statements very carefully. Each written statement normally covers the background information about the company and its products, union representation, etc; an explanation of the history and background of the dispute, including an account of the sequence and outcome of any relevant meetings or discussions; the arguments supporting or opposing the claim; and a brief summary of the case which brings together the essential points the arbitrator is being asked to consider. Relevant agreements, procedures or rules are attached as appendices. In the case of a job grading dispute, for example, full details are given of the grading scheme in operation, whereas in a disciplinary case details of any disciplinary rules or procedures are provided.

In certain circumstances, before the hearing date there may also be a site visit. This is highly likely in the case of differences between parties concerning the degree of skill required by a job, the physical conditions under which the work is carried out or the assessment of piece-work, prices or times. In all these cases it is of value for the arbitrator to see the work in progress.

The arbitration hearing

The procedure outlined below is standard practice in the use of voluntary arbitration to settle:

- trade disputes
- alleged claims of unfair dismissal

- an alleged unreasonable refusal by an employer to accept an employee's request for flexible work-ing.

The hearing is informal and confidential, the parties usually being represented by those responsible for conducting normal negotiations. It is usually completed in two to three hours, is held in private, and the procedure to be followed is a matter for the arbitrator. However, the stages of a typical arbitration hearing are:

1 The arbitrator explains his or her role and then reads out the terms of reference to ensure that both parties place the same interpretation on their scope or meaning.

2 The arbitrator checks that the parties have exchanged their written statements and have had suffi-cient time to give the statements proper consideration.

3 The arbitrator normally invites the party making the 'claim' or seeking to change the status quo (say, Party A), to put its case uninterrupted, and to include a critique of the written submission of the other party (say, Party B). This is usually done by one person, but other members of the team may be called upon to give supporting statements.

4 The arbitrator then invites Party B to ask questions on Party A's statement. Such questioning can be effected either directly by the leader of Party B in respect of Party A or through the arbitrator.

5 The arbitrator invites Party B to put its case uninterrupted, and to include a critique of the written submission of Party A. This again is ordinarily be carried out by one person but with other members of the team giving supportive statements.

6 The arbitrator then invites Party A to ask questions on Party B's statement. Again, such question-ing can be effected directly to the other party or via the arbitrator.

7 The arbitrator will then ask questions of each party in turn or put the same questions to both par-ties. A party to whom the question is directed may respond through the team leader or nominate another member of the team to respond. The person who answers the question may call upon another member of the team to make a supporting statement. Each time one party responds to a question, the other party is given the opportunity to comment on the response. One party can ask questions of the other through the arbitrator.

8 Before inviting the parties to make their closing statements, the arbitrator normally obtains a formal assurance from each party that everything it wished to say has been said, and that it has had suf-ficient opportunity to comment on or attempt to rebut what has been said by the other side.

9 The arbitrator will then invite each side to make its closing statement. These are normally taken in reverse order to the opening presentations. The formal (or closing) statement is a summary of the main points the party wishes the arbitrator to take into account in reaching his or her decision and should contain no new material. The arbitrator cannot accept any further evidence after the hearing.

The award
The arbitrator does not announce the award on the day of the hearing. The arguments of the parties are taken away and given serious consideration. The parties receive the award, via ACAS, usually within two to three weeks of the hearing. All awards are regarded as confidential to the parties and are not published unless the parties agree otherwise. A typical award is worded as follows:

The Award
Having given very careful consideration to the arguments very well presented to me, both orally and in writing, I award that:
THE JOB OF CLERICAL OFFICER IS CORRECTLY GRADED AT LEVEL 4

Arbitrators do not give reasons for their decisions because to do so could give rise to further dispute between the parties. They do, however, indicate the factors (or considerations) they took into account in reaching their decision (award). Those factors may be complex and manifold, and include the need for the parties to continue in a working relationship after the award, the need to bring the dispute to a final conclusion, the potential knock-on effects of an award on other groups of workers, the ability of the employer to finance the award, and the credibility of the negotiators, particularly where the employers' pay offer has been rejected, against the advice of the union negotiators, by the employees concerned. In short, these collapse to three major considerations: equity, economics and expediency (pragmatism).

A wise arbitrator (C. W. Guillebaud) once stated about arbitration that:

> If at all possible, neither side should be left with a strong feeling of resentment so that the dispute continues to rankle – for the arbitrator will not then have achieved the objective of settling the matter satisfactorily and improving relations for the future.

In other words, the arbitrator's award should seek to minimise aggregate dissatisfaction. In addition, the parties are not always interested in the rationale behind the arbitrator's decision since they have come to arbitration after a long process and by this time may well just be relieved that the matter has been resolved, and satisfied that they have been able to state all the arguments in favour of their position.

The award of the arbitrator is not legally binding – but it is virtually unknown for an award not to be implemented by the parties. It would be difficult (or require very exceptional circumstances) for one of the parties not to want to implement the award. They are morally bound to do so. After all, they have gone to the arbitration of their own volition, shaped the terms of reference for the arbitrator, selected the arbitrator and had every opportunity to state their case to the arbitrator.

COPING WITH INDUSTRIAL ACTION

Although every employer's focus is to concentrate on steps to avoid disputes turning into industrial action with sanctions, such disputes can and do happen. In this event it is essential that management implements a strategy and policy that maintains as much normality as possible. There is a set of strategic options available to management to minimise the likely disruption from the application of industrial sanctions to the organisation. However, not every one applies in every case to every organisation. They are to:

- keep materials and supplies coming in
- find alternative sources of labour
- maintain output or a level of service to satisfy demand
- maintain the distribution of the product or service to the customer.

Management must critically evaluate each of these choices. In the case of a retail organisation that has to keep supplies coming in, vital questions that have to be answered are:

- Will a picket be mounted?
- Who will unload and store the goods?

When considering an alternative supply of labour, the critical questions are whether the organisation can get hold of other staff and new part-timers. With respect to the maintaining of a minimum level of service the vital considerations are:

- Can orders be advanced or dealt with cumulatively?
- Is there any current overstocking that can be used up first?

As regards the distribution of the goods, operational issues include whether customers could themselves come to the organisation, and if so, whether they would be met by pickets. Could customers be telephoned when deliveries are being despatched? Could working hours be temporarily altered to expedite matters?

Imagine you are the manager of a transport operation. You believe that current negotiations with your employees are going to break down and the employees are going to impose industrial sanctions upon you. What key questions would you ask yourself with respect to the strategic options open to you?

Making sure that supplies keep coming and going is critical. If a business cannot continue to service the market or continue to receive materials, it will have difficulties maintaining output or some level of service. Recruiting an alternative workforce is more than just getting in extra people. It may be that the alternative workforce is already in your organisation. Managers and team leaders/frontline managers may be able to do the work of the potential strikers. Perhaps the work to be done can be covered by other workers who are members of other trade unions not involved in the dispute or who are not unionised at all. Maintaining output to satisfy demand is often possible in the period before the dispute starts. Overtime can be increased, production switched to other plants or companies, and priority tasks tackled first.

SUMMARY

- The distribution of collective bargaining in the UK fell from 70 per cent in 1984 to 40 per cent in 1998.
- A strategic choice for a management involved in collective bargaining is the level at which bargaining takes place – multi-employer level, company level, enterprise level, or some combination of these levels.
- Over the past 25 years the trend in bargaining levels has been towards decentralisation within organisations.
- There has been relatively little change in the scope of collective bargaining over non-pay issues among establishments that recognise trade unions.
- There has been a substantial increase in the proportion of unionised workplaces where pay bargaining does not take place.
- Untidy bargaining structures have been seen to have an adverse effect on the efficiency of organisations. Managements have tried to overcome this by introducing single union arrangements or single-table bargaining arrangements.
- Partnership agreements are a sophisticated form of employee relations in which management and trade unions commit themselves to share responsibility for meeting business objectives within a framework for jobs, pay security and good conditions of employment.
- The key principles underpinning partnership agreements are: a commitment to the success of the enterprise, recognising legitimate interests, a commitment to employment security, a focus on the quality of working life, transparency and adding value.
- Partnership agreements are said to bring benefits to employees, employers and trade unions, and they are now well established in organisations in every sector of the economy.
- Collective bargaining has ceased to be the dominant form of pay determination in the economy as

a whole. In 1998 just under half of all employees had their pay unilaterally set for them by management, either at a higher level in the organisation or at the workplace.

■ If agreement cannot be reached in the collective bargaining process and negotiations break down, there are a number of choices available to the employer – notably to refer to the matter to the disputes procedure, and/or to seek third-party intervention in the form of conciliation, mediation and arbitration.

■ Although the details of conciliation vary in each case, the process usually proceeds via a series of side meetings at which the conciliator explains the issues with each party, and a joint meeting at which the two sides can explain their positions face to face.

■ Arbitration involves the parties' determining the terms of reference for the arbitrator, selecting the arbitrator, presenting submissions to the arbitrator, attending an arbitration hearing and receiving and implementing the arbitrator's award.

■ In jointly agreeing to go to arbitration, the parties may decide to opt for pendulum arbitration in which, unlike conventional arbitration, the terms of reference confine the arbitrator's award to the employer's final offer or the employees' final claim, and in which no other settlement can be awarded.

■ If the breakdown of the collective bargaining process cannot be rescued by the use of the disputes procedure or by the use of third-party intervention, and the employees impose industrial sanctions, it is then important for management to implement a strategy and associated policies that will minimise the impact of such sanctions on the organisation.

FURTHER READING

CHAMBERLAIN N. W. (1951) *Collective Bargaining*. New York, McGraw-Hill.

CULLY M., WOODLAND S., O'REILLY A. and DIX S. (1999) *Britain at Work, as Depicted by the 1998 Workplace Employee Relations Survey*. London and New York, Routledge.

FLANDERS A. (1968) Collective bargaining: a theoretical analysis, *British Journal of Industrial Relations*, November.

HAYNES P. and ALLEN M. (2000) Partnership as union strategy: a preliminary evaluation, *Employee Relations*, Volume 23, No.2.

INDUSTRIAL PARTNERSHIP ASSOCIATION (1996) *Towards Industrial Partnership: A new approach to relationships at work*. London, IPA.

INDUSTRIAL PARTNERSHIP ASSOCIATION (1997) *Towards Industrial Partnership: New ways of work in British companies*. London, IPA.

INDUSTRIAL RELATIONS SERVICES (2002) When all else fails, *Employment Review*, January, No.719; pages 12–16.

JOHNSTONE S., WILKINSON A. and ACKERS P. (2004) Partnership paradoxes: a case study for an energy company, *Employee Relations*, Volume 26, No.5.

KELLY J. (2001) Social partnership agreements in Britain: union revitalisation or employer counter-mobilisation, in M. Martinez Lucio and M. Stuart (eds) *Assessing Partnership: The prospects for and challenges of modernisation*. Leeds, Centre for Industrial Relations and Human Resource Management.

MILLWARD N., BRYSON A. and FORTH J. (2000) *All Change at Work?* London and New York, Routledge.

MUMFORD K. (1996) Arbitration and ACAS in Britain: a historical perspective, *British Journal of Industrial Relations*, Volume 34, No.2.

OXENBRIDGE S. and BROWN W. (2002) The two faces of partnership? An assessment of partnership and co-operative employer/trade union relationships, *Employee Relations*, Volume 24, No.3.

TAYLOR P. and RAMSAY H. (1998) Unions, partnership and HRM: sleeping with the enemy, *International Journal of Employment Studies*, Volume 6, No.2.

TOWERS B. (1996) Collective bargaining levels, in B. J. Towers (ed.) *A Handbook of Industrial Relations Practice*. London, Kogan Page.

TRADES UNION CONGRESS (1998) *Partners for Progress: New unionism in the workplace*. TUC.

TRADES UNION CONGRESS (1997) *Partners for Progress*. TUC.

WEBB S. and WEBB B. (1902) *Industrial Democracy*. Longmans Green.

Negotiating (including bargaining)

THE PURPOSE OF NEGOTIATIONS

Negotiation involves two parties (such as individuals, companies, employers, trade union representatives, employee representatives) coming together to confer with a view to concluding a jointly acceptable agreement. It is a process whereby interest groups resolve differences between, and within, themselves. The term can therefore apply to a number of different situations ranging from, at one extreme, resolving a difference between two managers as to how a problem might be best solved, to, at the other extreme, a meeting with a trade union to determine the year's annual pay increase.

If both parties to an agreement do not have the same understanding about what they have agreed, they run the risk of spending time – time that could be used for more fruitful purposes – resolving disputes between themselves over whether one party, or the other, is behaving in accordance with what was agreed. Making an agreement commits the parties to behaving within its parameters until they agree jointly to change the terms of the agreement. So what has been agreed must be capable of effective implementation and operation.

Common elements

Negotiation involves two main elements :

- purposeful persuasion
- constructive compromise.

Each party attempts to persuade the other to accept its own case (request) by marshalling arguments backed by factual information and analysis. However, the probability that one party can persuade the other to accept its case (requests) completely is extremely low. If an agreement is to be reached, both parties must attempt to accommodate the demands of the other. To do so they must identify parameters

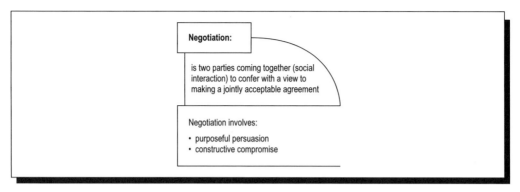

Figure 11   *The definition of negotiation*

of common ground within, and between, their requests of each other. Constructive compromise can then be made within these parameters. Compromise is only possible if sufficient common ground exists between the two parties. The overriding objective of any negotiation is for the parties to reach a mutually acceptable agreement and not to continue their differences nor to score debating points off each other. Negotiation is a problem-solving technique.

So we can define negotiations as:

> two parties coming together to confer with a view to making a jointly acceptable agreement by the use of purposeful persuasion and constructive compromise.

(See Figure 11.) This definition does not confine negotiation to set-piece bargaining situations. It demonstrates that a negotiating situation arises where any two parties have a difference but have a common need to reconcile it, and so have to meet together and through persuasion and compromise find an acceptable solution to their difference(s).

DIFFERENT TYPES OF NEGOTIATING SITUATIONS

Figure 12 below identifies four types of negotiating situations in which managers may find themselves:

- between managers – This involves a negotiated settlement to an issue usually confined to an individual (for example, establishing at an appraisal interview a manager's objectives for the coming year or resolving a difference between two managers as to how a problem with an employee might best be overcome)
- grievance-handling to resolve a complaint by an employee that the behaviour of someone else at the workplace has affected them unfairly, thereby causing feelings of injustice if not an intolerable situation – Grievances normally relate to individual employees, but if they are not handled with care, they can develop to concern a group of employees
- bargaining that results in a negotiated agreement to resolve issues of collective concern to employers and employees (for example, pay, hours of work, holidays and working practices) – It can also take place within the management team (or union teams) to establish a common position to be presented to the other party to the forthcoming bargaining sessions. This is often referred to as 'intra-organisational bargaining' (see below). However, bargaining can, and does, take place between management and individual employees (for example, in a non-union environment, particularly among middle management), resulting in a personal contract
- group problem-solving that results in a negotiated agreement to resolve issues such as the

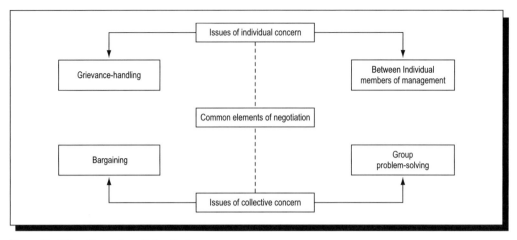

Figure 12 *Different types of negotiating situations*

conditions on which one party will co-operate with a second party in relation to action initiated by that second party.

Between individual managers

The most common negotiating situation in which employee relations managers/professionals are likely to find themselves is the one shown in the top right-hand quadrant of Figure 12 – negotiation with their management colleagues. Each day managers find themselves negotiating with their colleagues, either in the same management function or in another management function (for example, marketing, finance, sales, operations management). These managers can be of the same, higher or lower status than themselves. Negotiations between individual members of management are likely to be over such issues as:

- suggested courses of action (for example, how to deal with an employee complaint against management behaviour)
- the introduction of new employment practices and procedures (for example, the introduction of an appropriate incentive scheme)
- securing the allocation of additional financial, staffing and equipment resources to support the people function
- gaining the commitment of managerial colleagues to a proposed course of action, particularly in the context of employee relations initiatives.

Negotiations between individual managers involve parties protecting the same economic and political interests, so the style of negotiations in such situations is generally friendly and constructive, and certainly not adversarial.

Courses of action

Two or more managers may disagree as to how a problem should/might be resolved. In such situations each manager will seek purposefully to persuade the other of the merits of his or her proposed solution to the problem. If one is able to persuade the other that his or her proposed solution (or some compromise) is acceptable, that is the agreement that will be implemented to solve the problem. However, if managers with different views on how a problem might be resolved cannot be persuaded to accept one or other desired approach, or they cannot agree a compromise solution between them, a senior manager will have to intervene and impose a resolution to the problem.

Gaining resources

Employee relations managers also frequently negotiate with senior managers to gain resources to enable them to implement new policies, procedures and practices which they have devised on their own initiative or as requested by a more senior manager. In such circumstances, a junior manager seeks to persuade the senior manager to allocate the necessary resources. The outcome may be an agreement in which the junior manager obtains some resources – not perhaps what he or she would ideally like, but nevertheless sufficient to implement the new policies, procedures and practices. On the other hand, the senior manager may not be persuaded by the junior manager's arguments and may prefer instead to allocate resources to an alternative project that he or she considers to have a higher priority.

Gaining commitment

Managers in any management function and at any level of seniority cannot assume that their proposed actions, policies and arrangements will be accepted without question by their management colleagues. There is likely to be some opposition from those management colleagues who have different interests and priorities. Financial pressures may mean one manager's progress is another's hold-up, and such inter-departmental rivalries can be a problem in organisations. So if unanimous management commitment to, and support for, proposed changes to policy and/or strategy (for example, a major change in reward strategy or a new training and development strategy) are to be gained, some manager has to make a persuasive case that carries his or her colleagues along. An agreed management position to which all are committed (ie have bought into) is thus likely to emerge via the process of intra- or inter-management negotiation involving persuasion and often compromise.

Negotiation then is not – as is popularly thought – an activity confined to relationships between managers and employee representatives. It is a daily activity in which all managers, inside and outside the employee relations function, are involved. Negotiations take place day in and day out between managers of different and similar levels of executive authority and between the different managers from the different management functions. Nevertheless, some managers have difficulty viewing such circumstances as negotiating situations, preferring to regard them as a process of 'influencing others' and/or gaining the support/commitment of others.

> When were you last involved in a negotiating situation where the other party was a management colleague? What was the issue? What arguments did you use to persuade your colleague that your view of handling the issue might be the right one? What counter-arguments did your manager colleague put forward? How were your differences of approach to solving the problem overcome?

Grievance-handling

What is a grievance?

A grievance is a complaint, real or ill-founded, by an employee that the behaviour of management or that of another employee has impacted upon him or her in an unfair manner creating feelings of injustice. Such complaints may, however, be unjustified. If management believes the employee's complaint is unfounded, perhaps because the employee has simply misunderstood the situation, then management must explain to the employee why it considered this to be the case. Not to do so carries the danger of adding another complaint to the original one as well as sending a message to the employee that management is not taking his or her complaint seriously.

Grievances are important to the individual concerned. Each grievance has to be treated on its merit. One person's grievance cannot be traded off against that of another individual. Two separate grievances should not be linked. In managing grievances it is not good practice for management to say 'We shall concede the grievance of individual y if you will drop the grievance of individual x.' Individual x's grievance must be resolved before consideration is given to the complaint of individual y.

Grievance issues

Complaints about management's behaviour tend to come from individual employees and can range over a wide number of issues, such as that:

- a bonus payment has been calculated incorrectly
- a disciplinary penalty is too harsh
- promotion has been denied unreasonably
- access to a training opportunity has been refused
- the job is currently under-graded
- the employee has been sexually harassed/bullied by another employee or manager
- there are insufficient car parking spaces in the company car park
- working conditions – eg heating, lighting, space – are unpleasant
- overtime opportunities are restricted to particular individuals rather than distributed equally across all employees in the department/section
- a request for more flexible working arrangements has been unreasonably denied.

Although complaints about management behaviour usually come from individual employees, if they are not handled sensitively they can (and do) develop into collective employee complaints. The resolution of an employee grievance involves negotiation in that both management and the complaining employee seek to persuade each other that their own suggestion to resolve the grievance is the better one. However, such persuasion is rarely successful and a mutually acceptable solution will involve the parties' making concessions towards each other's positions.

Most grievances are not referred to the procedure

Most organisations have a grievance procedure. Employee relations managers must be familiar with this procedure. However, when an employee raises a grievance against management behaviour, the matter does not automatically trigger the full procedure. The vast majority of employee grievances are settled either informally or by a voluntarily negotiated and agreed settlement, before the procedure is triggered. Informal settlements can include an apology by the employer or perhaps an admission of error by the employer, who then rectifies the mistake that is the cause of the employee's complaint. Alternatively, the employer may explain to the employee why his or her grievance is ill-founded – an explanation that the employee then accepts.

What are the main issues of employee complaints in your organisation? Do these tend to get resolved informally, or do they require the full procedure?

Bargaining

In most academic literature, the words 'negotiation' and 'bargaining' are taken to be one and the same thing. This is incorrect. Bargaining is only one of a number of different negotiation situations in which a management may find itself. The tenor and style of negotiating in bargaining is likely to be more adversarial than in grievance-handling and group problem-solving situations (see below) since in this situation the representatives of the buyers and sellers of labour services are seeking to protect and advance the interests of of their constituents.

There are, however, different bargaining situations, which have been classified by Walton and McKersie in their classic book *A Behavioral Theory of Labor Negotiations* as:

- integrative bargaining

- distributive bargaining
- intra-organisational bargaining.

Integrative bargaining

Bargaining is a situation where the parties involved have a 'shopping list' of demands of each other. One party (usually the employees collectively) proposes a list of improvements to pay and other employment conditions (for example, a shorter working week, longer holidays) and the other (normally the employer or an organisation of employers) responds with a set of counter-proposals covering changes in working practices and changes in the pattern of working hours, etc.

For example, in the 2002/03 annual pay negotiations between the Fire Brigades Union and the Fire Service employers, the former had the following shopping list:

- an improvement in the basic pay for fire-fighters to £30,000 per year – an increase of 39.3 per cent
- emergency control staff to receive the same wage as fire-fighters
- fire-fighters working the retained and volunteer duty systems to be trained to the same standards as fire-fighters and to receive the same pay and conditions
- the introduction of the 'more appropriate and relevant' Fire Service National Pay Formula
- the settlement date to be 7 November 2002.

The Fire Service employers presented the following counter-shopping list:

- any improvement in pay to be subject to central government's providing the funding
- a commitment to national pay scales in the Fire Service
- the introduction of a new National Pay Formula, based on automatic indexation to pay increases in the economy as a whole, and which could accommodate special allowances without depressing national pay increases
- control staff conditions to be dealt with through job evaluation reflecting the employer's belief in the principle of equal pay for work of equal value
- an inquiry to be established by the government on the basis that this represented the only way of securing additional funding; the inquiry to examine pay and modernisation of working practices and to report in time for any new agreement to be implemented on 7 November 2002.

A bargaining situation involves issues of collective interest to the workforce, unlike an employee's grievance, which normally involves an issue of interest only to that individual. In many bargaining situations, a constructive compromise is achieved by the 'trading' of the items that each party has flagged up to the other for negotiation. In these situations identifying which items in their shopping list the parties are prepared to trade is a key activity in preparing for the bargaining (see below).

The parties come to an agreement in these bargaining situations by trading items in their respective shopping lists. The aim of the parties is to use trading to advance, or protect, their own interests and thus create new 'prices' (new rules) at which labour services will be bought and sold. This bargaining situation in which the parties accommodate each other's interests by trading items in their shopping lists with a view to both parties gaining something from the bargaining is categorised by Walton and McKersie as integrative bargaining.

In the 2002/03 Fire Service dispute, the employers traded:

- a wage increase of 16 per cent over 31 months, staring with 4 per cent from 7 November 2002, a

243

further 7 per cent from 7 November 2003, and a further 4.2 per cent from 1 July 2004, to give an annual pay of £25,000 for qualified fire-fighters

- a settlement date in future of 1 July
- a new National Pay Formula.

In return they received (gained):

- the New National Pay Formula to be subject to review
- an increase in the agreed 16 per cent above 4 per cent to be dependent on the modernisation of working practices with its achievements in intended efficiency validated by the Audit Commission
- the establishment of a Technical Advisory Panel to broker agreement in the case of local disputes over the introduction of alternative duty systems to the cherished two-shift system that had been in place for many years.

Distributive bargaining

In this situation one party presents a shopping list to the other side – which does not respond by tabling its own shopping list of demands. It is a situation in which one party wins and the other party loses. It is commonly referred to as the 'something for nothing' agreement. One party gains a concession from the other but trades nothing in return for gaining it. Until about ten years ago, especially in the public sector, this was the dominant outcome of collective bargaining, but in today's corporate environment, integrative bargaining outcome is much more common.

Distributive bargaining is nevertheless still to be found even in the private sector, as illustrated by the following an example taken from a bargaining outcome in a newspaper printing company in East Anglia. In 2003 the company in East Anglia received the following claim from the National Union of Journalists (NUJ) on behalf of its journalist employees:

- parity of pay rates with a competitor newspaper plus 5 per cent
- an increase in paid holiday entitlement
- sabbatical leave for staff employed by the company for a number of years
- consideration to be given to childcare arrangements in association with a nearby nursery
- the adoption of a new health care scheme
- the provision of a staff canteen
- an increase in the mileage rate above the present level of 43p per mile.

The company did not put forward a set of counter-proposals and entered into bargaining sessions with the NUJ. The eventual outcome was that the company conceded, with effect from 1 January 2003:

- a starting annual salary for trainee journalists raised to £16,600 on the satisfactory completion of training
- a minimum annual salary of £16,600 for senior journalists
- individuals whose salaries do not increase as a consequence of the changes to banding to receive an increase from 1 January 2003 of 2.6 per cent or £600, whichever is the greater.

In return for this increase in its labour costs, the company received from its journalists no concession in working practices. It was a classical 'something for nothing' agreement involving a transfer of scarce economic resources from the company to its employees.

Intra-organisational bargaining

The two different bargaining situations outlined above relate to the reconciliation of differences/interests between management and its employees' representatives. Walton and McKersie distinguished a third type of bargaining situation in which bargaining takes place within the two bargaining parties to arrive at a consensus as to what would be requested from the other party. They referred to this as intra-organisational bargaining. It deals with resolving conflict which occurs within each bargaining team. Usually the management team participating in bargaining has within it a number of different interest groups each of which may want something different (or have different priorities) in terms of concessions from, or concessions to, the other party. Disagreements within the management team can exist over the bargaining outcome aims, the items in the shopping list to be traded, the strategy and tactics to be adopted, and whether an offer from the other party should be accepted (see below).

These internal conflicts can occur before, during and at the end of the bargaining process. A consensus has to be struck within the bargaining team to resolve these internal differences. Intra-organisational bargaining within a management team can take place at a number of different levels:

- the workplace – The different interests here have to be accommodated and a common position agreed
- the company – All the different workplaces that make up the company have to reconcile their differences
- the industry – In multi-employer bargaining (or industry-wide bargaining) all the companies in the industry have to negotiate a common position acceptable to companies of different sizes, containing different components of the industry and having experience in differing degrees of product market competition
- the European level – In negotiating Framework Agreements under the EU social dialogue process (see Chapter 5), the public and private sector employers' organisations from each of the member states engage in bargaining to reach a consensus position with regards to negotiating with the ETUC.

The higher the level at which negotiations are to take place, the greater the number of conflicting interests there will be within the management team, and the greater the difficulty in establishing a common acceptable position. For example, UNICE/CEEP have 31 member organisations, while the British Printing Industries Federation, which bargains annually over pay and employment conditions with AMICUS (graphic, paper and media sector) has to bargain a position with over 1,000 member companies.

Attitudinal structures

An important part of the bargaining process is the attitude that the two parties adopt towards each other. The attitude may be adversarial or it may be co-operative or it may be of mutual professional respect and trust. The bargainers may change their attitudes towards each during the bargaining stages (see below), depending on factors such as changes in the economic environment and personalities. The bargainers may also attempt to influence the expectations of the other parties as to what the outcome of the bargaining might be, or, indeed, what their original proposal's offer might be.

An example of such behaviour by an employer is shown in the case study box below. Here the Chief Executive is clearly attempting to condition the employee to expect little in the way of improved wages and employment conditions in the forthcoming pay negotiations. As we have already noted, the style and attitude of the parties towards each other is also likely to vary depending on the negotiating situation in which the parties find themselves. All this points to the employee relations professional acquiring and developing the good practice of getting to know his or her opposite number on the other side. For example, how does he or she think? Is he or she prone to exaggerate? And so on.

Case study

The Chief Executive Officer reviews the prospect for the forthcoming negotiations

At a time when the company has been busy and the employees have seen much overtime, it is important to remember that this reflection of high levels of activity and 'just-in-time' requirements makes it more difficult than usual for us to plan output effectively. Because of our continuing over-capacity price competition remains fierce and margins continue to be eroded.

Our quarterly economic survey shows that in six of the last seven quarters we have achieved poorer margins. In the light of the increasing product market competition, an increase in the price of our products is impossible. Against such an uncertain economic background there is simply no ability to pay for any improvements in terms and conditions, and certainly no question of any reductions in working time through increases in holidays or a shorter working week.

Explain the difference between integrative, distributive and intra-organisational bargaining.

Group/joint problem-solving

This is a situation in which two or more parties negotiate the details whereby one party will co-operate with the other. Such negotiation takes place most commonly in a situation where management is endeavouring to initiate some action to resolve a problem of concern to both parties. Let us consider an example.

An organisation is currently performing comfortably in terms of sales, profitability, etc, but recognises that in the near future product market competition will become more intense. The top management has started to consider suitable policy initiatives that might be introduced to minimise any adverse consequences in terms of sales and so forth when the greater product market competition becomes a reality.

As a first step the organisation has decided to invite a team of consultants to examine its work organisation and systems and to produce a feasibility study on what action/policies it might introduce and what their effect might be on improving its future product market competitiveness. The management has committed itself to implement none of the report's recommendations until the workforce has been consulted and involved in thorough discussions on the report.

However, if the consultants are to gain a full picture for their report, they have to speak to and have the co-operation of the workforce. The company believes that the best way to achieve this is for the consultants to go into the departments and to speak to the employees on an individual basis. But the consultants will have to inform the supervisor/team leader and the representative of the employees of what they intend to do in the department. Supervisors/team leaders have accordingly been told to release employees from their workstation so that they can speak to the consultants.

The workforce has an interest in seeing the organisation's efficiency improve because it will enhance their job security. They are therefore prepared to co-operate with the work of the consultants – but they have some concerns. First, they know that in other firms where this consultancy organisation has done work, redundancies have been declared shortly afterwards. Second, the employee representatives are worried that management wishes them to have no role when the consultants are speaking to their constituents. They would prefer to be present at any interviews the consultants carry out with individual employees in the various departments.

The workforce is not against the use of consultants as a matter of principle – but its representatives have decided to approach the management about its concerns. The ensuing negotiations between the parties are over:

- whether the firm of consultants preferred by management to produce the feasibility report will be used or whether another firm of consultants could be brought in
- the procedure to be adopted by the consultants when in the departments – will they have direct access to employees? Will employee representatives be present at interviews?

The example illustrates the manner in which a group problem-negotiating situation operates. Management is normally seeking the co-operation of its workforce to some proposed action to gain information which can then be used to solve a problem jointly with the employees, to mutual gain. As a result, the management's negotiating style (attitude) will not be adversarial. Management wants something from its employees, so it will start by demonstrating to them that there is an advantage in co-operating. For management to bang the table and to be insulting in the negotiations toward the employee representatives would be inappropriate to the context and unlikely to secure management's primary objective, which is to gain employee co-operation with the work of the consultants.

> Has there recently been a joint problem-solving situation in your organisation? If there has, what was it about? What were the terms on which the employees co-operated? If there has been no joint prob-lem-solving situation in your organisation, why do you think that has been the case?

EMPLOYEE RELATIONS NEGOTIATIONS *V* COMMERCIAL NEGOTIATIONS

Negotiating situations in employee relations are very different from commercial contract negotiations. Many managers outside the employee relations function find it difficult to understand why employee relations negotiations involve so much quasi-theatrical behaviour and take so long to conclude. So it is important for employee relations managers to understand how employee relations negotiations are different from com-mercial contract negotiations. The main differences are summarised in the box below.

> Unlike commercial negotiations, employee relations negotiations:
>
> - involve an ongoing relationship
> - are carried out by representatives
> - are always conducted on a face-to-face basis
> - do not result in legally enforceable contracts
> - make more frequent use of adjournments
> - always result in an agreement.

Choice of negotiating partner

Commercial negotiations tend to be conducted on a more polite basis than those normally witnessed in grievance-handling or bargaining situations. In commercial negotiations, purchasers tend to buy from indi-viduals or organisations they prefer and sellers can give preferential deals to those they like. In employee relations negotiations, the parties cannot deal only with those they prefer. Each party selects its own representatives and management selects its best team to conduct the negotiations. In addition, the parties have to develop a professional relationship towards each other regardless of their feelings towards each other. Employee relations negotiations are always conducted by representatives of the parties who report back to constituents. Commercial contract negotiators are not accountable to constituents but usually to a line manager.

Face-to-face negotiations and adjournments

Many negotiations in the commercial field do not take place on a face-to-face basis. They may be undertaken by telephone (for example, telephone sales from call centres) or even by letter. Employee relations negotiations, however, always take place on a face-to-face basis. The use of adjournments is less common in commercial negotiations than in employee relations ones. In this latter case management (or union) negotiators may adjourn several times in bargaining situations – but usually on fewer occasions in grievance-handling – to consider a union (or management) proposal. Adjournments enable the parties to obtain and analyse more or new information, to reassess their objectives, aims, strategy and tactics, to regroup as a team where the negotiations are conducted via working parties, and, on occasions, to allow emotions to calm down.

Status of agreements

An important difference between employee relations and commercial negotiations is the legal status of the agreement that emerges. In the commercial contract world the contract outlining the conditions of the sale is legally binding and its contents can be enforced via the courts. The agreement that emerges from employee relations negotiations, as we saw in Chapter 1, is not legally binding. It is binding in honour only. Neither party can enforce its rights as stipulated in the agreement via the courts.

'No agreement'

In commercial negotiations, an outcome of 'no agreement' is quite acceptable – and quite common. Buyers and sellers may have every reason to conclude, after some negotiating, that a deal would not be in their interests and so amicably part and seek other suppliers or purchasers whose needs and terms are more acceptable. In employee relations negotiations, the aim – not just the possibility – is to reach an agreement and the outcome is always a new, or revised agreement, even if, on occasions, that agreement is unilaterally imposed by one party on the other.

Quality of future relationships

Grievance-handling, bargaining, joint problem-solving and intra-/inter-management negotiations all take place against an assumption that the parties mean to have an ongoing and permanent relationship. When the negotiations are over, the parties who have met on a basis of equality have to meet again the next day and continue their employer-employee relationship in which the employees are in a subordinate role. Employee relations negotiators, unlike their commercial contractor counterparts, cannot simply walk away from the party with which they are currently dealing and make a more favourable agreement with another party. For a motor car seller negotiating with a buyer, the relationship may well be confined to that one negotiation. Whether a sale is concluded or not, the parties are unlikely to meet again in a buyer/seller relationship, so one party can insult the other with impunity. By the same token, a cash buyer can use his or her bargaining power to obtain a discount on the price of the product or service he or she wishes to purchase.

The continuous relationship between employee relations negotiators at the workplace acts as a restraining influence on their behaviour during and after the negotiations. Each party must retain its dignity, preserve its professional self-respect and bear in mind the importance of preserving the quality of their future relationship. This means that management must avoid any implication that the outcome of the negotiation suggests that the employee and/or their trade union has 'lost' and that management have 'won'. Both parties must be able to leave the negotiations (whatever the negotiating situation) without losing face. Once the negotiations have been concluded, regardless of the outcome, the parties have to return to a constructive working relationship as soon as possible. For management to use its 'victory' over its employees to humiliate them is not good practice. To behave in such a manner will result in lower employee morale, increased absenteeism and a reduced quality of product or service to the customer.

In employee relations negotiations, the negotiators have always to bear in mind the importance of preserving the quality of their future relationships. Whatever the outcome of the negotiations and whatever the atmosphere in which they are conducted, the two parties have to be able to co-operate and work together 24 hours a day, five or more days a week, indefinitely, at the end of the negotiations. However, if the employee representative with which management has to deal is a national or regional one rather than a workplace representative, and therefore not someone who works on the premises and with whom a day-to-day working relationship has to be maintained, the need to maintain amicable relationships is less imperative because local management may not meet face-to-face with that particular employee representative again.

> List at least four ways in which employee relations negotiations are different from commercial contract negotiations.

STAGES IN THE NEGOTIATION PROCESS

All negotiating situations involve the stages shown in the bullet-point list below, although the length of time that each stage lasts and the degree of formality in each stage may vary. For example, a negotiating situation between managers on how to deal with a problem is unlikely to be written down except perhaps in the form of a letter and/or an internal memorandum to management colleagues. In all negotiating situations, the preparation stage lasts the longest time. The amount of time the two parties spend in actual bargaining, perhaps in a face-to-face situation across the table, is small relative to the total time spent by both sides in the whole negotiating process.

The stages in the negotiation process are:

- preparation and analysis
- presentation
- searching for and identifying common ground
- concluding the agreement
- writing up the agreement.

Preparing for bargaining

Selection of the bargaining team

The size of the management team will vary, but there are advantages in its being small and of an uneven number. If the team is small, it is easier to maintain. An odd number means that if the bargaining team has to take a vote to determine its position, there is always a majority view to prevail. A team of three will always at least split two to one whereas one of five will at least divide three and two. A team of two could divide one and one whereas one of four might split two and two. The management bargaining team should represent all major interest groups in the business.

At least three functions have to be carried out by a negotiating team who will work together under the guidance of its leader. The leader will be the main spokesperson and the principal negotiator in heading the negotiations. In addition, the leader will call for an adjournment if management considers one to be necessary, and will hold the chair during adjournments. It is the team leader who will enter corridor (private) discussions with the leader of the other side. The leader will also be responsible for finalising the agreement on behalf of management. Leaders require a number of attributes. They have to have good inter-personal skills to build the team as a coherent whole, and they have to be acquainted with the employees' attitudes and, if appropriate, the policies and problems of any organisation which represents the employees. It is imperative that the leader shows leadership and is respected by the other members of the team. In addition, the leader must be firm, be capable of exercising good judgement, be patient, be a good listener and be skilful in communicating ideas and getting points across.

The negotiating team also requires a note-taker whose role in negotiations cannot be stressed enough. The note-taker's role includes:

- in adjournments, informing the negotiating team whether the negotiations are making progress or just going round in circles
- advising the negotiators whether the agreed strategy and tactics (see below) are being observed
- recording the proposals made by the other party
- indicating whether the negotiating team has – say, through lack of concentration – missed an offer/proposal from the other side (If this is happening, the negotiating team can return to it in the next or subsequent bargaining sessions)
- ensuring that all issues are addressed; the note-taker summarises to the negotiating team what issues have been settled and what issues are still outstanding, and prevents issues that are on the negotiating agenda from being forgotten or overlooked
- supplying a complete and accurate record of what has been agreed, from which management drafts the agreement.

The team also requires a strategist whose role is to monitor the strategies of both sides and to identify and seek to confirm the anticipated basis of common ground and of constructive compromise for both sides. The strategist also provides any additional information or details that may be required by the team. In addition, he or she monitors and assesses any proposal as and when they are made by the other party.

Some negotiating teams also find it useful to have a member whose sole purpose is to listen to what is being said and to make no spoken contribution in the bargaining sessions. Other teams may also like to have a person whose role is to watch the body and facial reactions of the members of the other side when they are receiving proposals from management or making proposals to management. These reactions can convey useful information and reveal the extent to which the other party is committed to its own proposals and open to counter-proposals from the management side.

Regardless of the size of the management's negotiating team and the division of labour between them, it is imperative – prior to both the first meeting with the other side and to meeting again after an adjournment – that each member of the management team be given the opportunity to contribute to the discussion and agree on the bargaining objectives, strategy and tactics (see below). Ideally, the negotiating team should determine these issues. This provides each team member with an insight into the overall plan and strategy, and thereby generates commitment amongst the whole team to its objectives. So while the role of the team leader is most important during negotiations, the role of the whole team is very important in determining policies and strategies.

Team discipline

Members of the management team should conduct themselves during the negotiations in line with the agreed position(s) established in the analysis stage (see below) so that the team in the actual negotiations is united and purposeful. It is important before meeting with the other side that the team agree that only one member should speak at a time in the bargaining sessions and that the team leader should not be interrupted unless it is absolutely necessary. However, all members of the team should be prepared to speak when called upon to do so by the team leader. If members of the team other than the leader are to make a spoken contribution during the bargaining sessions, it should happen as part of a predetermined strategy, the leader having indicated to the other party that the new speaker is speaking by invitation from the leader.

It is also important before meeting with the other party that the team remind themselves of the importance of not disagreeing as a team in front of the other side, and that if team discipline begins to break down the leader should seek an adjournment so that the necessary action to re-establish discipline can be taken (even to the extent, if necessary, of excluding a member of the team from participating any further in the face-to-face negotiating sessions). The maintenance of team discipline is easier if all members are fully acquainted with the negotiating objectives and the necessary arguments and tradable items (see below) regarded as essential to achieving those objectives. It may help if before meeting with the other side the team has agreed a non-verbal method of communicating with each other (eg signals, passing notes, etc) during bargaining sessions.

The arguments from the management bargaining team have to be consistent and, despite any provocation or unprofessional behaviour on the part of the other side, should not deviate from the agreed format. If during negotiations the other side attempts to disrupt the discipline of the management team by trying to bring in another speaker from the management side against the planned sequence of contributors, the team leader must intervene immediately to make clear to the other side that their remarks be addressed to him or her. They should tell the other side to address all their remarks through them as the team leader. If a member of the management bargaining team begins to 'talk out of turn', the leader must carefully restrain him or her using appropriate language in the right tone of voice. It may, for example, only be necessary to tell the team member to keep quiet or to calm down for discipline to be restored – but if this does not work, an adjournment may be necessary during which discipline can be restored.

The members of the negotiating team must remain within their agreed roles and speak only when invited to do so, unless a change of plan is agreed during adjournments in the negotiations. However, the team members should endeavour to help each other out of difficulty if the team comes under pressure. Getting rattled transmits to the other side a clear message that management may not be totally united in its commitment to its case, and that unexpected gains may be made by playing on these perceived differences.

> What considerations should management take into account in selecting its team for bargaining with its employees' representatives? Justify your answer.

The analysis stage

A management negotiating team goes through three stages in preparing for bargaining. These are:

- analysis
- the establishment of aims to be achieved in the forthcoming negotiating sessions
- planning the strategy and tactics to achieve these aims.

The analysis stage of preparing for negotiations involves management undertaking research to collect information to substantiate its proposals to be put to its employees' representatives and/or to provide counter-arguments to the proposals from the other party. The employee relations professional must therefore be familiar with sources of information. Such information will be available from within the organisation (internal sources) or provided by outside organisations (external sources) such as the National Statistics Office, government departments, non-government organisations (eg ACAS, the Certification Office, the Health and Safety Executive), employers' associations, private research organisations (for example, Industrial Relations Services and Incomes Data Services) and academic institutions. Information from internal sources is likely to cover such issues as:

- the labour productivity trends
- profitability
- labour turnover
- absenteeism
- total sales
- investment
- pay changes
- orders pending
- cash-flow position
- employment trends.

Employers' associations are an important external source of information. They keep records about the types of agreements that exist in a sector and collect data on the size of pay increase settlements being granted by member companies. Many employer associations are also trade associations and as such collect information on the sector for a number of subjects – eg total sales figures, the balance of foreign trade (export/import trends) and unit labour costs.

The analysis stage also involves the management's negotiating team checking on the relevance to the forthcoming negotiation situation of existing agreements such as:

- collective or individual agreements
- custom and practice.

The employee relations manager should be familiar with the meaning and content of those policies that give effect to such rules, arrangements and accepted custom and practice.

In pay bargaining, purposeful persuasion arguments and counter-arguments usually relate to the company's ability to meet the employees' wages claim, labour market shortages and surpluses for particular occupations, pay relativities in terms of what other workers in other companies/other sectors are obtaining in wage increases (commonly referred to as the 'going rate'), changes in occupational and industrial/sector pay differentials (often referred to as the 'earnings league-table') and changes in inflation since the last pay increase was granted (ie the need to keep real wages at least maintained).

These arguments by employee representatives for improvement in wages and employment conditions are illustrated by the following trade union wage claim in an engineering company in the Midlands of the UK:

> Our 5 per cent wage increase is a justifiable claim on behalf of our members. Since the wages and condition settlement last year the rate of inflation, as shown by the Index of Retail Prices, has increased

by 1.5 per cent. Our members therefore require an increase of 1.5 per cent in wages to maintain their real purchasing power. You have been experiencing difficulty in recruiting labour over the last 12 months and the number of people leaving your employment has increased. This reflects the fact that your pay and conditions are out of line with those of your labour market competitors. To overcome this staff shortage problem and to make your pay rate competitive, our members require a further 2.5 per cent in addition to the 1.5 per cent inflation protection increase. The additional 1 per cent is justified by the increase in company's sales, profitability and productivity over the past 12 months. In addition, the company forecasts continuing growth over the coming year and has reported to its shareholders an average 4.5 per cent increase in sales and an average of 7.1 per cent increase in operating profits over the past 12 months.

A further example can be given of a wage claim to a company based in Cambridge:

A 3.8 percentage increase is claimed in line with increases nationally. Average weekly earnings for the whole economy rose by 3.7 per cent in the year to September, up from 3.6 per cent in August. A further 3 per cent increase on basic salary is justified by productivity increases, this increase to be applied and financed wholly through this year's productivity (self-financing). There have been many increases in productivity this year. Those that spring to mind are that the company has reduced staffing levels over the last two years from 550 to 500. In some areas, staffing levels have been reduced by 50 per cent, while mail room staff have taken on extra work – that of leaflet-counting. A further 1 per cent on basic salaries is justified by the 'Cambridge phenomenon', or as it is regularly described by the media, 'Silicone fen'. The people of southern Cambridgeshire know of its existence only too well. They have to pay its extra costs daily. The price of petrol is a good example. Cambridge Council already pay an allowance of 2 per cent and many other companies are being approached by staff to consider this when reviewing staff wages.

Those involved in annual pay bargaining must therefore be familiar with external sources of information covering inflation, pay trends and labour market indicators. Employee relations professionals – particularly those involved in bargaining – need to be knowledgeable about the extent and quality of information (data) available from the following sources:

- Industrial Relations Services
- Incomes Data Services
- *Labour Market Trends*
- the New Earnings Survey.

So what information can the employee relations professional find in these sources? It is important that, during your studies, you consult these sources frequently in their original.

Industrial Relations Services

The Industrial Relations Services (IRS), in its twice-monthly *Employment Trends*, provides information on employment trends and special features based on a survey of organisations, covering their employment policies and practices. It also contains a Pay and Benefits Bulletin which reviews trends in the general level of pay settlements (thus giving insight into the going rate) and reports on pay deals concluded in private and public organisations as well as those involving a whole industry.

In addition it summarises the latest pay awards, showing the name and size of the group of workers covered, the effective date and length of the agreement, and brief details of the main changes. Its datafile contains information on price changes (the Retail Price Index and hence the annual rate of inflation), on changes in average earnings (Average Earnings Index) and on future forecasts of annual rates of change in prices (future trends in inflation and real wage movements) and earnings. Furthermore, it contains a useful summary of the main statistics (inflation, average earnings, productivity/labour costs and an ability-to-pay factor, hours worked, unemployment and employment) used by collective bargainers to pursuade the other party of the merits of their claims.

Industrial Relations Services (IRS) also publishes a monthly *Pay Intelligence* updating service. It features key statistics from its pay databank, including settlement levels for the public, private manual, private non-manual, manufacturing and services sectors as well as the whole economy. It also contains a summary of the IRS monthly pay analysis and settlement chart, and a 'state of play' table detailing news and deals in key negotiations as well as the latest official inflation and earnings figures, together with the predictions of 10 leading forecasting organisations. The IRS pay databank is the only regularly published source of pay statistics independent of employers, trade unions and the UK government. Each year it records the details of pay settlements for some 1,500 bargaining groups covering more than 9 million employees across all sectors of the economy.

Incomes Data Services
The Incomes Data Services (IDS) *Report*, published twice-monthly, describes the changes to pay and conditions that are being agreed at company and industry level, and quickly and simply reports current developments in collective bargaining. Pay settlements are given in detail, and the latest statistics on wages, earnings and prices are reported and interpreted.

The IDS *Pay Directory* is published three times a year. It lists the wage rates, holidays, shift premium, etc, of a wide range of occupations in a variety of companies, and records the wage rates that apply in selected industries and the public sector. It also publishes studies twice-monthly which report on the results of research into single topics such as the pay of a particular group of workers, paid holiday entitlement, sick pay, pensions provisions, shift-premium pay, redundancy and absenteeism. Its *Top Pay Review*, published monthly, monitors the changes to the pay and benefits of executives and professionals and provides a comprehensive briefing on remuneration trends in companies and in the public sector.

Labour Market Trends
Labour Market Trends is a monthly publication and provides statistical information collected by the National Statistics Office on the labour market, of which the most significant is on employment, unemployment, unfilled vacancies and earnings. It also provides regular statistical information on inflation trends, being the official outlet for the Index of Retail Prices. In addition it provides information on changes in unit wage costs and on labour productivity for all employees for manufacturing, energy and water supply, production and construction industries, and for the economy as a whole.

New Earnings Survey
The New Earnings Survey (NES) is the most comprehensive source of earnings information in Great Britain. It is absolutely essential that you consult this source of pay data during your studies of employee relations. It is also essential reading for your pay and rewards studies. It is a survey of earnings of all those in employment in Great Britain carried out in April of each year. The survey is based on a 1 per cent sample of employees who are members of PAYE income tax schemes, and is designed to represent all categories of employees in businesses of all kinds and sizes. The sample each year comprises all those whose National Insurance numbers end with a specific pair of digits. The pair of digits method has been used since 1975. Employers are then contacted to give details on the identified employees. The method covers about 90 per cent of the sample. The remaining 10 per cent is obtained directly from large employers. This sample can include some employees not in a PAYE scheme. The coverage of full-time adults is virtually complete. The coverage of part-time employees is, however, not as comprehensive.

The NES provides an annual snapshot of earnings and hours worked analysed by gender (equal pay), industry (from which an earnings league-table can be calculated), occupation (skill differentials can be worked out from this series), age group, regions, county and collective agreements. Its results are published in six parts:

- Part A is a streamlined analysis giving selected results for full-time employees in particular wage negotiation groups, industries, occupations, age groups, regions and sub-regions.
- Part B provides analyses of earnings and hours for particular wage bargaining groups.
- Part C analyses hours and earnings for particular industries.
- Part D provides the same analysis for particular occupations.
- Part E provides the same analysis for regions and counties.
- Part F provides an analysis of the distribution of hours, joint distribution of earnings and hours, and an analysis of hours and earnings for part-time women employees.

The earnings data covers the level of earnings, the make-up of total earnings (basic pay, overtime pay, shift premiums, incentive payments, etc) and the distribution of total earnings (by decile, quartile and median).

> Take a look at the New Earnings Survey. Write a report on how pay and conditions in your organisation compare with the national average. How would you account for any differences found?

The identification of tradable items

The most important activity, however, for the management team in preparing for bargaining is the identification of the key issues involved in the forthcoming negotiations, and the identification from among them of which of these issues the team is prepared to trade. It also involves anticipating which of the issues the employees' side is prepared to trade on, and which it is not. By identifying possible tradable items, the management bargaining team establishes the parameters within which it expects to be able to identify common ground with its employees, and thereby the basis for a compromise agreement. In making these decisions about the possible tradable items, management weighs up the significance of the issues at stake for the protection and advancement of its, and its employees', economic interests.

In negotiations, at any given time, some of the issues are tradable and others are not. Let us give an example.

Management has just received a list of demands from its employees that includes a 2.5 per cent increase in basic rates, the introduction of a productivity bonus, an increase in holidays, changes to parental leave arrangements, and the removal of no-strike arrangements. After long consideration, management decides – because of market conditions – that any increase in basic rates and any removal of no-strike arrangements are not tradable items. However, it is prepared to trade the introduction of a productivity bonus if this can be made self-financing, an improvement in holiday entitlement and changes to existing parental leave benefits.

Having decided which items it is prepared to trade, the management negotiating team now starts the task of anticipating which issues it believes the employees (the union) will be willing to trade. In doing this, management must assess the strength of feeling of the employees about each of the items on the negotiating agenda, including whether they feel sufficiently strongly that at the end of the day they would be willing to impose industrial sanctions against the organisation. Let us say, for example, that management anticipates that the employees and their representatives feel most strongly about the introduction of a productivity bonus and gaining an increase in holiday entitlement (ie that these are their non-tradable items). So in this case, management anticipates that its employees are willing to trade basic pay rate increases, the no-strike clause and parental leave arrangements (that these are their tradable items) to obtain improvements in holiday entitlement and the introduction of a productivity bonus. Management thus sees a basis for agreement around a productivity bonus, an increase in holiday and parental leave changes, in return for retention of a no-strike clause and no change in basic rates.

Establishing bargaining aims

The next phase of the preparation stage is the establishment by the management negotiating team of the objectives it wishes to achieve in the forthcoming negotiations. This phase also requires management to anticipate the negotiating aims and objectives of its employees and/or their representatives. It is a task that can be done more competently if the management knows and understands what motivates the representatives of the workforce with which it has to deal. Getting to know them does not mean agreeing with their position. However, it is only by knowing 'what makes them tick' (for example, their attitudes, their reaction to pressures upon them, their personalities) that management can predict/anticipate with any reasonable degree of certainty:

- how the employees' representatives might react to management proposals
- the issues they are prepared to trade in bargaining
- the bargaining style they are likely to adopt
- the strategy and tactics they might develop.

By setting objectives, the negotiators know what they are trying to achieve. Negotiation is about compromise and flexibility so it is normally unrealistic to set inflexible objectives because that usually gives only two options – win or lose. Negotiators have to arrive at some sort of prioritised approach. It is standard practice for bargainers to establish three positions for each item involved in the negotiations. These positions are

- What would management ideally like to achieve?
- What does management realistically believe it can achieve?
- What is the least for which management will settle (the fall-back or sticking position)?

The fall-back position represents the lowest package for which management will settle. It is the minimum that can be accepted without failing to meet the negotiators' objectives. If this position cannot be achieved, management will prefer to enter into a dispute situation with its employees. It means that management is prepared to withstand industrial sanctions that the employees may take against them rather than settle for less than its fall-back position. Management as part of preparing for negotiations must therefore also draw up plans to minimise/offset any costs that may accrue to the organisation should a failure to agree result in industrial action by employees.

An aspiration grid

Having established its negotiating objectives, the next step for management is to anticipate the bargaining aims/objectives of the other party along the same lines – what is likely to be their ideal, realistic and fall-back position on each issue involved in the negotiating situation? Having considered which items it is prepared to trade, having anticipated the tradable items of the other party, having established its own bargaining objectives and having anticipating those of the other party, management can now construct an 'aspiration grid' that sets out the parameters for the expected outcome of the negotiation. Such a grid shows the issues management is prepared to trade as well as management's anticipation of the issues it expects its employees will be willing to trade. It gives the parameters within which the forthcoming bargaining might

Table 19   *An aspiration grid*

Items for negotiation	Management			Employees/Union		
	Ideal	*Real*	*Fall-back*	*Fall-back*	*Real*	*Ideal*
Basic rate Increase of 2.5 per cent	X	X	X	O	O	X
Introduction of productivity bonus	X	X	O	X	X	X
Increase in holiday entitlement	X	O	O	X	X	X
Changes to parental leave	X	O	O	O	O	X
Retention of no-strike clause	X	X	X	O	X	X

be expected to develop. It helps management identify the information it requires from the other party and the information management requires to convey to the other party.

An example of how an aspiration grid can be used is shown in Table 19 above. An **X** indicates that a party is not prepared to trade that item; an **O** indicates that the party is prepared to trade that item. This grid is based on the example outlined previously. If both parties have an **X** against the same item in their fall-back column, it indicates that there will be no accommodation on that issue and the expectation must be that the negotiations will break down. There can be no basis for an agreement. Management then would have to give consideration to whether it is prepared to bear the costs that a failure to agree would involve. If it decides it is not, management will have quickly to reassess its position on that issue.

The grid shows that, ideally, management would like to trade no items with the employees. However, it knows this is unrealistic. The grid shows that management has therefore established a 'realistic' position of wishing to trade increases in holiday entitlement and changes to the parental leave arrangements for no changes in pay and to the no-strike arrangements, and for there to be no productivity bonus introduced. The management fall-back position is to introduce a productivity-based bonus scheme, to increase holiday entitlement and to change existing parental leave arrangements in return for no increase in basic rates and the retention of the no-strike clause. The bottom line for the management negotiating team is to trade a productivity bonus, an increase in holiday entitlement and changes to parental leave arrangements in return for no increase in pay and retention of the no-strike clause.

The grid also shows what management expects to be the negotiating objectives of its employees' representatives. Management knows that the representatives would ideally like to trade no items. Management is of course aware that the employee representatives will view this as unrealistic. The grid therefore shows that management anticipates the employees' realistic bargaining aim to be one of trading pay and changes in existing parental leave arrangements in return for the introduction of a productivity-based bonus scheme, increased holiday entitlement and the removal of the no-strike clause. The grid further shows that the management negotiating team anticipates that the bottom line for the employees' representatives is likely to be to trade no increase in pay, no changes to the parental leave arrangements and the retention of the no-strike clause in return for the introduction of a productivity-based bonus scheme and an increase in holiday entitlement.

The grid thus suggests there is a basis for agreement between the parties. This is indicated in that the fall-back positions of the two parties do not have **X**s against the same issue. Management is not prepared to trade a basic rate of pay increase and the removal of the no-strike clause. Management anticipates that the employees are prepared to trade these issues. The employees are expected by management not to be prepared to trade the introduction of a productivity-based bonus scheme and an increase in holiday entitlement. However, management has assessed that it can live with trading these issues. The management negotiating team now has a structure of how the bargaining can be expected to develop and evolve. In the face-to-face sessions with the representatives of its employees it will have to pass information to them as to what issues management is prepared to trade and at the same time seek to gain information from the employees' side which confirms management's expectations as to what the employees are prepared to trade.

The aspiration grid enables a negotiating party to structure to its own position systematically and to record the expected outcomes of the other party's position. It sets out each side's objectives, known or anticipated, and their three positions. The grid gives an expected structure to negotiating sessions prior to their beginning. It indicates the information the parties require to obtain and transmit to each other during the forthcoming negotiating sessions to confirm (or readjust) their expectations of the other party's position. If information received during the negotiating sessions suggests that expectations about the other party's intentions are inaccurate, the aspiration grid has to be re-analysed and amended.

The aspiration grid gives management a picture of how the bargaining sessions are likely to develop. In the actual bargaining sessions, management can test out whether its anticipation of the employees' bargaining objectives is correct or must be reassessed by ensuring that the employees and their representatives receive clear information as to management's bargaining objectives.

If management enters bargaining without having established objectives, the probability of reaching an unsatisfactory outcome or entering into a dispute situation is increased. It is essential that in establishing its 'realistic' and 'fall-back' bargaining objectives, management takes proper, and due, account of the relative balance of bargaining power between itself and the employees (see Chapters 1 and 2). The management negotiating team must take all these factors into account. If the balance of bargaining power favours the employer, the aspiration grid will be different from one that relates to a situation in which the bargaining power lies with the employees and their representatives.

Planning strategy and tactics

The third phase of the preparation stage is when the negotiating team plans its strategy and tactics to deliver its bargaining objectives. This involves:

- deciding before meeting with the other party who is to speak, in what order, and on what issues
- anticipating arguments and counter-arguments.

Anticipating arguments and counter-arguments
An important part of planning the strategy and the tactics to achieve the bargaining objectives is to antici-pate the arguments mostly likely to be used by the other party against your case and to consider how they might be countered. In this regard it is helpful if a member of management negotiating team can play the 'devil's advocate' and probe management's case for its weak points, exploring how the employees' and/or their representatives' arguments against management's case might be exposed and answered. Plans can then be made as to how they might be responded to.

Communication with the team
During the negotiating sessions the team may find it necessary to communicate among themselves with-out the need to call for an adjournment. Any agreed method of communication will have to be non-verbal. Research shows that the most common method used in negotiating teams is the passing of notes.

In conducting negotiating, the preparation stage is the longest and most important stage in the process. If management's analysis of the information it has gathered – whether by interview techniques or from statistical data – is incorrect, it will establish inappropriate bargaining objectives and develop an unrealistic strategy and tactics, with the result that the chances of achieving its bargaining objectives will be significantly reduced. If it does achieve its objectives despite inadequate preparation, it is likely to be because management holds the upper hand in the relative balance of bargaining power stakes or by good fortune. Good luck, however, is not a management skill. A 'seat of the pants' approach to a bargaining situation is understandable – but any competent negotiator will tell you there is no substitute for preparation. The golden rule to remember when preparing for bargaining is: 'Failure to prepare is preparing to fail.'

If management fails to prepare adequately, however, disaster does not follow automatically. The situation can be rescued if management reassesses its negotiating analysis, objectives and strategy and tactics in the light of new information it gains and which was not available at the preparation stage. In short, it amends its original aspiration grid. Indeed, it is essential that management reassesses its bargaining objectives, its aspiration grid and the analysis upon which they are based every time it gains information it did not have, or did not take into account, when getting ready for the next negotiating session. During any negotiating adjournments, management should frequently monitor and review its negotiating objectives (including a review of the aspiration grid) in the light of how the negotiations are developing and progressing.

Failure to prepare is preparing to fail. Explain the importance of this statement for employee relations managers who are involved in negotiation.

SUMMARY OF PREPARATION FOR BARGAINING

There are three stages in preparing for bargaining:

- analysis
- establishment of aims
- strategy and tactics

Analysis
- the facts/sources of information of the incident, claim, etc
- any relevant rules (company) agreements or 'custom and practice'
- any relevant precedents or comparisons
- attitude of management on the issue(s)
- what issues are tradable? Which issues will the other party trade?
- significance of the issues for the employees, their representatives and their trade union

Aims
- ideal (like to achieve)
- realistic (hoped for)
- fall-back (must have)
- consider feasibility of aims against relative bargaining power

Strategy and tactics
- size of team
- who is to speak? In what order? On what subject?
- anticipation of most likely of the other side's arguments and counter to them
- be familiar with the meaning and intent of the agreements, procedures and rules of your organisation

Preparation is vital
Wrong analysis = Incorrect aims = Failure to achieve objectives

Golden rule
Failure to prepare
     is
Preparing to fail

The presentation stage

At the first meeting with the other side, if the negotiators are unknown to each other, it may be necessary to break the ice by the teams introducing themselves to each other. On the other hand, if the negotiators are well known to each other, some other form of general meeting might help to start things off on the right foot.

Management begins the meeting

If management is making the initial presentation, the leader of the management team first gives a general summary of its proposals by the use of such language as:

> We want to put to you today proposals in six areas – increased holidays, reduced working hours, increased pay, enhanced childcare facilities, changes in working practices, and the conditions surrounding the operation of the sick pay scheme ...

After informing the employee(s), or their representatives, of the issues it is going to raise, management then substantiates the case it has already outlined by adducing supporting facts and figures emphasising the rationale behind the proposals and trying to suggest its strength of feeling towards each of them. So the first part of the presentation stage of negotiating involves both parties' telling each other what they ideally would want from each other.

Although it is perhaps not common practice, it is good practice for each party to put on the table all the issues they wish to be dealt with in the forthcoming negotiation/bargaining sessions and not just to present its views on selected issues. This avoids the possibility of a set of long negotiating sessions over many issues ending in apparent agreement only for one party to then say 'Oh, by the way – we need to talk about [a new issue] as well.' Some negotiators believe there can be advantages in 'keeping something up your sleeve to hit them with later', but bearing in mind that the purpose of negotiation is to come to an agreement, this is a dangerous tactic because:

- The hidden issue might be a non-negotiable issue for the other side or one on which it is prepared to trade only if the alternative is no agreement at all. If this is the case, there is a high probability that the negotiations will break down, losing with them the issues on which an accommodation has already been made.

- It can destroy the mutual trust between the leaders of the respective negotiating teams. Negotiators do not like to have negotiated in good faith and to have openly raised all the issues to secure an agreement only to find that the other party has behaved differently.

- If one party behaves consistently in this way, the other party will become to regard it as part of that party's negotiating ritual and take it into account in future negotiating sessions. Any new alleged surprise thereafter hoping to evoke further improvements in the offer/claim by the other side is trumped.

At best, a management may get away with the 'keep something up your sleeve' tactic once. The employee relations professional should be an open negotiator who puts all his or her cards to be considered in any negotiation on the table from the outset.

Management receives proposal(s)

If management is receiving one or more proposals from its employees' representatives, it listens carefully to what they are saying and does not interrupt their presentation. When the employee side has completed its presentation, it is good management practice to avoid an unconsidered (ie knee-jerk) response. By the same token, it is unwise for management to respond with immediate counter-proposals unless they have been agreed beforehand. If management is receiving proposals for the first time, its response should be confined to asking questions to seek clarification of the employees' proposals so that it can be confident it genuinely understands what those proposals actually mean. Typical questions might be:

- What does the actual proposal on item X really mean? Could you please give us more details?

- What is the source of information on the statistic on wage rates/inflation rate, etc, that you have quoted?

- When you make reference to average earnings, what kind of average do you mean – mode, median, unweighted arithmetic?

It is essential that at the end of the presentation of the employees' proposals, management is 100-percent certain of what has been proposed and what the employees' proposals actually mean. It is therefore good practice, before the employees' presentation session concludes, for management to summarise back in a neutral manner what it understands has been proposed on behalf of the employees. At the end of the employees' presentation, management should arrange to meet with the employees at a future date so that a full and measured response to the employees' proposal(s) can be given.

We can illustrate this point by use of the following typical measured response from CEN Ltd to a list of demands from its employees for changes in their wages and employment conditions.

Case study

Response to wage claim

Thank you for your claim, which has been given very careful consideration by the company.

Before addressing the principal part of your claim – an increase in wage rates – I would like to deal with the other items that you put forward for consideration.

Increased holidays
Currently, all staff working for CEN enjoy five weeks' annual holiday. This compares favourably with other organisations across a range of industries, and in particular with the majority of our

---

competitors. It is also important to emphasise that holiday entitlement for one group of staff is not something that the company would decide in isolation. When we agreed to recognise the union for collective bargaining, it was made clear that being a member of a trade union would not bring any better, or worse, benefits to individuals. Similarly, those areas of the company that have chosen not to go down the collective bargaining route will likewise be no better or worse off.

Because the company can see no justification for increasing holiday entitlement across the board, we are therefore unable to agree to this aspect of your claim.

Sabbaticals
Similar arguments about common benefits also apply to this issue. However, we do note that in your claim you are not specific about how sabbaticals would operate. While we do not believe that such a system would be workable across the company, we are prepared to listen to any detailed ideas that you want to present before ruling this matter out completely.

Childcare provision
Again, this is an area in which you have provided no detail. For example, how many people would want to take advantage of any provision? Would those people be prepared to make a contribution to the cost? Clearly the company can see some advantages – staff retention, for example – that might flow from such a provision, but again it is not something that can be considered for one group of staff in isolation. What we propose, therefore, is that the personnel director carries out an evaluation of costs, local provision, etc, and that the matter is revisited as a potential company-wide benefit. If you would like to submit ideas, number of interested participants, etc, to this evaluation, the personnel director would be delighted.

Healthcare
Together with colleagues across the company you will, either tomorrow or Thursday, be receiving a letter from David Smith advising you of the company's intention in this area. As I am sure your colleagues in the union have advised you, this is something that the personnel director has been evaluating since earlier this year, and it has always been the intention that any scheme would be delivered across the group.

Canteen
We are afraid that this element of your claim cannot be accepted. There is no evidence to suggest that staff are prevented from taking a proper lunch break and there are numerous local outlets serving hot and cold food at affordable prices. The suggestion that staff are somehow forced down the road of eating unhealthy snacks does not stand up to any sort of close scrutiny. However, if you can provide evidence of any member of staff who is prevented from taking their lunch break on a regular basis, please do so. It will then be addressed.

Staffing levels
Management are not fully aware of any 'on-going crisis situation', but if you can provide details of your concerns, they will be looked at and responded to.

Motoring expenses
We do not understand your comment about an absence of motoring expenses. Any member of staff who uses his or her own car for business use is reimbursed at the rate of 33p per mile. We acknowledge that this might need to be reviewed and are prepared to discuss this with you. However, for the record, there is no Inland Revenue rate of 43p.

Air conditioning/pool cars
Please provide us with details of your concerns.

Investors in People
Your comments on the decision to apply for the IiP standard are noted. So far as job descriptions are concerned, Colin has already written to individuals about this and we now consider that this matter has been dealt with.

Pay
First of all we would like to make it clear that these negotiations are between CEN Ltd and Union X. Other companies within the Group will carry out their own negotiations and arrive at their own conclusions. We have no intention of linking these quite separate matters.

We are solely concerned with pay levels at our establishment and what is right for this business.

We note your comments regarding an increase of 5 per cent across the board because, you say, it is increasingly costly to live in Mid-Anglia. While we appreciate that gaining a foothold on the housing ladder in this region can be difficult, this does not apply to those already living here. For those individuals already resident in the area, the rise in the cost of living is 2.1 per cent. The Bank of England, in its latest inflation report, does not expect it to rise significantly above this level over the next two years. Clearly, such economic data has to be taken into account by the company when setting its budgets for both revenue and costs, particularly wage costs. For example, it is unlikely that our advertisers would accept an increase in our rates significantly higher than the prevailing rate of inflation. We therefore have to keep budgeted increases in revenue within inflationary targets, which limits our ability to budget for unsustainable increases in our costs.

For this reason, we are unable to accept your claim for an across the board increase of 5 per cent. However, we do understand the need to increase our overall salary rates for your group of employees so that they properly reflect the market in which we operate. We therefore propose to:

1   Increase the starting rate for trainees from £12,250 to £13,000 – an increase of 6.1 per cent. This would also mean that since 2000 the starting rate for trainees has increased by 27 per cent. We also intend to increase the final year rate for trainees from £14,250 to £15,000 – an increase of 5.3 per cent since last year and an increase since 2000 of 22 per cent.
2   At present, we have a 0–2-year qualified band of £14,250 to £15,750 and a 2+ years' qualified rate for seniors that starts at £15,500. It is our intention to abolish the 0–2-year qualified rate and simply have a senior staff rate instead.
3   With effect from 1 January next year, trainees will go on to the higher level (£15,000) once they have obtained their qualification. This usually occurs approximately 21 months after they commence training. Once they have satisfactorily completed their training they will move on to the newly established senior rate which, with effect from 1 January next year, will be £16,500 for senior qualified staff. This represents an increase of 6.45 per cent for 2+ years' qualified staff and 15.8 per cent on the starting rate for newly qualified staff. At the beginning of 2000 the starting rate for newly qualified staff was £11,750, so our proposals would represent an increase over three years of 40 per cent.
4   For individuals who fall outside the changes detailed, we propose to increase salaries in 2005 by 2.5 per cent. This, as in previous years, represents a rise above the prevailing rate of inflation. Overall, the changes we propose for next year will bring significant increases to over 50 per cent of our staff, the average increase for your members being 4.7 per cent.

So by the end of the presentation stage both parties will have put to each other their ideal positions. There is unlikely, at this point, to be much common ground between them. However, the issues to be resolved during the negotiating sessions will now be known to both parties, who can forthwith begin the task of seeking confirmation of their anticipated common ground.

Identifying common ground

The emphasis and tone of the negotiations now switches from concentrating on differences to identifying points of common ground that can form the basis of a possible agreement. The point has now been reached at which both parties must seek to confirm the expected common ground from which an agreement can be built. Each team has to obtain, in future bargaining sessions with other party, information that will enable it to confirm whether its expectations of the location of the common ground are correct.

Each subsequent bargaining session must be used constructively by both parties to gain this necessary information. Management must supply information to the other party so that the employees can assess the correctness of their expectations of management's position on the issues that are the subject of the negotiations. Negotiation sessions which do not provide the information needed by the two parties to confirm their anticipated areas of common ground are not a constructive use of time – negotiating sessions do happen in which neither party gains relevant information. This generally occurs when either party tries to:

- score points off the other
- lay blame
- issue threats
- shout down the other side or be sarcastic
- interrupt
- talk too much
- attack personalities on the other side.

Management can seek to confirm its expectations as to where the common ground with the other side lies by a number of techniques. The most important of these are:

- the 'if and then' technique, which involves using such language as 'If you are prepared to move closer to our position on issue Y, then we are prepared to move closer to your position on X' – A positive response to this means that X and Y have been identified as tradable items. The technique deliberately emphasises the requirement of the other side to move. It is a conditional offer
- open discussion within broad parameters – For example, management could indicate that an issue might be considered, but only in return for something – say, a different set of employee representative arrangements. Management would then outline these arrangements so that they form the basis of discussion and negotiation
- questioning (interviewing) for clarification of the other side's position
- watching the body language of other party (frowns, glances, nods, etc) as the members react to the proposals put forward
- listening carefully to what is being said, including any conditions placed on any offers/proposals (see below)
- every now and then summarising, using neutral language, the other party's position on an issue – This is particularly helpful if the issue concerned is complex. Such a summary might well begin with something like ' ... So what you are saying is that you understand our offer on issue X means that

[at this point there is a complex example given of how the party believes what the other party has proposed will operate], and we both have no problems with that.' Each separate negotiating meeting should begin with one or the other party's summary of the stage the negotiations have reached. Such a summary usually outlines the areas upon which agreement has been reached and the issues upon which an agreement has still to be reached

- linking the issues so that specific issues may together be precisely identified as ones the parties are prepared to trade or not – Linking issues also ensures that the negotiations maintain momentum

- seeking agreement in principle before discussing details – It is pointless discussing the details of, for example, how flexibility of employees between different tasks will operate if one party is totally opposed to employee flexibility.

If the use of the techniques outlined above and summarised in the box below draws out new information, an adjournment can be called – if thought necessary – to consider the implications of the new information, including whether there is a need to reassess negotiating aims (ie amend the aspiration grid), to reopen analysis or to revise strategy and tactics.

SUMMARY OF TECHNIQUES TO CONFIRM COMMON GROUND

- the 'if and then' technique
- open discussion
- asking questions, seeking clarification
- watching the body language
- listening to what is said, and how
- periodic summarising
- linking of issues
- looking for a general agreement before a detailed one

Listening for disguised messages
In negotiation situations, listening skills enable a negotiation team to decode signals hidden within the spoken language. Let us look at some example statements:

- 'At this stage, we are not prepared to consider that,' means 'That is a tradable item but at this stage it is not thought necessary to trade it.'

- 'We would find it extremely difficult to meet that demand,' means 'Meeting that demand would not be entirely out of the question.'

- 'I am not empowered to negotiate on that point,' means 'You will have to talk about that to my boss.'

- 'We can discuss that point,' means 'It is negotiable.'

- 'These are standard company terms,' means 'These terms are negotiable up to a point.'

- 'It is not our policy to make bonus payments – and even if we did, they would not be as large as 10 per cent,' means 'We will let you have 2 per cent.'

- 'It is not our normal practice to . . .' means 'We might . . . if you make it worth our while.'

There is information significant enough to confirm tradable items in these statements. If either negotiating team neglects to listen for the true meaning hidden within such statements, it may miss out on learning what it needs to know.

The importance of momentum

Confirmation of what is the common ground gives the negotiation sessions a momentum. If talks then become bogged down on a particular issue, the momentum can be sustained by switching to a new issue. This reinforces the importance of the negotiators' putting all issues on the table from the outset. A thorny issue can be returned to later, and if it is then the only outstanding issue to an agreement being secured, the parties are more than likely to readjust their attitudes towards that issue to a more accommodating one. Both sides are at that stage faced with a stark choice. Either an accommodation is reached on the one outstanding issue or no agreement is made – all the contributory agreements on issues that have been reached till then fall by the wayside. The party that has the stronger feelings on the remaining, but difficult, issue is thus faced with the very real possibility of throwing the baby out with the bathwater.

Outline the various techniques by which a management negotiating team can search for the common ground and thereby the basis for an agreement with representatives of the workforce. Which of these techniques do you consider to be the most important, and why?

Adjournment

In bargaining the use of adjournments is helpful in ensuring that the negotiating sessions are proceeding as planned. The number and frequency of adjournments depend upon the normal practice of negotiating sessions in the environment in which they are being undertaken. Although adjournments may be suggested at any time, there are at least three constructive uses of the ad hoc (as distinct from the scheduled) break:

- to give the parties an opportunity to withdraw and review progress among themselves or consider a proposal tabled by the other side

- to provide a break if the negotiations have reached an impasse or become bogged down in trivia or personal argument such that team discipline is in danger of breaking or has broken down

- to provide an opportunity for one or two members of each side to talk informally with each other away from the negotiating table in a manner that would not be appropriate in the formal bargaining sessions. This equally gives the leaders of the two teams a chance to meet away from the negotiating table to discuss, without commitment, what it would take to unblock the impasse. The words 'without commitment' are normally used in such situations to reassure the other members of the two teams that their leaders will not strike any formal deal without prior reference back.

Adjournments thus enable one or both parties to reconsider their position in private and are very much part of negotiating procedures. Their main purpose is to provide space in which to review and assess progress against the negotiating objectives and against the perceived objectives of the other party. They provide an opportunity to update the negotiating strategy in respect of how the negotiations are progressing. If the adjournment is taken to consider a specific proposal, it is important to remember that such adjournments create expectations of a response in the minds of the other party. Reading what is going on is vital, and keeping the mind focused on the negotiating objectives is essential. In such situations, the warning by Cairns (1996) is salutary:

> If the adjournment is to consider a new offer, don't take ten minutes to reject it and 50 minutes discussing sport or the previous night's TV. Management may get the signal that if you took an hour to consider their offer, they are close to an agreement.

Adjournments should also be sought by management whenever it has any doubts about how the negotiating session is progressing or whenever team discipline is about to break down (or has already broken down). The golden rule for management is: 'If in doubt, get out.'

Concluding the agreement

Entering this stage of the bargaining process is a matter of timing and judgement. The ability to recognise the best deal that in the circumstances can be reached and will be acceptable to the constituents represented is an important skill for the employee relations professional to acquire. In negotiating situations where increases in pay and other conditions are being offered in return for changes in working practices, the last item to be decided is what the amount of the increase in pay will be. There are a number of reasons for this.

First, the employer wants to know exactly what it is going to get in terms of increased work effort for the pay increase. It is only when an amount is on offer that the employer can make a considered judgement whether the 'price' for the changes in working practices gained is worth it. The same applies to the employees. It is only when they know what they have to do for it (ie the price they have to pay) that they can make a considered decision on whether the proposed pay increase offer is adequate compensation.

Second, if the pay issue is put on the table early in the negotiations, the negotiations themselves are likely to become deadlocked. The momentum to the negotiating session will come to a halt. Neither of the parties could accommodate each other's interests because they would not, at this stage, be able to assess whether the 'price' was worthwhile.

Third, by negotiating over pay after all other issues have been agreed, the negotiators are faced with a stark choice. If they cannot accommodate each other over pay, then the whole agreement collapses. What has been agreed concerning the other items in the respective shopping lists is withdrawn. The parties have to weigh up whether they want to 'throw out the baby with the bathwater'. Neither will want to see all its earlier hard work go to waste. Attitudes are thus more attuned to compromise than if there were more than one outstanding issue. Both sides also have to weigh up whether – if an agreement fails to materialise over the one outstanding issue of pay improvement – they are prepared to bear the costs that go with the other party's imposing industrial sanctions against them.

Factors to consider in concluding the agreement

There are a number of considerations management should bear in mind when closing the negotiations. First, it must be satisfied that all the issues have been discussed and agreed, and that both parties fully understand what they have accepted. If there is a misunderstanding over what has been agreed, the negotiating process must recommence. It is crucial that both sides have the same understanding of what they have agreed, or when the agreement is implemented the parties will become embroiled in frequent disputes over how one party or the other is interpreting and/or applying the agreement.

Second, management has to convince the other party that its final offer is final. Management must be extremely careful not to allow any suggestion that what is effectively a bluff is its final position or that what is genuinely its final position is no more than a bluff. A series of 'final offers' from management will destroy its credibility with the other party and undermine its ability to convince the workforce that the bottom line has been reached. Management gains little by telling its employees that there can be no further improvement on its offer if the threat of industrial pressure from the employees – for example, by a ballot supporting industrial action – brings a further concession. In such circumstances management has demonstrated to the other side that it has not reached its fall-back position and the employees will begin to expect even further improvement. When management tells the employees that its offer is final, then that must be the case.

The authors once heard a personnel director referring to the fact he always had four sets of final offers, each hidden away in one of his pockets. This may sound amusing, but when he pulls out these four offers he will destroy his negotiating credibility with the employees and their representative body. To tell them management has reached its final offer will not be believed, because what the director was saying was that he was prepared to raise his final offer at least four times. What would he do if the fourth offer were not believed? A management negotiator must retain the respect and credibility of the other party. 'Final final final' offers will not achieve this.

Third, management should avoid being rushed into concluding a final agreement, no matter how tempting the offer/proposal from other side sounds. Management must make sure it has all the information it requires from the employees (or their representatives) and then seek an adjournment. This will enable the management negotiating team to examine the final offer and to identify any potential problems that may have gone unnoticed before.

Writing up the agreement

Once management has an oral agreement, it should run through a summary of the proceedings with the employees' representatives noting precisely what has been agreed, and thereafter secure an agreement that what has been summarised is indeed what was agreed. It should then be written up in draft form. The written agreement should state:

- who the parties to the agreement are
- the date it was concluded
- the date upon which it will become operative
- which groups/grades of employees are covered by the agreement
- the contents (clauses) of the agreement
- the duration of the agreement
- whether the agreement can be reopened before this end date, and if so in what circumstances
- how disputes over its interpretation and application will be settled (through the existing grievance/disputes procedure?)
- which other agreements, if any, it replaces.

The written agreement should contain the signatures of representatives of the parties covered by the agreement.

Explain why recording the negotiating process is vital. Outline what techniques can be used for this purpose and what the advantages of each are.

The agreement is usually drafted by management and then sent to the other party, which will usually initial the clauses the wording of which it accepts. Only when both sides are happy with the wording will the agreement be printed and formally signed.

There are some pitfalls management should avoid when writing up the agreement. First, the team should check the wording very carefully. One word can make a big difference to the meaning of a clause in the agreement. There is, for example, a vast difference in meaning between a clause which states that 'the management may provide' and a clause that states 'the management will provide'. The first implies that in certain circumstances management may not provide. The second leaves no room for doubt.

Second, the team should retain full concentration in the latter stages of the negotiations. It is likely that by then the negotiating process will have been going on for some time. There is a danger that the management negotiators will relax once they have an oral agreement, thinking perhaps that the hard work is over. However, management should bear in mind that all too quickly the details of what was said in negotiations may be forgotten. What has been agreed will be what is down in black and white on the signed agreement.

Third, the agreement must be straightforward and easy to understand. Unless it is fully understood by both parties and its wording and intent clear, its operation will cause endless disputes over its interpretation and application.

Fourth, it is important for the management negotiating team to keep an accurate record of what was agreed. It may turn out to be management's only protection against an attempt by the other party to insert into the agreement something that was not agreed during the negotiations. Fortunately, attempts to 'cheat' when writing up an agreement are extremely rare among management and employees' bargaining representatives. To behave in this way would be to try to pull a fast one over the other side. A party may get away with this type of behaviour once – but the cost could be high in terms of lost professionalism and of lost trust with the other party.

So throughout the stages of negotiation there is a gradual movement towards common points of agreement. At the end of the presentation stage, there is little common ground between the parties, but at each subsequent meeting there should emerge – via an exchange of information – an increasing degree of common ground. Each meeting of the two parties should make progress towards a constructive compromise.

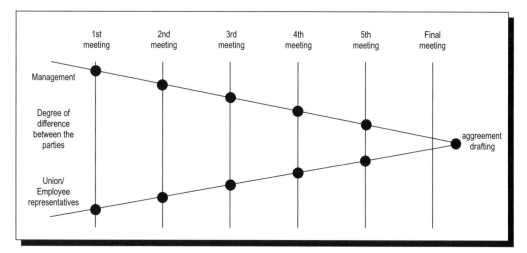

Figure 13 *The reconciliation of differences over time*

THE OUTCOME OF NEGOTIATIONS

The best outcome of the bargaining process is one in which both parties make some gains – the so-called win/win situation. This is normally achieved by professional negotiators who concentrate on achieving well-prepared objectives, on maintaining long-term relationships with their other party, on emphasising a prag-matic approach, and on making an agreement which meets the needs of both parties. However, the relative balance of bargaining power between the two parties still heavily influences the outcome of the bargaining regardless of the professionalism the management bargaining team displays.

The opposite outcome is the lose/lose situation which arises from a lack of professionalism on the part of the negotiators. The result is that:

- neither party achieves its objectives
- no agreement is secured
- long-term relationships are soured
- the constituents of the negotiators no longer respect/trust them
- both parties become disillusioned with the negotiating process.

A third possible outcome is the so-called win/lose situation in which one party dominates the other and secures something from the other party without giving anything in return. We saw above that where this is the outcome it is referred to as distributive bargaining. Such bargaining outcomes are characterised by an 'us and them' distinction between the parties. The bargaining teams' energies are directed towards victory ('I win, you lose'), a strong emphasis on immediate solutions regardless of their long-term consequences, sometimes even personalised conflicts rather than the considered assessment of facts, information and arguments, and little consideration of the quality of future relations between the parties after the negotiations are over.

SUMMARY

Negotiations can be defined as what happens when two or more parties come together to make an agree-ment by purposeful persuasion and by making constructive compromises.

- Four different negotiating situations can be identified – between managers, grievance-handling, bargaining and group problem-solving.
- The most common negotiating situation in which employee relations professionals are likely to find themselves is negotiating with their managerial colleagues over various issues – for example, to determine the appropriate course of action to solve a problem.
- Grievance-handling is resolving an individual employee's complaint that management behaviour (or that of another person) has impacted unfairly upon them.
- Integrative bargaining is where the parties involved reach an agreement by trading items in the list of demands they make of each other.
- Group problem-solving is a situation in which two or more parties negotiate the details whereby one party will co-operate with an action proposed by the other that is of common interest to both par-ties.
- The main differences between employee relations negotiations and commercial negotiations lie in the choice of negotiating partner, face-to-face relationships, adjournments, the status of agree-ments reached, and the need to consider the quality of future relationships.
- There are five stages to the bargaining process – preparation and analysis, presentation, search-ing for the common ground, concluding the agreement and writing up the agreement.

- The most important stage of negotiating is preparation and analysis, and its importance can be summed up in the sentence 'Failure to prepare is preparing to fail.'

- An aspiration grid shows the issues the parties expect to trade with each other and helps identify the common ground likely to be the basis of reaching a compromise agreement.

- There are techniques available to management through which it can confirm its expectations of where the common ground lies.

- These include the 'if and then' technique, questioning, body language, listening and summarising.

- In writing up the agreement, clear wording is important if future disputes over the interpretation and operation of the agreement are to be avoided.

FURTHER READING

CAIRNS L. (1996) *Negotiation Skills in the Workplace: A Practical Handbook*. London, Pluto Press.

INCOMES DATA SERVICES, *Pay Directory*, published three times a year.

INCOMES DATA SERVICES, *Report*, published twice monthly.

INDUSTRIAL RELATIONS SERVICES, *Employment Trends*, published twice monthly.

INDUSTRIAL RELATIONS SERVICES, *Pay Intelligence*, published monthly.

OFFICE FOR NATIONAL STATISTICS, *Labour Market Trends*, published monthly.

OFFICE FOR NATIONAL STATISTICS, *New Earnings Survey*, published annually in six parts.

WALTON R. E. and MCKERSIE R. B. (1991) *A Behavioral Theory of Labor Negotiations*, 2nd edn. New York, Ithaca.

WALTON R. E., CUTCHER-HERSHENFELD J. E. and MCKERSIE R. B. (1994) *Strategic Negotiations*, Cambridge, Mass., Harvard Business School Press.

Employee performance and behaviour

CHAPTER 10

CHAPTER OBJECTIVES

When you have completed this chapter you should be aware of and able to describe:

- **the development of disciplinary procedures**
- **how the law supports the use of disciplinary procedures and protects individuals from unfair treatment**
- **the importance of clear rules about conduct**
- **the importance of counselling to the disciplinary process**
- **how to use the disciplinary process to manage different disciplinary problems**
- **the importance of setting clear performance standards for individuals.**

INTRODUCTION

This chapter and the one that follows cover two related topics: discipline and grievance. Although they are to be dealt with separately it is important to recognise that both are a two-way process and concern complaints, real or imagined, by one party against another. Both are covered by a specific Code of Practice, which is examined in detail later in the chapter. However, because of the way that the law has intervened in the disciplinary process (unfair dismissal legislation), disciplinary issues have tended to have a much higher profile within organisations than grievances, which are not as legally regulated.

What is discipline?

Discipline is an emotive word in the context of employment. The dictionary offers several definitions of the word 'discipline', ranging from 'punishment or chastisement' to 'systematic training in obedience'. There is no doubt that discipline at work can be one of the most difficult issues with which a manager has to deal. It brings to the forefront matters relating to an individual's performance, capability and conduct, and in the context of employment, the most appropriate definition to adopt is (Collins Concise Dictionary):

> to improve or attempt to improve the behaviour, orderliness, etc, of by training, conditions or rules.

In this chapter we examine the practices and skills that are required if employee behaviour and performance is to be effectively managed. This includes the principles of discipline-handling, the characteristics of a fair and effective disciplinary procedure, the legal aspects of discipline and dismissal, and the monitoring and evaluation of disciplinary procedures. A fair and effective disciplinary procedure is one that concentrates on improving or changing behaviour, and not one that relies on the principle of punishment.

Management problems with the discipline process

Many managers have a problem with managing employee behaviour and performance because they believe that the methodology available to them – the disciplinary process – is cumbersome and ineffective or that the law on employment rights is heavily biased in favour of the employee. This can often result in problems being ignored because it is felt that effective action against individual employees either takes too long or is liable to mean an appearance before an employment tribunal at which the employee may well be successful. Many managers share this basic misconception, and it is the responsibility of the employee relations professional to advise and guide their managerial colleagues through what, to many, is a mine-field.

Good practice

It is important for managers, at all levels, to appreciate that the effectiveness of the business can be under-mined if issues relating to conduct, capability and performance are not handled professionally and consist-ently, or, even worse, if such matters are ignored altogether. This chapter looks inter alia at the concept of 'good practice' in relation to performance and behaviour at work, at the steps that have to be taken when managers are trying to alter existing behaviour or performance, and at how to ensure that all employees are treated fairly. 'Good practice' is a concept that many managers have difficulty with because it is a term that is difficult to define. In the context of discipline at work it is about acting with just cause, using pro-cedures correctly, acting consistently, following the rules of natural justice – it is all four of those things – and more. It is also about developing those good management habits which ensure that you do follow pro-cedure, you do act consistently and you do take account of the rules of natural justice when taking disci-plinary action. Good practice is therefore an important principle. Not only does it help to ensure fairness and consistency but it makes good business sense and can add value.

THE ORIGINS OF DISCIPLINARY PROCEDURES

Up to the beginning of the 1970s employers had almost unlimited power to discipline and dismiss individ-ual employees – and in many instances they were not slow to exercise this power. While it was possible for a dismissed employee to sue for 'wrongful dismissal' under the common law, it was rarely a practical option because of the time and heavy costs involved. The only time that employer power was likely to be restricted was where trade unions were present in the workplace and dismissal procedures were estab-lished through the collective bargaining process.

This changed with the Industrial Relations Act 1971. This Act gave individual employees the right, for the first time, to complain to an industrial tribunal that they had been unfairly dismissed. Industrial tribunals themselves had only been established in 1964, and so in 1971 were a relatively new feature of business life. They were renamed employment tribunals with effect from 1 August 1998 by the Employment Rights (Dispute Resolution) Act 1998, and this change has been carried through to all pre-existing enactments. As well as introducing the right not to be unfairly dismissed, the 1971 Act also introduced, in 1972, the Industrial Relations Code of Practice. This brought in the idea that there was a right and a wrong way to deal with issues of discipline. It was subsequently superseded by an ACAS Code of Practice on *Disciplinary Practice and Procedures in Employment*, and this has in turn now been superseded by a Code of Practice on *Disciplinary and Grievance Procedures* (see below).

The 1971 Act was a turning-point in the relationship between employer and employee. The relative informality of the then industrial tribunals and the fact that access to them did not depend on lawyers or money meant that for many employees the threat of dismissal without good reason disappeared or diminished. This does not mean that employees cannot be unfairly dismissed. They can. The law has never removed from management the ability to dismiss who it likes, when it likes, and for whatever reason it likes. All that has happened since 1971 is that where employers are deemed to have acted unreasonably and unfairly in dismissing employees, they can be forced to compensate an individual for the consequences of those actions. Most employers have accepted this legal intervention without serious complaint and seek to manage performance and behaviour issues in as fair a way as possible. Some clearly do not, and take a cavalier attitude to individual employment rights. Others suffer from a misconception as to what they can do and how the law impacts upon their actions.

THE CURRENT LEGAL POSITION

Up until 1996, the law relating to discipline and dismissal was contained in the Employment Protection (Consolidation) Act 1978. In August of that year the Employment Rights Act 1996 came into force, consolidating provisions contained in the 1978 Act together with provisions of the Wages Act 1986, the Sunday Trading Act 1994 and the Trade Union Reform and Employment Rights Act (TURERA) 1993. The Employment Relations Act 1999 and the Employment Act 2002 have made further changes.

The starting-point for the disciplinary process is to be found in section 1 of the 1996 Act, which deals with an employee's right to a statement of employment particulars. Section 3 of the Act states that any statement of particulars must also specify any disciplinary rules applicable to the employee or referring the employee to the provisions of a document specifying such rules which is reasonably accessible to the employee. The Employment Act 2002 has now inserted a further requirement that the statement must also include information about any procedures applicable to the taking of disciplinary decisions.

The section goes on to stipulate that the statement of particulars must also specify who an employee can appeal to if he or she is dissatisfied with any disciplinary decision that is made.

Sections 94 to 134 of the Act deal specifically with unfair dismissal and set out

- the legal definition of dismissal
- the specific reasons for which it is fair to dismiss an employee
- the position of shop workers who refuse to work on a Sunday
- the position of trade union officials
- the position of health and safety representatives
- the position of pension trustees.

Fair dismissals

There are three ways in which individuals can be legally dismissed. One: their employment is terminated with or without notice. This is the most common situation and includes circumstances in which somebody is summarily dismissed for gross misconduct or simply given notice of dismissal. Two: they are employed under a fixed-term contract and that contract comes to an end without being renewed. Three: they resign (with or without notice) because of the employer's conduct, a situation more usually known as 'constructive dismissal'. This book is not intended as a legal text and more detail on the meaning and applicability of these three definitions can be found in *Essentials of Employment Law* by David Lewis and Malcolm Sargeant (CIPD, 2004) or in the CIPD Employment Law Service, which has been specifically designed to aid all practitioners with the legal aspects of their work.

Subsection two of section 98 of the Employment Rights Act 1996 defines a number of reasons for which it can be fair to dismiss an employee. These are:

- lack of capability or qualifications
- bad conduct
- redundancy
- breach of a statutory provision.

Dismissals relating to 'capability' (ie poor performance or absence) and 'conduct' (ie poor behaviour), together with 'some other substantial reason' (which is explained below) are probably the most common and have the most links with the disciplinary process. However, to be considered fair reasons for dismissal they have to pass the test of 'reasonableness' set out in section 98 of the Employment Rights Act. This states in subsection 1 that:

> In determining ... whether the dismissal of an employee is fair or unfair, it is for the employer to show (a) the reason for the dismissal and (b) that it is either a reason falling within subsection 2 (see above) or that it is for some other substantial reason.

Subsection 4 then goes on to say that:

> the determination of the question whether the dismissal was fair or unfair, having regard to the reason shown by the employer, shall depend on whether, in the circumstances (including the size and administrative resources of the employer's undertaking), the employer acted reasonably or unreasonably in treating it as a sufficient reason for dismissing the employee; and that the question shall be determined in accordance with equity and the substantial merits of the case.

The requirement to act reasonably has been central to the operation of unfair dismissal legislation for some considerable time, and one of the acid tests that an employer defending a case at tribunal can be judged on is the quality and fairness of its disciplinary procedures. This concept is supported by the legal validity given to the ACAS Code of Practice on *Disciplinary and Grievance Procedures*, and by the case of *Polkey v A E Dayton Services Ltd* [1987] IRLR 503. In the *Polkey* case the House of Lords effectively stated that failing to follow a proper procedure was unlikely to succeed as an effective defence unless the employer could prove that the outcome would have been no different irrespective of the procedure followed – a prospect that was, according to their lordships, fairly remote.

The Employment Act 2002 has now taken the principle of procedural fairness a step further. It contains a section on dismissal and disciplinary procedures which details how disciplinary matters are to be handled. These procedures – the standard three-step dismissal and disciplinary procedure (see below) – are then referred to in a new section 98A of the Employment Rights Act 1996.

Standard (three-step) dismissal and disciplinary procedure

Step One
The employer must set down in writing the nature of the employee's conduct, capability or other circumstances that may result in dismissal or disciplinary action, and send a copy of this statement to the employee. The employer must inform the employee of the basis for his/her complaint.

Step Two
The employer must invite the employee to a hearing at a reasonable time and place where the issue can be discussed. The employee must take all reasonable steps to attend. After the meeting, the employer must inform the employee about any decision, and offer the employee the right of appeal.

Step Three
If the employee wishes to appeal, he/she must inform the employer. The employer must invite the employee to attend a further hearing to appeal against the employer's decision, and the final decision must be communicated to the employee. Where possible, a more senior manager should attend the appeal hearing.

The standard dismissal and disciplinary procedure will apply when an employer is contemplating dismissal (including dismissal on grounds of lack of capability, bad conduct, redundancy, non-renewal of a fixed-term contract and retirement). Failure to follow the above procedure when it applies will make any dismissal automatically unfair. For occasions (cases of gross misconduct, for example) on which it is not possible, or appropriate, to follow the standard three-step procedure, there is a modified two-step procedure that must be followed.

Modified (two-step) dismissal procedure

Step One
The employer must set down in writing the nature of the alleged misconduct that has led to the dismissal, the evidence for this decision, and the right to appeal against the decision, and send a copy of this to the employee.

Step Two
If the employee wishes to appeal, he/she must inform the employer. The employer must invite the employee to attend a hearing to appeal against the employer's decision, and the final decision must be communicated to the employee.

These changes are important, and it is vital therefore that employee relations professionals make themselves aware of the provisions of the 2002 Act.

Unfortunately, section 98A(2) then goes on to say that failure to follow a procedure shall not be unreasonable if the employer can show that he/she would have decided to dismiss had a procedure been followed. For some, this makes an important change to the principle established in the *Polkey* case.

Although the Act sets out minimum qualifying periods of employment for the acquisition of employment rights, these limits can be, and have been, changed. For example, on 1 June 1999 the minimum period of continuous service with an employee to qualify for unfair dismissal was reduced from two years to one year. It is always disturbing when we hear, as we do, managers talk of having a free hand to take whatever actions they like during an individual's first months of employment. Making distinctions about how to deal with performance or behaviour issues based on an individual's length of service is to invite the possibility of inconsistency to creep into the process and to lay the organisation open to legal challenge. To avoid this possibility it is prudent for all managers and employee relations professionals to ignore an individual's length of service and treat all disciplinary issues in exactly the same way.

DISCIPLINARY PROCEDURES
ACAS Code

The ACAS Code of Practice on *Disciplinary and Grievance Procedures in Employment* is of significant importance in the management and resolution of disciplinary issues. While breach of the Code of Practice is, in itself, not unlawful, its provisions and impact are central to the understanding of the disciplinary process. The latest edition of the code, which is issued under section 199 of the Trade Union and Labour Relations (Consolidation) Act 1992, came into effect in October 2004. Its importance to the statutory process is very clear, and although a failure to follow any part of the code does not, in itself, make a person or organisation liable to any proceedings, employment tribunals will take the code into account when considering relevant cases. Similarly, the code has also to be taken into account by the arbitrators appointed by ACAS to determine cases brought under the ACAS Arbitration Scheme (see section 212A of the Trade Union and Labour Relations (Consolidation) Act 1992).

Given such a very clear statement of the code's status, and taking into account the statutory underpinning of procedures by the Employment Act 2002, it is a foolish organisation that does not take seriously the need to invest time in ensuring that its own disciplinary procedure and practice are appropriate and meet the minimum requirements set out in the legislation.

Because of the importance that ACAS places on drawing up disciplinary procedures and company rules, it has produced a handbook *Discipline and Grievance at Work* which provides advice on dealing with disciplinary matters. The handbook, which at the time of writing was being revised, is based on the Code of Practice and looks at:

- the need for rules and disciplinary procedures
- handling a disciplinary matter
- holding a disciplinary hearing
- deciding and implementing disciplinary or other action
- the appeals process.

The disciplinary procedure

It has been the case for a number of years that a disciplinary procedure should be set out as follows:

- an oral warning
- followed by a written warning if the required improvement is not forthcoming
- followed by a final written warning if conduct or performance is still unsatisfactory
- and finally, dismissal.

Under this type of procedure, employers routinely recorded 'oral warnings' – but the latest ACAS advice is that discipline ought to fall into two categories: informal and formal. In the informal stage, which aims to replace the oral warning, no record would be kept, thus making it a genuinely 'oral' warning. Only if the oral (the verbal, informal) approach does not work are employers recommended to move into the formal stage. The formal stage, which provides for a written warning or final written warning, ought to be no different from an organisation's existing disciplinary code, but it is important to be aware of the three-step statutory approach to which we referred above.

Once a situation has entered the formal stage of a disciplinary process there are a number of important points to note. Firstly, it is essential that a record be kept of every disciplinary warning issued, and secondly, it is vital to advise individuals how long a warning will remain 'live'. 'Live' in this context indicates the length of time that a particular disciplinary sanction will stay on the record. Live warnings can be taken into account if further disciplinary issues arise, but warnings that have expired cannot. Many organisations will have different time-scales for different levels of warning – for example, a written warning might be live only for six months, whereas a final written warning might be live for 12 months. Finally, it is important that employees are advised of what will happen next if the desired changes to performance or behaviour are not made. One critical point to note at this stage is the rights that individual employees now have under Data Protection legislation. Under the provisions of this legislation, employees have the right to see anything that the employer holds in their personnel file, and this would include any notes made as part of the disciplinary process. It is therefore essential to ensure that a professional approach is taken to the writing of such notes and that they do not contain malicious or defamatory remarks.

The purpose and scope of a disciplinary procedure should be very clear. It should allow all employees to understand what is expected of them in respect of conduct, attendance and job performance, and set out the rules by which such matters will be governed. The aim is to ensure consistent and fair treatment for all.

> To what extent does your organisation's disciplinary procedure meet the criteria of clarity? Does it set out the time that individual warnings will be 'live', and is it capable of ensuring consistent and fair treatment for all employees? You may consider it worth reviewing your procedure against these benchmarks.

Principles underlying disciplinary procedure

When we examine handling discipline, you will note that the only way to ensure consistency is by taking a 'good practice' approach and recognising that a disciplinary procedure is more than just a series of stages. You should also recognise that there are a number of principles that underlie the procedure which are extremely important and help to ensure good personnel management practice. As with the mechanics of the procedure itself, ACAS offers guidance on good disciplinary procedures – which, it says, should:

- be in writing
- specify to whom they apply
- be non-discriminatory
- provide for matters to be dealt with without undue delay
- provide for proceedings, witness statements and records to be kept confidential
- indicate the disciplinary actions that may be taken
- specify the levels of management which have the authority to take the various forms of disciplinary action
- provide for workers to be informed of the complaints against them and, where possible, to see all relevant evidence before any hearing
- provide workers with an opportunity to state their case before decisions are reached
- provide workers with the right to be accompanied
- ensure that, except for gross misconduct, no worker is dismissed for a first breach of discipline
- ensure that disciplinary action is not taken until the case has been carefully investigated
- ensure that workers are given an explanation for any penalty imposed
- provide a right of appeal – normally to a more senior manager – and specify the procedure to be followed.

The right to be accompanied by a shop steward or other trade union official used only to apply to workplaces where there was a recognised union. However, the Employment Relations Act 1999 has now provided all workers with the statutory right to be accompanied at disciplinary and grievance hearings. The right applies where the worker is required or invited by his or her employer to attend certain disciplinary or grievance hearings, and when he or she makes a reasonable request to be so accompanied. In Chapter 3 we examined the concept of 'workers', and how certain employment rights had now been extended to apply to them. This right is one of them – and the statutory right to be accompanied applies to all workers, not just employees working under a contract of employment.

Whether a worker has a statutory right to be accompanied at a disciplinary hearing will depend on the nature of the hearing. When a problem first surfaces, employers often choose to deal with it initially by means of an informal interview or counselling session. So long as the informal interview or counselling session does not result in a formal warning or some other action it is often more appropriate to try to resolve matters with just the worker and the manager present. Equally, employers should not allow an investigation into the facts surrounding a disciplinary case to extend into a disciplinary hearing. If it becomes clear during the course of the informal or investigative interview that formal disciplinary action may be needed, then the interview should be terminated and a formal hearing convened at which the worker should be afforded the statutory right to be accompanied.

It is important to note that the right to be accompanied applies to every individual, not just union members, and it is of no consequence whether the organisation recognises unions or not.

The statutory right to be accompanied applies specifically to hearings which could result in:

- the administration of a formal warning to a worker by his or her employer (ie a warning, whether about conduct or capability, that will be placed on the worker's record)
- the taking of some other action in respect of a worker by his employer (eg suspension without pay, demotion or dismissal), or
- the confirmation of a warning issued or some other action taken.

After live warnings expire

Although it is to be hoped that any disciplinary problems within an organisation can be resolved at the earliest opportunity, and without recourse to all levels of the procedure, the world of work is not so simple. Many managers complain that having given an individual an oral warning or, in some cases, having got all the way through to final written warning stage, the problem to which the disciplinary action related resurfaces as soon as the warning ceases to be 'live'. It is then assumed, mistakenly, that the whole process must begin again.

This is not so – and three points must be considered. Firstly, for what length of time do warnings stay live? If it is for too short a time, you run the risk of only achieving short-term changes in behaviour . . . yet on the other hand you do not want it to be too long. A sanction that remains on an employee's record for an excessive period of time relative to the original breach of discipline can act as a demotivating influence. Secondly, has the warning been too narrow? Very often it makes more sense to issue a warning in such a way that an employee is left in no doubt that 'any further breaches of the company rules will result in further disciplinary action'. The ACAS Code of Practice makes it clear that the procedure may be implemented at any stage. If you have an employee against whom you constantly have to invoke the disciplinary procedure, or the offence is serious but does not amount to gross misconduct, then it may be appropriate to begin with a written rather than an oral warning. In extreme cases, a final written warning could be appropriate.

Gross misconduct

Before leaving procedural requirements it is necessary to examine what gross misconduct means. You will have noted above that according to the ACAS principles it is permissible to dismiss an individual without notice if he or she has committed an act of gross misconduct. Gross misconduct can be notoriously difficult to define and often difficult to prove, and ACAS very helpfully provides a list of actions that would normally fall into this category. These are:

- theft
- fraud
- deliberate falsification of records
- fighting

- assault on another person
- deliberate damage to company property
- serious incapability through alcohol or under the influence of illegal drugs
- serious negligence
- injury or damage
- serious acts of insubordination.

While that is quite an extensive list, it is also notable for its lack of clarity. For example, what is an act of serious insubordination? Would it cover the refusal to carry out instructions received from a supervisor? What is serious negligence, or serious incapability through alcohol?

The potential difficulties caused by this lack of clarity mean that whatever procedure you establish, it reflects the organisation's structure and culture: the norms and beliefs within which an organisation functions. This is where the writing of clear company rules is so important. Not only do such rules help to distinguish between ordinary and gross misconduct but they provide employees with clear guidelines on what is acceptable in the workplace, in terms of both behaviour and performance.

> How sure are you, that your organisation's procedure is working as it should? What criteria would you use to assess whether it is or is not?

RULES IN EMPLOYMENT

Rules should be written for the benefit of both employer and employee. Their purpose should be to define and make clear exactly what standards of behaviour are expected in the workplace. Typically, rules cover the following areas:

- time-keeping
- absence
- health and safety
- misconduct
- the use of company facilities
- confidentiality
- discrimination.

There are some (including ACAS) who would argue that rules about poor performance should also be included, but there are practical difficulties about writing rules in respect of poor performance. Individuals need to know what is expected of them with regard to performance, but this ought to be done through a clearly written job description that sets out their prime tasks and responsibilities and how their performance will be measured. Clearly, if rules relating to behaviour are broken and, as a consequence, performance is impaired – for example, drunkenness – it is easy to see a link between poor performance and rule-breaking, and that the disciplinary procedure might be used to correct the problem.

But if someone is simply not competent to carry out the tasks for which he or she has been employed, it is hard to see what sort of rule has been broken, notwithstanding the fact that the disciplinary procedure may be used as a means of correcting the problem. This, however, is a minor point. The important point is to ensure that the following principles are followed whatever rules are established:

- They are clear.
- They cannot be misinterpreted.
- They are able to distinguish between ordinary misconduct and gross misconduct.

However, notwithstanding the difficulties in writing rules about performance, many companies now include a section on (in)capability within their disciplinary procedures. Although many procedures content themselves with identifying the various procedural stages and a definition of 'gross misconduct', others are including sections such as in the following example.

CAPABILITY

We recognise that during your employment with us your capability to carry out your duties may vary. This can be for a number of reasons, the most common ones bring that either the job changes over a period of time and you have difficulty adapting to the changes, or you change (most commonly because of health reasons).

Job changes

a) If the nature of your job changes and we have concerns regarding your capability, we will make every effort to ensure that you understand the level of performance expected of you and that you receive adequate training and supervision. This will be done in an informal manner in the first instance and you will be given time to improve.

b) If your standard of performance is still not adequate, you will be warned, in writing, that a failure to improve and to maintain the performance required will lead to disciplinary action. If this were to happen, the principles set out in paragraph 2 above will apply. We will also consider a transfer to more suitable work if possible.

c) If we cannot transfer you to more suitable work and there is still no improvement after you have received appropriate warnings, you will be issued with a final warning that you will be dismissed unless the required standard of performance is achieved and maintained.

Personal circumstances

a) Personal circumstances may arise in the future which do not prevent you from attending work but which prevent you from carrying out your normal duties (eg a lack of dexterity or general ill health). If such a situation arises, we will normally need to have details of your medical diagnosis and prognosis so that we have the benefit of expert advice. Under normal circumstances this can be most easily obtained by asking your own doctor for a medical report. Your permission is needed before we can obtain such a report and we will expect you to co-operate in this matter should the need arise. When we have obtained as much information as possible regarding your condition, and after consultation with you, a decision will be made as to whether any adjustments need to be made in order for you to continue in your current role or, where circumstances permit, a more suitable role should be found for you.

b) There may also be personal circumstances which prevent you from attending work, either for a prolonged period or periods or for frequent short periods. Under these circumstances we will need to know when we can expect your attendance record to reach an acceptable level, and again this can usually be most easily obtained by asking your own doctor for a medical report. When we have obtained as much information as possible regarding your condition, and after consultation with you, a decision will be made as to whether any adjustments need to be made in order for you to continue in your current role or whether, if circumstances permit, a more suitable role should be found for you.

The importance of clear rules

Failure to be clear and failing to make a proper distinction between types of misconduct has caused many organisations to suffer losses at employment tribunals. It is no good having a very clear procedure, laying down the type and number of warnings that an individual should receive, if the rules that are being applied are imprecise or do not reflect the attitudes and requirements of the particular business. As Edwards (1994; page 563) says:

> How people expect to behave depends as much on day-to-day understanding as on formal rules. Workplaces may have identical rule-books, but in one it may be accepted practice to leave early near holidays; in another, on Fridays; in a third, when a relatively lenient supervisor is in charge; and so on.

There is also a need to ensure that rules reflect current industrial practice, as is illustrated by the following case (*Denco v Joinson* [1991] IRLR 63). The applicant, who was a union representative, had been dismissed for gross misconduct for gaining unauthorised access to his employer's computer system. He had gained access to a part of the system that would normally be inaccessible to him by using another employee's password. In his defence it was argued that 'he had only been playing around' with the system, and that there had been no intent to obtain information to which he was not entitled. Furthermore, that while he might have been doing something wrong, it was not 'gross misconduct' and could have been covered by a disciplinary warning. In upholding the dismissal for gross misconduct the Employment Appeal Tribunal (EAT) stated:

> The industrial members are clear in their view that in this modern industrial world if an employee deliberately uses an unauthorised password in order to enter or to attempt to enter a computer known to contain information to which he is not entitled, then that of itself is gross misconduct which *prima facie* will attract summary dismissal, although there may be some exceptional circumstances in which such a response might be held unreasonable.

In essence the EAT were making the same point that had been made some years earlier in *C A Parsons & Co Ltd v McLaughlin* (1978) IRLR 65 – that some things should be so obvious that it ought not to be necessary to have a rule forbidding it. However, for the avoidance of doubt, the EAT went on to say in the *Denco* case that:

> It is desirable, however, that management should make it abundantly clear to the workforce that interfering with computers will carry severe penalties. Rules concerning access to and use of computers should be reduced to writing and left near the computers for reference.

While the comments of the Employment Appeal Tribunal about certain things being obvious may seem perfectly reasonable, it should be remembered that employers have an absolute duty to demonstrate that they have acted reasonably when they dismiss somebody. In *Denco*, the EAT acknowledged that there might be circumstances in which an employer's particular response might be 'unreasonable' even about something which is supposedly obvious. The message is very clear. If something is not allowed, say so, and spell out the consequences of breaching the rule. Because technology, or the ownership of businesses, can change, what may have been acceptable once may now be frowned on. A classic example is Information Technology which, since the *Denco* case in 1991, has moved forward at a remarkable pace. Nowhere is this more evident than in the case of Internet access and the use of e-mail where personal use is difficult and time-consuming to monitor, but which if inappropriately used can bring an organisation into serious disrepute.

This has caused many organisations to rethink their policies on computer use and recognise that clear guidance must be given to employees. The following extract from an 'IT policy' is one example.

IT RESOURCES POLICY (extract)

Please read this document carefully.

Failure to comply with this policy may not only result in disciplinary proceedings (including summary dismissal for acts of gross misconduct) but may also result in criminal and/or civil liability for you and/or the Company. Breaches of those rules shown below will be considered by the firm to be acts of gross misconduct.

Business and non-business use of the firm's IT resources
The Company's IT resources, including but not limited to computer hardware, software, telephones, fax machines, voicemail, e-mail, intranet and Internet access (the 'IT Resources'), are intended primarily to assist you to conduct the Company's business in accordance with your duties as an employee of the Company.

You may make reasonable personal use of the Company's IT Resources provided that:

- you do so in your own time and it does not materially affect the amount of time you and your colleagues devote to your or their duties respectively.
- it does not interfere with or adversely affect the Company's business and/or reputation, and
- is in accordance with this policy.

You may use the IT resources in your own time for reasonable non-business purposes, but please note that you have no legal right to do so under the terms of your employment or otherwise. In any event, your use of the IT resources (whether for personal or business use) may be monitored. Use of the IT resources for non-business use remains subject to the Company's discretion and rules and regulations, and may be withdrawn by the Company on a temporary or permanent basis at any time.

Use of the Company's IT resources
Whether you use the IT resources for business or for personal use, there are things you must NOT DO and things that you MUST DO. These are listed below: . . .

As we stated above, there are a number of variables – such as technological developments – in the drafting of company rules, and the prudent employee relations professional will ensure that in his or her organisation they are the subject of regular monitoring so that they properly reflect the organisation's current values and requirements.

The need to be clear about the behavioural standards that are expected in any workplace, and the sanctions that will be applied for non-compliance, is particularly important in distinguishing between gross and ordinary misconduct. Frequently, organisations commit the error of making vague statements in their company rules to the effect that certain actions *may* be treated as gross misconduct or that the failure to do something *could* leave an individual liable to disciplinary action. For example, many rules on theft that we have seen simply state that 'Theft may be considered to be gross misconduct.'

This sort of wording can only leave room for doubt and confusion. If an employee stole a large sum of money from the company, there is little doubt that he or she would be charged with gross misconduct and, if the allegation was proved, dismissed without notice. What, though, would happen if the alleged theft were of items of company stationery or spare parts for machinery? Would every manager treat the matter as one of gross misconduct and dismiss, or would the value of the items taken be a consideration? Employee relations professionals must be aware of these potential contradictions when helping to frame rules that govern the employment relationship. If it is normal practice to turn a blind eye to the misappropriation of items like stationery, then this can cause problems when someone is accused of a more serious theft. We have already highlighted the importance of discipline being applied fairly and consistently. Company discipline can certainly be questioned if different managers are given the opportunity to apply different standards to the same actions. Allowing different managers to take a different view about the seriousness of certain acts of theft brings inconsistency into the process. It could prove very costly at an employment tribunal. One way to avoid this problem is to make positive statements – for example, that all theft will be treated as gross misconduct.

A better rule on theft might be:

> Theft: stealing from the company, its suppliers or fellow employees is unacceptable, whatever the value or amount involved, and will be treated as gross misconduct.

Using this style of wording should help to ensure that every employee in the organisation knows the consequences of any dishonest action on his or her part. Ensuring that managers apply the sanction consistently is another problem, and one we will deal with later in the chapter.

How often are the rules in your organisation reviewed, and when were they last updated? Do you know whether different standards apply to the application of the rules?

Theft, whatever standards different organisations might apply, is usually associated in the public mind with gross misconduct, notwithstanding the problems of definition that we have just outlined. The distinction between gross misconduct and other serious infractions of the rules can often be harder to identify. The first thing to acknowledge is that no clear distinction exists, but it is possible to apply common sense to the issue. For example, it is easy to understand that a serious assault on another person ought to be treated as gross misconduct, whereas poor time-keeping would not. While a consistent failure to observe time-keeping standards might ultimately lead to dismissal, the two offences clearly initially evoke different outcomes – namely, immediate dismissal in the first case and normally a verbal warning in the second. Perhaps one way in which a distinction might be drawn, therefore, is by reference to the expected outcome of the disciplinary process and to the relationship of trust that ought to exist between employer and employee.

Although not wishing here to explore the wider issues relating to the contract of employment, it is implied in every contract that for an employment relationship to be maintained there has to be mutual trust and confidence between employer and employee. When issues of discipline arise, that relationship is damaged. One of the purposes of disciplinary action is to bring about a change in behaviour, and if the offence is one of poor time-keeping, there is usually no question of a total breakdown of trust and the expected outcome of disciplinary action is of improved time-keeping and a rebuilding of the relationship. If the cause of the disciplinary action was a serious assault on another employee, perhaps a manager, however, a disciplinary sanction might bring about a change in behaviour or ensure that the offence is not repeated, but there is a high probability that the relationship of mutual trust and confidence might be damaged beyond repair, and it might be impossible for the employment relationship to be maintained.

HANDLING DISCIPLINARY ISSUES

The way in which managers and employee relations professionals approach disciplinary issues will be subtly different, depending on the nature of the problem. Most organisations will have some form of disciplinary procedure, and probably some company rules, but the use and application of the procedure may vary from company to company and from manager to manager. In some organisations disciplinary action is very rarely taken, either because standards are clear and accepted by employees or standards are vague and applied haphazardly. In others standards are maintained by an over-reliance on automatic procedures, which usually acts as a demotivating influence on the workforce.

The purpose of disciplinary procedures, according to the ACAS Code, should be to promote

> orderly employment relations as well as fairness and consistency in the treatment of individuals. They enable organisations to influence the conduct of workers and deal with problems of poor performance and attendance, thereby assisting organisations to operate effectively.

The principles of fairness and consistency are at the heart of 'good practice', and the aim of all managers should be to handle disciplinary issues in as fair and equitable a way as is possible. They should do this because it represents 'good practice' in terms of management skill, not just because of the influence of the law. If managers are only concerned with legal compliance, they will not be as effective as those who are driven by the need to operate 'good practice'. The law on unfair dismissal is now so ingrained into the fabric of the workplace that only by maintaining such standards does it cease to become an issue. Good managers have nothing to fear from the laws relating to individual employment rights. That is not to say the law should be ignored, but neither should it be feared. In an ideal world managers would act in such a way that they avoided accusations of unfair treatment. But this is not an ideal world and even the best managers can find themselves defending their actions before an employment tribunal – and this is why it is important for the concept of 'good practice' to become part of an organisation's ethos.

Not only does this allow the organisation to demonstrate consistent and fair treatment for all, but ensures that it meets its absolute duty to act reasonably as set out in section 98(4)(a) of the Employment Rights Act 1996. Furthermore, such an approach not only makes good business sense, it fits the concept of 'natural justice' that is so important in handling disciplinary issues.

The 1996 Act identifies the reasons for fairly dismissing an employee as (poor) conduct, (lack of) capability and 'some other substantial reason', and all of these would require the implementation of a disciplinary process in order for any action taken to be reasonable. However, before reaching for the disciplinary procedure, a good manager will consider whether some other route would be even more appropriate. Maintaining good standards of discipline within an organisation is not just about applying the rules or operating the procedure. It is about the ability to achieve standards of performance and behaviour without using the 'big stick'. One way this might be done, and to avoid becoming embroiled in the disciplinary process, is counselling, which could provide the required change in behaviour without making the individual concerned feel he or she was some kind of dissident.

Counselling

Counselling is more than simply offering help and advice. It is helping, in a non-threatening way, an individual to come to terms with a particular problem. The problem may be about performance, about time-keeping, about drug or alcohol abuse, or about another employee – for example, an accusation of sexual harassment. Counselling an employee, whatever the nature of the problem, needs careful preparation. In a situation involving the abuse of a drug or alcohol, managers may have the necessary skills to carry out such a sensitive task, but even if they conclude that specialist help is required, they can still help to bring the problem out into the open. In other cases, provided the problem is approached in a systematic way, this type of intervention may avoid disciplinary action.

One example of where counselling might be an appropriate first step would be in respect of an allegation of sexual harassment or bullying. Provided the complainant has not suffered any physical assault and, most importantly, that the complainant is happy for the matter to be handled in an informal way, counselling can be very helpful – not only to the alleged harasser but also to the victim. Without wishing to minimise or condone what can be a very serious problem in some workplaces, it can often be the case that the alleged harasser or bully does not realise that his or her behaviour or actions are causing offence or fear. Sitting down with individuals and explaining to them that some of their words or actions are causing distress to another employee can often be very effective. However, it is important not to leave it there but to monitor the situation and ensure that the behavioural change is permanent, and that the complainant is satisfied with the action taken and the eventual outcome. If not, you may find yourself dealing with a formal grievance or even a claim for constructive dismissal.

> Does your organisation's disciplinary code say anything about equal opportunities or discrimination? Is there, for example, a clear rule that says sexual harassment or racial discrimination will not be tolerated? Do you have a Code of Practice that gives guidance on how to manage these sorts of problems?

Similarly, if the problem concerns poor performance, 'good practice' would be to discuss the problem with the employee concerned rather than go straight into the disciplinary procedure. The first step would be to speak to the employee in private, explaining what aspects of performance were falling short of the desired standard and, most importantly, what actions were required by the employee to put matters right. The golden rule to remember is to set clear standards. If employees do not know what is expected of them, how can they deliver the performance that is required? Another step in this process might be to consider whether some additional training might be an option. All of this might be best dealt with under a formal appraisal scheme, if one exists within the organisation.

The formal approach

However, if after following the counselling route there are still complaints of harassment, or the quality of work being carried out still falls below standard, it may then be necessary to begin disciplinary proceedings. Again it is important to remember the principle of 'good practice'. The operation of the disciplinary procedure can often lead to managerial disenchantment because of the claim that 'it takes too long'. This is where the employee relations professional has a clear duty to advise and guide management colleagues. Because starting down the disciplinary path can, ultimately, lead to a dismissal, it is important to remember the requirement that in taking a decision to dismiss somebody you should act reasonably and in accordance with natural justice.

It is easy to understand the frustration a line manager might feel if the disciplinary process takes too long, but it is the employer who is in control of the process and can determine the timings. The question of fairness relates not to how long the process takes, but to the quality of the procedures followed. For example, say you had an experienced employee who was responsible for carrying out a very important task within the organisation and which had serious cost implications if it were not carried out efficiently. If the task was not being performed satisfactorily, the amount of time you could allow the employee to improve his or her performance would be limited. Alternatively, if the employee was inexperienced and performing a task that was less cost-sensitive and important, the time allowed for improvement should be longer.

It is also necessary to consider how long the substandard performance has been allowed to continue unchallenged, because it may be the case that a previous manager was prepared to accept a lower standard of performance. What is important in either of these scenarios is that the employee is made aware of the standard that is required and understands the importance of achieving that standard in whatever time-scale is agreed. Under the ACAS Code it is acceptable to miss out stages in the procedure, and this may be the more obvious solution if the consequences of the poor performance are so serious.

USING THE DISCIPLINARY PROCEDURE

Whatever the nature of the problem, once the decision has been taken to invoke the formal disciplinary procedure, it is important to ensure that its application cannot be challenged. The following guidelines, which are broken down into two stages, help to ensure a consistent and fair approach.

Preparing for the disciplinary hearing

Now that the Employment Act 2002 sets out minimum procedural standards for the conduct of dismissal and disciplinary meetings the preparatory process becomes particularly important. There are various steps that must be taken in preparing to conduct a disciplinary interview, and a number of points to consider – some of which are a statutory requirement:

1 Prepare carefully and ensure that the person conducting the disciplinary hearing has all the facts. This sounds straightforward, but it is not always possible to obtain all the facts. Frequently, the evidence of alleged misconduct is no more that circumstantial, particularly in cases involving theft. However, the guiding principle is to ensure that a thorough investigation takes place and that whatever facts are available are presented – including, where appropriate, written witness statements. Sometimes people will ask to remain anonymous when providing information during a disciplinary investigation, and this has to be treated with a great deal of care. If possible, seek some form of corroborative evidence and try to check whether the anonymous informant's motives are genuine.

2 Ensure that the employee knows what the nature of the complaint is. This again sounds straightforward, but is often the point at which things begin to go wrong. For example, it would not be sufficient to tell an employee that he or she is to attend a disciplinary hearing in respect of poor performance. He or she must be provided with sufficient detail in order to be able to prepare an adequate defence and so that the employer can demonstrate that it has met the statutory requirements set out in the procedure outlined above.

3 Arrange a suitable time and place for the interview. This would seem to be obvious but, as with so many things in employee relations, what may seem obvious to the specialist is not always apparent to the busy line manager. There is a tendency for managers to arrange meetings within their own offices where the potential for being interrupted is more pronounced or privacy less easily guaranteed. It is also important to remember that the employee might request an alternative date to the one suggested, particularly if the chosen companion or trade union official cannot attend.

4 Ensure that the employee knows the procedure to be followed. Simply because an individual was provided with a copy of the disciplinary code when he or she commenced employment does not imply that he or she knows the procedure to be followed. It is always wise to provide people with a new copy of the disciplinary procedure – not least because there may have been amendments since they received their original version.

5 Advise the employee of the right to be accompanied (see above). Where individuals work in a unionised environment this tends to be automatic, with an invitation to attend the meeting sent directly to the appropriate union official. However, in non-unionised environments people are not always sure who would be an appropriate person to accompany them, or whether they want to be accompanied at all. As a matter of good practice it is wise to encourage somebody to be accompanied, but a decision against it has to be respected. When that does happen, the fact that the employee wishes to attend the disciplinary interview alone should be recorded.

6 Enquire if there are any mitigating circumstances. What is or is not a mitigating circumstance will be dictated by each case. It is not for the employer to identify matters of mitigation, but it is

important to ask the employee who is facing a disciplinary sanction whether there are any particular circumstances that might account for his or her actions. Whether an individual manager accepts what may seem to be no more than excuses is a question of fact determined by individual circumstances. For example, an employee with a bad time-keeping record might be excused if he or she was having to care for a sick relative before attending work, whereas another employee might put forward a less acceptable excuse, such as a broken alarm clock.

7 Are you being consistent? This is where the employee relations professional can provide invaluable assistance to the line manager. Most line managers deal very rarely with disciplinary issues and may not be aware of previous actions or approaches that have been taken in respect of disciplinary issues. The employee relations professional can provide the advice and information that ensures a consistent approach.

8 Consider explanations. This is not the same as mitigating circumstances or excuses. This is the opportunity that you must give to an employee to explain his or her acts or omissions. For example, if the hearing was about poor performance, the employee might want to point out factors that have inhibited performance but which might not be immediately apparent to the line manager conducting the hearing. There may be issues around the quality of training received or the quality of instructions given.

9 Allow the employee time to prepare his or her case. The question here is how much time. It is important that issues of discipline are dealt with speedily once an employee has been advised of the complaint against him or her, but it is important for the employee not to feel unfairly pressured in putting together any defence that he or she may have.

10 Ensure that personnel records, etc, are available. This covers more than basic information about the individual and includes records relating to any previous disciplinary warnings, attendance, performance appraisals, etc.

11 Where possible, be accompanied. It is very unwise for a manager to conduct a disciplinary interview alone because of the possible need to corroborate what was said at some future time. It also helps to rebut any allegations of bullying or intimidation that may be made by a disgruntled employee.

12 Try to ensure the attendance of witnesses. This should not be a problem if the people concerned are in your employ, but can prove difficult when they are outsiders.

The importance of careful preparation cannot be stressed too strongly, for it is at this stage that things often go wrong. Where tribunals, for example, often express concern is in the preliminary stages of the disciplinary process. Employers are often criticised for failing to give sufficient information to the employee about the nature of the complaint against him or her. We have certainly found examples of employers who have deliberately withheld information to prevent employees from constructing plausible explanations for their conduct or actions. While this was never acceptable, it is clearly in breach of the statutory procedure and must not be allowed.

The disciplinary interview

Good preparation helps the second part of the process – conducting the actual disciplinary interview. There are a number of points to remember at this stage:

1 Introduce those present – not just on grounds of courtesy, but because an employee facing a possible sanction is entitled to know who is going to be involved in any decision. In a small workplace this may be unnecessary, but it can be important in larger establishments.

2 Explain the purpose of the interview and how it will be conducted. This builds on the need to ensure that the employee fully understands the nature of the complaint against him or her and the

procedure to be followed. As with any hearing, however informal, what it is for, what the possible outcomes are, and the method by which it is to be conducted are important prerequisites for demonstrating that natural justice has been adhered to. If it is apparent that, for whatever reason, the employer does not fully understand the nature of the complaint against him or her, you must halt proceedings until they are clear – even if this means postponing to another day.

3   Set out precisely the nature of the complaint and outline the case by briefly going through the evidence. This may seem like overkill, but it is important to ensure that there are no misunderstandings. It is important to ensure that the employee and his or her representative, if there is one, are given copies of any witness statements and afforded a proper opportunity to read them.

4   Give the employee the right to reply. Put simply: no right of reply, no natural justice.

5   Allow time for general questioning, cross-examination of witnesses, etc. If this did not happen, it would be difficult to persuade a tribunal that the test of reasonableness had been achieved.

6   No matter how carefully you prepare, or how well you are conducting a disciplinary hearing, things may not always proceed smoothly. People can get upset or angry and the whole process become very emotional. In such circumstances it might be advisable to adjourn and reconvene at a later date. If this happens, it is important to make it clear to the employee that the issue cannot be avoided and a hearing must be held.

7   Sum up. There is a need to be clear about what conclusions have been reached and what decisions are to be made, and for this reason it is better to adjourn so that a properly considered decision can be made. One of the biggest handicaps the employee relations specialist can face is the manager who pre-judges. It is not uncommon to be asked to assist at a hearing where the manager wishes to administer a particular, predetermined, type of warning. It is the job of the professional adviser to counsel against this approach.

Careful preparation and a well-conducted interview are not guarantees that individuals will not complain of unfairness, but they are essential if the test of reasonableness is to be satisfied.

MISCONDUCT DURING EMPLOYMENT

There are two distinct perpetrators of misconduct: the persistent rule-breaker and the individual who commits an act of gross misconduct. In most instances, dealing with the persistent rule-breaker is relatively straightforward, provided that the disciplinary code is applied in a sensible and equitable manner. Assuming that it has been possible to go through some form of counselling with the employee, but the required change in behaviour has not been forthcoming, it is likely that the only alternative is to begin the disciplinary process. The likely first step would be a verbal or written warning, followed, if necessary, by the subsequent stages in the procedure, leading ultimately to dismissal.

Although the dismissal of an employee is never an easy task for a manager, it can – if the steps outlined above are followed – be a relatively straightforward process. Furthermore, individuals who are dismissed for persistent infringements of the rules, for which they have had a series of warnings and the opportunity to appeal, rarely go to employment tribunals. It is difficult for an individual to claim that the employer acted unreasonably when he or she has been given a number of opportunities to modify his or her actions. The only complaint that an individual might have in such circumstances is that the procedure itself was unfair or had been applied contrary to the rules of natural justice. This could happen if some people were disciplined for breaches of the rules and others were not.

Imagine that your organisation had dismissed somebody for bad time-keeping and unauthorised absences, and the employee had challenged this in an employment tribunal. What evidence would you need to present in support of your organisation's action?

Gross misconduct

Gross misconduct, on the other hand, presents totally different problems for the manager. Earlier, some of the issues surrounding the concept of gross misconduct were examined, as was the need to be absolutely clear what breaches of the rules *will* mean, as opposed to *might* mean. For the manager who is called upon to deal with a case of alleged gross misconduct it is vitally important that all procedural steps are strictly adhered to, because mistakes can be costly. For obvious reasons managers are often under extreme pressure to resolve matters quickly. This is not just because it is much fairer to the accused individual that the matter is resolved, but because other colleagues may have already pre-judged the outcome. Pressure cannot always be avoided, but it is necessary that in such circumstances the requirement to prepare properly and conduct a fair hearing are not forgotten.

Some cases of gross misconduct are very clear-cut, and the employee concerned either admits the offence or there are sufficient witnesses to confirm that the alleged offence was committed by the employee in question. In such cases the first decision for the employer is to decide whether to treat the matter as gross misconduct, for which the penalty is summary dismissal without notice or pay in lieu of notice, or to take a more lenient line Such decisions are made easier if the company rules are clear and unambiguous about what constitutes gross misconduct. But in our experience, many cases of gross misconduct are not clear-cut and managers are very unsure about how to deal with them. Some of the cases in which we have been asked to assist include suspected theft of goods or money, suspicion of tampering with time-recording devices, suspected false expense claims or seeking payment of sick pay while fit for work. One reason why managers can be unsure about such offences is that some of them could lead to criminal charges being laid against the employee or employees concerned.

One way to approach this very sensitive issue is by ensuring that the 'Burchell rules' are applied. These rules relate to a case that was decided in 1978 involving an incident of alleged theft (*British Home Stores v Burchell* [1978] IRLR 379). The specific facts of the case are not particularly important, but it is significant because of the test of reasonableness that flowed from it. The Burchell test states that where an employee is suspected of a dismissable offence, an employer must show that:

■ the reason for dismissal was *bona fide* and not a pretext

■ the belief that the employee committed the offence was based on reasonable grounds – that is, that on the evidence before them, the employer was entitled to say that it was more probable that the employee did, in fact, commit the offence than that he or she did not

■ the belief was based on a reasonable investigation in the circumstances – that the employer's investigation took place before the employee was dismissed and included an opportunity for the employee to offer an explanation.

The implications of the Burchell test

Let us look at this test in a little more detail and try to relate it to events as they might take place in the working environment. Take the example of a suspected fraudulent expense claim. The first part of Burchell says that the reason for dismissal must be *bona fide* and not a pretext. This means not using the alleged offence as a convenient means of dismissing an employee whose 'face no longer fits' or who has a history of misconduct on which no previous action has been taken. The second and third parts of Burchell relate to the employer's belief in the employee's guilt and to the standards of the investigation carried out. As Lewis and Sargeant (2004; page 159) state:

> The question to be determined is not whether, by an objective standard, the employer's belief that the employee was guilty of the misconduct was well-founded but whether the employer believed that the employee was guilty and was entitled so to believe having regard to the investigation conducted.

Using the Burchell test in the case of a suspected fraudulent expense claim, the employer would have to be very diligent in assembling the evidence. What guidelines were laid down for the benefit of those allowed to claim expenses? What expenses had been accepted in the past? Were the same standards applied consistently to all staff? Had any other employee made a similar claim in the past without challenge? Assembling such an array of evidence is only likely to happen if there is a thorough investigation – but this is only the first part of the process: the employee is also entitled to offer an explanation. What do you do if the explanation is linked to the lack of guidelines about what is and is not claimable?

While the findings in the *Parsons* case (see above) – that some things are so obvious that they do not need a rule – is relevant, the seniority of the employee concerned might also be relevant. A 'reasonable' belief that a senior employee who regularly claimed expenses was acting dishonestly might be easier to demonstrate than a situation in which a junior employee was claiming expenses for the first time. We acknowledged above the uncertainties that sometimes can be encountered when the possibility of criminal proceedings is on the agenda. A question we are often asked is, can we dismiss somebody if we have asked the police to investigate with a view to prosecution? The short answer is 'yes' – provided that the Burchell test is followed. Quite properly, the burden of proof placed on an employer in such circumstances is totally different from the burden of proof imposed by the criminal justice system. In a criminal trial the prosecution must prove 'beyond all reasonable doubt' that an offence was committed. This is entirely reasonable when an individual's liberty is at risk – and it is why, under the Burchell test, you can dismiss somebody 'fairly' for dishonesty who might be found 'not guilty' in a criminal trial.

LACK OF CAPABILITY

This is the second of the fair reasons for dismissing an employee, and we must consider it under two sub-categories – firstly, lack of capability that is linked to an employee's inability to do the job, leading to unacceptably poor performance; and secondly, lack of capability that relates to an individual's inability to do the job because of poor health or sickness.

Poor performance

Advising a line manager who has a member of his or her team delivering less than adequate performance is very common for the employee relations specialist. Very often the initial step in this advisory role is persuading the line manager not to take precipitate action. It is not unusual for the personnel professional to be told by a manager that a particular employee is 'useless', and that the manager needs 'help to get rid of' him or her. Persuading a line manager not to launch into a formal disciplinary process without considering what other options are open is very important. Earlier, we looked at the question of counselling and noted that in the event of an ultimate dismissal, an employment tribunal would want to satisfy itself that the dismissed employee knew what standards were expected of him or her and that he or she had been given an opportunity to achieve those standards, and that all this had happened before any formal disciplinary procedures had begun. Another option might be the provision of alternative work for the employee concerned if he or she had demonstrated incapability at the present tasks.

Whatever options are taken, the employee is entitled, on grounds of fairness, to be told exactly what is required of him or her: what standards have been set and the time-scale in which he or she is expected to achieve them. During the period of time that an individual is being given to reach the desired standards, a good manager ensures that the employee is kept informed of his or her progress. This again is the operation of the principle of 'best practice' or good management habits.

One important point to remember in looking at capability is the obligations placed on employers by the Disability Discrimination Act 1995, the principal purpose of which is to protect disabled people from discrimination in the field of employment, and this issue is dealt with below.

Managing absence

This can be one of the most emotive issues that any manager has to face, and must at all times be handled with sensitivity by managers. There is always scope for disputes to arise in this difficult area, and it is important that the employee relations professional makes himself or herself aware of all the circumstances in which absences can occur – and where these involve legal rights, must ensure that he or she understands the scope of such rights. Time off work for domestic emergencies is one example.

Absence from work can occur for a number of reasons. Some – like holiday, bereavement or paternity leave – is normally arranged in advance and causes minimum disruption to the employing organisation. The absences that cause disruption within any organisation are those that are unplanned, because the employee concerned is sick, has simply failed to turn up for work or has experienced a domestic emergency. In so far as the second reason is concerned, it would be normal to treat this as a breach of the rules on unauthorised absence and deal with it as a case of misconduct.

One reason for unauthorised absence could be that an employee has failed to return from a authorised absence – say, a holiday – at the due time. Individuals returning late from holiday has become a much more widespread problem in recent years owing to the increase in overseas travel. For most individuals who return to work late in such circumstances the fault lies with delayed air flights or other travel problems. For some employers the disruption caused by a late return from holiday is minimal and they may treat it as no more than an irritation. But for others, particularly at a time of the year when large numbers of people are on holiday, the disruption caused can be very serious. Notwithstanding the fact that the cause of the problem (a late flight) was outside the employee's control, the employer might take the view that steps could have been taken to minimise the disruption – for example, an explanatory telephone call. Whether disciplinary action is taken in such circumstances will clearly rest on the facts of each individual case, but in any event action should follow the guidance given above for preparing and conducting a disciplinary interview, particularly in respect of mitigating circumstances and other explanations.

However, in most establishments the most widespread cause of absence from work is sickness or alleged sickness, and although it would be wholly unreasonable to treat a case of genuine sickness as a disciplinary matter, incapacity for work on health grounds can be a fair reason for dismissing an employee. For this reason the way in which an employer deals with health-related absences is very important.

Sickness absence

Dealing with sickness absence can be a minefield for any manager, but for the employee relations specialist who is expected to give clear and timely advice, it is even more so. Estimates of the cost to the UK economy of sickness absence currently hover around the £11 billion level, and absence really has therefore to be managed effectively. Unauthorised absence is usually a disciplinary matter, but most absences do not fall into this category. They are recorded as sickness. Without wishing to suggest that any employee deliberately seeks to be untruthful, notifying the employer of 'sickness' remains the most common reason for absence from work, and although the overwhelming majority of employees have minimal periods of sickness absence, most organisations nonetheless have individual staff whose sickness record is poor. Such people can consistently accumulate as many as 25–30 sick days per annum, through a mix of 'flu', 'migraine' and 'stomach upsets'. The British Airways dispute in the summer of 2004 centred on the company's determination to 'do something about rising sickness rates' and the unions' determination that this should not be linked to improvements in pay.

The second CIPD annual survey into employee absence, published in 2001, exposed high levels of 'hidden absence' among employees and found that up to a third of absences were not considered genuine. With employees taking an average of three days off per annum, the survey puts the annual cost of sickness absence at £487 per employee. Not surprisingly, 94 per cent of the survey respondents described sickness absence as a 'very significant business burden'. By the time of the 2004 survey (see the CIPD website www.cipd.co.uk) the annual cost of sickness absence had risen to £567 per employee per annum with absence levels at 4 per cent, or 9.1 working days per employee. One response the survey identified is that three quarters of employers had introduced changes to their policies on absence management over a two-year period.

In order to manage such a problem effectively, the starting-point has to be adequate record-keeping, and ACAS advise that 'records showing lateness and the duration of and reason for all spells of absence should be kept to help monitor absence levels'. Such records enable a manager to substantiate whether a problem of persistent absence is real or imagined. All too often the employee relations specialist who is asked for advice is expected to work with insufficient data. Managing absence is not just about applying rules or following procedure, it is about addressing problems of persistent absence quickly and acting consistently. This sends out a clear and unambiguous message to all employees that absence is regarded as a serious matter.

But how do you act rigorously and at the same time retain fairness and consistency? The most effective way is through the return-to-work interview. This has been shown to be the most effective method of controlling sickness absence. The employer demonstrates that absence matters, that it has noticed the employee's absence, and that it cares.

In their booklet *Discipline and Grievance at Work*, ACAS set out guidelines for handling frequent and persistent short-term absences which support the principle of the return-to-work interview and help to ensure a consistency of approach. Factors that must be taken into account are:

- Absences should be investigated promptly and the employee asked to give an explanation.
- Where there is no medical advice to support frequent self-certified absences, the employee should be asked to consult a doctor to establish whether medical treatment is necessary and whether the underlying reason for absence is work-related.
- If after investigation it appears that there were no good reasons for the absences, the matter should be dealt with under the disciplinary procedure.
- Where absences arise from temporary domestic problems, the employer in deciding appropriate action should consider whether an improvement in attendance is likely. It is also important to consider whether any of the absences should, or could, have been covered by the Maternity and Parental Leave (time off for dependants in an emergency) Regulations 1999. These regulations are discussed in more detail below.
- In all cases the employee should be told what improvement is expected and warned of the likely consequences if unwarranted absences continue.
- If there is no improvement, the employee's age, length of service, performance, the likelihood of a change in attendance, the availability of suitable alternative work and the effect of past and future absences on the business should all be taken into account on deciding appropriate action.

Persistent absence
Frequent short-term absences can be very difficult to manage and can be the cause of serious conflict between employees. When one individual within a work group is constantly absent, it is usually his or her colleagues who suffer. This is because they have to take on additional duties or alter their hours at short notice. It is they, not the management, who are inconvenienced and they are entitled to expect that their employer will do something to manage the problem.

Where doubt still remains about the nature of the illness, injury or disability, the employee can be asked if he or she is prepared to be examined by an independent doctor to be appointed by the company. Normally – unless there is some form of contractual provision which allows for this – an employee cannot be compelled to attend. However, with the growth of occupational sick pay schemes, many organisations have overcome this problem by building compulsion into their scheme rules. Very often, advising an employee that such an examination is required if attendance does not improve is sufficient to resolve the problem. Complications can arise when the injury or illness which necessitates the persistent short-term absences is genuine. It could never be reasonable to discipline individuals in such circumstances – but it can be fair to dismiss the employee concerned. When such a situation does arise it is absolutely imperative that a careful process of assessment and examination is carried out. This would include obtaining a comprehensive medical report setting out full details of the individual's capacity to work and the consideration of other options – part-time work, reduced hours, alternative work, etc.

All of the above makes good sense and is consistent with the principle of managing absence with a 'good practice' ethos. However, employee relations professionals must consider what other methods they can use for managing absence. These might include the introduction of flexitime and annual hours schemes so that employees could manage domestic commitments without resorting to 'taking a day off sick'. In short, employers might consider how they can become more family-friendly.

Long-term absence

The section above dealt with the persistent short-term absentee and noted that although some absences might not be genuine, many were. A similar problem arises in respect of employees whose absence is long-term. It is reasonable to presume that the majority of long-term absences are also genuine and would certainly be covered by some form of medical certification. Nevertheless, they still have to be managed, and again ACAS provides guidance. In their view, it is important that:

- The employee should be contacted periodically and [the employee] should maintain regular contact with the employer.
- The employee should be advised if employment is at risk.
- The employee should be asked if he/she will consent to his/her own doctor being contacted and be clearly informed of the employee's right to refuse consent, to see the report and to request amendments to it.
- The employee's doctor should be asked if the employee will be able to return to work, and the nature of the work that he or she will be capable of carrying out.
- On the basis of the report received, the employer should consider whether alternative work is available.
- Employers are not expected to create special jobs, nor are they expected to be medical experts. They should simply take action on the basis of the medical evidence.
- As with other absences, the possibility of an independent medical examination should be considered.
- Where an employee refuses to co-operate in providing medical evidence, he or she should be told, in writing, that a decision will have to be taken on the basis of what information is available, and that the decision may result in dismissal.
- Where the employee's job can no longer be kept open and no suitable alternative is available, the employee should be informed of the likelihood of dismissal.

This last point can be very emotive. Where you are dealing with an employee who has long service, has an exemplary work record, and is genuinely suffering from a serious illness or has been left unable to work by a serious illness, telling him or her that he or she is likely to lose the job can be very difficult – not only because the employer is genuine concerned about the impact of such a decision but because the employer is concerned about the possibility of legal action for unfair dismissal being taken against him or her.

In cases where illness or injury is obvious and the medical prognosis reasonably clear, following the ACAS guidelines will help ensure that the decisions made will stand up to external scrutiny. But what happens when the injury or illness is not so obvious? Bad backs and stress are two examples that spring to mind. Because the words 'stress' and 'backache' are used so loosely – even by doctors on medical certificates – an employer must deal with these cases both carefully and critically. The way forward may only emerge over time. Often both employer and employee will have to wait for many weeks, if not months, for further medical investigations to be carried out before the appropriate form of action can be decided. For personnel professionals this can be a difficult time. They are often under pressure from line manager colleagues to support a premature decision to dismiss so that a replacement can be recruited. The effective employee relations professional who has developed his or her influencing skills will be able to persuade colleagues that acting precipitately is not in the best interests of the organisation.

Disabilities and absence

It is possible that individuals who have contracted a serious illness, have suffered a serious injury or are suffering from 'stress' will be deemed to be suffering from a disability. So, whereas the above sections may contain useful advice in dealing with many types of absence, what happens if the reason for the absence is in respect of a disability covered by the Disability Discrimination Act (DDA)?

As part of the protection provided by the DDA, employers may have to make 'reasonable adjustments' to employment arrangements – and in the context of managing absence, section 4(2)(d) of the Act states that 'it is unlawful for an employer to discriminate against disabled persons by dismissing them or subjecting them to any other detriment'. Because the Act applies equally to existing employees as well as to new recruits, employers should be careful of initiating action in respect of employees with a permanent health problem without paying due regard to the legislation. Section 6(1) of the Act states that an employer has a duty to make 'reasonable adjustments' if an employee is disadvantaged either by the physical features of the workplace or by the arrangements for the work itself. The Code of Practice which accompanies the Act lists a number of 'reasonable adjustments' that an employer might have to consider. These could include:

- making adjustments to premises
- allocating some of the disabled person's duties to another person
- transferring the person to fill an existing vacancy
- altering the person's working hours
- assigning the person to a different place of work
- allowing the person to be absent during working hours for rehabilitation, assessment or treatment
- giving the person, or arranging for them to be given, training
- acquiring or modifying equipment
- modifying instructions or reference manuals
- modifying procedures for testing or assessment
- providing a reader or interpreter
- providing supervision.

Clearly, employers will not have to make 'reasonable adjustments' in respect of all 'sick' employees – only those who fit the Act's definition of disability. A 'disabled' person is a person with 'a physical or mental impairment which has a substantial and long-term adverse effect on [the] ability to carry out normal day-to-day activities' (section 1). This chapter is about discipline and not disability, but employee relations specialists must be aware that the disability legislation imposes challenges that must be taken into account when managing absence. Most importantly, it must be remembered that dismissal of a disabled employee is automatically unfair and on that basis will almost certainly be impossible to defend.

Absence and domestic emergencies

The Employment Relations Act 1999 amended the Employment Rights Act 1996 to provide employees with a right to take a reasonable amount of time off work to deal with unexpected or sudden emergencies. For example:

- if a dependant falls ill, or has been injured or assaulted
- when a dependant is having a baby (this does not include taking time off after the birth of a child)
- to make longer-term care arrangements for a dependant who is ill or injured
- to deal with the death of a dependant
- to deal with a disruption in care arrangements for a dependant
- to deal with an incident involving an employee's child during school hours.

The details of the time off right are contained in the Maternity and Parental Leave (time off for dependants in an emergency) Regulations 1999 and set out the circumstances in which an employee can use the provisions, and how the employee can, if necessary, enforce his or her rights. Essentially, the emergency for which an employee is claiming time off must involve a dependant of his or hers. A 'dependant' is the husband, wife, child or parent of the employee. The term can also include someone who lives in the same household as the employee – for example, a partner or elderly relative. It does not include tenants or boarders.

Neither the number of times an employee can be absent from work nor the length of the time off that can be taken is specified in the Regulations, but in most cases no more than one or two days should be sufficient to deal with the problem. The fact that the right is unpaid is, in most circumstances, going to limit the length of the absence anyway.

However, like any right it is open to abuse, by both unscrupulous employers or by employees acting in bad faith. Where an employee believes that he or she has suffered a detriment, or in extreme cases, been dismissed in seeking to take time off, he or she has the right to apply to an employment tribunal. If an employer believes that the right is being abused, he or she should deal with the situation according to the normal disciplinary procedures.

In the context of employee relations, however, this right could offer an opportunity to the employer. In Chapter 2 we declared that it was important for the employee relations professional to see the law as more than an object of compliance – that some rights could be seen as a minimum standard that could be enhanced by a progressive employer and that the pro-active employee relations professional can provide the evidence to support such an enhancement. And we said above that in order to reduce some absences, employers might have to develop more family-friendly policies. The right to time off for domestic emergencies could be the springboard for the development of such a policy.

Some other substantial reason

One other fair reason for dismissal set out in the 1996 Employment Rights Act, and that we need to consider, is 'some other substantial reason'. This concept was introduced into the legislation 'so as to give tribunals the discretion to accept as a fair reason for dismissal something that would not conveniently fit into any of the other categories' (Lewis and Sargeant, 2004; page 161). Dismissals for 'some other substantial reason' have, as they point out, been upheld in respect of employees who have been sentenced to a term of imprisonment, employees who cannot get on with each other, or where there are problems between an individual and one of the organisation's customers. Interestingly, the cases which Lewis and Sargeant quote all relate to the 1970s and 1980s – which might indicate that businesses are now less reliant on this rather vague concept. It is certainly the case that the more professional employee relations specialists, recognising that such issues and conflicts do arise, have amended their disciplinary procedures accordingly, and many organisations will have a rule relating to general conduct which may be worded in the following way:

> Any conduct detrimental to the interests of the company, its relations with the public, its customers and suppliers, damaging to its public image or offensive to other employees in the company, shall be a disciplinary offence.

It is easy to see how such a rule could be used to deal with any of the examples cited by Lewis and Sargeant. In the context of managing discipline, it is a much more systematic route. Some other substantial reason can, to the non-lawyer, be a rather vague concept, whereas being able to proceed against an individual for a breach of a specific rule is much clearer to everybody involved.

APPEALS

Every disciplinary procedure must contain an appeals process – otherwise, it is almost impossible to demonstrate that the organisation has acted reasonably, within the law. In common with every other aspect of the disciplinary process, it is important to ensure fairness and consistency within an appeals procedure which should provide for appeals to be dealt with as quickly as possible. An employee should be able to appeal at every stage of the disciplinary process, and common sense dictates that any appeal should be heard by someone who is senior to the person imposing the disciplinary sanction. This will not always be possible, particularly in smaller organisations, but if the person hearing the appeal is the same as the person who imposed the original sanction, then ACAS advises that the person should hear the appeal and act as impartially as possible. In essence, an appeal in these circumstances is going to be no more than a review of the original decision, but perhaps in a calmer and more objective manner.

As with the original disciplinary hearing, an appeal falls into two parts – action prior to the appeal, and the actual hearing itself. Before any appeal hearing the employee should be told what the arrangements are and what his or her rights under the procedure are. At the same time it is important to obtain, and read, any relevant documentation. At the appeal hearing the appellant should be told its purpose, how it will be conducted and what decisions the person or persons hearing the appeal are able to make. Any new evidence must be considered and all relevant issues properly examined. Although appeals are not regarded as an opportunity to seek a more sympathetic assessment of the issue in question, it is equally true that appeals are not routinely dismissed. Overturning a bad or unjust decision is just as important as confirming a fair decision. It is an effective way of signalling to employees that all disciplinary issues will be dealt with consistently and objectively.

Many organisations fall into the trap of using their grievance procedure in place of a proper appeals process. This is to be avoided wherever possible. The grievance procedure should be reserved for resolving problems arising from employment, and is covered in the next chapter. Finally, not only should appeals be dealt with in a timely fashion, the procedure should specify time-limits within which appeals should be lodged.

SUMMARY

In this chapter we have explained why managing employee performance and behaviour is such a key area. We have looked at the origins of disciplinary procedures and how they have developed over time. We have also provided an outline of the current legal position, but it is important to remember that this is not a legal text and it is important to check legal facts each time a performance or behaviour problem arises, because the law is constantly evolving.

Poor management of performance and behaviour can create employee relations problems, and we therefore make no apology for the stress placed on the importance of best practice and the need to act professionally. We have tried to reflect the realities of managing these issues within an organisational context, because discussions that we have had with managers from a whole range of organisations show that they can cause major employee relations problems – because breaches of rules are either ignored or treated with differing degrees of seriousness by different managers.

There is also an overwhelming business case for the effective management of employee performance and behaviour. More and more organisations are recognising the value that can be added by involving employees in the business and gaining their commitment to organisational objectives. Assuming that this is a trend that most organisations would wish to see continuing, an employee relations climate that recognises the rights and responsibilities of both parties to the employment relationship is absolutely vital.

Key points

- A fair and effective disciplinary procedure is one that concentrates in improving or changing behaviour, and not one that relies on the principle of punishment.
- There must always be a just cause for disciplinary action, whether it is misconduct, inability to perform the job in a satisfactory manner or some other reason.
- Good practice is an important principle because it helps to ensure fairness and consistency.
- The statement of particulars of employment must specify any disciplinary rules applicable to the employee, and must also include information about any procedures applicable to the taking of disciplinary decisions.
- There is a need for clear and unambiguous rules within the workplace, and both procedures and rules should be regularly monitored.
- It is important to discuss performance and behavioural problems with the employee (counselling) before using the disciplinary procedures.
- Disciplinary interviews should be prepared for thoroughly, and disciplinary interviews conducted in a professional manner.
- Employees are entitled to know the cause of complaints against them, entitled to representation, entitled to challenge evidence, and entitled to a right of appeal.
- Managing absence should be a priority for any organisation and appropriate policies established for the purpose.

FURTHER READING

ADVISORY, CONCILIATION AND ARBITRATION SERVICE (2001) *Discipline and Grievance at Work: The ACAS advisory handbook*. London, ACAS.

ADVISORY, CONCILIATION AND ARBITRATION SERVICE (2004) *Disciplinary and Grievance Procedures: The ACAS code of practice*. London, ACAS.

CIPD Employment Law Service

CIPD (2004) *Employee Absence: A survey of management policy and practice*.

EDWARDS P. (1994) Discipline and the creation of order, in K. Sisson (ed.) *Personnel Management: A comprehensive guide to theory and practice in Britain*. Oxford, Blackwell.

Employment Act 2002.

Employment Act 2002 (Dispute Resolution) Regulations 2004.

Employment Relations Act 1999.

Employment Rights Act 1996.

Employment Rights (Dispute Resolution) Act 1998.

LEWIS D. and SARGEANT M. (2004) *Essentials of Employment Law*. London, Chartered Institute of Personnel and Development.

Trade Union and Labour Relations (Consolidation) Act 1992.

Managing employee grievances

INTRODUCTION

A grievance is a complaint by an employee that the behaviour of management, or that of an employee, has been unfair and unjust in its application to him or her. Employee complaints may be genuine or they may be the result of a misconception or misunderstanding. In either case, settling them quickly and effectively is important. To the individual concerned, his or her grievance is important. In addition, an organisation cannot ignore employee grievances since the mishandling of an individual's grievance can escalate into a collective dispute. The objective of grievance management is to rectify matters that have gone wrong by:

- thoroughly investigating the situation
- identifying the cause of the employee's complaint
- taking appropriate action to resolve the complaint to the mutual satisfaction of the employee and the management
- resolving the grievance as quickly as possible.

A key aspect of fairness at work is the opportunity for the individual employee to complain about, and receive redress for, unfair treatment. In this chapter, the fundamentals of managing employee grievances, as an important element in the work of the employee relations professional, are examined. The 1998 Workplace Employee Relations Survey reported that in 95 per cent of workplaces the responsibilities of employee relations professionals included providing line managers with advice in managing employee grievances.

In managing employee grievances line managers require help, advice, support and expertise from the employee relations professional. Such assistance includes devising effective grievance procedures and then training line managers to operate the procedures in a fair, reasonable and consistent manner. In addition, it is good practice on the part of the employee relations professional to take responsibility for monitoring and reviewing the effectiveness – especially in terms of outcomes – of the operation of the grievance procedure.

THE BUSINESS CASE FOR RESOLVING GRIEVANCES

Employee grievances on a wide variety of issues (including discrimination, harassment and bullying) arise even in the best-managed organisations. If grievances are not dealt with, or handled quickly, they are likely to fester and harm the employment relationship. A grievance may also be felt by a group, as well as an individual, and, if left unresolved, may develop into a major collective dispute which is likely to bring in the involvement of a trade union. However, whether individual or collective, all employee grievances have the potential to damage the quality of an organisation's employee relations and thereby its competitive position and labour market image. The golden rule for management to remember in managing employee grievances is that they are important to those who express them, and must therefore be treated seriously.

Employee grievances are an outward expression of employee dissatisfaction which, if not resolved, can result in unsatisfactory work behaviour and performance, which in turn may have adverse consequences for the organisation's competitive position. Unresolved employee dissatisfaction gives rise to:

- employee frustration
- deteriorating interpersonal relationships
- low morale
- poor performance, resulting in lower productivity and/or a poorer quality of output or service
- disciplinary problems, including poor performance by employees
- resignation and loss of good staff (increased labour turnover)
- increased employee absenteeism
- withdrawal of employee goodwill
- resistance to change – if employees feel they have been treated badly, they are likely to oppose the introduction of change.

In addition, unresolved grievances can lead to employees who feel so strongly that their 'employment rights' have not been respected resigning their employment, and claiming to an employment tribunal a fundamental breach of contract amounting to constructive dismissal.

If an organisation has a reputation for a high level of employee dissatisfaction, it will be a disincentive for individuals or organisations to purchase goods and/or services from that organisation, believing that the goods and services are likely to be of poor quality. A reputation for employee dissatisfaction also gives an organisation a 'poor employer' image in the labour market. This image will accentuate the organisation's problems of recruiting and retaining the appropriate quantity and quality of labour services necessary to achieve its organisational objectives.

Organisations in which a significant number of employees experience feelings of unfairness will have relatively higher cost structures than in a competitor organisation that has absolute and relatively lower levels of employee dissatisfaction. The former organisation has a competitive disadvantage relative to the latter, which will be expressed in sales, revenue and profitability.

If an organisation does not address its employees' grievances, the quality of their working life is likely to be adversely affected. It is essential to the continued prosperity and wellbeing of the organisation that its employee complaints about management behaviour are addressed as quickly as possible and as near to their source as possible.

If the clear business case outlined above for the effective and professional management of employee grievances is to be a reality, then training for team leaders and supervisors to manage employee grievances effectively must be a high business priority. It is also important if the business/organisational benefits of effective grievance management are to be delivered that employees (both old and new) know to whom they can take their grievance. The 1998 Workplace Employee Relations Survey reported that the main source of information by which employees are usually made aware of the existence, and content, of a grievance procedure are in their letter of appointment (47 per cent of workplaces), the staff handbook (55 per cent of workplaces) or on a noticeboard (10 per cent of workplaces).

WHAT IS A GRIEVANCE?

A grievance usually arises because an aggrieved individual regards some management decision (or act of indecision) or behaviour on the part of another employee as unfair and unjust in its application to him or her. However, not all employee complaints are justified, in that the action complained of may be legitimate behaviour within the terms and spirit of a collective agreement between the employees and the management, within a company rule contained in the staff handbook or within the necessities of the business. If employee grievances are to be managed effectively, management must acquire and develop an ability to distinguish genuine from unfounded grievances, and in the case of the latter, explain clearly to the individual concerned why his or her complaint merits no action by management.

However, all grievances, whether genuine or unfounded, are important to the individual concerned and have to be treated on their merits. When management receives a complaint which appears frivolous, it is not good practice to reject it without at least an investigation into how it has arisen. If this reveals the employee's complaint to be ill-founded, this must be explained to the individual. By acting on the basis of just cause after investigation and then behaving in a fair, reasonable and consistent manner, management demonstrates to its employees that both unfounded and genuine complaints are treated seriously and in a businesslike manner.

Non-trading of grievances

In resolving employee grievances, management treats each one on its merits thereby accepting that the complaint is a serious issue for the individual concerned. An employee's grievance has to be dealt with independently of the complaint of any other employee. In managing employee grievances, management proceeds on the basis of one at a time. It resolves the individual's grievance on a particular issue (for example, denial of a training opportunity) and then moves on to settle another employee's grievance over a different issue. The employee relations professional should avoid falling into the trap of having to deal simultaneously with a whole list of different grievances over different issues from a number of different employees.

The effective resolution of grievances, unlike in bargaining, excludes a trade-off between employee complaints about employer or another employee behaviour. It is not good employment practice for management to settle one person's grievance in exchange for another employee's agreeing to drop his or her grievance. In grievance-handling management should resist the temptation to trade off one employee's grievance against another. In short, management does not say 'If you drop that employee's grievance over the lack of clean toilet facilities, we shall concede that employee's grievance over the lack of parking facilities.'

Complaints from individual employees can centre on many aspects of management behaviour. An employee complaint may be to the effect that the employer has acted in breach of a collective agreement (ie management is not applying it as the parties intended); tools and/or machinery have not been properly maintained; the canteen facilities are poor and inadequate; the workplace is too dark, too cold (or hot) and/or unhealthy; or the imposed disciplinary penalty is too harsh. Other areas of individual complaints by employees against management are likely to include that they have been passed over for promotion; they have been denied access to a training and development opportunity; their holiday allocation does not meet their family circumstances; a bonus has been paid late; a new working practice has been introduced without prior consultation; or their job is graded at an inappropriate level. Complaints by an individual employee against the behaviour of another employee are likely to centre on alleged bullying/harassment issues.

Industrial Relations Services in 2002 published the results of its survey into the handling of individual grievances (see IRS, No.759, September 2002). Its survey attracted usable responses from 75 organisations employing a total of nearly a quarter of a million people and ranging in size from 15 employees to 46,000. Around half of the 75 respondents had a single formal written procedure covering both individual and collective disputes, initiated by employees, while around a third operated an individual procedure only. This latter group of organisations is predominantly private sector and non-unionised. The survey also showed that one in six employers surveyed operated separate procedures for individual and collective grievances/disputes.

The top ten complaints raised by employees in the Industrial Relations Services' 2002 Survey are shown in Table 20. The issues of harassment and/or bullying was the top common source of grievance, followed by discipline, and then new working practices. The IRS 2001 Survey of grievance-handling had found the most common topic raised under grievance procedures related to pay and grading, whereas in its 1997 Survey complaints over the introduction of new working practices was top of the list. The 2002 Survey also revealed that typically in each organisation over the past year, complaints had been raised under the individual grievance procedure up to five times.

Table 20   *Top ten complaints raised by employees in the IRS Survey 2002*

Complaint	Percentage
Harassment/bullying	45
Discipline	27
New working practices	23
Grading	22
Discrimination	18
Work allocation/staffing levels	17
Non-pay terms and conditions	17
Pay	15
Health and safety	2
Miscellaneous	18

Of 1,000 people interviewed in 1998 for the IPD study of the psychological contract, 17 per cent reported they had been treated unfairly in the last 12 months on grounds of age, race, gender, disability, experience, qualifications or some other grounds. The highest proportion of complaints was found among young employees and among health service employees. The main stated reasons of alleged unfair treatment were:

- personality clashes   (19 per cent)
- lack of experience   (11 per cent)
- gender   (10 per cent)
- age   (8 per cent)
- lack of qualifications   (6 per cent)
- race   (4 per cent).

Many employee complaints are thus falling into what can broadly be described as 'equality' issues. Women employees are increasingly laying complaints before management that their jobs are inappropriately graded and paid. An increasing number of employee complaints are based on alleged injustice in that the behaviour complained of is motivated by a dislike of them on the grounds of their gender, race, creed, colour or disability. Harassment complaints can be more difficult to manage in that in some cases the alleged harasser/bully is also the manager of the employee making the complaint.

Employee grievances can be collective in that a group of employees have a common complaint relating to their employment or an individual has a grievance which has collective implications. All employees, for example, in an office may complain that the temperature is too high or too low, while employees collectively in the workplace may complain that their level of pay or bonuses seems unfair compared with those of different groups of employees in other sections of the organisation. Research indicates that the main causes of grievances raised by a group of employees centre on:

- the interpretation and application of an existing agreement
- pay and bonus arrangements
- organisational change
- new working practices
- grading issues.

Collective grievance procedures are not as universal as individual grievance procedures and tend to be associated with unionised workplaces. In the 2002 IRS Survey, most organisations had experienced few collective disputes in recent years.

What are the main sources of employee grievances in your organisation? How would you explain this pattern?

THE TAKE-UP OF GRIEVANCES

Employees who are unable to get their grievances resolved informally enter their complaint into the formal grievance procedure. This procedure aims to encourage employees who believe they have been treated unfairly to raise their complaint without fear of reprisal, and have it resolved as quickly as possible in order to prevent minor disagreements developing into serious disputes and to help build an open and trusting organisational climate. Managers need a knowledge and understanding of how to operate these procedures, and most organisations provide training in managing employee grievances for team leaders and other frontline managers. All organisations require effective formal complaints procedures in place to ensure that employee dissatisfaction is dealt with to mutual satisfaction – but they should avoid using them if it is at all possible for the grievance to be resolved informally. Activating the grievance procedure is costly in terms of management time.

Most employees' complaints against management behaviour do not reach the formal grievance procedure. Of the workplaces with formal grievance procedures surveyed in the Workplace Employee Relations Survey 1998, only 30 per cent reported they had been activated in the last 12 months. In the smallest workplaces, the corresponding figure was 20 per cent, and in large workplaces 79 per cent.

There are many reasons why employee complaints do not enter into formal procedure. First, something happens to make it unnecessary. As Torrington and Hall (2005) point out, the employee's dissatisfaction can disappear after a good night's sleep and/or after a cup of tea with a colleague. Second, employees merely want to get their dissatisfaction off their chests. The grievance is resolved simply by an appropriate manager's listening to the employee. 'A shoulder to cry on' provides sufficient satisfaction for the employee to withdraw his or her disapproval of management's behaviour.

Third, in times of high levels of unemployment, individuals are reluctant to raise their grievance formally, fearing that management may hold it against them and react by denying them promotion, access to training and development programmes and merit award payments. Fourth, employees may, in some cases, see little point in raising their grievance because they perceive the procedure is not a particularly effective mechanism for resolving problems. Fifth, some individuals are unwilling to express their dissatisfaction with management for fear of offending their immediate superior who may see the complaint as a criticism of his or her competence. Finally, it may be that employees have nothing to complain about. The IPD 1999 Survey of Surveys into worker dissatisfaction and insecurity found that the majority of British employees were satisfied with their jobs, did not feel insecure, and had a high level of commitment to their employer.

The IPD publication *Fairness at Work and the Psychological Contract* (1998) interviewed 1,000 people of whom only 10 per cent said they had made a formal complaint about the way they had been treated in their organisation. Indeed, only 28 per cent said they had ever made a complaint against their organisation. They either did not regard their treatment as unfair or they had no faith in or knowledge of any complaints procedure. Of the 10 per cent who had laid a complaint, one in five reported that the procedure in his or her organisation was fair in dealing with the complaint, while nearly one in three considered it unfair. This suggests that many of those who formally complained were unhappy with the operation of the grievance procedures. Although this level of dissatisfaction is perhaps an inevitable consequence of the failure to uphold some complaints, it is, at the same time, disturbingly high. The results may also help to explain why many of those who felt they had been unfairly treated did not follow up their grievance.

The lack of individual grievances being put formally into the grievance procedure does not mean that the quality (climate) of employee relations in an organisation is in good shape. However, employee dissatisfaction identified at an early stage can be settled quickly through informal discussions. Behaving in this way reduces considerably the probability of the employees' level of dissatisfaction reaching the point at which they are prepared to make a formal complaint against management behaviour.

A situation in which employee complaints are being suppressed because they feel that senior management will not act against a team leader/supervisor whose style of management is the cause of the grievance cannot be allowed to continue. Senior management might, for example, counsel the team leader/frontline manager on why his or her management style has to change or provide him or her with formal training after which his or her style should change for the better. If such action fails to produce a more constructive management style, management must either redeploy the team leader/frontline manager elsewhere or consider dispensing with his or her services. If employee complaints are shown, following thorough investigation, to be the result of a personality clash between the team leader/frontline manager and an individual employee, redeploying the individual to another area of employment may be the best option.

> Has the grievance procedure in your organisation been activated in the last 12 months? If it has, what were the issues and the groups of workers involved? If it hasn't, why do you think this is the case?

GRIEVANCE PROCEDURES

The grievance procedure provides the means by which individual employees process their complaint against management behaviour or that of another employee. In the former case, it informs the individual of the action he or she must take to raise a grievance and the steps management will take in giving it consideration.

A grievance procedure benefits employees because they know where they stand and know what to expect. The purpose of the procedure is to:

- ensure the fair and consistent treatment of employees
- reduce the risk of 'unpredictable' action
- clarify the manner in which grievances will be dealt with
- maintain a good employee relations environment
- help the employer to avoid disputes or costly legal action.

It can therefore be useful to define, in advance, the purpose of the policy. For example, the grievance procedure for Tyco Fire and Security and ADT Fire and Security starts with the following explanation of purpose:

> The purposes of this procedure are to ensure that you have an opportunity to raise formally with management any grievances relating to your job or complaints regarding the company or any member of the company. The company's aim is to ensure that your grievance or complaint is dealt with promptly and fairly by the appropriate level of the company's management.

Meanwhile, at Motherwell College the grievance policy and procedure states:

> *1.0 Introduction*
> This policy provides a mechanism whereby any grievance relating to employment within Motherwell College is settled fairly, consistently, quickly and as near to the point of origin as possible. This procedure is non-contractual.
>
> The following procedure is written to take account of individual grievances. It is not intended to form part of any collective grievance procedure.
>
> *2.0 Purpose*
> The purpose of this policy and procedure is to ensure that a common approach will be followed in respect of individual grievances within Motherwell College.

And the staff grievance procedure at the Scottish Prison Service states in its introduction:

1.2
From time to time staff may have individual grievances related to employment matters. This procedure is designed to enable managers and staff to resolve such issues quickly, effectively and fairly.

1.3
All grievances raised by employees will be dealt with confidentially and in private. This does not preclude discussions with other levels of management or trade union representatives to obtain or confirm information and to resolve the grievance.

Underlying principles

In managing employee complaints, management is guided by a number of principles – fairness, consistency, representation and promptness. Fairness is ensured in that the procedure:

- prevents management from dismissing the employee's complaint out of hand on the grounds that it is trivial, too time-consuming and/or too costly
- ensures that there is a full investigation by an unbiased individual to establish the facts of the case
- provides the employee with adequate time to prepare his or her case and to question management witnesses
- allows for the case to be heard by individuals not directly involved in the complaint
- provides for the right of appeal to a higher level of management and, in some cases, to an independent external body.

A grievance procedure with a clearly demarcated number of stages and standards of behaviour at each stage provides consistency of treatment and reduces the influence of subjectivity.

In raising a complaint, the procedure provides the individual with the right to be represented by an individual independent of the employer. Such a representative is usually internal to the organisation (for example, an employee representative, a shop steward, a work colleague) rather than external (for example, a full-time trade union official, a solicitor). The staff grievance procedure for the Scottish Prison Service, for instance, states:

> The individual raising the employment-related grievance is entitled to be accompanied/represented by a trade union representative or a fellow staff member of his/her choice at all formal stages of the procedure.

The promptness principle is achieved by the procedure's having a small number of stages, each of which has time limits for its completion. This enables the grievance to be resolved as quickly and as simply as possible.

To summarise, then, the grievance procedure ensures the right of an employee to complain if he or she experiences unfair treatment and, if he or she exercises this right, to be treated in a fair and reasonable manner consistent with the principles of natural justice. It provides that the individual employee is treated with dignity and respect. By establishing standards of behaviour and due process to resolve employee grievances in a peaceful and constructive manner, the grievance procedure thus provides 'order and stability' in the workplace.

Forms of procedure

The form of grievance procedures varies immensely. In a small non-union establishment, the procedure is likely to be written into the employees' contract of employment, of which the following language would be typical:

> If you have a grievance relating to your employment, you should raise it with your immediate supervisor.

In larger organisations, a grievance procedure is likely to be a clause in a collective agreement. However, in large and medium-sized unionised and non-unionised organisations, the grievance procedure is likely to be reproduced in the company handbook, or be available as a separate document, and a typical wording would be:

> If you have any grievance relating to your employment, you should raise it with your immediate supervisor. If the matter is not settled at this level, you may pursue it through the grievance procedure agreed between the company and the trade union representatives. Further details of such procedural agreements are maintained separately in writing and may be consulted on request to management.

The Employment Act 2002, however, imposes upon employers statutory dispute resolution procedures incorporated into every contract of employment, for employee grievances. It provides a model procedure of minimum standards for grievance-handling that is binding on employees and employers irrespective of workforce size (see below).

A typical procedure

A typical grievance procedure has a standard format of:

- a policy statement of the purpose of the procedure (see above)
- a statement of the scope of the procedure
- a statement of the general principles to be applied in its application
- a number of stages – At each stage, the aim is to identify action that stops the problem recurring or continuing. The number of stages in a procedure can range from two to five, but three stages are the most popular arrangement in practice (see IRS 2002 Survey)
- setting time limits by which each stage should be completed, so that a speedy resolution of the grievance can be secured
- setting out who are individuals to be involved at each stage
- providing a right to representation, for the employee laying the complaint against management, by an individual independent of the employer
- monitoring and review arrangements: these are usually encapsulated in the following statement:

> Organisation X will continue to examine and review existing grievance procedures to reflect the organisation's needs on the basis of experience and statutory obligations ...

In most organisations, procedures for managing employee complaints relating to health and safety provision, job grading (job evaluation scheme), sexual harassment and discrimination, and 'whistle-blowing' are normally separate from the general grievance/disputes procedure. Grievances about job grading, harassment, bullying, etc, are thus normally dealt with by means of a purpose-built procedure. Their degree of differentiation from the general grievance procedure depends on the volume of business and on the speed, efficacy and acceptability required by the parties. These specific procedures are discussed in greater detail later in the chapter.

Stages

There are a number of stages in a typical grievance procedure. Common factors to all the stages are:

- They spell out the details of who hears the case (eg the departmental manager, managing director) and the individuals to be present (eg the personnel manager, the line manger and the employee concerned) including who can represent the employee (eg a colleague, friend or shop steward).

- They explain the appeal mechanisms available to employees.
- They define the time limits by which the stages must be complete.
- They explain what will happen if the grievance is not resolved or remains unsettled.

This is illustrated in the paragraphs below, which reproduce a typical three-stage grievance procedure.

A TYPICAL THREE-STAGE GRIEVANCE PROCEDURE

Stage 1
If you wish to raise a formal grievance you should, in the first instance, raise it orally or in writing with your immediate supervisor or manager. Where a matter affects a group of employees, a spokesperson from amongst the group should raise the matter with the immediate supervisor/manager. The supervisor/manager will normally respond within five working days.

Stage 2
If the matter is not resolved at Stage 1 or within five working days, you or the spokesperson of a group may refer it in writing within three working days to the next level of management who may also involve a representative of the Personnel Department. You or the spokesperson should set out the grounds for the complaints and the reasons for the dissatisfaction with the Stage 1 response. A meeting will normally take place to consider the matter within seven working days of the request being made.

Stage 3
It the matter is not resolved at Stage 2 or within seven working days, you or the spokesperson may refer it in writing within three working days to the next level of management who may involve a representative of the Personnel Department. You or the spokesperson should set out the grounds for the complaint and the reasons for dissatisfaction with the Stage 2 response. A meeting will normally take place to consider the matter within 10 working days of the request being made. The decision of the Divisional Executive is the final stage of the procedure and will be given in writing.

Although the aim of grievance procedures is to reach a resolution of the employee complaint as quickly as possible, it cannot, however, be done with undue haste. As we have seen, a grievance procedure usually specifies how, and to whom, employees can raise a grievance and spells out the stages through which the complaint will be processed. To ensure a speedy settlement, time limits are specified by which each stage of the procedure must be completed (see above).

So in managing grievances management's objective is to settle the complaint as near as possible to the point of its source. If employee complaints are permitted unnecessarily to progress to a higher level, this principle is undermined. A professional employee relations manager ensures that his or her managerial colleagues, but particularly line managers, understand the limits of their authority when operating within the parameters of the grievance procedure. The procedure is a problem-solving mechanism, and the significance of each of the different procedural stages is reinforced when grievances are settled as near as possible to the point of origin.

Although defined stages through which a grievance can be processed are essential, there is no ideal number of stages. The number is a function of many factors, including the size of the organisation. However, natural justice principles would point to a minimum of two stages because this at least ensures one level of appeal from the immediate decision. Nor should the procedure contain too many stages, since this makes the process unduly long and is in conflict with the principle of resolving grievances as quickly as possible and as close as can be to their origin.

Do you have a grievance procedure in your organisation? If not, why not? If you do, how many stages does it have? Why does it have that number?

Time limits

An employee with a complaint wants his or her grievance settled as soon as possible, and is likely to regard it as the highest priority for the manager to whom the complaint is made. That manager, on the other hand, needs time to gather the facts, consult with other managers and consider what action to take – all of which has to be fitted around all the other tasks for which that manager is responsible. The idea behind a time limit is that it provides a manager with an opportunity to consider the problem seriously while at the same time also committing him or her to provide an answer within a fixed period of time. This relaxes the pressures on the employee or his/her representative, both of whom now know that if a satisfactory answer has not been provided at the end of the time limit, their complaint will proceed to the next stage.

The usual practice is to allow longer time limits for the completion for each successive stage. Internal stages time limits can vary from a low of 24 hours to a maximum of five days, but such limits are longer for external stages. Time limits alone do not ensure the expeditious handling of grievances but they are useful in establishing standards of reasonable behaviour by the parties. When the external stages of a grievance procedure are triggered, time limits for their completion again provide reassurance for the employee that inordinately lengthy delays in dealing with the complaint are not possible. Most of the criticisms against time limits (for example, loss of flexibility, undermining mutual trust or the issue is not dealt with properly at the lower levels) are avoided if there is a proviso in the procedure to permit, by mutual agreement, an extension of the time limits by which each stage of the process must be completed. The guiding principle is that the employee's complaint progresses quickly to the level needed to find a solution to the problem, and that managers do not 'sit on' grievances.

Employee representation

Fair and reasonable behaviour by an employer in managing employee grievances requires the employee to have the right to representation by an individual who can advocate his or her case. Representation assists the individual employee who may lack confidence and the experience to deal with his/her line manager or senior manager, especially those operating at the executive level (for example, the managing director). The individual's representative is independent of the interests of the employer and is not there merely to witness what management says to the individual. This employee's representative is, however, likely to be internal to the organisation. The 2002 research by IRS on resolving disputes at work revealed a wide range of practice in the role of the independent representative. It varied from acting as a silent witness to being a full-blown representative. In one organisation the role was to address the hearing, ask questions of the manager involved and the panel, and generally support the worker. At another organisation the employee representative could address the meeting on points of procedure, and could advise and generally represent the interests of the individual.

The Workplace Employee Relations Survey 1998 showed that only 4 per cent of the workplaces surveyed did not allow employees to be accompanied by a third party in grievance hearings. In workplaces where the employer permitted the employee to be independently accompanied, 41 per cent allowed them to choose whoever they wished to accompany them. The remaining half specified a variety of options, including a trade union official (45 per cent), a full-time official (27 per cent) and another work colleague (87 per cent). In workplaces where union members were present but there was no recognition of the union, nearly half (46 per cent) of managers said workers could be accompanied by anyone of their choosing. Of those who specified the options open to employees, full-time union officials were mentioned by 20 per cent of managers.

The Employment Relations Act 1999 gives workers a statutory right to be accompanied by a fellow worker or trade union official when they are required or invited by their employer to attend certain categories of grievance hearings and when they make a reasonable request to be so accompanied. The chosen companion has a statutory right to address the hearing and to confer with the worker but no statutory right to answer questions on the worker's behalf or to attend hearings in his or her place. Workers are free to choose an official from any trade union to accompany them at a grievance hearing, regardless of whether or not a trade union is recognised by the employer. However, the ACAS Code of Practice (see below) on *Discipline and Grievance at Work* recommends that where a trade union is recognised in a workplace, it is good practice for an official from that union to accompany the worker at a hearing.

What stage representation?

In many procedures representation starts at the second stage, after the individual has raised the complaint with his or her immediate manager. Representation then only becomes necessary if the employee is dis-satisfied with the response from the immediate manager and wishes to take the matter to a higher level of management. The assumption behind this is that a grievance is not a grievance if the individual employee's immediate manager resolves the problem.

However, there are employee relations managers who consider that employees should have representation from the very start of their complaint. In these circumstances the employee's first step is to take the grievance to his or her workplace representative (where he/she has one), rather than to his or her immediate superior, and persuade the representative that he or she has a genuine grievance and ask for representation in processing the complaint. The employee's representative then has an important responsibility to act as a useful 'filter' and sift the genuine grievances from the unfounded.

Equality of representatives

In the internal stages of the procedure, individual employees' representatives are also employees of the organisation. As employees they are in a subordinate position to management, who can give them instruc-tions, empower them, verify the quality of their work, monitor their time-keeping and initiate disciplinary action against them. In short, they are contracted to supply work to the employer.

However, when they are in the role of employee representative they interact with management as partners of equal status. The acceptance of this equality of relationship is recognised by management in that management has committed itself to a grievance procedure which sets out the 'players' to be involved in each stage of the procedure. When processing the grievance and the management and an employee's representative meet at the different stages, they do so on the basis of equality. So if, for example, as the third stage of the procedure stipulates, the employee's representative and the chief executive/managing director ultimately meet to try to resolve the grievance and the meeting is held in the managing director's office, they interact with each other as employee relations players of equal status. A professional managing director will always treat the employee's representative as such and ensure that he or she has the proper facilities (seating, appropriate space for documents, etc) to represent his or her 'client' in a businesslike manner.

The grievance procedure also protects the employee representative from a refusal by the representative's frontline manager/team leader to allow him/her to leave his/her job to represent his/her 'client's' interests. The procedure is management's acceptance that in certain circumstances the individual employee's role as an employee relations player takes preference over his or her role as an employee. If in managing grievances management and employee representatives are equal partners, then they have a joint responsibility for settling grievances.

This equality relationship in grievance-handling is difficult for some line managers to understand. Many find it hard to recognise employee representatives other than as employees of the company and therefore subject to their control and direction. Some managers will never come to terms with the status distinction, relative to management, between the individual as an employee representative and the individual as an employee under their supervision and direction. They feel that their authority is undermined by more senior managers treating employees, when wearing their representative hat, as equal. They find it difficult to understand why their senior managers show so much consideration and grant such facilities towards individuals who they perceive as merely employees of the organisation. It is, therefore, an important responsibility for the employee relations professional to ensure that the management involved in grievance-handling understands, and accepts, this equality of status in employee relations roles.

> When managing grievances, is the employee representative in relation to the appropriate manager representing management's interests in a superior, inferior, or equal status position? Justify your answer.

The operation of the procedure

The role of the employee relations professional

Grievance procedures are an integral part of the whole way in which an organisation is managed. They directly affect line management at all levels. Line managers have always had the main responsibility for operating the grievance procedure, assisted and advised by the employee relations professional. It is important that the employee relations professional does not take on board line managers' problems or responsibility for them. It has become standard practice in modern organisations for team leaders/frontline managers to manage people in partnership with human resource managers (Kelly and Gennard, 1997; Whittaker and Marchington, 2003; Renwick, 2003). The role of the employee relations professional in managing grievance is therefore to:

- identify line management training and development needs with regard to managing grievances
- devise and implement a training and development programme so that line managers can acquire and develop the skills necessary to become effective managers of employee grievances
- ensure that line managers have a clear understanding of the way in which grievance procedures are intended to operate
- devise a grievance procedure which conforms with 'good practice' and spells out what has to happen at each stage, and why
- promote awareness of 'good practice' in managing grievances amongst line managers
- ensure that employees are aware of their rights under the procedure
- promote a constructive grievance policy at board level.

The employee relations professional also has an important role to play in monitoring and reviewing the operation of the grievance procedure and for recommending revisions to its design or operation. This involves reviewing the outcomes of the grievance decisions taken following the procedure and assessing whether these outcomes have been those desired by the management interest – and if not, why not. (For example, is it because line managers are not undertaking a thorough investigation of the complaint?) This review and monitor function also requires the employee relations professional to analyse the subject matter of individual employee grievances, consider why the outcomes have been what they have, and check that the procedure has been applied in all cases fairly and consistently (ie that management has behaved reasonably in processing employee grievances). The IRS 2002 survey of the handling of employee grievances showed that 25 per cent of the 75 participating organisations monitored on a regular basis the outcome of resolving employee grievances. This compared with the same percentage in its 2001 survey, and 40 per cent of organisations in its 1997 survey.

The role of the line manager

The frontline manager remains a key player in the operation of a grievance procedure. The filing of a grievance by an employee may be seen by frontline managers as reflecting badly on their managerial competence. If grievance procedures are to operate effectively, senior management must reassure frontline managers that this is by no means necessarily the case. On the contrary, frontline managers should be encouraged by their own reporting managers to hear grievances. It is important that frontline managers become aware of employee dissatisfaction as early as possible. It is usually easier to resolve grievances informally in a manner satisfactory to individuals and their managers if they are handled as quickly and as close to the source of the complaint as possible.

The frontline manager has the least executive authority, and this limits his or her ability (as well as confidence) to make decisions without reference to a more senior manager. If a frontline manager/team leader frequently refers a grievance up to a superior, the employee will realise that a possibly quicker way of having his/her problem resolved is to short-circuit the first line manager and go directly to a superior. If this happens, the legitimate authority of the frontline manager becomes undermined. This then threatens the credibility of the procedure, since what has happened is effectively a reduction in the number of stages in the procedure. The ultimate impact is to remove the grievance from its source of origin, to slow the process down by having to refer the complaint back through its correct stages, to cause confusion, and to create bad feeling. To avoid this happening, the employee relations professional must ensure three things – that:

- everyone knows, within the procedure, the limits of their own and others' authority
- the procedures are operated consistently by line managers
- frontline managers have the authority to settle grievances.

In situations where union workplace representatives believe that frontline managers are unable to take a decision at the appropriate level, good practice requires management to insist that the procedure be followed. Management thereby demonstrates that it will apply the procedure consistently, and that its operation is understood by those managers who have a part to play in its operation. It is essential that frontline managers have the authority to deal with as many types of grievance as possible. The frontline manager/team leader has to be able to say 'yes' as well as 'no'.

It is equally important that frontline management continues to be involved in the settling of grievances even if the complaint proceeds beyond the stage at which they are formally involved. This can be achieved by their attendance at subsequent meetings or at the very least by being kept informed of the outcome as the grievance proceeds through subsequent stages of the procedure. It is bad management practice for a frontline manager to hear the outcome of an employee's complaint first from the employee himself or herself and/or from his/her representative.

Grievance records

When a grievance progresses to a higher stage in the procedure, documentation of what happened at the previous stage is necessary to those managers who now become involved for the first time and are not familiar with the issues involved. In practice, the extent to which records of grievances are kept varies widely. In some organisations the completion of grievance records is a required activity for frontline management. In others, only the personnel/HRM department keeps records. In yet others no documentation of any kind is kept except when an employee complaint progresses to the external stage of the procedure. The ACAS Code of Practice on disciplinary and grievance procedures advises that records be kept detailing the nature of the grievance raised, the employer response, any action taken, and the reasons for it.

Grievance records serve useful purposes for management. If there is a failure to agree at any stage, a written record clarifies the complaint, and the arguments put forward about it by the individual employee and/or his or her representative. Such a record is also helpful to those managers involved in the next stage of the procedure. If the record is agreed by both parties – as commonly completed by the manager concerned and countersigned by the employee and/or his or her representative – it is even more valuable. Grievance record forms assist the personnel/HRM function to keep in touch with the progress of unresolved grievances and to analyse trends in the use and outcomes of the grievance procedure. Analysis of the record will show where, and why, delays in the procedure frequently occur. When a resolution to an individual's grievance has been reached, a written and agreed statement helps ensure that there are no misunderstandings about what has been agreed. In the absence of an agreed statement, the parties may find that they have different versions of what they thought they had actually agreed. A written statement is also useful for communicating the outcome of the employee's complaint.

However, systems which require line management to keep records of grievances are not easy to maintain unless management keeps a watchful eye on matters. Some frontline managers who handle grievances complain that having to keep grievance records is an extra, irksome administrative chore. Grievance record systems at the frontline level will not operate effectively without the careful observation of more senior management.

Does your organisation keep grievance records? If not, why not? If it does, what information do the records contain, and why?

THE LAW
The Employment Relations Act 1999

The Employment Relations Act 1999 introduced the right for workers to be accompanied at grievance hearings. When the worker is required or invited by the employer to attend certain categories of grievance hearings and the worker reasonably requests to be accompanied, the employer must permit the worker to bring along a companion of his or her choice. The companion must be either a trade union official or a fellow worker. This right was based on the widespread practice of allowing a chosen companion to attend these key meetings.

Unsurprisingly, empirical evidence (for example, the Department of Trade and Industry Review of the 1999 Employment Relations Act, published in February 2003) suggests that the right has operated smoothly since its introduction in September 2000. Compliance has been high, and in its first two years of operation only 136 applications were made to employment tribunals of an alleged breach of this right. This figure is low, given the large number of qualifying hearings which occur each year. The evidence does not show that the granting of the right has been unworkable or difficult to apply. The Employment Act 2004 sets out in more detail the circumstances in which the companion is allowed to address a hearing beyond that of speaking to it at all and conferring with the employee.

The Employment Act 2002

This act sets out statutory disputes resolution procedures and the consequences of failure to comply with them. Its statutory grievance procedure complements the legal right to be accompanied in workplace hearings by a trade union official or fellow worker of the employee's choice. The 'model' statutory internal grievance procedure forms part of the implied terms of all employment contracts and is binding on employees and employers irrespective of workforce size. Except in certain circumstances, employment tribunals will not permit employees to submit complaints at all if the first step in the relevant grievance procedure (see below) has not been fulfilled or 28 days have not elapsed since the complaint was sent to the employer. The 2002 Act provides for the first time that employers are required to have procedures for dealing with employee grievances. These provisions are designed to encourage parties to avoid litigation by resolving their differences through proper internal procedures.

The 2002 Act sets out two statutory grievance procedures:

- a standard procedure
- a modified procedure.

The *standard procedure* has three steps:

1 The employee must set out the grievance and the basis for the grievance in writing and send the statement or a copy to the employer ('the statement of grievance').

2 The employer must invite the employee to a meeting to discuss the grievance. The meeting must not take place unless the employee has informed the employer of the basis for the grievance when the written statement under Step 1 was made. The employer must have had a reasonable opportunity to consider its response to that information before the meeting. The employee must take all reasonable steps to attend the meeting. After the meeting, the employer must inform the employee of its decision in response to the grievance and notify the employee of the right to appeal against the decision if not satisfied.

3 If the employee wishes to appeal, he or she must inform the employer. In such a case, the employer must invite the employee to attend a further meeting which the employee must take reasonable steps to attend. After the appeal meeting, the employer must inform the employee of its final decision.

The *modified procedure* is intended to apply where a dismissal has already occurred. An employee aggrieved by his or her dismissal now has to use this modified disciplinary procedure. The modified grievance procedure has two steps:

1 The employee must set out the grievance and the basis of it in writing and send the statement or a copy to the employer.

2 The employer must set out its response in writing and send the statement or a copy to the employee.

The modified statutory procedure is intended to apply to circumstances where a former employee has a grievance against his or her employer following the termination of employment. Examples of such grievances might arise from ex-employees who believed that they had not received their correct holiday or redundancy pay.

Under statutory grievance procedures, each step and action under the procedure must be taken without unreasonable delay; the timing and locations of meetings must be reasonable; meetings must be conducted in a manner that enables both employer and employee to explain their cases; and in the event of appeal meetings subsequent to the first meeting, the employer should, as far as is reasonably practicable, be represented by a more senior manager than attended the first meeting, unless the most senior manager attended that meeting.

The statutory model grievance procedure is not intended to affect any existing company agreements that are 'additional to' and not inconsistent with the new statutory procedure.

The ACAS Code of Practice

The ACAS Code of Practice on disciplinary and grievance procedures became operative on 4 September 2000. Although a failure to follow the Code does not render an employer liable to any proceedings, the Code is admissible in evidence and can be taken into account by employment tribunals. The Code provides practical guidance for employers, workers and their representatives on the statutory requirements relating to grievance issues; what constitutes reasonableness when dealing with grievance issues; producing and using grievance procedures; and a worker's right to bring a supportive companion to grievance hearings. The Code advises that when workers are choosing a companion they should bear in mind that it would not be reasonable to insist on being accompanied by a colleague whose presence would prejudice the hearing or who might have a conflict of interest. Nor does the Code regard it as reasonable for an employee to ask to be accompanied by a colleague from a geographically remote location when someone suitably qualified is available on site. It also advises that although employees are free to choose an official from any trade union to accompany them at a grievance hearing, regardless of whether the union is recognised or not, where a union is recognised in a workplace it is good practice for an official from that union to accompany the worker to a hearing. The Code further points out that it is good employment practice to allow the employee's companion to ask questions and participate as fully as possible in the hearing, and to be given a reasonable amount of time to confer privately with the employee.

> How has your organisation responded to the right of employees to be accompanied in grievance hearings? If it has not responded, why hasn't it? If it has reacted, in what way did it react, and why did it react in this way?

MANAGING GRIEVANCES

Much of an employee relations professional's time can be taken up in dealing with individual employees' problems or complaints. Most employee grievances are, however, dealt with satisfactorily before they reach the formal grievance procedure. For example, take the case of an employee who claims that he has received an incorrect amount of pay. There are a number of possible ways this might be resolved:

1   On checking, management accepts that the amount of pay due has been miscalculated and rectifies the matter immediately. The grievance is resolved to everyone's satisfaction.

   or

2   The payment is correct although the employee believes that he has been underpaid; there is no real grievance and either of two things might happen now:

   a) the situation is discussed and explained adequately and the matter is resolved

   b) the employer fails to explain the details to the satisfaction of the employee who still believes he has been treated unfairly (even though this is not the case). Now there is a possibility that a collective complaint might develop, and if this happens a simple problem is taken up to an inappropriate level

   or

3   The details of the complaint are accepted by the employer, who nevertheless fails to take correc-
tive action quickly . Another grievance arises which takes the place of the original. The employee
was relying on a correct payment to meet commitments but now cannot do so because the
company is 'hanging on' to his money.

The first possibility is obviously the preferred one because it puts right a genuine error promptly and
efficiently. Possibilities 2(b) and 3 carry the risk of generating feelings of mistrust and suspicion.

However, not all grievances are of as simple a nature and resolved so quickly. Management deals with all
grievances in a competent and systematic manner, which involves a number of stages:

■   hearing the grievance
■   preparing for a meeting with the employee and/or his or her representative
■   meeting with the employee and/or his or her representative
■   confirming the common ground between the employee and the management
■   resolving the grievance
■   reporting the outcome.

The grievance interview

The grievance interview enables an individual to state his or her complaint and management to discover,
and remove, the cause of the employee's dissatisfaction. From the interview, management collects the
facts of the situation, analyses the problem, and, if appropriate, decides the action to resolve the grievance.
Good management practice in preparation for a grievance interview is to check the employee's employment
record with the organisation. Although circumstances and time pressures may make this impossible, it is
worth remembering that an employee with a grievance against management may be angry and possibly
adopt an aggressive attitude. If this turns out to be the case, management must calm the individual down.
When an individual loses his/her temper, management has to guard against responding in a similar way or
being provoked into such a reaction. This can easily happen when faced with an aggressive employee critical of management's behaviour. Few people think rationally when they are angry.

Gathering information about an employee's grievance is extremely important. If incorrect, or insufficient,
information is collected, it is likely to lead to wrong analysis and an incorrect decision. Competent
interviewing, watching and listening skills are crucial in this regard.

By the end of the interview, the manager will have an understanding of the employee's grievance and
how he or she would like to see it resolved. If the employee's grievance is, for example, that she has
been denied access to a training opportunity, then the manager will explain to her why she has been
denied the opportunity. The employee, in turn, will also have the opportunity to explain to management
how she wishes to see the complaint dealt with, perhaps by enrolling her on the next available
appropriate training opportunity.

The 'why?' question is always the most difficult to which to gain answers since an individual always
presents a favourable view of his or her case, withholding information that weakens it. The golden rule,
however, is that the manager needs to gather all the facts, including those that might make the
individual's case against management less clear-cut.

Management requires all the facts. It has to make a decision on whether the employee's grievance is
genuine and well-founded, and if so, on what action to take. If the grievance interview fails to bring out
vital information, the manager may conclude wrongly that the employee does not have a genuine

complaint. On the basis of the information collected from the grievance interview the manager makes an assessment of the complaint/problem. He or she decides upon an appropriate course of action, explaining to the individual employee, to his or her representative and to managerial colleagues why he or she has decided upon that action.

Unfounded grievances

At the end of the interview, management may conclude that the grievance is unfounded because:

- the real problem is a clash of personality between the individual employee and his or her immediate manager, or
- the employee has misunderstood something crucial (for example, a company rule).

Grievances can be actual or unfounded, and distinguishing between them is an important responsibility of both employer and employee representatives. They have a common interest to avoid wasting time, resources, effort and emotion in putting inappropriate issues through formal procedures. However, as we have stressed throughout this chapter, all grievances are important to the individual concerned, so if management receives a complaint which it judges to be ill-founded, it is not good practice to dismiss it in an arbitrary manner. It should:

- find out why, and how, it happened
- explain clearly and openly why it is a complaint that merits no action.

This not only sets the record straight but also allows everyone to see that even an imagined rather than a real complaint is being handled seriously. For instance, some organisations have accepted employment conditions which include the option of changing the location at which individuals work. Local authorities, for example, with offices in towns across their areas sometimes need to move their officers around to cover short- or long-term absences, and this is usually set out in employment contracts and/or collective agreements. In this case, an employee required to move location but who did not wish to do so would not have a legitimate grievance. However, if the employee did raise a complaint, it would have to be discussed and resolved as early as possible. This would provide an opportunity to clarify the facts of the situation and to forestall the individual's building up a long-term resentment and thus damaging long-term relationships.

In the above case, because the grievance is imagined rather than real, management's action (ie relocation) is within the bounds of accepted behaviour. Nobody is acting contrary to the accepted way of behaving – even though the employee does not like the action that is taking place – and there is no real grievance to be settled. Nonetheless, the employee's case has to be heard and the issue dealt with, if only to clarify the situation. It is important that the issue is handled in a way which avoids the individual's feeling ignored or snubbed.

Genuine grievances

On the other hand, the manager may conclude – after interviewing the employee laying the complaint – that further information is required about the grievance before management's attitude to the issue can be established. (For example, what does the agreement say? What is company policy on the issue? Are there any witnesses or other people with relevant information that should also be interviewed?) In such circumstances management will make arrangements with the employee and his or her representative for a further meeting. Alternatively, following the grievance interview management may decide that the employee's grievance is genuine, be prepared to seek a resolution to the matter, but require time to prepare a considered response. In this situation, management will also try to make arrangements on when and where next to meet with the employee and/or his or her representative to resolve the issue.

Explain the importance of interviewing skills if the employee relations professional is to be competent in managing employee grievances.

Planning to meet with the employee and his/her representative

There are three main stages to preparing to meet with the individual employee and the representative in order to negotiate a settlement to the individual's grievance. These are :

- analysis (or the research stage)
- establishment of the aims as to how the grievance can be resolved while at the same time protecting management's interests
- planning the strategy and tactics to achieve the established aims.

Analysis

The analysis stage involves management's collection and consideration of relevant information to substantiate its proposals for resolving the individual employee's grievance. It also includes developing the argument(s) to be put to the employee and the representative to support management's case. In managing grievances the main source of relevant information is interviewing management colleagues and employees who are regarded as likely to have information (for example, they may have witnessed the incident about which the employee is complaining) relevant to the issue that is the subject of the complaint.

The analysis stage also involves management's checking whether the subject matter of the grievance has been complained of previously by employees, and if so, what the outcome was. Knowledge of such outcomes enables management to know whether any 'precedent' exists for dealing with the employee's grievance. Other important management activities in the analysis stage include asking:

- Are any company rules relevant?
- Is custom and practice relevant?
- Are any collective agreements or personal contracts relevant?

The most important activity for management in the preparation stage is the identification of the exact details of the employee's complaint. Some of these details are more important to the complainant's argument than others, and some of them are more significant to the management's view of the matter than others. Any agreement on a resolution may be reached by the parties' 'trading off' the importance of these details surrounding the issue but retaining certain principles. In making a decision about which 'details' to trade, management assesses their significance to the complaint and tries to anticipate which 'details' it believes the employee will be prepared to trade in return.

Let us assume that management has encountered a young male employee swearing in the presence of a frontline manager and suspended him from work for three working days without pay. The lad considers the penalty too harsh and with his representative approaches management to register this fact. In analysing the situation, management identifies three issues:

- the fact that he has been suspended
- the length of the suspension
- that there is to be no pay for the period of suspension.

From a management perspective, given the offence, for the employee to escape any disciplinary penalty would be unacceptable. However, before finally making this decision, management assesses how strongly the individual's work colleagues feel about the harshness of the disciplinary penalty. Would they, for example, be prepared to impose industrial sanctions against the company? If they would, how successful might such action be? So if it persists with retaining the initial penalty, management has to weigh up whether the grievance might not escalate into a collective dispute, and with it all the associated costs. If management concludes that the employees would not take the issue to a collective dispute, it can be confident in its view that the initial penalty can be upheld. But if the conclusion is the opposite, then management is likely to take the view that although the principle of the imposition of a disciplinary penalty cannot be compromised, the severity of the penalty might be reduced.

If management comes to this conclusion, it turns to consider the length of the suspension and lost pay. Again the management is unlikely to see the payment of wages during a period of the suspension period as a matter upon which a compromise can be made. If management assesses that to maintain this stance will not provoke a collective dispute, the non-payment of wages during a period of suspension will become non-negotiable. However, if management's assessment is that the employees feel strongly about non-payment, it will indicate that it is prepared to negotiate on the issue.

On the basis of the above analysis, management will hope to see a resolution based on some compromise on the length of the suspension in return for the retention of lost pay and some disciplinary penalty. Management has decided which details it is prepared to trade in the light of assessing its bargaining power relative to the group of workers concerned, should the individual's complaint of too harsh a disciplinary penalty develop into a collective dispute. Management has anticipated that the employee will accept the principle of suspension but will trade the details surrounding the length of the suspension and the lost pay.

The establishment of aims
Having completed its analysis, management then establishes objectives for the forthcoming meeting with the individual employee and his representative (we are still using the example above). Management establishes three aims:

- how it would ideally like the grievance to be resolved
- how it thinks the grievance can be realistically resolved
- what the least is for which management will settle (the fall-back position).

Management establishes these three positions for each of the issues involved in the employee's grievance. Having established its own aims/objectives, management turns its attention to anticipating the aims/objectives of the employee making the complaint: what is the individual employee ideally, realistically and minimally, expecting to achieve as a resolution to his grievance?

Management can now construct an aspiration grid (see Chapter 9) setting the parameters for the expected outcome for the forthcoming grievance-handling meetings. A possible aspiration grid for management is shown in Table 21. It shows that management would ideally would like to trade no details surrounding the grievance with the employee. However, management knows this is unrealistic and has established, on the basis of its analysis of the situation, a realistic position of some compromise around a retention of the suspension and no pay in return for a reduction in the period of the suspension from three days to two days. Its fall-back position is to retain the suspension and lost pay for a further reduction in the length of the suspension (to one day).

Table 21   *Aspiration grid: grievance centring on three days' suspension without pay*

Possible resolution to grievance	Management			Employee		
	Ideal	*Real*	*Fall-back*	*Fall-back*	*Real*	*Ideal*
3 days' suspension, pay restored	X	X	X	O	O	X
2 days' suspension, pay restored	X	X	X	O	O	X
1 day's suspension, pay restored	X	X	X	O	X	X
2 days' suspension, no pay	X	X	O	O	O	X
1 day's suspension, no pay	X	O	O	O	O	X

The grid shows that management anticipates that the employee expects management to be unwilling to compromise on suspension and the lost pay accompanying it. It also demonstrates that management anticipates that the employee will accept a reduction in the length of suspension, and that if a mutually acceptable solution is to be achieved, it will centre on this issue. It also shows that no problems are anticipated over the loss of pay issue because although management is not prepared to make compromises on this aspect of the grievance, management thinks the employee is.

The aspiration grid shows that there is a basis for a resolution to the employee's complaint that management has imposed too harsh a disciplinary penalty. In the fall-back position, although management is not prepared to compromise on the principle of the suspension, it is on its duration. However, it is not prepared to compromise on the 'no pay during suspension' issue. The employee is prepared to make compromises on the length of suspension and to accept no pay during the period of suspension. Through the use of appropriate techniques (see Chapter 9) during subsequent meetings, management will test whether the objectives of the employee (and his representative) are in reality as anticipated. Management will at the same time seek to pass on to the employee – by appropriately coded language and techniques – its attitude towards the issues of the length of the suspension and no pay during the period of suspension. Should new information come to light in subsequent meetings, the management team will have to review, and possibly amend, its aspiration grid.

Strategy and tactics
Having established its negotiating aims, management now moves to planning its strategy and tactics to realise those objectives. There are a number of issues for management to consider:

- who will speak for management and in what order
- communications methods within the management team (for example, the passing of notes)
- management's arguments and how these might in turn be countered
- an anticipation of arguments to be made by the employee in support of his case and how these might be countered.

The anticipation of the likely arguments to be used by the other side in support of its case and how management might counter them is particularly important. Insights into these sets of counter-arguments can be gained by a member of the management playing the 'devil's advocate' to probe management's case for weaknesses. In the light of this exercise, management can strengthen its case.

The preparation stage is the most important stage in managing employee grievances. The golden rule in preparing is: 'Failure to prepare is preparing to fail.'

However, even if management prepares inadequately, the situation might be saved if management re-assesses its analysis, aims and strategy in the light of new information which it failed, for whatever reason, to obtain while preparing its original case in response to the employee's complaint.

Meetings with the employee and his/her representative

In presenting its case to the individual employee and/or his or her representative, management outlines the matters it intends to raise, and then:

- presents a broad picture of its proposals for resolving the grievance
- gives the details of its proposals backed by supporting evidence
- summarises its proposals to resolve the grievance.

The employee will have stated his or her case at the grievance interview.

The parties now move on to seek confirmation of their expected common ground for the basis of a resolution to the employee grievance. There are a number of techniques management can use for this purpose – the 'if and then' technique, questioning for clarification, watching, listening, etc (see Chapter 9). However, information to confirm the expected basis for an agreement will not emerge if the meetings with the employee are destructive rather than constructive – if, for example, the parties merely blame each other for the grievance, if they keep interrupting each other, if one side attacks personalities on the other side, and so on. In most grievance-handling situations, adjournments are called most often to confirm facts or to speak to a witness who can confirm the facts, rather than because of the provision of significantly new information which requires the parties to reconsider their strategy and tactics and their objectives.

RESOLVING THE GRIEVANCE

If a manager is unable to find a resolution to the grievance, the matter can be referred to the next stage in the procedure at which a higher-level manager will prepare, present and try to find a mutually acceptable solution. When a grievance remains unresolved, the manager in passing the matter to the next stage must check that the complaint is taken up at that level, and not just lost sight of.

However, when a resolution to a grievance is found – but before finally accepting that the resolution has been agreed – management must:

- be convinced that the employee understands what has been agreed
- 'play back' to the employee what management understands the resolution of the grievance to actu-ally mean, in order to prevent any misunderstanding.

If this process reveals that the employee has indeed misunderstood what has been agreed, and that misunderstanding cannot be cleared up in further discussion, the negotiations will have to restart.

Once management has an oral agreement for the resolution of the employee's grievance, it should be written up. In many grievances this will take the form of an internal memo/letter to another manager and to the employee recording what has been agreed. For example, if the complaint was one of denial of access to a training opportunity and it is upheld via the grievance-handling process, a manager will write to the personnel or other appropriate department, reporting that (for instance) it has been agreed that the individual concerned should attend the next available appropriate training course. On the other hand, 'writing up' can – depending on the issue – take the form of a signed agreement by the manager concerned, the individual employee and his or her representative. The outcome is then reported to the appropriate interested parties. Clarity is important and the manner in which what has been agreed is recorded should leave no room for doubt.

> Outline the skills required of managers in successfully handling grievances. Which do you consider to be the most important, and why?

Specific issues/specific procedures

The grievance procedure deals with the broad range of complaints and problems. However, some areas of organisational life have their own specific list of potentially thorny issues. These include:

- job grading and evaluation
- complaints by one employee about the behaviour of another
- sexual harassment
- discrimination in promotion and advancement.

So while some employee complaints remain general grievances, others are best dealt with by specific procedures designed to deal with the type of difficulties inherent in certain issues.

> Does your organisation have special issues/grievance procedures? If so, what issues do they cover? Why do these specific procedures exist?

Job grading appeal procedures

Job evaluation helps determine the appropriate level of a job as measured against criteria such as decision-making, working conditions (for example, exposure to hazards, working in the open air as against in an office, etc), contacts with and outside the organisation, the degree of supervision received, the complexity of the work (for example, gathering and inputting data as opposed to gathering and then manipulating data to produce a report with recommendations) within the organisation's structure. The appropriate level in the structure influences the pay level and seniority associated with the job.

A grievance that centres on such an issue arises mostly when an individual claims that his or her job has changed relative to when it was last evaluated because it now carries greater responsibility for:

- people (in terms of supervising and training them)
- financial resources (increased budget, financial control)
- physical resources (modern high-tech expensive equipment)

and therefore warrants a higher grading and level of remuneration.

On the other hand, management may argue that the post has not changed in responsibility, and that what has changed is an increase in the volume of tasks, at the same level of responsibility. It therefore makes sense in resolving such a dispute to have a procedure tailored to cover the specific circumstances of job grading, including access to specialist and expert individuals.

In a typical job evaluation appeals procedure, the first stage normally requires the individual employee to discuss the basis of his or her appeal with his or her immediate line manager/team leader. The second stage normally requires the individual to complete a 'formal appeal form', which then goes before a meeting of a job evaluation appeals panel. The complainant, accompanied by his or her representative, presents a case to the appeals panel, as does the employer. The appeals panel will decided either to upgrade the job or to reject the appeal. The decision is usually communicated to the individual through his or her line manager. If the appeal is upheld, the decision will be implemented from the date of the panel's decision.

If the job-holder is dissatisfied with the decision of the appeals panel, he or she may request that the case goes to a third stage and be heard by an independent appeal body. At this stage the job-holder (assisted by his or her representative) will present the basis of the appeal, a member of the appeals panel will present justification for their decision, and the independent appeal body – which is usually chaired by an independent chairperson acceptable to both parties – will make a decision that is final and binding. In some organisations with job-evaluated grading structures, this means that individual grievances over job gradings are at the end of the day decided by arbitration.

A job evaluation procedure is relatively clear-cut and straightforward. It has the advantage over the standard grievance procedure of building in access to experts at each appeal stage and providing more specialist panels to hear the appeals.

Dignity at work

Harassment based on gender, race and disability, and bullying at work have received increasing attention in recent years as organisations and worker representative bodies have become more concerned about the dignity of individuals in the workplace. Many organisations have policies and procedures which link the complaints procedure on harassment and bullying with the existing grievance procedure rather than establishing separate arrangements for such complaints. Others have treated it as a specific issue. Both approaches work.

Harassment, in general terms is:

> Unwanted conduct affecting the dignity of men and women in the workplace. It may be related to age, race, disability, religion, nationality or any personal characteristics of the individual, and may be persistent or an isolated incident. The key is that the actions or comments are viewed as demeaning and unacceptable to the recipient . . .

Bullying may be characterised as:

> Offensive, intimidating, malicious or insulting behaviour, an abuse or misuse of power through means intended to undermine, humiliate, denigrate or injure the recipient . . .

Bullying or harassment may be what one individual does to another individual (perhaps by someone in a position of authority, such as a manager or frontline manager) or involve groups of people. It may be obvious or it may be insidious. Whatever form it takes, it is unwarranted and unwelcome to the individual. Bullying and/or harassing includes:

- spreading malicious rumours or insulting someone by word or behaviour
- copying memos that are critical about someone to others who do not need to know
- ridiculing or demeaning someone – picking on him/her or setting him/her up to fail
- unwelcome sexual advances – touching, standing too close, the display of offensive materials
- deliberately undermining a competent worker by overloading and constant criticism.

Bullying and/or harassment make someone feel anxious and humiliated. Feelings of anger and frustration at being unable to cope may be triggered. Some employees may try to retaliate in some way. Others may become frightened and demotivated. Stress, loss of self-confidence and self-esteem caused by bullying and/or harassment can lead to job insecurity, illness, absence from work and even resignation. Almost always, job performance is affected and relations in the workplace suffer.

Employers are responsible for preventing bullying and harassing behaviour. It is in their interests to make it clear to everyone that such behaviour will not be tolerated. The costs to the organisation may include poor employee relations, low morale, lower productivity and efficiency and, potentially, the resignation of staff. An organisational statement to all staff about the standards expected can make it easier for individuals to be fully aware of their responsibilities to others.

In organisations where a harassment policy exists, it is normal for a dual system to operate. The initial action is usually confined to the specifics of the complaint within the procedure laid down for managing harassment and/or bullying. If the problem cannot be resolved within the limits of the policy and is proved to be an issue that merits disciplinary proceedings, the disciplinary procedure is triggered.

When an employee complains that he or she has suffered harassment and/or bullying by another employee, whether a manager or not, he or she has a grievance. He or she is, in fact, making a complaint to management. In dealing with allegations of harassment and/or bullying the manager first conducts a thorough investigation to establish whether there is a *prima facie* case of harassment and/or bullying for the accused employee to answer. If the manager decides, on the basis of the investigation, that there is a case to answer, disciplinary proceedings are likely to be instigated against the accused employee.

However, this is conditional on the 'victim' agreeing to allow the issue to be taken to this stage. If the victim refuses to proceed any further with the matter, that is the end of it. If disciplinary proceedings are started against the accused individual, and the charge of harassment and/or bullying is upheld, an appropriate penalty will be imposed – up to and including, often as a last resort, dismissal of the employee. If, on the other hand, the manager decides that the harassment and/or bullying allegation has no foundation, the manager must explain fully to the 'victim' and his or her representative why this is the case.

So if a manager is sitting in his or her office and a woman employee comes in claiming that she has been sexually harassed, and that she has witnesses and wants action taken against the individual concerned, it is clear what the manager must do:

- investigate the claim thoroughly
- decide whether there is a case to answer
- if there is a case to answer and it cannot be settled amicably, and the 'victim' insists on pressing the complaint, initiate the disciplinary procedure
- if there is no case to answer, explain that carefully and sensitively to the 'victim'.

Different organisations define their acceptable standards of behaviour differently, particularly with respect to gross misconduct. In some organisations harassment and/or bullying is regarded as gross misconduct, carrying instant dismissal if proven. That this is the case will be spelled out to employees in the organisation's policy statement on sexual harassment and/or dignity at work. It is not the case in all organisations, however, for in some, lesser penalties can, and are, imposed on the harasser.

There are therefore good reasons for dealing with harassment and/or bullying complaints outside of the general grievance procedure. First, there is a reasonable chance that the person who is the subject of the complaint is the line manager of the employee making the complaint. This can make it difficult to resolve the grievance as near to the point of its origin as possible. Second, there is a link between grievance, discipline and harassment. The role of the employee relations professional in harassment/bullying complaints is to act as a catalyst for line managers to manage the issue by providing them with general expertise and support, including access to training programmes to handle dignity at work issues.

> Explain briefly the process you would adopt when dealing with a case of alleged sexual harassment or bullying by one employee against another.

Other areas

Other complex areas of employee complaint which justify having separate grievance procedures include discrimination in promotion and alleged unequal treatment in terms of pay, overtime, travel, etc. Each case is unique and requires thorough investigation before deciding whether the grievance is real or imagined, whether the offence is proven and whether informal or formal action through procedures is appropriate. All cases of grievance have to be handled with equal care. Procedures offer the means for management to behave in a fair, reasonable and consistent manner in managing grievances.

SUMMARY

This chapter began by examining the business case for resolving employee grievances, defining a grievance and identifying the issues which are most frequently the cause of employee grievances. It then went on to explain that the effective resolution of grievances, unlike bargaining, excludes a trade-off between different employee complaints about management behaviour. The chapter also explained the extent to which employees take up (or do not take up) grievances, analysed the underlying principles of a grievance procedure and described the main features of a 'typical' procedure (ie the number of stages, time limits, representation of employees, etc).

The chapter further examined the operation of grievance procedures and the role of employee relations professionals in managing employee grievances (for example, the promotion of 'good practice' in managing grievances among line managers). In addition, it outlined the legal framework surrounding grievance management. The chapter then went on to point out that many grievances are of a simple nature and are resolved quickly, but that this is not always the case. The managing of employee grievances involves a number of stages – hearing the grievance (the grievance interview), preparing to meet the employee (analysis, establishing aims, planning strategy and tactics), meeting with the employee and/or his/her representative, confirming, as the basis for a successful resolution of the grievances, the common ground between the employee and management, resolving the grievance, and reporting the outcome. The chapter also explained how crucial in managing employee grievances effectively it is that a manager be able to distinguish the genuine employee complaint from the unfounded one.

It was also pointed out in the chapter that the grievance procedure deals with the broad range of employee complaints and problems but that there are issues best dealt with by specific procedures designed to deal with particular difficulties that can arise in handling such issues. These include job grading and evaluation, complaints by one employee about the behaviour of another, sexual harassment, bullying and discrimination in promotion and advancement.

FURTHER READING

ADVISORY, CONCILIATION AND ARBITRATION SERVICE (1997) *Guide for Small Firms: Dealing with grievances*. London, ACAS.

ADVISORY, CONCILIATION AND ARBITRATION SERVICE (2001) *Discipline and Grievance at Work*, an Advisory Handbook. London, ACAS.

ADVISORY, CONCILIATION AND ARBITRATION SERVICE (2004) *Disciplinary and Grievance Procedures*. London, ACAS.

ADVISORY, CONCILIATION AND ARBITRATION SERVICE (forthcoming) *Bullying and Harassment: A guide for employers*. London, ACAS.

CHARTERED INSTITUTE OF PERSONNEL AND DEVELOPMENT (2004) Statutory disputes resolution proposals cause concern, *Impact*, Issue 6, February.

CULLY M., WOODLAND S., O'REILLY A. and DIX G. (1999) *Britain at Work as Depicted by the 1998 Workplace Employee Relations Survey*. London and New York, Routledge.

DEPARTMENT OF TRADE AND INDUSTRY (2003) *Review of the Employment Relations Act 1999*.

GAYMER J. (2004) Making a molehill out of a mountain, *People Management*, 26 February.

INDUSTRIAL RELATIONS SERVICES (2002) Don't nurse a grievance: resolving disputes at work, *Employment Trends*, No.759, September.

INSTITUTE OF PERSONNEL AND DEVELOPMENT (1998) *Fairness at Work and the Psychological Contract*. London, IPD.

INSTITUTE OF PERSONNEL AND DEVELOPMENT (1999) *How Dissatisfied are British Workers? A Survey of Surveys*. London, IPD.

JACKSON T. (2000) *Handling Grievances*. London, Chartered Institute of Personnel and Development.

KELLY J. and GENNARD J.(1997) The unimportance of labels: the diffusion of the personnel/HRM function, *Industrial Relations Journal*, Volume 28, No.1.

RENWICK D. (2000) HR line work relations: a review, pilot case and research agenda, *Employee Relations*, Volume 22, No.2.

RENWICK D. (2003) Line manager involvement in HRM: an inside view, *Employee Relations*, Volume 25, No.3.

RENWICK D. and GENNARD J. (2001) Grievance and discipline: a new set of concerns, in T. Redman and A. Wilkinson (eds) *Contemporary Human Resource Management*. London, Pearson Education.

ROLLINSON D., BROADFIELD A. and EDWARDS E. (1996) Supervisor and management styles in handling discipline and grievance: Part 2 – Approaches to handling discipline and grievance, *Personnel Review*, Volume 25, No.1.

TORRINGTON D., HALL L. and TAYLOR S. (2005) *Human Resource Management*, 6th edn. London, Prentice Hall/Financial Times; Chapter 25.

WHITTAKER S. and MARCHINGTON M. (2003) Devolving HR responsibility to the line: threat, opportunity or partnership?, *Employee Relations*, Volume 25, No.3.

Managing redundancies

INTRODUCTION

Over the past quarter of a century British business has been exposed to ever increasing competition in its own and world markets. In the 1960s, 1970s and early 1980s this tended to impact more heavily on manufacturing industry, which therefore experienced the greatest job losses. However, in the last 15 years this increase in competition has spread to the public and service sectors.

Notwithstanding the significant improvements in competitiveness of many UK businesses in the last decade, Britain has not always been successful in competing in overseas markets nor in defending home markets. In the 1970s and 1980s this supposed weakness of the British economy was variously blamed on trade union resistance to change, poor and badly trained management, too much or too little UK government spending, and a whole range of other economic and social factors. Since the mid-1990s, the view of Britain's economy has changed: now it is perceived, relative to our competitors' economies, as reasonably strong and stable. Yet despite this, we still see many organisations having to reduce their labour force. As always, there are a number of factors which are blamed: for example, an exchange rate that is too high, non-membership of the euro, a financial system that is geared to shareholder reward rather than capital investment.

The issue of exchange rates has long been a source of concern, particularly in the manufacturing sector, and has been blamed for many of the job losses that have been suffered. This bears out many of the points we outlined in Chapter 2 in respect of the corporate environment and its influence on employee relations. One example is the car maker MG-Rover which, in 2004, announced £100 million of cost cuts in an attempt to reduce some of its losses. In making their announcement the company attributed the losses to exchange rates which, they said, worked against the company. Although the search for cost cuts will be made across the whole business, it is likely that at some point there will be an impact on employment levels.

INCREASES IN REDUNDANCY

Every few years, the fluctuating nature of our economic life cycles means that we become used to hearing the words 'downturn', 'slowdown', and 'downsize'. At different times in the economic cycle different sectors of the economy are affected. For example, a survey published by the CBI in September 2004 showed growth prospects for the engineering industry at their strongest for nine years, which could have a positive impact on jobs. At the same time service sector companies reported a much more negative picture, with a slowdown in demand and an increase in costs. This could have a clear knock-on effect on jobs. We have talked elsewhere about the effects of globalisation, and there is no doubt that problems in the global market, increases in oil prices and instability in the Middle East can raise the spectre of large-scale redundancies. This is because global events like these can have an impact on sectors such as travel – airlines have been particularly hard hit – and it is therefore no surprise that a survey carried out by career consultants Penna Sanders & Sidney (*People Management*, 5 April 2001) found that 70 per cent of their respondents reported that either they or someone they were close to had been made redundant.

Very often we only hear about the large organisations and the mass redundancies, but always, whenever there are major job losses, there will be a cascade effect downwards to smaller businesses, who are somewhere in the supply chain or who are affected by changes in consumer spending. This means that the employee relations professional must always be alive to the potential for redundancy – and is the reason that we are devoting a whole chapter to redundancy issues.

THE LEGAL REGULATION OF REDUNDANCY

Prior to 1965 employees had no statutory protection in respect of redundancy. The 'right' of organisations to hire and fire at will was seen as one of those inalienable 'management rights' that were necessary if organisations were to compete successfully in a commercial world. However, by the beginning of the 1960s there was a widespread belief that economic growth was being held back because of a lack of labour mobility. The Redundancy Payments Act 1965 was part of the answer to this problem, and enjoyed the support of both major political parties as well as both sides of industry – a classic example of the postwar consensus that we mentioned in Chapter 3. The Act set out for the first time that a worker with a minimum period of service was entitled to compensation for the loss of his or her job through redundancy. Compensation was decided on the basis of age and length of service, and was subject to both a maximum and a minimum amount. The basic law in relation to redundancy compensation has not changed much in the intervening years, but there have been significant developments in respect of consultation, selection and the transfer of undertakings.

The definition of redundancy

In order to properly understand the way in which the law seeks to offer protection to those facing the loss of their employment, there are a number of factors which must be considered. The first of these concerns the definition of redundancy, which is set out in section 139 of the Employment Rights Act 1996. Principally, there are two ways in which a redundancy can occur, and these feature in section 139(1) as follows:

(a) The fact that [the] employer has ceased or intends to cease –
   i) to carry on the business for the purposes of which the employee was employed by him, or
   ii) to carry on that business in the place where the employee was so employed, or

(b) The fact that the requirements of that business –
   i) for employees to carry out work of a particular kind, or
   ii) for employees to carry out work of a particular kind in the place where the employee was employed by the employer, have ceased or diminished or are expected to cease or diminish.

To put that in everyday language: redundancy occurs when the employer closes down completely, moves premises, requires fewer people for particular jobs or requires no people for particular jobs. Redundancy can also occur when an individual has been laid off or kept on short-time for a period that is defined in sections 147 to 152 of the 1996 Act. Assuming that the reason an individual's employment comes to an end is within one of the statutory definitions, or that he or she has been laid off or kept on short-time, and assuming that he or she has a minimum period of qualifying employment, then he or she is entitled to a statutory redundancy payment.

Redundancy 'can mean different things to different people. Even as a specific legal concept, it has been the subject of differences and errors of interpretation' (Fowler, 1993). For that reason it is an area in which the employee relations professional must develop his or her skills.

The need for a redundancy policy and procedures

For personnel professionals, job security policies and the avoidance of redundancy are an increasingly important part of the employee relations framework. In Chapter 2, in examining the management of change we said that organisations have a continuing need to evolve, to constantly search for their distinctive capabilities. This in turn means a continuing process of change and leads to the inevitable weakening of employees' confidence in their employer's ability to maintain job security. Where redundancy is unavoidable, 'good practice' dictates that organisations have in place policies and procedures that enable them to deal with a difficult situation with sensitivity and equity. The employee relations specialist has a key role to play in this process in advising managerial colleagues as to the scope and extent of any policies, and in advising them how to manage the redundancy process.

Policies and procedures are important, not only because the law dictates certain minimum requirements but also because, like most activities connected with employee relations, there is a good business case for doing so. An essential element in the management of redundancy situations is the need to provide effective counselling and support for the redundant employee – support in terms of job-seeking, outplacement, etc. Of equal importance is the need to ensure that those who are to remain in employment, and who may be fearful for their future, are not ignored. Ignoring the 'survivors' is likely to produce a demotivated workforce that is prone to conflict with management.

REDUNDANCY AND THE MANAGEMENT OF CHANGE

In the context of redundancy we must look at what it is that causes firms to have to change and ask whether job losses have to be the inevitable result. In many cases, organisations have had no option but to declare redundancies – for example, for an urgent need to cut costs, or the failure to win an important contract. These are just two examples of where immediate action has to be taken. But redundancies could sometimes have been avoided if organisations had invested more time in human resource planning, training or skills development.

The lack of foresight shown by many business leaders is demonstrated by Duncan Brown of Towers Perrin (*People Management*, 22 November 2001), who reported on the 'boardroom rejection of a number of HR initiatives to do with recruiting and retaining top talent, including, ironically, one concerned with leadership development'. They were rejected, Brown reported, 'not on principle but for expediency'. In his view the 'traditional UK corporate response to a downturn – pay freezes and ... redundancies' – can often prove disastrous.

In a complex business world we have to recognise that business change will continue to lead to reduced workforces because organisations are under continuous pressure to:

- improve their effectiveness
- increase profitability
- reduce costs and remain innovative.

But businesses can be changed without wholesale job losses. Changes in markets have created a need for organisations to be much more responsive to their customers' requirements. In manufacturing, for example, consumers demand higher and higher standards combined with better value for money, but better long-term planning might indicate that costs, other than people ones, could be reduced – items such as uncontrolled purchasing, wasted information technology spending and bloated administration. But even here care must be taken. Sometimes there can be a knee-jerk reaction to perceived overspending or bloated administration. The government has announced plans to slim down the Civil Service by over 100,000 jobs, but there is a body of evidence which suggests that this is not practical – not because jobs must be saved *per se* but because there is insufficient evidence to justify the scale of job cuts. There is a belief in many quarters that a good proportion of the disestablished posts will reappear again in a different guise.

One example of how a business can take a measured approach to the management of change is the experience of Transport for London (reported by Griffiths in *People Management*, 12 August 2004). As Andy Cook, their Head of Corporate HR and Group Employee Relations, put it:

> We've got a potential funding gap of £1 billion if we don't meet all our aspirations … and we need to ensure that we are running as efficiently as we can.

Transport for London therefore had to embark on a change programme that involved job losses and staff redeployment, but – and this is the crucial part – it was not

> just about reducing costs and staff numbers – we have to make sure we've got the right skills mix to move forward.

Has your organisation had cause to declare any redundancies in the past two years? If so, could these have been avoided?

In Chapter 2 we looked in detail at the need for organisations to develop clear business strategies that would, in turn, help to identify what their people strategies ought to be and how they should manage change. For many, the answer has been to downsize the organisation or to introduce flexible working practices. According to Sparrow and Marchington (1998), these responses

> raise questions about the most appropriate organisational form. … Under the burden of economic and competitive pressure, a range of organisational strategies is aimed at competing not just on cost but on quality and speed of response.

Evidence suggests that had alternatives to redundancy been at the top of everybody's agenda, some of the large numbers of jobs that have disappeared over the past three decades might have been saved. For many senior managers the need to deliver very large productivity increases and cost savings made redundancy the only option (P. Lewis, 1993). Although this lack of choice has to be acknowledged, there are two reasons why employers ought to be considering alternatives to redundancy. One is that every organisation has to maintain some form of competitive advantage. Two, it is a reasonable presumption to say that competitive advantage is unlikely to be achieved and maintained without a committed and motivated workforce.

Decisions about redundancy, because they are often made to address an immediate and short-term problem, can create the entirely opposite wrong effect. They can engender a mood of disillusionment and cynicism that, if allowed to fester, can destroy any of the short-term financial gains of a redundancy exercise, together with any hope of gaining employee commitment to the future. Sparrow and Marchington (1998) make the point that in relation to downsizing and de-layering, immediate financial and performance measurements made today cannot assess the implications of correct or incorrect decision-making, as such decisions now tend to operate and be proved effective over a longer time-span.

Employee commitment

If employee commitment is to be obtained, together with high levels of motivation, then employees must feel secure in their employment, not afraid for their future. In 1983, when unemployment was running at over 3 million, Ron Todd – then General Secretary of the Transport Workers Union (TGWU) – commented that there were 3 million people on the dole, and another 23 million who were scared to death (Blyton and Turnbull, 1994). There is little evidence to suggest that the fear factor has gone away. In a 1996 report the IPD stated that 'insecurity has damaged people's commitment', a state of affairs that if not remedied had the potential to damage competitive performance. The Penna Sanders & Sidney survey is further evidence that redundancy remains a spectre that can affect an individual's perception of his or her job security. Although we can acknowledge that all businesses have to worry about competition, about retaining their competitive edge, about growth and even about survival, these worries could be eased if they knew they had a committed and loyal workforce. The challenge is how to overcome the fear factor and to achieve the necessary commitment that is so important.

Fear is often generated by a failure on the part of senior management to recognise the need for prompt and accurate communication when people's livelihoods are at risk. Linked to this need for timely communication is the need to ensure that when messages have to be communicated, they are done so in a way that will not cause distress to those affected. In today's technological age, the potential for poor communication is exacerbated by the use, or misuse, of mediums such as e-mail or text messaging. Sadly, there are a number of examples of organisations who have advised employees about impending redundancies by e-mail or text message – not always with bad intentions, simply through lack of foresight. One of the most common ways in which poor communication impacts on redundancy situations is during the course of a merger or acquisition. Company A will often signal an intention to bid for or merge with company B, and as part of its strategy to win shareholder approval for its plans will announce what savings can be expected if it is successful. These savings can often include a declared intention to downsize the workforce. The first the affected employees hear about it is through press announcements or e-mail messages. Fortunately, there are some good examples of how to do things properly, as the following case study demonstrates.

Case study

Working for Work

When Work Communications acquired Park HR, a rival recruitment advertising firm with a work-force of 115 spread around the country, Work knew it had to get the process of keeping everyone informed absolutely right. Getting things wrong would be an embarrassing and potentially costly lesson in how not to practise what it preached.

The deal meant further uncertainty for Park staff. In the months before the £4.6 million takeover, Park's parent company, SHL, had been embroiled in a long-running boardroom dispute that eventually saw the departure of its founder-members from the board. The directors of Work had stressed at the outset that they wanted to retain the structure of the business they were buying, but many employees at Park were understandably sceptical about such messages at that point. So Work launched a concerted internal communications offensive to inform them of any moves it might make after the takeover and calm any fears of 'wholesale changes'.

Unlike most firms involved in an acquisition, it decided not to use a PR agency. 'We felt that what was happening was a private affair,' explained Simon Howard, co-founder of Work. 'When these deals are announced, a lot of companies spend shed-loads of money on PR, but often the staff get no more than a note on their desk. There's a sense of "start as you mean to go on".'

Employees at Park were initially informed of the takeover via e-mail – a method that Howard says his team used carefully. 'We had to have a degree of caution. What we did was say that we'd put a paper pack on everyone's desks by the following morning in which we might say things that we wouldn't necessarily want outsiders to read,' he says. 'Although using e-mail was never going to be perfect, it did let us tell our people and competitors the bare facts of what was happening, so that they didn't find out through Chinese whispers.'

As well as the e-mail, staff received details of a specially designed website containing information about Work, biographies of the company's employees and a list of answers to frequently asked questions (FAQs).

But many employees were obviously still worried about their jobs and wanted direct contact with those in the know. So the website also gave people the chance to e-mail in further questions. From the responses he received, Howard says that his company was better able to gauge the general mood among Park's employees during the takeover.

'It's clear that we are all very worried about losing our jobs,' one employee wrote in an e-mail to the board. 'More importantly, I would like to know how you're going to make your decisions. In the past, Park has based a lot of decisions on who likes whom – not on how capable you are or how good you are at your job.'

Park had offices in London, Bristol, Birmingham, Manchester and Edinburgh. Many employees working outside London were concerned that they would be ignored, but Tracey Hyde, an account manager at the Manchester office, says that the regular contact she had with Work's board members was valuable.

'A lot of our reservations were addressed quickly, and the powers-that-be got round to individuals very quickly,' Hyde says. 'Working out of a regional office means you can be remote from the top people. The way we were contacted with personal letters made us feel that the board were taking our personal situations into account.'

Once the situation had been clarified, Work's directors set about meeting as many staff as they could, and Caroline Watson, a client relationship manager at Park in Edinburgh, says the directors' visits did more than provide a chance to meet the new board, they signalled a culture change. 'The communications programme showed us that there's a sense of openness and accessibility.'

A. Blyth, *People Management*, May 2003

There is no magic formula for achieving commitment, but a 1995 survey by the IPD and Templeton College, Oxford, identifies some important elements that can help management achieve this objective. One of these is trust, on which, says the survey, the psychological contract that the employer has with employees must rest. The employees will have trust if they are confident that the employer will continue to search for new customers and new markets, thus making it possible for their talents to be employed.

Clearly, as the survey points out, 'trust is vulnerable to the incidence of redundancy in an organisation', and serious questions are now being raised about some of the cost reduction, redundancy and downsizing policies that have been prevalent in recent years. This said, the survey caused some employers to declare that they would offer continual employment unless in the most exceptional circumstances. Where businesses find it impossible to underwrite job security they should commit to consulting on those strategic issues that can affect security of employment.

> Whether or not there have been redundancies in your own organisation, what do think is the current position in respect of employee security? Do you and your colleagues feel secure, or is there some concern about the future?

Much depends on the interaction that can be created between managers and the workforce as a means of fostering the levels of commitment and loyalty that are being sought. These sort of imperatives are the major reason that there has been such a concerted push by human resource specialists to integrate people management issues into strategic management. As Pettigrew and Whipp (1995) argue, one of the central contributors to competitive performance is the way in which people within a firm are managed. In employee relations terms this means creating a partnership between workers and their managers that is collaborative, not adversarial. There are a number of examples where employers and employees are prepared to negotiate and make agreements over job security – although these tend to be in unionised environments.

> Are you aware of any other arrangements of this kind? Is it something your organisation has considered?

POLICIES AND PROCEDURES

No matter what sort of strategic vision an organisation employs there will sometimes be no alternative to reducing the numbers employed. The possibility that this will occur is much higher now than it was 20 years ago. Good employee relations practice dictates a need for clear policies and procedures which allow redundancy situations to be dealt with in a professional and equitable manner. Not only are there legal regulations to be taken into account, but the psychological contract has to be maintained, and if there is no policy, the wrong decisions can be made – as Virgin Airlines discovered in the aftermath of the 11 September terrorist attacks.

Speaking at the 2004 European HR Forum, Virgin's Director of Organisational Development, Moira Nagle, explained how, less than a week after the attack, the airline decided to lose 25 per cent of their staff. But – and this is the key point – Virgin did not have any redundancy procedures. As a consequence, as Nagle freely admitted, they lost some very skilled employees ... many of whom have since been rehired.

> We thought getting people out of the door was the thing we needed to do [and] we probably lost some very skilled people we would have preferred not to lose.

Policy

A statement of policy on redundancy might, in some ways, be better classified as an organisation's statement of intent in respect of its commitment to maintaining employment. For example, a policy statement on redundancy might be set out as follows:

> The company intends to develop and expand its business activities in order to maintain its competitive advantage within our existing marketplace. It is also our intention to seek new products and markets,

provided they have a strategic fit with the rest of the business. To achieve these objectives we need the active co-operation and commitment of the whole workforce. In return our aim is to provide a stable work environment and a high level of job security. However, we also need to ensure the economic viability of the business in the competitive world in which we now have to operate. In such a world changes in markets, technology or the corporate environment may cause us to consider the need for reductions in staffing levels. In order to mitigate the impact of any reductions in staff, the following procedure will be adopted. . . .

Such a policy statement does not make any commitment to having no compulsory redundancies, but it is an important first step in recognising people as an important asset. There is a reasonable amount of evidence that suggests that the downsizing, re-engineering culture of the late 1980s/ early 1990s had a detrimental affect on businesses that needed to grow. A study by International Survey Research cites responses from a number of senior HR managers which found that downsizing went too far and the overall effect was negative (*People Management*, No.22, November 1996; page 15). We have already quoted the Sparrow and Marchington view that decision-making must be evaluated over a longer time-scale, and many organisations are now beginning to realise, as Virgin did, that they have lost valuable experiences and skills. Although Virgin appear to have rehired many of their key staff, this will not always prove possible, and valued employees once lost can prove difficult to replace.

Hendricks and Mumford in charting the rapid rise and fall of the re-engineering concept (*People Management*, May 1996) argued that it failed as a technique because many of its followers did not understand people and change management techniques. They pointed to evidence that re-engineering always took longer than expected, involved more resources than were available, and presented unforeseen problems. Developing a redundancy policy, or statement of intent, as described above, should be driven by an organisation's overall business strategy and can be an important first step in building that important management/workforce partnership. But even in the most strategically aware organisations, not everything (11 September, the war in Iraq) is predictable and there may be situations in which job losses cannot be avoided. This is where the procedure, mentioned in our example of a policy statement, comes into play.

Does your organisation have a redundancy policy? If it does, what does the policy say about job security?

Procedure

The first thing to say about a redundancy procedure, as with any other procedure, is that it has to fit the business. That is, it must be written and designed to cater for the individuality of each organisation. Draft procedures can be obtained from professional bodies like the CIPD or from commercial organisations like Croner's, but they should always be treated as guidelines or templates and be amended to meet individual organisation's requirements.

As a basic minimum there are a number of things that a redundancy procedure should cover, starting with alternative courses of action. Where the possibility of a reduction in employee numbers arises, management should begin a process of consultation. There are a number of legal rules relating to consultation which must take place with either trade unions, elected workplace representatives or individuals. The purpose of this consultation is to establish whether any potential job losses can be achieved by means other than compulsory redundancies. Some of the factors that would normally be considered at this juncture would be:

- a ban on recruitment (unless unavoidable)
- the retraining of staff

- the redeployment of staff
- restriction on the use of subcontracted labour, temporary and casual staff
- reduction in the amount of overtime working.

Depending on the nature of the business, other considerations might include a temporary lay-off, short-time working or even job sharing.

Early retirement

If there were any employees who were over normal retirement age, it might be necessary to insist on their immediate retirement, and at the same time it may be appropriate to ask for volunteers for early retirement. This is only an option if the business has its own regulated pension scheme – a state of affairs that is rapidly disappearing, and does need careful consideration. As an absolute minimum the pension scheme must allow for the payment of pensions early on grounds of redundancy, and most certainly allow for some form of early retirement, but there is usually a penalty in the form of a reduced pension. So for any individual to seriously consider such an option, early retirement must carry some form of financial inducement. In effect, the potential retiree is credited with more years of pensionable service than he or she has actually worked. The question of how many extra years to credit will depend on how near to normal retirement age a particular employee is and the ability of the employer to make the necessary payments into the fund. It is possible that the employer might have to make a substantial payment into the pension fund, more than a redundancy payment in many cases, to ensure that there is no detriment to the early-retired employee. Alternatively, the employer may have to provide a one-off lump sum that will take the employee up to an agreed date for receiving his or her pension.

It is important that these financial considerations are taken into account by the employee relations professional when asked, as he or she often is, to cost the available options for reducing the workforce. A further point to remember in considering early retirement is the position of pension trustees. Following the Maxwell scandal, trustees now have much more responsibility for the management of individual schemes. Whether to allow early retirement on redundancy grounds or to enhance the value of an individual's pension are not management decisions. They are trustee decisions. For the employee relations professional all of this means that the question of whether early retirement as an alternative to compulsory redundancy is an option has to be carefully costed and researched.

If a time comes when management has given very careful consideration to the alternatives discussed above but has concluded that the need for redundancies still remains, the next step in the procedure would be for management to give employees, or their representatives, written details of its proposals. This would include details of the criteria that management proposes to use for selecting individuals for redundancy.

Voluntary redundancy

Management may indicate at this stage that it is prepared to accept volunteers – but this must be subject to the company's need to retain a balanced workforce, with the appropriate mix of skills and knowledge. As P. Lewis (1993) and others have noted, the concept of voluntary redundancy has become the most widely accepted method of dealing with redundancy, and there are obviously a number of advantages in adopting the voluntary approach. Firstly, it can help to avoid some of the demotivating effects that redundancy inevitably has on an organisation.

Secondly, it can be cost-effective. Although persuading people to go, rather than forcing them to leave, will probably require higher individual payments (possibly in pension costs), the financial benefits of a redundancy exercise can begin to impact much earlier if a costly and time-consuming consultation exercise can be avoided. There is a danger that more people will want to opt out of work than was originally envisaged if a voluntary approach is adopted, and this can have unbudgeted cost implications. For this reason it is important, before paying extra costs in this way, for a comprehensive human resource planning exercise to be carried out in order to assess future labour requirements.

Another factor that must be considered before making any announcements about voluntary redundancy is an assessment of who might volunteer. It is the authors' experience that individuals who have volunteered, and then been refused, display a serious lack of commitment to any reorganisation precipitated by the redundancy situation. Avoiding this requires a careful evaluation of which individuals would be allowed to go, if they volunteered – and again it is the authors' experience that too many managers make assumptions about individuals within their teams. This is where the employee relations professional, in his or her role as objective adviser, can make a valuable contribution.

Compulsory redundancy

If the voluntary option is not feasible, because the wrong people are volunteering or insufficient numbers have come forward, the next step has to be compulsory redundancy. At this point in the procedure there should be an acknowledgement that the organisation would, as far in advance of any proposed termination date as possible, notify all employees that compulsory redundancies are proposed and that a provisional selection has been made. This part of the procedure fulfils a statutory requirement. The easiest and most non-contentious method of selection is 'last in, first out' (LIFO), but the Employment Appeal Tribunal has now challenged even this. In the case of *Blatchfords v Berger and Others* (2001) the EAT observed that

> it could not be said with certainty either that selection on the basis of LIFO would always be reasonable or that no reasonable employer today would adopt LIFO as the sole criterion.

Even if LIFO was deemed to be a reasonable selection process, it can nevertheless have significant downside effects. Using LIFO, for many organisations, might mean that they lose their youngest employees or those with the most up-to-date skills. For this reason many organisations have adopted a selection system that is based on a number of criteria such as attendance records, range of work experience, disciplinary records, etc. Such criteria, which have to be as objective as possible and be based on a system of points scores, tend to be looked on very favourably by tribunals It would be important to stress that any selection was provisional and subject to possible change following consultation with the employees affected.

Creating a points score

Once management has determined what criteria should be used, it is suggested that each employee should be scored by an appropriate number of points for each criterion (usually on a scale of 10). There should be clear guidance given to the manager/managers who are asked to make the decision on the number of points each individual will receive, and some thought should be given to weighting each criterion by a factor which would take into account the importance of that factor to the employer.

For example, you should decide which particular attribute or criterion is the most important, and then multiply that score by a factor of, for example, 5. The criterion that has the lowest importance might be multiplied by a factor of, for example, 1.

It is important that great care is taken in setting scoring guidelines. When all the scores have been calculated, those employees with the lowest scores will be the ones who should be selected for redundancy, but it is often the case that companies produce scores in this way but still feel unhappy about the results. In other words, they feel unhappy about dismissing certain employees even though those employees have scored badly. In such cases the employers should consider very carefully *why* they would be unhappy about selecting those employees. There may be an objective reason why they should be retained such that, had the selection criteria been drafted to take that reason into account, those employees would have scored more highly. An employee may be engaged in a particular project (eg to introduce information technology into the workplace), and as such the employer may be loath to choose that employee for redundancy. For this reason, the selection criteria should include whether or not someone is engaged on a particular project, and that particular criterion should be assigned an appropriate weighting factor. Alternatively, employees who have some unique or special skill that it is essential that the employer retain could be taken out of the pool for selection completely.

The important point is that such considerations have to be made when deciding on the type of system to be used. It is our experience that tampering with the results when they do not deliver the desired outcomes is more likely to lead to a legal challenge from those who are selected. Judge, in an interview for *People Management* (22 November 2001), made it clear that

> The key to devising a selection process that is seen to be fair and can withstand scrutiny by trade unions and employment tribunals is to be clear about the skills and experience the company will need in the future. This is only possible if business objectives are clear to all employees.

In summary, therefore, an employer should make a note of those objective criteria which it considers appropriate, decide upon a scoring system, and then decide upon the weighting factor for each criterion. A specimen matrix and score sheet (supplied by the CIPD Employement Law Service) is set out below.

Matrix and score sheet

Name:	Age:
Date of birth:	Years of service:
Department:	Job role:

Employee assessment

Criteria	Score out of 10	Weighting (maximum × 5)	Total
		X	
Skills		X	
Attendance		X	
Flexibility		X	
		X	
		X	
		X	
		Grand total	

Assessed by: .... **Checked by:** ....

Do you think that in your organisation line managers have sufficient information about the skills of the workforce and the future skill requirements of the business?

Assistance to redundant employees

Once the selection of individuals has been confirmed, it is important – particularly if the procedure is to be consistent with the policy – that an acknowledgement is made in respect of alternative employment. Of course, alternative employment is not always possible, nor is it always desired by those to be made redundant. Nevertheless, it is incumbent on the employer to make every effort to look for alternatives, and where they exist, to consider redundant employees for suitable vacancies. If the organisation, or the number of jobs to be reduced, is very small, options in respect of alternatives are very rare.

Nevertheless, the procedure has to set out the basis on which employees will be interviewed for any vacancies and the terms and conditions on which alternative jobs will be offered. Terms and conditions may be the standard terms for the job in question. They may be the terms previously enjoyed by the individual concerned or there may be some form of transition. These are all issues that the employee relations specialist must consider. Naturally, the procedure must say something about trial periods.

It would be normal practice for a redundancy procedure to set out what steps the organisation proposed to take in assisting the redundant employee who could not be found alternative employment within the business. Such steps should include provisions for paid time off to attend interviews, to seek retraining opportunities or to attend counselling sessions. This latter point will be dealt with in more detail later in the chapter.

Compensation for redundancy

Finally, the procedure might set out the basis on which employees will be compensated for the loss of their employment. There is a statutory entitlement to a minimum amount of redundancy pay, which is set out in section 162 (2) of the 1996 Act:

- one and a half weeks' pay for each year of employment in which the employee was not below the age of 41
- one week's pay for each year of employment that the employee was between the ages of 22 and 40
- half a week's pay for each year of employment under the age of 22.

No more than 20 years' service can be taken into account in calculating an individual's redundancy payment, and there is also a maximum weekly amount that an individual can receive, irrespective of how much they earn. This maximum amount is now reviewed by the UK government on an annual basis and uprated on an annual basis. However, some organisations are prepared to make enhanced payments in order to ease the trauma that redundancy can cause or to encourage volunteers to come forward. They can also pay for more than 20 years' service if they so wish, but it is important to remember that any enhancements, to either amounts or length of service, are entirely at the employer's discretion, unless there is a specific contractual arrangement. Employee relations professionals who are charged with drawing up a procedure should be aware of the pitfalls of setting out too much detail on compensation. It is important to ensure that the organisation retains some flexibility on the issue of enhanced payments. Whatever motives lie behind paying more than the statutory amount, no organisation can predict the future or the circumstances in which redundancies may occur. It is important therefore to ensure that any payments set out in a procedure document are not considered to be contractual.

ENTITLEMENT TO COMPENSATION

In the context of redundancy payments, the definitions of redundancy can be of particular importance. Before 1990 an employer had certain rights to reclaim part of any redundancy payment made to an individual employee, and although this rebate only applied to the statutory part of a redundancy payment, it was an important factor for an employer to take into consideration when considering an enhanced payment. With the ending of the rebate, employers now have to meet the total cost of all redundancy payments and as a consequence have become much more concerned with ensuring that any loss, or diminution of work, does actually justify a payment.

Business reorganisation

There are three sets of circumstances which an employer might argue create no entitlement to a redundancy payment. In the context of so much change management an employer might say that the events which led to an individual's leaving employment had nothing to do with redundancy but were simply the consequences of a legitimate and lawful business reorganisation which were unacceptable to the employee/s concerned. The likely scenario is that employees in such circumstances would resign and claim that they had been constructively dismissed. It is also likely that such an employee would argue that the 'work of a particular kind' that he/she had been carrying out had 'ceased or diminished' and that he/she was entitled to the statutory rights. This would then have to be resolved by a tribunal – the sort of case that Lewis and Sargeant (2004) describe as one of the tribunals' more difficult tasks. In the case of *Lesney Products v Nolan* [1977] IRLR 77, Nolan and some of his colleagues argued that the change from a long day shift with overtime to a double day shift was a diminution in the employer's requirements for work of a particular kind, and that they should have received a redundancy payment. The Court of Appeal held that such a change was a legitimate reorganisation based on efficiency, and that therefore no payment was due.

The employee's workplace

The second set of circumstances in which an employer might refuse to make a redundancy payment concerns the words 'in the place where the employee was so employed'. This raises the whole question of mobility clauses in the contract of employment, and how much the employer can rely on them. For example, if the contract stipulated that an employee could be required to work anywhere, a refusal to do so could lead to a dismissal for misconduct, but not for redundancy. For the employer to rely on the terms of a mobility clause to rebut a claim for a redundancy payment, there must be an express clause in the contract that allows an employer to ask an employee to work at a different location or locations. Even then it is by no means certain that the employer would win the argument.

In 1995 the Court of Appeal held that a clause contained in a contract of employment requiring an employee to work in such parts of the UK as her employers might dictate constituted unlawful sex discrimination within the Sex Discrimination Act 1975. The case in question, *Meade-Hill and Another v British Council*, revolved around the British Council's decision to require Ms Meade-Hill to accept the incorporation of a mobility clause into her contract as a consequence of a promotion. Although this particular case – which was decided in Ms Meade-Hill's favour – was more concerned with sex discrimination than redundancy payments, it is important because of statements made by the Court of Appeal in respect of mobility clauses generally. It commented that even if this particular mobility clause could not be justified in its present form, the objectionable aspects would disappear if it were modified in a relatively minor respect. In the court's view there was no great cause for celebration by employees as a result of this particular decision.

For most employee relations professionals the question of mobility is more likely to arise when the whole, or part, of a business is moving either to a new geographical location some distance from the present workplace or to new premises broadly within the existing geographical location. In order that an organisation can retain a degree of flexibility in terms of its location it is important to be clear about an employee's 'place of work'. For this reason it is important, when drawing up the employee's 'statement of terms and particulars of employment' as required by the Employment Rights Act 1996, to identify whether 'the employee is required or permitted to work at various places' (section 1 (4)(h)).

The case of *Blatchfords v Berger and Others* to which we referred above is a classic example of how important it is not only to issue a statement of terms but to be clear about where an individual can be expected to work. In the *Blatchfords* case the Employment Appeal Tribunal (EAT) examined whether a mobility clause could be implied in the employees' contracts of employment.

There were seven applicants to the employment tribunal, six of them secretaries and one a cashier. They were all employed by the Respondent (a firm of solicitors) at the same office in Holborn. They did not have written contracts of employment or section 1 statements. Blatchfords had two other offices in the Greater London area, one in South Harrow, the other at Croxley Green. Largely owing to the loss of an important client, the firm decided to amalgamate the Holborn and South Harrow offices and to close the Holborn office on 27 November 1998.

The six secretaries were offered the opportunity of relocating to the South Harrow office. Two initially said they were prepared to do so but then changed their minds. In the end all six refused. However, Blatchfords required them all to relocate and argued that there was an implied term in their contract requiring them to do so.

None of the seven Applicants took up employment at South Harrow but left the company's employment instead. They claimed unfair dismissal, but the tribunal found that the employer's requirement for them to relocate to South Harrow was, on the facts, a fundamental breach of their contracts – that is, they had been constructively dismissed. The employer's appeal to the EAT was also unsuccessful.

What does your contract say about mobility? Are there any circumstances in which the current wording could bring you into conflict with an employee?

Alternative employment

The third set of circumstances that might lead to refusal to make a redundancy payment is when the employee refuses an offer of 'suitable alternative employment'. In circumstances when the employee is offered a new contract of employment, to begin immediately, or within four weeks of the termination of the old contract, and the offer is unreasonably refused, there is no entitlement to a redundancy payment. However, the burden of proving that an offer is suitable lies with the employer. If the employee were to express the view that the proposed new job was inferior to the old one, it would be for the employer to demonstrate that it was not – and how an employer might do this has been the subject of many industrial tribunal cases. In *Hindes v Supersine Ltd* [1979] IRLR 343, it was argued that whether the proposed employment was 'substantially equivalent' to the former job was as objective assessment as any. In *Cambridge and District Co-op v Ruse* [1993] IRLR 156, the Employment Appeal Tribunal held that 'it is possible for an employee reasonably to refuse an objectively suitable offer of alternative employment on the ground of his personal perception of the job offered'. In this case Mr Ruse had refused an alternative job because he considered it represented a demotion and a loss of status.

It is very difficult to give absolute advice on such matters as alternative employment. The sensible employee relations specialist will deal with each case individually and on its merits. It may be that what is suitable for one employee may be totally unsuitable for another. One alternative is the provision within section 138 (3) of the legislation that allows for a 'trial period'. This gives the redundant employee an opportunity to try a new job for a period of four weeks, or such longer (specified) period as may be agreed to allow for retraining. If, having opted for a trial period, the employee decides at the end of it that the job is not suitable, a redundancy payment is still payable.

THE LAW AND CONSULTATION

Since the mid-1970s all member states of the European Union have been required to enact legislation which obliges employers to consult with workers' representatives about redundancy. This was generally assumed to mean consultation with recognised trade unions and was first implemented into the UK legal framework by sections 99 to 107 of the Employment Protection Act 1975. The relevant provisions are now contained in sections 188 to 198 of the Trade Union and Labour Relations (Consolidation) Act 1992.

During 1992 the European Commission claimed that there were imperfections within the UK legislation because:

■ there was no provision for consulting with employees in the absence of a recognised trade union

■ the scope of the UK legislation was more limited than was envisaged by the original European Directive (75/129/EEC)

■ there was no requirement that an employer considering collective redundancies had to consult workers' representatives with a view to reaching agreement in relation to the matters specified in the Directive.

The Commission's complaints were considered to be well-founded and amendments made by the Trade Union Reform and Employment Rights Act 1993 made it a requirement that consultations about proposed redundancies must include discussion and consultation about ways of avoiding dismissals altogether. This change to the legislation was considered to be insufficient, and in 1994 the European Court of Justice ruled that the UK could not limit the right to be consulted to representatives of recognised trade unions. As a response to this, additional regulations – the Collective Redundancies and Transfer of Undertakings (Protection of Employment) (Amendment) Regulations 1995 – were introduced and took effect from March 1996.

Further changes, in the shape of the European Directive on Information and Consultation of Workers at National Level (described in Chapter 3), are now due to take place. The main purpose of legislation arising from the Directive will be to:

■ recognise at an EU level the fundamental rights of employees to be informed and consulted on any decisions likely to affect them significantly

■ develop arrangements for anticipating and forestalling the social consequences that may arise from changes in the organisation and running of a company

■ strengthen the link between information and consultation on strategic and economic issues and consultation on how to address the social consequences arising therefrom.

Irrespective of what may or may not be on the horizon, what does this plethora of Directives, legislation and regulation mean in practical terms for the employee relations specialist? What is an employer required to do if there is a possibility that employees will be made redundant? The question has to be considered from two angles: collective redundancies and individual redundancies.

Collective redundancies

The Trade Union and Labour Relations (Consolidation) Act 1992 together with the 1995 Regulations oblige any employer wishing to make 20 or more redundancies to consult with 'appropriate representatives'. These appropriate representatives should be union representatives where there is a recognised union in the workplace, but where this is not the case there is provision for employees to elect representatives. Where employees do decide that they want some form of collective representation in such circumstances, the intention is that:

- Employers will have to make suitable arrangements for the election of employee representatives which ensure that an election is carried out sufficiently early to allow for information to be given and consultation to take place in good time.

- The number of representatives to be elected and the terms for which they are to be elected will be matters for the employer to determine, so long as the number of employee representatives is sufficient to represent all employees properly and the period of office is long enough to complete the consultation.

- The candidates for election must be members of the affected workforce at the date of election.

- No one who is a member of the workforce may be unreasonably excluded from standing for election.

- Everyone who is a member of the affected workforce at the date of election must be entitled to vote, and each person may cast as many votes as there are representatives to be elected.

- The election should be conducted in such a way that those voting do so in secret and that the votes given at the election are fairly and accurately counted.

- In the event of any dispute as to the validity of the election, any of the affected employees may complain to a tribunal and the burden shall be on the employer to show that the election conditions were complied with.

The timetable for consultation

Section 188(2) of TULR(C)A 1992 requires consultation about proposed redundancies to begin at the earliest opportunity, but in cases involving 20 or more people minimum time periods are a necessity. If the employer is proposing to dismiss over 100 employees, the consultation process must begin at least 90 days before the first dismissal takes effect. If the proposal is to dismiss less than 100, but 20 or more, the consultation process must begin no later than 30 days before the first dismissal.

Some commentators have expressed doubt about how the phrase 'proposing redundancies' should be interpreted, particularly as the Collective Redundancies Directive uses the phrase 'contemplating redundancies'. This is slightly different from the wording in TULR(C)A, which states that consultation must be 'with a view to reaching agreement'. Until two recent Employment Appeal Tribunal (EAT) cases, many commentators had argued that consultation must start before decisions over redundancies are made. Employers took a different line, arguing that it was not practical to consult over something that had not been decided. The EAT have now declared, in *Securicor v GMB* (2003 All ER (D)181) and *Dewhirst Group v GMB* (2003 All ER (D)175), that employers do not have to consult about the business reasons for the job losses before a decision is made. In both the above cases the decision to implement redundancies had been made before consultation started. That for the moment is where the law stands, but both cases could be challenged in a higher court, or the European Court of Justice may consider the UK's implementation of the Directive unlawful. Notwithstanding these legal arguments, it is still good employee relations practice to begin consultation as soon as possible if a satisfactory outcome is desired.

Information required by employee representatives

The timetable described above can only start to run once employees or their representatives have been provided with certain information:

- the reasons for the employer's proposals
- the numbers and descriptions of the employees to be dismissed
- the method of selection the employer proposes for dismissal
- the method of carrying out the dismissals the employer proposes, having due regard to any procedure agreement that might be in existence
- the period of time over which the programme of redundancies is to be carried out
- what method the employer intends to use in calculating redundancy payments, unless the statutory formula is being applied.

Should an employer fail to provide some or all of the information required, or the information that is provided is insufficient, the consultation period will be deemed not to have started. In such circumstances the employer faces the risk of a penalty being imposed (see below) for failing to consult at the earliest opportunity. It is difficult to give precise guidance on what, and how much, detail must be provided, but vague and open-ended statements will not be acceptable. For the employee relations specialist there has to be an acknowledgement that every case must be decided on its merits and will have to be researched.

It is no good relying on 'what happened last time'. That may not be good enough. In *MSF v GEC Ferranti (Defence Systems) Ltd* [1994] IRLR 113 the Employment Appeal Tribunal held that

> whether a union has been provided with information which is adequate to permit meaningful consultation to commence is a question of facts and circumstances. There is no rule that full and specific information under each of the heads [of the legislation] must be provided before the consultation period can begin.

They went on to confirm an earlier judgment which held that a failure to give information on one of the heads may be a serious default, but that there is nothing to say that it must be treated as a serious default.

Consultation must be genuine

For consultation to be deemed genuine it has to be evidently undertaken 'with a view to reaching agreement' with employees representatives. Three things have to happen. An examination has to take place of ways to avoid dismissals. If this is impossible, ways of reducing the numbers to be dismissed should be looked at. Finally, ways should be found of mitigating the consequences of any dismissals. How tribunals will measure whether these obligations have been fulfilled is open to question. It would be strange if the legislation, as amended, meant that the employer and the representatives have to reach an agreement. What is more likely is that employers must approach the discussions with an open mind and where possible take account of any proposals put to them by the representatives. This in itself can cause problems, insofar as the distinction between consultation and negotiation is concerned. Very often union representatives will see employer proposals as a matter for negotiation, and this can sometimes be a cause of conflict, particularly where an employer perceives that he or she has little room for manoeuvre.

Penalties for failing to consult

If there has been a failure to follow the proper consultation process, an application can be made to an employment tribunal for a declaration to this effect and that a 'protective award' should be paid. This is an award requiring the employer to pay the employee remuneration for a protected period. The legislation relating to protective awards is quite complex, but some of the important elements are that:

- the affected employee receives payment at the rate of one week's gross pay for each week of the 'protected' period
- unlike some compensatory awards, there are no statutory limits on a week's pay
- subject to certain maximums, the length of a protected period is at the employment tribunal's discretion – the test is, what is just and equitable having regard to the seriousness of the employer's default?
- the maximum periods are 90 days when 90 days should have been the consultation period, and 30 days when 30 days should have been the consultation period; in any other case the maximum is 28 days.

As P. Lewis pointed out (1993), the financial implications of protective awards can be quite significant because there are often substantial numbers of employees involved – and yet, according to a report commissioned by law firm Naborro Nathanson, around one in five companies was unsure about the requirements of the legislation (*People Management*, No.25, December 1996; page 7).

Employers with well-established redundancy procedures are unlikely to come into conflict with the law over a failure to consult. Notwithstanding this, the prudent employee relations specialist will keep the procedure under review in the light of any relevant tribunal decisions. The real problems arise for those organisations that do not have a procedure or who try to put together a procedure in a hurried and casual manner when redundancies are imminent. Such organisations might find that the price they pay for a lack of preparedness is extremely high. Tribunals have shown an increasing tendency to take a very narrow view of any special pleading by employers that there was no time to consult, and the guidelines set out by the Employment Appeal Tribunal in 1982 are still of very great relevance.

The EAT (in *Williams v Compair Maxam* [1982] ICR 156 EAT) stressed that:

- the employer should consult the union as the best means by which the management result can be achieved fairly and with as little hardship to employees as possible
- the employer should try to agree with the union the criteria to be applied in selecting the employees to be made redundant
- when a selection has been made, the employer should consider with the union whether the selection has been made in accordance with these criteria.

To be acceptable, non-consultation would have to be the result of some event that was quite out of the ordinary, but it would be very unwise to trust that circumstances you believe to be 'out of the ordinary' would be accepted as such by a tribunal.

Individual consultation

Consultation with trade unions and now with the wider constituency of 'employee representatives' has tended to attract most of the attention in studies of redundancy, and there is certainly a good deal of case law on the subject, but the necessity for individual consultation must not be overlooked. Many managers have fallen into the trap of assuming that when only one or two individuals are to be made redundant there is no obligation to consult or that consultation can be cursory. This is an incorrect assumption, and although there is no statutory framework for individual consultation as there is when collective redundancies are on the agenda, tribunals can still intervene. The Employment Rights Act 1996 identifies redundancy as a fair reason for dismissal (section 98 (2) (c)), provided that the employer has acted 'reasonably'. This requirement opens the door for an employee to claim unfair dismissal on the grounds that the employer, by failing to consult, has not acted reasonably. Although not giving rise to an employment tribunal claim, an article by Pickard in *People Management* (22 November 2001) provided a classic case study on 'How not to shed staff'.

> Nicky H has been made redundant three times in her working life, but the first occasion was the worst. She worked for a publishing company as head of the central marketing team, which acted as an internal agency. The first inkling that anything was wrong came from a colleague who heard via an e-mail that the team was to be disbanded in a reorganisation.
>
> Nicky immediately tried to see her boss, but was told he was tied up in meetings all day. When they did meet, he was accompanied by a woman she had never seen before.
>
> 'He told me I was out of a job,' she says. 'Then he said: "But that's not the point. The point is that you are completely incompetent. The team can't stand you, you have no management skills, and I don't know why we hired you – you can't even photocopy anything."
>
> 'I was then told I would be escorted straight to the HR department and would not be allowed to speak to my team. When I got to HR, the manager said she had no idea what was going on and offered me a box of tissues.'
>
> The incident came a few weeks after Nicky's three-month review, at which, she says, no criticisms were made of her competence. 'I have never felt like such a piece of trash in my life,' she says. 'I had bad dreams about that day for a year afterwards and it killed my confidence. To be treated like that in front of a complete stranger was absolutely horrendous.'
>
> She did manage to get a message to her team, however. They met her in the pub later and were sympathetic. But she could do nothing more, having been at the company for less than six months.
>
> Shortly afterwards, she took a low-level job at a friend's firm to help rebuild her confidence, until that suffered cash-flow problems and had to shed some staff. She then joined a major management consultancy, but again found herself a victim of cutbacks.
>
> This latest redundancy was a complete contrast to Nicky's earlier experience: she got three months' salary, outplacement support and backing from the company, which allowed her to send e-mails to contacts, kept in touch and invited her back for social events.
>
> With the help of the consultancy, she has now decided to start her own business giving style advice to executives. She could also offer a few tips on redundancy.

Most claims for unfair dismissal in respect of redundancy are in two areas: unfair selection and lack of consultation. If the scenario reported above had concerned an employee with the required length of service to register a claim for unfair dismissal, it is inconceivable that the employer's actions would have been judged anything other than unreasonable. But, as we stated in Chapter 10, 'good practice' demands that you operate reasonably and with just cause on every occasion – not just when you think an employee can make a claim against you. Too often we hear managers say, 'They [a member of staff] have only been here a few months – do I really have to go through all the procedure?'

Many employers have argued that because the redundancy only affected one or two individuals, consultation would not have made any difference. This defence has been virtually closed to employers since the decision of the House of Lords in *Polkey v A E Dayton Services Ltd* [1987] IRLR 503, but unwise and unprofessional employers still try to use it. In *Polkey* the House of Lords did not say that consultation was an absolute requirement, but that the onus is on the employer to demonstrate that consultation would have been 'utterly useless'. In the majority of cases it would be difficult to demonstrate the uselessness of something that had not been tried. What impact the changes introduced by the Employment Act 2002 will have on the *Polkey* principle (as we mentioned in Chapter 10) remains to be seen.

By far the best option for employers is to recognise that good employee relations would be best served by adopting a systematic approach to consultation whether the proposed redundancies are going to affect five people or 50 people. This means that you should always allow enough time for a proper consultation exercise even when it is only one or two people that are to be made redundant. You should give very careful consideration to the possibilities of alternative employment, even lower-paid alternative employment. You must allow people time to:

- consider their options
- challenge the need for redundancy
- propose their own alternatives.

The employer does not have to go along with any alternatives proposed but must be able to demonstrate that they were given careful and objective consideration. It is sometimes too easy to be dismissive about suggestions made by a potentially redundant employee, but the way in which you approach the question of alternative employment will very often determine a tribunal's view of your reasonableness. In one case in which we were involved the employer was found to have unfairly dismissed an employee because he had made assumptions instead of properly consulting. In this particular case the employer had assumed that the employee, who was a long-serving manager, would not be interested in a lower-ranked and lower-paid job, and so he had not discussed it with him. At the tribunal hearing the employee was asked by the Chairman whether he would have taken such a job – and he answered in the affirmative. As the Chairman explained to the employer, it was not about whether he should have been given the lower-paid job – that might not have been appropriate in the circumstances – but that it should have been discussed with him. That would have been 'reasonable consultation'. Good practice dictates that you should always allow for the possibility of error in the judgements that you make. We have seen too many managers make the arrogant assumption that they must be right. As Judge (*People Management*, 22 November 2001) put it:

> It is important not to assume someone is dead wood unless you can be sure that they have no potential to develop new skills. I have known people take on a second lease of life because of the challenge posed by a redundancy.

Are you confident, having read the sections on consultation, that you fully understand the legal requirements? Do you need to advise any of your colleagues of their obligations?

Transfers of undertakings

When the ownership of a business transfers, there is always the possibility that redundancies will be one of the results that flow from such a transfer. Under the Acquired Rights Directive of the European Union (Directive 77/187/EEC) member states are required to ensure, in broad terms, that all employees who are covered by employment protection legislation receive additional protection in respect of job security if the identity of their employer changes. This does not mean that an employer who acquires a new business is obliged to retain all the inherited employees irrespective of the commercial realities, but equally a new employer cannot just dispense with the old employees without just cause. Should employers find, on the transfer of a business, that there are sound commercial reasons for reducing the headcount, then subject to the normal rules on consultation and the operation of a fair selection procedure, the law will not stand in their way. What the law does insist on, however, is that the transferred employees' rights are retained. This means that if they had the requisite period of service with their old employer to qualify for a redundancy payment, the new employer cannot avoid making a redundancy payment to them. In the context of consultation, all the issues of representation and the right to information that we have noted above in respect of collective redundancies apply equally to transfers of undertakings.

POST-REDUNDANCY

The massive rise in unemployment in recent years has meant that more attention is now paid to the needs of redundant employees. In this section we look at the growth in both counselling and outplacement services, and in addition, the position of those employees that remain in employment, who may very well suffer from the so called 'survivors' syndrome'.

Counselling

We have decided to examine counselling and outplacement separately, notwithstanding that they overlap in many ways. In this section we analyse counselling in the sense that counselling can help employees come to terms with the fact that they have lost their job. Counselling in respect of personal skills, job search and financial planning is dealt with under 'outplacement'.

Although redundancy has become part of everyday life, the loss of one's job usually comes as a tremendous personal blow. Even when 'the writing is on the wall' and job losses in the organisation are known to be inevitable, individuals still hope that they will be unaffected. To misappropriate an advertising slogan made famous by the national lottery, they hope 'it will not be them'.

There can be a tendency for employers to want a redundancy exercise to be over and forgotten as quickly as possible, and this can manifest itself in a very uncaring attitude. The employee relations specialist should be reminding managerial colleagues that they have a continuing responsibility for their redundant employees and, as the CIPD guide on redundancy says, be providing displaced employees with a counselling service. Redundant employees can feel anger, resentment, and even guilt – emotions which, if not carefully managed, can inhibit an employee from moving forward to the next phase of his or her career – and this is where effective counselling becomes crucial. However, it is important to proceed cautiously, and earlier in this book, in another reference to counselling, we stressed the need for proper training. As Fowler (1993) said:

> Handling the first stage of redundancy counselling requires considerable skill, and should not be attempted by anyone who does not, as a minimum, understand the general principles of all forms of counselling.

Not every redundant employee will agree to or want counselling, but it is nevertheless important to understand its key purpose. If you talk to redundant employees, as we have done, you are struck by the violent mood swings that can occur during the initial post-redundancy phase. Depending on the personality of the individual concerned, the mood can swing from pessimism about the future to unfounded optimism, from anger at the former employer to a feeling that he or she has been given an opportunity to do something different. The objective of counselling is to bring all these emotions out into the open and to help individuals to make decisions about their future. It is not a panacea – it will not stop people being angry or feeling betrayed – but it might help them to view their future constructively.

For the employee relations specialist there is a further dimension to the provision of counselling. Not only is there a moral imperative but there are sound business reasons. Unless the organisation is closing down completely, there will be other employees left who you will want to build the organisation around. Richard Baker, Director of Human Resources at Hoechst Roussel, made a very valid point when he said (quoted by Summerfield in *People Management*, No.2, January 1996; page 31):

> People … never forget the way they are treated when they are made redundant, and neither do the friends and colleagues who remain behind.

Outplacement

Outplacement is a process by which individuals who have been made redundant by their employer are given support and counselling to assist them in achieving the next stage of their career. There are a large number of organisations offering outplacement services, but the range and quality of their services vary greatly and the employee relations specialist must research prospective suppliers carefully if a decision to use outplacement is taken.

Broadly, outplacement consultancies offer services on a group or individual basis which fall into the following general categories:

- CV preparation
- researching the job market
- communication techniques
- interview presentation
- managing the job search.

Each organisation operates differently, but in the best organisations the process probably starts with a personal counselling session with a trained counsellor. Once this has been carried out, the next step would be the preparation of the CV. This involves identifying key skills and past achievements so that the job-hunter can self-market from a position of strength. Step Three would be to make decisions about job search methods (cold contact, advertisement, recruitment consultants, etc) and contact development – for example, networking. Step Four would be to ensure that the key communication skills of letter-writing, telephone techniques and interview presentation were of a sufficiently high standard to enhance the job search. Where skills must be improved, the better consultancies will provide the necessary training at no extra cost. The final step is managing the actual job search, setting personal targets, keeping records of letters and phone calls, maintaining notes of interviews, and carrying out a regular job search evaluation.

Running alongside these basic services will be a range of support services, such as secretarial help, free telephone and office space and financial planning advice. What an individual gets will depend on the particular package that the former employer purchases on his or her behalf.

Of course, not every employer will be able to afford the cost of outplacement, particularly if large numbers of employees are affected by the redundancies. In such circumstances, organisations must consider what they can do to help from within their own resources or by using a mixture of internal and external resources. A classic example of a company that took its responsibilities seriously is evidenced by the following case study.

Case study

Rolls-Royce outplacement

When aero-engine company Rolls-Royce had to axe 4,800 jobs worldwide in the wake of the 11 September attacks on targets in the USA, it was well-placed to deal with the crisis.

Here in Britain, the company had set up six resource centres in early 2000 to handle an anticipated downturn in the market.

The centres, one at each at the company's main UK sites, provide a three-day career transition training programme leading to an Investors in People-recognised award and continuing, open-ended support and advice.

The centres take CIPD good practice as a model, and each is staffed with a manager, a counsellor, several other dedicated Rolls-Royce personnel and a flexible team from the company's two external outplacement providers, Capita Grosvenor and Winchester Consulting. The providers give access to national jobs databases with online search facilities.

Since the centres opened, hundreds of employees affected by cutbacks have used them for careers guidance, advice on writing CVs, training, and so on. 85 per cent have found new employment, typically after some weeks.

'One of the challenges was the reputation that resource centres have in other organisations,' says John McKell, Rolls-Royce head of employment policy. 'They are renowned for providing minimal provision to lower-paid workers in poky surroundings, while managers get executive packages. But at Rolls-Royce the service is gold-plated for everyone.'

The company has involved employees and unions from the start. In response to a proposal from union officers, it set up a resourcing committee by means of which employee and union representatives could review redundancy support. Several improvements, such as better communications, have resulted.

Even the TUC has recognised the value of good advice being made available to workers facing redundancy, and has produced a guide on how they can make the best use of the government's Rapid Response Service (RRS). RRS was established in 2003 and aims to help workers affected by major redundancies. Operated through local JobCentre Plus centres, it aims to help people into new jobs before they lose their current ones by providing specialist advice services.

Does your organisation have any sort of policy on counselling and outplacement? If not, who would make the decisions about what level of support to offer?

Survivors' syndrome

When people are forced to leave employment because of redundancy, those who are left behind can be affected just as much as those who have left. Anecdotal evidence we have gathered from the finance sector and local UK government indicates that disenchantment, pessimism and stress are the likely result of even a small-scale redundancy exercise. Survivors' syndrome, as it is called, can be minimised if, as we pointed out above, those who are to be made redundant are treated fairly and equitably, and there is a decision made to invest in an effective post-redundancy programme. This usually means a time commitment from senior managers and a good communications process.

The feelings referred to above are the result of two factors – one, that remaining employees are often asked to 'pick up' the work of their former colleagues, either directly or indirectly as the consequence of a reorganisation. In one local authority individuals had to reapply for their own jobs three times in three years following a series of redundancies and reorganisations. The second factor concerns communication. We have anecdotal evidence which suggests that in many organisations the remaining employees are not always communicated with effectively, thus providing an opportunity for rumour and disenchantment to thrive. Getting the message across about why redundancies were necessary and what happens next is vitally important – and yet most people we have spoken to identify poor communication as one of the principal causes of their dissatisfaction.

Blakstad and Cooper (1995) identify three sets of stimuli that can interfere with communications, one of which is internal stress. Internal stress can be caused by a number of variables, but one of the causes identified is 'group concerns'. The aftermath of a redundancy exercise is a classic example of 'group concerns', and yet many managers do not take it into account when communicating with the survivors. For the professional manager who wishes to minimise the effect of survivors' syndrome, communication and communication methodology must be carefully worked out. As Blakstad and Cooper (1995) say:

> While it is usually impossible to understand the individual concerns of each member of the [group], structuring the communication around an awareness of group tensions can be used to strengthen retention of messages.

Although communication with those left behind is vital, there is another option that is worthy of consideration, and that is counselling. Because redundancies are often cost-cutting exercises, many organisations are reluctant to hire counsellors to help with the aftermath. But a recent study by Professor John McLeod of the School of Social and Health Sciences at the University of Aberdeen suggests that it might be an investment worth making (reported by Blyth in *People Management*, 1 May 2003):

> The findings of more than 80 studies on workplace counselling show that 90 per cent of employees are highly satisfied with the process and outcome. Evidence suggests that counselling helps to relieve work-related stress and reduces sickness absence rates by up to half.

The following case study by Blyth indicates the effectiveness of such an approach.

Case study
The Royal Mail

Having made a loss after tax of £940 million in 2001/02, the Royal Mail announced one of the biggest restructures in British corporate history. In 2002 around 30,000 redundancies were announced, and more have been made since then.

Andrew Kinder was formerly principal welfare co-ordinator and chartered occupational psychologist for the Royal Mail, and now provides the same services from agency SchlumbergerSema. Describing the impact of such large-scale change on Royal Mail staff, he says: 'Many individuals find it hard to cope, some feeling that they have to work harder to secure their futures, others feeling deep concerns about why they kept their jobs. Royal Mail is committed to addressing these issues not only because they could have a negative effect on productivity but also because the organisation takes its legal duty of care to individuals very seriously. Reorganisations like this happen, and we as humans can't control change – but we can control how we respond to it. Counselling is a key aspect of the firm's efforts to empower employees to cope with change.'

Pauline Leech, head of information services in the Royal Mail's property division, has taken advantage of Kinder's counselling services. 'The team in which I work has been going through so much change that we felt it would be useful to bring in a counsellor,' she says. 'Andrew ran a session helping us develop a number of coping strategies. We talked about our feelings and behaviour, completed a questionnaire and discussed responses to situations. A drama triangle, involving three people playing the role of victim, persecutor and rescuer, was very interesting and gave an insight into different approaches to the same situation. It gave us a good insight into the pressure felt by colleagues. For me it helped to know that the firm cared enough to offer this support.'

SUMMARY

Redundancy is one of the most emotive issues that any manager can be called upon to deal with. Calling individuals into your office and informing them that they no longer have a job is never easy. For the employee relations specialist at the beginning of his or her career, managing a redundancy exercise can be just as traumatic as for the redundant employee.

No matter how experienced you become, managing redundancy is never straightforward, but in this chapter we have attempted to set the process into some sort of organised framework. Most redundancies occur because organisations have to change, and although we have recognised this, we nevertheless felt it important that employee relations specialists should be aware that there may be alternatives to reducing an organisation's headcount. In particular we stressed that in an era of constant change businesses need to retain their competitive advantage. This is unlikely to happen if their employees are constantly looking over their shoulders, fearing for their jobs. One of the challenges that all managers, whether or not they are personnel practitioners, will face in the twenty-first century is how to reconcile the need for organisational change with the individual's need for contentment and security at work.

Not only does the employee relations specialist have to understand the need for organisations to change, but he or she must understand that this has to be accommodated within a well-developed legal framework that directs and constrains his or her actions.

Finally, as we saw in the last part of the chapter, redundancy leaves survivors struggling in its wake, and these individuals must receive the highest levels of communication and consideration. They often experience a psychological state that is not unlike bereavement, and they will inevitably lose some degree of trust in their organisation or even in their immediate manager.

Key points

- The definition of when redundancy occurs is important because it determines an individual's legal right to compensation, consultation, etc.
- Redundancy should always be a last resort, and it is therefore important to have effective policies and procedures for dealing with a redundancy situation.
- Selection in redundancy situations must be objective and capable of withstanding external scrutiny.
- If employers do not wish to pay out large sums in compensation, they must ensure that they fulfil their statutory obligations. Evidence from numerous tribunal cases demonstrates that not consulting is the most expensive failure.
- People do not forget how a redundancy exercise was handled, and the professional personnel practitioner must take care to ensure that any redundancy exercise considers the needs of all individuals as well as those of the organisation.
- The 'survivors' of a redundancy are just as likely to be affected by its consequences as those who are actually made redundant, and it is therefore important that they understand why redundancy was necessary.

FURTHER READING

BLAKSTAD M. and COOPER A. (1995) *The Communicating Organisation*. London, Institute of Personnel and Development.

BLYTH A. (2003) The art of survival, *People Management*, Volume 9, No.9, May; pages 39–40.

BLYTON P. and TURNBULL P. (1994) *The Dynamics of Employee Relations*. London, Macmillan.

BROWN D. (2001) Lopsided view, *People Management*, Volume 7, No.23, November; pages 36–7.

FOWLER A. (1993) *Redundancy*. London, Institute of Personnel and Development.

GRIFFITHS J. (2004) Q & A: all change, *People Management*, Volume 10, No.16, August; pages 14–15.

HENDRICKS R. and MUMFORD E. (1996) Business process re-engineering RIP, *People Management*, Volume 2, No.9, May; pages 22–9.

JUDGE G. (2001) The judge who has to sit in judgement, *People Management*, Volume 7, No.23, November; page 32.

KAY J. (1993) *Foundations of Corporate Success*. Oxford, Oxford University Press.

LEWIS D. and SARGEANT M. (2004) *Essentials of Employment Law*. London, Chartered Institute of Personnel and Development.

LEWIS P. (1993) *The Successful Management of Redundancy*. Oxford, Blackwell.

PETTIGREW A. and WHIPP R. (1995) *Managing Change for Competitive Success*. Oxford, Blackwell.

PICKARD J. (2001) When push comes to shove, *People Management*, Volume 7, No.23, November; pages 30–5.

SPARROW P. (1998) New organisational forms, processes, jobs and psychological contracts, in P. Sparrow and M. Marchington, *Human Resource Management: The new agenda*. London, Pitman Publishing/Financial Times.

SPARROW P. and MARCHINGTON M. (1998) *Human Resource Management: The new agenda*. London, Pitman Publishing/Financial Times.

SUMMERFIELD J. (1996) Lean firms cannot afford to be mean, *People Management*, Volume 2, No.2, January; pages 30–2.

SUMMERFIELD J. and VAN OUDTSHOORN L. (2003) *Counselling in the Workplace*. London, Chartered Institute of Personnel and Development.

WATKINS J. (2003) Direct line, *People Management*, Volume 9, No.10, May; pages 42–3.

Managing health and safety

CHAPTER 13

CHAPTER OBJECTIVES

When you have completed this chapter you should be aware of and able to describe:

- **the nature of the institutions that formulate and introduce health and safety laws and regulations**

- **the legal framework under which organisations have to operate**

- **the duties imposed on employers and employees**

- **the role of trade unions in health and safety**

- **the importance of risk assessment.**

INTRODUCTION

Employee relations is concerned with gaining people's commitment to the achievement by an organisation of a series of business goals and objectives. This will only succeed if individuals believe that they are valued by their employer – and yet in many organisations employees can gain the impression that they do not really matter, that they are expendable. Such organisations may have a good reward system, may have effective systems of communication, may have well-trained line managers and effective policies to deal with a range of people issues, but in one key area they are found wanting. That key area is health and safety. The CIPD Professional Standards say that

> The underlying aim of health and safety is to promote the wellbeing of employees and others affected by the operation of any business, service or organisation. When a workplace is safe and people see that their wellbeing is respected, it is likely to improve morale and support other human resource policies. Work itself can have positive or negative long-term effects on employee health. It is an increasingly important aspect of health and safety to ensure that risks to physical or mental health are identified and controlled.

If, on the other hand, people consider that their health, safety or welfare at work is of little or no consequence to their manager, or worse, to the organisation as a whole, their commitment to the business will diminish. And yet, as the CIPD Standards go on to say,

> those organisations successfully managing health and safety recognise that health and safety policies align with their other human resource management policies.

Too often when the words 'health' and 'safety' are mentioned, many management teams raise a collective groan of despair.

Why is this? It is widely acknowledged that injuries and disease from workplace activity constitute a moral, legal and economic problem. The cost of accidents and disease to the country as a whole is extremely difficult to calculate, especially when a substantial proportion of accidents are of a minor nature and go unreported. Yet according to figures from the Health and Safety Executive, three quarters of a million people take time off work for what they regard as work-related illness. As a result more than 40 million working days are lost per year, of which 33 million are attributable to work-related ill health and 7 million to workplace injury. This has immense consequences for productivity within an individual organisation, but also for UK Ltd.

Nevertheless, it is not all bad news. Despite a clear distaste for health and safety legislation and the lack of popularity for the enforcement mechanisms, there is little doubt that we have come a long way in protecting the health and safety of the British workforce. In 1884 Her Majesty's Factories Inspector reported that 403 people were killed while at work in the country's factories. By the start of the present decade the Health and Safety Commission (HSC) statistics showed only 31 deaths in the manufacturing sector. In mining, HM Inspector of Mines reported 998 miners killed in 1884; in 2000 this had reduced to 6.

However, we must not be complacent. In the year 2003/04 there were still 235 fatal injuries to workers – a rate of 0.81 per hundred thousand workers. In addition, during the same period, employers reported over 150,000 other injuries – a rate of 614.1 per hundred thousand employees. Not only do these figures represent serious distress to those involved, and to their families, but also they are a drain on our national resources; current estimates put such costs at around £18 billion per year. Then there is the cost to an individual business if employees are injured or disabled at work. Even if there is no occupational sick pay scheme in place, statutory sick pay will be due, there is a cost in lost productivity, plus the cost of management time in carrying out an accident investigation, and finally, there is the possibility that an individual can claim damages through legal action. For more information on a range of health and safety statistics you are encouraged to visit the HSE website, www.hse.gov.uk.

Such is the concern at the ever mounting cost of a lack of awareness that (as reported by C. Taylor in *People Management*) the Health and Safety Commission has called

> for a compulsory duty on all organisations to investigate all reportable incidents, cases of ill health or even 'near misses' that could have resulted in injuries. The commission believes that the proposals can save the UK £1.8 billion a year, including £600 million for business, if employers turn their attention to those incidents not currently investigated.

Do you know how much accidents at work and sickness cost your organisation each year?

Because of the clear link between health and safety and employee commitment and productivity, it is important that personnel professionals play their part in creating a positive health and safety culture in the workplace. As a further extract from the CIPD Professional Standards emphasises,

> Health and safety is an all-embracing multi-disciplinary topic and requires a knowledge of a wide range of subjects such as law, risk/safety management, occupational health and hygiene, ergonomics and human factors.

How seriously is health and safety taken in your organisation? Is the individual with operational responsibility a senior manager or director?

THE HEALTH AND SAFETY AT WORK ETC ACT 1974

The statistics quoted above, on deaths at work, mean that it would be churlish to pretend that there have not been real increases in the standards of health and safety management, the major breakthrough coming at the beginning of the 1970s. The report of the Committee on Safety and Health at Work (the Robens Report) was published in 1972 and was directly responsible for the introduction of the present system of safety management. This came into being in 1974 when the Health and Safety at Work etc Act (HSW Act) set up new institutions and provided for the progressive revision and replacement of all health and safety law then existing.

Health and safety institutions

The Act created a number of institutions of which the two most important are:

- the Health and Safety Commission (HSC) – a body of up to ten people, appointed by the government after consultation with organisations representing employers, employees, local authorities and others, as appropriate. A recent innovation is that one of the present members of the Commission has been appointed to represent the public interest, which, given issues like rail safety, can be seen as a very progressive step. The HSC's primary function is to make arrangements to secure the health, safety and welfare of people at work, and the public, in the way undertakings are conducted – including proposing new laws and standards, conducting research, providing information and advice, and controlling explosives and other dangerous substances. It has a specific duty to maintain the Employment Medical Advisory Service, which provides advice on occupational health matters. It also has a general duty to help and encourage people concerned with all these matters
- the Health and Safety Executive (HSE) – a body of three people appointed by the Commission with the consent of the relevant Secretary of State. The Executive advises and assists the Commission in its functions. It has some specific statutory responsibilities of its own, notably for the enforcement of health and safety law. The Executive employs approximately 4,000 people including policy advisers, technologists, scientific and medical experts, and their best-known personnel, inspectors. They are all together collectively known as the HSE.

Local authorities also have statutory responsibilities for the enforcement of health and safety law, mainly in the distribution, retail, office, leisure and catering sectors. HSE liaises closely with local authorities on enforcement matters through the Health and Safety Executive/Local Authorities Enforcement Liaison Committee (HELA). An enforcement liaison officer network in HSE regional offices across Britain also provides advice and support for local authorities.

Ministerial responsibilities

Health and safety is regulated in the same way across the whole of Great Britain, and a number of different Secretaries of State are responsible to Parliament at Westminster for the activities of the HSC and HSE in different areas. Since July 2002 Ministers in the Department for Work and Pensions have taken responsibility for the HSC and HSE, although these bodies are separate from the Department itself. In most matters the Commission and Executive act by virtue of their powers and duties under the Health and Safety at Work etc Act and its associated legislation, or European legislation. In a few, they act under agreements as the agent of the Secretary of State concerned.

Secretaries of State have the power to direct the Commission in particular matters, and they themselves may introduce health and safety law, provided that they consult the Commission. In practice, the Commission has put forward to Ministers almost all health and safety proposals since the 1974 Act. In exercising their responsibilities for negotiating and implementing European health and safety law, Ministers have always looked to the Commission for help and advice.

Advisory committees

The HSE provides the Commission with policy, technological and professional advice. Other expert advice comes from the HSC's network of advisory committees. Some deal with particular danger areas such as hazardous substances and some with particular industries like construction or the railways. Each includes a balance of employer and employee representatives and, where appropriate, technological and professional experts. Each is serviced by the HSE. Their main function is to recommend standards and guidance and, in some cases, to comment on policy issues confronting the HSC or to recommend an approach to a particular new problem.

The Commission and Executive have links with other bodies, notably with the universities, engineering institutions and the National Radiological Protection Board, which has a national function in relation to ionising and other radiations. They also maintain close contact with professional and scientific societies – for example, the Royal Society, the British Occupational Hygiene Society, the Institute of Occupational Hygienists and the Royal Society of Chemistry – which make a major input into the development of the scientific and technical base of occupational health and safety in the UK.

One example of the research that is carried out in respect of health and safety issues, and which is very relevant to organisations with a mobile workforce such as sales representatives or delivery drivers, can be seen in the work of the Work-Related Road Safety Task Group. This group was set up by the Commission to consider occupational road risk. It is estimated that around 800 employees die every year when driving for work purposes. This equates to a quarter of all fatal road traffic accidents.

Fatigue is a major problem (as evidenced by the Selby rail crash), and if employees are travelling long distances and then attending high-pressure meetings it is unlikely that they will be getting sufficient rest. Failure to address the risks of excessive driving can lead to the courts' imposing heavy penalties. In one case at the Old Bailey, the directors of a haulage company were found to have been grossly negligent after one of their drivers fell asleep at the wheel and killed two people. The court held that the directors should have realised that the driver, who spent 60 hours a week behind the wheel, had failed to take proper breaks and was in a 'dangerously exhausted state'.

Another issue concerning drivers which has been addressed in the recent past is that relating to mobile phones. Although not specific to the workplace, the legislation on the use of hand-held mobile phones while driving has had to be taken into account by organisations who wish to keep in contact with their workforce.

> If your organisation employs individuals who drive as part of their work (sales representatives, van drivers, etc), what checks are made on their driving hours, or their use of mobile telephones, and are they encouraged to take breaks?

THE LEGAL FRAMEWORK: DUTIES IMPOSED BY THE ACT

The Health and Safety at Work etc Act applies to all work situations. The starting-point and main principle of the Health and Safety at Work etc Act is that it is those who create risk from work activity who are responsible for the protection of workers and the public from any consequences to their health or safety. The Act places specific responsibilities on employers, the self-employed, employees, designers, manufacturers, importers and suppliers. Associated legislation places additional duties on owners, licensees, managers and people in charge of premises. The main provisions of the Act express general duties – for example, upon employers to maintain a safe workplace, upon anyone who undertakes work activity to protect the public – and require that goods are designed so as to be safe and without risks to health. Employees are required to co-operate with their employers in taking care.

The general duties of employers

The Act imposes a duty on all employers to ensure, so far as is reasonably practicable, the health, safety and welfare at work of their employees. In particular, this duty includes:

- providing and maintaining plant and systems of work which are safe and without risks to health
- making arrangements for ensuring the safety and absence of risks to health in connection with the use, handling, storage and transport of articles and substances
- providing information, instruction, training and supervision to ensure the health and safety at work of all employees
- maintaining a workplace which is safe and without risks to health
- providing and maintaining the means of access to, and egress from, the workplace
- providing adequate welfare facilities
- for employers who employ five people or more, preparing, and keeping up to date a written statement of their policy showing how management intends to provide a safe working environment and also giving details of the organisational arrangements for carrying this out
- ensuring that non-employees (contractors, the general public, work experience staff, temporary staff, visitors, etc) are not exposed to any risks resulting from workplace activities
- providing free of charge to employees anything necessary, or required by law, in the interest of health and safety at work (personal protective equipment).

The general duties of employees

The Act also acknowledges the importance of employees' involvement in health and safety at work. Employees are required to:

- take reasonable care for the health and safety of themselves and others who may be affected by their acts or omissions
- co-operate with employers and any other persons so far as is necessary to enable them to carry out statutory provisions
- not intentionally or recklessly interfere with or misuse anything provided in the interests of health, safety and welfare.

As for managers or designated leaders, not only does the Act impose duties on them as ordinary employees but the Act also imposes extra duties on them. These other duties are in relation to their obligation to supervise the work of others, and the Act states that:

1   Where a person by his/her act or default causes another person to commit an offence, he/she, as well as that other person, may be charged with the offence.
2   Where an offence committed by a body corporate is shown to have been committed due to the consent, connivance or neglect of a director or senior manager, the director/senior manager, as well as the body corporate, shall be guilty of an offence.

Safety policy

One of the strict duties imposed on employers under the Health and Safety at Work etc Act is that organisations are obliged to have a safety policy that must be communicated to all employees. This does not mean that each employee must be given a copy, but that the policy must be prominently displayed where it can easily be seen. Some organisations manage this process by including a copy of the policy in the employee handbook; others have a specific 'health and safety' noticeboard. There is no laid-down format for a health and safety policy, but the HSE does provide guidelines (again available from its website) on what form a policy statement should take. An intrinsic part of the health and safety policy is the organisational arrangements that have been put in place for the actual management of safety issues. Such organisational arrangements will specify who, in the organisation, has what responsibilities for particular issues. This is a key document, because whereas the policy can be seen as a sort of 'apple pie and motherhood' statement, the organisational document clearly spells out who should do what. The following example of a policy statement and the organisational arrangements that flow from it demonstrate this point.

HEALTH AND SAFETY AT WORK ETC ACT 1974 – GENERAL POLICY STATEMENT

It is Company Policy to promote the highest standard of Health and Safety at all levels of business. The Policy is to do all that is reasonable to prevent personal injury and damage to property and to protect everyone (including our clients) from foreseeable hazards. In particular this Company has responsibility:

- to provide and maintain a safe and healthy working environment for employees, taking account of any statutory requirements
- to provide and maintain safe plant, equipment and systems of work, taking account of any statutory requirements
- to provide information, training and instruction to enable employees to perform their work safely and efficiently
- to make available all necessary and relevant safety devices, protective clothing and equipment and to supervise their correct use
- to maintain a constant and continuing interest in health and safety matters applicable to the Company's activities, in particular by consulting and involving employees and/or their representatives wherever possible
- to make reports and keep records taking account of statutory requirements.

Employees have a duty to co-operate in the operation of this Policy:

- by working safely and efficiently, having regard for others
- by meeting statutory obligations
- by promptly reporting incidents involving other employees, clients or plant, equipment, or working practices that have resulted or may result in injury or damage
- by observing company procedures and rules appropriate to securing a safe and healthy workplace
- by assisting in the investigation of accidents with the object of introducing measures to prevent a recurrence.

Signed

Managing Director

Organisational arrangements

Managing Director will be responsible for ensuring that Group Policy is carried out.

Competent person will advise the Managing Director on safety matters and formulate the Company's health and safety policy. He/she will draw up or assist in drawing up risk assessments and safe working practices and carry out safety audits.

Safety officer to be nominated, in writing, by operational managers and managers for each [department or location]. The Safety officer bears direct responsibility for health and safety and environmental matters. The Safety officer's duties include checking that regulations and Company safety policies are being complied with, and promoting the safe conduct of the work. The Safety officer may be the [departmental or site manager].

Operations manager and managers will be responsible for maintaining high health and safety standards in their areas of control, including appropriate consultation with staff and contact with local authorities. They will review accident reports and progress action, where appropriate. They will be responsible for ensuring that all employees in their department or section are instructed in the policy of health and safety, and that the arrangements are being applied effectively. They will be responsible for the maintenance of equipment and processes on which personal safety depends, and for the safe introduction of new materials, machinery and processes.

Safety representatives are [elected or appointed] for each [department or location] and will sit on the Safety Committee while carrying no additional responsibility. They will communicate safety concerns to their management and the Committee, and will keep a watchful eye on safety matters [in their department/at their site].

Individual employees will be responsible for complying with the Company's health and safety policy by observing the Company rules on such matters and taking reasonable care for the health and safety of themselves, other employees, or our clients.

The grievance procedure will be the means by which employees register a grievance to supervision on a matter of health or safety. The procedure provides for rapid consideration of any problem.

Arrangements: all employees are expected to study the detailed health and safety arrangements under the heading 'Organisation and Administration' applicable to their working location, or location being visited, which is available from their line manager.

Is it your organisation's practice to issue the policy to all employees? Are you sure that all the employees understand it? If you are not sure, should you be thinking of other ways of getting across the message of the organisation's safety intentions?

Some of the legal duties imposed by or under the Act are very specific. For example, a mine must always have two exits, or laboratories that offer particular services must be approved by the HSE. The duty to assess risks and take appropriate action is fundamental and absolute. Beyond that, many duties are expressed as goals or targets which are to be met 'so far as is reasonably practicable' or through exercising 'adequate control'. The phrase 'so far as is reasonably practicable' is key within the Health and Safety at Work etc Act. For example, employers must weigh up the costs of providing a safe system of work against the risk to health and safety if such a system was not provided. Only if the costs are grossly disproportionate to the risks can the safety precaution be considered unreasonable. Most everyday health and safety issues, however, will have 'reasonably practicable' solutions. The cost of keeping walkways and fire exits clear, for example, is not disproportionately high compared with the risk to safety.

The thinking behind this comes from a legal case, *Edwards v NCB* [1949], in which the judge stated:

> A computation must be made in which the quantum of risk is placed on one scale, and the sacrifice involved in the measure for averting the risk is placed on the other.

When calculating the cost against the risk, the size of the risk and the sacrifice that has to be made in order to reduce the risk, two factors must also be looked at. Firstly, what is the likelihood that injury will in fact be caused? (The greater the probability that an accident will occur, the greater is the duty to guard against it.) And secondly, what is the severity of the injury risked? Within the legislation you will come upon various words which qualify your legal duties:

- *absolute* – you have to do this (there is no choice)
- *practicable* – if it is feasible to do, you should do it
- *reasonably practicable* – it is a matter of weighing cost against risk.

These qualifications imply some degree of latitude or judgement over how far it is reasonable to go. To do something 'so far as is reasonably practicable' is, as we explain above, something of a balancing act, but it can also mean, for example, to ascertain and apply up-to-date good practice wherever it is established, since clearly it is always reasonably practicable to do that. Where good practice is not specified or obvious, it is reasonable to weigh the *seriousness* of the risk against the difficulty and cost of reducing or removing it. In such cases, risk-reducing measures must legally be pursued up to the point where the taking of any further steps would be grossly disproportionate to any residual risk. These rules are regardless of company size or economic circumstances.

In a very few cases the requirement of a regulation may be to do what is practicable or technically feasible. This means that whatever is specified must be done, regardless of the expense.

Regulations, codes of practice and guidance

The Health and Safety at Work etc Act provided that legislation passed before 1974 would be 'progressively replaced by a system of regulations and approved codes of practice'. At the time the Act came into force there were some 30 statutes and 500 sets of regulations. In carrying out the reform of the law, the general principle has been that regulations, like the Act itself, should, so far as possible, express general duties, principles and goals, and that subordinate detail should be set out in approved codes and guidance. In 1994 there was a 'Review of regulation', but it would be fair to say that the process of reform continues. Further change might result from the European legislative process, which sometimes imposes more detailed and specific requirements than would be envisaged under the Act, or alternatively, change might be driven by public pressure to provide safer workplaces.

The appropriate government Minister makes regulations normally on the basis of proposals submitted by the Commission once the consultation process about which we explained above has been exhausted. Such regulations have to be laid before Parliament, and, unless objection is made, proposals automatically become law 21 days after being submitted for parliamentary scrutiny.

Approved codes of practice (ACOPs) are approved by the HSC with the consent of the appropriate Secretary of State: they do not require agreement from Parliament. Approved health and safety codes have a special authority in law, as codes do in disciplinary and other matters. Failure to comply with the provisions may be taken by a court in criminal proceedings as evidence of a failure to comply with the requirements of the Act or of regulations to which the ACOP relates, unless it can be shown that those requirements were complied with in some equally effective way. Approved codes (which can be updated fairly easily) thus provide flexibility to cope with invention and technological change without a lowering of standards.

Other guidance is issued by the Commission or its advisory committees, or by the HSE, in effect as a notification of the standards its inspectors expect. Following HSC/E guidance is not compulsory and employers are free to take other action. In addition, the HSE issues a large volume of guidance adapted to the needs of local authority inspection. Each year the HSC and HSE publish over 350 documents giving information, advice and guidance about different sectors or processes; at any one time there are approximately 1,200 priced titles and 800 free titles in print, many of the latter additionally available on the HSE websites.

Other legislation

Some legislation existing prior to the 1974 Act remains in force, including legislation covering mines, railways and nuclear safety, and some parts of the Factories Act 1961 and the Offices, Shops and Railway Premises Act 1963.

Under the Nuclear Installations Act 1965, the Executive is the licensing authority for nuclear installations and it supervises mining qualifications under the Management and Administration of Safety and Health at Mines Regulations 1993. The Railway Inspectorate approves new railway works and changes to existing works by means of regulations made under the Transport and Works Act 1992.

European legislation

In recent years most legislation on health and safety has been introduced to implement European Directives – mainly directly promoting minimum standards for the health and safety of workers but also via measures designed to complete and maintain the Single Market or protect the environment. There is now a developed body of EU health and safety law. A key element is the Framework Directive (implemented in 1993 by the Management Regulations), which established broadly based obligations for employers to evaluate, avoid and reduce workplace risks, etc. EU Directives on health and safety are based on a set of common principles and themes, which is likely to follow the same format in the future:

- the avoidance of risks
- the evaluation of risks that cannot be avoided
- the necessity to combat and deal with risk at source
- the replacement of the dangerous by the non-dangerous or the less dangerous
- the need to give collective protective measures priority over individual protective measures.

In 1992 six major pieces of European legislation, known in the UK as the 'six-pack', came into being. The practical impact of this new legislation was not simply to add more requirements, but rather to make explicit what was already implicit in the Health and Safety at Work etc Act.

The 'six-pack' consists of:

- the Management of Health and Safety at Work Regulations 1992 (amended)

- the Workplace (Health, Safety and Welfare) Regulations 1992
- the Provision and Use of Work Equipment Regulations (PUWER) 1992 (updated 1998 – 'PUWER 98')
- the Manual Handling Operations Regulations 1992
- the Personal Protective Equipment at Work Regulations 1992 (PPE)
- the Health and Safety (Display-Screen Equipment) Regulations 1992 (DSE).

Do all your organisation's managers fully understand the responsibilities these regulations impose? What, if any, training do they receive?

The development of European Occupational Health and Safety legislation is underpinned by the concept of 'social dialogue' – explained in more detail in Chapter 5 – by which consultations are required with representatives of the employers, workers and governments across the member states. Britain plays a strong role in this process, the HSE providing experts to the various groups that are working on proposed legislation, as well as exchanging experience with equivalent regulators across Europe. This means that the UK is usually in a good position both to influence the formation of the legislation and, subsequently, to convert the resulting Directives into national legislation through our own policy process.

THE POLICY PROCESS

In developing policy, the HSE follows the principles of good regulation as adopted by the UK government under the following headings.

- Transparent – Legislation must be clear and easy to understand with aims written in clear and simple language; people and businesses are given an opportunity to comment and time to comply before introduction
- Accountable – The HSE/HSC answers to Ministers, parliament and the public for any legislation it proposes, with appeals procedures for enforcement actions
- Targeted – Legislation is focused on the problems and reduces adverse side effects to a minimum, where possible being goal-based, and regularly reviewed for effectiveness
- Consistent – New legislation is consistent with existing regulations in health and safety and other subjects, and compatible with international law and standards
- Proportionate – The effect which regulations have on people and businesses provides a balance between risk and cost, and alternatives to state regulation are fully considered.

In order to follow these principles it is incumbent on policy staff to take responsibility for considering a wide range of options during the development of any legislative initiative – whether these originate from the identification of an issue peculiar to Great Britain or from a European or international initiative. The starting-point is the collection of evidence to justify the intervention. Evidence can come from various sources, such as experience with the enforcement of existing legislation, scientific data and, if necessary, specially commissioned research. Alternative solutions, including non-legislative ones, are considered, their impacts assessed (see below), and associated existing legislation considered for contradictions or compatibility. The HSE must take particular care in order to ensure that its proposals do not discriminate unfairly against any person or group.

Once the alternative solutions have been developed, this analysis is made available to a wide range of interest groups and the public for their views. Such consultations frequently take place in two stages: the issue of a Discussion Document, in which the problem is described and views are sought on appropriate action; and of a Consultation Document, in which the details of the options are presented and views sought on practicability. The results of this policy development process and the consultations are then presented to the HSC for it to advise Ministers on the appropriateness of the regulations, if this is the option selected. If all agree that regulation is necessary, associated guidance is produced and issued well in advance of the implementation date of the regulations. This process is designed to obtain broad public support, avoid unintentional consequences, and produce a solution that is enforceable and that balances the risks, costs and benefits.

A current topic of concern to many individuals revolves around the liability of company directors for fatal accidents that are caused by a less than rigorous safety regime, and over whether such individuals should be prosecuted for 'corporate manslaughter'. This is a key issue for the government and the Commission as they try to bring home to the leaders of British industry their responsibility for leadership on risk management issues, and fits in well with wider initiatives, like moves towards greater social and environmental responsibility in business.

As part of this process the Commission issued guidance on 'Directors' responsibilities for health and safety' which set out what it thought directors ought to do to make sure that occupational risks are properly managed in their organisations. And 'organisations' in this context includes both companies and public sector employers. In 2002 the HSC for the first time laid out how companies can be prosecuted for breaches of health and safety law. A 'new enforcement policy' states under what circumstances prosecution should take place and what factors must be considered in decisions to investigate incidents. The HSC Chairman stated that the 'changes emphasise the central role of the director in health and safety'. The policy warns inspectors to ensure that they consider the role of the management chain, including individual directors and managers, in any possible offences. It also describes how to take action against them if evidence shows it is justified (see Lister in *People Management*, 7 February 2002).

The government has proposed the new criminal offence of 'corporate killing', but at the time of writing this has not translated into any legislative action. If such a new offence does get on to the statute-book, it is intended that it should cover those cases where a fatality is caused by 'management failure' that falls below standards that could reasonably have been expected. While the proposals have received considerable criticism from employers' organisations, there is little doubt that, following high-profile cases involving cockle-pickers and railway workers, something will happen sooner rather than later.

As with many other topics of current interest, details and guidance can be found on the HSE website.

Regulatory impact assessment

All proposals for legislation, and published guidance that will have the force of law, have to be supported by a 'regulatory impact assessment' (RIA) if they are going to have an impact on businesses, charities or the voluntary sector. This assessment:

- identifies the problems and the specific objectives of the proposals
- assesses the risks
- compares the benefits and costs of a range of options, including a 'do nothing' case, and non-regulatory solutions
- summarises who or what sectors bear these costs and benefits, and identifies any issues of equity or fairness
- considers the impact on small firms and any measures to help them comply
- sets out the arrangements for securing compliance, with details of sanctions for non-compliance

■ stipulates how the policy will be monitored and evaluated, so that results feed back into the process of policy development.

The impact assessment develops throughout the policy process: a draft accompanies the consultation document and feedback is used to refine the analysis. The final results are presented to Ministers, who sign a statement that having read the RIA, they are satisfied that . . . 'The benefits justify the costs.'

EVALUATION AND REVIEW

Plans for evaluation of the impact of the legislation are required before their introduction. These use the data gathered earlier in the process (to justify the intervention) to contribute to a definition of a baseline and to allow the impact of the regulations to be quantified. The success of the legislation will be judged against how well it meets its objectives. Legislation, once introduced, is normally evaluated against a pre-announced timetable. The aim is to repeat this process at intervals to discern whether the legislation should be modified or repealed. This avoids having a growing raft of archaic legislation – which could potentially be a problem thanks to Britain's long-unbroken legislative history.

In 1994 the Health and Safety Commission completed a comprehensive review of its regulation, at the request of Employment Department Ministers, to remove any unnecessary burdens on business as part of the government's wider 'deregulation initiative'. The review set a series of challenging and far-sighted recommendations which looked fundamentally at the law in place, how it was understood and interpreted, and how it was enforced. The recommendations were fully implemented by 1998 and have involved a series of actions and initiatives to improve the way the health and safety system is regulated.

ENFORCEMENT

For most personnel professionals, and their line manager colleagues, their principal contact with health and safety institutions is through the process of inspection. The main object of inspection is to stimulate compliance with health and safety legislation and to ensure that a good standard of protection is maintained. Inspectors have, and make use of, important statutory powers. They can enter any premises where work is carried out without giving notice. They can talk to employees and safety representatives, take photographs and samples, and impound dangerous equipment and substances. If the levels of health and safety standards being achieved do not satisfy them, they have several means of obtaining improvements:

■ advice or warnings

■ improvement or prohibition notices (the former requires a contravention of the Act to be remedied in a specific time, and the latter requires an activity to be stopped immediately, or after a specific time, unless remedial action is taken)

■ prosecution in the criminal law courts

■ in the case of a death resulting from a work activity, consideration of the possible charge of manslaughter – manslaughter investigations are a police responsibility

■ informal investigation of particular accidents or incidents, so as to learn lessons or prepare legal action.

Inspectors decide what enforcement action is appropriate in accordance with the Commission's published enforcement policy statement. Commission policy requires that enforcement action should be proportionate to the risk created; targeted on the most serious risks, or where hazards are least well controlled; consistent; and transparent. This policy is currently being revised and has been subject to a major consultation exercise in its own right.

The HSE was the first central government enforcing body to sign up to the Enforcement Concordat, which provides a blueprint for fair, practical and consistent enforcement of regulations and was a joint initiative by the Cabinet Office and Local Government Authority. As part of its commitment to this initiative, the HSC requires local authorities to follow its enforcement policy.

Prosecution

If an enforcement officer does decide to prosecute – because an organisation or an individual is contravening legislation, failing to comply with an improvement or prohibition notice, or committing any other specified offence, such as obstructing an enforcement officer or making false statements – he or she must take into account all the circumstances of the case, including its seriousness, the employer's record and the effectiveness of health and safety arrangements.

In most cases prosecutions are heard in magistrate's courts (lower courts) where, on a guilty finding, fines of up to £20,000 per breach for sections 2–6 of the Health and Safety at Work etc Act 1974 can be levied. For all other breaches of health and safety regulations, the fine in a lower court is limited to £5,000. Also, a lower court can impose community service orders or imprison individuals for up to six months. Offences heard in the lower courts are known as 'summary offences'.

All of these options are regularly exercised by the lower courts, and each year some 2,500 charges are laid against employers by the HSE and local authority inspectors (the Crown Office and Procurator Fiscal Service in Scotland). The fines can be substantial – because most incidents involve more than a single breach of legislation, a form of 'totting up' takes place. These fines etc can be levied against the organisation and/or individuals within it. In a serious case, the accused may be indicted to crown court, where the penalties are more severe – an unlimited fine or up to two years' imprisonment.

The HSE has a firm belief that where there are problems in persuading businesses to take a pro-active approach to health and safety, the organisation's stakeholders – eg customers, insurers, investors – can create pressure for improvements. This pressure is amplified by the HSE's policy of maintaining a database of convictions and naming, on its website, those convicted.

RISK ASSESSMENT

The most pro-active basis for managing health and safety at work is through the process of health and safety risk assessments – and it is a clear legal requirement that every organisation must carry out such assessments: there is no choice.

But for a risk assessment to have any meaningful benefit to an organisation and its employees, it must be more than a ritual exercise to satisfy a legal requirement. In the introduction to this chapter we said that gaining people's commitment to business objectives could be undermined if health and safety was not taken seriously. Where this happens, employer/employee relations are inevitably damaged because people perceive that they are undervalued as individuals. In the context of employee relations, risk assessment therefore becomes a vital tool in the process of gaining that commitment.

Looked at from this perspective, risk assessment becomes less of a chore and more a means of enhancing other employee involvement and participation initiatives. Success, however, will depend on the extent that you involve those who actually carry out the tasks within your organisation in the risk assessment programme. Sensible managers will take every opportunity to involve as many of them as possible in the programme because they understand that risk assessment is a pro-active exercise that will help their organisation avoid harming people and incurring losses.

Three factors underpin the requirement to carry out risk assessments:

- moral reasons – Not many people would wish to see others become ill, get injured or die through work activities they are responsible for. It is extremely upsetting for all concerned when a serious accident takes place. It is difficult to have to explain to the relatives/partners of an injured person what has actually happened. It is even more difficult to attend the funeral of someone who has been killed by the activities of your organisation. How do you face the bereaved family? What can you say?
- legal reasons – These are classed by some people as the 'CYA factor' (CYA standing for 'cover your a—'!). There is no doubt that the law is being tightened up with more and more specific regulations. The most recently introduced legislation includes a specific requirement to carry out risk assessments, and it is impossible to fully comply with the Health and Safety at Work Act without doing so
- economic reasons – There are enormous financial implications that stem from the mismanagement of health and safety at work. HSE studies have shown that in accident situations, uninsured costs heavily outweigh insured costs. The possible uninsured losses to be incurred through accidents at work and which have to be taken into account include such things as:
  - loss of key workers
  - loss of service to clients
  - damage to image (marketing) – for instance, when an organisation from the caring sector, such as a Health Service Trust, is featured in the media following work-related injuries or illness to staff or patients
  - damage to supplier relationship – if you are a total-quality organisation and you suffer accidents which are featured in the media, what is implied about your management control systems, and how would this be interpreted by your major customers?

Legislation requiring risk assessment

Although the personnel professional may not be directly responsible for the carrying out of risk assessments, the outcome of such assessments, or the failure to have them carried out, may impact on his or her work. This is because individual employees are likely to raise grievances, either formally or informally, about unaddressed health and safety issues. The resolution of such grievances then becomes part of the HR function. For this reason it is vitally important that HR professionals fully understand the legal framework of risk assessment and the methodologies involved.

The Management of Health and Safety at Work Regulations 1992 specify the overall requirement to assess every work activity and environment for risk. Other more specific regulations requiring risk assessments include:

- the Manual Handling Operations Regulations 1992
- the Personal Protective Equipment at Work Regulations 1992 (PPE)
- the Health and Safety (Display-Screen Equipment) Regulations 1992 (DSE)
- the Noise at Work Regulations 1989
- the Control of Substances Hazardous to Health Regulations 1999 (COSHH 99)
- the Control of Asbestos at Work (Amendment) Regulations 1998
- the Control of Lead at Work Regulations 1998
- the Fire Precautions (Workplace) Regulations 1997.

In general, risk assessment is only common sense – we would never cross a busy street without looking to see if it was safe to do so (an everyday example of risk assessment).

The Management of Health and Safety at Work Regulations stipulate the following general duty:

> The carrying out of suitable and sufficient risk assessment of all risks to the health and safety of employees and non-employees [*in fact anyone*] arising from the work activities, and the identification of the necessary preventive and protective measures to prevent injury.

A risk assessment that is suitable and sufficient is defined in the ACOP as follows:

- It should identify the significant risk arising out of work.
- It should enable the employer or self-employed person to identify and prioritise the measures that must be taken to comply with the relevant statutory provisions.
- It should be appropriate to the nature of the work and such that it remains valid for a reasonable period of time.

The duty to assess risks under these Regulations is general, referring to all eventualities arising at and from work. If a more specific Regulation – ie COSHH, DSE, PPE or Manual Handling, etc – applies to an activity or situation, it will not be necessary to repeat the existing risk assessment carried out for those Regulations, provided that:

- the assessment is still valid
- the assessment is 'suitable and sufficient'.

The various specific Regulations do not define how risk assessments should be carried out – they only guide us on what the outcome of risk assessment should be, and this gives us the flexibility of selecting a method that suits our organisation's particular needs. Similarly, there is no one method that will suit all organisations, and it is recommended that a method broadly fitting the needs of the organisation is taken and adapted to fit the specific situation.

In order to fully understand the process of risk assessment it is advisable to become familiar with the following definitions:

- A hazard is 'something with the potential to cause harm'.
- Risk is the likelihood that that potential to do harm will be realised.
- Risk assessment is a process of identifying the hazards in any work situation and making a competent judgement as to the likelihood of that hazard actually causing a risk of harm. It involves rating the severity of that risk and identifying measures to ensure that the risk is eliminated or, if that is not possible, adequately controlled so as to prevent harm.
- Preventive and protective measures are those measures that have to be taken as a result of carrying out a risk assessment. Some are dependent on the specific legislation involved, but HSE guidance is as follows:
  - if possible avoid the risk altogether
  - combat risks at source
  - wherever possible adapt the work to the individual (not vice versa)
  - take advantage of 'technological and technical progress'
  - risk-prevention measures must form part of a coherent policy and approach
  - those measures which protect the whole workplace and the people who work there or visit it must be given priority
  - workers must understand what they need to do.

Measures should form part of an approach that builds an active health and safety culture in the organisation. The combating of risk at source is an important point to grasp; all too often we treat the symptom rather than the root cause. If we regularly find water on the floor, yes, it is important to clean it up to prevent people slipping on it – but it is vital that we repair the real cause of the risk, the faulty tap (or question why the tap was there in the first place!).

Risk assessment methodologies

Methods of risk assessment vary from organisation to organisation and it is important to evaluate the method most suited to your organisation's needs.

The five-step approach

This is a very easy-to-use system published by the HSE. This well-thought-out form (HSE Leaflet IND(G) 163L) consists of one sheet that gives useful advice to guide the user through each of the five steps, and a second sheet with headings and prompts for each step, and a column under each heading to record your findings.

The five-steps are:

1 Look for hazards.
2 Decide who might be harmed, and how.
3 Evaluate the risks arising from the hazards and decide whether existing precautions are adequate or whether more should be done.
4 Record your findings.
5 Review your assessment from time to time and revise it if necessary.

This system should be suitable for most organisations. Some people have commented that it is not sophisticated enough. Experience demonstrates, however, that simple, effective systems usually deliver the required result because they are more likely to receive management buy-in.

Team-based risk assessment

Another easy-to-use form-based system ensures that the risk assessment process is a team activity. This system, developed by the Industrial Society, is founded on the logic that drives such initiatives as quality circles and product improvement groups. It harnesses people's creative powers and gets them involved not just with designing safer working practices but also with more productive and economic outcomes.

The process of team-based risk assessment has, as its objective, involving the people close to the action. In this respect it is similar to product improvement groups. The team study the method(s) being used to carry out an activity, or the features of a work area, by breaking the activity down into component parts (easily digestible chunks) and asking a series of questions about each stage. Firstly, are any hazards present? If so, do those hazards represent a risk, and if so, do we rate the risk as low, medium or high? Thirdly, are we using the most appropriate method, equipment or material for what we are trying to achieve and if we are, what controlling action(s) is/are necessary? Fourthly, how are the controls to be implemented, and when? Fifthly, who is involved? And finally, what monitoring is to be carried out, how often, and who is involved?

The team should be encouraged to estimate the cost of any changes required and the likely benefits of proposed changes.

Computer-based risk assessment systems

There are numerous examples of computer-based risk assessment systems. The important points to be considered when selecting such an option are:

- Will it fulfil the organisation's needs, and is it flexible enough for you to use in the organisation's risk assessment programme without having to utilise other more traditional methods as well?
- How difficult is it to operate, bearing in mind that you wish to involve those close to the action, and how long will it take to train them in its use?

A factor common to all systems is the need for some means of rating the risks assessed so as to allocate priorities for action (and available budget). A number of these feature the simple concept of applying 'low', 'medium' or 'high' to the assessed risk and concentrating on the 'highs' first, and so on. This will be perfectly adequate for most organisations that in general are fairly low-risk environments.

However, some organisations – owing to the nature of their processes, etc – have a number of inherent risks of varying severity which need to be classified and managed accordingly. Also, many managers are more comfortable with numerical rating systems. These are many and varied but have a common theme of:

- applying numbers to gradations of the severity of hazard potential, and to the gradations of the severity and likelihood of realisation of risk
- rating those numerical factors in a given circumstance
- multiplying these factors together to give a rating.

Points to bear in mind when designing or choosing such a system include not having too large a scale of gradation for hazard and risk. This will only confuse those attempting to use the system and lead to inconsistent results. Some people have an aversion to numbers and this could get in the way of successful risk assessment.

Experienced safety professionals would point out that many people who have carried out risk assessments have experienced some difficulty when rating risks. This difficulty centres on the assessors' tendency to focus on the potential severity of harm to be suffered from a hazard rather than assessing the likelihood of the risk's being realised, and thus marking everything as high-risk. Instead, separate judgements should be made of the level of severity of harm (injury or illness) and the likelihood that the risk will be realised.

What system of risk assessment is used in your organisation, and how often is it reviewed?

The process

Firstly, it is important to observe what is actually going on in the workplace. This means walking the job, observing, talking and listening to people. For instance, what is the 'normal' work activity? Does it comply with the operating manual, or has there been some 'drift'? What happens in pressurised/abnormal situations?

Secondly, look for any hazards. This includes anything with the potential to cause harm to people and provides an opportunity for employee involvement. Get the people working in that environment to help with this – those closest to the action are in the best position to know what really goes on and can help rate the severity of the hazard. As with any aspect of personnel, good records are vital – in this case, your findings.

Thirdly, do these hazards represent any risk? Are the hazards adequately controlled, or should more be done to prevent the 'potential to cause harm' from being realised? What is the severity of the risk? How many people could be affected? Who are they? Don't forget risks to visitors, contractors, customers, etc. Again it is vital that those who work in the area or use the equipment/methods are fully involved. Consider what might present a risk to any particularly vulnerable person such as new or expectant mothers, new employees, young persons.

Fourthly, design safe systems of work. Design protective and preventive measures to eliminate or adequately control any risks. Using the 'team' approach to do this is again vital. People will support what they have had a hand in creating. People are ingenious, and this is an excellent opportunity to tap the talent that undoubtedly exists. The result is often not only a safer method of working but also an improvement of service, efficiency and effectiveness.

Having done all of this, three further things must happen. Whatever safe system of work has been identified has to be implemented, and once implemented it needs to be monitored. Managers have to be encouraged to talk and listen to people and to look for evidence that the safest system is being used.

One methodology employed by many organisations is to use an initial process of self-assessment, as the following example in respect of display-screen equipment demonstrates.

Title: Display-Screen Equipment – Self-Assessment	*Date:*

Name: .... **Date:** ....

Main use of workstation? ....

How much time on average do your spend using a display screen each week?
(Please delete as appropriate)

Less than 5 hours	5 – 10 hours	10 – 20 hours	20+ hours

Do you touch type? Yes/No

Equipment present at workstation

Screen ☐	**Keyboard** ☐	**Mouse** ☐	**Other input device** ☐	**Printer** ☐
Chair ☐	**Lamp** ☐	**Phone** ☐	**Document holder** ☐	**Footrest** ☐
Desk ☐			**Other items** ☐	

Display Screen	Yes	No	Assessor
Are the display characters easy to read and of adequate size?	☐	☐	☐
Are the screen characters stable and free from flickering?	☐	☐	☐
Are there controls for brightness and contrast?	☐	☐	☐
Can the screen be tilted and swiveled easily?	☐	☐	☐
Can the height of the screen be adjusted?	☐	☐	☐
Is the screen free from uncomfortable glare and reflections?	☐	☐	☐
Is the screen regularly and adequately cleaned?	☐	☐	☐

Keyboard

	Yes	No	Assessor
Is the keyboard separate from the screen?	☐	☐	☐
Is the keyboard tiltable?	☐	☐	☐
Is there enough space in front for user to rest and wrists?	☐	☐	☐
Have you got a keyboard pad?	☐	☐	☐
Is the keyboard non-reflective?	☐	☐	☐
Is the layout of the keys easy to use?	☐	☐	☐
Are the keyboard symbols easy to read?	☐	☐	☐
Does the keyboard remain still on the work surface when in use?	☐	☐	☐

Work Surface or Desk

	Yes	No	Assessor
Does the surface have low reflection?	☐	☐	☐
Are you able to rearrange the layout of equipment?	☐	☐	☐
Is the document holder stable and adjustable?	☐	☐	☐
Is work positioned to lessen head/eye movement?	☐	☐	☐
Are all electrical cables/equipment in good condition?	☐	☐	☐
When in a sitting position are your legs clear of the underside of your desk?	☐	☐	☐

Work Chair

	Yes	No	Assessor
Is the chair stable?	☐	☐	☐
Does it allow ease of movement and a comfortable position?	☐	☐	☐
Can the seat be adjusted in height while sitting?	☐	☐	☐
Is the seat back adjustable both for height and tilt?	☐	☐	☐
Can you place your feet flat on the floor?	☐	☐	☐
If the answer to the above is no, do you have a footrest?	☐	☐	☐
Does the armrest help to achieve a comfortable position?	☐	☐	☐

Environment

	Yes	No	Assessor
Does the layout of your immediate work area allow you to do your job properly?	☐	☐	☐
Are you able to gain access to the equipment you need to perform your job properly without excess reaching, stretching or twisting?	☐	☐	☐
Is your workstation free from glare caused by internal lighting?	☐	☐	☐
Do windows have adjustable blinds/coverings?	☐	☐	☐
Is the work area free from excessive noise?	☐	☐	☐

Other items

	Yes	No	Assessor
Has health and safety training been provided in the aspects of using a workstation?	☐	☐	☐
Do you feel that you have received adequate training in IT skills?	☐	☐	☐
Have you received and understood the DSE information sheet?	☐	☐	☐
Do you know who to contact within the company if you wish to discuss any aspect of DSE?	☐	☐	☐
Are you aware of the accident/incident reporting procedure as documented in the H&S handbook?	☐	☐	☐
Do you suffer from any recurring discomfort which you believe is caused by the use of display-screen equipment?	☐	☐	☐

Assessor use only.
Notes and advice given to the user:

_____

_____

_____

_____

_____

Model Assessment and proposed action report:

| Workstation fig. 1 |

| Workstation fig. 2 |

Other comments:

_____

_____

_____

Proposed action:	Date for completion:

User's signature:	Date:
Assessor's signature:	Date:

Has your organisation introduced any new equipment, changed working processes or recruited new staff? If the answer to any of these is yes, have new risk assessments been carried out?

CONSULTATION WITH EMPLOYEES

In its booklet *Consulting Employees on Health and Safety – A guide to the law*, the Health and Safety Executive make the point that 'consulting employees on health and safety matters can be very important in creating and maintaining a safe and healthy working environment'. Notwithstanding the fact that, by law, employers must consult all of their employees on health and safety matters, the above sentiments support the theme that we have been pursuing in this chapter – namely, that by involving employees an employer can motivate them into having a greater awareness of health and safety issues. The upside of such motivation is likely to be a more efficient business as accidents and work-related illnesses decline.

By law, employers must consult all their employees on health and safety matters on the following matters:

- any change that may substantially affect their health and safety at work – for example, in procedures, equipment or ways of working
- the employer's arrangements for getting competent people to help him or her satisfy health and safety laws
- the information that employees must be given on the likely risks and dangers arising from their work, measures to reduce or get rid of these risks, and what they should do if they have to deal with a risk or danger
- the planning of health and safety training, and
- the health and safety consequences of introducing new technology.

In the context of consultation, one of the most important initiatives contained in the Robens Report (see page 356 above) was a significant role for trade unions in the management of health and safety. Section 2(4) of the Health and Safety at Work etc Act 1974 provides for the appointment of safety representatives when there is a recognised trade union in the workplace. 'Recognised' in this context means formally recognised for the purposes of collective bargaining, but it does not necessarily mean statutory recognition as set out in the Employee Relations Act 1999. Where a union is voluntarily recognised, that is sufficient to trigger their rights to a formal role in health and safety management.

Where safety representatives are appointed by a trade union, their activities are governed by the Safety Representatives and Safety Committees Regulations 1977 (SRSC Regulations) and employers cannot refuse to recognise them. Once appointed, they are entitled to be consulted over the making and maintenance of health and safety arrangements. Any employees not in groups covered by trade union safety representatives must be consulted by their employers under the Health and Safety (Consultation with Employees) Regulations 1996 (HSCER). The employer can choose to consult them directly or through elected representatives. If the employer consults employees directly, he or she can choose whichever method suits everyone best. If the employer decides to consult his or her employees through an elected representative, then employees have to elect one or more people to represent them. Figure 14 opposite demonstrates how the system works.

Basically, the difference between the roles of trade union safety representatives and elected representatives of employee safety (representatives elected by groups of employees not covered by trade union safety representatives) is as follows.

Under the SRSCR 1977 the duties of trade union safety representatives are:

- to investigate possible dangers at work, the causes of accidents there, and general complaints by employees on health and safety and welfare issues, and to take these matters up with the employer

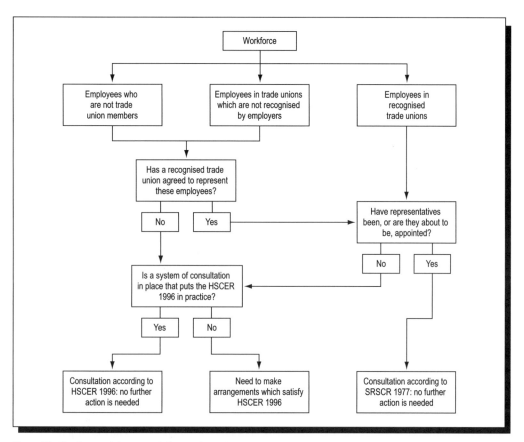

Figure 14 *Employee safety representation requirements*

- to carry out inspections of the workplace, particularly following accidents, diseases or other events
- to represent employees in discussions with health and safety inspectors and to receive information from those inspectors, and
- to go to meetings of safety committees.

The employer must set up a safety committee if two or more trade union safety representatives ask for one. The separate HSCER 1996 give elected representatives of employee safety the following duties:

- to take up concerns with employers about possible risks and dangerous events in the workplace that may affect the employees they represent
- to take up with the employers general matters that affect the health and safety of the employees they represent, and
- to represent the employees who elected them in consultations with health and safety inspectors.

Union safety representatives may be elected or appointed. and the SRSC Regulations stipulate that if an employer has received written notification from a recognised independent trade union of the names of the people appointed as union safety representatives, such persons have the functions set out in Regulation 4 of the SRSC Regulations. Although it is always preferable to have representatives who have an interest in safety management, so far as is reasonably practicable, union safety representatives will either have been employed by their employer throughout the preceding two years or have had at least two years' experience in similar employment. Employees cease to be union safety representatives for the purpose of these regulations when:

- the trade union which appointed them notifies the employer in writing that their appointment has been terminated
- they cease to be employed at the workplace
- they resign.

There is nothing in the legislation which stipulates the number of union safety representatives who can be appointed, but guidance notes published with the SRSC Regulations suggest appropriate criteria for assessment of the numbers. It is important to note that none of these functions imposes a duty on 'safety representatives', although they will be liable for the actions they take as ordinary employees.

Given the range of activities that representatives have to cover, it is in everybody's interests that they are well trained. Employers who consult representatives of employees on issues of safety have a duty to ensure that those representatives are provided with such training in respect of their functions as is reasonable in all the circumstances. The employer must also meet any reasonable costs associated with such training, including travel and subsistence costs.

Inspection

Regulation 5 of the SRSC Regulations entitles safety representatives to inspect the workplace at least every three months, but they must give reasonable notice in writing of their intention to do so. Of course, inspections may take place more frequently if the employer agrees. Additional inspections may be made if there has been a substantial change in the conditions of work or new information has been published by the HSC or HSE relevant to the hazards of the workplace. Inspections may also be conducted where, for example, there has been a notifiable accident or dangerous occurrence. The employer must provide reasonable facilities and assistance for the purpose of carrying out an inspection, including facilities for independent investigation by the union representatives and private discussion with the employees. However, there is nothing to prevent the employers or their representatives from being present during an inspection.

It is also important to recognise that a trade union safety representative or a representative of employee safety is entitled to time off, with normal or average pay, during working hours to perform his or her functions and to undergo such training as may be reasonable in the circumstances.

Safety committees

One of the most effective methods of creating a culture of health and safety is to create an effective safety committee. By 'effective' we mean a group of individuals (managers and employees) who have a genuine interest in safety matters meeting together on a regular basis to seek ways of improving the health, safety and welfare of the workforce. All too often safety committees are no more than talking shops – there because somebody thinks they ought to be. There is, however, a statutory underpinning of this process. Where at least two union safety representatives submit a written request, employers must establish a safety committee, but before doing so they must consult the union safety representatives who made the request and the representatives of recognised trade unions. Such a committee must be formed within three months of the request being made, and a notice must be posted stating the composition of the committee and the workplaces covered. Under section 2(7) of the Health and Safety at Work etc Act (HASAWA) 1974 the function of safety committees is to keep under review the measures taken to ensure the health and safety at work of employees.

Does your organisation have a safety committee? If it does, does the committee play a pro-active role in health and safety issues? If your organisation doesn't, how does the organisation communicate health and safety matters to the workforce?

Detriment

It should be noted that the Code of Practice advises employers, recognised unions and union safety representatives to make full and proper use of existing industrial relations machinery to reach the degree of agreement necessary to achieve the purpose of the SRSC Regulations and to resolve any differences. However, where an employee suffers a detriment as a result of health and safety activities, a complaint may be brought under section 100 of the Employment Rights Act 1996 (if the individual was dismissed) or section 44 of the Act. Section 100 states that health- and safety-related dismissals shall be regarded as automatically unfair. In such cases the compensation available for the aggrieved employee is not, as it is in ordinary dismissals, capped. This means that tribunals are free to decide the size of any award. The remedies available for infringement of section 44 mirror those available from detriment on trade union grounds, but in essence it means that any individual who believes that he or she has suffered a detriment could resign and claim unfair dismissal. In *Goodwin v Cabletel* (quoted in Lewis and Sargeant), a construction manager who had responsibility for health and safety matters on site was unhappy with one subcontractor and took an aggressive approach to dealing with the matter. The manager's employer, however, wished to be more conciliatory and imposed a detriment by demoting him. The manager resigned and claimed constructive dismissal. The EAT subsequently confirmed that protection extended to the way duties were carried out.

CURRENT AND FUTURE ISSUES

In June 2000 the HSC and the then Department for Environment, Transport and the Regions issued a strategy statement called *Revitalising Health and Safety*. This was designed to:

- inject new impetus into the health and safety agenda
- identify new approaches to reduce further rates of accidents and ill health caused by work, especially approaches relevant to small firms
- ensure that the UK approach to health and safety regulation remains relevant for the changing world of work over the next 25 years
- gain the maximum benefit from links between occupational health and safety and other government programmes.

The strategy statement followed a consultation which had been launched in 1999 and sought the views of all those with a stake in health and safety management. The Action Plan presented in the statement incorporated many ideas suggested in the consultation, and includes measures to:

- motivate employers through a ready reckoner of the benefits of good health and safety, a new challenge to industry on annual reporting and changes to the enforcement regime
- engage small firms more effectively, in conjunction with the Small Business Service, through a programme of tailored sector-specific guidance and support schemes
- put the government's own house in order through the removal of Crown immunity
- promote coverage of occupational health in local health improvement programmes and take action on rehabilitation
- secure greater coverage of risk concepts in education, both through the national curriculum and specifically for safety-critical professionals.

It also set some challenging targets for the country to achieve by 2010 which, if achieved, would:

- reduce the number of working days lost per 100,000 workers from work-related injury and ill health by 30 per cent
- reduce the incident rate of fatal and major injury accidents by 10 per cent
- reduce the incident of cases of work-related ill health by 20 per cent.

In support of this governmental strategic approach the HSC has produced its own Strategy for Workplace Health and Safety in Great Britain to 2010 and Beyond. Full details of this strategy can be seen on the HSE website at www.hse.gov.uk, but in general it consists of four strategic themes and key points to support them.

In addition the strategy will require both the Commission and the Executive to change the way in which they work, and during 2004/05 the Commissioners have undertaken to:

- take a more active role in the HSE's management committees
- engage and communicate with their stakeholders, and
- assume ownership of the strategic programmes.

Stress at work

Stress at work is one of the major concerns of managers because it seems to have overtaken 'bad back' as one of the major causes of absence from work. Figures from the HSE say that a very high proportion of the working days lost each year are stress-related. Time off through stress is clearly on the increase and can be extremely costly for any business. Richard Lister of the solicitors Lewis Silkin says that 'employers must take steps to alleviate stress in the workplace to avoid personal injury claims' (*People Management*, February 2002).

On 5 February 2002 the Court of Appeal (CA) overturned three judgments – and upheld one – against employers over claims for stress-related psychiatric illness. The judgments were made by county courts, as opposed to tribunals, and the ruling was an attempt by the CA to establish a consistent framework across the legal system for dealing with stress-related personal injury claims.

One of the cases that came before the Court of Appeal was *Barber v Somerset County Council*: the House of Lords (HL) handed down its judgment in this case on 1 April 2004. Although the HL reversed the CA judgment in the *Barber* case, more importantly the guideline principles set out by the CA in *Sutherland v Hatton (and related cases)* [2002], from which *Barber* was appealed, are said to still stand.

In essence, the various cases that have been before the Court of Appeal and the House of Lords have clarified the legal position of employers. The fact that all employers owe a legal duty of care to their employees is well understood, but it is now clear that injury to mental health is to be treated in the same way as injury to physical health.

Although there is no specific statute or other regulation controlling stress levels permitted in the workplace, broad principles therefore apply in the same way as they would to any personal injury claim. Stress claims have been notoriously difficult to prove – firstly, because the nature of the condition and the knowledge and foreseeability of injury have been tricky to establish, and secondly, because it has been difficult to find evidence of the cause of the stress itself.

Stress claims are also a comparatively recent phenomenon.

The 1995 case of *Walker v Northumberland County Council* marked the first major stress award in UK legal history. Following *Walker*, a number of successful claims were brought in which a previous mental breakdown had not occurred. What did and did not constitute a reasonably foreseeable risk of injury relied on the facts of each case and the views of the particular court. One notable case was *Lancaster v Birmingham City Council* [1999], in which liability was admitted when an employee had taken three periods of sick leave and had then been medically retired. The employer conceded that it had failed to act on complaints from Mrs Lancaster and had failed to give her the necessary training and guidance to do her job. The previous periods of sick leave meant that it was foreseeable that failure to act would result in injury.

It was against this background that Lady Justice Hale's judgment in the Court of Appeal in *Sutherland v Hatton* was hailed as the landmark workplace stress judgment. It attempted to clarify the law by setting out 16 clear guidelines under which employees could bring claims and employers protect themselves.

The 16 propositions put forward by Lady Justice Hale in the CA – which we have set out below – have received virtually unqualified approval from the House of Lords and remain standing.

THE 16-POINT CRITERIA FOR STRESS CASES

The Court of Appeal's criteria for stress cases are, in summary:

1) The ordinary principles of employers' liability apply.
2) There are no occupations which should be regarded as intrinsically dangerous to mental health.
3) The threshold question to be answered in any workplace stress case is whether this kind of harm to this particular employee was reasonably foreseeable.

   This test has two components:
   - there must be an injury (as distinct from occupational stress), and
   - this injury must be attributable to stress at work (as distinct from other factors).
4) Foreseeability depends upon what the employer knows (or ought to know) about the individual employee.
5) Factors likely to be relevant in answering the threshold question include:
   - the nature and extent of the work done, and
   - signs from the employee of impending harm to health.
6) The employer is generally entitled to take what it is told by its employee at face value, unless it has good reason to think to the contrary.
7) To trigger a duty to take steps, the indications of impending harm to health arising from stress at work must be plain enough for any reasonable employer to realise that it should do something about it.
8) The employer is only in breach of duty if it has failed to take steps which are reasonable in the circumstances.
9) The size and scope of the employer's operation, its resources and the demands it faces are relevant in deciding what is reasonable. Also relevant are the interests of other employers and the need to treat them fairly – for example, in any redistribution of duties.

10) An employer can only be expected to take steps that are reasonable.

11) An employer which offers a confidential advice service, with referral to appropriate counselling or treatment services, is unlikely to be found in breach of duty.

12) If the only reasonable and effective step would have been to dismiss or demote the employee, the employer will not be in breach of duty in allowing a willing employee to continue in the job.

13) In all cases it is necessary to identify the steps which the employer both could and should have taken before finding it in breach of its duty of care.

14) The claimant must show that the breach of duty has caused or materially contributed to the harm suffered. It is not enough to show that occupational stress alone has caused the harm – it must be attributable to a breach of the employer's duty.

15) Where the harm suffered has more than one cause, the employer should only pay for that proportion of the harm suffered which is attributable to its wrongdoing, unless the harm is truly indivisible. It is for the defendant to raise the question of apportionment.

16) The assessment of damages will take account of any pre-existing disorder or vulnerability and of the chance that the claimant would have succumbed to a stress-related disorder in any event.

It is not the case that one or other of the tests is more important – all 16 have to be looked at in each individual case.

As a matter of practicality, there are a number of positive steps which employers may take to meet the standard of care proposed in *Sutherland* and *Barberair*:

- Conduct a pre-employment health check so that vulnerable potential employees may be excluded from stressful roles.

- Include a clear policy on how to deal with stress in the company health and safety policy to show that the company is complying with the health and safety regulations by providing a safe working environment for employees that assists staff in following the set procedure.

- Put in force a bullying and harassment code and a clear complaints-handling procedure.

- Include stress in risk assessments.

- Monitor and record the hours employees work, and take action if they breach the benchmark set out in the Working Time Regulations 1998.

- Introduce health monitoring through a confidential advice line and/or regular company medicals.

HSE management standards

Against this background of a greater awareness on stress the HSE has developed standards of good management practice. These are part of a voluntary approach aimed at helping managers to measure their organisation's performance in tackling stress. Currently the subject of consultation, the standards – if they are adopted – are likely to be introduced on a voluntary basis, but will nevertheless be of tremendous persuasive influence in any litigation. They are likely to assist in the interpretation of legislation and the 'reasonable standard of care' that employers owe to employees. Compliance with these management standards will therefore assist in showing that an employer has met the reasonable standard of duty of care required.

There are six standards suggested by the HSE, and these are set out below. Employee relations practitioners would be well advised to make themselves familiar with their content because the standards will have a major impact on the management of absence which we discussed in Chapter 10.

THE SIX HSE STANDARDS

1 Demands
Includes issues like workload, work patterns and the work environment.

The standard is:

- [At least XX%* of] employees indicate that they are able to cope with the demands of their jobs, and
- Systems are in place locally to respond to any individual concerns.

States to be achieved:

- The organisation provides employees with adequate and achievable demands in relation to the agreed hours of work.
- People's skills and abilities are matched to the job demands.
- Jobs are designed to be within the capabilities of employees.
- Employees' concerns about their work environment are addressed.

* For the pilot exercise, a percentage of **85%** was used.

2 Control
How much say employees have in the way they do their work.

The standard is:

- [At least XX%* of] employees indicate that they are able to have a say in the way they do their work, and
- Systems are in place locally to respond to any individual concerns.

States to be achieved:

- Where possible, employees have control over their pace of work.
- Employees are encouraged to use their skills and initiative to do their work.
- Where possible, employees are encouraged to develop new skills to help them undertake new and challenging pieces of work.
- The organisation encourages employees to develop their skills.
- Employees have a say over when breaks can be taken.
- Employees are consulted over their work patterns.

* For the pilot exercise, a percentage of **85%** was used.

3 Support
Includes the encouragement, sponsorship and resources provided by the organisation, line management and colleagues.

The standard is:

- [At least XX%* of] employees indicate that they receive adequate information and support from their colleagues and superiors, and
- Systems are in place locally to respond to any individual concerns.

States to be achieved:

- The organisation has policies and procedures adequate to support employees.
- Systems are in place to enable and encourage managers to support their staff.
- Systems are in place to enable and encourage employees to support their colleagues.
- Employees know what support is available and how and when to access it.
- Employees know how to access the required resources to do their job.
- Employees receive regular and constructive feedback.

* For the pilot exercise, a percentage of **85%** was used.

4 Relationships
Includes promoting positive working to avoid conflict and dealing with unacceptable behaviour.

The standard is:

- [At least XX%* of] employees indicate that they are not subjected to unacceptable behaviours, eg bullying, at work, and
- Systems are in place locally to respond to any individual concerns.

States to be achieved:

- The organisation promotes positive behaviours at work to avoid conflict and ensure fairness.
- Employees share information relevant to their work.
- The organisation has agreed policies and procedures to prevent or resolve unacceptable behaviour.
- Systems are in place to enable and encourage managers to deal with unacceptable behaviour.
- Systems are in place to enable and encourage employees to report unacceptable behaviour.

* For the pilot exercise, a percentage of **65%** was used.

5 Role
Whether people understand their role within the organisation and whether the organisation ensures that no person has conflicting roles.

The standard is:

- [At least XX%* of] employees indicate that they understand their role and responsibilities, and
- Systems are in place locally to respond to any individual concerns.

States to be achieved:

- The organisation ensures that as far as possible the different requirements it places upon employees are compatible.
- The organisation provides information to enable employees to understand their role and responsibilities.
- The organisation ensures that as far as possible the requirements it places upon employees are clear.
- Systems are in place to enable employees to raise concerns about any uncertainties or conflicts they have in their role and responsibilities.

* For the pilot exercise, a percentage of **65%** was used.

6 Change
How organisational change (large or small) is managed and communicated in the organisation.

The standard is:

- [At least XX%* of] employees indicate that the organisation engages them frequently when undergoing an organisational change, and
- Systems are in place locally to respond to any individual concerns.

States to be achieved:

- The organisation provides employees with timely information to enable them to understand the reasons for proposed changes.
- The organisation ensures adequate employee consultation on changes and provides opportunities for employees to influence proposals.
- Employees are aware of the probable impact of any changes to their jobs. If necessary, employees are given training to support any changes in their jobs.
- Employees are aware of timetables for changes.
- Employees have access to relevant support during changes.

* For the pilot exercise, a percentage of **65%** was used.

Board responsibility

There are a number of issues that are being developed as part of the Revitalising Health and Safety Action Plan, and one aspect of this work is encouraging large organisations to adopt consistent ways to deal with health and safety issues in their published reports. Scrutiny by shareholders – and by the wider public – of how organisations perform on health and safety will help provide a benchmark, and the Chair of the HSC and Ministers have written to 350 of the top businesses in the country encouraging them to adopt the HSC's guidance on reporting. Once again, the guidance is available on the HSE website. There is no doubt that effective leadership from directors and senior managers is essential if organisations are to deliver the improved health and safety performance envisaged by the Revitalising Health and Safety strategy. As with most aspects of organisational behaviour, leadership from the top is vital if employee commitment is to be obtained.

SUMMARY

This chapter has tried to do a number of things. We have explained the approach which the HSC and HSE take in the development and enforcement of health and safety law, and noted that the system for enforcement is designed to achieve a high degree of accountability, with extensive use made of alternatives to regulation such as self-help guidance materials, promotion of good practice, awareness campaigns and advice. Where enforcement is deemed necessary there is a range of enforcement tools to allow the action to be proportional. The extensive negotiations which precede the introduction of European legislation, with its tripartite consultation, and the subsequent national system for developing legislation, including extensive consultation across industry and government, is intended to achieve consistency with existing legislation. The mature, yet still highly relevant, primary legislation in the form of the Health and Safety at Work etc Act (1974), with its goal-setting basis and powers to introduce supporting secondary legislation, allows the system of health and safety legislation to be targeted on those sectors or hazards which produce greatest risk.

We have stressed that it is important for safety to be taken seriously, and that if managers ignore safety policies and procedures the wrong message is sent out. What does it say about the organisation if, when employees break safety rules, they are not appropriately disciplined because management turns a blind eye in the name of expediency?

Overall, as the CIPD Standards state,

> By playing a central role in preventing accidents and illness at work and limiting the risk of adverse effects on other stakeholders, the personnel professional adds real value. Accidents and illness affect not only those directly involved. They impact on productivity, morale, the organisation's image and the bottom line, as downtime and the costs of insurance, investigation and possible legal penalties have to be met.

Safety is not, if it ever was, an option: it is a high priority for all.

Key points

- Systems should be in place which are designed to achieve a high degree of transparency on the need for legislation, through the inclusive nature of the composition of the Commission, the extensive use of consultation prior to introduction and the production of accessible and definitive guidance.

- At the organisational level you should understand that managing and creating a health and safety culture in the workplace can be considered under three main areas: principles of accident prevention, strategies, and techniques.

- Good management has to come from above. Employees have to see that their health, safety and welfare are part of the strategy of the organisation and are being taken seriously – that there is a balance between quality and production!

- Irrespective of whether theirs is a unionised or non-union organisation, employees need to be consulted, to feel part of the decision-making process, and to know that they are being listened to (effective communication).

- Any safety policy should be well communicated if it is to be understood.

- As personnel professionals you should be aware that commitment is the result of leadership. You can help develop this process by persuading line manager colleagues that they will help develop a safety culture by the way they act.

- You should be able to explain how important it is for everybody to have a clear understanding of their accountability and responsibility for health and safety and implementation, and how important it is to identify the hazards within the workplace.

FURTHER READING

HEALTH AND SAFETY EXECUTIVE (1998) *The Health and Safety System in Great Britain*. HSE Books.

HEALTH AND SAFETY EXECUTIVE (1999) *Reducing Risks, Protecting People*. HSE Discussion Document.

HEALTH AND SAFETY EXECUTIVE (2000/01) *Health and Safety Statistics*. HSE Books.

HEALTH AND SAFETY EXECUTIVE (2003) *Managing Health and Safety – Five Steps to Success*. HSE Books.

LEWIS D. and SARGEANT M. (2004) *Essentials of Employment Law*. London, CIPD.

LISTER R. (2002) The benefit of foresight, *People Management*, Volume 8, No.4; pages 20–1.

STRANKS J. (2001) *A Manager's Guide to Health and Safety at Work*. London, Kogan Page.

TAYLOR C. (2001) HSC demands tougher regulation of accidents, *People Management*, 14 June.

Index

Membership has its rewards

Join us online today as an Affiliate member and get immediate access to our member services. As a member you'll also be entitled to special discounts on our range of courses, conferences, books and training resources.

To find out more, visit www.cipd.co.uk/affiliate or call us on 020 8612 6208.

Also from CIPD Publishing . . .

People Resourcing

3rd Edition

Stephen Taylor

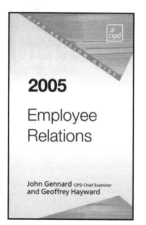

2005

Employee
Relations

John Gennard CIPD Chief Examiner
and Geoffrey Hayward

Need help studying for your exams?

The 2005 Revision Guides are here to help you!

Based on the experience and skills of the CIPD Chief and Associate Examiners, the 2005 CIPD Revision Guides provide comprehensive and relevant information and are an invaluable resource for students in the lead-up to their examinations.

The Revision Guides available include: *Employee Relations, Employee Reward, Employment Law, Learning and Development, Managing Activities, Managing Information, Managing in a Business Context, Managing People, People Management and Development, and People Resourcing.*

Students SAVE 20% when buying direct from the CIPD

To order, visit us online at www.cipd.co.uk/bookstore or call us on 0870 800 3366

The Guides include:

- advice on how to prepare for the exams;
- pointers on how to avoid common mistakes and how to maximise students' potential;
- advice on how to approach exam questions;
- examples of past exam questions with suggestions on how to answer (including examples from the May 2004 exam paper); and
- examples of responses students have given and explanations of why these were good, poor or average.

The Chartered Institute of Personnel and Development is the leading publisher of books and reports for personnel and training professionals, students, and for all those concerned with the effective management and development of people at work.